Integral Theory and Transdisciplinary Action Research in Education

Veronika Bohac Clarke
University of Calgary, Canada

A volume in the Advances in Educational Technologies and Instructional Design (AETID) Book Series

Published in the United States of America by
IGI Global
Information Science Reference (an imprint of IGI Global)
701 E. Chocolate Avenue
Hershey PA, USA 17033
Tel: 717-533-8845
Fax: 717-533-8661
E-mail: cust@igi-global.com
Web site: http://www.igi-global.com

Copyright © 2019 by IGI Global. All rights reserved. No part of this publication may be reproduced, stored or distributed in any form or by any means, electronic or mechanical, including photocopying, without written permission from the publisher. Product or company names used in this set are for identification purposes only. Inclusion of the names of the products or companies does not indicate a claim of ownership by IGI Global of the trademark or registered trademark.

Library of Congress Cataloging-in-Publication Data

Names: Clarke, Veronika Bohac, 1956- editor.
Title: Integral theory and transdisciplinary action research in education / Veronika Bohac Clarke, editor.
Description: Hershey, PA : Information Science Reference, 2019. | Includes bibliographical references.
Identifiers: LCCN 2017058223| ISBN 9781522558736 (hardcover) | ISBN 9781522558743 (ebook)
Subjects: LCSH: Action research in education. | Interdisciplinary research.
Classification: LCC LB1028.24 .I68 2019 | DDC 370.72--dc23 LC record available at https://lccn.loc.gov/2017058223

This book is published in the IGI Global book series Advances in Educational Technologies and Instructional Design (AETID) (ISSN: 2326-8905; eISSN: 2326-8913)

British Cataloguing in Publication Data
A Cataloguing in Publication record for this book is available from the British Library.

All work contributed to this book is new, previously-unpublished material. The views expressed in this book are those of the authors, but not necessarily of the publisher.

For electronic access to this publication, please contact: eresources@igi-global.com.

Advances in Educational Technologies and Instructional Design (AETID) Book Series

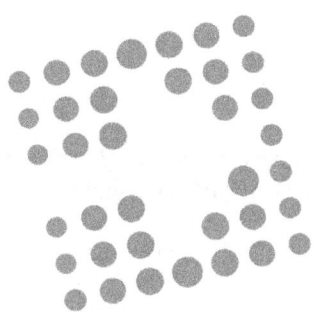

Lawrence A. Tomei
Robert Morris University, USA

ISSN:2326-8905
EISSN:2326-8913

Mission

Education has undergone, and continues to undergo, immense changes in the way it is enacted and distributed to both child and adult learners. In modern education, the traditional classroom learning experience has evolved to include technological resources and to provide online classroom opportunities to students of all ages regardless of their geographical locations. From distance education, Massive-Open-Online-Courses (MOOCs), and electronic tablets in the classroom, technology is now an integral part of learning and is also affecting the way educators communicate information to students.

The **Advances in Educational Technologies & Instructional Design (AETID) Book Series** explores new research and theories for facilitating learning and improving educational performance utilizing technological processes and resources. The series examines technologies that can be integrated into K-12 classrooms to improve skills and learning abilities in all subjects including STEM education and language learning. Additionally, it studies the emergence of fully online classrooms for young and adult learners alike, and the communication and accountability challenges that can arise. Trending topics that are covered include adaptive learning, game-based learning, virtual school environments, and social media effects. School administrators, educators, academicians, researchers, and students will find this series to be an excellent resource for the effective design and implementation of learning technologies in their classes.

Coverage

- K-12 Educational Technologies
- Online Media in Classrooms
- Social Media Effects on Education
- Hybrid Learning
- Bring-Your-Own-Device
- Educational Telecommunications
- Game-Based Learning
- Classroom Response Systems
- Instructional Design
- E-Learning

IGI Global is currently accepting manuscripts for publication within this series. To submit a proposal for a volume in this series, please contact our Acquisition Editors at Acquisitions@igi-global.com or visit: http://www.igi-global.com/publish/.

The Advances in Educational Technologies and Instructional Design (AETID) Book Series (ISSN 2326-8905) is published by IGI Global, 701 E. Chocolate Avenue, Hershey, PA 17033-1240, USA, www.igi-global.com. This series is composed of titles available for purchase individually; each title is edited to be contextually exclusive from any other title within the series. For pricing and ordering information please visit http://www.igi-global.com/book-series/advances-educational-technologies-instructional-design/73678. Postmaster: Send all address changes to above address. Copyright © 2019 IGI Global. All rights, including translation in other languages reserved by the publisher. No part of this series may be reproduced or used in any form or by any means – graphics, electronic, or mechanical, including photocopying, recording, taping, or information and retrieval systems – without written permission from the publisher, except for non commercial, educational use, including classroom teaching purposes. The views expressed in this series are those of the authors, but not necessarily of IGI Global.

Titles in this Series

For a list of additional titles in this series, please visit: www.igi-global.com/book-series

Educational Research in the Age of Anthropocene
Vicente Reyes (University of Queensland, Australia) Jennifer Charteris (University of New England, Australia) Adele Nye (University of New England, Australia) and Sofia Mavropoulou (Queensland University of Technology, Australia)
Information Science Reference • copyright 2019 • 352pp • H/C (ISBN: 9781522553175) • US $185.00 (our price)

Ubiquitous Inclusive Learning in a Digital Era
Ebba Ossiannilsson (Swedish Association of Distance Education (SADE), Sweden & International Council for Open and Distance Education (ICDE), Norway)
Information Science Reference • copyright 2019 • 300pp • H/C (ISBN: 9781522562924) • US $185.00 (our price)

Advanced Methodologies and Technologies in Modern Education Delivery
Mehdi Khosrow-Pour, D.B.A. (Information Resources Management Association, USA)
Information Science Reference • copyright 2019 • 959pp • H/C (ISBN: 9781522573654) • US $395.00 (our price)

Creating Caring and Supportive Educational Environments for Meaningful Learning
Kisha Daniels (Duke University, USA) and Katrina Billingsley (South University – High Point, USA)
Information Science Reference • copyright 2019 • 295pp • H/C (ISBN: 9781522557487) • US $185.00 (our price)

Business Community Engagement for Educational Initiatives
Mikhail Epshtein (College of Staten Island (CUNY), USA)
Business Science Reference • copyright 2019 • 325pp • H/C (ISBN: 9781522569510) • US $195.00 (our price)

Technology-Assisted ESL Acquisition and Development for Nontraditional Learners
Seda Khadimally (University of Phoenix, USA)
Information Science Reference • copyright 2019 • 304pp • H/C (ISBN: 9781522532231) • US $175.00 (our price)

Handbook of Research on Immersive Digital Games in Educational Environments
Aliane Loureiro Krassmann (Federal Institute of Education Science and Technology Farroupilha, Brazil) Érico Marcelo Hoff do Amaral (Federal University of Rio Grande do Sul, Brazil) Felipe Becker Nunes (Federal University of Rio Grande do Sul, Brazil) Gleizer Bierhalz Voss (Federal Institute of Education Science and Technology Farroupilha, Brazil) and Manuel Constantino Zunguze (Pedagogical University, Mozambique)
Information Science Reference • copyright 2019 • 695pp • H/C (ISBN: 9781522557906) • US $265.00 (our price)

701 East Chocolate Avenue, Hershey, PA 17033, USA
Tel: 717-533-8845 x100 • Fax: 717-533-8661
E-Mail: cust@igi-global.com • www.igi-global.com

Editorial Advisory Board

Lynn Bosetti, *La Trobe University, Australia*
Bence Ganti, *Integrál Akadémia, Hungary*
Marilyn Hamilton, *Integral City Meshworks, Inc., Canada & Findhorn Foundation College, UK*
Brad Kershner, *Independent Researcher, USA*
Barbara V. Meibom, *Institut für Führungskunst, Germany*
Petrea Redmond, *University of Southern Queensland, Australia*
Rica Viljoen, *Henley Business School, South Africa & Mandala Consulting Group, South Africa*
Ian Winchester, *University of Calgary, Canada*

List of Reviewers

Janice Beler, *University of Calgary, Canada*
Faye Bres, *Brio Institute, Canada*
Dave Carlgren, *University of Calgary, Canada*
Elizabeth Churchill, *University of Victoria, Canada*
Ema Clarke, *Independent Researcher, Canada*
Anne Daniel, *University of Calgary, Canada*
Brent Davis, *University of Calgary, Canada*
Brendan Gray, *University of Alberta, Canada*
Kathleen Kellock, *University of Calgary, Canada*
Krystyna Laycraft, *Brio Institute, Canada*
Jennifer Lock, *University of Calgary, Canada*
David Proctor, *Vancouver Island University, Canada*
Natalie Prytuluk, *University of Calgary, Canada*
Garette Tebay, *University of Calgary, Canada*
Bernita Wienhold-Leahy, *Thompson Rivers University, Canada*

Table of Contents

Foreword xvi

Preface xxii

Acknowledgment xxvii

Section 1
Integral Theory and AQAL as a Conceptual Framework and Research Methodology

Chapter 1
Methodological Pluralism and Graduate Student Research in Education 1
Brent Davis, University of Calgary, Canada

Chapter 2
Integral Meta-Impact: Integral Theory and Applying It With Meta-Theory Methodology for
Validation, Dynamic Insight, and Effectiveness 19
Simon Divecha, The University of Adelaide, Australia

Chapter 3
Legitimizing Integral Theory in Academia: Demonstrating the Effectiveness of Integral Theory
Through Its Application in Research 45
Veronika Bohac Clarke, University of Calgary, Canada

Section 2
Using AQAL in Research in Schools

Chapter 4
An Integral Analysis of International Mindedness 65
Avis Eileen Beek, University of Calgary, Czech Republic

Chapter 5
CoS and Effect: An Integral View 87
Dave Carlgren, University of Calgary, Canada

Chapter 6
An Integral Analysis of Bahamian Adolescents and Their Perspectives About a Future After High School 109
    M. Kathleen Kellock, University of Calgary, Bahamas

Chapter 7
An Integral Analysis of Mindfulness and Self-Compassion Among Adolescents 134
    Bernita Wienhold-Leahy, Thompson Rivers University, Canada

Chapter 8
Cultivating Compassion in an Upper Elementary School Classroom Community 160
    Garette Tebay, Parkland School Division No. 70, Canada

Chapter 9
An Integral View of Mindfulness Practices and the Perception of Challenge Within a High School Setting 182
    Anne Daniel, University of Calgary, Canada

Chapter 10
Promising Futures: An Integral Exploration of the Futures Thinking of High School Teachers 208
    Roy A. Norris, Louis Riel School Division, Canada

Chapter 11
Creating a Culture of Inclusion in Pre-Kindergarten: An Integral Analysis of Beliefs, Understandings, and Practices of Early Childhood Educators.. 238
    Natalie Anne Prytuluk, Edmonton Public Schools, Canada

Section 3
Application of AQAL in Practice Beyond the School System

Chapter 12
An Integral Theory Approach to the Feedback System in Supervising Doctoral Students in the Nordic Higher Education Context.. 271
    Cheryl Marie Cordeiro, University of Gothenburg, Sweden & The Norwegian Institute of Food, Fisheries and Aquaculture Research (Nofima), Norway

Chapter 13
An Integral Analysis of Wellbeing in Adults With Characteristics of High Functioning Autism...... 287
    Janice Marie Beler, University of Calgary, Canada

Chapter 14
The Development of Creativity: Integral Analysis of Creative Adolescents and Young Adults – Abstract, Introduction, Background, Theoretical Perspectives.. 314
    Krystyna Czeslawa Laycraft, University of Calgary, Canada

Chapter 15
Post-Adult Education Alternatives in 45 Years of Learning/Teaching: An Integral-Informed
Autoethnographic Reflection 339
  R. Michael Fisher, University of Calgary, Canada

Chapter 16
Reimagining Sustainability Leadership: Integral Action Research in a Non-Profit Organization 357
  Justin Robinson, Royal Roads University, Canada

Chapter 17
Integral Post-Analysis of Design-Based Research of an Organizational Learning Process for
Strategic Renewal of Environmental Management 383
  A. Faye Bres, University of Calgary, Canada

Compilation of References 408

About the Contributors 452

Index 455

Detailed Table of Contents

Foreword xvi

Preface xxii

Acknowledgment xxvii

Section 1
Integral Theory and AQAL as a Conceptual Framework and Research Methodology

Chapter 1
Methodological Pluralism and Graduate Student Research in Education 1
Brent Davis, University of Calgary, Canada

This chapter surveys the range of research attitudes and methodological positions that are represented in contemporary educational research. Oriented by integral methodological pluralism, the discussion includes an analysis of the diverse ways that research foci are conceived, the sorts of conceptual and methodological distinctions that are necessary to deal with different research attitudes, associations to broader categories of scientific study, types of intention manifest in educational research, and varied criteria for claims to truth. The chapter concludes with considerations of the nature and place of methodological pluralism in graduate-level research, specifically, and educational research, more generally.

Chapter 2
Integral Meta-Impact: Integral Theory and Applying It With Meta-Theory Methodology for
Validation, Dynamic Insight, and Effectiveness 19
Simon Divecha, The University of Adelaide, Australia

Integral theory presents as a theory of everything. As such, how do we validate its use while applying it as a methodology and investigating its blind spots? Meta-theory methodology can authenticate integral theory and provides a check on its comprehensiveness. The methodology draws on relevant mid-range theories and integral theory (a meta-theory itself) to refine and justify a study's methods while simultaneously applying theory to specific research. This rigor creates clarity and insight. Complex issues—for example, the concept of sustainability that illustrates this chapter—are characterized by many different (mid to meta, conceptual to applied) theoretical approaches. Meta-theory methodology assists to sift these, highlight critical points, and realize integral theory's promise.

Chapter 3

Legitimizing Integral Theory in Academia: Demonstrating the Effectiveness of Integral Theory
Through Its Application in Research 45
Veronika Bohac Clarke, University of Calgary, Canada

This chapter is based on the analysis of experiences of graduate students and professors using Integral Theory (IT) as transdisciplinary research framework, at a Western Canadian mainstream university. The traditional disciplinary orthodoxies, which had presented a formidable challenge to the acceptance of IT in mainstream academia, are briefly described. For example, not having a single disciplinary home, Integral academics do not fit into the traditional roles and their associated benefits. This applies both to professors and to graduate students. Integral students must continue to defend their research and professors must defend Integral teaching. Nevertheless, research is strengthened by an Integral worldview and a more complex understanding of the world. The chapter concludes with a specific discussion of how IT is employed to investigate multiple contexts of complex problems.

Section 2
Using AQAL in Research in Schools

Chapter 4

An Integral Analysis of International Mindedness 65
Avis Eileen Beek, University of Calgary, Czech Republic

The purpose of this chapter is to report on a study that examined contextual interpretations of international mindedness by International Baccalaureate (IB) Diploma Programme students in different school contexts in the Czech Republic. The conceptual framework was based on Wilber's integral theory and integral methodological pluralism, a novel application in the study of international mindedness. Using an empirical methodology, international mindedness was shown to be widely applicable, developmental, and experiential in nature. Through a hermeneutic phenomenological methodology, findings revealed the experience of international mindedness was characterized by the development of an intercultural identity, the ability to take alternate perspectives, and the capacity to resolve disconnection from important people in their lives. Contextual factors of privilege and exposure to diversity also influenced students' experience of international mindedness. Implications for improving education for international mindedness at the level of the school and the IB organization are discussed.

Chapter 5

CoS and Effect: An Integral View 87
Dave Carlgren, University of Calgary, Canada

The science that is done by students in grade school settings naturally differs considerably from that done by actual scientists. While much of this difference is attributable to differences in age and experience between the two groups, it may be possible to decrease the gap between the learner and the researcher in science. To explore this possibility, an educational design research (EDR) study was conducted from the perspectives of complexity and networks, communities of practice, and integral theory, the goal being to assess the potential outcomes of engaging learners in a student-led science conference called the celebration of science (CoS).

Chapter 6
An Integral Analysis of Bahamian Adolescents and Their Perspectives About a Future After High School 109
M. Kathleen Kellock, University of Calgary, Bahamas

Adolescents in high school are faced with many opportunities and challenges, which may direct their future path towards higher education and career development. The future orientation among Bahamian adolescents was looked at from an integral lens. The beliefs and goals Bahamian adolescents had for their future were explored and included present actions and plans students proposed to realize these goals. Further, the expectations adolescents perceived others had for them and the perceptions they held for themselves, including outside influences and systems that impact adolescents' implementation and realization of their goals were identified. The use of Wilber's integral methodological pluralism, supported by mixed methods research, gathered phenomenological, hermeneutical, and empirical data from members of the school and the community involved in a private high school in the Commonwealth of The Bahamas. Studies on future orientation with adolescents in other countries provided a comparison for and offered additional insight into the phenomenon of college and career readiness.

Chapter 7
An Integral Analysis of Mindfulness and Self-Compassion Among Adolescents 134
Bernita Wienhold-Leahy, Thompson Rivers University, Canada

This case study focused on teaching self-compassion to adolescents through a mindfulness program. Self-compassion involves being kind towards oneself, understanding that we are all part of common humanity, and mindfulness. This multi-methods study was grounded in integral theory, which examines self-compassion through multiple lenses with both qualitative and quantitative methodologies. The findings indicated that a mindfulness program teaching self-compassion had many benefits to students, including increased mindful awareness and focused attention; emotional awareness and regulation; self-awareness, self-kindness, and self-acceptance; resiliency and growth mindset; compassion, acceptance, and forgiveness for others; and a belief it could reduce bullying in schools. Mindfulness programs in the school context will need to be introduced slowly over the next several years as students, parents, teachers, and administrators all have to understand the importance of these skills before they can be implemented into the classroom.

Chapter 8
Cultivating Compassion in an Upper Elementary School Classroom Community 160
Garette Tebay, Parkland School Division No. 70, Canada

This chapter explored the notion that compassionate behaviors can be learned or cultivated among elementary school students through mindfulness practice in the classroom. Integral theory served as the conceptual framework for the research questions, the methodology, and the analysis. The investigation thus unfolded as a narrative inquiry using a mixed methods approach and informed by integral methodological pluralism to relate the story of one classroom. Increased self-awareness, happiness, and calm were observed in the students and teacher alike as a result of mindfulness practice. The integral analysis determined that these positive effects were persistent for all involved and pointed to the potential benefits of adopting mindfulness practice at the system level.

Chapter 9
An Integral View of Mindfulness Practices and the Perception of Challenge Within a High School
Setting 182
    Anne Daniel, University of Calgary, Canada

The purpose of this chapter was to examine how mindfulness-based strategies are taught within four different classroom settings in a large urban high school and how they impact students' perceptions of challenge. Two different approaches toward mindfulness training were represented in the four classrooms: the first derived from an explicit, outcomes-based approach within a Yoga class setting with a focus on awareness of personal experience; the other was embedded and implicitly connected to the subject discipline of natural science with a focus on situated being. Integral methodological pluralism (IMP) was used to gather data from multiple viewpoints: phenomenological interviews, structural analysis of language frequency and comparisons, ethnographic observations, and hermeneutic interviews. Integral theory was used to analyze the data and identify the individual and cultural themes. Systemic influences are discussed in connection with these findings, and implications for implementation of mindfulness in relation to perception of challenge are explored.

Chapter 10
Promising Futures: An Integral Exploration of the Futures Thinking of High School Teachers 208
    Roy A. Norris, Louis Riel School Division, Canada

Teachers spend their working days preparing young people for the times to come. Teachers also imagine a wide variety of ideas about possible, probable, and preferable futures. This chapter explores how teachers feel and think about the potential futures for themselves and their students, and how teacher perceptions of futures inform their teaching practices. The study sets integral theory as the basis for the methodological pluralism and analytical blending which are sustained throughout this trans-disciplinary study as a whole. The findings show that although high school teachers envision many possible futures, they are most likely to trust shorter term empiric predictions, and they rarely think about futures more than a few years away. Learning more about how often, how deeply, and how optimistically teachers envision possible futures matters because teachers are educating the people who will become adults in all versions of the near futures.

Chapter 11
Creating a Culture of Inclusion in Pre-Kindergarten: An Integral Analysis of Beliefs,
Understandings, and Practices of Early Childhood Educators.. 238
    Natalie Anne Prytuluk, Edmonton Public Schools, Canada

The purpose of this study was to understand how beliefs, understandings, and pedagogical practices of early childhood educators affect, and are affected by, their relationships with children, classroom team members, parents, and colleagues, as they create an inclusive culture in a pre-kindergarten classroom. To explore this research problem from multiple perspectives, integral theory was selected as the conceptual framework, and a multi-methods exploratory sequential design was employed using integral methodological pluralism. Data about educational experiences, culture, behaviors, and systems, were collected from five early childhood educators in pre-kindergarten classrooms in four urban schools, followed by a questionnaire of classroom practices, document analysis, and a focus group. Findings revealed that important factors for creating an inclusive classroom culture included: early childhood educators' positive beliefs toward inclusion; a social constructivist theoretical perspective; and the ability to build strong relationships with children, parents, and colleagues.

Section 3
Application of AQAL in Practice Beyond the School System

Chapter 12
An Integral Theory Approach to the Feedback System in Supervising Doctoral Students in the
Nordic Higher Education Context.. 271
*Cheryl Marie Cordeiro, University of Gothenburg, Sweden & The Norwegian Institute of
Food, Fisheries and Aquaculture Research (Nofima), Norway*

Feedback giving makes an important part in the context of higher education thesis writing, in particular, doctoral thesis writing supervision. In the past decade, European level standardization higher education policies have encouraged a pedagogy paradigm shift towards a more student-centered learning approach. Within the Nordic context of higher education, feedback giving from supervisor to student has often been studied from the perspective of the supervisor, as a small part of the overall doctoral degree program. This study uses findings from foundational pedagogy literature in the field of Nordic pedagogy studies in combination with empirical data findings from interviews, and maps elements of the doctoral thesis writing feedback system from an integral pluralism approach. The integral model of a feedback system to a doctoral thesis supervision is novel for the Nordic pedagogy literature and it is meant as complement to the current canon of literature on Nordic pedagogy.

Chapter 13
An Integral Analysis of Wellbeing in Adults With Characteristics of High Functioning Autism...... 287
Janice Marie Beler, University of Calgary, Canada

Quality of life is generally assessed through objective measures including conditions relating to material living, productive activity, health measures, education levels, and economic standing. In contrast, wellbeing is a complex process involving subjective evaluation of the qualities and experiences that make life good. Research is plentiful with studies exploring autism and quality of life. Less information is available relating to wellbeing and autism, especially from first person perspectives. This research explored how autism characteristics shape understanding and experiences of wellbeing in individuals with characteristics of high functioning autism. The study made use of a multi-method research framework, integral methodological pluralism (IMP), based on Ken Wilber's integral theory, for gathering and understanding knowledge from diverse perspectives, styles, and methodologies. Findings contributed towards a more coherent and inclusive understanding of personal wellbeing in high functioning autism.

Chapter 14
The Development of Creativity: Integral Analysis of Creative Adolescents and Young Adults –
Abstract, Introduction, Background, Theoretical Perspectives 314
Krystyna Czeslawa Laycraft, University of Calgary, Canada

The purpose of this chapter was to investigate creativity in adolescents and young adults and its role in psychological development. For this qualitative research, hermeneutic phenomenology/ontology linked with the narrative/biography methodology was chosen. To interpret the data, the pattern models of creativity were generated, by applying the concepts of complexity science, especially self-organization, with the theory of positive disintegration and the psycho-evolutionary theory of emotions. It was discovered that the process of creativity in young people is intertwined with the strong emotions of passion, curiosity, enthusiasm, and delight. These emotions are the driving forces that generate order and complexity not only in the creative process but also in overall psychological development. The presence of these strong emotions often contributes to lesser tension in young people's development, including a greater ability to integrate their experiences, to take their psychological development into their own hands, and to find direction for their future.

Chapter 15
Post-Adult Education Alternatives in 45 Years of Learning/Teaching: An Integral-Informed
Autoethnographic Reflection 339
    R. Michael Fisher, University of Calgary, Canada

The author critically examines the directional trends that education has gone through in the last 45 years of his teaching and learning experiences, primarily in Alberta, Canada (1972-2017). He argues that, formerly, Alberta was at the leading edge of positive progressive change, before neoliberal ideology invaded Education. Through use of autoethnographic reflection and sociocultural and political contextualization of his educational experiences, the author elaborates the necessity of adopting a holistic-integral alternative path to research and teaching outside of institutionalized mainstream education systems. His emphasis on the affective domain, for example the importance of fear in education, is accompanied by his applications of developmental notions of "post-adult," transdisciplinary, and integral theoretical work. The purpose of the chapter is to demonstrate, through his own life, a model of potential guidance for teachers, who are questioning how best to negotiate their own careers within the challenges of 21st century neoliberalism and cascading global crises.

Chapter 16
Reimagining Sustainability Leadership: Integral Action Research in a Non-Profit Organization 357
    Justin Robinson, Royal Roads University, Canada

This research explored how the stakeholders of Integral Without Borders (IWB)—an international think tank and NGO focused on applying integral metatheory to sustainable development—might reimagine sustainability leadership to increase their collective capacity for wise and transforming action in the world. Applying an integral action research methodology in the context of an action research engagement model, eight individual interviews, two focus groups, and an open space lab were conducted with participation from an international cohort of IWB's stakeholders. The study identified fertile territories from which the possibility space for sustainability leadership might be expanded, specifically "four Rs" of integral transformation praxis: (1) revive, (2) reidentify, (3) recode, and (4) reconfigure. Recommendations relevant to IWB's specific leadership goals and development as an organization were also proposed.

Chapter 17
Integral Post-Analysis of Design-Based Research of an Organizational Learning Process for
Strategic Renewal of Environmental Management 383
    A. Faye Bres, University of Calgary, Canada

This chapter is based on a design-based research study of organizational learning and on a subsequent integral analysis of how and why organizational learning did, and did not, occur in the study. Integral theory is applied to deepen the understanding of how human organizations learn and adapt as complex adaptive systems made up of nested, operationally closed groups and individuals. The level of development and learning potential of an organization, as holon, can be understood as an emergent property resulting from the coordination of function and action of the unities that make up the system, even given that the levels of development and learning potentials of the groups and individuals in an organization are not consistent across the organization. The advantages of combining complexity and integral theory are explored, as both are understood to provide different, complementary interpretations of whole human systems.

Compilation of References 408

About the Contributors 452

Index 455

Foreword

The following book is a superb overview of Integral Theory (or more technically, Integral Metatheory)—an introduction to its basics, why this approach seems to be so important, and specific examples of research using it focused on education and extended into life in general. Although, in its specific present-day form, I am generally regarded as its founder (presented in 26 books, all still in print, published over the last 50 years and now translated into some 25 foreign languages), there are today thousands of bright individuals and scholars around the world who have contributed to its enhancement, elucidation, and further evolution. This book is a terrific example of exactly that.

Still, especially when viewed through the lens of most current trends in academia, many of the tenets of Integral Metatheory are quite controversial. There seem to be several reasons for this. The first, of course, is that the core elements of Integral could simply be wrong or misguided (or twisted or prejudiced), and thus right-minded folks everywhere would react with appropriate negativity. Another possible reason is itself very controversial, and this refers to the various developmental stages that have been fairly rigorously investigated by different developmental models. Let me explain this by giving a little bit of theoretical background here.

One of the things that makes Integral a "meta-theory" in many ways, and not just a straightforward theory, is that where theories adjust their contents based on how well they represent and unify many different facts, meta-theories attempt to represent and unify many different theories themselves. Theories unify facts, meta-theories unify theories (which unify facts). When it comes to developmental stages, for example, I examined over 100 different developmental theories and models—from the East as well as the West, and taken from premodern and modern and postmodern times—which were models that each contained anywhere from 4 to 30 stages of development (this overall analysis, and charts of all of these 100 models, can found in my book *Integral Psychology*). Through a systemic meta-analysis of all of them, I arrived at around 16 major overall stages that seemed to most faithfully reflect the core elements of those models (most of which were individual theories that themselves were based on a great deal of evidence or facts).

What virtually all of them had in common was the central idea that human beings are not born with all of their skills and capacities fully formed and already functioning, but rather those qualities emerge and develop over time, and further, the course of that development in many cases can be researched, analyzed, and categorized. And if you do carefully research that development, then in most cases you will find that it unfolds through a series of stages, levels, or degrees of development, and you can arrange those stages in terms of the "amount" of development a stage displays, with each senior stage becoming more and more encompassing or more "whole." (We see this in general evolution itself, where there is a sequence that runs from "atoms to molecules to cells to organisms"—which clearly represent increas-

Foreword

ing degrees of wholeness, with each of those stages moving beyond, yet also including or enfolding, its predecessor, and you cannot reverse or skip any of those stages.) Most of the developmental models had stages just like that, and what was notable about them is that, although these stages manifested themselves in very different ways in virtually every culture they were tested, when it came to the general stages themselves, they were usually cross-cultural—and you couldn't alter their sequence with any amount of social conditioning (just as you can't have molecules before you have atoms, or cells before molecules). Some of these models were tested in up to 40 different cultures (including Amazon rain forest tribes, Australian aborigines, and Harvard professors), and no major exceptions were found (although a few cultures had minor variations in a sub-stage or two). The overall evidence for these major stages is quite compelling, and I believe that now the burden of argument has switched from proving that they exist to proving that they don't.

Most of the more complete models traced development in a series that was composed of "holons," and this is exactly why they display a sequence of increasing developmental wholeness. "Holon" is term coined by Arthur Koestler (1967) that means "a whole that is a part of a larger whole." Virtually everything in the universe is a holon of one sort or another. The evolutionary sequence that I just gave is composed entirely of holons (a whole atom is part of a molecule, a whole molecule is part of a cell, a whole cell is part of an organism, and so on). Most human developmental sequences are like that, composed of holons that are the whole of one level but become simply a part of the larger, more mature holon at the next level.

Carol Gilligan, for example, studied moral development in women and found that it moves through four very broad stages (each of which, I add, is a holon). Stage one she called "selfish," since the woman tends to care only for herself (hence we also call this general stage "egocentric"). Stage two she called "care," since the woman extends care from herself to a larger group (her clan, her tribe, her nation, her religion, etc., a stage that, since it's group oriented, we also call "ethnocentric")—but this doesn't mean she stops caring for herself, it's just that care itself is a holon, it becomes a part of increasingly more inclusive wholes, and in this case it becomes part of a larger group. The next stage she found to be, not care (confined to her group), but what she called "universal care"—the woman extends care to all groups, to all humans, and attempts to treat everybody fairly regardless of race, color, sex, gender, or creed (hence, we also call this "worldcentric"). Finally, the woman integrates, into an even larger whole, both her masculine and feminine modes of thinking, which Gilligan called "integrated" (and we also call "integral").

Holons everywhere.... In most cases, this is the result of the simple additive nature of existential realities. You really do need letters before you can have words; and you do need words before you can have sentences; and you need sentences before you can have paragraphs. There's really no way around those simple realities of addition—you definitely cannot have sentences before you have words—and this is why almost anywhere you look in the universe, you find holons, and this certainly seems to include human development as well. Or it does at least according to virtually every single one of the 100 developmental models that I studied.

Of those 4 to 30 stages that those models contain, the most common and widespread models worldwide tended to agree on around 6-8 major stages of development that they felt were central (truly worldcentric). Here's the kick. If we look at what those models take as being the two or so highest or most developed stages that their evidence supports, these highest stages are indeed be the "biggest" holons in the sequence—they are the most whole, or the most unified, or the most integrated, or the most inclusive, or the most systemic. These highest stages, in other words, are truly inclusive and integral. This is true of everybody's models from the genius Jean Gebser (whose highest stage he called "integral-aperspectival") to Jane Loevinger, who has perhaps the most widely adopted developmental model in the world (whose highest stage she called "integrated"). So here's the kick part (which is an aspect of what makes any of these models controversial): according to most models, only around 5% of the population presently reaches those stages of adult development.

This cuts against virtually every major current in our present culture, from the popular to the academic—a current of "diversity" and "multiculturalism" and "inclusion"—the idea that all individuals are absolutely equal in every way. But these studies are not denying that at all. Rather, what they are doing is simply providing direct evidence that those values—of embracing diversity and inclusion—are actually values that only emerge at these higher stages. Human beings are certainly not born with values of inclusion. Nor, these models show, do the earlier stages of development have anything like those values. Even looking at Gilligan's simple four stages, you can see that, if your aim is overcome notions of ethnocentric superiority and privilege, you need to develop past any ethnocentric stage itself—which is fully stuck in those kinds of thinking—and instead reach worldcentric stages or higher. These models all value diversity and inclusion, they simply point out that a human is not born with those values, but rather they are values that emerge only at some of the very highest stages of human development that exist.

This amounts to an elitism, to be sure, but it's an elitism to which all are equally invited. According to virtually every one of these models, these developmental stages are available to literally every human being alive. These stages do not represent different kinds or classes or types of people; nobody is "in" or "at" a stage, all of these stages are in everybody. People definitely distribute in a specific way, with a very general percentage of any given population skewing toward each stage at any given time (with individuals themselves moving up and down through a large range of the developmental spectrum under different circumstances; the stages themselves unfold in a very specific sequence, which cannot be reversed or skipped, but people are all over the place, although they tend to have their center of gravity at just one or two levels at any given time, with development itself being the overall general transformation of that center of gravity to greater and greater holons).

There is a strange thing about those two highest levels. (And, by the way, when I say "highest" I mean only the highest of those most commonly recognized 6-to-8 stages. A few models, including Integral, recognize the possibility of three or four even higher stages, which will become more widespread as development and evolution continues.) But most developmental researchers have found that these two stages involve a truly profound, wholly unprecedented, and incredibly far-reaching transformation, something not seen at any of the earlier stages. As Clare Graves, a pioneering developmentalist, pointed out, all of the earlier stages (six or so of them in Graves's model) think that their truth and values are the only real truth and values that there are; everybody else might be well-intentioned, but they are fundamentally mistaken, confused, or just plain wrong. But with the emergence of these two higher stages, there is a dramatic shift—Graves called it "cataclysmic" and "a monumental leap in meaning." Namely, these higher stages don't think any of the earlier stages are simply wrong or mistaken; rather, they view all of the earlier stages as having a genuinely significant existence, and thus need to be fully included in any truly comprehensive and adequate view of the world. If nothing else, these stages are all irreplaceable components of an overall human development. In other words, it really is the case that a truly "inclusive" stance in a very real sense is what marks these higher stages. These two or so higher

Foreword

stages are so dramatically different from earlier ones that Graves's followers call all of the earlier stages "1st tier" and these higher, truly inclusive stages "2nd tier."

One of the things that definitely seems to continue becoming "larger and larger" with increasing development is the capacity to take perspectives. Some models actually define a major stage or level of development as being "the addition of a new and wider perspective that a person can take." Thus, Gilligan's first stage, the selfish, can seriously take only a 1st-person perspective (hence, selfish or egocentric); her second stage—care—adds the capacity to take a 2nd-person perspective and thus extend care to others (to a "you" or "thou," thus expanding her perspective to a whole group, or ethnocentric—but not yet to *all* groups, which happens next); her third stage, universal care, adds a 3rd-person perspective (which can indeed take an objective, 3rd-person, universal perspective, thus expanding care to all groups, to all humans, with a "universal care," or worldcentric). Loevinger's model as well as Susann Cook-Greuter's have empirically tracked this development up to and including a 7th-person perspective (in 2nd tier).

When you can take that many different perspectives—and actually see the world through those many different lens—this is truly being able to "see the world through another's eyes" or "walk a mile in their shoes," and hence more and more perspectives start to carry meaning and value. The more perspectives a person can take, the broader and more inclusive their worldview becomes. And these new perspectives are viewed very seriously, as disclosing genuinely new and significant dimensions of reality that need to be taken carefully into account. Academically, this starts to show up as an increasing expansion from disciplinary to interdisciplinary to multidisciplinary to transdisciplinary (to integral), as each one of those takes on more perspectives and attempts to find a larger and larger unity-in-diversity among them.

Integral Metatheory is an explicitly 2nd-tier integrated metatheory. This is not the modernist dream of a great, grand, single metanarrative that forces all other approaches into its own folds. It is rather an integrated embrace of multiple epistemologies, multiple methodologies, and multiple ontologies, all given coherent room within its giga-inclusive 2nd-tier framework. It deliberately adopts a 7th-person perspective, and looks at the world—including all of its various 1st-tier disciplines—through a 2nd-tier lens (and even makes room for several yet higher stages, or 3rd tier). Whether it succeeds or not in this endeavor is certainly open to debate, but the fact that it is intentionally grounded in those holistic dimensions—and their genuinely inclusive nature—is a necessary, if not sufficient, item that needs to be kept in mind when judging any validity that it may (or may not) have.

Individuals who have gained a bit of wisdom in their lives will often say things like, "Nothing human is alien to me," or "To understand all is to forgive all." Those are quintessentially Integral expressions. When it comes to inclusiveness, it's common to say, among Integralists, that "Everybody is right." The general idea is that every major discipline has at least some truth, because no human brain is capable of producing 100 percent error (or, as I jokingly put it, "Nobody is smart enough to be wrong all the time"). Thus, each major discipline has some degree of truth in it—it is "true but partial." The main academic question thus becomes not, "Which of these approaches is right, versus all the others which are wrong?" but "How can they all fit together?"

This, anyway, is what Integral Metatheory attempts to do. One way to look at this developmentally is that, according to some models, cognitive development in its major higher stages moves from "systemic" (which embraces large systems of data), to "meta-systemic" (which examines and differentiates those systems into a vast multicultural diversity), to "paradigmatic" (which takes many of those differentiated items and integrates them into large inclusive paradigms), to "cross-paradigmatic" (which then examines and integrates those many different paradigms into even more inclusive arrangements). Integral

Metatheory has not only examined items like the 100 major different developmental models (looking for integrative frameworks), it has done essentially the same across a large swath of academic disciplines, sociology to philosophy to science to spirituality. The resultant cross-paradigmatic framework is called "Integral" or sometimes "AQAL," which is short for "all quadrants, all levels, all lines, all states, all types," which refer to the basic dimensions that this Metatheory has found are the minimal requirements to be able to produce integrative frameworks in any area (thus, for example, the "levels" aspect of that AQAL list refers to the levels or stages of development or evolution that any holon has undergone, and since essentially everything displays some sort of evolutionary unfolding, that's a dimension that needs to be included in any comprehensive understanding of it).

Integral's extremely generous embrace of virtually all human disciplines across virtually all epochs of human evolution ("Everybody is right") is perhaps the main item that indeed makes it rather controversial. The criticism here is almost always from those who fully applaud their own particular discipline, or approach, or methodology, but simply do not accept any of the other disciplines or approaches that Integral happily embraces. The most common Integral response to that criticism is that it is a criticism coming directly from 1st-tier (although that, in itself, doesn't mean the criticism is wrong—just not very adequate). A more adequate criticism involves: "First, accept as real ALL of the elements in the AQAL list, and then show us a better way to integrate them all than the Integral framework provides—and we'll definitely listen."

As I previously noted, the most common, widespread degree of development now being expressed by a majority of academic opinion is in the very general vicinity of a stage called "pluralistic" by Integral and "relativistic" by Graves—it's the "meta-systemic" that was just mentioned, and drives many of the "multicultural" and "diversity" and "inclusion" movements. These movements tend to have a great deal of difficulty with Integral views, because diversity in general rejects all hierarchies, with no exceptions, whereas Integral points out that there are two very different types of hierarchies: "dominator hierarchies" and "growth hierarchies." Dominator hierarchies are all the wretched things that multiculturalists say about them, and Integral joins that condemnation. But there are also growth hierarchies, which are the natural nested hierarchies that evolution itself produces everywhere—"atoms to molecules to cells to organisms" is a natural growth hierarchy. Notice that molecules don't hate atoms, or oppress them, or marginalize them—if anything, molecules love atoms, they literally embrace them. Most healthy human growth and development occurs, as we've noticed, through natural nested hierarchies, where each higher stage is not more domineering or controlling, but is literally more inclusive and more embracing—holon by larger holon by even-larger holon. Gilligan's stages, for example, are more and more inclusive, with each higher stage genuinely including much more diversity.

The problem with most multicultural and diversity movements—which claim to be absolutely "inclusive"—is that they will actually include you only if you accept their specific viewpoint. But, bless their hearts, they have not yet figured out how to genuinely include those views that fundamentally disagree with theirs—an *actual* inclusion eludes them. In fact, they maintain that they don't have to talk to such views or even listen to them, they can completely ignore them and even deny them a chance to speak (as, for example, openly evidenced in Berkeley's protests). This indeed is a deeply 1st-tier stance—it's definitely moving in the right direction, it wants to be truly inclusive, but it's just not inclusive enough. Only at the next major stage—2nd tier and the beginning of truly integral or integrated stages—does consciousness finally figure out how to be truly inclusive or integrated. Many academic disciplines remain in those essentially fragmented, divisive, 1st-tier dimensions, and have a great deal of difficulty seeing any merit in approaches other than what their own silos provide.

For better or worse, you won't find that difficulty with Integral. So I invite you, in the following pages, to settle back and see how a specific problem can be approached with multiple, well-recognized, seemingly exclusive epistemologies and methodologies that actually can be brought together in a coherent and cross-paradigmatic stance, with the result that a much more comprehensive, truly inclusive, and fruitful result can be obtained. It's a big, big, very big world out there, and Integral invites you to embrace it all.

NOTE

The purpose of a Foreword is to provide the general contours of the subject matter of the book - in this case Integral Theory and specifically Ken Wilber's meta-framework. Readers who wish to learn more about Ken Wilber's analysis of Carol Gilligan's work (see *Sex, Ecology and Spirituality*) or about Ken Wilber's Integral model and how Gilligan's work relates to it (see *Integral Spirituality*), are invited to consult the sources listed below. Ken Wilber's recommendation for readers who wish to know more about Gilligan's view of women's development is in the 'Additional Reading' section.

Ken Wilber
Summer 2018
Denver, Colorado

REFERENCES

Koestler, A. (1967). *The ghost in the machine*. London: Hutchinson.

Wilber, K. (1995). Sex, ecology, spirituality: The spirit of evolution. Boston, MA: Shambhala, P. 802, where Carol Gilligan's 1982 book In a different voice (Cambridge: Harvard University Press) is specifically discussed.

Wilber, K. (2006). *Integral spirituality* (p. 12). Boston, MA: Shambhala.

ADDITIONAL READING

Gilligan, C. (1985). In a different voice: Women's conceptions of self and of morality. In H. Eisenstein & A. Jardine (Eds.), *The future of difference*. New Brunswick, NJ: Rutgers University Press; Retrieved from http://sfonline.barnard.edu/sfxxx/documents/gilligan.pdf

Preface

There have been a number of philosophers in the past century, who thought integrally, but Integral Theory as a specific theoretical and conceptual model has been developed by the American philosopher Ken Wilber. The model is also referred to as AQAL ("all quadrants, all levels, all lines, all states, all types"). Integral Theory or AQAL was from its inception an inclusive theory, in a time of traditional disciplinary boundaries. Ken Wilber therefore developed the theory outside of the traditional academic context, and has been refining it over the past 50 years. As the chapters in this book disclose, the theory has been adopted by scholars in various academic disciplines (E.g., education, business, nursing), and these scholars generally had to fight ontological battles in their academic institutions in order to get their discipline-crossing work accepted.

The researchers who have contributed to this book have also contributed to the legitimization of Integral research in mainstream academia, by reporting on Integral research that they have completed and successfully defended in a rigorous thesis examination process. The University of Calgary's Werklund School of Education made the bold decision to offer a doctoral program in Curriculum – Integral Theory, and nine members of this doctoral cohort have contributed chapters to this book. In addition, two PhD graduates from the University of Calgary report on their research in this book. Professors from The University of Calgary, University of Gothenburg, and The University of Adelaide report on their Integral work at these mainstream, research universities. And finally, Integral researchers who broker and develop the relationships between educators, academia and various systems outside of academia report on their research and experiences.

With the growing recognition in academia, think tanks and research agencies, of the importance of interdisciplinary and even transdisciplinary research, Integral Theory is slowly entering the academic mainstream. In spite of the bold example of the University of Calgary program, Integral Theory still defies easy categorization within the mainstream research approaches, and therefore is generally not included in major methodological overviews. The title of this book, for example, categorizes Integral Theory under the general term "action research", in order to make it more searchable and "recognizable" to academic audiences. While Integral Theory can certainly be used to design, implement and analyze Action Research projects, as one of the chapters indicates, Integral Theory encompasses more than just one methodological approach.

Integral Theory is defined as a meta-theory, which integrates all current research paradigms and their methodologies into a coherent framework. This framework facilitates the design and implementation of transdisciplinary research design and analysis. A number of the chapters in this book focus on transdisciplinarity in detail, but for the purpose of this Introduction, a simple description of transdisciplinarity

Preface

would be research that deliberately crisscrosses the boundaries of specific disciplines in a back-and-forth manner, (not merely pooling the results of an inquiry from two different disciplinary perspectives), or, as many of the doctoral researchers have referred to transdisciplinarity in their chapters in AQAL terms, it is "the Quadrants talking to each other".

As such, AQAL can be seen as a very complex tool, daunting for researchers (particularly individual researchers) to use. The chapters in this book demonstrate through concrete examples how Integral Theory has been applied by academic researchers. Of particular value are the specific descriptions of how researchers have dealt with the challenges of using Integral Theory for research design and analysis. The authors in this volume have doctoral degrees from mainstream universities, and still continue to use Integral Theory in their work in universities and other educational institutions. It will become clear in reading this book, that Integral Theory can be immensely practical and useful for educators working in school districts and in other applied educational contexts, as well as to psychologists or business consultants. The book unfolds in three parts.

Section 1 introduces Integral Theory and specifically Ken Wilber's AQAL model, as a conceptual framework and a tool for implementing methodological pluralism.

In Chapter 1, "Methodological Pluralism and Graduate Student Research in Education," Brent Davis describes, with insight and precision, the evolution of just how Integral Methodological Pluralism is becoming understood by academic researchers. Davis then illustrates the process of understanding and application of Integral Methodological Pluralism with reference to the teaching and supervision of doctoral students conducting Integrally informed research.

In Chapter 2, "Integral Meta-Impact: Integral Theory and Its Application With Meta-Theory Methodology for Validation, Dynamic Insight, and Effectiveness," Simon Divecha takes a closer look at the philosophical and theoretical underpinnings of Integral Theory as a Meta-theory. Divecha illustrates the application of Integral Theory and its pluralist methodology to the example of sustainability, and offers a critique and recommendations for optimal use of Integral Theory for transdisciplinary research.

In Chapter 3, "Legitimizing Integral Theory in Academia," Veronika Bohac Clarke describes the traditional disciplinary context in academia, and then describes some of the perspectival challenges to the acceptance of Integral Theory as a framework for transdisciplinary research. Bohac Clarke then discusses the practical challenges facing Integral researchers, both in designing, implementing and defending their research. Finally, Bohac Clarke identifies some of the benefits of using Integral Theory and Integral Methodological Pluralism.

Section 2 represents doctoral research done in school systems across Canada and in international settings, by doctoral students who were members of the cohort in an Integral based program, at the University of Calgary. It should be noted, that many of the authors identify themselves by their academic affiliation rather than their institutional affiliation, in order to maintain anonymity of their research sites.

In Chapter 4, "An Integral Analysis of International Mindedness," Avis Beek investigated the international mindedness of International Baccalaureate (IB) Diploma Programme students in two schools in the Czech Republic. Beek collected and analyzed quantitative and qualitative data, using Integral Methodological Pluralism. Beek found that while the experience of international mindedness can be characterized by the development of an intercultural identity and the ability to take alternate perspectives, the contextual factors of privilege and exposure to diversity also had a significant impact on the students' sense of international mindedness.

In Chapter 5, "CoS and Effect: An Integral View," Dave Carlgren describes a project that was undertaken in a private school to enable students to work and think as "real" scientists do in the field. The study was conducted from the perspectives of Complexity and Networks, Communities of Practice, and Integral Theory as the meta-framework, with the goal of assessing the potential outcomes of engaging learners in a student-led science conference called the Celebration of Science (CoS).

In Chapter 6, "An Integral Analysis of Bahamian Adolescents and Their Perspectives About Their Future After They Complete High School," Kathleen Kellock investigated the future orientation among Bahamian adolescents in high school. Kellock used Integral Methodological Pluralism, to gather phenomenological, hermeneutical and empirical data from members of the school and the community involved in a private high school in the Commonwealth of The Bahamas. Kellock identified the beliefs and goals that Bahamian adolescents had for their future, including the present actions and plans through which the students proposed to realize these goals.

In Chapter 7, "An Integral Analysis of Mindfulness and Self-Compassion Amongst Adolescents," Bernita Wienhold-Leahy reports on her study, which focused on teaching self-compassion to adolescents through a mindfulness program. This multi-methods study examined self-compassion through multiple lenses with both qualitative and quantitative methodologies. The findings indicated that a mindfulness program teaching self-compassion had many benefits to students, but would need to be introduced slowly over the next several years so that all involved would understand the importance of these skills before they could be implemented school-wide.

In Chapter 8, "Cultivating Compassion in an Upper Elementary School Classroom Community," Garette Tebay explored the notion that compassionate behaviours can be learned or cultivated among elementary school students through mindfulness practice in the classroom. Using Integral Methodological Pluralism, to relate the story of one classroom, Tebay found positive effects, which were persistent for all involved and pointed to the potential benefits of adopting mindfulness practice at the system level.

In Chapter 9, "An Integral View of Mindfulness Practices and the Perception of Challenge Within a High School Setting," Anne Daniel examined how mindfulness-based strategies are taught within four different classroom settings in a large urban high school, and how they impact students' perceptions of challenge. Integral Theory was used to gather and analyze the data and identify the individual and cultural themes. Daniel noted the significant systemic influences, which helped to explain some of the findings and highlight implications for implementation.

In Chapter 10, "Promising Futures: An Integral Exploration of the Futures Thinking of High School Teachers in a Technology-Rich Learning Environment," Roy Norris uses Integral Theory as the basis for the methodological pluralism and analytical blending which are sustained throughout his transdisciplinary study of how teachers feel and think about the potential futures for themselves and their students. Norris reports that teachers rarely think about futures more than a few years away. He recommends developing teacher capacity via training in long-term futures thinking, which would allow teachers to consider much larger problems and challenges confronting cultures, over longer time spans.

In Chapter 11, "Creating a Culture of Inclusion in Pre-Kindergarten: An Integral Analysis of Beliefs, Understandings, and Pedagogical Practices of Early Childhood Educators," Natalie Prytuluk reports on her study to understand how beliefs, understandings, and pedagogical practices of early childhood educators affect, and are affected by, their relationships with children, classroom team members, parents, and colleagues, as they create an inclusive culture in a pre-kindergarten classroom. Using Integral

Preface

Methodological Pluralism, Prytuluk collected data about educational experiences, culture, behaviours and systems, from five early childhood educators in pre-kindergarten classrooms in four urban schools. Prytuluk's findings identified important factors for creating an inclusive classroom culture.

Section 3 features Integral research done in various educational settings outside of the school system.

In Chapter 12, "An Integral Theory Approach to the Feedback System in Supervising Doctoral Students in the Nordic Higher Education Context," Cheryl Cordeiro reports on a pedagogy paradigm shift towards a more student-centred learning approach in Nordic higher education institutions. Specifically, based on her research, Cordeiro maps elements of the doctoral thesis writing feedback system from an integral pluralism approach. Cordeiro proposes the Integral Model of a feedback system to a doctoral thesis supervision, as a new addition to Nordic pedagogy.

In Chapter 13, "An Integral Analysis of Wellbeing in Adults With Characteristics of High Functioning Autism," Janice Beler reports on her unique approach to investigating well-being and autism, from first person perspectives. Beler used Integral Theory to investigate how autism characteristics shape the understanding and experiences of well-being in individuals with characteristics of high functioning autism. Beler's findings pointed towards a more coherent and inclusive understanding of personal well-being in high functioning autism.

In Chapter 14, "The Development of Creativity: Integral Analysis of Creative Adolescents and Young Adults," Krystyna Laycraft used Integral Theory as the organizing framework for the research and analysis of creativity in adolescents and young adults and its role in their psychological development. On the basis of her analysis, Laycraft developed models of creativity of young people by combining the concepts of complexity science, particularly self-organization, with the Theory of Positive Disintegration and the Psycho-Evolutionary Theory of Emotions.

In Chapter 15, "Post-Adult Education Alternatives in 45 Years of Learning/Teaching: An Integral-Informed Autoethnographic Reflection," Michael Fisher uses autoethnographic reflection and socio-cultural and political contextualization of his own educational experiences, to arrive at the conclusion that adopting a holistic-integral alternative path to research and teaching is necessary outside of institutionalized mainstream education systems. For mainstream application, Fisher stresses the importance of developmental notions of "post-adult," transdisciplinary and integral theoretical work, when guiding teachers to negotiate their career trajectories.

In Chapter 16, "Reimagining Sustainability Leadership: An Integral Analysis of One Non-Profit Organization," Justin Robinson reports on a project using Integral meta-theory to investigate a complex self-study process of an NGO organization to reimagine sustainability leadership to increase their collective capacity for wise and transforming action in the world. Robinson's findings explore promising areas for expanding the possibility space for sustainability leadership.

In Chapter 17, "Integral Post-Analysis of Design-Based Research of an Organizational Learning Process for Strategic Renewal of Environmental Management," Faye Bres reports on an Integral analysis of a study of organizational learning, which she designed and conducted using the Design Based Research (DBR) approach. Bres conducted 3 iterations of the research and analyzed findings identified through DBR. Bres noted gaps that could not be explained using DBR, and analyzed these data using Integral Theory for a more contextually comprehensive explanation.

In these 17 chapters, the authors demonstrate the utility and promise of Integral Theory as a meta-framework for methodological pluralism and transdisciplinary research. The chapters feature a diverse array of research problems, which had been approached through the Integral Theory meta-framework, and the resultant research implementation processes that had been utilized. In addition to illustrating how research problems have been approached "Integrally", these chapters also describe in real and practical terms, how the researchers dealt with the challenges of doing Integral research, "on the ground".

Veronika Bohac Clarke
University of Calgary, Canada

Acknowledgment

This book has been from the beginning a joint effort of a large number of dedicated individuals who made a commitment to help bring it to the light of day through their voluntary contributions.

I wish to thank Ken Wilber, who made the offer to write the superb Foreword to the book.

I am grateful for the serious scholarly effort that each author dedicated to the creation of their chapter.

Finally, this book would not have been possible without the hard work of peer reviewers.

Section 1
Integral Theory and AQAL as a Conceptual Framework and Research Methodology

Chapter 1
Methodological Pluralism and Graduate Student Research in Education

Brent Davis
University of Calgary, Canada

ABSTRACT

This chapter surveys the range of research attitudes and methodological positions that are represented in contemporary educational research. Oriented by integral methodological pluralism, the discussion includes an analysis of the diverse ways that research foci are conceived, the sorts of conceptual and methodological distinctions that are necessary to deal with different research attitudes, associations to broader categories of scientific study, types of intention manifest in educational research, and varied criteria for claims to truth. The chapter concludes with considerations of the nature and place of methodological pluralism in graduate-level research, specifically, and educational research, more generally.

INTEGRAL THEORIES

Some years ago, a story entitled "Study links obesity to a virus" appeared on the front page of my morning newspaper (Vancouver Sun, 2007, pp. A1 & A6). The article was brief but compelling – partly because it was written with the usual assurance of scientific reporting, and partly because it offered hope for a growing problem in the provocative suggestion of "an obesity vaccine."

Coincidentally, several pages later, there was another piece that presented a different window into roots of obesity. Entitled "Are your friends making you fat?" (Vancouver Sun, 2007, p. E1), this report's answer was that, yes, it seems that they are. Based on social network analyses, the article offered insight into how tacit norms are established and implicit permissions are enacted among friends.

Of course, like any critical reader, I recognized each story to be partial – and my skepticism was no doubt amplified by a culture of caution in the modern academy. We have been trained to watch out for claims of simple causes and singular solutions to complex problems. I thus reacted with a barrage of "What about?" questions. What about increasingly sedentary lifestyles? Accelerating consumption of processed foods laced with high fructose corn syrup? Growing stress and other pressures on emotional health? Permissive and indulgent parenting? Simple overeating?

DOI: 10.4018/978-1-5225-5873-6.ch001

At the same time, I felt destabilized. The pair of articles opened a space of tension for me as I thought about my long-time habit of assuming obesity was almost entirely a psychological issue. Had I been ignorant and cruel in the assumption that responsibility for one's body-mass index rests mainly with the individual? Had a succumbed to the manipulations of a weight-loss industry that had been using pop psychology and cultural mythology to prey on unwitting victims? How much unnecessary emotional distress and unjustified social stigma had been borne by persons carrying extra weight?

The issue of obesity isn't an outlier around such matters, of course. Clearly, it's a phenomenon that is subject to conflicted and potentially damaging reads. But, as a teacher and an educational researcher, I have encountered similar diversities of interpretation – and similar damaging consequences – around perspectives on intelligence, attentiveness, behavior, and personality. In particular, I have vivid memories of a heated staffroom discussion around how I, as a new teacher, should make sense one student's acts of aggressive disinterest in my math class. Opinions ranged from "He's just a bad kid" to "You just need to make the questions more relevant," when the "real" issue unfolded to be a complex mix of physiological and interpersonal matters that had relatively little to do with my classroom.

It might seem that the lesson of such experiences is that we should all embrace complexity. I for one, however, have never been particularly good at doing that. Neither, for that matter, has modern schooling – which, for as long as I've been part of it, has been oscillating between a traditional impulse for standardization and a progressive insistence on personalization. To complicate matters, the past few decades have seen a new tension arise between nurturing the individual psyche and attending to collective ethos.

This context of competing foci has contributed greatly to my interest in efforts to integrate diverse habits of interpretation and disparate claims to truth – that is, to shift the terms of engagement away from the simplistic binary of "fact vs. fiction" and toward such matters as means of deriving truth, modes of representation, intentions of utilizing truths, and strategies to avoid false claims.

Ken Wilber's (1995, 1996, 2000) integral theory is by far the most popular of the genre, and it forms the basis of this discussion. His main strategies for drawing together perspectives and conclusions is to create a matrix by crossing axes that span the continua of "interior–exterior" and "individual–collective." These axes are not offered as actual fault lines of the universe, but rather as perceptual tools that are useful for highlighting how different habits of seeing and different strategies for looking give rise to different sorts of observation. The resulting four-quadrant matrix, along with a sampling of phenomena associated with those quadrants, is illustrated in Figure 1.

Figure 1. The four quadrants of Ken Wilber's Integral Theory

	individual	
	SUBJECTIVE	OBJECTIVE
interior	thoughts, emotions memories, states of mind, perceptions, immediate sensations	material body (including brain), visible and measureable behavior, competencies, skills	exterior
	shared values, meanings, language, relationships, cultural background	systems, networks, technology, government, the economy, the natural environment	
	INTERSUBJECTIVE	INTEROBJECTIVE
	collective	

Given the range of phenomena that falls into the scope of the model, it is perhaps not surprising the one of the most common criticisms of Wilber's Integral Theory is that it aims to be about everything. That assessment isn't entirely fair, as the intention is not to collect all possible phenomena and perspectives into a single box. Rather, the model is better considered as a framework to juxtapose current strategies of looking at a phenomenon. Consider, for example, obesity. When treated as an objective "it" (i.e., placed in the upper right quadrant), obesity might invite attempts to isolate causes and diagnose symptoms aimed at curing it. When located in the intersubjective "we" realm (i.e., in the lower left quadrant), it is a phenomenon that summons considerations of complicity and situatedness – and, as current studies of body shaming would illustrate, actions in response are less about what it is and more about who we are. And so on. Phrased differently, the model is not intended to offer a totalized vision of reality but to reveal partialities and blind spots associated with any claim to truth, while urging consideration of what other perspectives might have to offer.

LOOKING INSIDE THE QUADRANTS

As indicated in Figure 1, Wilber uses pronouns as a shorthand labels for the different categories of phenomena that arise using his "interior–exterior" and "individual–collective" axes.[1] I find his vocabulary useful. However, as an educational researcher, I prefer some minor modifications in terminology. These are presented in Figure 2.

These alternatives aren't offered as refinements or corrections; they are intended merely as phrasings that are fitted to the specific interests and responsibilities of educational researchers. For instance, in place of Wilber's "individual–collective" axis, I find it more useful as a researcher to distinguish between individuality (i.e., associated with those phenomena that tend to be seen as well-bounded and integrated unities) and collectivity (i.e., associated with those phenomena that are seen to arise in the interactions of agents or parts).

Similarly, instead of Wilber's "interior–exterior" axis, I find it more productive to think in terms of a continuum across the sorts of reports that arise, ranging from the mainly empirical to the mainly interpretive. As for the sorts of phenomena that fall into the resulting quadrants, as a researcher my

Figure 2. A re-wording of Wilber's quadrants in terms of key research decisions and prominent epistemologies

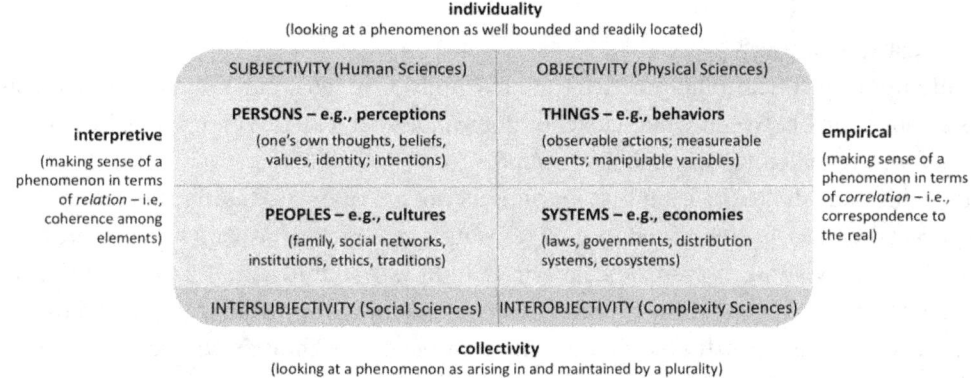

preference is for the more descriptive labels of Things and Systems (instead of "It" and "Its") on the empirical side, and the more inclusive Persons and Peoples (instead of "I" and "We") on the interpretive side. Framing phenomena in terms of Things and Systems involves an objectification – and when objects are researched, there is typically an expectation of empirical description or rational explanation. In a parallel manner, characterizing research interests as Persons or Peoples invokes senses of agency and usually entails a willingness to address muddied and shifting subjective and intersubjective realities; hence the emphases on interpretation at that end of the inquiry spectrum.

As it turns out, within the world of educational research, each of the quadrants can be loosely associated with a distinct science[2] of the modern era. I highlight these alignments in the following brief commentaries on the foci in each of the quadrants.

Things and the Physical Sciences (Upper Right Quadrant, Individuality ∧ Empirical)

One of the most powerful realizations in the modern, humanist era was that almost any phenomenon could be treated as a thing – that is, objectified, or in Wilber's terms, made an "it." Each thingified it – the stone, person, trajectory, collision, logical deduction, or whatever – could then be analyzed and compelled to surrender its secrets through controlled, documented, and replicable interventions using methods developed across the physical sciences and analytic philosophy.

A main purpose of research oriented by this quadrant's sensibilities is predictability. Hence, regarding the interests of educational researchers, the sorts of phenomena that lend themselves to this quadrant's manners of seeing/perceiving and looking/inquiring are those that have some sort of static or stable quality across observations, measures, and/or manipulations. Arguably, there are relatively few such phenomena in the very dynamic and frequently unpredictable spaces of learning – and the list of candidates seems to be dwindling steadily as theories and observations complexify. A century ago, behavior, attention, and intelligence were seen by the establishment to be objectifiable. Today, only sub-elements or highly controlled aspects of these phenomena continue to be seen in this light. Conversely, new vistas have opened that appear to lend themselves to being treated as things – such as, for example, brain activity, conceptual metaphors, and emotional well-being, all of which are objects of study across evolving neuroscientific and physiological methods.

Persons and the Human Sciences (Upper Left Quadrant, Individuality ∧ Interpretive)

Does teaching cause learning?

Much contemporary educational practice (and research) is at least partially based on the assumption that there is a causal link between what a teacher does and what a student learns. A little over a century ago, that belief was revealed to be on shaky ground.

Key to this shift was the realization that learning is not a matter of "taking things in," but of "ongoing construal" – an endlessly iterative dance of refining one's web of associations in order to maintain coherence with one's dynamic circumstances. This insight was shared across a range of new interpretive perspectives, including phenomenology, pragmatism, existentialism, structuralism, and psychoanalysis. Collectively, these domains constituted the first major wave of the "human sciences." Across this movement, "truth" was recast not in terms of empirically derived fact, but more toward the pragmatic "what works." That is, in terms of personal theories of the world, each human derives idiosyncratic truths from a unique pool of experience. The critical feature of those truths is immediate utility, not scientific generalizability. Concisely, everyone makes their own coherent senses of the world – and a person's subjective sense can resiliently defy objective evidence.

Within education, that associated evolution in sensibility might be characterized as a shift in core metaphor from objects to agents. In terms of knowledge and teaching, this shift is enacted as a move away from generalizable, delivery-oriented insights toward specific, actor-oriented strategies. The transition was marked by the emergence of "authentic" and "progressive" educational movements in the 20th century, distinguished by their disdain for standardized practices and their interests in personal engagement, developmental variations, learner differences, and the possibilities afforded by aligning learning with individual curiosities and goals.

Peoples and the Social Sciences (Lower Left Quadrant, Collectivity ∧ Interpretive)

Persons, of course, do not exist in vacuums, but are parts of peoples – that is, families, social circles, cultures, and other collectives. Perhaps oddly, this commonplace realization didn't figure prominently into educational practice or research until about 50 years ago when an array of collectivist-oriented issues pressed into the educational imagination, spurred by various social justice movements, emergent critical discourses, situated theories of learning, and the burgeoning social sciences.

Pivotal in the early stages of this movement was the conviction that "all knowledge is socially constructed." That is, humans live together in shared hallucinations; coherent worlds arise through intricate networks of postulates and inferences. These collective hallucinations carry with them criteria for truths, codes of ethical action, and compelling issues. And, to surprising extents, the critical element in their viability and perpetuation is shared commitment among members, not correspondence to empirical reality … as is especially evident in the current array of world religions.

Among educational researchers, prominent themes of inquiry associated with this quadrant have included interrogation of discourses used to frame identity and to deploy power, strategies around participation and engagement in collective process, and the promotion of social justice.

Systems and the Complexity Sciences (Lower Right Quadrant, Collectivity ∧ Empirical)

One of the unsettling insights to arise among researchers in the social sciences (in the Peoples quadrant) was that, often, human collective action unfolds in manners disturbingly similar to systems involving non-human actors. For instance, studies of settlement patterns show that the invisible rules that govern human intrusion into new territories seem to be indistinguishable from the rules that guide smoke particles as they deposit on a ceiling. Similarly, the rules that operate in traffic jams seem virtually identical to those governing clogged plumbing. There are other disturbing similarities between many human and non-human systems when it comes to such matters as distribution of wealth/resources, establishing member hierarchies, and altruism – despite persistent and pervasive beliefs that such phenomena rely on higher-order thinking skills.

It turns out that the impacts of individuals' higher-order thinking are often washed out in the space of collective action. In such instances, it is frequently useful to think in terms of "systems" – that is, in terms of phenomena interacting with phenomena, potentially giving rise to emergent systems that exhibit new, transcendent properties and behaviors that are not manifest in parts or agents on their own.

Among educational researchers, systems-based investigations have proven useful for examining the roles and impacts of governing policies, resource distribution, and other structures that operate without a centralized controller or operator. The category also includes biological systems – indeed, any phenomenon that might be productively understood through ecosystemic metaphors.

LOOKING BETWEEN THE QUADRANTS

While tables and grids can serve as powerful conceptual tools, they carry an inherent risk, especially when employed as a principal visual metaphor in a theory that aims to integrate diverse perspectives. Well-defined lines, grids, and regions might support an impression that distinctions are imagined to be real and stable.

As already emphasized, distinctions offered by the Integral model are better considered perceptual tools than actual fault lines. That is, within the model, each border between quadrants should be understood as a hazy and shifting heuristic convenience rather than dividing line. In this context, a border is as much a connection as a separation. With this point in mind, I turn now to the specific meanings and implications of each of the four borders that arises in the Integral model. Key aspects of these borders are summarized in Figure 3, and more detailed discussions follow.

The Border Between Right ("Empirical") Quadrants: Things and Systems

The quadrants on the right share what might be called "an obligation to physical evidence." Hence their associations with forms of objectivity – that is, with evidence, with an assumption of stable laws that govern phenomena, and with explanations that are rooted in those laws.

In practical terms, the border between the two quadrants on the right side has to do with whether a phenomenon under study is reducible or irreducible. The Upper Right quadrant is concerned with those phenomena that can be decomposed to fundamental parts that are governed by fundamental laws. Typically assumed to obey the laws of physics, these phenomena are viewed as inherently decomposable and

Figure 3. Some of the key distinctions between adjacent quadrants

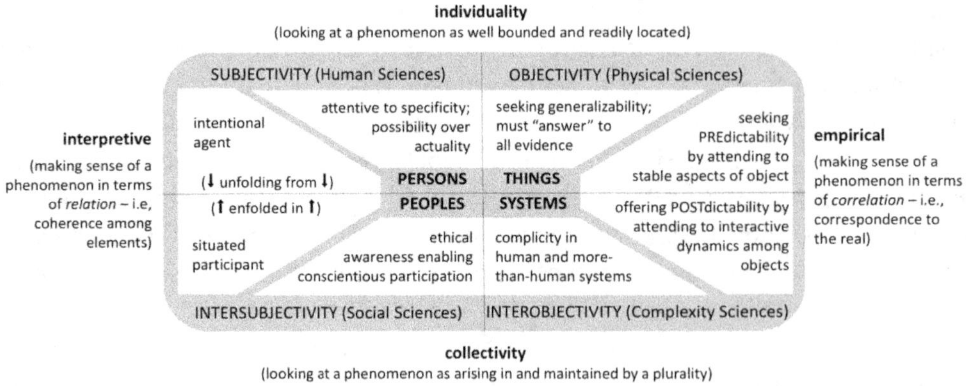

predictable. That is, a sufficiently accurate set of measurements at a given instant, coupled to a sufficient understanding of the relevant laws, should enable an observer to anticipate what will happen next with confidence – at least to within the limitations of measurement tools and acceptable margins of error. The sensibility at work here is evident in the word statistics, which derives from the Greek *statikos*, "causing to stand, hold still." Having a thorough knowledge at one, still instant is sufficient for knowing what will unfold in subsequent instants.

The Lower Right quadrant also embraces the use of statistics, but in a very different sense and for very different purposes. Oriented more by Darwinian dynamics than Newtonian mechanics, in this case observations and measurements are combined to afford vibrant renderings of systems rather than static portraits of things. These systems often defy predictability, largely because they "learn." Just because they behaved one way in the past doesn't mean they'll behave the same way in the future. That said, these systems are still constrained by laws of the universe – and so, while they may not be predictable (literally: "able to say before"), they are usually postdictable (i.e., "able to say after"). That is, they are comprehensible, but not in the manner that meshes with the traditional schooling's desire for control.

The Border Between Left ("Interpretive") Quadrants: Persons and Peoples

In contrast to the Right quadrants and their obligation to observable and measurable happenings, truths associated with Left quadrants do not need to be anchored to any objective reality. Rather, personal, social, and cultural truths are typically sustained in the face of contrary evidence and often even when the agent's or group's very existence is at risk. What matters most is not a match to physical reality but coherence within a web of contruals.

On this count, the border between the two quadrants on the left signals a complementarity. Peoples (i.e., Lower Left) are recognized to unfold from and be enfolded in Persons (i.e., Upper Left). Thus, the individual is seen as a situated participant in a grander whole through the lenses of the Lower Left quadrant, and more as a self-defined intentional agent through the lenses of the Upper Left. Phrased differently, the Upper Left quadrant is concerned more with individuals' construals of reality, and so is anchored to idiosyncratic experiences and concerned with personal identity, choice, and so on. The Lower Left quadrant is associated with collective realities and distributed knowledge, articulated in concerns with collaborative action and shared situations.

The Border Between Upper ("Individuality") Quadrants: Persons and Things

With regard to phenomena associated with the two upper quadrants, there is a tendency to see them in isolated, self-contained, and well-defined terms. In the Upper Right quadrant, Things are seen in terms of themselves, not as elements in grander systems. In the Upper Left, Persons are regarded as coherent (or, at least, coherence-seeking) unities, not as agents in grander social systems or representatives of cultural systems. To be clear, however, the suggestion is not that objects and psyches are regarded as hermetically sealed, independent forms; it is simply that they are often regarded, typically engaged, and usually studied as well-bounded, non-overlapping phenomena.

That said, the border between the two quadrants is strongly reflective of the contrast between Traditional (Standardized) and Progressive (Authentic) Education. In the Upper Right quadrant, which might be aligned with Traditional sensibilities, the emphasis is on actuality, generalizable samenesses, and correlations between causes and effects. In the Upper Left, more fitted to Progressive Education, the emphasis is on possibility, difference, and the inevitability of idiosyncratic interpretation.

Given the prominence of this contrast in contemporary educational thought, it's worth pausing for a moment to reflect on the way that such tensions can sometimes occupy the collective imagination. The Traditional–Progressive (or Standardized–Authentic) dichotomy is often presented as spanning the full spectrum of educational possibility – when, in fact, it is indicative of only one strip that runs across the much broader landscape of educational thought.

The Border Between Lower ("Collectivity") Quadrants: Peoples and Systems

Anyone wanting to make sense of the major developments in educational thought over the past few decades would be well advised to look at the phenomena and discourses associated with the Lower quadrants. These are the homes of emerging interests into the situated, distributed, shared, embedded, nested, systemic, and ecosystemic aspects of education.

Even with those shared interests, however, the border that sits between the lower quadrants is as substantial as the one that marks the separation of the upper quadrants. The focus in the Lower Left quadrant is on intersubjective phenomena – that is, those phenomena that arise in and are amplified through habits of interpretation. Its major themes since the 1970s have included race, culture, gender, and social class. Around these matters, it is argued, we must see ourselves as not as passive or powerless observers, but as conscientious participants capable of effecting change through new ways of making sense of things.

In contrast, the focus in the Lower Right quadrant is on interobjective phenomena – that is, nested, overlapping, and interlacing systems that may include us, but that most often transcend us. As exemplified by efforts to respond to climate change, species decline, ocean acidification, and so many other happenings in more-than-human systems, we humans are prone to categorical errors in this quadrant – thinking, for example, that personals acts of driving less, changing lightbulbs, and choosing paper grocery bags are somehow appropriate responses.

They're not. Rather, they are indicative of categorical errors. The crises mentioned in the previous paragraph are problems that have arisen on the levels of nation-states and the species, and so responses that operate on individual and social levels simply can't come close to addressing them. In contrast, action on the cultural level – such as formal schooling – are more fitting. They are matters to be taken up at the systemic level, cutting to the core of what schooling is all about.

It would be an understatement to say that formal education has not yet found its way into such issues. The current educational system simply doesn't know how to think or act in the spaces articulated by the Lower Left quadrant.

LINKING RESEARCH INTERESTS AND ATTITUDES TO RESEARCH METHODOLOGIES

Early in my academic career, I was assigned to teach a graduate-level course on research methods that had been designed by someone else. I still recall the spike in anxiety as I read through its standardized outline. Following a methodology-of-the-week format, students were expected to tour through a dozen perspectives through self-contained introductions to phenomenology, survey research, case studies, hermeneutics, quasi-experimental investigations, ethnography, narrative inquiry, and so on. Moreover, although novices to educational research, they were expected to take principal responsibility for these introductions. To boot, the culminating assignment was a "protoproposal" through which participants were to demonstrate abilities to integrate research interests and methodological traditions.

I smelled disaster. How, exactly, were novice researchers supposed to move from a disjointed smorgasbord of perspectives to well-designed inquiries?

Thankfully, just before the term started I chanced to have lunch with a colleague in another faculty (Social Work) who had been assigned a similar course. Her approach was not to focus on methodologies, but on categories of phenomena and research interests that "called forth" different strategies for investigation. Introducing me to Integral Methodological Pluralism (IMP; Wilber, 2006; Esbjörn-Hargens, 2009), she explained how she was able to teach a course that – she claimed – not only offered students a more integrated overview of the methodological landscape, but that helped course participants appreciate how their particular interests aligned with different academic traditions and research sensibilities.

Key to IMP is the realization that not only are multiple categories of phenomena (i.e., Things, Persons, Peoples, and Systems), there are distinct positionings for examining them. Each can be looked at from the inside or from the outside. I summarize these positionings in Figure 4, signifying inward-looking perspectives with a mirror icon and outward-looking attitudes with a magnifying glass icon.

Upper Right, Studying Things: Logic/Argument and Experiment/Measurement

The classical distinction between research attitudes in the modern era is between argument-driven, inward-looking rationalism and evidence-seeking, outward-looking empiricism. The former is obligated to deduction, using impeachable logic to knit ever-more-sophisticated truths from foundational premises. The latter is obligated to evidence, operating from standards of repeatable experiments that give stable and generalizable results.

In my undergraduate studies in the sciences, rationalism was exemplified by mathematics and empiricism by physics. While I can't claim that any of my professors ever asserted this to be case, my sense was that the complementary pair was assumed to mark the boundaries of all respectable research. Good inquiry, that is, could be driven by either compelling argument or rigorous experimentation. Ultimately, when enough was known about the phenomenon at hand, rational and empirical approaches would mesh around a logical account of observed evidence. As noted in a previous section, a few centuries ago it

Figure 4. Fitting foci of studies to 8 regions of research methodologies

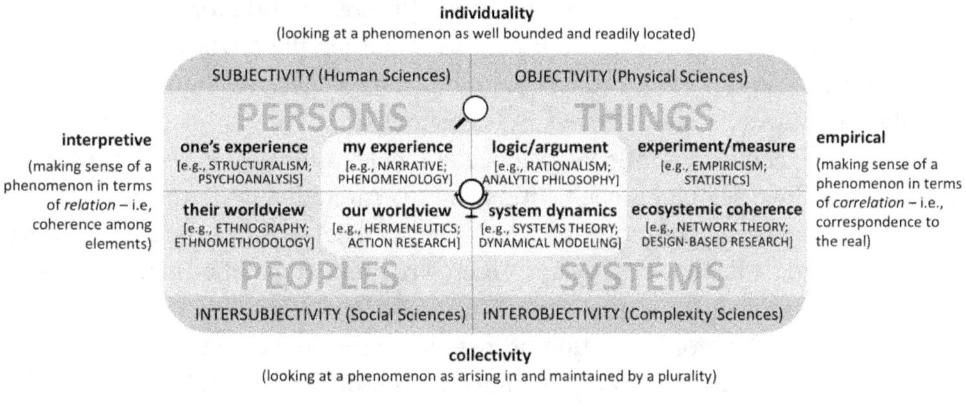

was assumed that all phenomena would eventually surrender to this logico-scientific attitude. Indeed, the belief persists in many domains.

At present, most examples of this sensibility within educational research are associated with neuroscience and behavioral psychology, with important insights emerging around, for example, brain plasticity, neural function, cognitive load, different memory systems, extrinsic and intrinsic motivations, learner diversity, and personal agency. At classroom levels, quasi-experimental approaches have afforded important insights into task structures, feedback strategies, and interpersonal dynamics. On larger scales, survey approaches and other statistics-based strategies have been effective helping develop policies that are attentive to but not constrained by public belief and opinion. Things start to get more dubious at grander scales, however, as might be exemplified by high-stakes international comparison testing that generate much interest but uneven or non-existent correlations with standards of living, human rights, general well-being, opportunity, and other matters of vital human interest.

The list goes on. What is essential, however, is a conceptual commitment interpreting the phenomenon at hand in terms of a stable, objectifiable Thing. If that metaphoric frame can be assumed, then logical and/or experimental methods are a fit.

Upper Left, Studying Persons: My Experience and One's Experience

With its focus on Persons, it would be reasonable to conclude that the Upper Left quadrant is the domain of psychology. And, indeed, the mid-20th-century break of developmental and cognitive psychologies from more empirical behavioral and experimental psychologies would support that perception. But, in fact, the methods and emphases that most define this quadrant come from outside psychology proper. They are rooted in domains that arose in large part as critiques of or responses to the highly empirical leanings of psychology in the late 1800s and early 1900s, including European structuralism and North American pragmatism.

A persistent "problem" with schooling was a major motivator of these critiques. In the early 1900s, as educational research became more systematic, more and more commentators began to state what is now obvious: students who are subjected to virtually identical learning circumstances inevitably learn very different things at very different rates – even when those students are of similar ages, have similar interests and abilities, and come from very similar backgrounds. That is, standardized teaching in no way correlates to standardized results.

The tools to make sense of this phenomenon were found in evolutionary biology, as Piaget and others offered accounts of learning in terms of construing coherence of personal experiences rather than the commonsensical-but-indefensible "taking things in." It took a while for the notion to take hold in educational research, but it emerged as the dominant sensibility in the 1970s and 1980s with the rise of (radical) constructivism, theories of embodied cognition, and perspectives informed by psychoanalysis. Methodologically, this research was oriented by structuralism, as investigators focused on different categories of experience, contexts, subtle variation, and other influences on personal sense-making.

It was also informed by research into perception and interpretation undertaken by 20th-century phenomenologists, who offered a methodology that enabled researchers to interrogate their own experiences and habits of interpretation. Phenomenology also figured prominently in the emergence of narrative and autobiographical methods that arose in the late-20th century.

Perhaps to be expected, the rapid evolution of methodologies in the Upper Left "persons" quadrant has helped to open research into personal growth and empowerment, including topics associated with grit, resilience, positive psychology, flow theory, fixed/growth mindset, and meditative practices such as mindfulness.

Lower Left, Studying Peoples: Our Worldview and Their Worldview

It may seem odd, but it has only been over the last half-century or so that investigations of schooling as a social and cultural institution began to figure prominently into educational research. The shift was at least in part supported by the co-entangled rises of the social sciences and cultural studies in academia, of critical perspectives in the media, and of human rights movements in the public sphere.

The major methodological influence in this quadrant was inward-looking hermeneutics, which might be roughly defined as the coupled study of what we believe and why we believe it. Hermeneutics arrived in several guises, including critical theory and critical pedagogy, which focused gazes on mythologies of schooling, especially around matters of race, class, and gender.

Outward-looking ethnographic methods were taken up at the same time, initially used to examine the cultures of classrooms, schools, and communities, and more recently adapted in comparisons of educational attitudes across religions and nations.

Educational researchers with interests that land in the Lower Left quadrant have also adopted and adapted methodologies from literary theory, linguistics, political science, economics, and other social science domains. Typically employing elements from both hermeneutics and ethnography, some of these approaches also intersect with the Upper Left (e.g., autoethnography) and Upper Right (e.g., value-added theory) quadrants.

Lower Right, Studying Systems: System Dynamics and Ecosystemic Coherence

As already mentioned, formal education hasn't figured out what to do with systems-based research, and that might help to explain why educational research lags behind most other academic domains in its embrace of complexity science, ecology, and related discourses.

That lag may be tethered to the inherently conservative nature of public schooling, a cultural project that almost always seems to chase rather than lead societal evolution. Consequently, investigations informed by ecological, systems, and complexity theories have tended to unfold on the fringes of current educational research. Nevertheless, the past decade has seen sharp increases in systems-informed studies of classrooms, schools, curricula, and school districts, as well as explosive interest in design-based research, a methodology rooted in complexity sensibilities.

COUPLING METHODOLOGY TO INTENTION

The previous section dealt with clusters of methodologies as they nest within different categories and modes of interpreting phenomena of relevance to formal education. Absent in that discussion was consideration of the sorts of intention that might be driving research. Three distinct and fairly obvious levels of intention within educational research come to mind:

- **Description/Exploration:** What is this? What's going on?

- **Explanation/Analysis:** Why is this happening?
- **Intervention/Activism:** What might be done?

I've represented these levels in Figure 5, which is intended as a sort of overlay for Figure 4. Each of the eight methodological attitudes flagged in Figure 4 might be engaged with any of the above intentions. While these intentions need not unfold in sequence, it turns out that they usually do.

For example, within my home domain of mathematics education, a prominent (and for an extended period, the dominant) topic of inquiry over the past 40 years has been the relationship between teachers' disciplinary knowledge and student learning. The first 20 years of research was concerned with finding some sort of relationship between the two constructs, which proved worrisomely elusive. Then, in the late 1990s, the emphasis shifted to explanation as investigators realized that sorts of mathematical expertise needed by teachers is distinct from the expertise of mathematicians, engineers, and others. More recently, over the past decade or so, the emphasis has shifted to interventions, through such efforts as structuring courses for teachers and studying their impacts on teaching practices.

Significantly, and tying back to the previous section, differences in intention do not necessarily entail shifts in methodology. For instance, an ethnographic study of a school culture might just as well be focused on characterizing what's going on as seeking to better understand the interpersonal and social dynamics that drive an observed phenomenon.

CRITERIA FOR CLAIMS TO TRUTH

How is the truthfulness of a claim assessed?

It sometimes seems that the only researchers to have figured this out reside in the Upper Right Things quadrant. And that makes sense insofar as "truth" is understood as an object that is portable and that lasts – in which case measures of validity, reliability, and the other standards of the physical sciences are all that are needed. However, the truths associated with the other quadrants are typically more situation-dependent and can have quite limited shelf lives. How might one judge the claims emerging from these quadrants?

Figure 5. Levels of intention in educational research

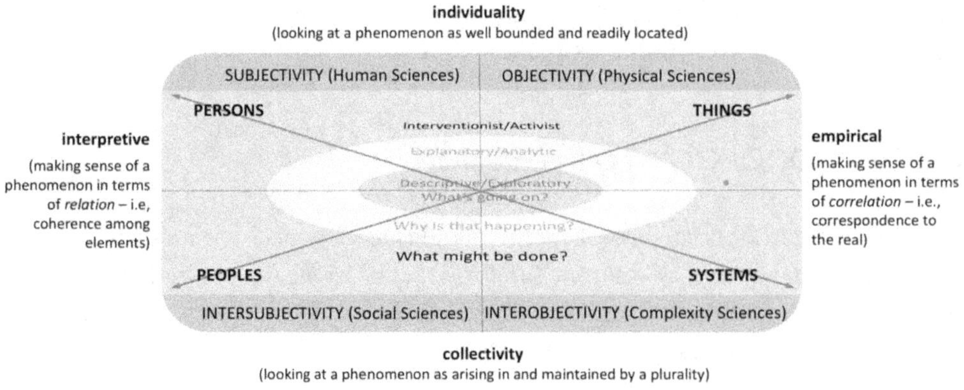

Figure 6. Some criteria for claims to truth

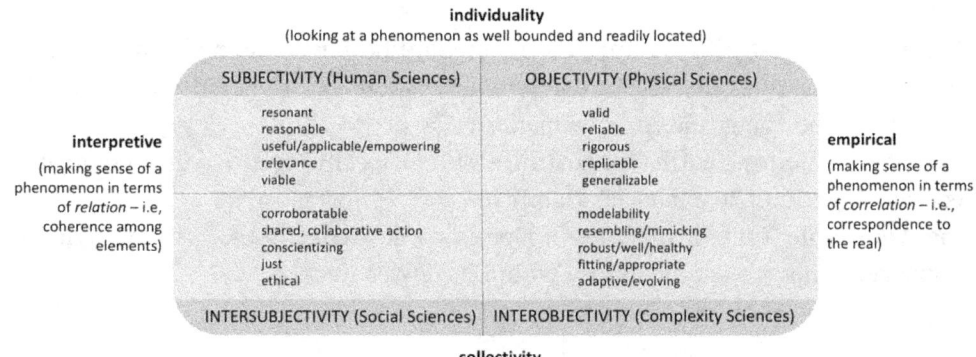

The answers aren't settled here. What is apparent is that criteria vary from phenomenon to phenomenon and from methodology to methodology. At the risk of oversimplifying current discussions and debates, I have collected some quadrant-specific criteria in Figure 6, and elaborate some them below.

Truths About Things:

- **Valid:** The research investigating what it claims to be studying?
- **Reliable:** The same result obtained when the methods are repeated?
- **Generalizable:** The result applicable beyond the specific conditions under which it was obtained?

Truths About Persons:

- **Viable/Relevant:** The claim perceptible and coherent? Does it make sense within the subject's world of experience? Does the claim matter to the person?
- **Credible/Resonant:** Does the claim "feel" right? Does it occasion reflection or provoke new or deeper insight?
- **Useful/Empowering:** Does the claim enable the person to do something that wasn't previously doable? Does it expand the space of the possible?

Truths About Peoples:

- **Corroboratable and Coherent:** Do others support the insight? It is consistent with the circumstances, the traditions, the technologies, etc.?
- **Activating:** Does the insight support and motivate shared, collaborative action, especially action toward improving circumstances of work/community/existence?
- **Conscientizing:** Does the insight help to raise awarenesses of circumstances? Does it trigger awarenesses of self-limiting biases among participants? Does it prompt thinking/acting in more ethical and just ways?

Truths About Systems:

- **Model-Ability/Mimic-Ability/Manipulability:** Can the phenomenon be modeled? Once modeled, and governing rules discerned, can similar systems be triggered into being? Can they be manipulated by modifying rules or information?
- **Robustness/Well-Being/Health (Inward Fitness):** Does knowledge of the system and/or the system's ecology contribute to enhanced viability?
- **Evolving/Adaptable (Outward Fitness):** Does the knowledge of the system's dynamics contribute to enhanced fitness to and flexibility within its environment?

METHODOLOGICAL PLURALISM

The preceding discussions underscore that there are many species of knowledge and truth in formal education. Consequently, the teacher and the educational researcher must be able to assume and mediate multiple perspectives. There are few situations in the life of an educator in which singular truths can operate.

This sensibility is now well represented in the educational research literature. Unfortunately, it has been operationalized less well. For example, it is most commonly enacted as "mixed methods" or "multi-method" research, through which both "quantitative and qualitative" data are gathered.

As a researcher devoted to methodological pluralism, I confess to being horrified at how frequently I encounter the qualitative/quantitative distinction. Far from indicating an enlightened view, I see the pervasive belief that research is made better by complementing counts and measures with descriptions as embodying a profound methodological ignorance. Indeed, from where I sit, arguably the most important contribution of IMP to educational research is its demonstration of the conceptual vacuum that surrounds the qualitative/quantitative dichotomy.

The matter doesn't end there, however, as there are many ways to enact a methodological pluralism. To this point, in our work with graduate students whose research involves multiple perspectives, Veronika Bohač Clarke and I have noticed four distinct attitudes: disciplinarity, crossdisciplinarity, interdisciplinarity, and transdisciplinarity.

Disciplinarity: Quadrant, Disciplinary, and Methodological Absolutism

We define disciplinarity as a tendency to frame or interpret any and all phenomena through the lenses of just one quadrant. Most often that quadrant is the Upper Right, and the attitude is signaled by a demand for scientific rigor or an insistence that dyads such as "quantitative vs. qualitative," "subjective vs. objective," and "theory vs. practice" are hard and fast dichotomies (as opposed to, say, complementarities).

That said, we have also encountered people whose lenses are drawn from only the Upper Left and/or Lower Left quadrants. The strongest marker of the former is a relativistic attitude, accompanied by an avowal that nothing trumps one's personal truths. The latter is often articulated as some variation of "All knowledge is socially constructed."

More subtly, rigid disciplinary attitudes tend to show up as impulses to criticize and reject rather to listen and engage. For example, when interpretations of a phenomenon from outside one's discipline are offered, the disciplinarian might meet them with questions of the "How is this wrong?" variety, rather than more open-minded queries, such as "How is this right?" or "What might I have to learn here?"

Crossdisciplinarity: Quadrant, Disciplinary, and Methodological Centrism

Admittedly, we don't encounter very many rigid disciplinarians in the field of education. Grappling as educators must with so many sorts of truth, such a narrow approach is not just difficult to maintain; it's utterly impractical.

More common is a willingness to acknowledge the relevance and viability of other perspectives and interpretations, but that comes with a tendency to reframe those insights through the lens of a preferred discipline or quadrant. This habit is often accompanied by an inability (or perhaps reluctance) to move far afield from the sorts of insights that are typical of the preferred frame.

In practical terms, crossdisciplinary attitudes tend to show up as a limited openness. Instead of the disciplinarian's skeptical "How is this wrong?", the crossdisciplinarian's questions tend more toward "How might this add?", "How can I use this?", or "Does this align with what I am learning?" There is a reluctance to leave home, but there is a willingness to consider and learn from what's going on in neighbors' yards.

Interdisciplinarity: Quadrant, Disciplinary, and Methodological Integration

For beginning researchers, one of the common consequences of disciplinary and crossdisciplinary attitudes is that questions and interests are often forced to fit familiar frames and methods. Such tendencies begin to ease with the emergence of more interdisciplinary attitudes.

The interdisciplinarian may continue to identify strongly with home disciplines or domains, but this identification is mitigated by an awareness of the epistemological constraints of any single perspective. The researcher becomes more conscious and mindful of the inevitability of perspectival biases, which is usually articulated not just as a willingness to situate research interests in other domains but a realization that other sensibilities must be engaged for nuanced understandings.

Such realizations don't necessarily translate into direct personal engagement with other perspectives and methodologies, however. A strong identification with one's home quadrant is often maintained, most often explained or rationalized in terms of needs for theoretical depth and/or methodological expertise. It's thus typical for researchers at this stage to draw on insights and embrace challenges from other perspectives, but unusual for them to engage directly or extensively with perspectives or strategies from other domains.

Transdisciplinarity: Quadrant, Disciplinary, and Methodological Pluralism

Arguably, the best any one person can do is to be interdisciplinary, at least in the individualistic world of graduate studies. In the grander research world, however, there is ample opportunity – and, arguably, abundant obligation – to adopt a transdisciplinary attitude.

Most commonly, transdisciplinarity is defined it terms of teams of disciplinary experts who come together around a common problem or concern (cf. Choi & Pak, 2006). This attitude entails multi-perspectival interpretations of the phenomenon at hand, whereby different perspectives and strategies are engaged simply because it makes no sense to do otherwise.

To be clear, it is impossible for an individual to be transdisciplinary. True transdisciplinarity is based on deep expertise across many domains, and so it requires a team. What can be developed on the individual level, however, are nuanced appreciations of where others are coming from, the possibilities that can arise through joint inquiry, and a humility in one's own contributions to such shared efforts.

EDUCATIONAL RESEARCH AND METHODOLOGICAL PLURALISM

For reasons that aren't entirely clear even to me, ever since encountering those two articles on obesity (that were mentioned at the start of the chapter), my antennae have been up for other news on the topic. Most recently, I've noticed a spate of reports on Lower Right Systems takes on the obesity epidemic. Nation's health care systems and entire economies are beginning to creak under the strain of excess body weight; toxins and stimulants that humans have let seep into the more-than-human world may be playing unanticipated roles in triggering or blocking physiological impulses and other biologically based mechanisms; some appetite suppressants and artificial sweeteners may be having the opposite of their desired effects as they interrupt gut flora, signaling systems, and other of the body's complex subsystems; thought-to-be "nutritional" foods may be contributing to the problem, in large part because they may not be all they're cracked up to be when recent human evolution is taken into consideration. The list goes on.

Against this backdrop, no one needs to argue for the utility and relevance of transdisciplinarity and methodological pluralism. It clearly makes no sense to think otherwise. Yet, even though the array of issues and concerns within education is at least comparable to those that surround obesity, calls for transdisciplinarity and methodological pluralism are not especially common among educational researchers. In fact, across my three decades of experience, I've encountered consistent calls in only two domains: curriculum studies and the learning sciences.

Perhaps that should be expected. For its entire history, educational research has drawn most of its foci, frames, and methods from other domains, as evidenced in the habit of labeling areas of educational research by tagging the word "educational" onto the names of other fields (e.g., educational psychology, educational philosophy, educational leadership). Curriculum studies and learning sciences are exceptions to this rule. They are home grown; they have arisen among and are focused on phenomena that are of specific interest to educators.

It would be inappropriate to extrapolate from that subjective observation to a recommendation for collective action. At the same time, I feel it would be inappropriate not to suggest that educational researchers' entrenched habit of borrowing from other domains might not be complemented by looking as much in the mirror as through the window.

To illustrate this point, and to sum up the discussion, a few years ago I participated in a research collective that sought to better understand how "spatial reasoning" was being studied within and across different disciplines (Bruce et al., 2017). Among our many findings, it was noticed that (1) spatial reasoning was a prominent focus of research in many domains, (2) educational researchers were aware of and drawing extensively from those domains, and (3) none of those domains seemed to be aware of or attending to the synthesizing efforts and substantial results of educational researchers.

We were initially taken aback, even offended, until we paused to consider the location of educational research in the grander landscape of academic inquiry. Our domain is a nexus. Unlike colleagues in many other disciplines, we rarely have the luxury of a narrow focus and a single methodology. As educational researchers, we have an obligation toward and an opportunity for methodological pluralism, and this need+possibility should be a core topic of discussion from the beginnings of programs designed to initiate new participants into the domain. Educational research is not a physical, human, social, or complexity science. It is an integral research domain.

REFERENCES

Bruce, C., Davis, B., Sinclair, N., McGarvey, L., Hallowell, D., Drefs, M., ... Woolcott, G. (2017). Understanding gaps in research networks: Using "spatial reasoning" as a window into the importance of networked educational research. *Educational Studies in Mathematics, 95*(2), 143–161. doi:10.100710649-016-9743-2

Choi, B. C., & Pak, A. W. (2006). Multidisciplinarity, interdisciplinarity and transdisciplinarity in health research, services, education and policy: 1. Definitions, objectives, and evidence of effectiveness. *Clinical and Investigative Medicine. Medecine Clinique et Experimentale, 29*(6), 351–364. PMID:17330451

Esbjörn-Hargens, S. (2008). Integral ecological research: Using IMP to examine animals and sustainability. *Journal of Integral Theory and Practice, 3*(1), 15–60.

Wilber, K. (1995). *Sex, ecology, spirituality*. Boston, MA: Shambhala.

Wilber, K. (1996). *A brief history of everything*. Boston, MA: Shambhala.

Wilber, K. (2000). *Integral psychology: Consciousness, spirit, psychology, therapy*. Boston, MA: Shambhala.

Wilber, K. (2006). Integral Methodological Pluralism. In *Integral spirituality: A startling new role for religion in the modern and post-modern world*. Boston, MA: Shambhala.

KEY TERMS AND DEFINITIONS

Complexity Sciences: Those domains of inquiry that are focused on *learning systems* – that is, forms and phenomena that are self-organizing, self-referencing, self-maintaining, and dynamically coupled (i.e., shaping and being shaped by) their situations/contexts.

Crossdisciplinarity (Methodological Centrism): A research attitude exemplified by a tendency to frame research strategies and insights through the lens of a single academic attitude or domain, but tempered by an openness to complementary strategies and insights from other perspectives.

Disciplinarity (Methodological Absolutism): A research attitude exemplified by a tendency to frame or interpret phenomena through the lenses of a single academic attitude or domain.

Human Sciences: Those branches of inquiry that are focused on phenomena associated with individuals, with particular emphasis on perception, cognition, and consciousness.

Interdisciplinarity (Methodological Integration): A research attitude exemplified by a strong alignment with a single academic domain, coupled with active incorporation of methods and insights from other domains in an effort to develop more nuanced insights and to mitigate possible perspectival bias.

Physical Sciences: Typified by physics and chemistry, domains of inquiry associated with an attitude and approach to knowledge generation that is particularly well fitted to mechanical phenomena and that is oriented by expectations of predictability and replicability.

Social Sciences: Those branches of inquiry that are focused on cultures and societies, typically founded on the rejection of an individual/collective dichotomy.

Transdisciplinarity (Methodological Pluralism): A research approach in which teams of disciplinary experts combine their diverse perspectives, methods, and domain knowledge to address a common problem or concern.

ENDNOTES

[1] This chapter is organized around a number of distinctions, none of which are radical dichotomies. To signal the sort of distinction being made, I use three different notations: –, |, v. The horizontal bar (–) signifies a continuum, highlighting shades of gray between poles. The logical "and" (Λ) signifies the intersection of two emphases in thinking. The vertical bar (|) points to border-defining qualities between mostly similar attitudes. The plus sign (+) points to a combining of categories of interest or research foci.

[2] In the conceptualization stages of this chapter, I used the word *epistemology* rather than *science* in this section. While I do not consider the words synonymous, I have opted for the latter for reasons explicated in Davis, Sumara, and Luce-Kapler (2015).

Chapter 2
Integral Meta-Impact:
Integral Theory and Applying It With Meta-Theory Methodology for Validation, Dynamic Insight, and Effectiveness

Simon Divecha
The University of Adelaide, Australia

ABSTRACT

Integral theory presents as a theory of everything. As such, how do we validate its use while applying it as a methodology and investigating its blind spots? Meta-theory methodology can authenticate integral theory and provides a check on its comprehensiveness. The methodology draws on relevant mid-range theories and integral theory (a meta-theory itself) to refine and justify a study's methods while simultaneously applying theory to specific research. This rigor creates clarity and insight. Complex issues—for example, the concept of sustainability that illustrates this chapter—are characterized by many different (mid to meta, conceptual to applied) theoretical approaches. Meta-theory methodology assists to sift these, highlight critical points, and realize integral theory's promise.

1. INTRODUCTION

There is no doubt that we are now in a state of global emergency. This unprecedented worldwide crisis is a symptom of a much deeper problem: the current state of our consciousness; how we think about ourselves and our world. We have the urgent need, and now the opportunity for a complete rethink ... Ervin Laszlo and David Woolfson in Thomas Berry, Dreamer of the earth (2011)

Ken Wilber ... highlighted how serendipitous it is that integral frameworks are emerging at the same time that humanity is being confronted with complex issues like climate change... it is no mere coincidence that such post-national problems are arising at the same time that integrative approaches are being developed to provide global solutions. Sean Esbjörn-Hargens, Executive editor introduction, Volume 5(1) Journal of Integral Theory and Practice (2010a)

DOI: 10.4018/978-1-5225-5873-6.ch002

Integral theory (Wilber, 2000a, 2005), sometimes referred to more formally as an *all quadrants, all levels* (AQAL) framework, is a prominent foundation for research. Practitioners are attracted by its ability to map and model an understanding across broad, wide-ranging and divergent fields. It promises to assist in navigating the complexity. As a '*Theory of Everything*' (Wilber, 2000b) it has significant appeal as it appears suited to multi-scale scopes and disparate perspectives that difficult and important topics (such as sustainability) can present. Additionally, it helps to identify suitable research approaches (Esbjörn-Hargens, 2010b; Marshall, 2012).

A theory of everything has obvious relevance across society. It may address the full spread of our human, ecological, organisational, social, political, cultural, ethical, historical and future development, transformation capacity-potentials and present awareness issues at play around priority areas of concern. Consequently, integral theory investigation has broad appeal for any field that is characterised by our own and other's perspectives, alongside cultural-style influences and shared unconscious biases, as well as (often) more obvious economic or scientific drivers as significant and important influences. The Integral theory section (1.4) of this introduction outlines the theory and its widespread use.

Despite the appeal of integral theory, it presents something of a conundrum. If the theory is comprehensive and we are using it for the insights and clarity it provides how can we simultaneously check its validity? The very appearance of completeness could mask bias or analytical blind spots.

1.1. Methodology Outline

This chapter is a structure to deal with multiple theories, meta-theory (including integral) and a meta-theory methodology. It outlines: 1) The promise of integral theory 2) A validation framework 3) Meta-theory methodology for application and research 4) Illustrates utilisation. The chapter's structure is:

- The next section 1.2 Theory and meta-theory sets the framework for the usefulness of these analytical approaches.
- The 1.3 Meta-theory section provides a short definition of this type of theory and its usefulness.
- Section 1.4 Integral theory overview is an outline of integral and its applications.
- Section 1.5 A sustainability case is a practical short example. This multifaceted concept - many theoretical and practical approaches can be applied to it - is used to illustrate the whole chapter.

The Meta-theory methodology section (2) sets out how to systematically undertake analysis and validation:

- Section 2.1 Building meta-theory and 2.2 Meta-theory development and testing outline the framework's first steps.
- Section 2.3 Summary and application into integral theory describes the process of applying the review from the previous steps.

Section 3 Discussion considers how meta-theory methodology can assist a researcher:

- 3.1 Integral on integral considers how an integral framework alongside meta-theory can deepen analysis and support conclusions drawn from these analytical processes.

- The 3.2 Integral time triangulation section outlines a process to strengthen analysis over the time taken to do the research.
- The final meta-theory methodology phase – see Discussion and Conclusions (sections 3 and 4) – considers how results apply and theory changes or is built from this process.

The Conclusion section draws together arguments for these approaches.

1.2. Theory and Meta-Theory

Theory offers promise to deliver from three broad perspectives. Firstly, theory provides a framework for analysis to more readily compare differences of opinion and clarify the relative benefits of different approaches. Secondly, theory can help us use methods that are more efficient and reduce errors when we try to solve problems – by building on current theory. Through developing or refining a single integrated body of knowledge we are able to more clearly differentiate between competing (or seemingly mutually exclusive) theories. Thirdly, theory can provide clear explanations to use in practice – good theory advances our knowledge. It focuses research and investigation on critical questions and creates understanding (Van de Ven, 1989; Wacker, 1998). Meta-theory has a role across all three of these areas and particularly number two.

1.3. Meta-Theory

Meta-theory, as the name implies, means abstracting theory from examining other theories and models, looking for the synergies, conflicts and generalities to develop a holistic overarching framework. It can help to synthesise, structure knowledge, control for biases and place mid-range theory in a wider context (Edwards, 2009, p. 39; Finfgeld, 2003; Paterson & Canam, 2001, pp. 91-95). It can assist us to navigate and prioritise, clarify and resolve sources of bias and create options for action – ultimately aiding us to improve worldwide conditions (Edwards, 2009; Taylor, Irvin, & Wieland, 2006; Wallis, 2010). Integral theory, introduced below, illustrates this process.

1.4. Integral Theory Overview

Ken Wilber (2000c, 2005) argues that the sum of human knowledge can be used to find critically essential keys to explain physical, psychological and metaphysical realms and that a composite map of such knowledge can "turn out to be surprisingly simple and elegant" (Wilber, 2007, p. 16). Wilber calls the resulting map Integral Theory. Integral theory encompasses the growth and evolution of today's society from both individual and group perspectives. It holds that for any given phenomena there are four quadrants – individual and collective mapped over subjective and objective. Development can occur in stages across each of these quadrants, for different aspects of any whole (lines) and transitory states (e.g. conscious and unconscious), along with enduring types (e.g. Myers-Briggs personality style), completing the picture. Integral theory proposes that these 5 elements – quadrants, levels, lines, states and types – can be used across human issues (Wilber, 2000a, 2000c, 2005).

Integral theory explicitly sets out a core focus on valuing both subjective and objective perspectives (Ballard et al., 2010; Slaughter, 2002). Its acronym AQAL encompasses all quadrants and all levels plus all lines, states and types concepts (Marshall, 2012; Wilber, 2005). Within this, primary aspects are:

1.4.1. Quadrants

- Subjective and objective aspects of any phenomena. Integral theory argues that trying to describe phenomena - for example, the difficulty of explaining decision-making and action from a purely objective perspective - is akin to a flatland – divorcing meaning and purpose from human activities, business or society endeavours (Slaughter, 2002; Wilber, 2000c). Consequently, the framework explicitly recognises such objective perspectives alongside the subjective factors - those that are less immediately quantifiable and/or are non-measurable.
- Individual and collective influences or facets of a phenomenon. Individual values and personal financial motivation are clear factors to be considered within many investigations. For example, see the 2.5 A sustainability case section below. Equally – within a business, organisation or society more generally – collective systems including culture-style influences or shared or tacit value systems, are in existence. In the more measurable objective sphere, business capital expenditure prioritisation or country economic policy provide direction to, and influence on, decisions (Divecha, 2014; Edwards, 2009; Riedy, 2005).

The subjective and objective aspects above both have individual and collective facets. Consequently, the combinations are a four-part structure - the quadrant part of AQAL (all quadrants). Together, there are four possible combinations of such perspectives and concepts – individual and collective subjective, i.e. subjective and inter-subjective, and individual and collective objective, i.e. objective and inter-objective (Ballard et al., 2010; Esbjörn-Hargens, 2010d; Wilber, 2005). Integral theory organises these combinations into a two by two matrix (Wilber, 2000b). These quadrants can be thought of through the metaphor of lenses. That is, there can be a singular or plural focus and any issue can be considered subjectively as well as from a more measured and quantifiable perspective - objectively (Divecha & Brown, 2013; O'Brien & Hochachka, 2010). The four quadrants are:

- The Upper-Left usually representing individual-subjective viewpoints (for example personal meaning, emotions)
- The Lower-Left usually representing collective-subjective viewpoints (inter-subjective - for example worldviews, culture and shared values)
- The Upper-Right usually representing individual-objective viewpoints (for example objective reality – measurements made of a human brain when the subject is undertaking a specific behaviour)
- The Lower-Right usually representing collective-objective viewpoints (inter-objective - for example objective reality – visible social structures such as the economic system).

1.4.2. Levels

- Levels stand for development and stages or levels. Such levels are often outlined for individuals (and can be described across all the integral quadrants above). An example of such levels for an individual is that development unfolds in a defined, identifiable and invariable sequence - through specific stages or orders - within which people construct and understand themselves (and the world) within describable parameters. As a person shifts, from one stage to a new order, the new level includes previous orders and thus must be more complex to support this more comprehensive understanding. A person would thus make sense of themselves and the world in a holistic manner when at a particular stage and then, in a subsequent order, this prior understanding forms part (but not all) of their new meaning-making (McCauley et al., 2006). That is, the new meaning-making stage transcends and includes the previous steps - it transcends its previous level of knowledge but still includes this knowledge (van Eijnatten, 2004; Wilber, 2000a). Such cognitive stages are similarly linked to physical perspectives - for example perceptions and objective statements about why we should, or should not, act on climate change and/or peoples' ways of defining sustainability (Divecha and Brown, 2013; Lynam, 2014).

1.4.3. States, Lines, Types

Other aspects of integral theory are states, lines and types. In brief:

- States are temporary manners of being or external conditions.
- The concept of multiple lines is common in developmental hierarchies that may include cognitive, moral and emotional development. For example, Kohlberg's (1981, 1984) moral development and Cook-Greuter's (1999) ego development could be regarded as such separate lines of development.[1]
- Types describe typically fixed preferences. For example, a person's Myers-Briggs type, it is argued, does not change. However, the non-preferred way of being may be learned (McCaulley, 1990).

Integral theory's proponents hold that utilising all elements in any situation increases the likelihood of better understanding and/or successful outcomes (Esbjörn-Hargens, 2006; Wilber, 2005).

Integral theory can be, and is, applied to a wide range of human endeavour including sustainability and related topics, leadership, management, organisations and future studies. For example, McCauley, Drath, Palus, O'Connor and Baker (2006) argue that integral theory, applied to leadership, could expand the scope of research such that it encompasses complex social interactions and more holistic perspectives. Chris Riedy (2005), Barrett Brown and I (2013) and Richard Slaughter (1998) argue that an analysis of sustainability based on objective measured criteria alone (e.g. economic cost) is limited - incorporating human considerations, such as motivation and worldviews, is critical (Esbjörn-Hargens, 2010c; O'Brien & Hochachka, 2010). Combining objective perspectives, with the more subjective aspects of society, is important for better outcomes - social processes are necessary to implement technological solutions (Bradbury, 1998; Divecha, 2014). With integral theory's broad promise, it is not surprising it has found widespread uses across extensive fields with an estimated 35 to 50 academic disciplines using this framework in applied, conceptual and theoretical endeavours, including constructive critiques and development of theory along with the application of it (Esbjörn-Hargens, 2010b; Forman & Esbjörn-Hargens, 2008).[2].

Using integral theory's quadrants, stages, lines, states and types can help to clarify relationships, reveal factors that are underemphasised and structure disparate conceptualisations against each other for a deeper understanding. As a meta-theory, it can be applied to and categorise phenomena - including theories and the concepts that are used with such models. This organising ability and the clarity that may arise from it raise a number of questions. These include:

- How do we use such overarching theory while remaining open to critiques such as the theories are not as all-encompassing as promised?
- How do we build and test comprehensive theory while concurrently using and applying developed meta-theory for the insights it can offer?

1.5. A Sustainability Case

Sustainability provides a good illustration of a field to which meta and integral theory investigation can be useful. Sustainability related issues are inherently complex and the scope that can be examined is vast. Limiting this scale to an organisation, frameworks such as social, environmental sustainability can be closely linked to individuals (such as leaders), organisational policy, stakeholders, customers, layers of governance frameworks within which the organisation operates, and external social and economic drivers (Divecha, 2014; Divecha & Brown, 2013; Edwards, 2009; Esbjörn-Hargens, 2010c). Within an organisation's limits, and the factors that are relevant to such an entity, research fields that can be considered are broad. These include geographic and physical scales, social, economic and environmental valuing, as well as timescales, history and future orientation. There are collective and individual beliefs to address. Expectations or perspectives that make up these perceptions may be conscious and/or based on data or, equally, unconscious or unquestioned. Moreover, when such phenomena and related theories are compared to each other some are paradoxical (Divecha, 2014, pp. 103-106). Critical, evidence based, comparison is vital.

2. META-THEORY METHODOLOGY

A meta-theory presumes that several theories ... are adequate but apply under different conditions; it attempts to specify those conditions and the relationships among theories. Andrew Van De Ven and Scott Poole, Toward a general theory of innovation processes (2000)

In the introduction to this chapter, it is clear that there is the potential for significant interplay between theories. This opens questions into how different perspectives may be relevant. There may be relative rankings or specific reasons for a theory's applicability. Naturally, research of this nature seeks to identify the most important factors. However, any particular framework may be more or less applicable depending on specific circumstances, timing or individuals. Meta-theory methodology lets us better understand the relationships between theories and investigate the topics theory is applied to at greater depth.

For example, with respect to sustainability, good theory should have coherent principles that help us to understand, explain, predict or initiate effective action. Theories inevitably have a scope and domain and a set of circumstances and conditions within which they were developed. As such, they are likely to suffer at least some limitations arising from these contexts (Adler & Borys, 1993; Van de Ven & Poole, 2000; Van de Ven, 1989). One example is the contexts in which economic theories about energy efficiency adoption were developed and, subsequently, the gap between action and theory documented. Testing, comparing and working with the paradoxes that become evident can separate out the circumstances or conditions within which the theory has been designed. This is a strength of meta-theory. It highlights the framework and parameters theory seeks to be relevant within. It can introduce new terms to resolve the tensions or understand inherent paradoxes.[3] This is exciting as it promises to create a more encompassing picture, more capable of understanding complexity. Meta-theory allows us to compare and contrast such conditions or contingencies or contradictions, illuminating where the theory, and models derived from these theories, hold (Poole & Van de Ven, 1989; Van de Ven & Poole, 2000). It also allows us to test existing meta-theory and its usefulness (Edwards, 2009).

Thus, a meta-theory methodology lets us test a meta-theory (such as integral theory) as well as apply the meta-theory to the phenomena we are investigating. Advantages include:

1. Using meta-theory to synthesise existing theory and incorporate the mid-range theory developed or tested from the case studies can produce a comprehensive analysis (Finfgeld, 2003).
2. Analysis can help to make sense of research by looking at the ways theory operates within the research as well as seen through the case studies. It helps to explain the nature and structure of this knowledge and how it is constructed (Paterson & Canam, 2001, p. 95).
3. Meta-theory includes analysing for the core premises on which its theoretical concepts are based. It explores the frameworks or lenses that researchers were using when they created their theories. This should enable us to describe and explain the approaches – as well as predict and control for implicit or explicit biases and place the theories in a larger context (Edwards, 2009, p. 39; Paterson & Canam, 2001, pp. 91-93; Ritzer, 1992 cited in Paterson & Canam, 2001; Edwards, 2009; and, Taylor et al., 2006).

Meta-theory is defined as conceptual research – it uses theory as its data[4] and clarifies the conditions or contingencies of such theory (Edwards, 2009, p. 38; Van de Ven & Poole, 2000). However, there is significant latitude within this definition. The scale of meta-theory varies based on the concepts and phenomena it is seeking to analyse. For example, conceptual research looking at economic theories may create meta-theory that helps to define and clarify circumstances and paradigms that distinguish different viewpoints within such research - e.g. an economic meta-theory assessing behavioural, evolutionary, neo-classical and other distinct viewpoints on exchanges, markets and goods. Similar research on the implementation of energy efficiency within organisations could include what was considered the meta-theory above but is now a mid-range theory for further meta-theory building. Such further meta-theory building might add additional theoretical components such as organisational change, governance, cultural and psychological theories. The economic meta-theory has now become an object (data) in a meta-theory of organisational and household energy efficiency implementation.

2.1. Building Meta-Theory

Steps to build meta-theory can help to ground the discussion above. Edwards (2013) develops the methodology as cycles for building and testing both mid and meta-theory. The interlocking cycles help to define, and redefine, the theories - Figure 1 illustrates the dependencies and development cycles.

Another manner in which this can be conceptualised is to consider meta-theory as a Holon – a whole that is part of another whole (Divecha, 2014, pp. 84-86; Koestler, 1967, p. 48). Using this mental model, for example, economic theory can be a holon that informs energy efficiency economic meta-theory. Energy efficiency economic meta-theory, alongside big picture psychological and organisational theory applied to understanding energy efficiency could then be considered a set of holons, theories, that then inform a meta-theory on the energy efficiency perspectives relevant to sustainability. This conceptualisation builds on Edwards' (2009, p. 40) "holarchy of sense-making" by explicitly recognising that "overarch-

Figure 1. The research cycles of building and testing middle-range and meta-theory
Source: Adapted from Misunderstanding Metatheorizing (Edwards, 2013).

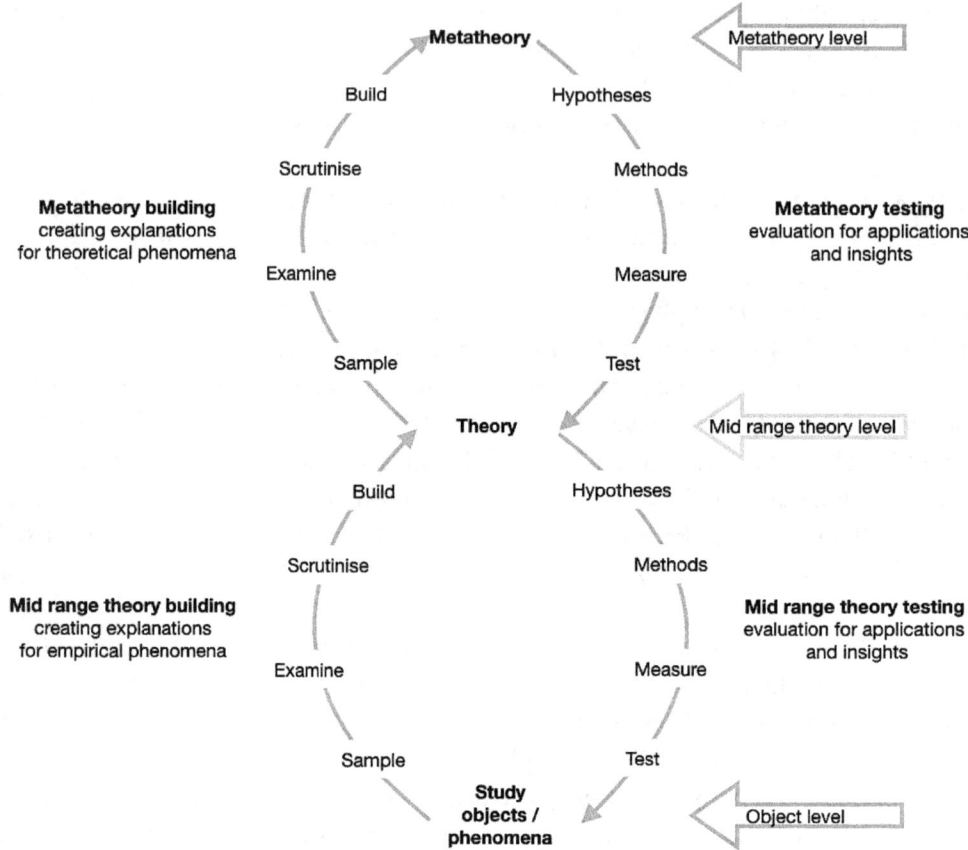

ing big pictures" - the meta-theoretical level – exists at different scales for different practitioners and circumstances.[5] Figure 2 illustrates this relationship.

This interplay of meta-theory and mid-range theory - theory that is meta-theory from one perspective and mid-range when serving another purpose - describe a group of scales of theory and models.

A further sustainability example may assist understanding. Such considerations with respect to organisations often include measurable objective perspectives such as pricing, profit and market failures (e.g. Stern & UK Treasury, 2007) alongside society engagement. Some significant overarching models arise from such aspects of sustainability (for example see Divecha, 2014). Such overarching models can become mid-range theory for a further meta-theory analysis that, for example, incorporates more subjective sustainability theory (e.g. theory related to developmental levels such as Divecha and Brown, 2013; Lynam, 2014) with the frameworks drawn from pricing, profit and market failure analyses.

The discussion above shows that mid-range and meta-theory distinctions and delineations can sometimes suggest that the two categories are independent of each other or generate confusion around overlaps. The next subsection - Meta-theory development and testing - seeks to further clarify this.

Figure 2. Theory that is appropriate and relevant for the particular investigation: A meta-theory and holons perspective
Source: Divecha, A climate for change (2014).

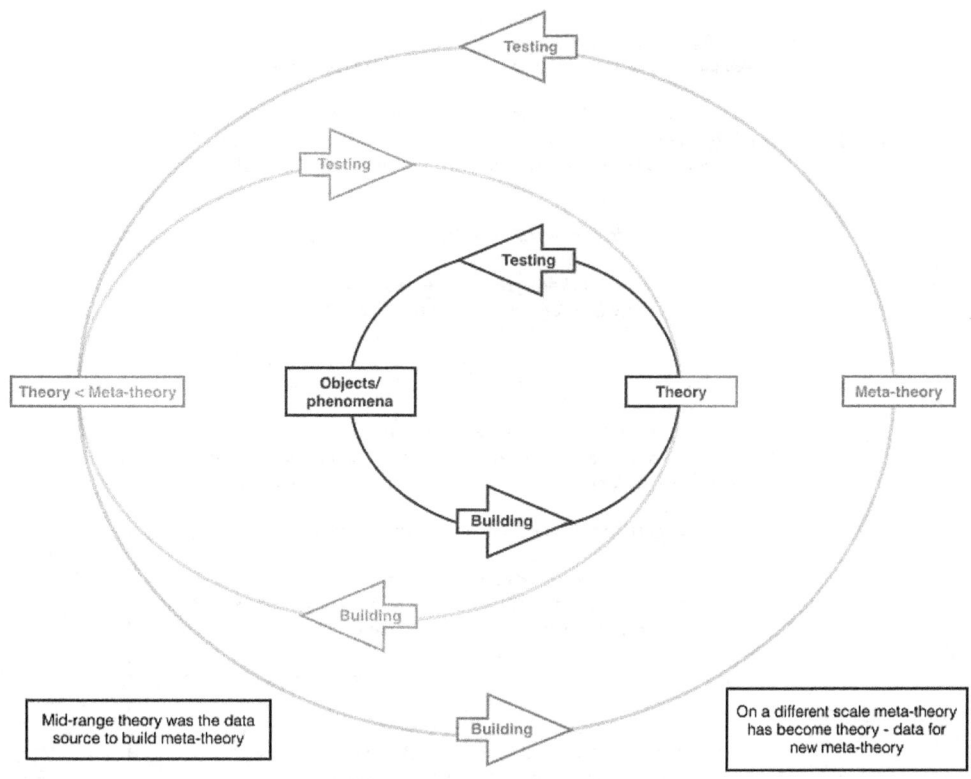

2.2. Meta-Theory Development and Testing

Metathoretical research is the systematic and deliberative study of theories and their constituent conceptual lenses. Mark Edwards, Organizational transformation for sustainability (2009, p. 2)

This subsection outlines methodology for testing and developing meta-theory. Edwards (2009) describes this methodology for the purposes of a systematic study of theory and building meta-theory from such a study.

This methodology has seven research phases.[6] The first phases set the context and boundaries of the research – phases one and two. The study design is detailed and then a multiparadigmal review follows – phases three and four. Edwards argues the multiparadigmal review is distinct from simply identifying the paradigms related to the theories under review. Rather, such a review looks at theories in depth and sources from a range of materials where that theory is used. This aims to identify multiple perspectives to discover all appropriate paradigms and lenses through which to view the theories, rather than just a more limited existing framework underlying these theories. A review like this includes, but is not limited to, understanding the conditions or contingencies in which such theories are useful.

The results are then analysed and meta-theory is built – phases five and six. The final stage looks at the implications of this meta-theory to be considered and then the process and meta-theory (personal

Figure 3. Multiparadigm review steps
Adapted from Edwards, *Organizational transformation for sustainability* (2009, pp. 92-100) and Divecha, *A climate for change* (2014).

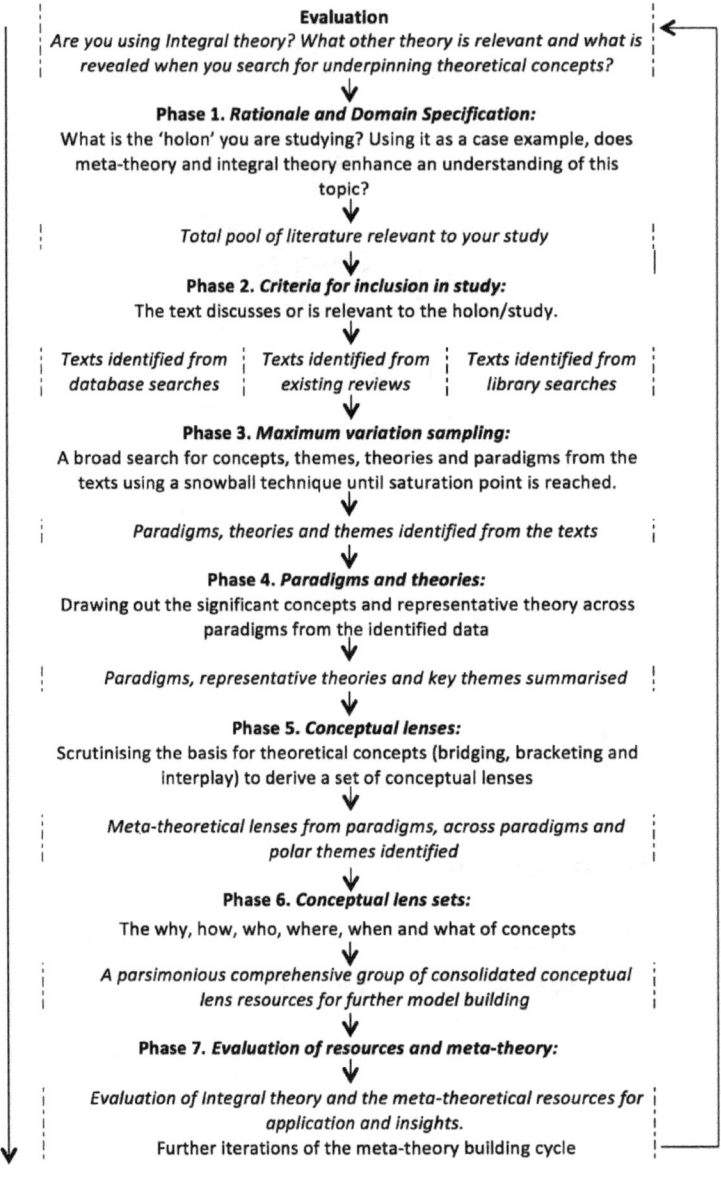

reflection for those involved in its development as well as the actual results) is evaluated – phase seven. Figure 3 illustrates these phases for an integral and meta-theory review of a topic and the figure notes provide further detail.

Figure 3 notes:

Phase 3: Snowball sampling draws on grounded theory methodology (Strauss & Corbin, 2008, p. 148). The search for texts concludes on reaching saturation point - additional texts do not reveal new themes and theories (Strauss & Corbin, 2008, p. 318).

Phase 4: Multiparadigm identification analyses the major themes, conceptual layers and paradigms in the texts to classify explicit or implicit frameworks in the theories and theme texts. A text can span several such paradigms. For example, investigating sustainability within an organisation many texts may exhibit a capitalist paradigm - viewing sustainability as a product and mediated by economic incentives, barriers and models. Within each paradigm it is likely there are a large number of representative theories and key themes that illustrate these frames. During this phase the theories and themes are identified and documented alongside the paradigms.

Phase 5: Conceptual lenses: Phase 4 is likely to identify a large variety of intersecting and overlapping themes alongside the commonalities and contradistinctions within each paradigm. In order to structure this and clarify the differences and synergies, this phase brackets the themes and theories into conceptual lenses. It also examines the interplay between the paradigms, theories and themes to derive additional conceptual lenses so those lenses that may span more than one paradigm are not overlooked.

Bridging and bracketing themes and theories, seeks to identify lenses that were characterising concepts as the theories were formed. For example, within the capitalist paradigm example above core conceptual lenses may be found in theories such as a profit lens (used to describe themes from the text related to maximising profit as determining behaviour). An investment case lens is broader. It comprises issues such as net present value, priorities and risk that are considered within the profit assessment.

Influences contributing to a theory or theme may span several paradigm categories. Perspectives can also appear to be mutually exclusive when viewed through particular structures and interplay analysis attempts to identify these conceptual dichotomies. To continue with the economic example an examination may reveal rational-irrational perspectives. That is, commonly in these theories there is a classically rationalist view that we make decisions based on maximising our economic outcomes versus a much more subjective approach centred around our desires and beliefs (Divecha, 2014, pp. 124-128).

Phase 6: Conceptual lens sets: In undertaking the steps outlined it is likely that there are a significant number of conceptual lenses. Consequently, there may be a wide range of interpretations possible from the multiplicity of lenses. To evaluate integral theory's application, there is a need to rationalise, structure and synthesise further. As a general rule, strong theory building uses the minimum number of concepts possible (parsimony), to communicate and explain phenomena at a given scale of analysis and application (abstraction), while still aiming to provide a comprehensive explanation (Wacker, 2008; Whetten, 1989). The abstraction, comprehensive and parsimony principles apply to the meta-theory analysis as it involves building theory and it is helpful to simplify, where possible, the conceptual lenses. Whetten's (1989) organising structure - see Table 1 - is useful for clarity and is used to group phase 5's conceptual lenses into sets.

For example, several of the lenses from phase 5 may be well described by a why type objective-subjective lens set. This could incorporate the rational-irrational style approaches to economics illustrated above plus other similar underpinning structures present from the analysis. The lenses that comprise such a lens set may cross one, some or all the identified paradigms.

Table 1. Structuring conceptual lenses by research focus

Key Question	Meaning	Focus
What, where	What factors are mediating	The structures
How	How does this happen	The processes mediating such action
Who, when	Who is responsible and when	Time and human context factors
Why	Why is action occurring or not occurring	A focus on underlying causes
Why, how, who, where, when and what	Concepts that cut across multiple categories and include facets of our lenses thus not reducible to single categories	Multifaceted conceptual lenses

Source: A climate for change (Divecha, 2014).

2.3. Summary and Application Into Integral Theory

A multiparadigmal review to this point, phases 1 to 6, analyses and clarifies conceptual frameworks underpinning the original research holon. For example, the research may have been undertaken to better understand integral theory and its potential usefulness in addressing this research holon. That is, an aim of the multiparadigm review may have been to inform our knowledge and understanding of the research holon through examining the links between integral theory and it.

Integral theory is founded on a vision to include "matter, body, mind, soul and spirit", as it appears in "self, culture and nature" within a genuine theory of everything (Wilber, 2000c, p. xii). From this starting point, a concern arises that integral theory may not necessarily be designed for application to any specific area of research. Consequently, it may be difficult to apply to, or it may not help greatly deepen our understanding of, a particular specific topic under investigation.

There are at least two responses to this concern. The first is that, as a theory of everything, integral would naturally apply to the area of research under investigation. The second is that practical analysis and research may demonstrate integral's usefulness - a range of researchers and practitioners are already applying integral theory to a wide set of fields (see the Introduction section of this chapter). Examining the conceptual lens sets from a multiparadigmal review, against integral theory's quadrants, levels, lines, states and types structure, should assist in developing links. Creating such conceptual lens sets within Whetten's organising structure assists with such a comparison. A comparison of these lens sets with integral theory can comprise part or most of phase 7 of the meta-theory methodology - Evaluation of resources and meta-theory.

To undertake such a phase the conceptual lens sets are visually mapped against the relationships with integral theory. That is the derived conceptual lens sets are placed within an integral quadrant, levels, states, lines and types diagram. Some of these sets may clearly, directly or indirectly, map onto an integral theory framework - for example the review may have found why type objective-subjective perspectives. These are common in organisational sustainability fields. From the example in the Phase 6 note above, aspects of an objective-subjective lens set may be present in the objective profit lens and somewhat subjective investment case lens. An objective-subjective lens set may also encompass other theories and themes from the phase 5 conceptual lens analysis and it maps quite directly to the integral quadrants' objective and subjective poles.[7]

Strengths of this evaluation include seeing what fits well with integral theory's descriptors, the areas that are more loosely described by the theory's map and conceptual lens sets that may appear to exist outside of the integral theory structure. The mapping exercise helps to answer questions such as those at the end of the Integral theory overview subsection of this chapter (if such questions were part of the initial multiparadigmal review conceptualisation and its phase 1). Moreover, with numerous theoretical and practical approaches there will be competing truths, multiple interpretations and contexts that shift, dimensionally and through time. There are also overlaps and intersections so this effort to rationalise such lenses and group them against a strong open framework like integral theory can help reduce confusion. Additionally, the review may reveal dynamics between lenses, dynamics that impact and affect an integral theory analysis of the research topic and theoretical structures where something more than integral may be useful. This chapter returns to the usefulness of these dynamics in its concluding section.

3. DISCUSSION

We live in a world awash with information, but we seem to face a growing scarcity of wisdom. And what's worse, we confuse the two. We believe that having access to more information produces more knowledge, which results in more wisdom. But, if anything, the opposite is true — more and more information without the proper context and interpretation only muddles our understanding of the world rather than enriching it. Maria Popova, Wisdom in the age of information (2014)

3.1. Integral on Integral

Integral presents some clear advantages and obvious challenges. With respect to this chapter's illustrating example, by reviewing how sustainability issues manifest within the organisations, a large-scale theory like this should let us examine effective action correlated with integral theory. That is, the theory may highlight key points and correlations that enhance our understanding of sustainability and this, in turn, builds confidence that integral theory framework is likely to be a useful structure (e.g. for change, implementation of initiatives and understanding of such issues).

As introduced initially (see Integral theory overview - section 2.4), a study's design informed by integral theory may have blind spots - missing perspectives not encompassed by the theory's framework. These can arise if they are not explicit within integral theory and/or if they not considered within the original theory or subsequent discussion of it. As a theory of everything it should be expected that integral is an all-encompassing framework covering everything – evidence fits within it. On the other hand, mechanisms to inquire into it, should the theory be incomplete, are clearly desirable. Consequently, methods to test the validity of this theory and determine if there are concepts or structures that may sit outside of it are valuable.

Two such methods are primarily triangulation and - as discussed in the Summary and application into integral theory, section 3.3 - meta-theory methodology. Integral theorists additionally argue using multiple methods replicates at least some of the numerous perspectives for phenomena examination. There are eight theoretical methodologies (internal and external perspectives on the universe as a whole) that Wilber holds as important when considering totality (Paulson, 2008; Wilber, 2006). Figure 4 illustrates these.

The eight zones approximately correspond to looking as (zones 1, 3, 5 and 7) and looking at (zones 2, 4, 6 and 8) theoretical perspectives across each quadrant. That is, there are two methodologies for first (zone 1&2), second (zone 3 & 4), third individual person (zone 5 & 6) and third person group (zone 7 & 8). Esbjörn-Hargens (2006) argues that integral research, at the very least, would include one first,

Figure 4. Eight Methodological Zones
Source: (Esbjörn-Hargens, 2014; Wilber, 2006)

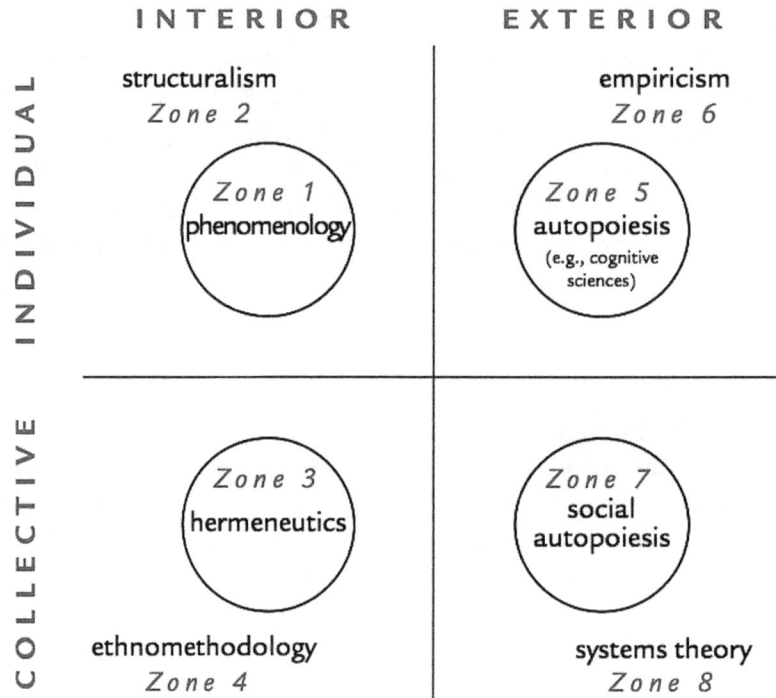

second and third person methodology - that is three or more approaches. For example, in the first person upper-left quadrant, looking as yourself (a first person perspective on yourself), methodology could be considered as phenomenology. Where as looking at yourself, in this same quadrant (a third person perspective on yourself), methodology would be a structural assessment technique (Esbjörn-Hargens, 2006, 2014; Hedlund, 2010).

With respect to the sustainability example, upper-left methodologies may be relevant. Practitioners, over timescales during which they consider the research topics, could look as themselves through techniques such as journaling and research note taking. That is, consciously study their own subjective experience (Küpers, 2008). Looking at themselves there are numerous assessments (e.g. Washington University Sentence Completion Test style assessments: McCauley et al., 2006) as well as type assessments (e.g. Myers-Briggs: McCaulley, 1990) that may be relevant and insightful for the research.

Second person, the lower left quadrant, methodology samples include techniques such as one-on-one interviewing - looking as individuals in the group. For the sustainability example that illustrates this chapter this may be discussing sustainability perspectives and interpretive analysis of that material. In the course of such interviews, a practitioner may be observing themselves and the interviewee - during both the interview and reflecting back on it (e.g. as recorded in research notes). Such a participant-observer technique can add to the analysis of the interview material and can be regarded as looking at the interviews and perspectives within them - a third person observation of the practitioner and the interviewee's interactions (Esbjörn-Hargens, 2006, 2014). The observation might extend to viewpoints on the practitioner's own and the interviewee's body language and presence (in person or video interviews).

Integral Meta-Impact

Third person research may be principally analysis of existing theory, such as the meta-theory methodology, and case studies. For example, a practitioner might undertake a meta-theory review across, say, socio-economic approaches to sustainability. That theorist could then choose to evaluate the developed meta-theory alongside conceptual lenses developed from other sustainability meta-theory reviews - for example, Divecha's (2014) Multi-paradigm Review of Energy and Edwards' (2009) Organisational Transformations for Sustainability. This would triangulate results from the three analyses against each other using integral theory quadrants (see the 2.3 Summary and application into integral theory section above).[8]

Thus, meta-theory / integral research has a multilayered approach - it uses multiple methodologies, covering first, second and third person approaches. It includes methodologies that address the research from each of these person perspectives across the subject matter. This strengthens wide scale investigation such as the type of sustainability research that illustrates this chapter. Research may span across meta-theory to case study, individual perspectives and more. Organising these multiple approaches through integral theory's quadrants assists to mesh and triangulate this data (Esbjörn-Hargens, 2006). Multiple methods are far more likely to be appropriate across these different landscapes and comparing conclusions and inferences with each other helps to validate the outcomes.

The multiple method approach carries some risk. A principle issue is that it may result in trying to encompass too great a scope at the risk of not enough depth to the research (Hedlund, 2010). For a given subject matter, it may be appropriate to apply a considerable part of the effort developing depth with respect to one or two of these first, second and third person techniques. Timescales over which the research is conducted may also mitigate risk and applying such techniques throughout all phases (possibly years of research) may further inform such work (Hedlund, 2010).

Notwithstanding such issues, it should also be recognised that the scope of many multifaceted and complex societal studies (e.g. sustainability) is inherently large. Consequently, attempting to limit investigation within narrow research methods also presents difficulties.

3.2. Integral Time Triangulation

As mentioned above, a second aspect of triangulation/quadrants/multiple methodologies is the time taken for the research - a practitioner's (first person) perspective, and the fields of theory and practice they draw on, is changing during the course of the research. In my experience, with respect to a sustainability example, this is particularly noticeable in the case of the divergent action logics sustainability perspectives - integral upper-left quadrant levels. Over a period of eight years, I undertook sustainability research that investigated, in part, the integral theory levels (action logics) associated with sustainability (Divecha and Brown, 2013; Divecha, 2014 chapter 4). Early coding of interview material associated with this research included a code used when I was uncertain about the action logics or felt that the examples were unclear. Over time, not only did my own understanding of this material deepen (aided by the personal action logics stage shifts), but additional theoretical contributions also clarified the application of such theory to my data (and vice versa).

Notable theoretical developments during this example sustainability research include the combining of stages and states with respect to a person's action logics (O'Fallon, 2010). This combination can be regarded as third person research for its theoretical contribution (while also having a significant first-person impact on my own capabilities). These developments enable clearer decision-making and correlation between theory and observed perspectives. For example, O'Fallon's (2010) revised methodology and model helps to discern how action logics relate to sustainability. However, this development (at approximately the halfway point of the eight-year research period) meant that the revised theory could be retrospectively used to question and validate previous action logics sustainability coding. The iterative process means that two separate third person methodological lenses were used to triangulate the correlation of interviewee sustainability statements with action logics. Alongside this, the first-person reflection (in part prompted by my engagement with these new theoretical structures) and personal action logics change assisted the research. In addition, interaction with others about the data and interpretation of it - such as Divecha and Brown (2013) - provides further reference points and a second person perspective on the research.

Consequently, triangulation with an integral theory framework using quadrants, stages, types and states lenses has an additional dimension related to time.

4. CONCLUSION

Democratic decisions can sometimes lead to incongruities. To the extent that this is a feature of the real world, its existence and reach are matters for objective recognition. Inconsistencies arise more readily in some situations than in others, and it is possible to identify the situational differences and to characterise the processes through [which] consensual and compatible decisions can emerge. Amartya Sen, The possibility of social choice (1999)

Finding ways to sustainably govern and manage ... systems [have] become ever more difficult as they have become increasingly interlinked, and as the size of human populations and the level of economic development have both increased. Addressing this complexity must in turn overcome historical academic divisions between ecology, engineering and the social sciences, the tendencies of social scientists to build simplified models of complex systems in order to derive ideal types of governance, and an over-reliance on a limited set of research methods to study social and environmental systems. Elinor Ostrom and Michael Cox, Moving beyond panaceas (2010)

Many topics of prominence, issues significant for the types of flourishing futures people commonly envision, are characterised by complexity. They are interlinked and interdependent, subject to change over time, are affected by charismatic, brilliant and chaotic individuals' input, social norms, human fears and values, philosophical thought and multiplicity of other similar and divergent influential factors. The combination of chaotic and complex interactions results in volatility - confounding us with positive as well as detrimental shifts.

Throughout this chapter sustainability is a wonderful example of such a deep multifaceted and sometimes nebulous topic. As an illustration, for just one important area of this, climate change, we have great knowledge yet are simultaneously struggling. The scale, depth and scope of change required to address this global phenomenon is quantifiable and relatively clear (at least from a risk management perspective). However, there is much more to this topic than risk. A casual examination of approaches will quickly reveal a depth of innovation, outstanding leadership, difficult intransigence, hostile opposition and extraordinary creativity and social progress. There are abundant profitable and cheap technology solutions, non-adoption of such solutions on a large scale, perplexing movement that is not anywhere near the speed an economic rational analysis would suggest should occur and many more, always shifting, paradoxical actions, theories and outcomes.

In short, there are dynamic processes at play and consequently this chapter illustrates dynamic methodology to apply meta and integral theory for insight, clarity and action. It proposes comprehensive analysis to deliver simple, parsimonious yet not simplistic insight. As highlighted in this chapter, alongside theories, practices and themes, timescales and change can become data for analysis. The research practitioners are part of this process - their understanding changes and their meaning making may transform as well as the fields of study relevant to their research shift. The theory examinations alongside personal perspectives, changes and the interplay between multiple theories, actions and the research are all relevant to investigations. The practitioner's interventions with their research topics, data, others and engagement over the course of such research are, likewise, important pieces relevant to addressing these sorts of moving interconnected systems, structures, understandings and issues. A meta-theory and integral model offers potential for insight and some clarity within such complexity.

For example, in applying a process like this to sustainability and climate change I outlined a theoretical lens - integral action loops (Divecha, 2014). The dynamic integral action loops analysis that resulted from a study involving integral theory and meta-theory methodology has the potential to shift more static frameworks to those that assist us to work with the key catalysts. Integral action loops may reveal fulcra present in a given situation, or group, as well as assist to evolve long-term strategy setting. Integral action loops additionally help to bridge a conceptual separation from climate change and what it can do for us, as opposed to the more traditional viewpoint that only considers climate and what we are doing for and to it. Meta-theory analysis revealed these perspectives.

Such developments are not limited to climate change. A dynamic lens, like integral action loops, is relevant to fields as diverse as terrorism or the global economy (Reviewers, 2014). That is, meta-theory alongside integral and a theoretical development approach can allow us to address movement through time, synthesise complexity and open insights into non-linear change.

A meta-theory methodology delivers us a framework to better enable the significant promise many encounters through integral theory analysis. It allows us to engage with multifaceted problems through a multi-theoretical and integral approach. Additionally, it helps us to illuminate the gaps - for ideas, insights and creating movement within ourselves and with respect to planetary topics and pressing problem areas. I would hope such contributions prove as rewarding for the research practitioners who engage in these types of analysis as they are for what these investigations may do for our world.

REFERENCES

Adler, P. S., & Borys, B. (1993). Materialism and idealism in organizational research. *Organization Studies*, *14*(5), 657–679. doi:10.1177/017084069301400503

Akiyama, T., Li, J., Kubota, J., Konagaya, Y., & Watanabe, M. (2012). Perspectives on sustainability assessment: An integral approach to historical changes in social systems and water environment in the Ili river basin of central Eurasia, 1900–2008. *World Futures*, *68*(8), 595–627. doi:10.1080/02604027.2012.693852

Ballard, D., Reason, P., & Coleman, G. (2010). Using the AQAL framework to accelerate responses to climate change. *Journal of Integral Theory and Practice*, 5(1).

Barrett, R. (2006). *Building a values-driven organization: A whole system approach to cultural transformation*. Butterworth-Heinemann. doi:10.4324/9780080461687

Benefiel, M. (2003). Irreconcilable foes? The discourse of spirituality and the discourse of organizational science. *Organization*, 10(2), 383–391. doi:10.1177/1350508403010002012

Bradbury, H. (1998). *Learning with the natural step: Cooperative ecological inquiry through cases, theory and practice for sustainable development (PhD)*. Boston: Boston College.

Cacioppe, R. (2000). Creating spirit at work: reNvisioning organization development and leadership – Part II. *Leadership and Organization Development Journal*, 21(2), 110–119. doi:10.1108/01437730010318200

Cacioppe, R., & Albrecht, S. (2000). Using 360 degree feedback and the integral model to develop leadership and management skills. *Leadership and Organization Development Journal*, 21(8), 8. doi:10.1108/01437730010379249

Cacioppe, R., & Edwards, M. G. (2005a). Adjusting blurred visions: A typology of integral approaches to organisations. *Journal of Organizational Change Management*, 18(3), 230–246. doi:10.1108/09534810510599399

Cacioppe, R., & Edwards, M. G. (2005b). Seeking the holy grail of organisational development: A synthesis of integral theory, spiral dynamics, corporate transformation and action inquiry. *Leadership and Organization Development Journal*, 26(2), 86–105. doi:10.1108/01437730510582536

Chesterman, D. (2001). Learning from research perspectives in collaborative working. *Career Development International*, 6(7), 378–383. doi:10.1108/EUM0000000006058

Cook-Greuter, S. R. (1999). *Postautonomous ego development: A study of its nature and measurement (Ph.D.)*. Cambridge, MA: Harvard University.

Davis, N. T., & Callihan, L. P. (2013). Integral methodological pluralism in science education research: Valuing multiple perspectives. *Cultural Studies of Science Education*, 8(3), 505–516. doi:10.100711422-012-9480-5

Dawson-Tunik, T. L., Commons, M., Wilson, M., & Fischer, K. W. (2005). The shape of development. *European Journal of Developmental Psychology*, 2(2), 163–195. doi:10.1080/17405620544000011

Dean, K. L. (2004). Systems thinking's challenge to research in spirituality and religion at work: An interview with Ian Mitroff. *Journal of Organizational Change Management*, 17(1), 11–25. doi:10.1108/09534810410511279

Dent, E. B. (1999). Complexity science: A worldview shift. *Emergence*, 1(4), 5–19. doi:10.120715327000em0104_2

Divecha, S. (2014). *A climate for change: An exploration towards Integral Action Loops to apply our knowledge for sustainability success (Ph.D.)*. Adelaide Business School, The University of Adelaide.

Divecha, S., & Brown, B. C. (2013). Integral sustainability: Correlating action logics with sustainability to provide new insights into the dynamics of change. *Journal of Integral Theory and Practice*, *8*(3-4), 13.

Divecha, S. (2014). *A climate for change: An exploration towards Integral Action Loops to apply our knowledge for sustainability success* (Ph.D.). Adelaide Business School, The University of Adelaide. Retrieved from https://greenmode.files.wordpress.com/2015/03/simon-divecha-thesis-reviews-print.pdf

Edwards, M. G. (2005). The integral holon: A holonomic approach to organisational change and transformation. *Journal of Organizational Change Management*, *18*(3), 269–288. doi:10.1108/09534810510599425

Edwards, M. G. (2009). *Organizational transformation for sustainability: An integral metatheory*. London, UK: Routledge.

Edwards, M. G. (2013). Misunderstanding metatheorizing. *Systems Research and Behavioral Science*.

Esbjörn-Hargens, S. (2005). Integral ecology: The what, who, and how of environmental phenomena. *World Futures: The Journal of General Evolution*, *61*(1), 5–49. doi:10.1080/02604020590902344

Esbjörn-Hargens, S. (2006). Integral research: A multi-method approach to investigating phenomena. *Constructivism in the Human Sciences*, *11*(1), 79–107.

Esbjörn-Hargens, S. (2010a). Executive editor's introduction. *Journal of Integral Theory and Practice*, *5*(1), 4.

Esbjörn-Hargens, S. (2010b). An overview of integral theory: An all-inclusive framework for the twenty-first century. In S. Esbjörn-Hargens (Ed.), *Integral theory in action: applied, theoretical, and constructive perspectives on the AQAL model*. New York: SUNY Press.

Esbjörn-Hargens, S. (2010c). An integral overview of climate change: Why truth is not enough. *Journal of Integral Theory & Practice*, *5*(1), 1–42.

Esbjörn-Hargens, S. (2010d). An ontology of climate change: Integral pluralism and the enactment of multiple objects. *Journal of Integral Theory and Practice*, *5*(1), 143–174.

Esbjörn-Hargens, S. (2014). *TetraDynamics: Quadrants in action*. Sebastopol, CA: MetaIntegral Foundation.

Finfgeld, D. L. (2003). Metasynthesis: The state of the art, so far. *Qualitative Health Research*, *13*(7), 893–904. doi:10.1177/1049732303253462 PMID:14502956

Forman, M., & Esbjörn-Hargens, S. (2008). *The academic emergence of integral theory: Reflections on and clarifications of the 1st Biennial Integral Theory Conference*. Retrieved 4 April, 2014, from http://www.integralworld.net/forman-hargens.html

Gladwin, T. N., Kennelly, J. J., & Krause, T. N. S. (1995). Shifting paradigms for sustainable development: Implications for management theory and research. *Academy of Management Review*, *20*(4), 874–907. doi:10.5465/amr.1995.9512280024

Gladwin, T. N., Kennelly, J. J., & Krause, T. N. S. (1996). Toward eco-moral development of the Academy of Management. *Academy of Management Review*, *21*(4), 912–914. doi:10.5465/amr.1996.15867658

Gómez, S. V. (2008). *From functional literacy and development to integral literacy and sustainable development. In Signposts to literacy for sustainable development.* Hamburg, Germany: UNESCO Institute for Lifelong Learning.

Gordon, G., & Esbjörn-Hargens, S. (2007). Are we having fun yet? An exploration of the transformative power of play. *Journal of Humanistic Psychology, 47*(2), 198–222. doi:10.1177/0022167806297034

Haigh, M. (2013). AQAL Integral: A holistic framework for pedagogic research. *Journal of Geography in Higher Education, 37*(2), 174–191. doi:10.1080/03098265.2012.755615

Hedlund, N. H. (2010). Integrally researching integral research: Enactive perspectives on the future of the field. *Journal of Integral Theory & Practice, 5*(2).

Hochachka, G. (2005). Integrating interiority in community development. *World Futures: Journal of General Evolution, 61*(1N2), 110-126.

Hochachka, G. (2008). Case studies in integral approaches in international development. *Journal of Integral Theory and Practice, 3*, 58–108.

Ingersoll, R. E., & Marquis, A. (2014). Understanding Psychopathology: An Integral Exploration. Pearson Higher Ed.

Irwin, R. R. (1996). Narrative competence and constructive developmental theory: A proposal for rewriting the *Bildungsroman* in the postmodern world. *Journal of Adult Development, 3*(2), 109–125. doi:10.1007/BF02278776

Koestler, A. (1976). The ghost in the machine (2nd ed.). London, UK: Hutchison.

Kohlberg, L. (1969). Stage and sequence: The cognitive developmental approach to socialization. In D. Goslin (Ed.), *Handbook of socialization: Theory and research*. New York: Rand McNally.

Kohlberg, L. (1981). *The philosophy of moral development: Moral stages and the idea of justice*. San Francisco, CA: Harper & Row.

Küpers, W. (2005). Phenomenology and integral pheno-practice of embodied well-be(com)ing in organizations. *Culture and Organization, 11*(3), 221–231. doi:10.1080/14759550500204142

Küpers, W. (2008). Embodied "inter-learning": An integral phenomenology of learning in and by organizations. *The Learning Organization, 15*(5), 388–408. doi:10.1108/09696470810898375

Landrum, N. E., & Gardner, C. L. (2005). Using integral theory to effect strategic change. *Journal of Organizational Change Management, 18*(3), 247–258. doi:10.1108/09534810510599407

Landrum, N. E., Gardner, C. L., & Boje, D. M. (2013). A values-based and integral perspective of strategic management. *The Journal of Values Based Leadership, 6*(1), 9.

Laske, O. E., & Maynes, B. (2002). Growing the top management team. *Journal of Management Development, 21*(9), 702–727. doi:10.1108/02621710210441685

Laszlo, E. (2007). *Science and the akashic field: An integral theory of everything*. Inner Traditions/Bear & Co.

Laszlo, E., & Woolfson, D. (2011). The WorldShift 2012 declaration: A declaration of global emergency and emergence. In E. Laszlo & A. Combs (Eds.), *Thomas Berry, Dreamer of the Earth: The Spiritual Ecology of the Father of Environmentalism*. Inner Traditions International.

Locander, W. B., Hamilton, F., Ladik, D., & Stuart, J. (2002). Developing a leadership-rich culture: The missing link to creating a market-focused organization. *Journal of Market-Focused Management*, 5(2), 149–163. doi:10.1023/A:1014048111158

Lynam, A. (2014). *Embracing developmental diversity: Developmentally aware teaching, mentoring, and sustainability education* (Ph.D.). Prescott College in Sustainability Education. UMI Dissertation Publishing.

Marshall, P. (2012). The meeting of two integrative metatheories. *Journal of Critical Realism*, 11(2), 188–214. doi:10.1558/jcr.v11i2.188

McCauley, C. D., Drath, W. H., Palus, C. J., O'Connor, P. M. G., & Baker, B. A. (2006). The use of constructive-developmental theory to advance the understanding of leadership. *The Leadership Quarterly*, 17(6), 634–653. doi:10.1016/j.leaqua.2006.10.006

McCaulley, M. H. (1990). The Myers-Briggs Type Indicator: A measure for individuals and groups. *Measurement & Evaluation in Counseling & Development*, 22(4), 181–195. doi:10.1080/07481756.1990.12022929

Millar, C. C., Choi, C. J., Russell, E. T., & Kim, J. N. B. (2005). Open source communities: An integrally informed approach. *Journal of Organizational Change Management*, 18(3), 259–268. doi:10.1108/09534810510599416

Montuori, A. (2013). *Complex Thought, An overview of Edgar Morin's intellectual journey*. Retrieved from https://metaintegral.org/sites/default/files/Complex_Thought_FINAL.pdf

Morin, E. (2008). *On complexity*. Cresskill, NJ: Hampton Press.

Neal, J. A., Lichtenstein, B. M. B., & Banner, D. (1999). Spiritual perspectives on individual, organizational and societal transformation. *Journal of Organizational Change Management*, 12(3), 175–186. doi:10.1108/09534819910273757

O'Brien, K. (2012). Global environmental change II: From adaptation to deliberate transformation. *Progress in Human Geography*, 36(5), 667–676. doi:10.1177/0309132511425767

O'Brien, K., & Hochachka, G. (2010). Integral adaptation to climate change. *Journal of Integral Theory & Practice*, 5(1).

O'Fallon, T. J. (2010). *The collapse of the Wilber Combs matrix: The interpenetration of the state and structure stages*. Paper presented at the 2010 Integral Theory Conference, JFK University. Retrieved from http://www.pacificintegral.com/docs/statestagesofallon.pdf

Ostrom, E., & Cox, M. (2010). Moving beyond panaceas: A multi-tiered diagnostic approach for social-ecological analysis. *Environmental Conservation*, 37(4), 451–463. doi:10.1017/S0376892910000834

Paterson, B. L., & Canam, C. (2001). *Meta-study of qualitative health research: A practical guide to meta-analysis and meta-synthesis* (Vol. 3). London, UK: Sage Publications, Inc. doi:10.4135/9781412985017

Pauchant, T. C. (2005). Integral leadership: A research proposal. *Journal of Organizational Change Management, 18*(3), 211–229. doi:10.1108/09534810510599380

Paulson, D. S. (2002). *Competitive business, caring business: An integral business perspective for the 21st century*. New York: Paraview Press.

Paulson, D. S. (2008). Wilber's integral philosophy: A summary and critique. *Journal of Humanistic Psychology, 48*(3), 364–388. doi:10.1177/0022167807309748

Piaget, J. (1954). *The construction of reality in a child*. New York: Basic Books. doi:10.1037/11168-000

Pielstick, C. D. (2005). Teaching spiritual synchronicity in a business leadership class. *Journal of Management Education, 29*(1), 153–168. doi:10.1177/1052562903260027

Poole, M. S., & Van de Ven, A. H. (1989). Using paradox to build management and organization theories. *Academy of Management Review*, 562-578.

Popova, M. (2014). *Wisdom in the age of information*. Retrieved 5 Nov 2017, https://vimeo.com/105692521

Reams, J. (2005). What's integral about leadership? A reflection on leadership and integral theory. *Integral Review, 1*, 118–131.

Riedy, C. (2005). *The eye of the storm. An Integral perspective on sustainable development and climate change response (Ph.D.)*. Sydney, Australia: University of Technology. Retrieved from http://adt.lib.uts.edu.au/public/adtNNTSM20050603.101829/

Riedy, C. (2008). An integral extension of causal layered analysis. *Futures, 40*(2), 150–159. doi:10.1016/j.futures.2007.11.009

Riedy, C. (2011). Futures of the climate action movement: Insights from an integral futures approach. *Journal of Futures Studies, 15*(3), 33–52.

Ritzer, G. (1992). Metatheorizing in sociology: Explaining the coming of age. *Metatheorizing, 6*, 7–26.

Robledo, M. A. (2013). Building an integral metatheory of management. *European Management Journal, 32*(4), 535–546. doi:10.1016/j.emj.2013.10.008

Scharmer, O., Arthur, W. B., Day, J., Jaworski, J., Jung, M., Nonaka, I., & Senge, P. (1999). Illuminating the blind spot: Leadership in the context of emerging worlds. Academic Press.

Sen, A. (1999). The possibility of social choice. *The American Economic Review, 89*(3), 349–378. doi:10.1257/aer.89.3.349

Slaughter, R. A. (1998). Transcending flatland: Implications of Ken Wilber's meta narrative for futures studies. *Futures, 30*(6), 519–533. doi:10.1016/S0016-3287(98)00056-1

Slaughter, R. A. (2002). Futures studies as a civilizational catalyst. *Futures, 34*(3-4), 349–363. doi:10.1016/S0016-3287(01)00049-0

Slaughter, R. A. (2003). *Integral Futures: A new model for futures enquiry and practice*. Indooroopilly, Australia: Foresight International. Retrieved from http://www.foresightinternational.com.au

Steingard, D. S. (2005). Spiritually-Informed management theory. *Journal of Management Inquiry*, *14*(3), 227–241. doi:10.1177/1056492605276841

Stern, N. H., & Treasury, U. K. (2007). *The economics of climate change: the Stern review*. Cambridge, UK: Cambridge Univ Pr. doi:10.1017/CBO9780511817434

Stewart, C. C. (2008). Integral scenarios: Reframing theory, building from practice. *Futures*, *40*(2), 160–172. doi:10.1016/j.futures.2007.11.013

Strauss, A. L., & Corbin, J. M. (2008). Basics of qualitative research: Techniques and procedures for developing grounded theory (3rd ed.). London, UK: Sage Publications.

Taylor, B. C., Irvin, L. R., & Wieland, S. M. (2006). Checking the map: Critiquing Joanne Martin's metatheory of organizational culture and its uses in communication research. *Communication Theory*, *16*(3), 304–332. doi:10.1111/j.1468-2885.2006.00272.x

Tourki, Y., Keisler, J., & Linkov, I. (2013). Scenario analysis: A review of methods and applications for engineering and environmental systems. *Environment Systems & Decisions*, *33*(1), 3–20. doi:10.100710669-013-9437-6

Van de Ven, A. H. (1989). Nothing is quite so practical as a good theory. *Academy of Management Review*, *14*(4), 486–489. doi:10.5465/amr.1989.4308370

Van de Ven, A. H., & Poole, M. S. (2000). Toward a general theory of innovation processes. In A. H. Van de Ven, H. L. Angle, & M. S. Poole (Eds.), *Research on the Managment of Innovation: The Minnesota Studies*. New York: Ballinger, Harper and Row.

van Eijnatten, F. M. (2004). Chaordic systems thinking; Some suggestions for a complexity framework to inform a learning organization. *The Learning Organization*, *11*(6), 430–449. doi:10.1108/09696470410548791

Volckmann, R. (2005). Assessing executive leadership: An integral approach. *Journal of Organizational Change Management*, *18*(3), 289–302. doi:10.1108/09534810510599434

Voros, J. (2008). Integral futures: An approach to futures inquiry. *Futures*, *40*(2), 190–201. doi:10.1016/j.futures.2007.11.010

Wacker, J. G. (1998). A definition of theory: Research guidelines for different theory-building research methods in operations management. *Journal of Operations Management*, *16*(4), 361–385. doi:10.1016/S0272-6963(98)00019-9

Wacker, J. G. (2008). A conceptual understanding of requirements for theory-building research: Guidelines for scientific theory building. *The Journal of Supply Chain Management*, *44*(3), 5–15. doi:10.1111/j.1745-493X.2008.00062.x

Waddock, S. A. (2001). Corporate citizenship enacted as operating practice. *International Journal of Value-Based Management*, *14*(3), 237–246. doi:10.1023/A:1017548722646

Wallis, S. E. (2010). Toward a science of metatheory. *Integral Review*, *6*(3).

Whetten, D. A. (1989). What constitutes a theoretical contribution? *Academy of Management Review*, *14*(4), 490–495. doi:10.5465/amr.1989.4308371

Wilber, K. (2000a). *Integral psychology: Consciousness, spirit, psychology, therapy*. Boston: Shambhala.

Wilber, K. (2000b). *A theory of everything: An integral vision for business, politics, science, and spirituality*. Boston: Shambhala.

Wilber, K. (2000c). *A brief history of everything* (2nd ed.). Boston: Shambhala Publications.

Wilber, K. (2005). Introduction to integral theory and practice. *AQAL Journal of Integral Theory and Practice*, *1*(1), 38.

Wilber, K. (2006). *Integral spirituality: A startling new role for religion in the modern and postmodern world*. Boston: Integral Books.

Wilber, K. (2007). *The integral vision: A very short introduction to the revolutionary integral approach to life, god, the universe, and everything*. Shambhala Publications.

Young, J. E. (2002). A spectrum of consciousness for CEOs: A business application of Ken Wilber's Spectrum of Consciousness. *The International Journal of Organizational Analysis*, *10*(1), 30–54. doi:10.1108/eb028943

KEY TERMS AND DEFINITIONS

Holon: Any whole that is a part of another whole.

Meta-Theory: Encompassing theory that takes an overarching perspective of more specific theories and is constructed from and tested by the analysis of other theories.

Models: Theoretical descriptions, for example, of systems and concepts. See Footnote 4 for further details.

Paradigm: A perspective reflecting a general way of thinking about a fundamental set of assumptions, theories and/or methods.

Paradox: Describes a contradiction. This can be a simplified and polarized view of the world or a theoretical concept with either/or distinctions.

Sustainability: A term that encompasses multiple different perspectives and typically addresses one or more of the following three conceptual questions: 1) What are we trying to sustain? 2) For whom or what? 3) For how long?

Triangulation: With respect to integral and meta-theory this is the use of multiple different methods and data sources to cross check theory and conclusions.

ENDNOTES

[1] The concept of lines and development can become confusing. In part, this is due to overlaps between models and metrics - calibrated measures of stage vs. descriptions of increasing maturity, ego or moral levels. Such multiple lines can be measured in an instrument (metric). See Stein (2009) for a discussion incorporating models and metrics and the measurement of multiple lines, such as through Dawson-Tunik, Commons, Wilson and Fischer's metric (Dawson-Tunik, Commons, Wilson, & Fischer, 2005).

[2] Examples include: adult development and play (Gordon & Esbjörn-Hargens, 2007); integral ecology (Esbjörn-Hargens, 2005), broad application to leadership research (Pauchant, 2005), management, organisations, leadership and change (Barrett, 2006; Benefiel, 2003; Cacioppe, 2000; Cacioppe & Albrecht, 2000; Cacioppe & Edwards, 2005a, 2005b; Edwards, 2005; Küpers, 2005, 2008; Landrum & Gardner, 2005; Laske & Maynes, 2002; Locander, Hamilton, Ladik, & Stuart, 2002; Neal, Lichtenstein, & Banner, 1999; Paulson, 2002; Reams, 2005; Scharmer et al., 1999; Volckmann, 2005; Young, 2002); management and sustainability (Gladwin, Kennelly, & Krause, 1995, 1996; Waddock, 2001); management more generally (Landrum, Gardner, & Boje, 2013; Robledo, 2013); software (Millar, Choi, Russell, & Kim, 2005); development (Hochachka, 2005, 2008; Irwin, 1996); complexity (Dent, 1999); scenario analysis (Stewart, 2008; Tourki, Keisler, & Linkov, 2013); futures (Riedy, 2008; Slaughter, 2003; Voros, 2008); spirituality and business (Dean, 2004; Pielstick, 2005; Steingard, 2005); collaborating (Chesterman, 2001); education (Davis & Callihan, 2013; Haigh, 2013); sustainability assessment, water and social systems (Akiyama, Li, Kubota, Konagaya, & Watanabe, 2012); development and literacy (Gómez, 2008); climate change, understanding, adaptation and transformation (Esbjörn-Hargens, 2010d; O'Brien, 2012; O'Brien & Hochachka, 2010; Riedy, 2011); psychopathology (Ingersoll & Marquis, 2014) and many more areas such as art, criminology, environmental philosophy, intersubjectivity, medicine, music therapy, politics, psychotherapy and counselling (Esbjörn-Hargens, 2006).

[3] For an in-depth discussion of energy efficiency and meta-theory application see Divecha (2014) Chapter 3.

[4] A note on data: Some meta-theory analysis distinguishes between theory and models. Van de Ven and Poole (2000) categorise data sources used for meta-theory development in such a way. Models are defined as being derived from theory describing a system – with relationships, events and actions – through which an operation's phenomena are described and understood. Examples of models include Piaget's theory of children's stage development (Piaget, 1954 see other chapters in this book for a discussion of such stages). Depending on the research topic this distinction may not add additional clarity. For example, research often ranges across territory defined as both theory and models with the terminology changing with the scale of phenomena considered. Theories and models, in cases like these, are thus the data for meta-theory development and testing. The meta-theory methodology then explicitly draws such theory and model data. This combined theory and model approach is the methodology presented in this chapter.

[5] In another example Marshall (2012) discusses the similarities and differences between two meta-theories - integral theory and critical realism (metaRealisim). One way of framing this discussion is to view each of these two meta-theories as a holon each of which becomes data for meta-theory

building. Similarly Esbjörn-Hargens (2010d) could be considered as developing meta-theory from meta-theories (e.g. critical realism and integral theory). There are other large-scale theories that are integrative approaches (Esbjörn-Hargens, 2010d; Riedy, 2011). Some of these, for example the work of Ervin Laszlo (2007) and Edgar Morin (Montuori, 2013; Morin, 2008), could also be meta-theory 'data' which combined with integral theory 'data' builds meta-theory. However, meta-frameworks such as critical realism, and the recent (2010-2017) growing discussion and synthesis between these and integral theory, are outside the scope of this chapter.

[6] This methodology is developed by Divecha (2014) based on Edwards' (2009, pp. 92-95) methods. It is adapted with two significant changes. The first is that Edwards (2009) outlines the methodology for phase 5, multiparadigm analysis, using bracketing and bridging. This terminology - bracketing and bridging - involves grouping and summarising the themes within a specific identified paradigm to identify the core conceptual lenses within it. It then, through bridging, looks for conceptual lenses that are shared across different paradigms. Edwards cites the outline of this technique to Schultz and Hatch (1996). However, Schultz and Hatch go further to describe a method they label as interplay. Interplay identifies both conceptual lenses that are shared across paradigms, as well as looking for contrasts. Such contrasts could serve to highlight conceptual lenses specific to a paradigm that may not be shared, or may be contradicted, by another paradigm - for example apparent paradoxes between theories (Poole & Van de Ven, 1989). Consequently, for studies with such apparent paradoxes, the interplay method is a useful addition to Edwards' meta-theory methodology. The second change to combine Edwards' last two phases, numbers 7 & 8. This is done as the implications and evaluation of meta-theory research appear to be interdependent and an artificial separation may not help to develop an integrated perspective.

[7] It is likely that multiple conceptual lens sets are revealed by this work. In conducting a multiparadigmal review for organisational transformation (as a window on sustainability challenges) Edwards (2009) identifies 24 different lenses broadly grouped under 6 categories. I conducted a multiparadigmal review over organisational approaches to energy efficiency and found 20 conceptual lens sets across the 5 categories from Table 1 (Divecha, 2014 Chapter 3).

[8] Note that a multiparadigmal review can surface perspectives relevant to all of the eight methodological zones in Figure 4. That is, this is not simply 3rd person analysis but when described within research it often has these 3rd person characteristics. Consequently, it is labeled in this way for simplicity in this chapter.

Chapter 3
Legitimizing Integral Theory in Academia:
Demonstrating the Effectiveness of Integral Theory Through Its Application in Research

Veronika Bohac Clarke
University of Calgary, Canada

ABSTRACT

This chapter is based on the analysis of experiences of graduate students and professors using Integral Theory (IT) as transdisciplinary research framework, at a Western Canadian mainstream university. The traditional disciplinary orthodoxies, which had presented a formidable challenge to the acceptance of IT in mainstream academia, are briefly described. For example, not having a single disciplinary home, Integral academics do not fit into the traditional roles and their associated benefits. This applies both to professors and to graduate students. Integral students must continue to defend their research and professors must defend Integral teaching. Nevertheless, research is strengthened by an Integral worldview and a more complex understanding of the world. The chapter concludes with a specific discussion of how IT is employed to investigate multiple contexts of complex problems.

INTRODUCTION

This chapter stems from my experience of supervising, to successful completion, 17 doctoral theses (both EdD and PhD) based on Integral Theory. As such, I am writing this chapter for potential researchers, particularly those, who may be situated in mainstream academia, and who are considering using Integral Theory in their research design and/or analysis. The description of Integral Theory and, specifically AQAL, which is offered in this chapter, could therefore be more accurately considered as an *interpretation* from a researcher, for researchers "doing Integral on the ground." Unlike the many highly theoretical analyses and critiques of AQAL that are available in Integral publications, this chapter takes a very practical, applied approach to conducting Integral research within the disciplinary confines of mainstream academia.

DOI: 10.4018/978-1-5225-5873-6.ch003

Background: Challenges to the Use of Integral Theory in the Traditional Academic Disciplinary Context

A brief account of the current context of mainstream universities is provided to explain the cautious and conservative reception of Integral Theory as a legitimate research framework.

Driven by neoliberal algorithmic governmentality, Western universities currently find themselves locked into public competition with each other. Big data, targets and research funding are some of the key elements in this academic race. In response, universities have been sacrificing creativity for efficiency, curiosity for strategy, and streamlining their research agendas toward a few research goals with strategically high probability of gaining research funding. In this climate, working with currently acclaimed research methodologies is strategically more conducive to winning the race, than trying out new strategies that have little or no track record.

While this chapter is based on experiences from one university, where Integral research has been given some opportunity to grow in one Faculty, I have had conversations with colleagues from numerous other Canadian universities to check my perceptions, and similar views were noted with respect to the importance of strategically positioned research and strong track record. Furthermore, having graduated 17 doctoral students whose thesis research was based on Integral Theory, I had 17 opportunities to witness the deep reservations that external examiners - scholars from top Canadian universities - expressed about transdisciplinary research and Integral Methodological Pluralism, particularly at the doctoral student level.

Specifically, I have observed two sources of resistance to the use of Integral Theory, and they appear to be related to the nature of the graduate programs themselves. At the doctoral level, the resistance of supervisors and examiners centers around traditional definitions of disciplines, ontologies and epistemologies. A doctoral student is generally expected to choose one discipline/ontology/epistemology and base their thesis research on it. Ontological pluralism is still mistrusted by traditional academics. Methodological pluralism is discouraged on the basis that it is difficult for one student to carry out, and even more difficult to defend.

At the master's level, particularly in the course based programs with capstone research projects, there is a learned tendency to follow templates and to follow closely the generally accepted dogma reproduced in research textbooks. The idea of trying out, or even trying to understand, a new research approach that is not covered in the traditional textbooks, tends to be seen as threatening and therefore is generally resisted by the students.

Beyond the graduate students' program-related challenges, there are also challenges to both professors and students in terms of their suitability or eligibility for research funding, which is still defined by disciplinary boundaries. Since they have no disciplinary home, they have a questionable academic identity within the organization, which often puts them at a disadvantage for research funding. This has direct implication for track record: no track record – no funding; no funding-no track record.

Brief History of Disciplinary Orthodoxies in the Academic Context

Before even addressing the issue of methodological pluralism, it is useful to delve ever so briefly into the context of the rise and fall of the dominance of popular ontologies, and the impact this has had on the classification of types of methodologies.

In the dim past, the first ontology was characterized as the Subjective ontology – "the world is what I perceive, the truth is subjective." This was the *only* ontology in its day, and the work of the great classical philosophers exemplify this world view. Even within this initial world view or ontology, there were nuances shaped by historical contexts, and many of these nuances were religious in nature. There were various labels attached to this ontology, depending on the specific disciplinary stance of each major thinker. Labels such as Existentialism or Idealism did much to confuse the matter and continue to make it far more mysterious than it needs to be for present day doctoral students.

The Subjective ontology received a decisive blow from the scientific revolution and modernity – the new version of enlightenment – which completely discredited the Subjective world view. The new ruling ontology was characterized as Objective – "the world is what can be measured, the truth is objective." There were labels attached to this ontology as well (Reductionism, Positivism, etc.) adding again some mystery – but there was no doubt that the Objective ontology was the *only* ontology. The Objective research and thinking continued to evolve, not only into Post-Positivism, but also, by the 1990s, into a new world-view that enabled the understanding of systems and complexity. This new world view, which is characterized as Inter-Objective –" the truth is what systems enact", does not use reductionist thinking, and does not break up objects of research into smaller constituent parts. Instead, it studies the behavior and evolving interactions within and among systems. This significant difference initially seemed to escape notice, since it was still considered "Science" and therefore Objective.

The last active remnant of the Subjective ontology was the work of the phenomenologist Edmund Husserl (1990, [1928]). From about the mid-1900s, the survivors of the Subjective- bashing evolved into Post-Modernists (Foucault, 1997), and promoted their own world view –characterized as the Intersubjective ontology – "the truth is what groups agree is true". They vigorously criticized the Subjective view (Derrida 1984), but for a time tolerated the fact that Science held its own ontology. Objective science, being the only ontology, did not seem particularly aware of Post-Modernist thought. However, at this point, a Post-Modernist effort ensued to recognize the existence of *two* ontologies: Relativism (Intersubjective ontology) and Positivism or Post-Positivism (Objective ontology). Paradigm wars ensued, played out in public fora such as the American Educational Research Association (AERA) and eventually, even if just to stop the bad press, the existence of the two world views was accepted. It is still up to debate whether the Objectivists really accepted the Intersubjectivists as equal partners, or even as serious researchers, but the public acrimony desisted. The acceptance of two ontologies, instead of just a single monolithic ontology that explained everything, was a huge development in academic research thinking.

The pragmatic outcome of this momentous compromise was that the two opposing world views became characterized and represented by two methodological silos "Qualitative" and "Quantitative" research methods.

These two silos each contained methodological families from two ontological paradigms thrown together and somehow assumed to be homogeneous. In spite of huge ontological differences, the Subjective and Intersubjective paradigm methodologies were now somehow equivalently "Qualitative". The same occurred with the "Quantitative "methodologies, which subsumed the methodological families of the Objective and Interobjective paradigms. Politically, these two "containers" still represented two opposing methodological camps.

At this point graduate students would say, for example, that they are conducting a qualitative study, and pick "constructivism" as the epistemology because it covers a multitude of sins, and avoid the discussion of ontology altogether. Crotty (1998) offered a "work-around" for avoiding the ontological issue, which was gratefully embraced by many graduate students.

Science continued to function separately (with the exception of Grounded Theory research) from the qualitative research side, until Johnson and Onwuegbuzie (2004) among others, began to propose the idea of using methodologies from both camps in one research study. More wars ensued, until Mixed Methods Research (MMR) was grudgingly accepted as a legitimate approach to research. To facilitate this legitimation, MMR proponents worked exceedingly hard to prescribe the exact approaches to mixing the methods. One question that they could not initially answer without a great deal of difficulty was the question about the ontology of a Mixed Methods study. Was there one, were there two, what were they, what role did they play, etc.

While this debate still raged on, Integral theory (AQAL) came on the research scene as a transdisciplinary research framework. Having developed AQAL and Integral Methodological Pluralism (IMP) outside of the political confines of academia, Wilber (2000a, 2000b, 2006) had no problem with proclaiming that there are several ontologies, not just two. In this way, IMP went beyond the Pragmatism of MMR, and enacted Integralism as a way of bringing together all existing ontologies. IMP also suggested that each ontology has its own appropriate set of methodologies, not just the two sets – Qualitative and Quantitative. This notion was initially (and is still) met with outrage, derision or confusion. Attempts to understand IMP from traditional disciplinary perspectives expressed a need to classify IMP under a simple, existing banner – "action research", "qualitative study", "MMR", "case study". The general agreement seemed to be that whether IMP is legitimate or not, it is just too complex to be practical. Interestingly, in Europe transdisciplinarity was really gaining momentum at around the same time (Nicolescu, 2001). Nicolescu's description of transdiciplinarity as knowledge that flowed across, between and beyond disciplines certainly was consistent with the notions underlying the structure of AQAL and IMP, but another remarkable consistency, was demonstrated in Nicolescu's notion of levels of Reality:

Disciplinary research concerns, at most, one and the same level of Reality. Moreover, in most cases, it only concerns fragments of one level of Reality. On the contrary, transdisciplinarity concerns the dynamics engendered by the simultaneous action of several levels of Reality. (1997, p. 3).

These similarities were noted by at least one Integral researcher (McGregor, 2015b).

Interpreting the Integral Model (AQAL) as a Research Tool

This section provides a basic description and interpretation of the Integral model (AQAL), as it is used by doctoral students in their research, at a mainstream research university – in this case the University of Calgary. The description of the specific research design and implementation approaches used by the doctoral students follows in the subsequent section.

The Integral Model is built on two foundational elements – the Quadrants and the Levels. This backbone is then elaborated and unfolded through the inclusion of Lines, States and Types. For the purpose of understanding and employing AQAL in research, the doctoral students have found the following three sources most practically useful: *A Brief History of Everything* (Wilber, 2000a), *Integral Psychology* (Wilber, 2000b), and *Integral Spirituality* (Wilber, 2006). Wilber's *Integral Spirituality* (2006), for example, provides, in addition to a concise description of the model, three very useful Appendices which further contextualize the model in western thinking. As such, these three sources were the primary basis of the interpretations and applications of AQAL to real life doctoral research.

THE QUADRANTS

The Quadrants represent the intersection of fundamental perspectives through which people perceive the world: singular, plural, inside, and outside. The intersection produces the characteristic Integral quadrant map or framework, consisting of the four fundamental world views, also referred to as primordial perspectives by Integral writers (Esbjörn-Hargens, 2006, 2009, 2010): Subjective (inside+singular), Objective (outside+singular), Intersubjective (inside+plural), and Interobjective (outside+plural). These world views are the ontologies that define the perspective taker's truth and reality. Thus, from the Subjective perspective or ontology, the truth is in the eye of the beholder, while from the Objective perspective or ontology, the truth is what is observable and measurable by scientific methods, regardless of whether the subjective observer sees it or not. From the Intersubjective perspective or ontology, the truth is what we (you and I, the group, etc.) agree on, and this agreement modifies the group members' individual subjective truths. From the Interobjective perspective, the truth is what greater systems do, generally independently of what individuals and groups believe, perceive or do. This seemingly simple quadrant map, shown in Figure 1, is invaluable in creating a clear and coherent big picture of the major world views or ontologies which doctoral researchers are required to navigate.

THE LEVELS

The Levels refer to the evolving levels of mental and psychological development over the lifetime of an individual or a group. Wilber (2000b) compared the conclusions of a number of key developmental theorists such as Fowler, Kegan, Kohlberg, Gilligan, etc. (Wilber, 2000b, pp. 197-217), and found fundamental coherence among them. In terms of describing the developmental levels for use in his model, Wilber referred to Loevinger's seminal work (Loevinger, 1985) and Cook-Greuter's continued elaboration of developmental levels (Cook-Greuter, 2004) for level definitions, which were based on statistically valid and reliable large-scale data.

In agreement with Piaget, the Levels develop in sequence, and levels cannot be skipped. It is, however, possible, to access the previous levels at will. It is helpful to think of the developmental levels as levels of complexity that the individual or group can comprehend and embody. As a number of Integral thinkers (Cook-Greuter, 2013) have reminded those who apply Integral Theory – "higher" levels of development should not be associated with higher levels of human attainment or enlightenment, but rather, they should be seen as evolutionary adaptation to the specific contexts within which the individuals or

Figure 1. Integral quadrant ontologies
(Adapted from Wilber, 2006 and Esbjörn Hargens, 2006, 2009).

UL: Interior Individual SUBJECTIVE What *I* feel, experience Contents of my mind - invisible	UR: Exterior Individual OBJECTIVE What *one (it)* does Behavioral, observable, measurable
LL: Interior Collective INTER-SUBJECTIVE How *we (you and I)* understand each other Cultural	LR: Exterior Collective INTER-OBJECTIVE What *they (its, systems)* do Social

groups live. For example, an individual who was born and has grown up in a totalitarian regime would not have encountered a context that would allow for more complexity than what is rigidly defined by the controlling system.

Wilber also decided to use colours to denote the levels, instead of the traditional labels derived from psychology. The colours were intended to facilitate the use of the model, and indeed that is the case in my experience in working with doctoral students. On the other hand, the usage of colours was one of the distractions, if not detractions, in final oral defences. From the traditional perspective, the use of colours was not seen as academically appropriate. Nevertheless, the use of colours to denote developmental levels was seen as legitimate in business literature. Wilber collaborated for some time with Beck & Cowan (1996), who developed the model of Spiral Dynamics based on the work of Clare Graves (1970), using colours to denote developmental levels. In subsequent years, a number of Integral researchers continued to develop and refine the characterizations of developmental levels (Cook-Greuter, 2014, Spence & McDonald, 2010).

Using even the basic characterizations of the developmental levels provides a fairly accurate general impression of the developmental levels of the individuals or groups being studied, however, the access to reliable tools for testing and interpreting developmental levels remains a critical requirement for integral researchers.

Figure 2 serves as a simple illustration of developmental levels as used in AQAL, by describing three of the levels at which human societies currently operate, with the greatest proportion of the population being at the Amber level, and the smallest proportion at the Green level (Wilber, 2000b).

THE LINES

The lines could be thought of as a number of discrete intelligences expressed by individuals or groups, such as cognitive, interpersonal, psychosexual, emotional and moral lines. These intelligences also possess developmental levels. In this way, depending on personal or contextual characteristics one can express and embody each intelligence at a different level. Wilber identifies the cognitive intelligence as being the determining factor in the capacity for handling complexity. Wilber plotted the developmental lines on a developmental level grid, to obtain a visual psychograph of an individual (Wilber, 2006, pp. 10, 24-25).

The Lines represent the component of AQAL, which can provide more fine-grained knowledge of the interactions between individuals or groups and their contexts within the Quadrants. An analysis of an individual's developmental lines can be very revealing, and can potentially provide answers to research

Figure 2. Simplified adaptation of Wilber's (2000b, pp. 48-53; 2006, p. 69) conceptual map, showing three of the developmental levels of consciousness.

Level 6 Green *Meta-systemic/Pluralistic*	Worldcentric, informational, relativistic, individualistic, human rights, pluralism, tolerance, sensitive self.
Level 5 Orange *Formal operational/rational*	Sociocentric, multiplistic, conscientious, competition, reason, science, democracy, capitalism, strive-drive, achiever self.
Level 4 Amber *Concrete operational mythic*	Ethnocentric, absolutistic, truth force, totalitarian regimes, monarchies, authoritarian religions, discipline, conformist rule/role.

participants' questions, such as: "How can someone so smart be so stupid?" As with the Levels themselves, a reliable and accessible analytical tool is crucial for a proper Integral analysis. These kinds of tools, which require expert interpretation, are usually beyond the means of graduate students to access.

THE STATES

The physiological and psychological states of consciousness, which are transient and generally go unnoticed in individuals' daily lives, unless they affect one's feeling, thinking, actions, or decision-making. An obvious example would be a drunk driver causing an accident. A driver could also cause an accident by falling asleep. There are less dramatic examples of States, such as being stressed, being in a meditative state, daydreaming, etc. The States are mutually exclusive, so one cannot be drunk and sober, or awake and asleep, at the same time. Altered states of consciousness can be involved in the individual meditative explorations of non-dual states, or, in a less immediately noticeable way, altered states can be used to manipulate large groups, as has been demonstrated throughout history in political or religious rallies. The States can affect human motivation for action, and thus can provide another source of fine-grained information about a situation.

THE TYPES

Most societies have been categorizing – or type casting - their members into various categories, from biological (blood types), to social (social castes), to psychological (personality types), to essential (various versions of Zodiacs). Examining the "types" that are being applied in particular contexts can bring some very fine-grained insights, for example in an intercultural study context.

In western society, type casting has become sometimes automatic (the "dumb blonde", for example, having been around in the group consciousness for far too many years). In a seemingly more benign example, a typical conversation at the water cooler might be:
"The boss just yelled at me."
"And what do you expect – he's an Aries!"
The typing can create expectations and even enable behaviour in others. This may not be an insignificant contribution to the unfolding of a research problem.

Thus, typing is an ongoing as well as evolving area that deserves Integral researchers' attention. For example, from a biological standpoint one might say there are two gender types – male and female. From a psychosocial standpoint, there are transgender types and various evolving expressions of gender types that will most certainly create new and different social expectations as well as judgments.

CONCLUDING REFLECTIONS ON AQAL

In conclusion, my colleagues and I have noted that there is a certain predictable learning curve associated with AQAL. The first time doctoral students read a book on AQAL, such as *Integral Psychology* (Wilber, 2000b) or *Integral Spirituality* (Wilber, 2006) –they react in quick succession from "Is this a self-help book?" to "What did he say?" The seemingly straightforward language hides a multitude of meanings, and most students report that they had to read the books twice or three times before they understood them. The first level of understanding, of course, is the intellectual or theoretical understanding. The students do not gain an embodied understanding of the model until they actually try to apply it to research, and then again they go through stages of deeper, applied understanding.

The first elements that students apply are the Quadrants and Levels, with the latter three components of AQAL being relegated to "details". It is not only much later, in the analysis stage, that students begin to access the Lines, States and Types. Before this happens, however, some students go down the theoretical rabbit hole of imagining that there must be 4 mini quadrants within each quadrant, and begin to construct an AQAL edifice worthy of the Kabbalistic Tree of Life, with a mini tree in each Sephirah. This exercise is unnecessary, however, since the use of the other three AQAL components – Lines, States and Types – actually fill in the finer grained details of the research problem in each Quadrant.

Finally, it is important to reiterate my previous comments about the accessibility of instruments and proper interpretations of developmental levels and lines. This is where the genesis of AQAL outside of the academia has negative consequences: the experts who are developing and refining reliable analytical tools for measuring developmental levels are not receiving salaries or research grants from an academic institution, and therefore must sell their products – thereby making them inaccessible to many graduate students. Making Integral Theory more commonplace in academia may create opportunities for institutional funding for doctoral students for this type of analysis.

Application of AQAL in Doctoral and Post-Doctoral Research Studies

This section addresses the translation of the AQAL map into the research context. After describing how AQAL can be used to systematically sort out ontologies and research paradigms, this section elaborates on specific applications of Integral Methodological Pluralism (IMP) in research design, implementation and analysis.

Integral Methodological Pluralism (IMP) as a Framework for Understanding and Defending Research Design

AQAL provides a logical and coherent framework for mapping out ontologies, as was illustrated in the previous section. In developing Integral Methodological Pluralism (IMP), Wilber (2006, Pp. 36-37) identified research paradigms, which were consistent with each quadrant ontology. The research paradigms, in the Kuhnian sense include epistemologies and methodologies. In keeping with Kuhn's (1970) characterization of paradigms, Wilber identified exemplar methodologies in each quadrant. Thus the framework of IMP provides a coherent map that links the ontologies, epistemologies and methodologies within each quadrant. This is an extremely useful tool for researchers, and particularly for doctoral candidates, since without this big picture map, shown in Figure 3, doctoral students found it challenging to navigate the plethora of (often synonymous) ontologies and epistemologies, and to demonstrate a coherent alignment between their chosen methodologies, the ontology, epistemology, and the research questions.

The current use of the designations "qualitative" and "quantitative" research overgeneralizes and conflates the ontologies and epistemologies from the Upper and Lower Left quadrants into the qualitative silo, and from the Upper and Lower Right quadrants into the quantitative silo. This overgeneralization has resulted, for example, in the current tendency to treat phenomenology and hermeneutics as epistemologically equal. This overgeneralization is also becoming particularly unhelpful in the growing area of

Figure 3. IMP: Ontologies and epistemologies in quadrants ontologies
(Adapted from Wilber, 2006 and Esbjorn Hargens, 2006, 2009)

UL Existentialism	UR Realism
Inside + singular Interior Individual	*Outside + singular* Exterior Individual
Rationalism Idealism Subjectivism	Positivism, post-positivism Empiricism Materialism Reductionism
(Monism of mind)	(Monism of matter)
LL Relativism	**LR Pluralism**
Inside + plural Interior Collective	*Outside + plural* Exterior Collective
Constructivism Interpretivism Critical interpretivism (Enactment of pluralism of mind)	Systems theory → complexity theory (Enactment of pluralism of material and human systems)

systems and complexity studies. "Quantitative" methodologies tend to be equated with the reductionist epistemology of the Upper Right quadrant, which operates by breaking things apart and studying the constituent parts. Complex systems, however, by definition cease to exist when they are broken apart (Varela et al, 1974). IMP goes beyond the left-hand side vs right hand side differentiations, and makes finer distinctions between the upper and lower quadrants within each side.

Wilber further refined the characterization of the methodologies in each quadrant by identifying an *inside* (e.g., the "feel" of the ontological experience) and an *outside* (e.g., the "look" of an ontological experience). Therefore, for example, within the Subjective ontology, the inside/feel would refer to the phenomenological experience, while the outside/look would refer to the observation or reflection of that experience by the experiencing subject. Wilber assigned Zones to these inside and outside stances, so that Zone 1 would represent the actual feelings that the subject experienced, while Zone 2 would be the reflections on those feelings and experiences. Figure 4 illustrates the Zones within each quadrant, and their associated methodologies.

The Zone characterization is helpful for graduate students in designing their research. Still using the Subjective, Upper Left quadrant ontology as an example, they can identify in specific terms whether they intend to investigate the feel of a lived experience (through phenomenological interviews) or whether they intend to observe that individual's lived experience (autobiography or biography) or reflect on that experience (autoethnography or narrative analysis). Similarly, in the Lower-Left quadrant Intersubjective ontology, for example, the researcher could clearly separate the Zone 3 hermeneutic meaning making, from the Zone 4 case study or ethnographic observation of the meaning making within groups.

Another useful aspect of the AQAL and specifically IMP framework, is its capacity to track the ontological and epistemological drift in methodologies, as they evolve over time. For example, Grounded Theory (GT) methodology, as developed by Bernie Glaser and Anselm Strauss (1967) began from an objectivist ontological stance in the Upper Right quadrant, as a systematic inductive generation of

Figure 4. IMP Zones and associated methodologies.
Loosely adapted from Wilber, 2006, P. 37.

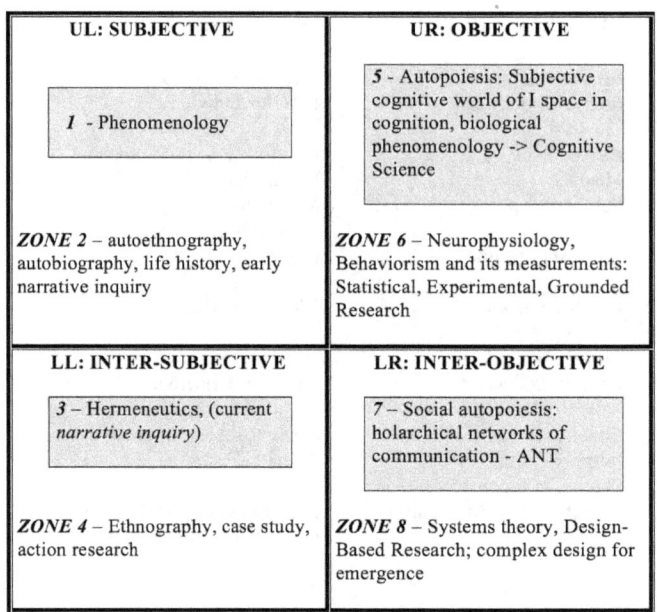

theories from systematically obtained data. Over the years GT evolved into an intersubjectively driven epistemology and methodology (Charmaz, 2014) in the Lower Left quadrant. Similarly, the currently hermeneutic methodology driving Narrative Inquiry (Connely & Clandinin, 1990) migrated into the Lower Left Intersubjective ontology from the Upper Left Subjective approaches of Narrative Analysis and Structuralism. This movement is illustrated in Figure 5.

In addition to mapping and making sense of evolving methodologies, the IMP map is a useful tool for mapping "big names" in research methodology literature, as well as mapping the writings of key theorists (Davis et al, 2015). Such maps are absolutely invaluable for doctoral students preparing for their Candidacy or thesis defence exams.

IMPLEMENTING RESEARCH DESIGN BASED ON THE IMP FRAMEWORK

This section provides a step-by-step description of research design, implementation and analysis as used by doctoral students in their research studies.

Identifying the Research Problem

At this stage, the researcher identifies the overall umbrella problem – not a problem to fix, but a research problem to investigate. The problem statement should be a sentence or a question, which would characterize the overall research problem. I used to call it the "bumper sticker statement", but the new generation of researchers are more familiar with Tweets than bumper stickers. From experience, researchers should not proceed to formulating research questions until they are able to characterize the overall research problem succinctly.

Figure 5. Evolution of methodologies (UL to LL and UR to LL Methodological Families)

UL: SUBJECTIVE Methodological Family	UR: OBJECTIVE Methodological Family
Zone 1 **Phenomenology** – Husserl, Varela, Moustakas, Van Maanen, **Zone 2** **Autoethnography** – Goldschmidt, Carolyn Ellis **Autobiography** - Gusdorf, (1980), Benstock, (1988), Gilmore (2002), Norman Denzin (1989) **Life history** – Butler (1964), Thomas and Znaniecki (1920), - Goodson, Bulmer **Narrative inquiry**	**Zone 5** - Subjective cognitive world of I space in cognition → **Cognitive Science** biological phenomenology – "neurophenomenology" - F. Varela **Zone 6** – Neurophysiology, **Behaviorism** and its measurements; **Statistical** - George Beam (2012), Groves, R.M et al (2009) **Experimental** – Cronbach (1957), Campbell and Stanley (1963) **Grounded Research** –Glasser, Strauss, Corbin, Stake
LL: INTER-SUBJECTIVE Methodological Family	LR: INTER-OBJECTIVE Methodological Family
Zone 3 **Hermeneutics** – Dilthey, Heidegger, Gadamer, **Narrative inquiry** – Jean Clandinin **Zone 4** **Ethnography** - Geertz, Wolcott, **Case study** – Yin, Merriam, Flyvbjerg, Stake, **Action research** – Kurt Lewin (1944), Chris Argyris, Paulo Freire **Participatory Action Research** (PAR), Cher Hendricks, **Grounded Research** - Kathy Charmaz (grounded theory from Constructivist perspective)	**Zone 7** – *Social autopoiesis*: holarchical networks of communication - **Actor Network Theory** (ANT) – Bruno Latour **Zone 8** – Systems theory, Complexity: **Design-Based Research** – Barab, Sandoval, Brown, Collins **Complex design for emergence** – Stacey, Levy, Black, Brent Davis

Four Quadrant View of the Research Problem

Once the research problem is identified, but before the research questions are generated, the researchers must ask themselves what their Kosmic address is – what is their own "home quadrant" and "home level" (Wilber, 2006, pp. 40-41). This exercise is an important requisite of Integral researchers, which is also referred to as reflexivity (Hendricks, 2017). This refers to an exercise of self-reflection about which quadrant and which level the researcher is most likely situated in, or for which they have most preference. This ensures that researcher bias is examined before research questions are formulated.

Researchers then imagine the research problem at the crossroads between the four quadrants, and ask themselves how the problem would be viewed from each perspective, and what would be the main research question asked about the problem from each perspective. At the end of this exercise, researchers have one major research question about the problem in each quadrant, as indicated in Figure 6.

The placement of the appropriate questions in each quadrant is the key step in the research design. Ontology (quadrant) defines the world view, the world view dictates epistemology (overall approach to the research), and consequently the methodology. If the world view is Subjective, for example, one clearly could not use a statistical methodology.

Figure 6. Designing research questions in quadrants.

Research statement – umbrella statement describing the research problem.
Major research questions – at least 4 but no more than 8 – provide avenues for investigating the problem.

UL - Subjective	UR - Objective
Question 1 -Methodology/method	Question 2 -Methodology/method
LL - Intersubjective	**LR - Interobjective**
Question 3 Methodology/method	Question 4 Methodology/method

A word of clarification needs to be said here about two terms that can mean quite different things, yet are used interchangeably in the research literature, depending on how each author understands and defines the terms. The two terms are: conceptual framework and theoretical framework.

I use the "*Conceptual framework*" to mean a map underlying all the elements of the research design, including the problem, the research questions, and the methodologies that will be used to answer the questions. So AQAL, as an organizing framework or map for the research design, is the conceptual framework for the research project.

I use "*Theoretical framework*" as the theoretical model or theory that describes some aspect of the research problem. So this element deals with some aspect of the content of the investigation. It can influence the design, if it dictates the kinds of questions that you will ask, but it is often used in the *analysis of the findings*. The theoretical framework is associated with one particular quadrant ontology, so it is possible to employ four different theoretical frameworks in the analysis. For example, Intersubjective (LL) data gathered in classrooms pertaining to a research question focused on inclusive classrooms, might be first analyzed for themes, and the themes might be further analyzed in relation to the components of Bourdieu's theory of social space, power and practical reason (Bourdieu, 2011). At the same time Interobjective (LR) district and national system policy data in the same research could be analyzed using Complexity theory (Morin, 1992) to elucidate the relationships and patterns of influence between them.

Matching Methodologies to Research Questions

Given that IMP indicates exemplar research methodologies in each ontological quadrant and zone, the researchers then select the methodologies that are suitable to supporting their research questions in each quadrant. Once the methodologies are selected, specific questions are identified. For example, if in the Upper Right (UR) quadrant, questionnaires about adoption of technology in the classroom are selected, then specific questions for the questionnaire are developed and tested. If the methodology is a focus group interview in the Lower Left (LL) quadrant, then specific questions for the focus group interview are developed. The strength of this approach is the clear line from ontologies to methodologies, to research questions, to specific instrument questions. This approach is illustrated in Figure 7.

A question that always arises at the point of implementation of the research design is: "which quadrant do we start with?" Some researchers try to follow the specifically designated order of data collection and analysis that is elaborated in Mixed Methods Research (Johnson & Onwuegbuzie, 2004). This approach is fine, but could become unnecessarily constraining. Because the logic of lining up the ontologies, research questions and methodologies is already built into the IMP framework, it is quite acceptable to be more intuitive about the starting point. The context of the research problem may also influence the researcher's decision as to which quadrant and research question to explore first. For example, it might be helpful to begin with a questionnaire to get an overall big picture of what various participant groups are actually doing, with respect to the research problem. From this big picture, a more informed set of questions for the LL quadrant focus groups might be designed, followed by yet more specific questions directed at individuals in the UL. The findings about what people do, how groups makes sense and what individuals experience – for example with respect to a research problem about inclusive classrooms – can then be contrasted with a policy analysis (LR) and interviews with policy makers. The policy perspectives may then be taken back to the LL groups such as school staffs. Some of these decisions about which quadrant to address next, are made on the basis of the analysis from previous quadrants. So, for example, it might become clear that the views of the policy makers may need to be gathered first, before developing interview questions for the focus groups (LL) in the schools.

Analysis and Findings

Each data set is first analyzed separately, using the appropriate analytical tools for the data gathering methodology that was used. The initial set of data and findings should not be mixed with other analyses from other quadrants. A clear view of what the problem looks like from each perspective should first be obtained. Thus, for example, UR data would be analyzed using statistical techniques ranging from simple percentage analysis to t-tests, etc., depending on the context, amount of data, and the question asked. Eventually, these findings would be expressed in a number of overall themes. In the same way, UL and LL data would be analyzed for themes, using the appropriate theme and reduction process. Eventually the researchers end up with themes in all four quadrants, which address the research questions posed in each quadrant.

What's Transdisciplinary About it: Quadrants Talking to Each Other

At this point, it becomes clear that themes from the various quadrants interact with each other – oppose, reinforce, explain. The doctoral students dubbed this process "the quadrants talking to each other". In many cases, this discussion among the quadrants (findings gathered through various disciplinary methodologies) can yield surprising explanatory power and insights. Ideally, the researchers would go back to the contexts and data sources that showed strong quadrant interactions, and conduct a subsequent round of inquiry. In the real-life world of doctoral students, a second round of research is beyond the scope and availability of time and resources. Figure 8 illustrates the transdisciplinary phenomenon of "Quadrants talking to each other".

Figure 7. Hypothetical example of progress from research questions to methods to specific questions.

Problem Statement: How have inclusive classrooms been implemented in District A?	
UL: SUBJECTIVE	**UR: OBJECTIVE**
Question 1 -> What is your personal experience of the inclusive classroom or school? Method: -Student interviews – phenomenological -Teacher interviews - phenomenological -Principal interviews –phenomenological -Parent interviews - phenomenological Specific questions designed to capture each person's subjective experience	Question 3 -> What are the observable behaviours, practices and learning results in the classrooms and schools? Methods: -Student questionnaires -Teacher questionnaires -Student achievement results -Student discipline record per school Specific questions designed for each questionnaire
LL: INTERSUBJECTIVE	**LR: INTEROBJECTIVE**
Question 2 -> What happens in your inclusive classroom? Method: -Interviews with teachers about their approach to running an inclusive classroom. -Focus group interviews with students about how they work with other students in the classroom. -Classroom observations. Specific questions designed to capture group meaning making.	Question 4 -> What is the policy impact on the schools in the district, and on the district, in the provincial, national and global context? Method: -District and school policy analysis -Government targets for the district -Funding for the district -Student demographics -Student-teacher ratios -Interviews with district administrators/policy makers Specific questions about the influences of various systems on the district administration and planning

CONCLUSION: BENEFITS, CHALLENGES, AND IMPLICATIONS OF USING AQAL IN ACADEMIC RESEARCH

Benefits, Challenges, and Implications of Using AQAL

AQAL is a framework that can support a research design that investigates problems from multiple ontologies and research paradigms. A full spectrum map of the research problem can identify clashes of perspectives, discrepancies between developmental levels – for example between teachers, parents and administration, or between schools and central office, etc.

The richness of data also increases the complexity of the analysis. It is certainly possible to add the analysis of developmental lines – perhaps to clarify the actions of administrators in this hypothetical example. The addition of every subsequent element of AQAL will also increase the complexity of the overall analysis and the sheer quantity of data, so clearly some decisions need to be made as to how much data is enough. Analyzing school administrators' developmental lines may not be necessary when studying ongoing policies such as inclusive classrooms, however, in a turbulent situation where inclusive classrooms constitute a new policy, studying the administrators' approach may be significant.

Figure 8. Quadrants talking to each other

IMP - INTEGRALISM - Accounts for perspectives from all 4 quadrants *co-arising* at the same time. All perspectives and their *interactions* are identifiable. Themes from one quadrant influence themes in other quadrants and vice versa.	
UL Existentialism *Inside + singular* Interior Individual Rationalism Idealism Subjectivism (Monism of mind)	**UR Realism** *Outside + singular* Exterior Individual Positivism, post-positivism Empiricism Materialism Reductionism (Monism of matter)
LL Relativism *Inside + plural* Interior Collective Constructivism Interpretivism Critical interpretivism (Enactment of pluralism of mind)	**LR Pluralism** *Outside + plural* Exterior Collective Systems theory → complexity theory (Enactment of pluralism of material and human systems)

Any introduction of a significant change in the research context can, of course, be added to the research design. Using the IMP map, any additional research questions can be easily tracked. This makes IMP useful in studying complex systems. It should become clear, that the more fully the capacity of the model is utilized, the more complex the data and analysis become. The limit of what one researcher can manage (without becoming superficial) can be reached very quickly. The need for employing research teams becomes obvious.

There are several benefits to research teams, whether there is one member per quadrant or more.

1. Each quadrant perspective is authentically represented, from formulating research questions, to employing the data collection and analysis tools at an appropriate level of expertise and sophistication.
2. The amounts of data are more manageable if each team handles one quarter.
3. The discussion next steps, as well as the transdisciplinary discussions between the quadrants talking, is usually superior in terms of monitoring researcher bias, than an individual reflexivity exercise.

In the case of doctoral students, currently I use a built-in system of regular reviews of the research project with members of the doctoral cohort, who stand in the place of the transdisciplinary team. Graduate student research team investigating a common problem for their Integral thesis project, would certainly be worthy of exploration.

Legitimizing AQAL in Academic Research

While transdisciplinarity (Choi & Pak, 2006; Volckman, 2014) is becoming recognized as the way to go in research, certainly by big think tanks and research funding organizations (Altass & Wiebe, 2017), in real life academia disciplinary orthodoxies continue to rule. Not having a single disciplinary home means one does not fit into the traditional role descriptions and faculty research funding rubrics. This applies both to professors and to graduate students.

An additional concern is that, as funding organizations increasingly use the term "transdisciplinary", academic research teams hunting for grants will put together politically and financially influenced research designs, which are often compromise positions.

Finally, there are journals, such as the Open Access journal *Sustainability*, where forward-thinking articles from around the world are published, but many universities only "count" publications in top tier journals (conservative, with 2-year submission to publication time line, and acceptance rate under 10%).

Transdisciplinary research in general, and Integral research in particular, face the Amber and Orange level challenges of traditional disciplinary orthodoxies, and algorithmic governmentality that are prevalent in western universities today.

However, as the work of the doctoral cohort in Integral Theory has demonstrated, it is possible to do legitimate transdisciplinary research in mainstream academia. The research projects carried out by these doctoral students were individual endeavours, and as such, were limited in magnitude. The next step would be to organize thesis research projects for "transdisciplinary teams" of four doctoral students, and to work out in detail the mechanism for structuring, enacting and analyzing such projects.

It is becoming very clear in today's research contexts that research problems are complex – no longer can researchers simply "isolate the problem", study it out of context, and provide a solution. Therefore, research designs must provide the capacity to gather complex data and understand the complex relationships that constitute the research problems (Davis & Sumara, 2008). AQAL and Integral Methodological Pluralism provide a coherent conceptual framework for handling complex problems – a research framework whose time has come (Watkins & Wilber, 2015; McGregor, 2015a)

REFERENCES

Altass, P., & Wiebe, S. (2017). Re-imagining Education Policy and Practice in the Digital Era. *Journal of the Canadian Association for Curriculum Studies*, *15*(2), 48–63.

Beck, D., & Cowan, C. (1996). *Spiral Dynamics: Mastering Values, Leadership and Change*. Malden, MA: Blackwell Publishers, Inc.

Bourdieu, P. (2011). *Outline of a Theory of Practice*. Cambridge, UK: Cambridge University Press.

Charmaz, K. (2014). *Constructing Grounded Theory: a practical guide through qualitative analysis* (2nd ed.). London: Sage.

Choi, B. C., & Pak, A. W. (2006). Multidisciplinarity, interdisciplinarity and transdisciplinarity in health research, services, education and policy: 1. Definitions, objectives, and evidence of effectiveness. *Clinical and Investigative Medicine. Medecine Clinique et Experimentale*, *29*(6), 351–364. PMID:17330451

Connely, M., & Clandinin, J. (1990). Stories of Experience and Narrative Inquiry. *Educational Researcher*, *19*(5), 2–14. doi:10.3102/0013189X019005002

Cook-Greuter, S. (2013). Assumptions Versus Assertions: Separating Hypotheses from Truth in the Integral Community. *Journal of Integral Theory and Practice*, *8*(3&4), 227–236.

Cook-Greuter, S. R. (2004). Making the case for a developmental perspective. *Industrial and Commercial Training*, *36*(7), 275–281. doi:10.1108/00197850410563902

Cook-Greuter, S. R. (2013). *Nine levels of increasing embrace in ego development: A full-spectrum theory of vertical growth and meaning making*. Retrieved from: http://www.cook-greuter.com/Cook-Greuter%209%20levels%20paper%20new%201.1%2714%2097p%5B1%5D.pdf

Crotty, M. (1998). *The Foundations of Social Research: Meaning and perspective in the research process*. London: SAGE Publications.

Davis, B. & Sumara, D. (2008). Complexity as a theory of education. *Transnational Curriculum Inquiry*, *5*(2).

Davis, B., Sumara, D., & Luce-Kapler, R. (2015). *Engaging minds: Cultures of education and practices of teaching*. Routledge. doi:10.4324/9781315695891

Derrida, J. (1984). Deconstruction and the other. An interview with Jacques Derrida. In R. Kearney (Ed.), *Dialogues with contemporary continental thinker*. Manchester, UK: Manchester University Press.

Esbjörn-Hargens, S. (2006). Integral research: A multi-method approach to investigating phenomena. *Constructivism in the Human Sciences*, *11*(1), 79–107.

Esbjörn-Hargens, S. (2009). An overview of Integral Theory. *IntegralPost*. Retrieved from https://integrallife.com/integral-post/overview-integral-theory

Esbjörn-Hargens, S. (2010). An ontology of climate change: Integral pluralism and the enactment of multiple objects. *Journal of Integral Theory and Practice*, *5*(1), 143–174.

Foucault, M. (1997). *Subjectivity and Truth. In Ethics: Subjectivity and Truth* (pp. 87–92). New York: The New Press.

Glaser, B. D., & Strauss, A. K. (1967). *The Discovery of Grounded Theory*. Chicago: Aldine.

Graves, C. (1970). Levels of Existence: An Open System Theory of Values. *Journal of Humanistic Psychology*, *10*(2), 131–155. doi:10.1177/002216787001000205

Hendricks, C. (2017). *Improving Schools Through Action Research: A Reflective Practice Approach* (4th ed.). Pearson.

Husserl, E. (1990). *On the Phenomenology of the Consciousness of Internal Time (1893–1917)* (J. B. Brough, Trans.). Dordrecht: Kluwer. (Original work published 1928)

Johnson, R. B., & Onwuegbuzie, A. J. (2004). Mixed Methods Research: A Research Paradigm Whose Time Has Come. *Educational Researcher*, *33*(7), 14–26. doi:10.3102/0013189X033007014

Kuhn, T. (1970). *The Structure of Scientific Revolutions* (2nd ed.). Chicago: University of Chicago Press.

Loevinger, J. (1985). Revision of the sentence completion test for ego Development. *Journal of Personality and Social Psychology, 48*(2), 420–427. doi:10.1037/0022-3514.48.2.420 PMID:3981402

McGregor, S. L. T. (2015a). Integral dispositions and transdisciplinary knowledge creation. *Integral Leadership Review, 15*(1). Retrieved from http://integralleadershipreview.com/12548-115-integral-dispositions-transdisciplinary- knowledge-creation/

McGregor, S. L. T. (2015b). The Nicolescuian and Zurich approaches to transdisciplinarity. *Integral Leadership Review, 15*(2). Retrieved from http://integralleadershipreview.com/13135-616-the-nicolescuian-and-zurich-approaches- to-transdisciplinarity/

Morin, E. (1992). From the concept of system to the paradigm of complexity. Journal of Social and Evolutionary Systems, 15(4), 371-384.

Nicolescu, B. (1997). *La Transdisciplinarité*. Paris, France: Rocher. Retrieved from http://perso.club-internet.fr/nicol/ciret

Nicolescu, B. (2001). *Manifesto of transdisciplinarity*. Albany, NY: State University of New York Press.

Spence, K. K., & McDonald, M. (2010). Linking Developmental Action Logics to transformational leadership behaviours. *Journal of Integral Theory and Practice, 5*(4), 94–111.

Varela, F., Maturana, H., & Uribe, G. (1974). Autopoiesis: The organization of living systems, its characterization, and a model. *Bio Systems, 5*(4), 187–196. doi:10.1016/0303-2647(74)90031-8 PMID:4407425

Volckman, R. (2014). Generativity, Transdisciplinarity, and Integral Leadership. *The Journal of New Paradigm Research, 20*(3-4), 248–265.

Watkins, A., & Wilber, K. (2015). *Wicked & Wise: How to Solve the World's Toughest Problems*. Chatham, UK: Urbane Publications.

Wilber, K. (2000a). *A Brief History of Everything* (2nd ed.). Boston, MA: Shambhala Publications, Inc.

Wilber, K. (2000b). *Integral psychology: Consciousness, spirit, psychology, therapy*. Boston: Shambhala Publications, Inc.

Wilber, K. (2006). Integral Methodological Pluralism. In *Integral spirituality*. Boston, MA: Integral Books.

KEY TERMS AND DEFINITIONS

Action Research: Often carried out by teacher researchers, Action Research is an exploration of interventions in the school context, with the ultimate aim of improving student learning. This exploration usually occurs in cycles, with the teacher researcher reflecting on what has occurred during each cycle.

Conceptual Framework: This term is used differently by different researchers; therefore, each researcher has to define how they use it in their work. I use the *conceptual framework* to mean a map underlying all the elements of the research design, including the problem, the research questions, and the methodologies that will be used to answer the questions. As such, AQAL, as an organizing framework or *map for the research design*, would be the conceptual framework for the research project.

Integral Methodological Pluralism: In integral methodological pluralism (IMP), four research paradigms are identified, which are consistent with each of the four quadrant ontologies of AQAL. The research paradigms include epistemologies and methodologies. Wilber identified exemplar methodologies in each quadrant. Thus, the framework of IMP provides a coherent map that links the ontologies, epistemologies and methodologies within each quadrant.

Integral Theory (AQAL): The integral model or AQAL, as designed by Ken Wilber, is a conceptual framework built on two foundational elements – the quadrants and the levels. This backbone is then elaborated and unfolded through the inclusion of Lines, States and Types. The quadrants represent the intersection of fundamental perspectives through which people perceive the world: singular, plural, inside, and outside. The intersection produces the characteristic integral quadrant map or framework, consisting of the four fundamental world views or ontologies. The levels refer to the evolving levels of mental and psychological development over the lifetime of an individual or a group. Each ontological (quadrant) view can be enacted at whichever developmental level the viewers who occupy the quadrant have attained.

Metatheory: AQAL serves as an organizing framework for ontologies, epistemologies, and methodologies. Since these are also the foundational points of departure for theorists, AQAL is also a coherent framework for organizing theories.

Ontological Pluralism: The four quadrants of AQAL represent the four basic world views, or ontologies. The ontologies are Subjective (inside+singular), Objective (outside+singular), Intersubjective (inside+plural), and Interobjective (outside+plural). These world views are the ontologies that define the perspective taker's truth and reality. Thus, from the Subjective perspective or ontology, the truth is in the eye of the beholder, while from the Objective perspective or ontology, the truth is what is observable and measurable by scientific methods, regardless of whether the subjective observer sees it or not. From the Intersubjective perspective or ontology, the truth is what we (you and I, the group, etc.) agree on, and this agreement modifies the group members' individual subjective truths. From the Interobjective perspective, the truth is what greater systems do, generally independently of what individuals and groups believe, perceive or do. Ontological pluralism means not only that there are four perspectives/ontologies, rather than the currently accepted two, but that all four perspectives co-arise in the contexts of individuals and groups.

Theoretical Framework: This term is also used differently by different researchers; therefore, each researcher has to define how they use it in their work. I use *theoretical framework* as the theoretical model or theory that describes some aspect of the research problem. So this element deals with some aspect of the *content* (not design) of the investigation. It could influence the design, if it requires that particular kinds of questions need to be asked in a specific quadrant, but its major role in the *analysis of the findings*. A theoretical framework is associated with one particular quadrant ontology, so in IMP it is possible to employ four different theoretical frameworks in the analysis.

Section 2
Using AQAL in Research in Schools

Chapter 4
An Integral Analysis of International Mindedness

Avis Eileen Beek
University of Calgary, Czech Republic

ABSTRACT

The purpose of this chapter is to report on a study that examined contextual interpretations of international mindedness by International Baccalaureate (IB) Diploma Programme students in different school contexts in the Czech Republic. The conceptual framework was based on Wilber's integral theory and integral methodological pluralism, a novel application in the study of international mindedness. Using an empirical methodology, international mindedness was shown to be widely applicable, developmental, and experiential in nature. Through a hermeneutic phenomenological methodology, findings revealed the experience of international mindedness was characterized by the development of an intercultural identity, the ability to take alternate perspectives, and the capacity to resolve disconnection from important people in their lives. Contextual factors of privilege and exposure to diversity also influenced students' experience of international mindedness. Implications for improving education for international mindedness at the level of the school and the IB organization are discussed.

INTRODUCTION

As our human experience becomes increasingly globalized, diverse individuals are much more able to influence one another. This contemporary experience is rich in collaboration and ingenuity that rightly advances our planet towards a peaceful and sustainable existence. However, the complexity of these exchanges is often challenged by that which divides us whether it be geography, language or politics. The aspiration to be *internationally minded* suggests that through respectful intercultural understanding, there is a way of being that allows us to acknowledge our differences and work together towards the greater good. Reasonably, education across diverse settings must play a role in the development of international mindedness. The aim of this research was to explore how education in different contexts is responsive to this increasingly significant worldview of international mindedness.

DOI: 10.4018/978-1-5225-5873-6.ch004

Integral theory was employed in this research as a novel and rigorous means of studying the complex construct of international mindedness. The integral approach aims to incorporate insights of all the existing research methodologies in an integrative way so that new possibilities can be realized (Oral, 2013). Inquiry into the multifaceted and complex construct of international mindedness was enriched through this holistic and all-encompassing approach. As integral theory provides a conceptual and methodological structure that is appropriate to virtually all contexts at any scale (Esbjörn-Hargens, 2009) it was well suited to frame this context-sensitive study of international mindedness. Perhaps most fitting to this research, integral theory is about connection. To Ken Wilber (2000a), integral means:

...to integrate, to bring together, to join, to link, to embrace. Not in the sense of uniformity, and not in the sense of ironing out all the wonderful differences, colors, zigs and zags of a rainbow-hued humanity, but in the sense of unity-in-diversity, shared commonalities along with our wonderful differences. (p. 2)

Context and Purpose

The context of this study was to examine international mindedness through the lens of schools offering the International Baccalaureate (IB) Diploma Programme. The IB is a non-profit international educational organization founded in 1968, providing programmes for students aged 3 to 18 in close to 150 countries (IBO, 2016). The organization is dedicated to guiding young people in the development of international mindedness. The aim of all IB programmes is to "develop internationally minded people who, recognizing their common humanity and shared guardianship of the planet, help to create a better and more peaceful world (IBO, 2013, p. 1).

More specifically, the purpose of the study was to examine contextual interpretations of international mindedness of IB Diploma Programme students in two distinct school contexts in the Czech Republic. The C-School can be described as a national school whose student body is primarily Czech, the majority of whom attended Czech government schools in the past. The majority of the teaching faculty are also Czech. The I-School is an international school that enrols students mainly from expatriate families and a smaller number of Czech citizens. It has a much more diverse student body and teaching faculty in terms of past school experiences.

Research Design

As an integrally informed inquiry, examination of the construct of international mindedness occurred through the distinct yet intersecting perspectives of the integral quadrants. The research was initiated with questions posed and literature reviewed from the perspectives of the integral quadrants. The study proceeded from the UR to the UL to the LL quadrant with the findings in each quadrant informing the subsequent. Implications for practice and further research emerged through the lens of the LR quadrant.

As integral theory acknowledges and includes insights from all valid forms of research (Esbjörn-Hargens, 2009), this integral research was enacted through methodological pluralism. In particular, integral methodological pluralism was employed in this study through empirical and hermeneutic-phenomenological research methodologies. Quantitative and qualitative methods were undertaken. Figure 1, outlines the research questions, literature review focus, methodology and methods and findings of the study.

Figure 1. Research questions, literature review outline, methodology and methods undertaken in the research

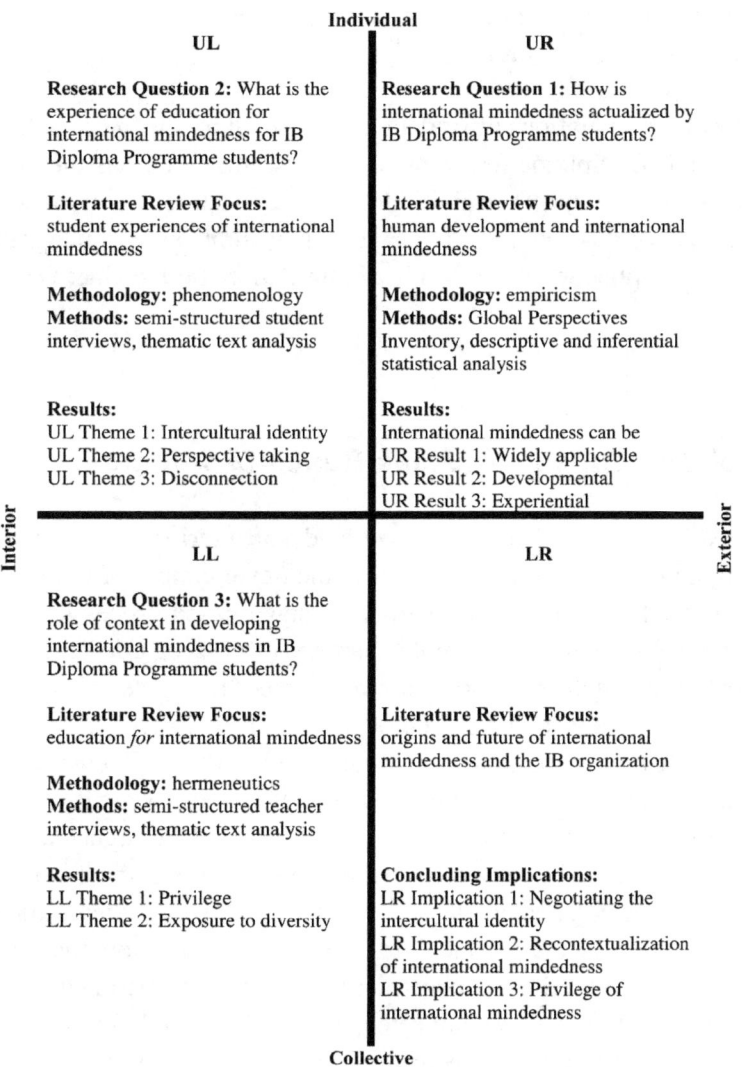

Significance

This study was well positioned to explore aspects of international mindedness and its contextual interpretations not already documented in the literature. In a major study on international mindedness commissioned by the IB, it was noted that the organization is striving to broaden their range of knowledge on the topic to allow for increased critical reflection (Singh & Qi, 2013). International education scholars have called for an appreciation of the potential for different local interpretations of international mindedness (Doherty & Mu, 2011; Drake, 2004; Lai, Shum & Zhang, 2014; Lee et al., 2014). Haywood (2007) summarized this position well:

The educator's role is not to direct students towards a particular style of international-mindedness, but is instead to encourage a predisposition towards international-mindedness in general that will allow students to develop their own responses and channels of expression...There can be many distinct ways of educating for international-mindedness. (p. 85)

In investigating local interpretations of student international mindedness in diverse contexts such as national and international IB Diploma Programme schools, this study has the potential to help educators recognize the relevance of international mindedness across diverse school contexts and how it can be nurtured. The objective of this chapter is to provide an example of how integrally informed research can be applied as a novel application of the study of international mindedness.

BACKGROUND

UR: International Mindedness as Stage-Based Development

The UR individual exterior view regards objective study of interior realities with attention drawn to the behavioural. Insight was be gained by examining the development of human constructs similar to international mindedness. These are often regarded as stage-based processes occurring as part of an individual's personal development. For example, Gardner (1981) regarded the entire course of human development as a continuing decline in egocentrism whereby the egocentric child grows to eventually recognize that one's perspective is not be shared by all persons. Bennet's (2004) model of intercultural sensitivity described a shift along a continuum from ethnocentrism towards ethnorelativism. He suggested a progressive construction of reality that accommodates and is sensitive to differing cultures and points of view (Bennet, 1986). Gudykunst (1994) proposed we proceed through four stages in the development of cultural competence namely unconsciously incompetent, consciously incompetent, consciously competent and unconsciously competent. Heyward's (2002) matrix of intercultural literacy is suited to application in international mindedness as it charted progressive development through mono-cultural, cross-cultural and intercultural levels. His constructivist model assumed new meanings are created as previous experiences are reinterpreted, reconnected, and realigned in light of new experiences.

International mindedness, like the aforementioned related constructs, can also be regarded as a stage-based developmental process. A number of researchers have described international mindedness as a process of developing widening perspectives. Harwood and Bailey (2012) developed a conceptual framework to monitor and evaluate the development of international mindedness in students that progresses from the individual outwards to the broader world. Singh and Qi (2013) offered a circle of influence model to represent the progressive levels of engaging with oneself and the surrounding environment. Their model suggested the individual is centrally located, surrounded in expanding circles that progress from the school/immediate environment, the local/national and finally the global signifying that the local and the global are never separate. Skelton (2007) proposed international mindedness is a continuum representing the development of the very complex relationship between self and other.

In this research it was proposed that an integral view of international mindedness and a stage-based model of human development could also help understand the universal nature of the construct. Within all four integral quadrants, levels of development occur in progressive stages whereby each level represents greater complexity. The integral levels represent the general movement of a widening identity and have a nested quality (Esbjorn-Hargens, 2009; Skelton, 2007). Each new level emerges, there is a shift from *me* (egocentric) to *my group* (ethnocentric) to *my country* (sociocentric) to *all of us* (worldcentric) to *all beings* (planetcentric) and finally to *all of reality* (Kosmoscentric) (Esbjörn-Hargens, 2009). As higher levels emerge and develop, they include constituents of the earlier worldviews, adding new and more differentiated perceptions such that they "transcend and include" (Wilber, 2000b, p. 27).

Of particular importance in this discussion of student international mindedness is the shifting worldview that Wilber (2000b) has suggested begins to occur during adolescence with the emergence of the capacity for formal operations. He described the transition as follows:

The self decenters once again: my group is not the only group in the universe, my tribe is not the only tribe, my god is not the only god, my ideology is not the only ideology. I went from egocentric to ethnocentric by decentering my ego into the group; now I go from ethnocentric to worldcentric by decentering my group into the world. (p. 170)

The individual external view of the UR quadrant supports the notion that international mindedness can be regarded as a stage-based and pervasive process of development whereby the individual can take on widening perspectives.

UL: Context and the Experience of Student International Mindedness

The UL individual interior view regards subjective study of interior realities with attention drawn to what is experiential or intentional. The UL individual interior view warranted analysis of reported feelings, impressions and personal involvement of students' experience of international mindedness. Unfortunately, there seems to be a dearth of research into the first hand subjective experience of student international mindedness, a gap that this research will attend to. However, several studies have been conducted that reveal the role of context in the individual experience of student international mindedness.

Sriprakash, Singh and Qi (2014) conducted interviews with IB Diploma Programme students in schools in China, Australia and India. For the Chinese students in a public school emphasizing patriotic education, the experience involved mediating local and global priorities. The Australian students' lived experiences of international mindedness were transformed through the cultural and linguistic diversity in their learning environments. Everyday experiences of poverty and social exclusion as well as religious and linguistic diversity shaped the experience of international mindedness for the Indian students. Thompson (1998) and Hayden and Thompson (1995) conducted a set of studies in which international school students were surveyed to indicate which factors supported the development of international mindedness. Students placed greatest importance upon the formal and informal contact with their peers. Less emphasis was placed upon importance upon the curriculum, school programmes and faculty and administration. IB Diploma Programme students in Ontario, Canada were surveyed about their views on international mindedness revealing that it is regarded as less integrated on a personal level and more compartmentalized by school subject (Tarc & Beatty, 2012).

The individual interior view of the UL quadrant supports the notion that context plays a significant role in student experience of international mindedness.

LL: Education for International Mindedness

The LL regards inter-subjective study of interior realities with attention drawn to the relational or cultural aspects of phenomena. Through the UL view, it was acknowledged that contextual influences shape the experience of international mindedness. The LL collective interior perspective merits investigation of the shared purpose of education *for* international mindedness. Hill (2013) has proposed the following description of education for international mindedness:

Education for international-mindedness is the study of issues which have application beyond national borders and to which competencies such as critical thinking and collaboration are applied in order to shape attitudes leading to action which will be conducive to intercultural understanding, peaceful co-existence and global sustainable development for the future of the human race. (p. 11)

Hill's description reminds educators that education for international mindedness is for all students in all settings; there is not one particular context best suited to its development. Emphasis is placed on the nature of the education programme that a school offers. Roberts (2003) suggested that international mindedness is not the result of students attending a diverse international school nor can it be entirely attributed to other cultural, economic, and social factors. Skelton (2007) offered that schools educating for international mindedness need to:

Be open and willing to discuss difference in every aspect of school life; to value those whose growing sense of the 'other' and its relationship to their own self is important; to create structures and systems with which respect for others is a fundamental part of the school ethos, including the way teachers work with students, each other and parents; and, most importantly, to model in our own moment by moment mindfulness that which we hold of value. (p. 388)

The goals of this type of education have been echoed in other arenas outside the IB. In 1995, at the United Nations Educational, Scientific, and Cultural Organization's (UNESCO) International Conference on Education, national ministers of education of member states accepted broad aims for international education in all schools (UNESCO, 1995). These aims included the promotion of a sense of universal values for a culture of peace, civic responsibility, intercultural understanding, respect for cultural heritage and protection of the environment. Haywood (2007) offered that a school committed to international mindedness should focus on specific objectives including building an interest in the natural and human world, having open and tolerant attitudes towards other ways of life, understanding the common value of the earth's environment, recognizing the interconnectedness of human affairs and possessing awareness of respectful and caring human values for the well being of all people. A study of IB Diploma programmes in Hong Kong revealed education for international mindedness in schools was faced by contextual challenges but was being addressed by situated programme adaptations (Lai et al., 2014). The authors called for more school-based support for teachers to "explore different models and pedagogies that are appropriate for their particular teaching contexts" (p. 94). This echoes Haywood's (2007) proposal that each school could and should develop its own model of education for international mindedness rooted in its own circumstances.

In supporting students in becoming internationally minded, an education programme for international mindedness can be described in different ways. In doing so, interpretations of international mindedness can evolve that are unique to each educational context.

LR: The IB and the Future of International Mindedness

The LR collective exterior view regards the inter-objective realities of education for international mindedness with attention drawn to the social systems and processes that support its actualization. Specific to education, the LR perspective embodies the system of factors in the classroom and institutions and the social and political realities surrounding them (Murray, 2009). This provides a fitting evaluative perspective to better understand the role the IB Organization plays in the development of student international mindedness. In particular, the origins of international mindedness in the IB were explored to illuminate the organization's vision and responsibility in education for international mindedness.

The mutually beneficial interchange between national systems and international education is becoming commonplace making outright distinctions between the two increasingly difficult (Plotkin, 2013). Fundamentally, education for international mindedness has meaning in national as well as international schools when one considers the "intellectual and cultural mobility not only of the individual but, most of all, of thought" (Belle-Isle, 1986, p. 28). Both students attending relatively mono-cultural national schools and those attending more diverse international schools are ill served if not aware of their local, national and international context (Hayden & Thompson, 2013). Ian Hill, the former Deputy Director General of the IB, noted that international and national schools could adopt an international perspective either through curricular adaptations or offering an international programme such as the IB (Hill, 2000; Hill 2006).

The IB was originally conceived in 1968 through the IB Diploma Programme to serve the needs of students attending international schools. As true pioneers of international education, the original aims of the programme were to:

- Provide a school-leaving diploma that would be recognized for university entrance around the world with common curriculum and examinations
- Promote critical thinking skills...via a balanced programme in the humanities, experimental sciences and experiential learning
- Provide a perspective that would promote international understanding, prepare students for world citizenship and promote peace. (Hill, 2002, p. 18)

It is understood that an academic school leaving qualification must be highly rigorous in order to align with university entrance criteria set by post secondary institutions from around the world. However, despite the initial aims of the IB Diploma Programme, it been critiqued as "being content heavy, overly assessed and still focused too heavily on traditional disciplinary knowledge" (Tarc, 2009, p. 123). The original intentions of the promotion of critical thinking and international understanding, aspects of becoming internationally minded, risk being overshadowed. Furthermore, whilst the IB asserts international mindedness is manifested in the components of multilingualism, intercultural understanding and global engagement (IBO, 2013) there is limited guidance for teachers as to how this might be enacted in an IB classroom. The IB has made efforts to be responsive to such criticisms. The organization has asserted that "subject aims, objectives, content and assessment criteria are written in order to develop international mindedness while, at the same time, ensuring that teachers have enough choice to make the course locally relevant and grounded" (IBO, 2015, p. 6).

When Hill (2000) first put forth the seminal view of education *for* international mindedness, it would seem the ideals of international understanding had shifted from being solely associated with the type of educational institution to the actual process of education taking place (Hill, 2012). With the rapid expansion of IB programmes in national government schools around the world, international mindedness was seemingly no longer synonymous with pre-university elite international schools. IB programmes today, regardless of the school context, are meant to encourage students to "address humanity's greatest challenges in the classroom and beyond…to explore global and local issues, including…aspects of the environment, development, conflicts, rights and cooperation and governance, critically consider power and privilege and recognize that they hold the earth and its resources in trust for future generations" (IBO, 2013, p. 7).

Humanity faces turbulent economic, political, social and environmental issues on a planetary scale. These are complex problems as they are "multi-dimensional, non-linear, interconnected, far from equilibrium and unpredictable" (Kuhn, 2008, p. 182). Greater systemic engagement is required to understand the issues involved and, optimistically, prevent such problems from occurring. One hopes that being internationally minded facilitates the easing of these issues.

The future of IB and international mindedness is similarly situated in the complex "realm of the unknown unknowns" (Snyder, 2013, p. 7). The IB, in assuming responsibility for the delivery of programmes for education for international mindedness, is beginning to enter this era. The organization is going through a period of rapid expansion, serving a diverse array of public and private, national and international, face-to-face and online school contexts that are very different from the international schools it served at its inception. The IB, in its belief that education must cross "disciplinary, cultural, national and geographical boundaries" (IBO, 2013, p. 1) acknowledges the complexity of developing an international mindset. However, as Snyder (2013) has pointed out "there is often no guiding central hand in the evolution of the system" (p. 12). As the IB continues to develop education programmes for international mindedness, the organization will need to continue to explore mechanisms that embrace the complexities of our increasingly globalized experience. Snyder (2013) has further noted "what the center can do is create a fertile environment that embraces the emergent nature of complex systems and work to create processes that maximizes the flow of feedback between and across levels" (p. 12). The inherent diversity of an international education organization like the IB ensures adaptability and transformation. A balance must be struck between redundancy (the source of stability in a system) and the promotion of diversity (the source of creativity) such that these elements can "co-exist in productive tension" (Davis & Sumara, 2009, p. 40). The IB must acknowledge that international mindedness is constantly evolving and the mechanisms employed to develop it should do the same.

METHODOLOGY

Research Questions

The purpose of this research was to give perspective to contextual interpretations of international mindedness of IB Diploma Programme students. To achieve this, three research questions were addressed:

- How is international mindedness actualized by IB Diploma Programme students?
- What is the experience of education for international mindedness for IB Diploma Programme students?
- What is the role of context in developing international mindedness in IB Diploma Programme students?

Data Collection

Integral research is grounded in Ken Wilber's (2006) integral theory incorporating perspectives of different research methodologies. The notion that each of the multiple perspectives that we engage with through each methodology is "true but partial" (Esbjörn-Hargens, 2010, p. 145) is supported by a view of epistemological pluralism. The integral ontology is multiple or, in Wilberian terms, "transcends and includes" (Wilber, 2000b, p. 27). Research within this pluralist epistemological stance occurs through integral methodological pluralism.

In integral methodological pluralism, each methodology that can be employed to engage in human inquiry discloses some facet that other methodologies cannot (Esbjörn-Hargens, 2006; Wilber, 2006). Integral methodological pluralism has been identified as a specific form mixed methods research (Esbjörn-Hargens, 2006, p. 89). Fundamentally, mixed methods research incorporates "a diversity of perspectives, voices, values and stances..., honours complexity alongside diversity and difference, and thereby resists simplification of inherently contextual and complex human phenomena" (Greene, 2006, p. 97). Johnson & Onwuegbuzi (2004) described the mixed methods research as that which "mixes or combines quantitative and qualitative research techniques, methods, approaches, concepts or language into a single study" (p. 17).

A quantitative empirical approach was most appropriate for the perspective of the UR research question. The Global Perspectives Inventory (GPI) (Braskamp, Braskamp & Engberg, 2014) was selected and administered to students. A qualitative hermeneutic phenomenology suited the exploration of the UL and LL research questions through semi-structured student and teacher interviews. The conceptual framework of integral theory provided the point of interface for the mixing or interrelating of the quantitative and qualitative data (Creswell & Plano Clark, 2011).

Limitations and Delimitations

There were a number of limitations with this study. There were restrictions in terms of school research sites and the participants. Potential research sites were limited in number and size due to constraints of time and geography. The sample size in the study was very small and results cannot be generalized to entire populations. In the collection of quantitative and qualitative data, there may have been barriers due to language, cultural bias, comprehension levels, participant focus and the degree to which participants responded candidly.

There were several delimitations in the research. The research was framed around the IB organization's interpretation of international mindedness. The research questions were intended to gain insight specifically on the IB Diploma Programme student experience of international mindedness. IB Diploma Programme students in their penultimate year of secondary school and teachers with at least two years of IB teaching experience were involved.

FINDINGS

UR: International Mindedness is Widely Applicable, Developmental and Experiential

Quantitative data was collected and analyzed from an UR integral quadrant perspective through an empirical methodology. The GPI was employed in this study to explore the first research question from the individual–exterior integral perspective: How is international mindedness actualized by IB Diploma Programme students? The GPI is composed of three scales that assess intercultural maturity (the process of becoming capable of functioning in situations with cultural perspectives different from one's own) and three scales that assess intercultural communication (the way people are able to effectively understand and communicate in diverse situations) (King & Baxter Magolda, 2005). Statistical tests were conducted to determine if the means for each scale for the national C-School and international I-School were significantly different from one another. The analysis failed to detect any statistically significant differences between the two groups of participants for any of the six scales of the GPI. This supports the perception of international mindedness as widely applicable across diverse contexts.

The GPI scales also assess the development of epistemological processes, identities and interpersonal relations and the acquisition of knowledge, attitudes and skills (Merrill, Braskamp & Braskamp, 2012). Statistical tests were conducted and it was revealed that participants from both schools scored lower on development scales and higher on acquisition scales. This suggests participants had:

- Acquired an understanding and awareness of cultures but had a less-developed view of the importance of cultural context in judging what is important to know and value;
- Acquired emotional confidence when in situations with cultural perspectives different from their own but had a less-developed acceptance of their own cultural background; and
- Acquired a desire for engagement with others with cultural backgrounds different from their own more but had a less-developed sense of interdependence and social concern for others (Merrill et al., 2012; Braskamp, Braskamp & Engberg, 2014).

This outcome would suggest that although the participants are gaining skills that support having a global perspective, the growth of related psychosocial processes was happening differently.

Finally, statistical relationships between the six scales of the GPI were explored and only weak correlations were observed between the scales with one exception. A "desire for exposure to people with cultural backgrounds different from their own" was associated with an increase in the "acquisition of emotional comfort with situations that are different from or challenge their own cultural norms" (Merrill et al., 2012, pp. 357–358). This result indicates that as individuals engage with people different from themselves, they are more comfortable respecting perspectives different from their own suggesting the development of international mindedness involves both experiential and contextual mechanisms.

UL: International Mindedness Involves Intercultural Identity, Perspective Taking, and Disconnection

It was intended that qualitative data collected and analyzed from UL and LL integral quadrant perspectives would enrich the empirical findings from the UR quadrant. Informed by a hermeneutic phenomenological methodology, exploration of the more textured subjective involvements of the participants occurred. This was addressed by the second research question of the study: What is the experience of international mindedness for IB Diploma Programme students?

Multiple elements shape our cultural self-identity. The C-School student participants made reference to the influence of historical oppression and vulnerability as to how Czechs perceive themselves today. They and their teachers regarded the development of a sense of cultural identity for young Czechs to be in flux. The I-school student participants typically found it difficult to self-identify with one specific culture. They described being influenced in varying degrees by their families' cultures, the cultures of the places where they had lived in the past and the cultures of the schools they attended. For many participants in the study, articulating an understanding of their cultural self-identity was particularly challenging as their identity was shaped by diverse influences.

Although their school peers might also be experiencing a process of cultural identity development, the resulting self-identity is a unique mélange for each individual student based on factors such as family, places lived, languages spoken, and so on. It is proposed that the students possess an intercultural identity. According to Dai (2009) an intercultural identity is the internalization of diverse cultural elements. The resulting identity is broader than the original and, importantly, remains receptive to further transformation. For the most part, the student participants were not able to objectively regard this intercultural identity. This finding is consistent with the UR result where it was revealed that students could stand to further develop an awareness and acceptance of their unique identities.

Perspective taking is the ability to "consciously put oneself into the mind of another individual and imagine what that person is thinking or feeling" (Decety, Chen, Harenski & Kiehl, 2013, para. 2). Student participants from both schools were able to describe impactful experiences where they demonstrated the consideration of other perspectives. They shared stories of experiences with intense themes including bullying, poverty and racism. In school, participants described how the alternative perspectives of their peers influenced them and how they were able to objectively notice their peers taking on the perspectives of others as well. Having openness to the points of view of others was considered helpful in forming one's individual point of view.

Students recognized their growth in the area of perspective taking. For example, some students reflected on experiences they had when they were much younger when they saw themselves as less able to take on other perspectives. In retrospect, they recognized their former inability to see things from others' point of view suggesting there is a developmental aspect to the ability to take on perspectives. Perspective taking develops while individuals are increasingly able to take on mutual roles (Steinberg, Vandell & Bornstein, 2010) a competence that builds with cognitive maturity acquired through adolescence (Choudhury, Charman, Bird & Blakemore, 2007; Hoffman, 2008). Once again, this finding is consistent with the UR result in that young people are acquiring the abilities associated with becoming internationally minded yet, as adolescents, the psychosocial processes are still developing.

Students from both schools said they have had experiences where they felt their international education separated them from important people in their lives not having the same experience. Disconnection was revealed as an aspect of the experience of international mindedness. They spoke about difficult feelings and experiences, which they resolved in different ways. In some cases resolution was through a path to reconnection and for others new connections formed to replace the disconnections. Often, they spoke about how their school experiences helped them rebuild a new sense of connection. For the students in this study, feelings of disconnection arose primarily because they were having a significantly different school/life experience than other members of their community, their peers or their parents.

In describing these experiences, it was apparent that the challenges students faced required new ways of being. Skelton (2007) pointed out that the way we cope with these difficult situations impacts our "willingness to be open and our energy to explore what is uncomfortably new rather than rest with what already exists" (p. 385). The student participants in this research were able to learn from feelings of disconnection. As they faced and resolved challenging situations, their ability to make meaning evolved.

LL: International Mindedness Is Influenced by Privilege and Exposure to Diversity

The students in this study perceived advantages to being IB Diploma Programme students and receiving an international education. Many of the students talked about their appreciation of the exceptionality of their international education experience and the advantages this has afforded them over others in terms of being internationally minded. This privilege was perceived on several levels including where they lived, the school they attended and their family background.

These findings reinforce the aspiration for international education and in particular international mindedness to be considered less exclusive (Bunnell, 2006; Carroll, 2003; Hallinan, 2004; McKenzie, 2004; Resnik, 2009). This underscores concerns that the experience of becoming a global person is limited to those with privilege that have greater access to media, technology and consumer capital (Rizvi & Lingard, 2000). Bunnell (2006) advised there was a need for, "a movement towards a wider discourse with groups outside the exclusive world of 'internationally minded schools'" (p. 167).

From the perspective of the LL quadrant, participants believed contact with diversity was an essential contextual factor impacting international mindedness. Students at both schools regarded extrinsic factors such as exposure to diversity and being surrounded by likeminded people as more impactful in the development of international mindedness than the IB Diploma experience. More specifically, students asserted that the experience of diversity through interactions with people from backgrounds different from their own facilitated the development of international mindedness.

Diversity exposure happened in different ways. At the I-School it was through daily contact with and connections between with teachers and particularly their school peers. This also happened at the less diverse C-School but to a smaller extent. Diversity exposure occurred for C-School students through school-sponsored travel such as service trips, student exchanges and summer schools as well as contact with the small number of the School's teachers from abroad. This theme is consistent with the UL result that suggested there is a context-driven experiential aspect to the development of international mindedness. All participants acknowledged that to whatever degree they had been exposed to diversity, they felt positively impacted by it. In particular, students regarded this as influential in the ability to take alternative perspectives.

It has been noted in the literature that no specific school context is necessary to develop international mindedness in students (Cambridge, 2002; Hayden & Thompson, 1995; Haywood, 2007; Hill, 2000; Lineham, 2013; Roberts, 2003; Schwindt, 2003; Thompson, 1998). However, the findings in this research suggest that exposure to diversity has a significant impact on the perception of being internationally minded. As one C-School participant aptly explained, "it's hard to be open minded about something that you've never come into contact with before." The challenge of diversity exposure is much greater in national schools with a more culturally homogeneous study body and in particular those schools with limited student travel opportunities. Seefried (2006, p. 7) has noted:

In the national schools, with a diverse or homogeneous population, the IB has had to find ways to encourage effortful, mindful and conscious modes of thought to promote not only tolerance but a celebration of cultural differences to prepare its students to successfully navigate the multicultural world they live in and to become productive global citizens. (p. 7)

REFLECTIONS ON INTEGRAL RESEARCH

Integral methodological pluralism, based on the conceptual framework of the integral model is unquestionably comprehensive in its approach to inquiry. According to Wilber (2006), an approach that leaves out any of the eight fundamental and irreducible methodologies (i.e. the eight integral zones) is a "less-than-adequate approach according to available and reliable human knowledge at this time" (p. 33). This inclusion works to ensure the comprehensiveness of integral research.

However, integral research has been criticized as "…so densely detailed, that after a time one can no longer see through it…" (McKinnon, 2009, p. 92). In practical terms, the resources required to conduct a full eight-zone project are considerable. In this project Esbjörn-Hargens' (2006) interpretation was employed in that integral research can be scaled to include first-, second- and third- person methodologies from at least three integral zones. Although tremendous insight could be gained from a full eight zone integral inquiry, scaling was a necessary measure. Additionally, aspects of the integral AQAL model including levels, lines, states and types were not emphasized in this stage of the research. Wilber has stated that research can also be integrally informed whereby the full integral model informs the research but does not include all eight methodological zones (as cited in Hedlund, 2010). Scaling has been similarly employed to differing degrees in a number of doctoral dissertations involving integral research (see Alisat, 2013; Kohls, 2014; McAlpine, 2015; McKinnon, 2009; Presely, 2014; Ross, 2011; Yuen, 2013).

This act of scaling propels researchers on a continued programme of inquiry. In the same way that each of the four quadratic perspectives that we engage with is "true but partial" (Esbjörn-Hargens, 2010, p. 145), the conclusions drawn from this integral research can be regarded as "true but partial". Through the use of the other methodological approaches representing the other integral zones as well as the assignment of integral levels along specific developmental lines, this examination of international mindedness can be extended for a deepened understanding of the phenomena.

IMPLCATIONS FOR FURTHER RESEARCH AND PRACTICE

UR/UL: Support for Intercultural Identity Negotiation

As globalization accelerates the extension of our social relations, recognition of our common humanity becomes more and more relevant. This requires an acceptance and openness to transformation as we are increasingly exposed to multiple sources of cultural identity. Individuals who possess an intercultural identity have a "constructive way of being a member of our increasingly integrated communities, both local and global" (Kim, 2008, p. 360). In supporting students in the negotiation of an intercultural identity, numerous contextual factors play a role. The results of this research are relevant but insufficient. This research could inform a parallel design for future exploration of intercultural identity formation. Through the outside methodological zone of the UR quadrant (empiricism) and the inside zone of the UL quadrant (phenomenology) there is much to be learned about the nature of the intercultural identity and its formation. Although beyond the parameters of this study, integral theory's AQAL model of "all quadrants, all levels, all lines" (Wilber, Patten, Leonard & Morelli, 2008, p. 9) may provide a suitable metric for the charting of ascending growth through *levels* of complexity achieved along specific lines of development (Esbjörn-Hargens, 2007). Additionally, the inside zone of the LL quadrant (hermeneutics) can be employed to investigate the role of context in intercultural identity formation. Further research is required in determining how the intercultural identity emerges and how it can be supported through international education programmes.

LL: Recontextualization of International Mindedness

The educational philosophy of global IB programmes is intended to reflect international mindedness in a way that accommodates local understandings. The enactment of this type of global policy into local practice involves recontextualization, a creative process of interpretation and translation (Braun et al, 2011, p. 586). Bernstein (2000) described recontextualization as a mechanism to delocate a discourse, relocate it and refocus it. This recontextualization of educational policy is typically undertaken by education authorities at the governmental level (Singh, 2002). However, as the IB functions independently of any outside authority, individual schools can be more involved in this process of local recontextualization (Doherty & Mu, 2011). Since the enactment of international mindedness is so influenced by local contextual factors, thorough investigation of local recontextualizations of international mindedness is warranted (Lai, Shum and Zhang, 2014). For example, it has been noted that teacher attitudes can impact how an education for international mindedness is approached in the classroom (Bent, 2009; Doherty and Mu, 2011; Gigliotti-Labay, 2010). Parent attitudes can also impact this recontextualization (Drake, 2004; Bunnell, 2009, Lee et al. (2012). Through recontextualization, the IB's central parameters regarding the education for international mindedness can be better adapted to local situations. Ultimately, this enhanced collaboration between the macro and micro views can only increase the development of student international mindedness.

LR: Extending the Privilege of International Mindedness

Perhaps the most significant result that emerged from this research was this theme of privilege. Student participants in this study perceived themselves to be in a position of privilege due to the opportunities afforded to them as students of a programme of international education. They were highly appreciative of the IB Diploma Programme providing them with a globally respected and rigorous university entrance qualification. However, many of the student participants also recognized that just having the opportunity to become internationally minded placed them in a position of considerable privilege. As one participant from the I-School noted, "if you're not allowed to have that freedom [to be internationally minded] then I don't feel like there is a way for you to be as internationally minded as somebody who does have that sort of freedom."

The IB organization's commitment to an educational for international mindedness is evidenced in its mission statement (IBO, 2013):

The International Baccalaureate aims to develop inquiring, knowledgeable and caring young people who help to create a better and more peaceful world through intercultural understanding and respect. To this end the organization works with schools, governments and international organizations to develop challenging programmes of international education and rigorous assessment. These programmes encourage students across the world to become active, compassionate and lifelong learners who understand that other people, with their differences, can also be right.

As revealed in this research, IB students are aware of the privilege afforded to them. If the mission of the IB is to truly be impactful in its endeavour to "create a better and more peaceful world", its scope of influence must extend. George Walker, the Director General of the IB from 1999-2005 has proposed that the "IB message" can be spread through partnerships with other educational associations, professional development for IB as well as non-IB educators, expansion of digital technologies to influence a wider audience and consultancy work with governments and other organizations aspiring to integrate international dimensions into their programmes (2011, p. 15). In order to overcome the exclusiveness of the IB programmes these types of initiatives must be explored both at the global organizational and local operational levels. By acknowledging and addressing the "IB privilege" we build our capacity to truly enact the ideals of the organization's mission.

CONCLUSION

In this study, results were revealed through the four integral quadrants. In exploring contextual interpretations of international mindedness in this way, themes emerged that built upon one another. The first UR result uncovered in the course of this research was the wide applicability of international mindedness and the final LL theme related to the experience with diversity. The pairing of these two themes of universality and diversity exposes the challenge the IB faces in helping students become internationally minded in different educational contexts. Walker noted, "At the heart of international education lies a fundamental tension between human unity and human diversity. Learning to live with this ambiguity is the essential challenge of international mindedness" (2004, p. 12). In many ways, this is the challenge humanity faces as we are confronted by increasingly complex global problems. Noddings (2005) advised, "…we have to think carefully about the merits of diversity and those of unity or universality and how to achieve an optimal balance between the two" (p. 3). In embracing diversity do we limit our capacity to find our commonalities and what is universal? Alternatively, in seeking what is universal, does the relevance of our diversity become diminished? These questions remain to be answered.

In conclusion, it is appropriate to draw on the wisdom of Ken Wilber (2000a), the father of integral theory, who is equally a visionary in promoting awareness of our common humanity.

If we remain merely at the stage of celebrating diversity, we ultimately are promoting fragmentation, alienation, separation and despair. You go your way, I go my way, we both fly apart…It is not enough to recognize the many ways in which we are different; we need to go further and start recognizing the many ways in which we are also similar. (p. 112)

REFERENCES

Alisat, L. (2013). *Gifted boys' experience of giftedness in alternative high school settings: Implications for practice and programming* (Doctoral Dissertation). Retrieved from http://theses.ucalgary.ca/bitstream/11023/548/2/ucalgary_2013_%20alisat_laurie.pdf

Belle-Isle, R. (1986). Learning for a new humanism. *International Schools Journal, 11*, 27–30. Retrieved from http://www.johncattbookshop.com/books/international-schools-journal

Bennet, M. (2004). Becoming interculturally competent. In J. Wurzel (Ed.), *Toward multiculturalism: A reader in multicultural education* (pp. 62–77). Newton, MA: Intercultural Resource Corporation. Retrieved from http://www.idrinstitute.org/allegati/IDRI_t_Pubblicazioni/1/FILE_Documento.pdf

Bennett, M. (1986). A developmental approach to training for intercultural sensitivity. *International Journal of Intercultural Relations, 10*(2), 179–196. doi:10.1016/0147-1767(86)90005-2

Bent, M. (2009). *A peaceful partnership? A case study of three IB English A1 teachers' conceptions of peace education at an IB World School in Peru* (Doctoral Dissertation). Retrieved from ProQuest Dissertations and Theses Global. (Order No. MR59633)

Bernstein, B. (2000). *Pedagogy, symbolic control and identity* (revised ed.). Lanham, MD: Rowman and Littlefield.

Braskamp, L., Braskamp, D., & Engberg, M. (2014). *Global perspective inventory (GPI): Its purpose, construction, potential uses, and psychometric characteristics.* Retrieved from https://gpi.central.edu/supportDocs/manual.pdf

Braun, A., Ball, S., Maguire, M., & Hoskins, K. (2011). Taking context seriously: Towards explaining policy enactments in the secondary school. *Discourse (Berkeley, Calif.), 32*(4), 585–596. doi:10.1080/01596306.2011.601555

Bunnell, T. (2006). The growing momentum and legitimacy behind an alliance for international education. *Journal of Research in International Education, 5*(2), 155–176. doi:10.1177/1475240906065600

Bunnell, T. (2009). The International Baccalaureate in the USA and the emerging 'culture war'. *Discourse (Abingdon), 30*(1), 61–72. doi:10.1080/01596300802643090

Cambridge, J. (2002). Global product branding and international education. *Journal of Research in International Education, 1*(2), 227–243. doi:10.1177/147524002764248158

Carroll, G. (2003). The reification of international education. *IB Research Notes, 3*(4), 2–5. Retrieved from http://www.bath.ac.uk/ceic/ibru/

Choudhury, S., Charman, T., Bird, V., & Blakemore, S. (2007). Development of action representation during adolescence. *Neuropsychologia, 45*(2), 255–262. doi:10.1016/j.neuropsychologia.2006.07.010 PMID:16962147

Creswell, J. W., & Plano Clark, V. L. (2011). *Designing and conducting mixed methods research*. Retrieved from https://books.google.com/

Dai, X. (2009). Intercultural personhood and identity negotiation. *China Media Research, 5*(2), 1–12. Retrieved from http://www.thefreelibrary.com/Intercultural+personhood+and+identity+negotiation.-a0215410902

Davis, B., & Sumara, D. (2008). Complexity as a theory of education. *Transnational Curriculum Inquiry, 5*(2), 33–44. Retrieved from http://ecs210.uregina.wikispaces.net/file/view/Complexity+as+a+Theory+of+Education.pdf

Decety, J., Chen, C., Harenski, C., & Kiehl, K. A. (2013). An fMRI study of affective perspective taking in individuals with psychopathy: Imagining another in pain does not evoke empathy. *Frontiers in Human Neuroscience, 7*, 489. doi:10.3389/fnhum.2013.00489 PMID:24093010

Doherty, C., & Mu, L. (2011). Producing the intercultural citizen in the International Baccalaureate. In F. Dervin, A. Gajardo, & A. Lavanchy (Eds.), *Politics of interculturality* (pp. 165–188). Newcastle upon Tyne, UK: Cambridge Scholars Publishing.

Drake, B. (2004). International education and IB Programmes: Worldwide expansion and potential cultural dissonance. *Journal of Research in International Education, 3*(2), 189–205. doi:10.1177/1475240904044387

Esbjörn-Hargens, S. (2006). Integral research: A multi-method approach to investigating phenomena. *Constructivism in the Human Sciences, 11*(1), 79–107. Retrieved from https://metaintegral.org/sites/default/files/Integral%20Research%20foundational%20article.pdf

Esbjörn-Hargens, S. (2007). Integral teacher, integral students, integral classroom: Applying integral theory to education. *AQAL: Journal of Integral Theory and Practice, 2*(2), 72–103. Retrieved from https://foundation.metaintegral.org/JITP

Esbjörn-Hargens, S. (2009). *An overview of integral theory: An all-inclusive framework for the 21st century*. Integral Institute (Resource Paper No. 1).

Esbjörn-Hargens, S. (2010). An ontology of climate change: Integral pluralism and the enactment of environmental phenomena. *Journal of Integral Theory and Practice, 5*(1), 183–201. Retrieved from https://foundation.metaintegral.org/JITP

Gardner, H. (1981). *The quest for mind*. Chicago, IL: University of Chicago Press.

Gigliotti-Labay, J. (2010). *Fulfilling its mission? The promotion of international mindedness in IB DP programmes* (Doctoral Dissertation). Retrieved from ProQuest Dissertations and Theses Global. (Order No. 3438266)

Greene, J. (2006). Toward a methodology of mixed method social inquiry. *Research in the Schools, 13*(1), 93–98.

Gudykunst, W. (1994). *Bridging Differences, Effective intergroup communication*. London, UK: Sage.

Hallinan, B. (2004, October). *Is international education a form of global elite reproduction of privilege, or is it a force for global progress?* Paper presented to the Education for International Mindedness Conference, Düsseldorf, Germany. doi:10.1177/1475240906065600

Harwood, R., & Bailey, K. (2012). Defining and evaluating international-mindedness in a school context. *International Schools Journal, 31*(2), 77–86. Retrieved from http://www.johncattbookshop.com/books/international-schools-journal

Hayden, M. C., & Thompson, J. J. (2013). International mindedness: Connecting concepts to practice. In L. Stagg (Ed.), International mindedness: Global perspectives for learners and educators (pp. 185–204). Academic Press. Retrieved from http://urbanepublications.com

Haywood, T. (2007). A simple typology of international-mindedness and its implications for education. In M. C. Hayden, J. Levy, & J. J. Thompson (Eds.), *The handbook of research in international education* (pp. 78–89). London, UK: Sage.

Hedlund-de Witt, N. (2013). *Coding: An overview and guide to qualitative data analysis for integral researchers*. Integral Institute (Resource Paper No. 1). Retrieved from https://foundation.metaintegral.org/JITP

Heyward, M. (2002). From international to intercultural: Redefining the international school for a globalized world. *Journal of Research in International Education, 1*(1), 9–32. doi:10.1177/147524090211002

Hill, I. (2000). Internationally-minded schools. *International Schools Journal, 20*(1), 24–37. Retrieved from http://www.johncattbookshop.com/books/international-schools-journal

Hill, I. (2002). The history of international education: An International Baccalaureate perspective. In M. C. Hayden, J. J. Thompson, & G. Walker (Eds.), *International education in practice: Dimensions for schools and international schools* (pp. 16–25). Oxford, UK: Routledge.

Hill, I. (2006). Do International Baccalaureate programs internationalize or globalize? *International Education Journal, 7*(1), 98–108. Retrieved from http://www.johncattbookshop.com/books/international-schools-journal

Hill, I. (2013). The emergence of international-mindedness. *International School, 15*(2), 9–11. Retrieved from http://www.johncatt.com/downloads/pdf/magazines/ismag/is15_2/is15_2.pdf

Hoffman, M. L. (2008). Empathy and prosocial behaviour. In M. Lewis, J. M. Haviland-Jones, & L. F. Barrett (Eds.), *Handbook of emotions* (3rd ed.; pp. 440–455). New York, NY: Guilford.

IBO. (2013). *What is an IB education?* Cardiff, UK: International Baccalaureate Organization. Retrieved from http://www.ibo.org/globalassets/digital-tookit/brochures/what-is-an-ib-education-en.pdf

IBO. (2015). *Diploma Programme: From principles into practice.* Cardiff, UK: International Baccalaureate Organization. Retrieved from http://www.follettibstore.com/main/home

IBO. (2016). *Facts and figures.* Retrieved from http://www.ibo.org/about-the-ib/facts-and-figures/

Johnson, R., & Onwuegbuzie, A. (2004). Mixed methods research: A research paradigm whose time has come. *Educational Researcher, 33*(7), 14–26. doi:10.3102/0013189X033007014

Kim, Y. Y. (2008). Intercultural personhood: Globalization and a way of being. *International Journal of Intercultural Relations, 32*(4), 359–368. doi:10.1016/j.ijintrel.2008.04.005

King, P., & Baxter Magolda, M. (2005). A developmental model of intercultural maturity. *Journal of College Student Development, 46*(6), 571–592. doi:10.1353/csd.2005.0060

Kohls, M. (2014). *The unintended quest: An examination of transcendence and personal change in high-risk non-traditional athletes* (Doctoral Dissertation). Retrieved from ProQuest Dissertations and Theses Global. (Order No. 3643109)

Kuhn, L. (2008). Complexity and educational research: A critical reflection. *Educational Philosophy and Theory, 40*(1), 177–189. doi:10.1111/j.1469-5812.2007.00398.x

Lai, C., Shum, M., & Zhang, B. (2014). International mindedness in an Asian context: The case of the International Baccalaureate in Hong Kong. *Educational Research, 56*(1), 77–96. doi:10.1080/00131881.2013.874159

Lee, M., Leung, L., Wright, E., Yue, T., Gan, A., Kong, L., & Li, J. (2014). *Research Summary: A study of the International Baccalaureate Diploma in China: Programme impact on student preparation for university studies abroad.* Cardiff, UK: International Baccalaureate Organization. Retrieved from http://www.ibo.org/globalassets/publications/ib-research/dp/chinasummaryinenglishweb.pdf

McAlpine, K. (2015). *Doing the right thing to protect children in Tanzania: An explanatory theory of the basic psychological process of doing the right thing and a practical theory to enable more and better protection of children* (Doctoral Dissertation). Retrieved from ProQuest Dissertations and Theses Global. (Order No. 3688840)

McKenzie, M. (2004, October). *Prep for the planet: Effective internationalism in practice.* Paper presented to the Education for International Mindedness Conference, Düsseldorf, Germany. Retrieved from https://scholar.google.com

McKinnon, D. (2009). Uncovering and understanding the spirituality and personal wholeness of school educators (Doctoral Dissertation). Retrieved from ProQuest Dissertations and Theses Global. (Order No. 304832727)

Merrill, K., Braskamp, D., & Braskamp, L. (2012). Assessing individuals' global perspective. *Journal of College Student Development, 53*(2), 356–360. doi:10.1353/csd.2012.0034

Murray, T. (2009). What is the integral in integral education? From progressive pedagogy to integral pedagogy. *Integral Review*, *5*(1), 96–134. Retrieved from http://integral-review.org/pdf-template-issue.php?pdfName=vol_5_no_1_murray_what_is_the_integral_in_integral_education.pdf

Noddings, N. (2005). *Educating citizens for global awareness*. New York, NY: Teachers College Press.

Oral, S. B. (2013). An integral approach to interdisciplinary research in education. *International Journal of Educational Research*, *4*(1), 1–13. Retrieved from http://www.journals.elsevier.com/international-journal-of-educational-research/

Presley, S. (2014). *How leaders engage in complexity leadership: Do action logics make a difference?* (Doctoral Dissertation). Retrieved from ProQuest Dissertations and Theses Global. (Order No. 3611483)

Resnik, J. (2009). Multicultural education – Good for business but not for the state? The IB curriculum and global capitalism. *British Journal of Educational Studies*, *57*(3), 217–244. doi:10.1111/j.1467-8527.2009.00440.x

Rizvi, F., & Lingard, B. (2000). Globalization and education: Complexities and contingencies. *Educational Theory*, *50*(4), 419–426. doi:10.1111/j.1741-5446.2000.00419.x

Roberts, B. (2003). What should international education be? From emergent theory to practice. *International Schools Journal, 22*(2), 69–79. Retrieved from http://www.johncattbookshop.com/books/international-schools-journal

Ross, M. (2011). *The evolution of education: Use of biofeedback in developing heart intelligence in a high school setting* (Doctoral Dissertation). Retrieved from ProQuest Dissertations and Theses Global. (Order No. NR81527)

Schwindt, E. (2003). The development of a model for international education with special reference to the role of host country nationals. *Journal of Research in International Education*, *2*(1), 67–81. doi:10.1177/1475240903002001607

Seefried, M. (2006, October). *Scholastic communities and democracy: The role of ethics in international education*. Speech presented at IB Africa/Europe/Middle East Regional Conference. Retrieved from http://www.ibo.org/contentassets/7adb995cb97e43ed8216a173aa4bcffe/ethics-in-international-education-en.pdf

Singh, M., & Qi, J. (2013). *21st century international mindedness: An exploratory study of its conceptualisation and assessment*. Cardiff, UK: International Baccalaureate Organization. Retrieved from http://www.ibo.org/globalassets/publications/ib-research/singhqiibreport27julyfinalversion.pdf

Singh, P. (2002). Pedagogising knowledge: Bernstein's theory of the pedagogic device. *British Journal of Sociology of Education*, *23*(4), 571–582. doi:10.1080/0142569022000038422

Skelton, M. (2007). International mindedness and the brain: The difficulties of becoming. In M. C. Hayden, J. J. Thompson, & J. Levy (Eds.), *The SAGE handbook of research in international education* (pp. 379–389). London, UK: Sage. doi:10.4135/9781848607866.n32

Snyder, S. (2013). The simple, the complicated, and the complex: Educational reform through the lens of complexity theory. In *OECD Education Working Papers* (No. 96). Paris, France: OECD Publishing. doi:10.1787/5k3txnpt1lnr-en

Sriprakash, A., Singh, M., & Qi, J. (2014). *A comparative study of international mindedness in the IB Diploma Programme in Australia, China and India.* Cardiff, UK: International Baccalaureate Organization. Retrieved from http://www.ibo.org/globalassets/publications/ib-research/dp/international-mindedness-final-report.pdf

Steinberg, L., Vandell, D., & Bornstein, M. (2010). *Development: Infancy through adolescence.* Retrieved from https://books.google.com/

Tarc, P. (2009). What is the 'international' in the International Baccalaureate? Three structuring tensions of the early years (1962–1973). *Journal of Research in International Education, 8*(3), 235–261. doi:10.1177/1475240909344679

Tarc, P., & Beatty, L. (2012). The emergence of the International Baccalaureate Diploma in Ontario: Diffusion, pilot study and prospective research. *Canadian Journal of Education, 35*(4), 341–375. doi:10.5116/ijme.4dfb.8dfd

Thompson, J. J. (1998). Towards a model for international education. In M. C. Hayden & J. J. Thompson (Eds.), *International education: Principles and practice.* London, UK: Kogan Page.

United Nations Educational Scientific and Cultural Organization (UNESCO). (1995). *Declaration and integrated framework of action on education for peace, human rights and democracy.* Paris, France: UNESCO. Retrieved from http://unesdoc.unesco.org/images/0011/001128/112874e.pdf

Walker, G. (2004). International Education and the International Baccalaureate. *Phi Delta Kappa Fastbacks, 522,* 7–34. Retrieved from http://pdkintl.org/

Wilber, K. (2000a). *A theory of everything: an integral vision for business, politics, science, and spirituality.* Boston, MA: Shambhala Publications.

Wilber, K. (2000b). *A brief history of everything* (2nd ed.). Boston, MA: Shambhala Publications.

Wilber, K. (2006). *Integral spirituality.* Boston, MA: Shambhala Publications.

Wilber, K., Patten, T., Leonard, A., & Morelli, M. (2008). *Integral life practice: A 21st century blueprint for physical health, emotional balance, mental clarity and spiritual awakening.* Boston, MA: Integral Books.

Yuen, C. (2013). *Mathematics anxiety learning phenomenon: Adult learner's lived experience and its implications for developmental mathematics instruction* (Doctoral Dissertation). Retrieved from ProQuest Dissertations and Theses Global. (Order No. NS23075)

KEY TERMS AND DEFINITIONS

Integrally Informed Research: Research that is epistemologically and methodologically informed by integral theory and aspects of the AQAL model.

Intercultural Understanding: The capacity to value one's own culture and be aware, respectful, and curious of other cultures.

International Baccalaureate: A non-profit international organization that offers international education programs with for students ages 3–18.

International Baccalaureate Diploma Program: A rigorous two-year course of study offered in IB accredited schools leading to an international academic school leaving qualification.

International Education: Education concerned with international mindedness.

International Mindedness: An outlook of being globally engaged through intercultural understanding that compels individuals to work towards peace, equality, and sustainability.

International School: A school that places emphasis on an international education program with a student body and teaching faculty is mostly culturally and linguistically diverse.

National School: A school following a national education program with a mostly culturally and linguistically homogeneous student body and teaching faculty.

Chapter 5
CoS and Effect:
An Integral View

Dave Carlgren
University of Calgary, Canada

ABSTRACT

The science that is done by students in grade school settings naturally differs considerably from that done by actual scientists. While much of this difference is attributable to differences in age and experience between the two groups, it may be possible to decrease the gap between the learner and the researcher in science. To explore this possibility, an educational design research (EDR) study was conducted from the perspectives of complexity and networks, communities of practice, and integral theory, the goal being to assess the potential outcomes of engaging learners in a student-led science conference called the celebration of science (CoS).

INTRODUCTION

In current educational practice, a distinction has arisen in the realm of science. There is now a significant gap between the practice of science and science education (Anderson & Krathwohl, 2001; Barnett, 2000; Healey & Jenkins, 2006). While the majority of previous research on this topic has been directed at identifying and working to remediate the differences in how science is conducted by college undergraduate students and by researchers, it may be instructive to wind back the proverbial clock somewhat further and investigate what is occurring in grade school science classrooms. Such a perspective may prove useful in designing an intervention that can introduce students to the practices, conventions, and communities associated with being a scientist. This study investigates one such possible intervention.

Relevant here is research carried out in the United Kingdom by Beau Lotto, who with his research group descended on a fifth grade elementary school classroom armed with bees and the desire to help students to be creative. In what became known as the Blackawton Bees Project (Schenk et al., 2011), students were first encouraged to learn about bees and then to design and implement experiments on them; soon they were pushing the boundaries of previous work and, with some assistance, conducting real scientific research. This project demonstrates the potential for grade school students, who have relatively few intellectual and creative constraints, to operate as research scientists. Further, from the

DOI: 10.4018/978-1-5225-5873-6.ch005

students' perspective, this opportunity will have provided an understanding of what it means to practise science as opposed to simply learning about it. So it was in the Blackawton Bees Project that, through the process of learning about bees, working with researchers, conducting experiments, and seeing their work published (as it eventually was), the students were also introduced to the range of actions and essential elements involved in contributing to the scientific community.

In my own science education practice, I have observed that the experiments recommended for and conducted in many classrooms follow a highly prescriptive model. Typically, this model involves the use of a textbook or other source that provides a list of materials, a set of procedures, and a series of questions intended to guide students toward certain conclusions. Frequently, an understanding of the conclusions from the textbook experiments is required in order to advance to the next topic, so the significance is revealed in subsequent pages to prevent any child from being left behind. Furthermore, most of the experiments are designed to verify previously determined results, a situation that is not the typical of experiments that researchers conduct for publication in scientific journals. Using the textbook commonly assigned to physics students in the province of Alberta (Ackroyd, 2007) provides a particularly illustrative example: in it, the acceleration due to gravity, g, is validated in no fewer than 11 ways, none of which is representative of approaches currently used by actual scientists.

Finally, while many classrooms model the scientific method in the conduct and presentation of an experiment, in that the instructions serve to communicate certain requirements of the thought processes involved, these exercises lack a fundamental component of what makes science humanity's most powerful knowledge-generation tool. This missing piece is the peer-review process, through which a potential contribution to the body of scientific knowledge is subjected to rigorous scrutiny by other members of the scientific community prior to publication and dissemination for wider public engagement. The present study has accordingly been designed to help fill this gap in science education.

Context

The sample for this study was drawn from a small school in Calgary, the largest city in the province of Alberta and third largest in Canada. This school was chosen both for its convenience and because of the openness of its founders and directors to new pedagogical approaches. The inclusion of classes from Grades 6-10 allowed for the involvement of a considerable number of students and was at the same time consistent with the school's desire to stage a research-focused conference. All of the students in these grades were eventually required to participate in what became known as the "Celebration of Science" (CoS). The school was entering its third year of operation when the project was initiated, at which time the estimated student population was around 200 students. This school employs expert teachers whose classes may be at any level; thus a biology teacher, for example, is expected to offer biology classes to students from Grades 1 to 12. The breadth of teaching responsibilities in this regard is significant because it meant that the teachers' roles changed over the course of this study.

Purpose

This study was conducted in order to address the following research questions.

1. Can participation in a school science conference encourage students to become active in the scientific community?

2. What role might such a conference play in the evolving science education paradigm?
3. How might engaged participation in a complex community of scientific practice benefit students' scientific discourse and encourage their participation in the subject? (This question is addressed in Carlgren, 2017.)

These three questions speak to key aspects of the current climate, practice, and culture of science education. The origin of and rationale for this study will be further discussed below. The ultimate goal was to use an integral framework, along with concepts relating to complexity and communities of practice, to gauge the viability and the possible advantages and practicality of implementing a student-led conference on science.

Significance

Unlike many other empirical studies, this one was not intended to establish a *truth*. The intent, rather, was to search for *meaning* in actions, interactions, products, and interpretations associated with the implementation of the Celebration of Science conference at the target school. The findings may be of interest to practicing educators, educational theorists and researchers, and anyone else involved with science education. Because these findings are not stated as empirical certainties, it is left to the reader to assess the significance and usefulness of any particular result or interpretation.

BACKGROUND AND THEORETICAL PERSPECTIVES

A brief note is in order before exploring the theoretical perspectives. This chapter covers numerous paradigms and frameworks with which readers may be unfamiliar, but it is beyond the scope of this paper to present them in detail. Recommendations for supplementary readings have accordingly been provided in a separate section at the end of the chapter.

Complexity and Networks

Modern complexity theory originated in the 1940s and 1950s in the context of systems theory and cybernetics. Most of this early research proceeded from a Newtonian perspective, in the context of which simple equations and linear models are applicable, and it therefore failed to represent adequately the nuances of realistic systems (Joas, 1996) open to external stimuli. The realization that then-current theories were inadequate for modeling reality led to the development of the field of cybernetics, which introduced the concepts of positive and negative feedback as fundamental principles of open systems. It was soon noticed that these concepts were applicable to open systems in fields as diverse as finance, healthcare, ecology, and various social sciences. Researchers such as Lorenz, Mandelbrot, and Prigogine (Pielke, 2013) approached the analysis of complexity from a mathematical standpoint in order to make valuable contributions to chaos theory, fractal geometry, and complex modeling, respectively.

Another important contribution was made by Kaput et al. (2005), who distinguished three fundamental components of complex systems, namely that

- the individual components do not fully explain the behaviour that emerges from the their interactions;
- a system is inherently non-linear, its evolution being motivated by feedback; and
- a system operates simultaneously on multiple levels and time scales.

The application of these principles to an educational setting faces challenges posed by entrenched assumptions regarding the very nature of knowledge and reality. Thus, for instance, if knowledge exists as an objectively perceived "substance," the advent of the Internet represents an educational conundrum in terms of the very availability of knowledge. This is because, inasmuch as traditions of educational practice have influenced how the *acquisition* of knowledge is conceived, the Internet has forced a re-definition of the roles and requirements of educators as something other than knowledge experts. Since these considerations may be understood as a kind of post-modernist critique, I note that this critique is intended here to invite discussion of subjectivist epistemologies.

While they have only been applied in the field of education relatively recently, and were initially confronted by numerous practices grounded firmly in objectivist traditions, subjectivist epistemologies have often been the primary focus in the development of educational theory in recent years. Particularly relevant in this context is the emergence of constructivism and constructionism as distinct educational paradigms, though the literature occasionally conflates them. It will be useful to make clear at this point what is intended by each term in the present discussion.

From the perspective of constructionism, or social constructionism, knowledge acquisition occurs through social interactions with objects. Thus Fish (1990) argued that "all objects are made and not found" and that "the means by which they are made are social and conventional" (p. 186). The implication is that the social makeup of a society and culture provides the backdrop for individuals' interpretive skills, beliefs, and behaviours, all of which significantly influence the interpretation, and subsequent "knowledge value," of objects. Fish called this experience of immersion in a culture a "publicly available system of intelligibility" (p. 186). Geertz (1973) offered another interpretation:

Thinking consists not of "happenings in the head" (though happenings there and elsewhere are necessary for it to occur) but of traffic in what have been called, by G. H. Mead and others, significant symbols—words for the most part but also gestures, drawings, musical sounds, mechanical devices like clocks, or natural objects like jewels—anything, in fact, that is disengaged from its mere actuality and used to impose meaning upon experience. (p. 45)

For a constructionist, then, knowledge is in essence socially constructed and requires the maintenance of social systems. Schwandt (1994) drew on previous work to illustrate this distinction:

Kenneth and Mary Gergen also challenge the idea of some objective basis for knowledge claims and examine the process of knowledge construction. But, instead of focusing on the matter of individual minds and cognitive processes, they turn their attention outward to the world of intersubjectively shared, social constructions of meaning and knowledge. Acknowledging a debt to the phenomenology of Peter Berger and Alfred Schutz, Kenneth Gergen (1985) labels his approach "social constructionism" because it more adequately reflects the notion that the world that people create in the process of social exchange is a reality sui generis.

Table 1. Categorizations and illustrations of simple, complicated, and complex problems

Baking a Cake	Sending a Rocket to the Moon	Raising a Child
Cakes will likely turn out the same provided that the recipe is followed each time.	Launching one rocket increases the reliability of future rockets.	Raising one child provides experience, but no assurance of future success.
Expertise is not required, though it may be helpful.	Multiple experts are required from various fields.	Expertise may contribute to success, but it is neither necessary nor sufficient.
Each time the recipe is followed, the cake will turn out the same.	There are many similarities among rockets.	Each child is unique and must be treated as an individual.
Good recipes are good every time.	Resolution of problems leads to a high degree of certainty in the results.	Results continue to be uncertain.

Source: Adapted with permission from Glouberman and Zimmerman (2002)

Contrary to the emphasis in radical constructivism, the focus here is not on the meaning-making activity of the individual mind but on the collective generation of meaning as shaped by the conventions of language and other social processes. (p. 127)

Constructivism differs fundamentally from constructionism in that, from the former perspective, knowledge is acquired individually and depends in large part on the history, experiences, intelligence, influences, and similar factors that inform the viewpoint of the person acquiring the knowledge.

What these distinct epistemological viewpoints contribute to this discussion is a framework that takes into account the complexity inherent in the relationship between the context and the learner as well as the evolutionary adaptations and dynamic interchanges among contexts and learners. Within the current cultural paradigm of scientific realism (which is highly empirical and linear), which contests the notion that that which can be observed and measured is all that exists (Haggis, 2008), the creation of such a complex epistemology is often avoided. It is for this reason that complexity science plays such a significant role in this study.

There are also fundamental distinctions to be made among simple, complicated, and complex systems, as illustrated in Table 1 (adapted from Glouberman & Zimmerman, 2002). A simple system is one amenable to an algorithmic approach or formula. A complicated system combines multiple simple systems or algorithms, and a complex system is one that *may* be amenable to algorithmic approaches, but not to the extent of producing substantial solutions or models.

Consistent with Kuhn's (1970) conception of a paradigm shift as a new way of viewing and interacting with the world, the embrace of complexity theory may constitute a paradigm shift in education. In this study, the incorporation of concepts relating to complexity altered the perspectives of students and teachers and their interactions and products and thus proved a useful interpretive tool. Complex systems allow an enhanced capability to visualize, depict and analyze connections that was previously unreachable

There have naturally been many shifts in educational thinking over time, which Davis, Sumara, and Luce-Kapler (2013) have usefully categorized into four prominent *moments*, each associated with a significant paradigm in educational thinking and practice. The *standardized moment* encompasses empiricism, rationalism, linearity, objectivism, and standardization, many of which concepts remain part of current educational practice worldwide. The *authentic moment* marks an expansion to include constructivism, post-modernism, deconstruction, existentialism, and associative learning; *democratic citizenship* further extends the paradigm to include cultural studies, globalization, poststructuralism, distributed cognition, and situated learning. Finally, *systemic sustainability* practices incorporate complexity science, network theory, nonlinear dynamics, systems theory, nested systems, and lifelong learning. These scholars insisted that their categorizations are neither rigid nor developmental, but that they should rather be viewed as nested sets of practices wherein each subsequent moment includes all that existed before and adds further insights and epistemological and ontological ramifications.

Howe (1998) similarly characterized the epistemological evolution through the latter part of the twentieth century in terms of three paradigms that he labeled *interpretivist, post-modernist*, and *transformationist*. In the terms just discussed, the interpretivist paradigm would encompass the standardized moment; the post-modernist paradigm would include much of the authentic moment and aspects of the democratic citizenship moment; and the systemic sustainability moment resembles interpretivist paradigms, though there are differences. Howe (1998) described the role of transformationalists as "working out defensible conceptions of knowledge and rationality that have contingent human experience as their basis" (p. 15), a post-modernist claim (in that it questions fundamentally the current narrative of belief) that bears comparison to aspects of the systemic sustainability moment. Because it is an emerging paradigm that at the same time includes all previous efforts and ways of thinking, the transformationalist movement deserves serious consideration in current research practices as a way of understanding complexity and dynamic systems. It is for this reason that complexity serves as a framework for this study. This framework has also proved crucial for understanding the impacts of feedback at multiple levels, the emergence of new characteristics, behaviours and physical creations, and the manifestation by individuals (students, teachers, etc.) of new characteristics and behaviours.

Integral Theory

Without belabouring the point in a volume dedicated to the subject, integral theory (IT) is a metatheory that takes into account "literally everything that all the various cultures have to tell us about human potential—about spiritual growth, psychological growth, social growth" (Wilber, 2007, p. 1) for the purposes of description, categorization, and/or analysis. IT is useful for determining the assumptions being made about actions, events, or objects, and it provides ontological and epistemological tools for the deep examination of certain types of questions. In short, it is an incredibly powerful framework for revealing both what is known and what remains beyond the reach of an existing paradigmatic perspective.

The application of IT begins with what can be described in terms of the initialism AQAL, which stands for "all quadrants, all levels" and proceeds to "all lines, all states, all stages, and all types," though AQAL encapsulates the concept adequately. Four quadrants make up AQAL in a manner akin to a coordinate axis of x and y variables (Figure 1). The upper left (UL) quadrant describes the interior, or subjective, aspects of a distinct item, concept, or other entity and thus includes any feelings or reflective processes on the part of the individual. The upper right (UR) represents the exterior, or objective, qualities of the individual and includes empirical and measurable quantities. The lower quadrants parallel the upper ones but describe groups rather than individuals. Thus the lower left (LL) describes the interior, or subjective, view of a collective in which the individual resides or participates and thus includes such cultural notions as traditions, languages, and laws. The lower right (LR) likewise extends the UR into the group realm, this time by including societies, countries, clubs, teams, and other empirically measurable associations.

Continuing through the acronym, AL represents the maximal level of the current developmental capability. In the predominant model of integral theory, that of Ken Wilber, such *levels* fall along an

Figure 1. The Four AQAL Quadrants

The "I" Quadrant Individual/Interior, Intentional **Subjective** First Person Language	**The "IT" Quadrant** Individual/Exterior, Objective **Behavioural** Third Person Language
The "WE" Quadrant Collective/Interior **Intersubjective** **Cultural** Second Person Language	**The "ITS" Quadrant** Collective/Exterior **Interobjective** **Social/Institutions/Systemic** Third Person/people Language

evolutionary continuum extending from the animalistic or reptilian to the non-dualistic or enlightened. It will be useful to review here four other aspects of IT that will be important to the discussion below.

- *Lines* refer to individuals' abilities, characteristics, and/or talents and include many of Gardner's multiple intelligences, examples being the spiritual line (aspects that facilitate progression toward enlightenment) and the cognitive line (the ability to take perspectives). These lines are generally considered to run perpendicular to the levels. By way of example, a spiritual figure such as the Dalai Lama would be expected to display a more advanced spiritual line but a less advanced kinaesthetic line in comparison with an accomplished athlete.
- Transient and temporary, or can be induced by means of psychoactive compounds or through meditative practices. Common states include waking, sleeping, and dreaming, while atypical, altered states may provide a glimpse of what could be possible were a development to continue along a certain line. Ayahuasca, a hallucinogenic drink used in parts of Central and South America, is one means of achieving the latter kind of state.
- Developmental *stages* represent progress along any particular line, a straightforward example being the aging process, which proceeds from highly egocentric infancy to ethnocentric adulthood with the distinction between self and others.
- Lastly, *types* represent general groupings outside the rest of the AQAL framework, common examples being the masculine/feminine dichotomy and the Enneagram personality types are common examples.

Because it is not feasible to examine each of these aspects in the course of a research study, the scope here is limited to the first quadrant and the levels and lines. Stages also receive consideration at certain points in what follows, but types do not. IT itself, as a metatheory, "acknowledges the multiplicity and irreducibility of approaches to social reality and calls for their integration. Integration is the process of building connections among theories rather than unifying or deconstructing them" (Renert, 2011). These theoretical considerations, in addition to their significance in the analysis presented below, also provide the necessary background for the introduction of the one other framework deployed here, communities of practice.

Communities of Practice

The cognitive anthropologists Lave and Wenger first developed the concept of a *community of practice* in 1991 by broadening the scope of their earlier notion of *situated learning*. Wenger (1998) further proposed the incorporation of three interrelated concepts, *joint enterprise, shared repertoire*, and *mutual engagement*, according to which individuals engaged in an enterprise should share a similar purpose, common resources, and an interest in maintaining group norms. The work of a contemporary scientist involves more, however, than simply belonging to a community of practice. Thus Luo (2009), taking up the notion of the "collaboratory" (collaborative laboratory) coined by William Wulf, observed that

A collaborator is seen as having a community component consisting of various communities of practice. Collaboratory members participate simultaneously in communities of practice within their local academic communities and with collaboratory members from other organizations. (p. 2)

From this perspective, the position of a scientist within multiple communities of practice can be more readily modelled by combining the notions of complexity and communities of practice than using the latter in isolation. In this study, students were introduced to a few aspects of the scientific community of practice through research, writing a journal-style paper, and participation in a conference. These processes, which mimic the actions of scientists within a broader community, constitute the novel element of this research. Students are often taught about science, but, I argue, they are rarely taught the inclusive and collaborative experiences unique to actually carrying out and legitimizing scientific thought.

RESEARCH DESIGN OVERVIEW

This study was conducted using an *educational design research* (EDR) methodology well suited to capturing the emergence of the new phenomena that were the primary focus. EDR, also referred to as design-based research, differs from traditional empirical research methods in a number of key ways, as can be seen in the objectives identified by the Design-Based Research Collective (2003) for research using this methodology.

First, the central goals of designing learning environments and developing theories or "prototheories" of learning are intertwined. Second, development and research take place through continuous cycles of design, enactment, analysis and redesign. Third, research on designs must lead to sharable theories that help communicate relevant implications to practitioners and other educational designers. Fourth, research must account for how designs function in authentic settings. It must not only document success or failure but also focus on interactions that refine our understanding of the learning issues involved. Fifth, the development of such accounts relies on methods that can document and connect processes of enactment to outcomes of interest. (p. 5)

Such a system of research differs significantly from the traditional ways in which hypotheses are created and tested. In an educational setting, which involves engaging with individuals who have unique histories, personalities, interests, and so on, manipulating only a single variable seems an unacceptable oversimplification. EDR studies, by contrast, are not intended to produce universal truths but rather meaningful insights, even if only into one specific context.

METHODS

The Research Problem

My own experience of nearly 14 years as a science teacher is consistent with the findings of studies describing a widening gap between the science done by grade-school students and that done by career scientists. While many science textbooks focus on the scientific method, students also need to explore other aspects of science. Thus, as discussed, scientific knowledge is not created by individuals but through a process in which the results of a study pass through the crucible of peer review before publication makes them available for broader public scrutiny and possible acceptance. The focus here is accordingly on how publication in a journal and presenting research at a conference can demonstrate to students what it means to adhere to ontological scientific principles and to build on a history of previous concepts and thereby to engage the community of scientific practice.

The Research Questions

As a first step in this exploration of scientific participation, three focusing questions were formulated:

1. Can students' active participation in a community of scientists be promoted through the development of a school conference dedicated to science?
2. Does this approach deserve inclusion within the evolving science education paradigm?
3. Can engaged participation in a complex community of scientific practice facilitate students' discourse regarding science and participation in research as scientists (Carlgren, 2017)?

Data Collection

Datum was collected using mixed methods in a manner that covered the four areas of examination suggested by Bloomberg and Volpe (2012), namely contextual, perceptual, demographic, and theoretical. Surveys of participating students were conducted at the outset in order to gather contextual and demographic information, including scientific affiliations and relations within their families and their parents' income and educational levels. Another survey, modeled on the Conceptions of Science Questionnaire developed by Kind, Jones, and Barmby (2007), generated numerical results for a range of questions. In addition, the "Draw A Scientist Test-Checklist" (DAST-C) was used to provide a secondary measure of students' conceptions of scientists and science; specifically, students were given a sheet of paper and are asked to sketch their idea of what a scientist looks like, without any other guidance or instruction. The checklist took into account three aspects of the resulting drawings in terms of their adherence to stereotypical norm, namely appearance, location, and activity as measured on a four-point scale used to produce a quantitative score.

Subjective data was also collected in the form of student work (i.e., preliminary and final copies of written work), feedback sheets and commentary from mentors, notes from researchers, and anecdotal comments by students and mentors. The subjective aspects of these assessments satisfied the Bloomberg and Volpe's perceptual and theoretical areas of examination.

Limitations and Delimitations

Limitations

The most significant limitation of this study was the relatively small amount of data that was collected and analysed. As with any study, the amount data is directly proportional to the depth of the analysis and insight possible and to the complexity of the conclusions that can be drawn. Other limitations included the relatively small sample and therefore its representativeness in terms of demography. Again, however, the purpose of an EDR study is not to identify truth per se but rather meaningful insights. This study, it is hoped, has done so in some small way.

Delimitations

I decided at the outset to reduce the data collection and analysis by forgoing a full parental demographic survey, and subsequently chose as well to disregard the results of the students' demographic survey because this information was more clearly indicated by the DAST-C and Conceptions of Science Questionnaire. Other delimitations were primarily a consequence of the changing nature of the tasks for teachers. The iterative nature of EDR, though, allows for choices and changes to be made as new information and perspectives emerge over the course of a study. Consultation with mentor teachers guided a large number of such choices during the present research, as will be seen in the following discussion. Overall, because this study combined an EDR methodology with mixed methods, the possibilities for data collection were vast, so I selected information directly applicable to the focusing questions and disregarded other potentially useful data.

EXPLORING THE ISSUES

Analysis of Findings

The quadrants described above constitute one structural tool used in the presentation of the findings of this study. In the following four sections of this paper, the perspective from one quadrant and the associated information and perspectives are discussed along with such interpretive considerations as the possibility of more than one interpretation.

Empirical Data (Upper Right Quadrant)

Empirical data was collected using the DAST-C and the Science Conceptions Questionnaire and from rubrics and mentors' feedback. These classes of data are presented individually below.

DAST-C

The checklist provided with the DAST-C was used to generate scores from 0 to 3 representing, respectively, nonexistent, sensationalized, traditional or stereotypical, and "broader than traditional" (Farland-Smith, 2012) appearance, locations, and activities depicted in the students' drawings of scientists. Separate assessors also rated the drawings, and the scores were collated for the 42 student assessments. The average scores were 1.82 for appearance, 1.02 for location, and 1.17 for activity, situating the participants' views of scientists somewhere between typical and sensationalized. A significant factor in the seemingly low scores was students' failure to include one or another element; such omissions were scored as 0 and thereby lowered the average for that element. Thus, for example, 22 of 42 students did not include a location, and 16 of 42 depicted no recognizable activity. In short, the DAST-C results showed that students often did not consider including a location or activity when sketching a scientist and that those who did tended toward traditional and stereotypical views of scientists.

Conceptions of Science Questionnaire

The Conceptions of Science Questionnaire provided a wider field for analysis than the DAST-C because it contained a fairly large number of questions (50) targeting specific conceptions of science; these were rated on a five-point Likert scale. This questionnaire was adapted slightly from the one developed by Kind, Jones, and Barmby (2007) so as to reflect North American terminology (i.e., "math" in place of "maths") and to correct a typographical error. It shares some items with the Relevance of Science Education and the 2003 Programme for International Student Assessment (PISA) questionnaires. In order to ensure reliability internally as well as with the Conceptions of Science Questionnaire, Cronbach's α was calculated and compared with the results from the original study following the recommendation of Gay, Mills, and Airasian (2006). The data from each study can be found in Table 2.

Kind, Jones, and Barmby considered a Cronbach's α score of 0.7 or higher to be internally reliable. A comparison of the results of their study with those presented here demonstrates that the questionnaire is a reliable measure of students' conceptions of science.

The questionnaire used in this study features assessments of seven distinct categories that contribute to a student's conception of science, namely learning science in school, self-concept regarding science, experimental work in science, science outside of school, future participation in science, importance of science, and general attitudes towards science. The results for the 932 students assembled by Kind, Jones, and Barmby and for the students who participated in this study are shown in Table 3.

Lower scores on the Likert scale correspond to relatively more positive conceptions of science. The ranges have been included to show that there appeared to be students who consistently failed to understand the rating system or who held extremely polarized views of science. The data from Table 3 can

Table 2. Cronbach's α for the questionnaire used by Kind, Jones, and Barmby (2007) and for the one used in this study

Measure	Kind, Jones, and Barmby	This Study
Learning science in school (6 items)	0.92	0.79
Self-concept in science (7 items)	0.85	0.80
Practical work in science (8 items)	0.89	0.79
Science outside of school (6 items)	0.87	0.71
Future participation in science (5 items)	0.88	0.75
Importance of science (6 items)	0.72	0.66
General attitude towards school (12 items)	0.85	0.88

Table 3. Average results by category

Category	Kind, Jones, and Barmby Mean Result	Mean Result	Range for This Study
Learning science in school	3.06	2.02	3.50
Self-concept in science	3.24	2.17	3.43
Experimental work in science	3.95	1.78	3.25
Science outside of school	2.64	2.52	4.00
Future participation in science	2.38	2.91	3.71
Importance of science	3.50	1.81	3.40
General attitudes toward science	3.32	1.75	3.83

be interpreted to suggest that there was a relatively wide range of student conceptions of science within this sample specifically and that these conceptions were largely more positive than those of the general population of students (with the exception of the category of future participation in science). This finding is important for establishing the context of the target school as it pertains to the generalizability of this study.

Mentor Feedback

The final piece of empirical data came from the feedback that the mentors provided to students as their writing and presentations evolved toward the completed product. The mentors worked with a range of students from Grades 6 to 10, and only the data collected from those who kept diligent records of their comments, rubric sheets, and student submissions were taken into account. As a result, only 42 student participants (of a possible total of 90) working with 3 mentors (of 5) were represented. Feedback on student draft writing and retained rubrics was coded into six categories based on the target of the comment, namely scientific content, science-specific writing elements, clarity, grammar/spelling, style and format, and citations and references. As students were required to adhere to APA style guidelines in their writing, many of the comments addressed changes in the latter two of these categories. A summary of the data is presented in Table 4.

The findings shown in Table 4 provide the basis for a number of interesting comparisons, similarities, and questions. To begin with, Mentor 2 commented much more than the other two mentors on *Science-Specific Writing Elements*. The following is a representative example excerpted from the original work:

Student writing: Manipulated variable: Unsure

Responding variable: Unsure

Feedback: you need to know this before you begin your expt! Remember, manipulated is the one you select/change, while responding is the one(s) that change as a result.

Table 4. Number of elements of each type of feedback provided by mentors

Mentor	Scientific Content	Science-Specific Writing Elements	Clarity	Grammar/Spelling	Style and Format	Citations and References
Mentor 1 (14)	53	75	55	135	97	30
Mentor 2 (13)	42	229	50	166	88	101
Mentor 3 (15)	40	61	51	169	97	125
TOTALS	135	365	156	470	282	256

Note: the parenthetical numbers below the mentor titles represent the number of students under the direction of each mentor.

Because the process being written about is a scientific experiment, certain characteristic elements of the writing align to yield the necessary scientific thought. Mentor 2 seems to have provided relatively more feedback of this type for the simple reason that this was an area of particular personal interest.

Another notable feature of the data in Table 4 are the similarities among mentors with regard to the total number of certain types of comments (apart from the already noted exception). Here Mentor 1 represented an exception in terms of a decreased focus on Citations and References owing to a lack of familiarity with APA formatting requirements and (as indicated through personal communication).

This section, then, has summarized briefly some of the quantitative and empirical data collected for this study. The analysis and such subjective data as changes that the feedback and revision processes revealed reside in a different quadrant, the Upper Left, to which the discussion now turns.

Motivation, Mentors, and Feedback (a Possible Upper Left)

Motivation

Student motivation is difficult to assess under the best of circumstances. A number of factors are worthy of consideration in this respect here. As the study commenced, the first change in the planned procedures to engage students in the research and the science conference was agreed upon by the science department teachers. Specifically, at a meeting with the teachers prior to implementation, it was decided that the entire project would be mandatory for all students, would extend from September to June, and would neither be graded nor play any role in course requirements or evaluation. These decisions had a decided impact on the project overall and its end products and on the students' relationships with their mentor teachers throughout the process. Mandating participation in the Celebration of Science (CoS) for all students in Grades 6-10 obviously created a different environment in terms of overall engagement compared with voluntary participation. This mandate does not, however, speak to the motivation of the students, especially since there was no grade connected with the process or student outcomes. Rather, student motivation appears to have been tied to a combination of two factors, *choice* and *freedom* on the one hand and students' relationships with their mentors on the other.

Student choice is one of the core tenets of the school in which this study took place. As an example, Fridays at the school are devoted entirely to teacher-led "options" that can involve anything from knitting to Minecraft Modding, dominoes, WW II weaponry, Harry Potter trivia, or martial arts demo team practice. The school was founded on the notion that students should make the decisions that affect their studies, and they have embraced this approach. So also students had opportunities for choice in the CoS project, and it was my observation as a researcher that this ability to choose provided students with a much-needed opportunity to focus on an area and style that suited them. Thus they were allowed to select both the type of research to be conducted (experimental or pure research) and the topic. This freedom of choice with respect to topic naturally meant that mentors had to be able to work on a wide variety of projects, but this approach also seems to have been crucial for maintaining the students' motivation. In other words, the participating students seem to have been motivated by the provision that, rather than being assigned topics or projects keyed to their grade levels or areas of specialization in science, they were free to make choices, choices that indeed often produced surprising results.

Another important consideration regarding student motivation is the student-mentor relationship. The assignment of mentors was essentially random, having been done alphabetically by last name. Perhaps surprisingly, relationships grew between mentors and students as the requirements for the project and methods of communication became clear in the context of conversations about the students' areas of interest. During these conversations, both mentors and students acted as knowledgeable contributors, and the former came to be recognized for knowledge and abilities that extended beyond the specifics of the school's curriculum. Teachers who served as mentors also learned about students' work habits and were able to make choices regarding deadlines and requirements that fit with their particular schedules, needs, and restrictions.

At work in this process was an interesting dynamic that merits further discussion. In my experience in the classroom, individual students are rarely catered to in terms of scheduling and the submission of materials. However, in the CoS work, it was done by all mentors with at least one student. Additionally, the meetings between mentors and students were usually conducted at mutually-agreed times, such as during lunch or the short breaks between classes. Under these circumstances, negotiation and discussion served as the primary means for determining the rate of student progress, with the mentor teachers taking into account the predetermined dates and students' schedules. The interaction between the mentor and student, the requirement to complete the project, the somewhat extra-curricular nature of the project, and the mutual agreement between mentors and students helped to create tangible foundational experiences for both the teachers and the students. It appears that these processes, together with the general feedback targeted at individual growth, fostered the relationships between mentors and students. As befits the UL quadrant, a specific type of data would have been required relating to introspection on the part of both the mentors and the students in order to define these elements more specifically. As such data was not collected in this study, doing so constitutes an avenue for future research.

Mentors

It has just been seen that mentors influenced the students' levels of motivation over the course of the CoS. Also significant in this respect were the guidance that the teachers offered and their unique specialties. The concept of the mentor teacher arose in the context of the school's complicated teaching schedule. As previously mentioned, specialist teachers provide instruction in their areas of expertise to a broad range of age groups, covering Grades 2 to 12. They accordingly switch grade groupings three or four times through the school year, for example from Grades 4 to 5 to 6, in order to cover certain topics of specialization within the prescribed curriculum. In light of this complexity with regard to scheduling, and given that the project was to last through most of the school year, the teachers decided that there was no need for the assigned groups of students to belong to the same class. Accordingly, the students were separated alphabetically into groups for assignment to mentors, with approximately equal numbers of students in each group. Since the assigned groups of students were diverse in terms of both their grade levels and their topics of choice, teachers were no longer able to play the traditional role of the sole possessor of knowledge in the classroom, the "sage on the stage," a state of affairs characteristic of Howe's (1998) "standardized moment." Instead, mentor teachers began to provide guidance and recommendations to students regarding written sources, writing elements, experimental techniques, and research directions, behaviour more aligned with Howe's "authentic moment" and possibly the "systemic sustainability moment" as well.

The science team also modified the original study concept in the use of handbooks. Specifically, the decision was made to compile and disseminate all of the information pertaining to the completion of either an experimental- or research-focused project, including expectations, deadlines, and helpful resources and examples, before the students engaged in the writing component of the project. With the expenditure of considerable effort, handbooks were created for the experimental and research projects at two different reading levels along and a third handbook for parents. The distribution of these documents to all students and parents established a common language and pool of resources and shared expectations. In the context of the UL quadrant, these documents provided a support mechanism to which each student or parent could turn for information. Contracts, guidelines, and deadlines were all intended to foster in individual students the perception that the structural needs of their projects were already in place, thus enabling independent investigation of the topic of choice. This is, however, only one possible interpretation of the function of these documents.

Feedback

Rubrics were also created to align with each of the milestones (i.e., deadlines) associated with each type of project. These rubrics allowed mentors to provide feedback in a way that promoted the growth of individual students as each draft, research proposal, and completed project was read and assessed individually. Additionally, students were encouraged to work at their own pace and to submit items prior to deadlines or as they were completed. As mentioned, students in some cases negotiated for more time owing to external pressures; but others returned work before the final due date. This asynchronicity may also speak to the issues covered by the UL quadrant, as each student received feedback in a timely fashion according to when he or she submitted work. Admittedly, this effect of the UL may be subtle, but it seems no less significant than others discussed here, especially when contrasted with the typical classroom requirement that all of the students hand in all of their assignments at the same time. Finally, the component of time plays a role in this context, for, since the project spanned the majority of a school year, students received frequent reminders of upcoming deadlines but were otherwise free to establish their own pace of progress through the work. So again, time played, not a restrictive role in this aspect of the project, but rather in its abundance created the space for choice, freedom, and individuality in the students' work.

APA, Community, and the Conference (One Lower Left)

The concerns associated with the Lower Left (LL) quadrant center on the internal perspective of a collectivity, such as an emerging community or culture. Four such matters are worthy of note in this section: Writing in APA format, community, handbooks and the conference.

Writing in APA Style

Perhaps counter-intuitively, the formatting requirements of the APA style guide, though they imposed restrictions, seem also to have guided the students through a certain method of thought. For some of them, the process of citing authors and conducting research that involved reading and writing about what others had done was a new experience. Previously at the school, all that had been required of students with regard to their English writing skills was to state their ideas; formatting was not considered. Introducing students to APA formatting, style guides, the Online Writing Lab at Purdue, and to the very concept of rhetorically constructing a reasoned argument using material that had been researched and properly cited—all of this extended their learning significantly. Students more than once expressed the opinion that they had through their projects learned about the broader community of scientists, the value of research, and the strength of an argument built upon the supportive work of others with more experience. Thus, for example, one sixth-grade student, when assigned a small research task in class, asked whether he could complete it in APA format because doing so "allows me to see my thoughts better." The structure of APA format also required students to write in a way that models much of the material that they were reading for their research, further deepening the connection with the community of scientists in which they were attempting to participate.

Community

In some situations, the work of the students extended beyond the expertise of their assigned mentor teachers and other specialists were sought out to provide specialized guidance. By way of example, one student working on a problem in group theory was paired with a biology specialist with little background in the subject; the latter therefore contacted a PhD mathematician on the school's staff to assist her with the calculations involved while she provided feedback on the scientific aspects of the writing. Here again, direct and indirect interactions among teachers, mentors, students, and scientists appear to have contributed to a sense of community for the students.

A further aspect of community was reflected in the students' discussions of their individual projects in classes or during their spare time. Their shared goal of completing their work aligned well with Wenger's (1998) three requirements for communities of practice, namely a joint enterprise, mutual engagement, and shared repertoire, which were introduced above. In short, the common experiences of requirements, deadlines, and the task in general seem to have contributed significantly to a sense of community among the students.

Handbooks

Building briefly on this point, the handbooks, rubrics, and associated requirements played roles in the LL quadrant by creating a shared repertoire of expectations. Since the students each conducted individual research on topics of their own choosing, the handbooks were key components in creating a sense of community through the shared standard to which all of the students were held.

The Conference

The Celebration of Science (CoS) itself also played an important role in building a community and providing students with a sense of belonging to something greater than their school. The variety of guest speakers, presenters, workshops, and demonstrations made possible by the staff created an atmosphere of exuberance and joy. Guests often attended the student presentations, including parents, many of whom said that they saw value in the events of the CoS and that the conference helped them to appreciate the learning that had occurred even in the midst of any frustration that they may have experienced at home during the process. The day of the conference was thus the prime moment when the sense of community, both within the student body and between it and the broader scientific community of science, became palpable. As a side note, the school administration elected to continue the CoS in the following year and extended it to include all subject areas and students up to Grade 12, thus creating even more opportunities for connections to form between the participants and the broader community.

Missing Pieces: The Lower Right (LR)

At a certain point during this study, I became aware that a set of words or terms seemed to be deeply embedded in the project. I first tried to make sense of these apparently disconnected concepts by creating a network diagram, but when this approach revealed no significant relationships, I turned to a Venn diagram in which groups of terms were associated in terms of common guiding ideas (Figure 2).

Venn Diagram

Figure 2 lists a number of illustrative components, including the titles of each of the three circles. The concepts of guidance/support, community and choice/freedom were perceived as fundamental to the success of this project, but none of them fell within the two central overlapping regions, nor did any of the terms used to describe more specific components of the study. Regarding the region in which Choice/Freedom and Community overlap, I suggest that extending the CoS to incorporate all academic subjects may shift the "topic" element so that it would fall within the overlap. Inclusion of "topic" in this area would also raise considerations associated with the LR quadrant, as a cross section of societal issues would be available for presentation rather than only those of one community or sub-culture. Mentors would fall within the region where all three circles overlap if students were allowed to choose their own, and their own (external) experts as well. Reconfiguring the conference along these lines could highlight the LR while also putting the mentors forward as the linchpin of the entire undertaking. This concept, and implementing student choice with respect to mentors, both warrant further study.

Figure 2. Venn diagram of interactions and essential elements (Carlgren, 2017)

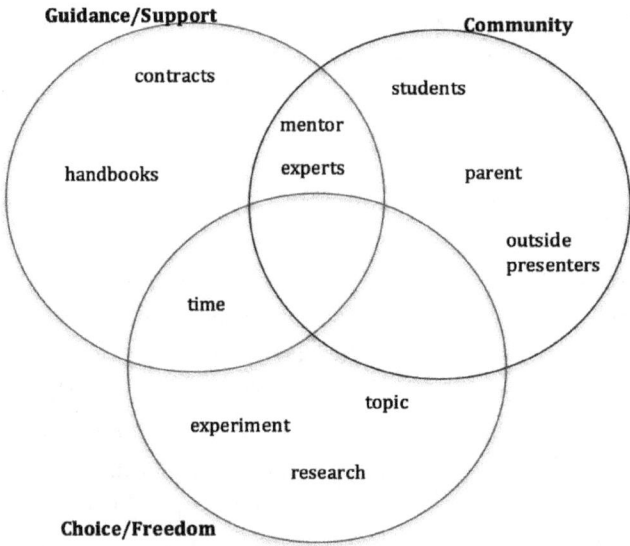

The (Missing) Lower Right

Beyond the Venn diagram, it is also worth considering whether the LR is relevant to contemporary pedagogical and scientific contexts. The relationships among the narratives that structure science, society, and schooling of course merit far broader and deeper investigation, both synchronic and diachronic, than can be offered in this paper or even in this book. Key considerations include how the teaching of science has become embedded in the public mindset and created patterns, habits, and sets of beliefs that surround and contain current practices; the role, if any, of science as a tool for generating knowledge in creating these patterns; and the extent to which current practices in science and science education are, in the context of societal expectations, beneficial to all members of the various stakeholder groups. All of these considerations represent potential avenues for future discussion, action, and research.

CONCLUSION AND IMPLICATIONS

I conclude this paper with a discussion of some of the implications of the findings presented here from the perspective of recommendations for practice, research, and growth.

Recommendations for Practice

The use of mentors and of handbooks and rubrics as well as the asynchronicity in the student's long-term projects as described in this study have implications for the construction of communities. Events that require the coordination of a large number of students may benefit from consideration of these elements, as each facilitates a distinct type of learning for the participating staff, mentors, and students. In hindsight, various sorts of events, such as sports competitions, could benefit from and influence this discussion. In many sports participants receive instruction or mentoring and individual feedback from coaches who are interested in their success, are encouraged to practice independently (the element of asynchronicity), are assessed according to some scale (usually a competition of some sort), and are the focus of a community that forms through a shared repertoire of activities and experiences. The common practice of teaching (increasingly) large numbers of students in a regimented fashion based on lectures may be suitable in some contexts, but alternative approaches, some of which can be included as regular events in the school year, have the potential to foster a broader range and greater depth of individual learning. In more abstract terms, contemplation about ontology and epistemology and the fundamental purpose of a given intervention and alternatives to it may serve as the basis for significant and salutary changes in pedagogy.

Recommendations for Research

Factors that influence the formation of communities, especially those that extend beyond the typical classroom setting, are one obvious area for future study suggested by the foregoing discussion. The practice of connecting students with experts and members of the broader community was found to foster productive relationships and to promote learning, and further research using similar interventions could help to pin down the extent to which students garner increased meaning through such interactions with the world beyond the classroom. Furthermore, questions relating to the absence of the LR are of particular interest in the context of recent upheaval in the U.S. science education landscape. With the Next Generation Science Standards (NGSS) mapping a course into previously undiscovered territory, it would be particularly useful to have a better idea of the possibilities of coordinating LR considerations with curricular alignment.

Recommendations for Growth

Instability and change, then, often encourage growth by creating the necessity to adapt, as can be seen in contexts ranging from education to, for instance, spirituality or evolution. While the tendency within any organization or system is to maintain established routines and habits, often unquestioningly, the post-modernist position provides a salutary corrective in its insistence on the value of challenging the dominant narrative. At the same time, the post-modernist approach often leads stagnation in the effort to deal with the implications of the view that all conceptions of reality, knowledge, and truth are equally valid. The fundamental recommendation here is that educators leverage the opportunities created by evolving practices, that they begin to look beyond traditional lectures to an approach that is more student-focused, individualized, and based on choice, and that their goal be to create new meaning rather than to seek a quantifiable truth. From the perspective of integral theory, growth in these respects might be represented by a change in level as a result of, as it were, forcing development in the cognitive line (which is responsible for the choice of perspectives) by means of changes in teaching styles and various forms of feedback. As Andrews (2014) has written,

To be effective teachers we need to awaken and excite our slumbering souls, to rediscover a sense of wonder. As Dag Hammerskjold once said, "We die on the day when our lives cease to be illuminated by the steady radiance, renewed daily, of a wonder, the source of which is beyond reason." The good

news is that the children, according to Swiss psychologist Alice Miller, are "messengers from a world we once deeply knew, but have long since forgotten." (p. 4)

Perhaps, then, the main take-home lesson of the present study comes in the form of a call to educators to seek personal meaning through their practice of teaching, in part by trying new methods and remaining "unbalanced" rather than settling into comfortable routines. For the school that was the target of this research, "Cos" had a very real effect.

REFERENCES

Ackroyd, J., Anderson, M., Burg, C., & Martin, B. (2007). *Physics*. Toronto: Pearson Canada.

Anderson, L. W., & Krathwohl, D. (2001). *A taxonomy for learning and assessing: A revision of Bloom's taxonomy of educational objectives.* New York: Longman.

Andrews, B. (2014). *The soul only avails: Teaching as a spiritual act.* Retrieved from: http://uuneedham.org/wp-content/uploads/2014/02/Teaching-as-a-Spiritual-Act.pdf?x34068

Barnett, R. (2000). *Realizing the university in an age of supercomplexity.* Maidenhead, UK: Society for Research into Higher Education and Open University Press.

Bloomberg, L. D., & Volpe, M. (2012). *Completing your qualitative dissertation: A road map from beginning to end.* Thousand Oaks, CA: SAGE.

Carlgren, D. (2017). *Integral exploration of the engagement of a scientific community of students in a school conference* (Unpublished dissertation). University of Calgary, Calgary, Alberta, Canada.

Davis, B., Sumara, D., & Luce-Kapler, R. (2013). Engaging minds: Cultures of education and practices of teaching (3rd ed.). New York, NY: Routledge.

Design-Based Research Collective. (2003). Design-based research: An emerging paradigm for educational inquiry. *Educational Researcher, 32*(1), 5–8. doi:10.3102/0013189X032001005

Dunne, J., Williams, R., & Martinez, N. (2002). Food-web structure and network theory: The role of connectance and size. *Proceedings of the National Academy of Sciences of the United States of America, 99*(20), 12917–12922. doi:10.1073/pnas.192407699 PMID:12235364

Farland-Smith, D. (2012). Development and field test of the modified Draw-a-Scientist test and he Draw-a-Scientist rubric. *School Science and Mathematics, 112*(2), 109-116. doi:.1949-8594.2011.00124.x doi:10.1111/j

Fish, S. (1990). How to recognize a poem when you see one. In D. Bartholomae & A. Petrosky (Eds.), *Ways of Reading: An Anthology for Writers* (2nd ed.; pp. 178–191). Boston, MA: Bedford Books of St. Martin's Press.

Gay, L., Mills, G., & Airasian, P. (2006). *Educational research: Competencies for analysis and applications.* Columbus, OH: Pearson.

Geertz, C. (1973). *The Interpretation of Cultures*. New York, NY: Basic Books.

Glouberman, S., & Zimmerman, B. (2002). Complicated and complex systems: What would successful reform of Medicare look like? In P.-G. Forest, G. P. Marchildon, & T. McIntosh (Eds.), Romanow Papers: Changing Healthcare in Canada, Vol. 2. Toronto: University of Toronto Press.

Gouy-Pailler, C., Achard, S., Rivet, B., Jutten, C., Maby, E., Souloumiac, A., & Congedo, M. (2007). Topographical dynamics of brain connections for the design of asynchronous brain-computer interfaces. *Proceedings, Annual International Conference of the IEEE: Engineering in Medicine and Biology Society, 2520-2523*.

Haggis, T. (2008). "Knowledge must be contextual": Some possible implications of complexity and dynamic systems theories for educational research. *Educational Philosophy and Theory*, *40*(1), 158–176. doi:10.1111/j.1469-5812.2007.00403.x

Healey, M., & Jenkins, A. (2006). Strengthening the teaching-research linkage in undergraduate courses and programs. *New Directions for Teaching and Learning*, *107*, 45–55. doi:10.1002/ti.244

Howe, K. R. (1998). Values in evaluation and social research. *Evaluation and Program Planning*, *23*(3).

Joas, H. (1996). *The creativity of action*. Chicago: University of Chicago Press.

Kaput, J., Bar-Yam, Y., Jacobson, M., Jakobson, E., Lemke, J., & Wilensky, U. (2005). *Planning documents for a national initiative on complex systems in K-16 education*. Retrieved October 31, 2014 from http://www.necsi.edu/events/cxedk16/cxedk16.html

Kind, P., Jones, K., & Barmby, P. (2007). Developing attitudes towards science measures. *International Journal of Science Education*, *29*(7), 871–893. doi:10.1080/09500690600909091

Kuhn, T. (1970). *The structure of scientific revolutions*. Chicago: University of Chicago Press.

Luo, A. (2009). Supporting participation in communities of practice by scientists from developing countries—The case of high energy physics. *Proceedings of the American Society for Information Science and Technology*, *45*(1), 1–11. doi:10.1002/meet.2008.1450450288

Onella, J.-P., Saramaki, J., Hyvonen, J., Szabo, G., Lazer, D., Kaski, K., ... Barabasi, A.-L. (2007). Structure and tie strengths in mobile communication networks. *Proceedings of the National Academy of Sciences of the United States of America*, *104*(18), 7332–7336. doi:10.1073/pnas.0610245104 PMID:17456605

Pielke, R. A. (Ed.). (2013). *Climate vulnerability: Understanding and addressing threats to essential resources*. New York: Academic Press.

Renert, M. A. (2011). *Living mathematics education* (Doctoral dissertation). University of British Columbia, Vancouver, Canada.

Schenck, D., Coles, J., Fraquelli, L., Airzee, S., & Wishy, A. (2011). Blackawton Bees. *Biology letters*, *7*(2), 168-172.

Schwandt, T. A. (1994). Constructivist, interpretivist approaches to human inquiry. In N. K. Denzin & Y. S. Lincoln (Eds.), *Handbook of Qualitative Research* (pp. 118–137). Thousand Oaks, CA: Sage.

Wenger, E. (1998). *Communities of practice: Learning, meaning and identity*. Cambridge, UK: Cambridge University Press. doi:10.1017/CBO9780511803932

Wilber, K. (2007). *Integral Spirituality*. Boston, MA: Integral Books.

ADDITIONAL READING

Crotty, M. (2012). *The Foundations of Social Research: Meaning and Perspective in the Research Process*. London: SAGE.

Wilber, K. (2007). *Integral Spirituality*. Boston, MA: Integral Books.

KEY TERMS AND DEFINITIONS

Communities of Practice: A community of practice encompasses a set of individuals who, through sharing a repertoire, common purpose, and mutual engagement, form a cohesive group.

Complexity: A description of a behavior of a system that demonstrates key aspects of *emergence, response to feedback*, and *being greater than the sum of its parts*. A complex system is one that cannot be broken down into constituent elements for the purpose of understanding the system as a whole. A complex system differs from a complicated system in that the latter is exactly equal to the sum of its parts. An example of a complicated system is an automobile, and of a complex system any vertebrate animal.

Paradigm: This term, more recently modified by Thomas Kuhn, describes the predominant mindset of a group, culture or society. It includes methods, standards, and ways of thinking that govern the legitimacy of contributions by an individual to a larger group.

Post-Modernism: A state of development characterized by the questioning of pre-existing narratives that drive behavior in the world. Post-modernists are often known for being highly skeptical and showing a proclivity for understanding narratives as social constructs and interpretations that are highly subjective, though this is of course itself a subjective, and potentially morally relative, claim.

Science: An ambiguous term that simultaneously describes a subject of study in school and a method for the generation of knowledge of the natural world through the procedural iterations of hypothesis creation, experimentation, observation, and revision.

Chapter 6
An Integral Analysis of Bahamian Adolescents and Their Perspectives About a Future After High School

M. Kathleen Kellock
University of Calgary, Bahamas

ABSTRACT

Adolescents in high school are faced with many opportunities and challenges, which may direct their future path towards higher education and career development. The future orientation among Bahamian adolescents was looked at from an integral lens. The beliefs and goals Bahamian adolescents had for their future were explored and included present actions and plans students proposed to realize these goals. Further, the expectations adolescents perceived others had for them and the perceptions they held for themselves, including outside influences and systems that impact adolescents' implementation and realization of their goals were identified. The use of Wilber's integral methodological pluralism, supported by mixed methods research, gathered phenomenological, hermeneutical, and empirical data from members of the school and the community involved in a private high school in the Commonwealth of The Bahamas. Studies on future orientation with adolescents in other countries provided a comparison for and offered additional insight into the phenomenon of college and career readiness.

INTRODUCTION

When adolescents leave high school they encounter a variety of opportunities available to them. These opportunities and choices must align with how they perceive their personal future and the future for their local, regional or national regions. In reflection, high school students contemplate whether or not they are in possession of the skills, knowledge and experiences to prepare them for a life outside the confines of a secondary school, irrespective of their completion or graduation from high school. Today, many

DOI: 10.4018/978-1-5225-5873-6.ch006

students are faced with the harsh reality that gaining admission into college or university, obtaining a degree or qualifications, finding employment and achieving financial sustainability are not guarantee, nor certainties (Bangser, 2008; Baum, Ma, & Payea, 2013).

Context

Historically, the past generations of citizens in The Bahamas have adjusted to societal changes including the emancipation of slavery, the desegregation of schools and national independence. Today students are confronted with the harsh realities of high youth unemployment, overpopulation, and extreme crime, as well as travelling abroad to pursue educational aspirations, and then compete for employment in a job market where there is a saturation of particular professions.

The Bahamian National Education Committee's (NEC) Vision 2030: Shared Vision for Education (National Education Committee, 2015) devised a national plan for Bahamian education through the years until 2030, which aims to provide quality education and produce multiple pathways to graduation. This plan will "foster academic excellence, social responsibility and equip students with multiple literacies that will enable them to make meaningful contributions as nation builders who are globally competitive" (National Education Committee, 2015, p. 8). For those adolescents, who are about to embark on a life post-high school, it is essential for them to explore their own plans and aspirations for the future, and chart the course, which will take them there. The Bahamas' Ministry of Education, Science and Technology (MOEST) has foreseen that young Bahamians will need to possess skills and qualifications which will help increase the numbers of a qualified and skilled workforce, furthering the economic and social development of the country. As such, local educational institutions are implored to provide individuals with opportunities "to enhance or expand his skill set for use in the labour market or to acquire knowledge or skills to enhance his personal life" (National Education Committee, 2015, p. 14). Schools should teach new types of skills and knowledge so as to help their students keep abreast with the changes and advancements in the careers and jobs of today and tomorrow.

Many high school students in the Commonwealth of The Bahamas will, upon graduation, further their education by attending college, university or other institutions of higher learning, as a continuation of their learning experience in preparation for their futures.

Purpose

The purpose of the study was to explore the forthcoming plans, beliefs and perceptions held by Bahamian adolescents enrolled in an established private school on the island of New Providence, about their future life in college/university or in the workforce after they complete high school. Additionally, the study examined the views and insight of teachers and parents from this school community regarding college and career readiness of high school students. The study uncovered the concerns that adolescents, and those influencing them, have about the future of their nation and their role in it, especially when some young people plan to return from colleges and universities abroad to seek gainful employment at home.

Significance

Minimal research has been undertaken in the Commonwealth of The Bahamas that has addressed the personal reflections of Bahamian adolescents regarding their perceptions for their own future and the future of their nation, and nothing using an integral lens. When high school students complete, and hopefully graduate from secondary school, many of them will either enroll in local colleges or technical and vocational institutes, seek local employment, or travel abroad to attend university. There has been a traditional belief in the country that when students from private high schools graduate, they will either attend college or university for two to four years, or more, before commencing their career path and enter the workforce. It is postulated that what students are taught, including the skills and expertise they acquire and learn while in high school will influence their understanding of their own experiences and their perceptions of personal readiness as they orient themselves for the future. As such, do these adolescents perceive themselves to possess the skills and knowledge to be ready for the next phase of their life?

BACKGROUND

The aim of this literature review looked at related perspectives surrounding the choices and decisions that adolescents make, the beliefs and expectations held by adolescents about their future, and the role and influence others have on young people as they orient themselves toward the future. There exists considerable research on adolescents and the perception they hold for their own future and a future that is more global in scale.

Selected Review of the Literature

Adolescence and Developmental Characteristics

Adolescence is a time when young people grow and mature both socially and developmentally. It is a time when young people make plans, set goals, and assess their personal beliefs and aspirations for their future. It is in this developmental stage that adolescents continue to explore and construct images of a future by relating to different domains and contexts. The content of these domains may be personal or social, realistic or ideal, and reality-based or fantastic (Seginer & Lilach, 2004).

Erikson (1963) saw adolescence as a period of development, a "no man's land between childhood and maturity" (p. 340), which following the onset of puberty to the attainment of adulthood, and terminates legally at the age of majority usually 18 years of age (Colman, 2006). Lewin (1939) recognized that adolescence is a period of transition in which people of all ages address their expectations, hopes and fears for the future. However, the time with which adolescence ends is not only a biological change, but a social change as well (Arnett, 2000). The demarcation of adolescence at the age of 18 years is fitting as it is "a good age marker for the end of adolescence and the beginning of emerging adulthood, is appropriate as it is the age at which most young people finish secondary school, leave their parents' home, and reach the legal age of adult status in a variety of respects." (Arnett, 2000, p. 477)

Beliefs and Aspirations

For some adolescents, there remains an uncertainty as to what they want to be when they grow up, or what to do after they graduate from high school. Unfortunately, many young people are not fully aware of the skills, the knowledge required for and the process of fulfilling their desired or aspired career. The choice of a future career may change with the cognitive and social development of adolescents as the consideration of possibilities factor prominently with young people. Developing personal self-efficacy becomes of paramount importance in an adolescent's achievement as it guides him or her to select more desirable goals for his or her future (Cunnien, Martin Rogers, & Mortimer, 2009). Additionally, some adolescents are mutually interested in their own personal futures as well as global and social futures. Arguably, the fundamental task of education today is not just to prepare students for the future, but equip them to create a future they want to live in (Eckersley, 1999).

Actions and Future Considerations

Young people are genuinely interested in their future prospects, and as adolescents develop and mature, their attention and apprehension for their own personal interest in their own future also intensifies. Consideration for the future provides the motivation for the attainment of goals in adolescents. Kerpelman and Eryigit (2008) believed a positive outlook and perception of the future allowed adolescents to imagine better possibilities in the future for themselves. This optimism toward the future may motivate behaviors that enable adolescents to achieve their goals by solving problems, tolerating frustrations, or maintaining flexibility (Neblett & Corina, 2006). Chen, Christmas-Best, Titzmann, & Weichold (2012) suggested that the manner in which individuals react to changing circumstances and adapt to new environments will affect and alter the choices and actions adolescents make in the future, which will influence the rest of their lives.

Expectations for Adolescents

Today, a high school diploma is no longer adequate to meet the needs and demands for the careers of the future. Many of these new careers are greatly influenced, supported and evolve in a technology-based economy (Bangser, 2008). The high schools of today must ensure that adolescents are afforded with the opportunity to explore a wide variety of career options, if they are to compete and be competent in a future world that is fast becoming more and more digitally enhanced and advanced (Bassett, 2005).

Some students and parents expect that the school and the educational system will provide the curriculum, courses and training for adolescents to be college ready upon high school graduation. Rojewski and Kim (2003) have suggested that the increased academic rigor in high school curricula and rising college entrance requirements, have polarized some college-bound and work-bound students. Young people also expect that when they graduate from university they will have the knowledge and training to enter into the workforce. Unfortunately, finding work in their desired field or in their home community may not be possible.

Systems of Influence

There are many systems that exist and operate in society today. The family, a high school, a place of worship, and the community are examples of systems, which are a part of an adolescent's life. Regardless of an awareness of systems and the complexity of these arrangements, people are shaped by them and in turn, influence them as well. "Today's students will go through their lives better prepared to make decisions that are good for them, beneficial to others, and helpful to the planet" (Goleman & Senge, 2014, p. 41).

The systems that have a great influence on adolescents while they are in high school include the school, the educational system, the community and the admission policies of colleges and universities. The collaboration and alignment of standards in both high school and post-secondary educational institutions will be required to help young people elevate their academic skills and develop greater college knowledge and readiness (Hooker & Brand, 2010). Therefore, in order for international students to be college ready and meet the requirements of foreign postsecondary educational institutions, the curriculum standards must be addressed and aligned so that international students have the skills, knowledge and credentials to apply to schools in other countries.

The Future and Future Orientations

When exploring the words future and adolescence similar meanings arose. The origin of the word, future, is derived from the Latin *futurus*, from a base meaning of "grow or become" (Oxford Dictionaries, 2014) or "going to be" (Waite, 2012, p. 294). The origin of the words adolescence and adolescent, come from the Latin verb *adolescere* meaning "to grow up" (Kegan, 1994, p. 19; Oxford Dictionaries, 2014) or "to mature" (Waite, 2012, p. 9). It is during adolescence when the social and cognitive development of young people causes them to 'grow, mature and become' a new self. This new self then continues to progress, grow, mature and become, in the years following high school. The similarity in the base meaning of the two words, future and adolescence, 'to grow', makes a poignant argument to address the relationship between these two concepts.

Numerous international studies have revealed various themes associated with future orientations with children and adolescents. Numri (1991) suggested that the planning for the future transcends any age and that these perceptions are often reflected in young people's personal hopes and fears. It is during this developmental stage "when planning for the future increases, as youth are pressed to find roles and to develop identities and self-definitions that will propel them towards their future adult life" (Schmid, Phelps & Lerner, 2011, p. 1127). Lindfors, Solantaus and Rimpela (2012) suggested that pictures of our future "act as a mirror of our times, reflecting the ideological and political values and ethos of society and its social and cultural norms" (p. 992), which may provide a roadmap and compass guiding us toward possible futures for self and society.

Individuals, and adolescents in particular, form an idea and a picture on what their future will be like. Future orientation is constructed by studying the transition of adolescents into adulthood in modern cultural settings, regardless of their nationality or ethnicity (Seginer & Lilach, 2004). Future orientation literature uncovers and explores common themes in the three main life domains of school enrolment, military service, higher education, work and career, marriage and family, as well as seeing how the individual depicts the future for themselves, others and the community (Seginer & Lilach, 2004; Seginer & Halabi-Kheir, 1998). In 1998, Seginer and Halabi-Kheir's study with Israeli adolescents showed that across age groups and gender, adolescents of different ethnic groups construct their future orientation with a strong emphasis on depicting a future on normative roles and expectations, such as attending school, getting a job, getting married and having a family. Other adolescents viewed their future from a broader perspective, which addressed the concerns, moods and emotions of the personal self, of others and the wider community.

The milestone of high school graduation acts as a path for adolescents to drive themselves to chart their own course and create their own map for their future. In the future, education in both secondary and postsecondary institutions will look very different and will reflect the skills needed for the new careers and occupations of the economy and society (Conley, 2014). Educational institutions and systems should investigate the perspectives adolescents have toward the future in order to provide the best educational practices. Exploring the many perspectives held by an individual or an organisation allows for understanding situations in the world and relationships with others (Wilber, Patten, Leonard & Morelli, 2008), which can help educational institutions and systems create curriculum and educational practices that best serves young people and prepares them for an ever evolving and changing world.

The future conjures a plethora of emotions perceived and imagined by young people. It can be tentative, unpredictable, and expansive. It may encompass ideas and thoughts they have about their community and nation, in addition to their beliefs on the sustainability of the planet. Thoughts of the future may also be more egocentric in nature addressing personal aspirations and dreams for continued education and training, potential employment and beginning a family. The future for some young people is something anticipated, and for others it is looked upon with dread. It is during adolescence that many young people contemplate their future and their role as citizens in the world to be. The hopes and fears that young people have for the future influence what they are prepared to do in the present and what they are prepared to work towards (Dunne & Edwards, 2010). For adolescents, awareness for the future can be an exciting prospect, a path and territory uncharted.

For adolescents, a future after high school opens doors for further education, career aspirations and family. Schmid, Phelps and Lerner (2011) recognized that "adolescence is a time when planning for the future increases, as youth are pressed to find roles and to develop identities and self-definitions that will propel them towards their future adult life" (p. 1127). During the high school years "young people see themselves in regard to 'the future' and why 'futures' processes are so valuable for them" (Gidley & Hampson, 2008, p 274).

Mapping a future requires consideration for possible, probable and perceived futures. Orientation to the future is complex, which varies from person-to-person within numerous contexts and reflects the individual's anticipation of events (Kerpelman & Eryigit, 2008). The aspirations and anxieties of adolescents and their future examined the influence of family, education, health, work and career (Lindfors, et al, 2012; Numri, 1991; Seginer, 2008; Seginer, 2003; Seginer & Halabi-Kheir, 1998; Seginer & Lilach, 2004). Additionally, more problematic circumstances involving global and social threats such as violence, unemployment, economic uncertainty and political unrest (Nikolayenko, 2011; Numri, 1991; Poole & Cooney, 1987; Seginer, 2008) were also identified.

College and Career Readiness

What does it mean to be college ready and possess college knowledge? The perception of college and career readiness is dependent on the developmental maturity of individual and the expectations of others. Within the context of a high school, adolescents can contemplate, explore and investigate options and personal interests (Conley, 2014), acquire the content knowledge, skills and expertise needed to understand and influence their own experiences and perceptions of personal readiness for life after high school. David Conley (2011), founder of the Educational Policy Improvement Center (EPIC) presented a definition and model of college readiness, which would project the necessary skills, knowledge and attributes required of adolescents as they prepare for a future after their experience in high school (Conley, 2008, 2011, 2014).

Within Conley's well-established framework, the skills and content adolescents are required to possess in order to prepare them for college and university are addressed and incorporated in the high school curriculum and other programs of instruction. Conley (2014) believed that a high school student is deemed *college ready* when all facets or keys of his framework are mastered and attained. Although some students may not successful grasp all keys, it does not mean that they are incapable of gaining acceptance into a college or university. Although this framework may only be a predictor of college readiness, some adolescents may struggle a little more when they get into college (Conley, 2014).

College readiness is both complex and contextual, and is a culmination of both educational and personal experiences (Conley, 2008). The complexity of possessing college knowledge and readiness for adolescents, while they are in high school, is essential for their future aspirations. Edmunds (2012) noted that it would take more than students taking the right academic courses such as the rigorous courses and programmes offered by the American College Board SAT and Advanced Placements courses, or the International Baccalaureate Diploma. Students will also be required to develop academic behaviors and skills that are aligned with college expectations (Edmunds, 2012). Conley (2014) deemed students were ready for college and career when they could "qualify for and succeed in entry-level, credit-bearing college courses leading to a baccalaureate degree, a certificate, or career pathway-oriented training programs without the need for remedial or developmental course work" (p. 51), or were able to enroll and succeed in a two- or four- year postsecondary institution without the need for remediation (ACT, 2011). Bassett (2005) added that to be college and career ready meant a young person would need to possess proficiencies required in their perceived real world such as being "globally competent" or "culturally literate." Urich and Mackenzie (1985) believed that the student who understands dialectical thinking and some of the important concepts of social science and who comprehends the meaning of social change is most likely to perform competently in the future (p. 92). Regrettably, not all adolescents will have all the real-world skills when they graduate from high school, but through personal growth, experience and interaction with others they can develop the necessary skills to facilitate a greater degree of success for future aspirations (Davis & Murrell, 1993).

When high school students identify their plan and aspirations for the future they are better able to make decisions and preparations to help them realize these goals when they graduate (Conley, 2014). At one time, obtaining a high school diploma was sufficient, however, many high school graduates today do not have the skills nor possess the credentials to qualify them for many of the emerging careers and occupations (Conley, 2014). Offering students better guidance and aligning the high school curriculum with the expectations of university and vocational training can present young people with a variety of options from which to pursue.

In a Belgian study, Germeijs and Verschueren (2007) suggested that adolescents be given decision-making strategies, which are helpful when exploring, investigating, selecting and pursuing a career. Hirschi, Niles and Akos (2011) suggested vocational and career planning and training to be a fundamental task that young people should develop during adolescence as these learned skills could transcend through the rest of their lives. Adolescents in the developed, industrialized world have more information available to them on a variety of possible career options, the necessary training required and the institutions of higher education that can help facilitate this plan. The access to information and the knowledge gained creates an increased perception of readiness, which is beneficial to students, as they will spend less time and money floundering in areas of schooling and employment that no longer are an interest to them (Vuolo, Mortimer, & Staff, 2013).

Additionally, cultural factors may influence an individual's career path. Lee, Rojewski and Hill (2013) led a study with adolescents in South Korea that implied that as adolescents prepare for their future, planning for a career favors highly in their shift from high school to postsecondary education, work and adult life. It is during this transition that they often defer making decisions about a future career until they have gathered more information about the current and future labour markets.

During adolescence, young people are at a crossroads of a developmental period transitioning them to adulthood when they plan for and anticipate the next phase of their life where they can explore more adult roles and responsibilities.

THEORETICAL PERSPECTIVES

Integral Theory

Ken Wilber's integral framework, in particular the AQAL model, the acronym for "all quadrants, all levels, all lines, all states, and all types" (Wilber, 2006) provided a guide to explore the phenomena of college and career readiness and the perception of personal and nationwide futures from participants at an established private high school in the Commonwealth of The Bahamas. Integral theory provides a "big picture" (Martin, 2008, p. 155) for the research of a phenomenon and aids in "the creation of a map that extends the awareness of perspectives" (p. 160). It is interested in the participatory relationship through which multiple ways of knowing and the many dimensions of reality occur through various methods of inquiry and this can be done by drawing on the many elements of quadrants, levels, lines, states, and types (Esbjörn-Hargens, 2011). Incorporating more elements of AQAL broadens our scope and strengthens our ability to understand people and see things more clearly from many perspectives (Wilber, Patten, Leonard, & Morelli, 2008). Esbjörn-Hargens (2011) believed that by drawing on the five elements of the AQAL model, it could offer educators an effective guide to pedagogical design, classroom activities, evaluations, courses and curriculum.

Wilber suggests that AQAL is only a map, a cartogram, a diagram to be interpreted for and by the individual who or the organization, which chooses to use it (Wilber, 2006). Like any map, the cartographer, or mapmaker, outlines the essential elements and components for consideration, which are open for interpretation by the user of the map. The path or route the individual chooses to follow, along with the intervening obstacles and opportunities he or she meets along the way are integrated within the experience of the journey.

It is through an integral view that we can have "a better perspective or understanding of how any phenomenon can be understood" (Tassett, 2010, p. 98). It was through this integral lens, that a better comprehension of how students, teachers and parents, perceived a phenomenon such as college/university and workforce preparedness.

Figure 1. Integral enactment as applied to the context of this study

WHO (Participants)	HOW (Methods)	WHAT (College and Career Readiness)
Student	Demographic Questionnaire Interview Document Analysis	High school courses School initiatives
Teacher	Demographic Questionnaire Interview	High school courses School initiatives
Parent	Demographic Questionnaire Interview	School initiatives
Education Policy Maker	Demographic Questionnaire Interview Document Analysis	Educational policy School initiatives

Integral Theory
AQAL Model

Integral Methodological Pluralism

Esbjörn-Hargens (2006) identified that one of the strengths of using an integral theory framework is that it is "scaleable" whereas the researcher can select from "as few as three different methodologies or as many as eight" (p. 89). Wilber's (2006) integral methodological pluralism includes eight fundamental perspectives and eight fundamental methodologies. Wilber (2006) acknowledged that using the AQAL model, or using integral methodological pluralism is only one way, but a more comprehensive and integral way in which to offer more depth and insight into a phenomenon. The use of integral methodological pluralism presented an opportunity to use multiple methodologies that were the best and most "functional fit" for the phenomenon being researched. Integral methodological pluralism is "a collection of practices and injunctions guided by the intuition that 'Everyone is right!' and each practice or injunction enacts and therefore discloses as different reality" (Esbjörn-Hargens, 2006, p. 86). Wilber (1995) explained that everybody is possession of "important pieces of the truth, and all of those pieces need to be honored, cherished and included" (p. 48).

Using integral methodological pluralism opens opportunities to employ a variety of methods and methodologies for a research problem. Therefore, the phenomenon of college and career readiness was addressed in all four quadrants in the AQAL model and then looked at from the inside and outside, the internal and external, of both individuals and collectives. Esbjörn-Hargens (2010) introduced the idea that a greater enactment of integral theory was possible through integral enactment theory. This extension of integral theory addresses the enactment of a phenomenon from the diversity of ontology (the what), epistemology (the who), and methodology (the how) (Esbjörn-Hargens, 2010). In order to see a phenomenon from many perspectives through the use of many methodologies, integral methodological pluralism offers an approach in which this can be accomplished. While many people see the same phenomenon in different ways, and enact them differently in diverse situations, their realities may clash and interfere with one another, yet they are all necessary in which to give a more genuine picture of a phenomenon. Figure 1 shows how integral methodological pluralism, with its many methodologies and methods of data collection (the how) was used within integral theory to capture the voices (the who) of those involved (the students, teachers, parents and policy makers) in the research to achieve college and career readiness (the what).

Integral enactment identifies who, the how, and the what of a phenomenon to ensure triangulation (Figure 1). Adapted from Esbjörn-Hargens, S. (2010). On ontology of climate change: Integral pluralism and the enactment of multiple objects, *Journal of Integral Theory and practice,* 5(1), 157. The model responds to the context and participants of this study.

METHODS

The Research Problem

This research investigated what Bahamian adolescents, from an established private school, believed about their readiness for life after high school. High school students approaching their final years of secondary education, often contemplate whether they will meet the requirements to enroll in and gain acceptance to tertiary education institutions including local colleges, universities, or technical and vocational institutes. In the Commonwealth of The Bahamas, some young people must travel overseas to pursue their tertiary education, whereas some youth will go directly into the local workforce.

The Research Questions

The research questions were positioned within the four quadrants of an integral framework (see Table 1), which addressed the perspectives of participants from the inside and outside, and from a first-, second-, and third person perspectives.

Question 1: What beliefs do adolescents have about their life at college/university or in the workforce after they complete high school?

Question 2: What are adolescents doing to prepare themselves for their life at college/university or in the workforce after they complete high school?

Questions 3(a): What expectations do others (i.e., teachers and parents) have for adolescents and their life at college/university or in the workforce after they complete high school? (b) What personal expectations do adolescents have for themselves and their life at college/university or in the workforce after they complete high school?

Question 4: What systems (i.e., school board, Ministry of Education) have an influence determining adolescents' readiness for their life at college/university or in the workforce after they complete high school?

The placement of the research questions as seen from within the conceptual framework of the integral theory AQAL model (Table 1), which encompasses perspectives from adolescents and their community.

The four quadrants become the housing unit for all aspects and experiences of the individual. Within each quadrant of Wilber's (2006) integral framework, various aspects and elements of an individual can be placed. These elements identify and include the individual's stage and state of consciousness, including their character or personality type. The level of development of an individual is also mapped from

Table 1. Research questions in the four quadrants of the AQAL model

	INTERIOR	EXTERIOR
INDIVIDUAL	UPPER LEFT (Experience) 1. What beliefs do adolescents have about their life at college, university of in the workforce after they complete high school?	UPPER RIGHT (Behavior) 2. What are adolescents doing to prepare themselves for their life at college, university or in the workforce after they complete high school?
	I / WE	IT / ITS
COLLECTIVE	3. (a) What expectations do others (i.e., teachers and parents) have for adolescents and their life at college, university or in the workforce after they complete high school? (b) What personal expectations do adolescents have for themselves and their life at college, university or in the workforce after they complete high school? LOWER LEFT (Culture)	4. What systems (i.e., school board, Ministry of Education) have an influence determining adolescents' readiness for their life at college, university or in the workforce after they complete high school? LOWER RIGHT (Systems)

an array of developmental theories and characteristics, including cognitive, interpersonal, emotional, self-identity and needs.

The upper two quadrants, the upper left (UL) and the upper right (UR), address the singular and personal experiences, feelings, and behaviors of the individual, whereas the lower two quadrants, the lower left (LL) and the lower right (LR) address elements of the individual within the collective. The upper right (UR) focuses on the exterior of the individual, in particular the behaviors and consciousness of an individual, including the developmental identity of adolescence to adulthood. In the upper left (UL), the interior of the individual addressed. This includes the intentional actions, the thoughts, feelings, and the sensations of the individual in any experience or phenomenon, such as the beliefs and aspirations held by young people concerning their perception of readiness for the future. The lower left (LL) addresses the cultural influences of an individual from the collective perspective, including expectations from self and others regarding adolescents' future decisions and concerns. Within this quadrant, an individual becomes aware of the shared values and feelings, and worldviews of a particular group (Wilber, 2006). The lower right (LR) addresses the social components and educational systems that are a part of an individual's life and influence and affect the choices that adolescents make pertaining to their future. Wilber (2006) advised that to be as integral as possible, all four quadrants must be used to show the growth, development and evolution of an individual (p. 23). It is the focus of the upper left quadrant, the behaviors and consciousness of the adolescent, which will offer a significant contribution to the study as it shows how "the self unfolds from egocentric to enthnocentric to worldcentric" (Wilber, 2006, p. 23). This transformation and growth of the individual to group awareness, in the upper left, permits the expansion of social systems to evolve into complex systems in the lower right (Wilber, 2006).

Data Collection

This research study endeavored to map the territory on the phenomena of college and career readiness and the perceived futures of Bahamian adolescents using multiple methodologies and a mixture of qualitative and quantitative data collection, which supported the intent to develop a more inclusive and more integral research study on college and career readiness. Phenomenological and hermeneutical data was collected by means of semi-structured interviews and interpretation of written documents, including those from the school and the Bahamian Ministry of Education. The interviews addressed and supported the main research questions, which were nested in the four quadrants of the integral framework. These methods of data collection drew on first- and second-person perspectives from the participants. Empirical data was obtained from a questionnaire that highlighted the demographics of the participants involved in the study. Additionally, information on the students' academics records (i.e., GPAs, PSAT and SAT scores) were gathered, assessed and paired with the students' perceptions, and the information published by the American College Board surrounding the issue of college and career readiness. Documents on school and national educational goals, policies, initiatives, and plans were examined, which identified the systems and organizations that the adolescents were entrenched in. Empiricism and systems theory data collection focused on the third-person perspectives of the participants and the domestic and international education systems affecting Bahamian adolescents.

Limitations and Delimitations

Limitations

There are over 200 schools, including pre-schools, within the Bahamian school system. One hundred and sixty-eight are fully maintained by the government and 99 are independent or private schools. One third of the public schools are positioned on the island of New Providence and two thirds are on the outer, or Family Islands (Bahamas Ministry of Education, 2015). The study used a small sample size, which took place at an established independent high school on the island of New Providence, a small island in the northwest quadrant of the Bahamian archipelago. Restricting the study to one school eliminated the valuable information that could have been obtained from other private and public schools in the country. Further expansion of this study to include participants from other high schools, trade/vocational institutions, and tertiary institutions in The Bahamas would help to disclose additional perceptions held by other students in the nation.

Gathering additional input from the school's decision makers and more from the nation's educational policy planners, including current college-going students would add an additional layer on the map and provide more depth to the study.

Delimitations

The key delimitation with the study was that it took place in a singular private high school. Despite the many other independent secondary schools on the island of New Providence, they did not have a large student population base or sizable teaching faculty needed for this study. As such it was selected as the most functional fit for this study. Public secondary school students and teachers were not interviewed in this study despite the fact that their input and observations would be meaningful.

In using grade 11 and 12 students, their parents and high school teachers only, the contributions of other adults and students from additional grade levels was restricted regardless of the value to promote a culture of college in high school, which should also include the participation from students of multiple grade levels.

EXPLORING THE ISSUES

Analysis of Findings

Qualitative data was gathered through phenomenological interviews from 22 high school students (grades 11 and 12) and from 23 adult participants. Semi-structured interviews allowed the researcher to build on predetermined questions in order to explore topics that arose in the interview process (Merriam, 2009). Quantitative data was obtained from demographic questionnaires administered to each participant. Additionally, school records and educational documents were analysed. The interviews were transcribed and the use of Nvivo, a software program, helped to sort, code and align participant interview transcripts and questionnaire responses into themes.

The student participants ranged in ages 15–18, and came from three different countries. Four percent of the students were third-generation college going students, 15% were second-generation college going students, and 18% were the first in their immediate family to pursue a university degree. The adult participants ranged in ages 21–50+, and came from eight different countries. Eighteen adult participants were the first in their family to attend university, whereas four were second-generation university graduates. Some adults held Bachelor's, Master's or Doctorate degrees. Others had certificates and diplomas from Community Colleges or Teacher's College. There was only one adult participant whose highest attainment was that of a high school diploma.

The altitude (level of consciousness) of the participants and the topography of the educational landscape were determined from the perspective of the researcher and the responses provided during the interview questions. The "altitude markers" or "levels of development" (Wilber, 2006, p. 67) of amber (traditional, mythic, egocentric and conformist), orange (rational, ethnocentric, pragmatic and modern) or green (pluralistic, multicultural and postmodern) was assigned to each participant and theme that emerged in the study. There were two student participants perceived to be at the amber/orange altitude/level, 12 at the orange altitude/level, and eight with the green altitude/level. Likewise, there were ten adults identified to be at the orange altitude/level, and 13 with a green altitude/level. Wilber (2016) refers to these levels as "the basic maps that human beings use to make sense of their world" (p. 16). While the designation of altitudes is not exact or constant it does provide an examination into the degree of consciousness of each participant and emergent theme.

Research Questions Explained

The answers to the research questions reflect the responses provided by the participants, including data collected from the school and education documents.

Beliefs and Aspirations of Adolescents

Question 1: What are adolescents doing to prepare themselves for their life at college, university or in the workforce after they complete high school?

Students are aware that there are several requirements in place for high school graduation and that there are academic courses and standardized examinations provided that help in their advancement to become more university ready, including enrolling in advanced and honours courses that they perceive will strengthen their college application. Many students have taken advantage of the numerous opportunities available to them pertaining to learning about colleges and universities in the United States and Canada. Although additional higher education institutions in the Caribbean and in the United Kingdom are possible options for students, these schools are not greatly promoted and students undertake to research these schools on their own. They are researching universities to undercover the climate and culture of tertiary education institutions and are using technology to investigate students' perspectives of college life from current college students. Students are aware that they are requiring additional qualifications to get into some schools in the United Kingdom, and fail to meet the standards for some American and Canadian colleges.

Actions, Future Preparations and Concerns

Question 2: What are adolescents doing to prepare themselves for their life at college/university or in the workforce after they complete high school?

Student participants had very different beliefs about their future life after high school. Some were excited about the prospect of attending university in upcoming months, whereas others were apprehensive about being able to fit in and being away from home. The majority of students were aware that the local university was insufficient to meet their college and career aspirations. The students worried that in the future there would not be career opportunities or openings for them in The Bahamas and that they had to be prepared to stay abroad and seek employment elsewhere. They were also aware that the present state of the nation created cause for concern about their safety and financial security, and that they were anxious about the direction their country was going or would be in the future.

The adult participants, teachers, parents and an educational consultant, were concerned that students were not ready for the demands and rigor expected of college and university. They were equally aware that, based on their perceptions, the adolescents did not possess the work ethic or skills to begin a career immediately after high school. The parents believed that their children needed to study abroad in order to get the credentials for their specific career aspirations because the local institutions of higher education were insufficient to meet those needs. They were also aware that the students were less likely to return upon completion of a university degree because of the limited employment opportunities in the country. Both the parents and teachers believed that because the students lived in an insular society they would be in for a rude awakening and culture shock when they were required to live abroad to study.

Expectations for Adolescents

Question 3: What expectations do others have for adolescents and their life at college/university or in the workforce after they complete high school? What personal expectations do adolescents have for themselves and their life at college/university or in the workforce after they complete high school?

The students perceived that by taking the national examinations a year earlier than most students in the country would afford them the opportunity to take advanced courses while in high school, thus exposing them to the rigor and academic expectations of college-level courses. The 11th grade students perceived that college would be easier and would offer them more time during the day to focus on their studies, compared to the hectic and demanding schedule they face in this grade level. The 12th graders, who were exposed to college-level courses anticipated that life in university would be challenging. They believed that because many of them lived a sheltered life and they felt that being exposed to new cultures, interacting with new people, and the expectation and need to be more independent was more worrisome then the demanding academic expectations required of college or university. Many also perceived that because they had achieved pleasing academic results and were engaged in a various extra-curricular pursuits they were entitled to receive a scholarship, which would help offset the cost of a university education. The absence of personal financial planning for further education, and the expectation that outside agencies would bankroll a child's college education was disconcerting. For many, the acquisition of a scholarship was perceived, by both parents and students, to be the only means for many young people to even contemplate pursuing tertiary education.

Systems of Influence

Question 4: What systems have an influence determining adolescents' readiness for their life at college/university or in the workforce after they complete high school?

The Ministry of Education in The Bahamas aspires to ensure that all students in the country are afforded a standard curriculum. However, some schools have established relationships with the American College Board, the International Baccalaureate or the Cambridge International Examinations (I.G.C.S.E.), in order to provide an opportunity for an additional international standardized curriculum. Additionally, students need to be exposed to 21st century skills, including practical applications in all subjects and the need to deviate from more traditional curriculum delivery, which appears to be dated and relies mainly on local and hidden knowledge for some national subjects, if they are to achieve success at tertiary education institutions both locally and abroad.

The research questions and a summation of students' responses are shown in Table 2.

EMERGING THEMES

Twenty-four smaller themes emerged from the semi-structured interviews, demographic questionnaires and the interpretation of student, school and educational written documents. These themes showcased the evolving nature of education, society and culture in the Commonwealth of The Bahamas including the potential for development for young people in The Bahamas, its education system and the country

Table 2. Research questions and summation of participant responses including research findings

Upper Left The "I" Quadrant	Upper Right The "IT" Quadrant
INTERIOR-INDIVIDUAL (INTERSUBJECTIVE) **BELIEFS/PERCEPTIONS**	**EXTERIOR-INDIVIDUAL (OBJECTIVE)** **BEHAVIORIAL/ACTIONS**
RESEARCH QUESTIONS & PARTICIPANT COMMENTS FOCUSED IN THE (**UL**) QUADRANT: *What beliefs do adolescents have about their life at college, university or in the workforce after they complete high school?* • college will be fun, exciting, wild, a party; a growing experience • college will be easier, "more chill" than high school (i.e., grade 11 has been tough; AP courses "no joke") • college will be harder, more challenging • excited and apprehensive about being away from home; no parents • an exciting experience; a learning experience; "it's going to change me. I don't think I'm going to come out the same person that I went there." • teachers, school and parents put a lot of demands on students (i.e., school work, extra classes, coursework, study for examinations) • local college doesn't support many college aspirations or career fields • preparing/studying for new careers not yet heard of in this country	RESEARCH QUESTIONS & PARTICIPANT ACTIONS FOCUSED IN THE (**UR**) QUADRANT: *What are adolescents doing to prepare themselves for their life at college, university or in the workforce after they complete high school?* • taking required and recommended courses (B.G.C.S.E.s, SATs, APs) • taking additional courses (i.e., college courses, personal improvement or self-interest courses) • fulfilling high school graduation requirements for institution; for nation (i.e., obtaining required GPA, cumulative 2.0 grades 10-12; school attendance record; community service hours/service learning) • participation in extra curricular activities (i.e., well rounded individual; aids in admissions and scholarship applications) • talking to college representatives; teachers; guidance counselors; former students, friends, relatives in college • researching colleges (i.e., admissions offices, YouTube, blogs, Skype) • researching potential scholarships • academic recognition (i.e., school and national awards; bragging rights for individual and the school)
Lower Left The "WE" Quadrant	Lower Right The "ITS" Quadrant
INTERIOR-COLLECTIVE (INTERSUBJECTIVE) **CULTURAL/INSTITUTION**	**EXTERIOR-COLLECTIVE (INTEROBJECTIVE)** **SOCIAL/ EDUCATION SYSTEMS/POLICIES**
RESEARCH QUESTIONS & PARTICIPANT COMMENTS FOCUSED IN THE (**LL**) QUADRANT: *What expectations do others have for adolescents and their life at college, university or in the workforce after they complete high school?* • some students need remedial courses after high school • not ready; not mature enough • national academic standards may not be to par with colleges abroad (i.e., mathematics, sciences) • in for a culture shock; rude awakening • resources/measures in place; students must chose to use them • crime is scaring them away • no job opportunities (i.e., brain drain) *What personal expectations do adolescents have for themselves and their life at college, university or in the workforce after they complete high school?* • take fewer courses; set own timetable • need to be more independent (i.e., cook food, do laundry) • necessary step to prepare for further education; career • norm; expectation; after high school you matriculate to college	RESEARCH QUESTIONS & SYSTEMS FOCUSED IN THE (**LR**) QUADRANT: *What systems have an influence determining adolescents' readiness for their life at college, university or in the workforce after they complete high school?* • The Government of the Commonwealth of The Bahamas (i.e., Ministry of Education, Science and Technology— MOEST— National Diploma Programme) • local, regional and international post-secondary schools, colleges and universities (i.e., admissions requirements) • foreign governments (i.e., student visa applications) • scholarship committees, organizations and personnel (i.e., financing college)

as well. The themes included issues surrounding the provision of curriculum, educational standards and assessment; the mechanisms for college/university; literacy in the country; perceived competition for future employment; brain drain; issues affecting family dynamics; poverty; stereotypes towards the young; peer pressure; national crime; and environmental issues. These themes were merged and condensed to form four encompassing themes.

Discussion of Themes

Four central themes transpired from the twenty-four emerging themes to create a map of the territory of the phenomena of college and career readiness, and the perceptions of Bahamian adolescents for their future life after high school. These themes transpired from smaller themes to address the research problem and have directly impacted the students positively and negatively.

Promoting a College-Going Culture

There exists a real possibility and opportunity for young people, in both independent and public schools in The Bahamas, to consider and aspire to pursuing postsecondary education whether it is obtained locally or abroad. The provision of guidance counseling sessions in some high schools aids in the facilitation of college and career aspirations throughout the high school experience although this is not always the case in every school.

Promoting a college-going culture was positioned in all four quadrants as it addressed the expectations of students, parents, teachers and policy makers in promoting a belief that all students in The Bahamas can have aspirations for tertiary education. This in turn will cause various stakeholders to act to make this a reality in all high schools in the Bahamian archipelago. To prepare students with the skills needed in the 21st century in order to meet the requirements of evolving careers and diversity in the workforce, they will need advanced learning, often provided by tertiary education. Advocating for a plan that promotes a national college- or university-bound initiative may alter the generations of university graduates in the nation. This in turn will increase the country's standard and quality of development.

The Importance and the Value of Education

While *the importance and value of education* is connected to the theme of *promoting a college-going culture*, it has implications not only in the familial setting but that of the institution and society. What a society or culture values and aspires to is directly affected to its importance on education for all citizens, from preschoolers to the elderly. Investment in tertiary education, in particular increasing the number of graduates with college and university degrees, has been attributed to the success, growth and development of nations globally.

The original importance placed on education in The Bahamas "was designed to provide minimal literacy and sound moral training rather than social mobility or even useful skills" (Craton & Saunders, 1998, p. 29). The general need and importance of education to create an educated workforce was sufficient in the past, but today the workforce and the skills required for the 21st century surpasses that of previous generations. For many young people today, the acquisition of a college or university degree is paramount in order to fulfill their aspirations for the future.

State of the Nation

The state of the nation described the concerns and events within The Bahamas that are impacting and plaguing the nation. National issues such as crime, family dynamics and poverty, peer pressure, literacy and education, and environmental issues gave cause for some young people planning not to return to the country upon completion of their tertiary education abroad, thus contributing to the brain drain the country has experienced and is perceived to occur in the upcoming years. Furthermore, an increase in young people attaining university degrees will improve The Bahamas' adult literacy rate, diversify the skill set and knowledge base acquired in the national workforce, and inculcate an aspiration for future generations of adolescents to pursue a college education. Capitalizing on the human capital and seeking innovation in the nation may mitigate the alarming trend of brain drain currently experienced in country. The young people want change, they want a better "Bahamaland," they want a future that is sustainable and filled with possibilities, and one that welcomes them and their ideas for change and progress.

Recognition of Perceptions

The perception of pursuing a college or university degree has been instilled as a social norm for many high school students. The school curriculum is one that coordinates and offer's college-level courses for students to take while in high school. The perception that "certain people" in society will pursue professional careers and others will be steered towards more vocational trades has been instilled in the culture and traditions of the nation. This perception is perceived to be perpetuated for generations and as such has created as self-fulfilling prophecy for many young adults who seem destined by their economic and social position in society. Equally, the perception that many national issues are not just beliefs held by the participants but realities they are faced with on a regular basis.

The perceptions of participants have acted as the orienting arrow in the compass positioning the other larger themes in this study including promoting a college-going culture, the importance and value of education, and acknowledging the present state of the nation. These themes are interconnected and encompass the other smaller themes that emerged from the study, which in turn have impacted the lives of the participants involved to some degree.

IMPLICATIONS AND CONCLUSION

The territory of an established private high school in the Commonwealth of The Bahamas, which promotes a college-going culture, was mapped to show the degree of readiness students, teachers and parents perceive adolescents have surrounding the phenomenon of college readiness. As with most maps, the cartographer creates a projection that best suits his or her needs or that of their patron. Mapping elements and layers are added or removed to showcase the most significant components. Each person thus draws their own cognitive map to reflect what is most significant or important for them and draws on their personal experiences and encounters to help create the image of their landscape from their perspective.

Ken Wilber's AQAL model and David Conley's Keys to College and Career Readiness provided frameworks for this study. Wilber's AQAL model presented an ideal framework as it afforded the opportunity to gather multiple perspectives using a variety of methods. Even though only two components of the model were used, quadrants and levels, they were enough to provide a perspective and a picture of the landscape, and as such added more elements on the map of college and career readiness from the perspectives of an education policy maker with the Ministry of Education, and students, teachers, and parents from an established private high school in the Commonwealth of The Bahamas. Conley's Keys to College and Career Readiness provided an overview of the content, skills and knowledge high school students needed to aid in their transition to university, college or the workforce upon the completion of high school. Looking at the phenomenon and the perceptions held by participants through an integral lens provided a greater understanding whether or not students were deemed ready to undertake the next phase of their life and ready to embark on the future.

Recommendations for Educational Practice

This study increased awareness about perceptions held by adolescents, their parents and teachers about future education and career options. This knowledge may guide educators, school administrators and national educational policy makers to consider alterations, changes or additions to a national curriculum to help guide and aspire more students in the nation to pursue a postsecondary education. Education and readiness for the future will look very different than it does now in both the secondary and postsecondary arenas as it is likely to be much more data driven (Conley, 2014). In the future, schools will likely gather more information on a wider range of student attributes, including behaviors, aspirations, challenges, and interests designed to help students determine how ready they are for particular types of colleges and for specific programs of study at those types of colleges and universities (Conley, 2014). Additionally, concerns for the future direction of the national curriculum may identify any gaps that may exist in the current system, and recognize challenges students face everyday as they prepare for their futures after high school. There is more to the story, more to the map, more of the territory and landscape to explore. The more people who tell their lived experiences will help to develop a more comprehensive, more insightful and more integral map.

Recommendations for Educational Research

College and career readiness is a major issue influencing in the future life of high school students. Although college and career readiness was only one aspect of the current study, it was a major issue factoring in the future life of Bahamian adolescents. The multiple perceptions and perspectives unearthed in the study provides curricular considerations for teachers, school administration and education policy makers to promote a college going culture in all secondary schools of The Bahamas.

Longitudinal studies that tract the student participants from this study, as they engage in their freshman year at university, would provide additional insight into this phenomenon. Equally, acquiring additional student input from other schools, both public and private, would add more information to help high school administrators and teachers plan for and direct other students who are considering a future that involves enrollment in university. Ideally, tracking and re-interviewing the student participants and additional students would provide greater understanding into the phenomena of college and career readiness and the perspectives of Bahamian adolescents about their future life. This data will help direct and create educational initiatives that will be beneficial and helpful to high school students in the Commonwealth of The Bahamas as they transition from high school to college and then the workforce. Understanding why students return or do not return to work and live in The Bahamas would be valuable information for government officials and educational institutions. Tracking these students as they proceed through the next two- to four years of college or university may prove helpful when creating new national educational initiatives. A longitudinal study of this type has not yet been undertaken in the Commonwealth of The Bahamas.

CONCLUSION

This study looked at the altitudes of all participants and the perspectives of numerous themes that were positioned in the four quadrants of Wilber's (2006) AQAL framework. The altitude markers of amber, orange and green assigned to participants and the orange and green altitudes given to emerging and central themes constructed a map of the phenomenon of college and career readiness from the perceptions of Bahamian adolescents, their teachers and parents from an established private high school in the Commonwealth of The Bahamas. The integral framework permitted the use of numerous maps gathered from individuals, collectives and systems to help identify and solve problems and challenges in places like our schools and country.

Wilber (2006) recognized that an individual position themselves within a phenomenon, which is dependent on their personal perspective and their level of consciousness or altitude. By eliminating any of the perspectives found in the quadrants, these viewpoints only will provide us with "fragmented, partial, broken view of reality" (Watkins & Wilber, 2015, p. 275), which will continue to perpetuate and stifle the provision of education, developmental advancements, a skilled workforce and earning potential for individuals in the years to come. Currently, we only have partial truths. We have not yet embraced the perspectives of all quadrants, or embraced the levels and diverse lines that are associated with the moral, ethical and developmental aspects of education in The Bahamas.

The education system in the Commonwealth of The Bahamas is multi-dimensional and thus will require the multiple perspectives of individuals and collectives to identify and explain better the condition and culture of education at this time in history. These perspectives and altitudes helped to uncover and provide a more accurate positioning of the participants and the state of education in The Bahamas to improve upon and create a new map and territory of the phenomenon of college and career readiness itself.

The map is only a representation of what is out there, what is available, what is real for an individual. Maps show only partial elements, the perceived elements of the territory. In more contemporary geographic tools and technology the use of layers places many maps on top of others to give a more comprehensive look at a "part" of the territory. To show the entire landscape we would need to have everyone's map, for every experience, and at multiple times throughout their lives. Combining maps, experiences and viewpoints from others—and their many perspectives—can help to discover more truths, more reality and more elements of the territory.

The gleanings from this study has provided an extension to the knowledge and understanding of the future of education and the Bahamian nation, and what it means to be college and career ready from the perspectives of adolescents, teachers, parents and policy makers within the context of a private high school in The Bahamas.

REFERENCES

ACT. (2011). *The condition for college and career readiness*. ACT, Inc. Retrieved from http://www.act.org/research/policymakers/cccr11/pdf/ConditionofCollegeandCareerReadiness2011.pdf

Advanced Placement. (2015). *College Board/International*. Retrieved from http://international.collegeboard.org/programs/advanced-placement

Arnett, J. J. (2000). Emerging adulthood: A theory of development from the late teens through the twenties. *American Psychologist, 55*(5), 469–480. doi: 066X.55.5.469 doi:10.1037//0003

Bahamas Ministry of Education. (2015). *Vision 2030: A shared vision for education in the Commonwealth of The Bahamas*. Retrieved from http://media.wix.com/ugd/29b6ce_3065a2357e31432f839d0eecea6dee3e.pdf

Bangser, M. (2008). *Preparing High School Students for Successful Transitions to Postsecondary Education and Employment*. National High School Center.

Bassett, P. F. (2005, September). Reengineering schools for the 21st century. *Phi Delta Kappan, 76–78*, 83. Retrieved from http://eric.ed.gov/?id=EJ725351

Baum, S., Ma, J., & Payea, K. (2013). *Education Pays 2013: The Benefits of Higher Education for Individuals and Society*. The College Board. Retrieved from http://trends.collegeboard.org/sites/default/files/education-pays-2013-full-report.pdf

Bethel, K. (1999). *Educational reform in the Bahamas. In Educational Reform in the Commonwealth Caribbean*. Washington, DC: Organization of American States. Retrieved from http://www.educoea.org/Portal/bdigital/contenido/interamer/BkIACD/Interamer/Interamerhtml/Millerhtml/mil_beth.htm

Bloomberg, L. D., & Volpe, M. (2012). *Completing your qualitative dissertation a road map from beginning to end* (2nd ed.). London, UK: Sage Publications, Inc.

Cambridge Assessment International Education. (2017). *Cambridge IGCSE curriculum*. Retrieved from http://www.cambridgeinternational.org/programmes-and-qualifications/cambridge-secondary-2/cambridge-igcse/curriculum/

Chen, X., Christmas-Best, V., Titzmann, P. F., & Weichold, K. (2012). Issue editor's notes: Youth success and adaptation in times of globalization and economic change. *New Directions for Youth Development, 135*(135), 1–10. doi:10.1002/yd.20022 PMID:23097358

Colman, A. M. (Ed.). (2006). *Oxford Dictionary of Psychology* (2nd ed.). Oxford, UK: Oxford University Press.

Conley, D. T. (2008). Rethinking college readiness. *New Directions for Higher Education, 144*(144), 3–13. doi:10.1002/he.321

Conley, D. T. (2011). *Redefining College Readiness* (Vol. 5). Eugene, OR: Educational Policy Improvement Center.

Conley, D. T. (2014). *Getting ready for college, careers, and the common core: What every educator needs to know*. San Francisco, CA: Jossey-Bass.

Craton, M., & Saunders, G. (1998). *Islanders in the stream: A history of the Bahamian people, Volume two: From the ending of slavery to the twenty-first century*. Athens, GA: The University of Georgia Press.

Cunnien, K. A., Martin Rogers, N., & Mortimer, J. T. (2009). Adolescent work experience and self-efficacy. *The International Journal of Sociology and Social Policy, 29*(3/4), 164–175. doi:10.1108/01443330910947534 PMID:19750144

Davis, T. M., & Murrell, P. H. (1993). Turning teaching into learning: The role of student responsibility in the collegiate experience. *Higher Education Report, 8*. Retrieved from http://files.eric.ed.gov/fulltext/ED372703.pdf

Dunne, S., & Edwards, J. (2010). International schools as sites of social change. *Journal of Research in International Education, 9*(1), 24–39. doi:10.1177/1475240909356716

Eckersley, R. (1999). Dreams and expectations: Young people's expected and preferred futures and their significance for education. *Futures, 31*(1), 73–90. doi:10.1016/S0016-3287(98)00111-6

Edmunds, J. A. (2012). Early colleges: A new model of schooling focusing on college readiness. *New Directions for Higher Education, 158*(158), 81–89. doi:10.1002/he.20017

Education Act, §§46–17 & 29 (2001).

Erikson, E. H. (1963). *Childhood and Society* (2nd ed.). New York, NY: W. W. Norton & Company, Inc.

Esbjörn-Hargens, S. (2006). Integral research: A multi-method approach to investigating phenomena. *Constructivism in the Human Sciences, 11*(1), 79–107.

Esbjörn-Hargens, S. (2010). An ontology of climate change: Integral pluralism and the enactment of environmental phenomena. *Journal of Integral Theory and Practice, 5*(1), 183–201.

Esbjörn-Hargens, S. (2011). *Integral teacher, Integral students, Integral classroom: Applying Integral theory to education*. Retrieved from http://nextstepintegral.org/wp-content/uploads/2011/04/Integral-Education-Esbjorn-Hargens.pdf

Germeijs, V., & Verschueren, K. (2007). High school students' career decision-making process: Consequences for choice implementation in higher education. *Journal of Vocational Behavior, 70*(2), 223–241. doi:10.1016/j.jvb.2006.10.004

Gidley, J., & Hampson, G. (2008). Integral approaches to school educational futures. In Alternative Educational Futures: Pedagogies for Emergent Worlds. Sense Publishers.

Goleman, D., & Senge, P. (2014). *The Triple Focus*. Florence, MA: More Than Sound.

Hirschi, A., Niles, S. G., & Akos, P. (2011). Engagement in adolescent career preparation: Social support, personality and the development of choice decidedness and congruence. *Journal of Adolescence, 34*(1), 173–182. doi:10.1016/j.adolescence.2009.12.009 PMID:20074789

Hooker, S., & Brand, B. (2010). College knowledge: A critical component of college and career readiness. *New Directions for Youth Development*, *127*(127), 75–85. doi:10.1002/yd.364 PMID:20973075

Kegan, R. (1994). *In Over Our Heads: The Mental Demands of Modern Life*. Cambridge, MA: Harvard University Press.

Kerpelman, J. L., Eryigit, S., & Stephens, C. J. (2008). African American adolescents' future education orientation: Associations with self-efficacy, ethnic identity, and perceived parental support. *Journal of Youth and Adolescence*, *37*(8), 997–1008. doi:10.100710964-007-9201-7

Lee, I. H., Rojewski, J. W., & Hill, R. B. (2013). Classifying Korean adolescents' career preparedness. *International Journal for Educational and Vocational Guidance*, *12*, 25–45. doi:10.1002/j.2164-5884.1933.tb00117.x

Lewin, K. (1939). Field theory and experiment in social psychology: Concepts and methods. *American Journal of Sociology*, *44*(6), 868–896. doi:10.1086/218177

Lindfors, P., Solantaus, T., & Rimpelä, A. (2012). Fears for the future among Finnish adolescents in 1983–2007: From global concerns to ill health and loneliness. *Journal of Adolescence*, *35*(4), 991–999. doi:10.1016/j.adolescence.2012.02.003 PMID:22353240

Martin, J. A. (2008). Integral research as a practical mixed-methods framework: Clarifying the role of integral methodological pluralism. *Integral Research as a Practical Mixed-Methods Framework*, *32*(2), 155–164.

Merriam, S. (2009). *Case Studies as Qualitative Research. In Qualitative research: A guide to design and implementation* (pp. 26–43). San Francisco, CA: Jossey-Bass. Retrieved from http://www.aea267.k12.ia.us/system/assets/uploads/files/1527/qualitative_research.pdf

National Education Committee. (2015). *Vision 2030: A shared vision for education*. Retrieved from http://media.wix.com/ugd/29b6ce_3065a2357e31432f839d0eecea6dee3e.pdf

Neblett, N. G., & Corina, K. S. (2006). Adolescents' thoughts about parent's jobs and their importance for adolescents' future orientation. *Journal of Adolescence*, *29*(5), 795–811. doi:10.1016/j.adolescence.2005.11.006 PMID:16427693

Nikolayenko, O. (2011). Adolescents' hopes for personal, local, and global future: Insights from Ukraine. *Youth & Society*, *43*(1), 64–89. doi:10.1177/0044118X09351281

Nurmi, J. E. (1991). How do adolescents see their future? A review of the development of future orientation and planning. *Developmental Review*, *11*(1), 1–59. doi:10.1016/0273-2297(91)90002-6

Oxford Dictionaries. (2013). Retrieved from https://www.oxforddictionaries.com/

Poole, M. E., & Cooney, G. H. (1987). Orientations to the future: A comparison of adolescents in Australia and Singapore. *Journal of Youth and Adolescence*, *16*(2), 129–151. doi:10.1007/BF02138916 PMID:24277319

Rojewski, J. W., & Kim, H. (2003). Career choice patterns and behavior of work-bound youth during early adolescence. *Journal of Career Development*, *30*(2), 89–108. doi:10.1177/089484530303000201

Schmid, K. L., Phelps, E., & Lerner, R. M. (2011). Constructing positive futures: Modeling the relationship between adolescents' hopeful future expectations and intentional self regulation in predicting positive youth development. *Journal of Adolescence, 34*(6), 1127–1135. doi:10.1016/j.adolescence.2011.07.009 PMID:22118506

Seginer, R. (2003). Adolescent future orientation: An integrated cultural and ecological perspective. *Online Readings in Psychology and Culture, 6*(1). doi:10.9707/2307-0919.1056

Seginer, R. (2008). Future orientation in times of threat and challenge: How resilient adolescents construct their future. *International Journal of Behavioral Development, 32*(4), 272–282. doi:10.1177/0165025408090970

Seginer, R., & Halabi-Kheir, H. (1998). Adolescent passage to adulthood: Future orientation in the context of culture, age, and gender. *International Journal of Intercultural Relations, 22*(3), 309–328. doi:10.1016/S0147-1767(98)00010-8

Seginer, R., & Lilach, E. (2004). How adolescents construct their future: The effect of loneliness on future orientation. *Journal of Adolescence, 27*(6), 625–643. doi:10.1016/j.adolescence.2004.05.003 PMID:15561307

Tasset, T. (2010). An integral exploration of leadership. *Journal of Integral Theory and Practice, 5*(2), 96–116.

The Government of The Bahamas. (2011). *Bahamas General Certificate of Secondary Education (BGCSE)*. Retrieved from http://www.bahamas.gov.bs

Urich, T. R., & Mackenzie, D. G. (1985). Educating students for life after high school: Where does vocational education fit? *NASSP Bulletin, 69*(481), 89–94. doi:10.1177/019263658506948114

Vuolo, M., Mortimer, J. T., & Staff, J. (2013). Adolescent precursors of pathways from school to work. *Journal of Research on Adolescence, 24*(1), 145–162. doi:10.1111/jora.12038 PMID:24791132

Waite, M. (Ed.). (2012). *Paperback Oxford English Dictionary* (7th ed.). Oxford, UK: Oxford University Press.

Watkins, A., & Wilber, K. (2015). *Wicked and wise: How to solve the world's toughest problems*. Chatham, UK: Urbane Publications.

Wilber, K. (1995). *Sex, ecology and spirituality: The spirit of evolution*. Boston, MA: Shambala Publications.

Wilber, K. (2006). *Integral Spirituality: A Startling New Role for Religion in the Modern and Postmodern World*. Boston, MA: Integral Books.

Wilber, K. (2016). *Integral meditation: Mindfulness as a path to grow up, wake up, and show up in your life*. Boulder, CO: Shambala Publications.

Wilber, K., Patten, T., Leonard, A., & Morelli, M. (2008). *Integral life practice: A 21st Century Blueprint for Physical Health, Emotional Balance, Mental Clarity, and Spiritual Awakening*. Boston, MA: Integral Books.

KEY TERMS AND DEFINITIONS

B.A.I.S.S.: The Bahamas Association of Independent Secondary Schools (B.A.I.S.S.) comprises 13 independent (private) secondary schools on the island of New Providence, The Bahamas. This organization began in the 1980s and was a precursor to the now defunct Headmasters Association, which formed in 1950. The B.A.I.S.S. focuses on Christian principles and the operational considerations of academics, sports and culture within the independent secondary schools on New Providence.

Chapter 7
An Integral Analysis of Mindfulness and Self-Compassion Among Adolescents

Bernita Wienhold-Leahy
Thompson Rivers University, Canada

ABSTRACT

This case study focused on teaching self-compassion to adolescents through a mindfulness program. Self-compassion involves being kind towards oneself, understanding that we are all part of common humanity, and mindfulness. This multi-methods study was grounded in integral theory, which examines self-compassion through multiple lenses with both qualitative and quantitative methodologies. The findings indicated that a mindfulness program teaching self-compassion had many benefits to students, including increased mindful awareness and focused attention; emotional awareness and regulation; self-awareness, self-kindness, and self-acceptance; resiliency and growth mindset; compassion, acceptance, and forgiveness for others; and a belief it could reduce bullying in schools. Mindfulness programs in the school context will need to be introduced slowly over the next several years as students, parents, teachers, and administrators all have to understand the importance of these skills before they can be implemented into the classroom.

INTRODUCTION

Social and emotional difficulties often manifest early in students' lives, and these difficulties can have a direct effect on their academic, emotional, and social wellbeing (O'Connell, Boat, & Warner, 2009). In fact, half of the lifetime cases of psychiatric disorders are evident by the age of 14, and three-fourths by age 25 (Kessler, Berglund, Demler, Jin, & Merikangas, 2005). These problems can persist into adulthood and create psychological burdens for the individuals and economic burdens for society.

DOI: 10.4018/978-1-5225-5873-6.ch007

Prevention of social and emotional difficulties can benefit both the individual and society; subsequently, educating for building resiliency may prevent or lower these emotional difficulties. Given the statistics noted above, it would seem logical that by building resilience during adolescence, the rates of mental health issues may be reduced. Recent research has found that self-compassion helps build resiliency and increases psychological wellbeing (Neff, Kirkpatrick, & Rude, 2007). In fact, a meta-analysis of fourteen studies on self-compassion has shown that an increase in self-compassion lowers levels of mental health symptoms (Macbeth & Gumley, 2012).

Teaching self-compassion, if built within the regular school curriculum, could become a critical method of instilling resilience and wellbeing in adolescents. Mindfulness can help adolescents reduce emotional distress, promote emotional balance, improve attention, and contribute to motivated learning (Broderick, 2013). This case study combined multiple developmental perspectives to study self-compassion in a high school context. This study could inform school districts to include mindfulness programs into the regular school curriculum.

Context

The British Columbia (BC) curriculum is currently undergoing a change, and the teaching of social and emotional learning, which includes increasing emotional regulation, attention, and stress management skills, has been included in cross-curricular competencies and also within subject-specific curricula (BCEd, 2014a). The "big ideas" in the new physical and health education curriculum are building an awareness of how the body works so that students are more knowledgeable about how to increase physical, mental, and emotional wellbeing. The goal is to teach students to take responsibility for their actions, be self-regulating, make ethical decisions, accept consequences, empathize with others, recognize and appreciate diversity, defend human rights, and contribute in social, cultural, and ecological causes. Intervention strategies that connect the teaching of self-compassion to these cross-curricular competencies and "big ideas" in subject-specific curriculum can be powerful ways to increase wellbeing and resiliency in adolescents.

Purpose

The purpose of this case study was to assess the impact of a mindfulness program on self-compassion with adolescents in one school in British Columbia. Self-compassion involves three main elements: self-kindness (being kind to oneself rather than self-critical), common humanity (seeing oneself within a larger society), and mindfulness (being aware of one's thoughts and feelings in the present moment and not allowing them to overwhelm) (Neff, 2003a). Self-compassion also enhances compassion for others by recognizing connectedness with others and by promoting prosocial behaviours, and it is an important aspect of emotional intelligence by monitoring one's emotions to guide thinking and behaviour to help cope with stress.

In mindfulness practice, one learns to pay attention and focus the mind on the present moment non-judgementally and with acceptance (Kabat-Zinn, 2003). A core part of mindfulness programs is to be aware of and regulate thoughts and emotions and build an awareness and understanding of oneself with compassion for oneself and others. This awareness has resulted in students having more emotional self-control, displaying an increase in prosocial behaviours, and displaying a decrease in problem behaviours (Durlak, Weissberg, Dymnicki, Taylor, & Schellinger, 2011).

The intervention method used for this research study is the "Learning to BREATHE" program (Broderick, 2013). This program is designed to develop mindfulness, which helps to enhance emotional regulation, strengthen attention, aid in academic performance, increase stress management skills, and empower adolescents as "they grapple with the psychological tasks of adolescence" (p. 13). It is hoped that by developing a mindfulness program to teach components of self-compassion within the BC curriculum, self-compassion and therefore emotional wellbeing among students will increase.

Integral theory (Wilber, 2007) was used as a framework to view multiple perspectives of adolescent development to determine if the mindfulness program increased student self-compassion, emotional regulation, and self-awareness and acceptance, and if self-compassion impacts student behaviours, mindset, and compassion for others. Integral theory or All Quadrants All Levels (AQAL) was used as a framework as it includes many different points of view with which to study self-compassion.

Significance

Since this is the first known research study that measured self-compassion in adolescents in this particular school district following a mindfulness program, this research may influence if mindfulness should be taught within the school district. Also, this research increased the body of knowledge surrounding intervention programs that may influence student mindfulness, compassion for others, and mindset. Most importantly, this study measured the effects of a mindfulness program on self-compassion and resiliency in adolescents, which will hopefully increase wellbeing amongst the research subjects.

BACKGROUND

The purpose of this literature review is to describe the elements of self-compassion (Neff, 2003a), to situate the elements of self-compassion within integral theory (Wilber, 2007), and to assess the implication of teaching self-compassion through a mindfulness program to adolescents. A mindfulness program can be implemented into the BC curriculum and may increase students' self-compassion, which may increase students' resiliency and wellbeing, and reduce susceptibility to mental health disorders. This research will add to existing literature on mindfulness programs that teach elements of self-compassion in high school students.

Selected Review of the Literature

Elements of Self-Compassion

Self-compassion is a concept brought into mainstream research by Kristin Neff (2003a) about a decade ago, and it involves a non-judgmental understanding of one's own suffering and failure without being overly self-critical while being kind to oneself. Self-compassion involves three main elements: self-kindness (being kind to oneself rather than self-critical), common humanity (seeing oneself within a larger society), and mindfulness (being aware of one's thoughts and feelings in the present moment and not allowing them to overwhelm).

Self-kindness means being aware of oneself, one's strengths and weaknesses, with acceptance and understanding. To accept our mistakes means we are not self-critical and self-judging (Neff, 2011). By using sympathetic rather than judgmental language to express empathy towards ourselves, we can actively comfort ourselves as we would others. Self-kindness allows people to see themselves accurately without judgment or criticism, which should aid in the development of an authentic, healthy self-identity.

A common humanity suggests that we are all human, and we are all fallible (Neff, 2011). This means that defeat and suffering are part of the human condition. Self-compassion means that we comfort ourselves when we make mistakes; wrong choices are part of human nature and are not to be criticized. Through a growth in self-compassion, one is able to handle negative situations and feel more in control of one's suffering. To look at one's suffering nonjudgmentally and accept one's own faults means to acknowledge that everyone suffers, and everyone is human.

Mindfulness is the "awareness that emerges through paying attention on purpose, in the present moment, and nonjudgmentally to the unfolding of experience moment by moment" (Kabat-Zinn, 2003, p. 145). It is to experience the way things are and not to judge them. A conscious awareness exists in the unfolding of experiencing the here and now (Neff, 2011). Mindfulness is an awareness of awareness or meta-awareness, but it also entails an *acceptance* of the way things are (Kabat-Zinn, 2003). This does not mean we become apathetic towards the way things are and not try to improve our life's circumstances. Rather, mindfulness allows us to see the way things are, to take steps to improve the situation, and to recognize and accept when changes are not possible (Neff, 2011). However, it is sometimes difficult to change what goes on inside our heads: our thoughts, feelings, and emotions. These are the automatic thoughts we cannot control, but they can control us (Goleman, 2006). When we are aware of our thoughts as only thoughts, they can lose their control of our mind. A conscious awareness becomes a calm foundation to experience life (Neff, 2003a). By reducing sensory input and sitting quietly, one can begin to pay attention to inner feelings, experience these feelings, and bring them into conscious awareness (Neff, 2011).

Self-compassion is different than self-esteem. Self-esteem is dependent on how well we *think* we are doing in the world and causes us to compare ourselves to others. Self-esteem is heavily reliant on the "*perceived* judgments of others," which leads to competition, as we try to look better than others. In addition, adolescents rely very heavily upon the perceptions of their peers who may become more important than their parents (Neufeld, 2004). This reliance on the perceived opinions of others makes self-esteem very vulnerable and easily shattered. If we do not think we are better than others, we feel a negative self-worth, or we lower our expectations of ourselves (Neff, 2011). Social comparison also affects our relationships; we tend to distance ourselves from people we deem as being better than us. If we feel others are better than us, we feel threatened. This may cause people to pick on or lash out at others that are better than themselves and may be responsible for bullying behaviours (Neff, 2003a). Instead of self-esteem, we should be striving for self-compassion and self-acceptance for who we are to have a healthy self-identity. If our self-worth and belonging is "grounded in simply being human, we can't be rejected or cast out by others. Our humanity can never be taken away from us, no matter how far we fall" (Neff, 2011, p. 69).

Situating Within Integral Theory

Ken Wilber's (2007) integral theory incorporates five elements: quadrants, levels, lines, states, and types. It has been termed AQAL, "All Quadrants, All Levels," and is a way of mapping development within the quadrants, to strive for higher levels, along different lines, while being aware of states and types.

Integral theory was the framework chosen to integrate many different epistemological perspectives to build a comprehensive contextual framework to determine if a mindfulness program increased self-compassion and resiliency in adolescents. It is to look within a person and from without; it is to see multiple perspectives to integrate these perspectives into one integrated structure (Wilber, 2007). Through Wilber's integral theory, self-compassion was studied as a way to increase levels of consciousness along four lines of development: cognitive, emotional, self-identity, and interpersonal lines within the four quadrants. The framework of integral theory is a post-metaphysical approach, which emphasizes an *awareness* of how things are. This means that adolescents have to experience phenomenon for themselves rather than just be presented with information, and mindfulness is a way for adolescents to increase awareness. It is how our minds become conscious about phenomenon within our own bodies, minds, cultures, and systems to see it as a complete whole.

The four quadrants of integral theory are the individual-exterior (UR) or objective quadrant, which includes the physical body and bodily systems; the individual-interior (UL) or subjective quadrant, which includes feelings and emotions; the collective-interior (LL) or intersubjective quadrant, which includes relationships and culture; and the collective exterior (LR) or interobjective quadrant, which includes society and systems (Wilber, 2007). These quadrants all develop simultaneously and are interwoven into each other into a true integral framework (Esbjorn-Hargens, 2009). The integral model (AQAL) further organizes the quadrants into lines, levels, states, and types. This framework allowed the flexibility to include many different viewpoints to study adolescents along several lines or streams of development while maintaining a structure within which to study one phenomenon: self-compassion. Self-compassion is viewed from the four quadrants to see the "big picture." The integral theory is necessary to have an all-encompassing view of self-compassion from the individual to the societal level.

Levels of Development

Stages or levels of development are milestones of growth and development that represent a more complex way of being; each level is considered a stage or wave of development (Wilber, 2007). In this study, several lines of development were incorporated, but only one level of development: the level of consciousness. As you will see, it is imperative that adolescents increase their awareness or level of consciousness from the second to third order of consciousness (Kegan, 1994).

Consciousness is a way of knowing, and how we make sense of what we know (Kegan, 1994). Metacognition is reflecting and being aware of how the mind operates and how an individual processes information (Blatner, 2004). It is more about thinking about how one is thinking. Levels or orders of consciousness reflect levels of awareness of a person's environment (Kegan, 1994). It transforms their way of looking at the world.

Kegan (1994) stated that adolescents are in the unique position where adult expectations surpass the adolescents' order of consciousness. Between the ages of twelve and twenty, adolescents are transforming between second and third orders of consciousness; therefore, most adolescents are at a lower order of consciousness than adults' expectations of them. The third order of consciousness incorporates a cross-categorical knowing, which supposes that adolescents will surrender their own needs and desires for the better good of the family, school, or community. A third order of consciousness expects adolescents to balance others' points of view with their own; they can understand and care about the opinions of others and suppress their own self-interest for the greater good. This higher order of consciousness is not necessarily reflected in the minds of today's adolescents. According to Kegan (1994), if adolescents do not acquire this third order of consciousness, they are *in over their heads* as teachers and parents have higher expectations of them.

Environments that challenge adolescents to become aware of themselves within their expanding social world may foster this new conceptual thinking and help them to become morally and socially responsible members. Adolescents today require experiences that will bridge their thinking from the second to the third order of consciousness (Kegan, 1994). A mindfulness program that teaches self-compassion may offer students the experiences that will expand their thinking to increase their levels of consciousness; this teaching of self-compassion may be the bridging that is critical to transform adolescents from the second to the third order of consciousness.

Lines of Development

Wilber (2007) stated that people develop levels of development along different lines of development at different paces. The lines of development are not necessarily discrete lines, but are more like streams, and taken together, form an integral map along different dimensions of biological, emotional, and interpersonal growth (Wilber, 2007). There are at least a dozen lines of development, and four lines of development for building self-compassion were chosen: cognitive, emotional, self-identity, and interpersonal. Through a mindfulness program, the level of consciousness along the lines of development may increase, and therefore, adolescents would be more able to reach the third order of consciousness that society expects of them. As one increases a level of consciousness along the lines of development, one grows in self, interpersonal, and global understanding and gains greater capacity for love, compassion, and connection.

According to Wilber (2007), the cognitive line is awareness and is necessary for all other lines of development, "Cognition delivers the phenomena with which the other lines operate" (Wilber, 2007, p. 65). One's feelings and emotions must all follow the cognitive line because, in order to have feelings and emotions, one must first be aware of them. According to Piaget (1964), adolescents are beginning to enter into the final, fourth stage of cognitive development called the formal operational stage. Gradually, as adolescents mature, cognition is gained as they construct information for themselves through experiences, social transmission, and equilibration. Increasing along the cognitive line of development is essential to self-compassion; adolescents need to first become aware of themselves in order to understand their strengths and weakness with acceptance and understanding. Through mindfulness practice, adolescents can become aware of their inner thoughts, pay attention to them, and assimilate them into their knowing which can assist adolescents to develop from the second to the third order of consciousness along the cognitive line of development.

In the cognitive line, one learns to be aware of one's thoughts and emotions, while in the emotional line, it is about the ability to regulate feelings and emotions so emotions do not disrupt oneself and one's relationships; it is about how the mind can monitor and regulate physiological actions in the body. Goleman (1995) has suggested that we have two minds: the rational and the emotional minds. The prefrontal cortex (PFC) controls the thinking, rational mind, which is important for forethought and impulse control. The amygdala triggers emotions like fear and panic; it is the "flight or fight" response, which is controlled by the emotional mind (Goleman, 1995). When one is emotionally charged, the amygdala reacts and the emotional part of the brain becomes over-active. In adolescence, the amygdala is activated even quicker, and the messages from the PFC telling it to slow down are not used as much (Siegel, 2013). This is why adolescents have an increased emotional tendency. If adolescents learn how their mind controls their emotions and body, they can learn to send messages to the amygdala instructing it to quiet down, enabling themselves to bounce back quicker from adversity (Davidson & Begley, 2012). Teaching adolescents to think about their emotions and behaviours in a non-critical way is a core element in self-compassion. Through mindfulness practice, adolescents can become aware of their thoughts as just thoughts, and they can better manage their thoughts. The higher the level of consciousness along the emotional line of development, the better one is able to regulate emotions.

If adolescents are better able to control their emotions, they may see themselves without judgment; therefore, they may be able to increase along the self-identity line of development. According to Loevinger's theory of ego-development (1976), adolescents develop from the conformist stage to the conscientious stage along a self-aware level. At the conformist stage, adolescents have strong group identifications with moral codes to follow, strong desires for social acceptance, and sensitivities to individual differences. They are prone to stereotyped sex roles, and they value niceness, helpfulness, and cooperation. Belonging is very important for security. The transformation to the conscientious stage is marked by an increase in self-awareness and an appreciation of multiple possibilities. At the conscientious stage, adolescents are able to see others' points of view, evaluate long-term goals, and have a sense of responsibility. Adolescents must become self-aware so they no longer conform to the standards of the group, but self-evaluate and form their own self-reflective standards. This transition from the conformist stage to conscientious stage is important to healthy adolescent self-identity. In order to reach this milestone, adolescents need to appreciate multiple possibilities in a situation, have a sense of responsibility, internalize rules, and self-evaluate their goals and ideals. Self-compassion may be the bridge between the conformist and the conscientious levels that may allow adolescents to become self-aware, make mistakes, and be kind to themselves as they reach a healthy self-identity.

If adolescents are better able to see themselves authentically and recognize perspectives of others, their ability to connect with and formulate relationships with others may increase. An increase in the levels of consciousness in the interpersonal line of development should increase positive emotions, empathy, and therefore, positive relationships. As Goleman (1995) stated, interpersonal development is the ability to recognize emotions in others; it is the ability to empathize. The art of relationships is, in large part, a skill in managing emotions in others. Through mindfulness practice, students may become more aware of the workings of the mind and how this might influence behaviours, and therefore, relationships. Increasing levels of consciousness or awareness along the interpersonal line of development should help adolescents develop empathy and compassion for others. It entails multiple perspectives, between the inner and outer selves, and to see others nonjudgmentally as imperfect human beings with acceptance and compassion, which requires a higher level of consciousness, to be aware of their own needs and the needs of others.

Adolescents are expected to see themselves as part of a larger community and make decisions to benefit the greater good (Kegan, 1994). Unfortunately, most adolescents' level of consciousness is at a lower level than is expected. Increasing the level of consciousness along the cognitive, emotional, self-identity, and interpersonal lines of development may help adolescents to become more integrated and better equipped to navigate their social world. This study examined how mindfulness program could be the bridging necessary to increase adolescent development from the second to third level of consciousness.

Four Quadrants of Integral Theory

Adolescents need to develop from the second to the third order of consciousness to be able to balance their own needs with the needs of the greater society (Kegan, 1994). They need to increase levels of consciousness along the four lines of development in order to build self-compassion and therefore resiliency and wellbeing. The level of consciousness and lines of development are integrated within the four quadrants of integral theory to map out a framework within which to anchor a mindfulness program to teach self-compassion to increase resilience in adolescents.

Connecting Body and Mind: The Upper Right Quadrant

The upper right quadrant is the exterior-individual quadrant; it is to look at the individual from the outside, the concrete body (Wilber, 2007). In order to influence their behaviours, adolescents must first be aware of how their mind influences their behaviours; therefore, increasing a sense of self-awareness is necessary. A core process in self-compassion is self-awareness, a conscious awareness of the self in relation to the body and mind (Neff, 2011). Mindfulness is a way of being in the present moment without judgment, and it increases emotional balance to allow for self-awareness (Kabat-Zinn, 2003). The focus of mindfulness is to develop an awareness of inner experiences: thoughts, feelings, and sensations, and to observe them nonjudgmentally. Consciousness is the experience that comes out of the senses, feelings, perceptions, and attention to an object (Varela, Thompson, & Rosch, 1992). Through the senses, the mind interacts with the environment, and, mediated by the brain, elicits behaviours, and, reciprocally, behaviour and experience alter the brain functions and mental perceptions. This bidirectional communication between the mind and body means that the mind is "embodied" (Maturana, Thompson, & Varela, 1987). An embodied mind is to be aware of the body's physical properties, how they affect the mind, and how the mind affects the body. Living as embodied beings means that our mind is integrally aware of our body and its effects on behaviours and perceptions of experience. Increasing one's awareness of the mind-body connection increases one's awareness of the self.

As levels of consciousness increase, it is expected that adolescents become more aware of the relationship between their minds and their bodies. Research has shown a negative effect between self-compassion and automatic thoughts (Akin, 2012). In addition, Longe et al. (2010) found self-compassionate thoughts activated the same areas of the brain as compassion and empathy towards others, and self-criticism was associated with PFC activity that leads to more error processing and behavioural inhibition. Wilber (2007) stated that the more one practices mindfulness, the faster one develops through levels of consciousness, and self-awareness increases.

Connecting Mind and Self: The Upper Left Quadrant

The upper left quadrant is the interior-individual or the individual's thoughts, feelings, and sensations (Wilber, 2007). Being aware of emotions, feelings, and internal experiences is an essential element of self-compassion, and emotional regulation is the ability to effectively process emotions (Goleman, 1995). Self-compassion has been shown to help with emotional regulation to reduce stress and increase psychological wellbeing (Newsome Waldo, & Gruszka, 2012). Through mindfulness, one can reduce activity in the amygdala, and the brain can perceive thoughts and emotions less judgmentally (Davidson & Begley, 2012).

Research has shown that self-compassion may buffer against emotional difficulties. For instance, Hope, Koestner, and Milvavskava (2014) found self-compassion was associated with an increase in life satisfaction and a decrease in negative affect. In addition, Raes (2011) found self-compassion was a buffering effect on emotional problems such as depression. Leary, Tate, Adams, Allen, and Hancock (2007) also found subjects high in self-compassion could handle negative experiences better because they had lowered negative emotions, were able to make themselves feel better after the negative events, and they saw these events as not being any worse than what others experience. In support of this research, Neely, Schallert, and Mohammed (2009) found self-compassion helped students manage negative emotions following disappointment. Emotional regulation may aid adolescents to slow down their thinking, and they may be able to view themselves more accurately.

Identity can be viewed as an ongoing story that we construct about ourselves from our past and present experiences (Warin & Muldoon, 2009). People with identity problems often tell themselves negative narratives which can increase rumination, a negative core belief that a person thinks about over and over (Alloy et al., 2012). Self-compassion means being honest with ourselves about the stories we construct, allowing ourselves to make mistakes, and being kind to ourselves (Neff, 2003a). Hall, Row, Wuensch, and Godley (2013) found those low in self-compassion were more self-critical and undervalued themselves whereas those high in self-compassion were able to perceive themselves more accurately, reported lowered perceived stress and depressive symptoms, were able to accept responsibility for their actions, and were less likely to ruminate about negative events. In addition, Raes (2011) found self-compassion had a buffering effect against depression because it reduced rumination. The more one increases in self-compassion, one can learn how to regulate emotions, analyze internal thoughts, and form alternative responses to a negative narrative. Self-compassion is based on our internal language, which means that our self-talk is not self-critical (Neff, 2003a).

Adolescents are more susceptible to "internal pressure for social conformity and sensitivity to social comparison" (Broderick, 2013, p. 15). Breines and Chen (2012) found subjects with higher self-compassion engaged in more upward social comparison, which meant they preferred to be with others better off than themselves, which can provide inspiration for change. Contrarily, subjects low in self-compassion preferred a lateral or downward comparison; they chose to engage with others who were either the same or were worse off than themselves, which does not lead to self-improvement motivations. With self-compassion, adolescents may be able to see themselves authentically and nonjudgmentally, and they can confront negative aspects of the self with kindness and motivation for change.

Resiliency is the ability to bounce back from defeat (Davidson & Begley, 2012). Self-compassion has been shown to increase resiliency by aiding in mastery performance, helping to develop a growth mindset, and increasing perseverance. A growth mindset is a belief that one's qualities can change and grow through effort (Dweck, 2006). Hope et al. (2014) found self-compassion was associated with coping in the face of defeat or disappointment in goal progress, and it has been shown to be positively associated with goal pursuit and mastery performance; they concluded self-compassion is associated with an increase in learning because it frees students from harsh self-criticism, and it enables students to cope in the face of failure. Neff, Hsieh, and Dejitterat (2005) also found self-compassion was associated with mastery goals, as subjects had more perceived competence, and self-compassion was negatively associated with task-avoidance and fear of failure. In addition, Breines and Chen (2012) found after subjects were taught to use a self-compassionate approach to viewing a personal weakness, they viewed their personal weakness as more changeable. Those high in self-compassion have an increased ability to cope with negative events, and they viewed their faults as more changeable (Hope et al. 2014; Neff et al., 2005). These studies showed that self-compassion aided subjects to persevere in the face of failure and to see their individual traits as more changeable, both core concepts in building resiliency.

Connecting the Self to Others: The Lower Left Quadrant

The lower left quadrant is the interior-collective or the individual within a group or culture; it is the collective 'we' (Wilber, 2007). It is where a sense of social awareness is formed within the school, family, and community. A core component of self-compassion is to develop the ability to see oneself within a larger society (Neff, 2003a). According to Goleman (2006), we are wired to connect; our brains are designed to be sociable. As children develop, they are able to reflect on their environment and experiences facilitating cognitive flexibility, emotional control, and concern for others (Zelazo & Lyons, 2012). Self-compassion has been associated with increased interpersonal relationships and compassion with others.

Through mindfulness, adolescents can become aware of themselves within a larger community, which can increase their relationship skills and compassion for others. By paying attention, we can sense someone else's inner state; we empathize with others. To increase levels of consciousness, it is important to see oneself in relation to others and to view oneself from their perspective. Research has shown that self-compassion has been correlated to greater interpersonal relationships skills. For example, Yarnell and Neff (2013) found higher levels of self-compassion were associated with greater authenticity in interpersonal relationships, higher likelihood to compromise, and higher levels of wellbeing in relationships. In another study, Akin (2010) found self-compassion could diminish self-critical tendencies, and subjects recognized their interconnectedness with others. A study by Crocker and Canevello (2008) showed the more self-compassion a subject had, the more social supports they showed their roommates. Neff and Beretvas (2012) showed self-compassion was associated with positive relationships traits with their romantic partners. More specifically, subjects high in self-compassion reported feeling worthy, happy, and being able to express opinions. In addition, those high in self-compassion were perceived as being more kind, caring, and more accepting of their partners.

Self-compassion has been shown to build empathy and a willingness to help others, and it could help rebuild connections with others. For example, Welp and Brown (2013) found subjects high in self-compassion were more willing to help a victim. In another study, Lindsay and Creswell (2014) found college students who experienced increased feelings of self-compassion also increased prosocial behaviours. More significantly, Breines and Chen (2012) found after teaching a self-compassionate approach to previous negative transgressions, subjects were motivated to make amends and not to repeat the transgression. This research is significant as it suggests that self-compassion training can lead to motivation to help others. With self-compassion, one develops empathy, or a concern for others, which helps in interpersonal relationships.

Connecting the Self to Society: The Lower Right Quadrant

The lower right quadrant is the collective-exterior or interobjective, the systems in which people live (Wilber, 2007). The school is the first and most significant place where students are socialized and where children are taught how to function within their broader society. In order for a program to be implemented within a system, that program should prove a systemic benefit to the students. Implementing an intervention strategy that incorporates elements of self-compassion could be a critical method of building wellbeing and buffer against mental health problems in adolescents. In fact, a meta-analysis of 213 school-based social and emotional learning (SEL) programs found students who received SEL programs had increased prosocial behaviours and decreased problem behaviours (Durlak, Dymnicki, Taylor, Weissberg, & Schellinger, 2011). "If self-compassion interventions do turn out to be successful, it may be that schools should start placing greater emphasis on the development of students' self-compassion to help them cope with the difficulties of growing up" (Neff & Mcgehee, 2010, p. 237).

Many self-compassion interventions have suggested that self-compassion interventions can improve resilience and wellbeing amongst adolescents. Bluth and Blanton (2012) found mindfulness and self-compassion promoted wellbeing in adolescents. In another research study, adolescents were taught mindfulness and self-compassion in an after school setting. Results indicated that mindfulness, self-compassion, perceived stress, and life satisfaction improved. Self-compassion was negatively related to perceived stress (Bluth, Roberson, & Gaylord, 2014). Recently, a program specifically designed for teaching self-compassion to youth called *Making Friends with Yourself* was developed. Research on this program found that the adolescent intervention group had significantly greater self-compassion, life satisfaction, and lower depression, anxiety, and perceived stress than the control group (Bluth, Gaylor, Campo & Mullarkey, 2015). Research seems to support the effectiveness of teaching self-compassion to increase resilience and wellbeing in adolescents, yet research in this area is in its infancy.

The "Learning to BREATHE" (L2B) program has shown promising results using elements of both mindfulness and SEL and is the program taught in this study. The L2B program has been adapted from Mindfulness-Based Stress Reduction (MBSR) program developed by Kabat-Zinn (2003) to a program easily incorporated into school curricula. The L2B program's focus is to develop social-emotional learning (SEL) to recognize emotions, values, and strengths to fostering empathy, relationships building, and responsible decision making (Broderick, 2013). Research on this program has shown a reduction in negative affect and increased calmness, self-acceptance, and emotional regulation in the research group as compared to controls (Broderick & Metz, 2009). A study conducted within a regular school classroom showed that participants showed greater gains in emotion regulation skills such as awareness of emotions and regulation strategies (Metz et al., 2013). The L2B also showed a significant reduction in self-report rates of anxiety (Potek, 2012). These results suggest the "Learning to BREATHE" program is effective in teaching social and emotional skills.

British Columbia is currently in the process of changing the curriculum to fit more with today's learners and the needs of society, and teaching self-compassion can be easily incorporated into the new BC Education Plan (BC Ministry of Education, 2012b). Creating a learning environment for self-compassion steeped in the new BC curriculum is an opportunity to develop curricula that can be transformational for the education system and beneficial for the students.

THEORETICAL PERSPECTIVES

Integral Methodological Pluralism

Integral theory stresses viewing a phenomenon from a variety of perspectives and combining different epistemologies into one comprehensive and effective format (Wilber, 2007). The integral theory integrates views of growth and development from the inside and outside of all four quadrants; therefore, viewing eight perspectives. These eight perspectives include inside and outside views of the "it" (the body or body systems), "its" (the system in which "it" lives), "I" (the individual), and "we" (the culture or relationships with which the individual resides), which suggests both quantitative and qualitative methods. Integral Methodological Pluralism (IMP) includes all eight viewpoints and their distinct epistemological approaches and methodologies. To use IMP as a framework implies using all eight paradigms. To leave one out is not true IMP (Esbjorn-Hargens, 2006).

Research Design Overview

Integral Methodological Pluralism (IMP) suggests a multi-methods approach to research (Esbjorn-Hargens, 2006). Therefore, both qualitative and quantitative methodologies were used to look both objectively and subjectively at self-compassion and whether it should be taught to adolescents.

Qualitative methods were used for the upper left, lower left, and lower right quadrants and quantitative methods for the upper right quadrant. In the upper left quadrant, the interior/subjective view was identified and interpreted through student journal writing, and the exterior/objective view was studied through individual student interviews. In the lower left quadrant, the interior/subjective view was studied through student interviews, and the exterior/objective view was studied through student focus group discussions and teacher and Certified Educational Assistant (CEA) interviews. In the lower right quadrant, the interior/subjective view of the educational system was studied through teacher and administrator interviews, and the exterior/objective view was through superintendent interviews to discuss policies and procedures around teaching SEL and mindfulness in schools. The upper right quadrant represents a more objective view of the individual from the inside and outside, and four questionnaires were administered: the Mindful Awareness Attention Scale (Brown & Ryan, 2003), the Self-compassion Scale (Neff, 2003b), Compassion Scale (Pommier, 2011), and Mindset Quiz (Dweck, 2006). The interior/subjective view measured the students' levels of the four questionnaires, and the exterior/objective view was shown through statistical evidence of a change between pre-and post-tests of the various scales.

Integral Methodological Pluralism is to view a phenomenon from eight different perspectives. This study was a broad overview of self-compassion within the high school context by collecting data on all eight perspectives of integral theory. The current study answered questions, lead into unanticipated directions, and provoked additional thoughts about self-compassion, social and emotional learning, and mindfulness in education.

METHODS

The Research Problem

Adolescence is a critical time of development when young people push boundaries and create both challenges and catastrophes (Siegel, 2013). This often creates social and emotional difficulties for adolescents. The predominant research problem guiding this study was if a program teaching mindfulness and self-compassion could raise adolescents' resilience and aid in buffering against emotional difficulties.

Table 1. Research questions divided into the four quadrants of integral theory

UL 2. Did student resiliency increase? a. In what ways did students perceive the three components of self-compassion: mindfulness, self-kindness, and common humanity? b. In what ways did students report a change in emotional regulation? c. Was there an increased sense of self-awareness?	UR 1. Did students report a change in the self-report questionnaires? a. Mindfulness Awareness Attention Scale b. Self-compassion Scale d. Mindset Quiz e. Compassion Scale
LL 3. Was there a change in classroom or school culture? a. In what ways did students perceive compassion towards others? b. In what ways did student interpersonal relationships change?	LR 4. What are the benefits to teaching self-compassion within school curricula? a. What were teacher/administrator perceptions regarding the implementation of SEL and mindfulness programs within BC curricula? b. Does self-compassion and mindfulness fulfill the requirements on social and emotional learning mandated by the new BC curriculum?
5. What are the gender differences in self-compassion?	

Source: Wilber, 2007

The Research Questions

The research questions and sub-questions were divided into the four quadrants of Integral Theory as shown in Table 1.

Data Collection

The "Learning to BREATHE" program was taught to 83 students in four classes in one Catholic high school. Qualitative and quantitative data was collected using several methods. Prior to the teaching of the L2B program, all students filled in the Self-Compassion Scale, Compassion Scale, Mindful Attention Awareness Scale, and the Mindset Quiz. A pre-test/ post-test design assessed the impact of the program on the subject population. Research participants completed an ongoing journal as a data collection method, but more importantly, as a method for students to reflect and integrate knowledge. Student focus groups were conducted at the end of the program to collect data on the shared understanding of self-compassion, to evaluate the program, to elicit the students' opinions, and to introduce new areas of study (Jarrell, 2000). Fourteen students were interviewed to provide in-depth information on student feelings and thoughts about self-compassion and the mindfulness program. Teacher and CEA interviews looked at their perceptions of the program and class culture. The classroom teacher, administrator of the private Catholic school, the superintendent of Catholic schools, and the assistant superintendent of public schools were also interviewed for knowledge about school policies and procedures surrounding the teaching of social and emotional learning as prescribed by the new BCEd initiative (2012a).

Limitations

There are several limitations to this research study as it was conducted in one Catholic school in one city in British Columbia. The results of this study cannot be generalized to the adolescent population outside of this context. First, the students who attend a private Catholic school may be demographically different than those students who attend other schools in BC. Second, this case study was conducted in relatively small city; therefore, the results cannot be generalized to the adolescent population throughout BC.

Delimitations

I chose to conduct a case study with only four classes to limit the amount of data collected. The relatively short curriculum was feasible considering the time limit to teach and collect the data. Even though this case study was limited to the chosen population and was conducted in a short amount of time, this is one of the first studies on self-compassion in the school setting.

EXPLORING THE ISSUES

Analysis of Findings

In order to contextualize the findings from this large amount of data, the four quadrants of the integral theory were used to organize the results. Within each quadrant, the data was examined with both an inside and an outside lens. The data from student journals, interviews, and focus groups were analyzed using themes or reoccurring patterns (Miles, Huberman, & Saldana, 2014) using QSR® NVivo 10 program. The questionnaire data was analyzed using the IBM SPSS Statistics 22 program.

UR Findings: Quantitative Results

Questionnaires to test students' mindful awareness, self-compassion, compassion for others, and mindset were distributed, collected, and analyzed. Pre-and post-test differences in the questionnaires using paired sample T-tests were used to find two significant results. According to the results of the Mindset Quiz, students' mindset changed from a fixed to a growth mindset after the program, $t(57) = 4.04$, $p=.00016$. According to the Compassion Scale, compassion for others increased significantly between pre-and post-test, $t(54) = 2.35$, $p=.023$. These results suggest that mindset and compassion for others changed as a result of the program.

UL Findings: Connecting Mind and Self

The UL quadrant is the subjective-interior or your thoughts, feelings, and emotions. For the themes of the UL quadrant, the data was narrowed to two main themes: awareness and self-awareness. These themes were further narrowed to three subthemes: emotional regulation, effects on behaviours, self-kindness, and self-acceptance.

Awareness

Twenty-three of the students wrote in their journals and nine of the students interviewed stated that the mindfulness practice affected their awareness; some students just noticed their surroundings, thoughts, and feelings more. Many students wrote that they became more aware of their thoughts, which affected their emotional awareness and regulation.

Emotional Regulation

Twenty-five of the students wrote in their journals and twelve of the students interviewed stated they felt the program made them more aware of and able to regulate their emotions. Their understanding of emotional regulation had a positive effect on their thoughts.

Effects on Behaviours

Many students stated that mindfulness helped them with a focused attention, which helped in academics, sports, and other activities. Twenty students stated that a more focused attention helped them with their academics. Seventeen students stated that a focused attention helped them in their sports activities. Six students stated that mindfulness helped with chores. Being mindful seemed to help the students be more aware and focused on their surroundings, more aware of their emotions; therefore, more able to regulate their emotions which affected their behaviours and their successes in their activity.

Self-Awareness

Nine students stated in their journals and six students stated in their interviews that mindfulness helped them become more aware of their mind/body connection. Becoming more self-aware may allow students to be more cognizant of their thoughts and feelings, which may make them more aware of how they think about themselves, how they treat themselves, and how to accept themselves.

Self-Kindness

Twenty students wrote in their journals and all the students stated in their interviews that learning about self-compassion made them think more kindly towards themselves and saw ways they could improve their situation. The point of self-compassion is for students to become more self-aware, so that they can see themselves as authentic beings, with flaws and inadequacies, to improve the situation where they can, and to accept themselves with kindness.

Self-Acceptance

Fourteen students wrote in their journals and two stated in their interviews that self-compassion allowed them to see themselves accurately, to accept themselves as part of common humanity, to be able to make changes where they thought changes could be made, and to be grateful for what they have. Most students did not view self-acceptance with apathy and a lack of concern, but as a way to view themselves accurately to make changes to improve the situation.

LI Findings: Connecting the Self to Others

A core component of self-compassion is to develop the ability to see oneself within a larger society (Neff, 2003a). The two main themes that came out of the data were compassion for others and conforming to the group. The subthemes were compassion for others, classroom culture, conforming to the group (peer pressure), and technology.

Compassion for Others

Twenty-five students during focus groups and twelve students during their interviews stated that self-compassion and common humanity could increase compassion for others. Some students stated that compassion for others would increase as they would be less judgmental and more forgiving of others' mistakes. Students learned that as members of common humanity, all people make mistakes, and understanding, accepting, and forgiving are important concepts for students to practise getting along with others.

Improved Classroom Culture

Forty-two statements by students declared that they thought the program might have improved classroom culture. Some students mentioned behaviours they noticed in themselves and their classmates that changed were being more caring and listening more. Other students noticed less negative or rude comments about other people in the halls and less gossip. Many students stated that learning about common humanity could reduce bullying in schools because there is more of an awareness that we are all human, we all make mistakes, and we need to be less judgmental of others. Students reported they was more caring for others, listening of others, and more awareness of bullying behaviours.

Conforming to the Group

Sixteen focus group statements and four students in their interviews stated that peer pressure to conform was a big stumbling block for many students, and it stopped them from participating in the mindfulness practices in class. They reported that they felt very aware and self-conscious about participating in the mindfulness practice, and it influenced their participation. Even if students felt a mindfulness practice might benefit them, they seemed to succumb to peer pressure.

Technology

Seventeen students reported that technology such as video games, texting, social media, and other technological activities were deterrents or distracted students from a mindfulness practice. Students also reported that social media messages contradicted the self-compassion teachings, as negative information from social media influenced them to also be more negative, and idealized figures made them feel less accepting of themselves.

Lr Findings: Connecting Self-Compassion to Education

The lower right quadrant is the objective exterior view of the "Its," the system within which "It" lives. It is to view the teaching of self-compassion from a systemic point of view, to look at society and the educational system of BC to see if and how a mindfulness program could be incorporated into the regular school program, and how it fits with the new BC Education Curriculum mandated by the BC Ministry of Education. The data was organized into two themes, social and emotional skills and systemic challenges. The data was further divided into subthemes of build resilience, interpersonal relationships, classroom application, and staff buy-in.

Build Resilience

The teacher, administrator, Catholic superintendent, and public superintendent all stated that there is a need for social and emotional learning to be included in the curriculum to build resiliency to enable students to cope better with life's difficulties. They stated that healthy decision making and persevering to achieve goals are necessary to cope in school, but also throughout their lives. Teaching skills to persevere and cope will increase resiliency, which is important as many students seem to experience mental health issues.

Skills to Increase Interpersonal Relationships

Skills that increase interpersonal relationships will help students to get along with others which is crucial, both in their personal and professional lives. The school administrator and Catholic superintendent both felt managing interpersonal conflicts was an important life skill for students to learn. These competencies have been mandated to be included in the new BC education curriculum.

Classroom Application

The administrators all felt the competencies in the new curriculum are important and benefit the students, but classroom application would be challenging. They see the implementation of the new curriculum to be either incorporated into the Physical Education, Personal Planning, or Religion (for Catholic schools) classes or ideas to be shared by master teachers already teaching these skills in the classroom. The school administrator and public superintendent stated that these skills need to be spread throughout the classes, and ideas about teaching the skills will be shared amongst teachers. The school administrator and public superintendent believed the new curriculum can be incorporated throughout the classes by sharing information with other teachers and seeing first hand how these skills can help students settle down to help them learn.

Staff Buy-In

All the administrators were unanimous in deeming that convincing the teaching staff of the importance of implementing social and emotional learning in the classroom as being the main challenge. Teachers need to feel comfortable practising social and emotional skills themselves, and they need professional development in this area to be able to teach them to students. Teachers need to be educated about social and emotional learning, but according to the interviewees, professional development in this area will happen slowly over the next couple of years as teachers are coping with the new curriculum as a whole. Even though all administrators feel social and emotional learning is very important for students to learn, and it should be taught in the classroom, the challenge is convincing the teachers of its importance, and this needs to be done slowly and methodically so that teachers "buy-in" to the concept and, in the process, may learn some social and emotional skills themselves.

The Integral Model: An Analysis of Perspectives

IMP was used as a methodology to bring the eight zones together into one comprehensive format. This section is where IMP becomes messy, yet dynamic. All eight different views of IMP were integrated to see the larger picture: how all the quadrants, levels, and lines were interrelated. In Figure 1, the themes and sub-themes in the different quadrants are linked, and the lines seem to converge in three main areas: awareness, compassion towards others, and building resiliency.

Awareness

Through a mindfulness practice, a person becomes more aware of the body/mind connection, which allows the mind to become more aware of its influence on thought processes and behaviours. The students reported that they became more aware of their thoughts, and of how their thoughts affect their emotions, and how that influences their actions and behaviours. Many students stated that they were not even aware of their thoughts and emotions before the mindfulness practices. Students reported that they were more self-aware and able to accept themselves for who they are; however, they also reported that focusing on the present moment is difficult as they have so many stressors and pressures in their lives.

Awareness of thoughts helped students to let go of their negative thoughts, to focus more attention to their activity, and to be kind to themselves. Self-acceptance is to view oneself with nonjudgmental awareness; students identified self-acceptance as a new concept, something that is difficult to do, as adolescents compare and self-evaluate themselves against their peers and images on social media. The students reported a greater awareness of their bodies, thoughts, and themselves, which allowed them to focus more attention on their activities.

Compassion for Others

The administrators all felt that fostering more compassion for others is important for today's youth. Both qualitative and quantitative results showed that compassion for others increased as a result of the program. Students reported that they were more accepting of others' faults and that class culture had changed. The students acknowledged others as members of common humanity, with faults and inadequacies, and they were more able to accept others' mistakes with nonjudgment, acceptance, and forgiveness. Students

Figure 1. Integral map of themes and connections between quadrants

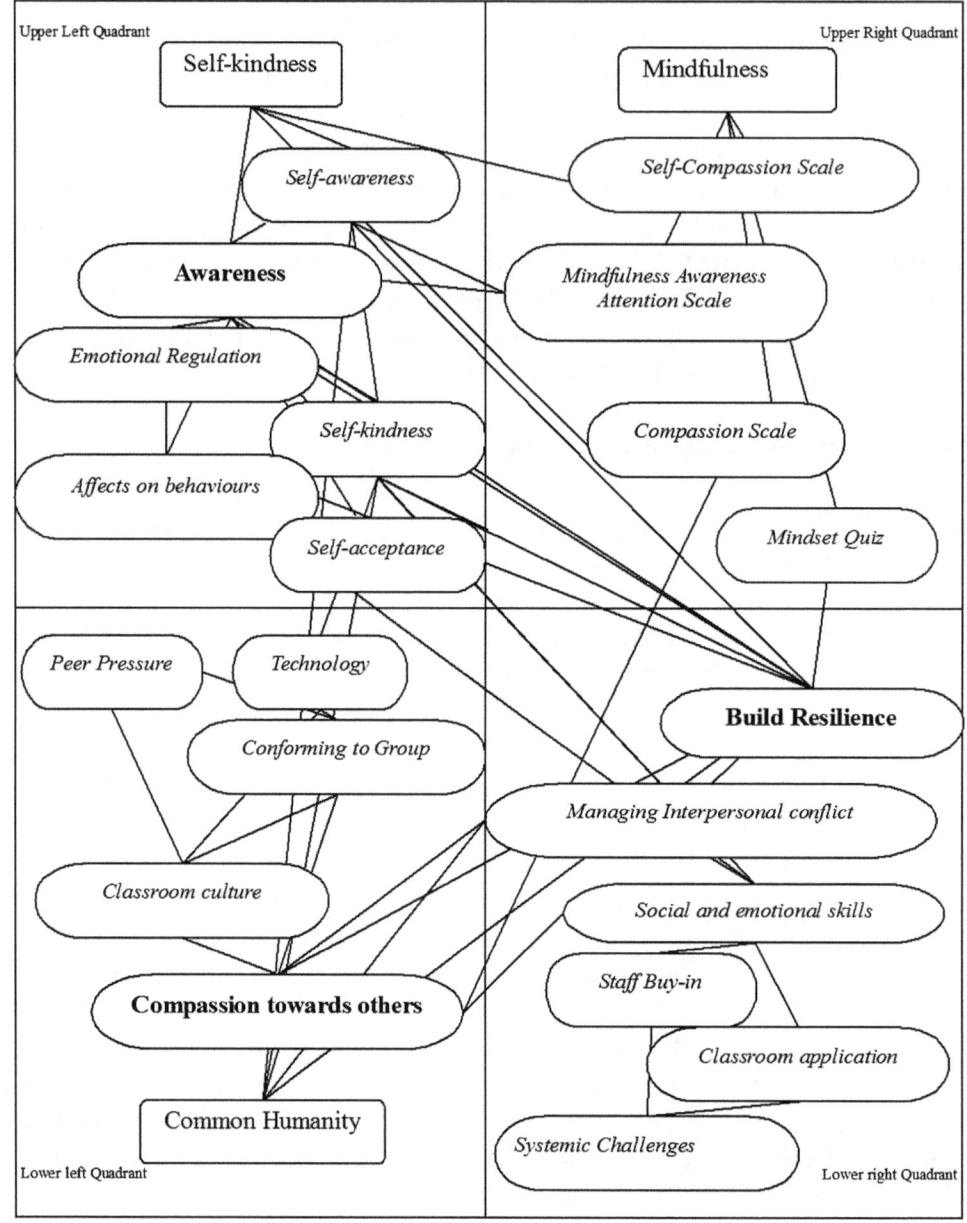

learned to have more compassion for others who might be experiencing stressful times in their lives. Students reported that they believed students were kinder to each other and listened more. In addition, many students reported in their journals, interviews and focus groups that learning self-compassion could reduce bullying in schools. Some students became more aware of bullying behaviours, including the bully himself, and others reported that they might be more willing to stop bullying behaviours if they noticed them. Interpersonal skills and compassion for others is important for students to navigate their world; the results seemed to show that students' compassion for others increased.

Building Resilience

Many students stated that learning about self-compassion and mindfulness aided them to become more resilient. This was shown in the way they did not give up when faced with challenges. Persevering with goals was a core competency the administrators deemed important for students to learn, and results indicated that students increased in growth mindset, which had been shown to be positively associated with goal pursuit and mastery performance (Dweck, 2006). Students forgave themselves for mistakes and self-evaluated to know that they could make different choices and do better next time.

Emotional regulation is a major skill in social and emotional learning and a core competency in resiliency. Students stated that they learned how emotional regulation enabled them to be in control of their emotions so they did not get overwhelmed and give up. Results of the data showed that students learned how to become more aware of and able to regulate their emotions, so they are more able to control their reactions which aids in rational decision making, perseverance in the face of difficulties, and emotional resiliency.

Many students believed that learning self-compassion could help buffer people against mental health issues. They believed self-compassion could reduce negative thoughts and self-criticism, which could decrease depressive symptoms, self-harming behaviours, and suicidal ideations. From the students' view, this program could benefit students by building resiliency to reduce mental health problems.

Levels and Lines of Development

Through the teaching of self-compassion, it was hoped that the students' level of consciousness would increase from the second to the third order according to Kegan's levels of consciousness (1994). According to Kegan, the third level of consciousness incorporates a cross-categorical knowing. At this level, adolescents need to surrender their own needs for the better good of the community. Could the third order of consciousness be realized in students through a mindfulness program? In order for students to reach the third order of consciousness, they should develop along several lines of development.

Lines of Development

The four lines of development identified for building self-compassion were cognitive, emotional, self-identity, and interpersonal. The analysis showed how students' perception and practice of self-compassion affected their development along these lines.

Through the teaching of a mindfulness program, the students seemed to increase along the cognitive line; students became aware of their mind-body connection, their inner thoughts, and how their minds influenced their emotions and their behaviours. They stated that they had more focused attention and better ability to think before they reacted. They became more aware and self-aware of the mind/body connection, how their thoughts effected their emotions, and how their emotions could affect their behaviours.

In addition, many of the students stated that the mindfulness practices helped them be more aware of their emotions so that they were better able to regulate them and not negatively affect their behaviours, which showed that the students increased along the emotional line of development. It is about having a cognitive awareness of their emotional reaction and an ability to monitor their emotional reaction to a given situation.

To develop along the self-identity line of development, adolescents need to develop from the conformist stage to the conscientious stage of ego-development along a self-aware level (Loevinger, 1976). According to the results of this study, the students are still in the conformist stage, but a sense of self-awareness is clearly emerging in their responses. Students could see themselves accurately with faults and inadequacies, but they were able to see those faults as changeable. Students were able to talk to themselves with reassurance rather than criticism, so they could bounce back from difficulties. To move into the conscientious stage, students must have "an awareness of oneself as not always living up to the idealized portrait set by social norms" (Loevinger, 1976, p. 19). This point is very important, as adolescents are very hard on themselves if they do not live up to the norms their peers or social media deem important. It seems that practising self-compassion may be a step towards increasing along the self-identity line of development.

Learning about common humanity seemed to help students increase along the interpersonal line of development as students' compassion for others increased; they learned to be nonjudgmental and accepting of others' mistakes as part of common humanity, and they were more forgiving to others when mistakes were made. Developing along these lines of development seemed to have also increased students' level of consciousness.

Levels of Consciousness

Kegan (1994) proposed that adolescents need to develop from the second to third order of consciousness, and there needs to be a bridging for adolescents to gain the third order of consciousness. A program teaching self-compassion through mindfulness could be the bridging the students require. The results of this study showed that students learned skills to build resiliency, such as awareness, self-awareness, emotional regulation, attention, and self-acceptance. These are skills important in the third order of consciousness: "identify inner motivations" (self-awareness), "hold onto emotional conflict internally" (emotional regulation), "be psychologically self-reflective" (self-acceptance), and have a "capacity for insight" (awareness) (Kegan, 1994, p. 27). A mindfulness program may be a way for students to develop from the second to the third order of consciousness.

Analyzing the data through the IMP framework was messy but informative. It is to integrate all the zones or points of view, to see the big picture, and to analyze how self-compassion affected the students in this research study. In IMP, all the themes were linked together to see the "big picture" of teaching self-compassion. The results indicated that students' awareness, compassion for others, and resiliency increased. The results did seem to show increased levels of development along the cognitive, emotional, self-identity, and interpersonal lines to increase students' level of consciousness from the second to the third order.

CONCLUSIONS AND IMPLICATIONS

Implications

Bringing self-compassion and mindfulness into schools to teach our children and youth to care for themselves and others is not just a "good idea," but it is necessary and very timely, as our classrooms are changing and become more diverse. The BC Ministry of Education mandated that social and emotional skills be incorporated into the classroom (2014b). The administrators deemed these competencies are important for students to learn; these skills can help increase student resiliency and therefore wellbeing. One method of teaching these skills is through mindfulness and self-compassion. The implication is that both students and teachers need to buy into the importance of teaching social and emotional skills in the classroom. Both students and teachers require a balance between challenge and support, so they do not become *in over their heads,* and mindfulness in education just becomes another "good idea" that was never implemented properly.

Recommendations for Practice

One of the recommendations is to have students learn a mindfulness practice within the regular school curriculum. If taught in earlier grades and throughout the school year, then a mindfulness practice will become part of their day-to-day practice and they will not be so self-conscious about practising. Making mindfulness applicable not only in school, but in the real world would be very important to have the students "buy-in" to a mindfulness practice.

Another recommendation is to offer professional development opportunities for teachers to become aware of the benefits of social and emotional learning and mindfulness, to learn these skills themselves, and to implement them into the curriculum. At the moment, teachers are overwhelmed with the new curriculum, and adding social and emotional skills to their already full plate would be too challenging at the moment. Teachers require a balance between support and challenge; we need to start where the staff are at right now, and convince them of the necessity of teaching these skills to fully embrace the "new ideas" in education. Professional development in this area has begun, but it will be slowly incorporated within the curriculum. The challenge is to meet the teachers where they are at, encourage them to grow in social and emotional skills themselves, and support them to effectively teach these skills to their students.

Conclusion

From the results of this study, there are grounds for teaching self-compassion and mindfulness in schools. First of all, social and emotional learning and mindfulness benefit the students. Students reported many positive results from the mindfulness program: increased awareness and focused attention; increased emotional awareness and regulation; increased self-awareness, self-kindness, and self-acceptance; increased growth mindset and ability to persevere; increased compassion, acceptance, and forgiveness of others, and a belief that it could reduce bullying.

Secondly, the teaching of social and emotional learning has been mandated by the BC government, and it will need to be incorporated into the regular school curriculum in the near future. Social and emotional learning skills are currently taught in both public and private sectors by many master teachers, but it will need to be more formally taught in the future. Staff buy-in and classroom application were the biggest challenges that face teachers in embracing social and emotional learning in the classroom. It is important for teacher education and professional development to teach SEL and mindfulness to the teachers first, so that they can learn the nuances of mindfulness before they bring them into the classroom.

REFERENCES

Akin, A. (2012). Self-Compassion and Automatic Thoughts. *Hacettepe University Journal of Education*, 421–10.

Alloy, L. B., Black, S. K., Young, M. E., Goldstein, K. E., Shapero, B. G., Stange, J. P., ... Abramson, L. Y. (2012). Cognitive vulnerabilities and depression versus other psychopathology symptoms and diagnoses in early adolescence. *Journal of Clinical Child and Adolescent Psychology*, *41*(5), 539–560. doi:10.1080/15374416.2012.703123 PMID:22853629

BC Ministry of Education. (2012a). *Enabling innovation: Transforming curriculum and Assessment*. Retrieved from: http://www.bced.gov.bc.ca/irp/docs/ca_transformation.pdf

BC Ministry of Education. (2012b). *Overview to BC's curriculum transformation plans*. Retrieved from: http://www.bced.gov.bc.ca/irp/docs/overview.pdf

BC Ministry of Education. (2014a). *Transforming curriculum and assessment: Physical and health education – Draft*. Retrieved from: https://curriculum.gov.bc.ca/sites/curriculum.gov.bc.ca/files/pdf/phe_learning_standards.pdf

BC Ministry of Education. (2014b). *Transforming curriculum and assessment: Social studies – Draft*. Retrieved from: https://curriculum.gov.bc.ca/sites/curriculum.gov.bc.ca/files/pdf/ss_learning_standards.pdf

Blatner, A. (2004). The developmental nature of consciousness transformation. *Revision*, *26*(4), 2–7. doi:10.3200/REVN.26.4.1-14

Bluth, K., & Blanton, P. W. (2014). The influence of self-compassion on emotional well-being among early and older adolescent males and females. *The Journal of Positive Psychology*, 1–12. PMID:25750655

Bluth, K., Gaylord, S. A., Campo, R. A., Mullarkey, M. C., & Hobbs, L. (2015). Making friends with yourself: A mixed methods pilot study of a mindful self-compassion program for adolescents. *Mindfulness*, *6*(6), 1–14. PMID:27110301

Bluth, K., Roberson, P.N.E., & Gaylord, S.A. (2014). A pilot study of a mindfulness intervention for adolescents and the potential role of self-compassion in reducing stress. *Explore (New York, NY)*.

Breines, J. G., & Chen, S. (2012). Self-compassion increases self-improvement motivation. *Personality and Social Psychology Bulletin*, *38*(9), 1133–1143. doi:10.1177/0146167212445599 PMID:22645164

Broderick, P. C. (2013). *"Learning to BREATHE": A Mindfulness Curriculum for Adolescents to Cultivate Emotional Regulation, Attention, and Performance*. New Harbinger Publications, Inc.

Broderick, P. C., & Metz, S. (2009). "Learning to BREATHE": A pilot trial of a mindfulness curriculum for adolescents. *Advances in School Mental Health Promotion*, *2*(1), 35–46. doi:10.1080/1754730X.2009.9715696

Brown, K. W., & Ryan, R. M. (2003). The benefits of being present: Mindfulness and its role in psychological well-being. *Journal of Personality and Social Psychology*, *84*(4), 822–848. doi:10.1037/0022-3514.84.4.822 PMID:12703651

CASEL. (2013). *Effective social and emotional learning programs: Preschool and elementary school edition. Collaborative for Academic, Social and Emotional Learning*. KSA-Plus Communications Inc. Retrieved from: www.casel.org

Crocker, J., & Canevello, A. (2008). Creating and undermining social support in communal relationships: The role of compassionate and self-image goals. *Journal of Personality and Social Psychology, 95*(3), 555–575. doi:10.1037/0022-3514.95.3.555 PMID:18729694

Csikszentmihalyi, M. (1990). *Flow: The psychology of optimal experience*. New York: Harper Collins Publisher.

Davidson, R., & Begley, S. (2012). *The emotional life of your brain: How its unique patterns affect the way you think, feel and live – and how you can change them*. London: Penguin Books.

Durlak, J. A., Dymnicki, A. B., Taylor, R. D., Weissberg, R. P., & Schellinger, K. B. (2011). The impact of enhancing students' social and emotional learning: A mata-analysis of school-based universal interventions. *Child Development, 82*(1), 405–432. doi:10.1111/j.1467-8624.2010.01564.x PMID:21291449

Dweck, C. S. (2006). *Mindset: How we can learn to fulfill our potential*. New York: Ballentine Books.

Esbjörn-Hargens, S. (2006). Integral research: A multi-method approach to investigating phenomena. *Constructivism in the Human Sciences, 11*(1-2), 79–107.

Esbjörn-Hargens, S. (2009). *An overview of integral theory: An all-inclusive framework for the 21st century*. Integral institute: Resource paper no. 1, 1–24.

Goleman, D. (1995). *Emotional intelligence: Why it can matter more than IQ*. New York: Bantam Books.

Goleman, D. (2006). *Social intelligence: The revolutionary new science of human relationships*. New York: Random House Publishing.

Hall, C. W., Row, K. A., Wuensch, K. L., & Godley, K. R. (2013). The role of self-compassion in physical and psychological wellbeing. *The Journal of Psychology, 147*(4), 311–323. doi:10.1080/00223980.2012.693138 PMID:23885635

Hope, N., Koestner, R., & Milyavskaya, M. (2014). The Role of Self-Compassion in Goal Pursuit and Wellbeing Among University Freshmen. *Self and Identity*, 1–15.

Jarrell, M. G. (2000). Focusing on focus group use in educational research. *Annual Meeting of the Mid-South Educational Research Association*.

Kabat-Zinn, J. (2003). Mindfulness-based interventions in context: Past, present, and future. *Clinical Psychology: Science and Practice, 10*(2), 144–156. doi:10.1093/clipsy.bpg016

Kegan, R. (1994). *In over our heads: The mental demands of modern life*. Cambridge, MA: Harvard University Press.

Kessler, R. C., Berglund, P., Demler, O., Jin, R., Merikangas, K. R., & Walters, E. E. (2005). Lifetime prevalence and age-of-onset distributions of DSM-IV disorders in the national comorbidity survey replication. *Archives of General Psychiatry, 62*, 93–602. PMID:15939837

Leary, M. R., Tate, E. B., Adams, C. E., Allen, A. B., & Hancock, J. (2007). Self-compassion and reactions to unpleasant self-relevant events: The implications of treating oneself kindly. *Journal of Personality and Social Psychology, 92*(5), 887–904. doi:10.1037/0022-3514.92.5.887 PMID:17484611

Lindsay, E. K., & Creswell, J. D. (2014). Helping the self help others: Self-affirmation increases self-compassion and pro-social behaviors. *Frontiers in Psychology, 5*, 1–9. doi:10.3389/fpsyg.2014.00421 PMID:24860534

Loevinger, J. (1976). *Ego development: Conceptions and theories.* San Francisco: Jossey-Bass Inc.

Longe, O., Maratos, F. A., Gilbert, P., Evans, G., Volker, F., Rockliff, H., & Rippon, G. (2010). Having a word with yourself: Neural correlates of self-criticism and self-reassurance. *NeuroImage, 49*(2), 1849–1856. doi:10.1016/j.neuroimage.2009.09.019 PMID:19770047

MacBeth, A., & Gumley, A. (2012). Exploring compassion: A meta-analysis of the association between self-compassion and psychopathology. *Clinical Psychology Review, 32*(6), 545–552. doi:10.1016/j.cpr.2012.06.003 PMID:22796446

Maturana, H. R., Thompson, & Varela, F. J., (1987). *The tree of knowledge: The biological roots of human understanding.* Boston: Shambhala Publications Inc.

Metz, S. M., Frank, J. L., Reibel, D., Cantrell, T., Sanders, R., & Broderick, P. C. (2013). The effectiveness of the "Learning to BREATHE" program on adolescent emotion regulation. *Research in Human Development, 10*(3), 252–272. doi:10.1080/15427609.2013.818488

Miles, M. B., Huberman, A. M., & Saldana, J. (2014). *Qualitative data analysis: A methods sourcebook.* Los Angeles, CA: Sage Publications.

Neely, J. E., Schallert, D. L., Mohammed, S. S., Roberts, R. M., & Chen, U. (2009). Self-kindness when facing stress: The role of self-compassion, goal regulation, and support in college students' wellbeing. *Motivation and Emotion, 33*(1), 88–97. doi:10.100711031-008-9119-8

Neff, K. D. (2003a). Self-compassion: An alternative conceptualization of a healthy attitude toward oneself. *Self and Identity, 2*(2), 85–101. doi:10.1080/15298860309032

Neff, K. D. (2003b). Development and validation of a scale to measure self-compassion. *Self and Identity, 2*(3), 223–250. doi:10.1080/15298860309027

Neff, K. D. (2011). *Self-compassion: The proven power of being kind to yourself.* New York: Harper Collins.

Neff, K. D., & Beretvas, S. N. (2013). The role of self-compassion in romantic relationships. *Self and Identity, 12*(1), 78–98. doi:10.1080/15298868.2011.639548

Neff, K. D., Hsieh, Y. P., & Dejitterat, K. (2005). Self-compassion, achievement goals, and coping with academic failure. *Self and Identity, 4*(3), 263–287. doi:10.1080/13576500444000317

Neff, K. D., Kirkpatrick, K., & Rude, S. S. (2007). Self-compassion and its link to adaptive psychological functioning. *Journal of Research in Personality, 41*(1), 139–154. doi:10.1016/j.jrp.2006.03.004

Neff, K. D., & McGeehee, P. (2010). Self-compassion and psychological resilience among adolescents and young adults. *Self and Identity*, *9*(3), 225–240. doi:10.1080/15298860902979307

Neufeld, G., & Maté, C. (2005). *Hold on to your kids: Why parents need to matter more than peers.* Toronto: Vintage Canada.

Newsome, S., Waldo, M., & Gruszka, C. (2012). Mindfulness group work: Preventing stress and increasing self-compassion among helping professionals in training. *Journal for Specialists in Group Work*, *37*(4), 297–311. doi:10.1080/01933922.2012.690832

O'Connell, M. E., Boat, T., & Warner, K. (2009). *National research council (US) and institute of medicine (US) committee on the prevention of mental disorders and substance abuse among children, youth, and young adults: Research advances and promising interventions.* Washington, DC: National Academies Press.

Piaget. (1930). *The child's conception of physical causality* (M. Gabain, Trans.). Kegan Paul, Trench, Trubner & Co.

Pommier, E. A. (2011). The compassion scale. *Dissertation Abstracts International. A, The Humanities and Social Sciences*, *72*, 1174.

Potek, R. (2012). *Mindfulness as a school-based prevention program and its effect on adolescent stress, anxiety and emotion regulation* (Doctoral Dissertation). Retrieved from ERIC. (ED537610)

Raes, F. (2011). The effect of self-compassion on the development of depression symptoms in a non-clinical sample. *Mindfulness*, *2*(1), 33–36. doi:10.100712671-011-0040-y

Siegel, D. (2013). *Brainstorm: The power and purpose of the teenage brain.* New York: Penguin Books.

Varela, F. J., Thompson, E., & Rosch, E. (1992). *The embodied mind: Cognitive science and human experience.* London: MIT Press.

Warin, J., & Muldoon, J. (2009). Wanting to be 'known': Redefining self-awareness through an understanding of self-narration processes in educational transitions. *British Educational Research Journal*, *35*(2), 289–303. doi:10.1080/01411920802043000

Welp, L. R., & Brown, C. M. (2013). Self-compassion, empathy, and helping intentions. *The Journal of Positive Psychology*, *9*(1), 54–65. doi:10.1080/17439760.2013.831465

Wilber, K. (2007). *Integral spirituality: A startling new role for religion in the modern and postmodern world.* Boston: Integral Books.

Yarnell, L. M., & Neff, K. D. (2013). Self-compassion, interpersonal conflict resolutions, and wellbeing. *Self and Identity*, *12*(2), 146–159. doi:10.1080/15298868.2011.649545

Zelazo, P. D., & Lyons, K. E. (2012). The potential benefits of mindfulness training in early childhood: A developmental social cognitive neuroscience perspective. *Child Development Perspectives*, *6*(2), 154–160. doi:10.1111/j.1750-8606.2012.00241.x

Chapter 8
Cultivating Compassion in an Upper Elementary School Classroom Community

Garette Tebay
Parkland School Division No. 70, Canada

ABSTRACT

This chapter explored the notion that compassionate behaviors can be learned or cultivated among elementary school students through mindfulness practice in the classroom. Integral theory served as the conceptual framework for the research questions, the methodology, and the analysis. The investigation thus unfolded as a narrative inquiry using a mixed methods approach and informed by integral methodological pluralism to relate the story of one classroom. Increased self-awareness, happiness, and calm were observed in the students and teacher alike as a result of mindfulness practice. The integral analysis determined that these positive effects were persistent for all involved and pointed to the potential benefits of adopting mindfulness practice at the system level.

INTRODUCTION

The development of compassion and the attitudes and behaviours associated with it is a multi-faceted and complex process. For this reason, research into the concept requires a model that takes into account multiple perspectives in a systematic fashion. Integral theory provides a framework for just this sort of model in regard to the elaboration of research questions and data collection methods and the interpretation of the collected data. This study has accordingly employed integral theory as a means to arrive at a well-rounded understanding of compassion as it was fostered through mindfulness practice in a classroom combining students from grades four and five.

Mindfulness strategies are becoming increasingly common in classrooms as a means to enhance the well-being of both teachers and students (Albrecht, Albrecht, & Cohen, 2012). Their popularity runs counter to the tendency in Western societies to view individuals' inner worlds as inconsequential and to leave interior, subjective ideations to clinical settings, such as the interactions between a student and a school counsellor. The focus in classrooms has rather been on the exteriorization of students' feelings

DOI: 10.4018/978-1-5225-5873-6.ch008

as behaviours through citizenship education (Marrero, 2007). The present study was designed to explore the effectiveness of mindfulness practices in promoting the development of wisdom, compassionate attitudes, and an ethic of care in a classroom community.

Context

This study took place in a vibrant northern community that, having experienced significant growth over the past decade, can been described as a boom town. The school division consists of 15 schools, and the study took place in one for kindergarten to grade 6 students. The school itself has experienced a fair amount of change over the last few years. Its student population was at one point one of the largest in the division, but the opening of a new school in the fall term during which this study took place reduced enrolment by about half, resulting in many staff changes and a shift in the school's programming and overall culture.

Purpose

This study was designed to explore the concept of compassion by introducing mindfulness practice in a classroom and investigating its effects on the attitudes and behaviours of the members of the classroom community and through them on the broader community. A further goal was to explore the social environment of the school and its position within the educational system in terms of the creation of compassionate learning environments.

These concepts and contexts were also examined through the inclusive lens of integral theory, which "is a way of knowing that helps one strive for the most comprehensive understanding of any phenomenon" (Marquis, 2007). This systematic framework facilitated examination of the interconnections among various perspectives that were identified in the course of the study.

Significance

This study is of particular note owing the use of integral theory throughout the research process. In the analysis of the data, this approach allowed for the analysis of individual perspectives, both in isolation and also in relation to other perspectives, through the integral model known as "all quadrants all lines" (AQAL, explained below). The benefits of this theory for a study like this one were well described by its originator, Wilber.

What is the point of using an Integral map or model? First, whether you are working in business, medicine, psychotherapy, law, ecology or simply everyday living and learning, the Integral Map helps make sure that you are "touching all the bases." If you are trying to fly over the Rocky Mountains, the more accurate map you have, the less likely you will crash. An Integral Approach ensures that you are utilizing the full range of resources for any situation, with a greater likelihood of success. (Wilber, 2005)

Not only does the analysis presented in this study "touch all the bases," but it also facilitated a comprehensive examination of the connections among the various aspects of the issues under discussion so that a holistic picture could emerge. This approach to the organization and analysis, then, provided the basis for an investigation of the phenomenon of compassion and its promotion through mindful practice from a variety of perspectives and methodologies.

BACKGROUND

Mindfulness Programs

Mindfulness is a relatively new concept in educational contexts. Its use traces back to Kabat-Zinn's (1994) development of a "Mindfulness-Based Stress Reduction" program for adults, which generated interest in finding a way to bring the benefits of mindfulness to children. The following table represents mindfulness programs that have been developed for use in classrooms with school-aged children, all of which adapted Kabat-Zinn's program to suit the needs of a specific group of students.

Mindfulness-based programs like these and other mindful practices help to develop compassionate behaviours. Mindfulness is the fifth of Armstrong's (2011) twelve steps towards a more compassionate life. Likewise, a study of the effects of loving-kindness meditation showed that it increased compassionate behaviours towards target strangers as well as feelings of compassion towards others (Hutcherson, Seppala, & Gross, 2008).

This study originated in efforts to conceptualize compassion in the classroom through the lens of each quadrant in the AQAL framework. These quadrants represent simultaneously the four domains of ontological reality in addition to an epistemology, a methodology, and a synthesis of the being, knowing, and doing/living that arise interdependently within each (Snow, 2007). To the upper left quadrant, which is the realm of an individual's inner workings, belong the introspective elements of mindfulness. The upper right quadrant is the locus of outward, observable behaviours associated with compassion and developed through mindfulness. The lower left quadrant is the locus of relationships that develop and change through mindfulness practice in the classroom. Lastly, the contemporary call for the systemic adoption of mindfulness practices in schools, and impediments to their adoption, belong to the lower right quadrant.

Table 1. A review of mindfulness programs for schools

Name of Program	Resources	Goal of Programming
Mindful Schools (mindfulschools.org)	• Online training through a variety of courses for developing personal mindfulness practice and incorporating mindfulness in schools • Access to online community of mindfulness educators and practitioners	Benefits said to include attention, emotional regulation, adaptability, compassion, calm, and resilience
.b Curriculum (mindfulnessinschools.org)	• A series of ten lessons teaching mindfulness skills • For use with 11- to 18-year-old students	Benefits said to include greater well-being, fulfilled potential, increased concentration and focus, coping with difficult mental states, and improved coping skills
Smiling Mind Education Program (smilingmind.com.au)	• A series of online modules and guided meditations designed for use in schools • 79 modules over 249 sessions and including lesson plans for teachers	Benefits said to be proven to help students with sleep, well-being, managing emotions, and school behaviour. The site also lists stress management, increased resilience and creativity, improved decision-making, and a sense of calm, clarity, and contentment
MindUP Curriculum	• Book includes three components of study, including lessons in the four pillars of neuroscience, mindful awareness, positive psychology, and social-emotional learning	Benefits are packaged as promises that children will learn about their brains through developmentally appropriate neuroscience to teach self regulation, self-awareness, and self control. Children will learn to take three three-minute brain breaks daily to help improve planning and focus on work. The program also encourages mindful action in the world to promote pro-social behaviours

In the classroom, mindfulness meditation can be used to develop such interior attributes as self-awareness, self-regulation, and compassion (Meiklejohn et al., 2012). These characteristics associated with the upper left quadrant have been described in terms of actions or states that cannot be contrived but must rather produced by nature. In this compassionate state are found natural expressions of wisdom, mindfulness, and compassionate action (McClain, Ylimaki, & Ford, 2010) that correspond with an ethic of care. Because compassion involves caring for others and wanting the best for those under care, any goals regarding education must be consistent with the production of competent, loving, and lovable people (Noddings, 1995).

Viewed through the interior subjective lens of the upper left AQAL quadrant, mindfulness represents a means for individuals to develop a compassionate interior world. Such an intentionally deliberate way of being in the world can seem out of alignment with fast-paced, goal-oriented Western societies (Kabat-Zinn, 2003), it may seem counterintuitive in today's classrooms is to prepare students to thrive in their results-driven reality.

The results of a randomized, controlled pilot trial in sixth grade classrooms that compared such a program with a stress reduction program that did not incorporate mindfulness suggested that mindfulness practice did indeed have a significant impact the behaviours of individual students with respect to externalizing problems and countering attention deficits (Britton et al., 2014). The focus in such studies has tended to be on individuals' negative behaviours rather than on cultivating positive behaviours (Schonert-Reichel & Lawlor, 2010). From the perspective of the upper right quadrant, the aim of this study was to nurture positive emotions.

When looking at mindfulness in a classroom, the teacher's perspective on the classroom community as its leader is naturally of particular importance. In contemporary classrooms, the teacher's role includes bringing shared experiences to students' attention. From a mindfulness perspective, doing so involves ensuring that they are in the present moment, suspending judgment so that the class can explore these experiences meaningfully from various perspectives (Langner & Moldoveanu, 2000). Teachers comfortable with allowing their students the freedom to lead the way in their learning while remaining mindfully present themselves have the capacity to build a thorough understanding of their students' true positions (Kabat-Zinn, 2009).

Viewing mindfulness as a path to compassion through the lens of the classroom community—which in terms of the AQAL means concentrating on the lower left quadrant— the members of a compassionate classroom community are well equipped to consider the wellbeing of others and are thus prepared to live and learn together in a meaningful way (McClain, Ylimaki, & Ford, 2010). Experiences associated with the lower left quadrant increase appreciation for the worth for all humanity, helping students to expand their social focus and interconnectedness of being (Hurley, 2014). Today's classrooms are diverse and complex communities. From a systemic perspective—associated with the lower left quadrant—teachers need to be ready to respond to the wide range of their students' learning needs (Vacarr, 2001).

The value of the perspective represented by the lower left AQAL quadrant can be increased further through collaboration with neuroscience, cognitive science, developmental science, and education. Davidson et al. (2012) have identified four interrelated considerations regarding mindfulness in the context of this systemic perspective: the individual involved in the system, the neural substrates, psychological functioning, and the behavioural outcomes of education. Mindfulness is relevant to all four of these considerations at the system level, since contemplative practices in educational settings can both complement and add value, beyond cultivating social emotions, by inducing plastic changes in the brain and by enhancing educators' professional development in ways that foster the qualities desired in teachers and students alike (Davidson et al., 2012).

Through consideration of each AQAL quadrant, this framework for compassionate action proceeds from the individual and interior change to exterior behavioural change and then beyond to other individuals and the wider world (Orr, 2014). Cultivating wisdom and compassion in our schools is of utmost importance because doing so lays the groundwork for change and for building communities whose members cherish one another (Orr, 2014; McClain, Ylimaki, & Ford, 2010).

Theoretical Perspectives

The four quadrants have been introduced as a means to organize the information that provides the basis for this study. Wilber's (2007) model goes beyond this simple framework to incorporate levels, lines, states, and types that contribute to its robustness. It is for these reasons that this model was chosen to inform the present study from conception to analysis.

Levels of Consciousness

This component of AQAL organizes individuals and societies into developmental levels among which an individual or group can move in stages or waves (Wilber, Patten, Leonard, & Morelli, 2008) Wilber (2000) derived these levels through a meta-analysis of theories of development and human cognition associated with such widely respected authorities aligning their approaches to demonstrate their fundamental agreement with his descriptions of developmental-level fulcrums. Wilber later incorporated colours of the spectrum, from infrared through magenta, red, amber, orange, green, teak, turquoise, indigo, violet, ultraviolet, and clear light, into his model for ease of use. In Wilber's conception, since there is no "highest" level, the use of colour helps to avoid the impression that an individual must achieve a certain level, or that the levels reinforce a hierarchy rather than merely indicating differences in altitude or perspective that are not linear but nested, with level transcending and includes the others.

One of the developmental theories that Wilber (2006) considers in his meta-analysis is Keegan's (1994) orders of consciousness, according to which life stages can be described in terms of five levels of consciousness, namely intermediate, instrumental, social, self-authoring, and self-transforming. The first of these levels is occupied mainly by younger children, who are mystified when others have opinions that differ from their own. Older children, aged seven to ten, usually occupy the second instrumental level, which is less as it were magical than the first, being more mechanical and associated with fixed laws and a tendency to view the world in relation to how it affects "me." According to Keegan, most adults reside at the third level, which is characterized by a consciousness of "me" as well as something greater, "us." Some individuals advance to a self-authoring consciousness, being able to mediate among various rule systems and to show deep empathy for others when making decisions. Only a relative few achieve self-transforming consciousness, a level of wisdom that allows an individual to maintain mindful participation while navigating the world.

Developmental Lines

Multiple factors inform the development of consciousness. These factors do not arise across all four AQAL quadrants simultaneously; rather, multiple lines of development may exist within a given quadrant that together determine an individual's level, such as cognition, needs, self identity, values, emotions, aesthetics, morals, interpersonal relating, kinaesthetic learning, and spirituality (Wilber, Patten, Leonard, & Morelli, 2008). An integral psychograph can be used to illustrate the relationship between the levels and lines (Wilber, 2007, p. 58). The lines are not conceived as rigid but rather as fluid, like waves or streams; thus it is possible to conceptualize development in a framework that, when applied to a classroom setting, provides insight into the kinds of activities that will facilitate advancement to a more complex level of meaning-making (Cook-Greuter, 2004).

Methods are available within the field of psychology for measuring the levels and lines of development, in particular the Washington University Sentence Completion Test created by Loevinger (1985). This description and assessment has been used and adapted by other researchers for use in leadership development (Cook-Grueter, 2004) and in comprehensive integral therapy (Marquis, 2008).

States and Types

States of consciousness are ephemeral, rather than being developmental; most are exclusive and able to persist through all levels of consciousness. This study looked at meditative states and the state of compassion through the practice of mindfulness. According to Wilber (2007), these kinds of states can be attained through training or practice. Types represent horizontal differences that do not exist within any hierarchy. A type generally remains the same as an individual evolves through levels of consciousness; it is a description of texture rather than a structure (Wilber, Patten, Leonard, & Morelli, 2008).

RESEARCH DESIGN OVERVIEW

The use of integral methodological pluralism (IMP) in the design of this study made it possible for what could have been a flat narrative to blossom into a robust investigation that captured not only the stories of the children in the classroom but also those of the teacher, the school, and the district. The use of IMP facilitated the gathering of data from various perspectives and exploration of the interconnectedness among these perspectives. The study also allowed for an exploration of the interplay between the narrative and empirical data gathered by the teacher and through students' self-assessment.

Methods

IMP, then, was used in this study as a systematic means to develop a multiple-method study. Integral theory unites the non-dual philosophies of the East with the critical philosophies of the West, and the two ontological divisions, interior/exterior and objective/subjective, yield four perspectives on the nature of reality (Snow, 2007). As discussed above, these quadrants, which together define AQAL, simultaneously represent four domains of ontological reality, epistemological knowing, a methodology, and a framework for synthesizing the being, knowing, and doing/living that arise interdependently within the quadrants (Snow, 2007).

IMP facilitates a holistic approach to research by embracing multiplicity in being, knowing, and doing, thereby allowing for a sophisticated view of a given phenomenon from various perspectives (Esbjörn-Hargens, 2010). The present study was conceived using the methodologies of the IMP model as umbrellas for dozens of other, distinct methodologies (Esbjörn-Hargens, 2006). In particular, narrative inquiry served as a means to explore the exterior perspectives of students' individual journeys in mindfulness as well as the exterior perspective of the classroom community as transmitted through the teacher's narrative. Empirical data on individual compassionate behaviours collected from exterior and interior perspectives were represented and another, was explored through participatory research. Finally, systems theory was also employed.

Esbjörn-Hargens (2006) made clear that all eight perspectives are not necessary for a study to be consistent with IMP. The necessary components, rather, are first-, second-, and third-person perspectives; a valid study might include as few as three perspectives or more than eight when multiple methodologies are employed as it were per umbrella (Esbjörn-Hargens, 2006). This study accordingly explored seven of eight perspectives through the students' and teacher's first-person voices, the teacher's second person observations of her students, and the researcher's observations regarding meetings with the teacher. The third-person perspective situated the classroom in the context of the policies and practices of the school and district.

Narrative Inquiry

The story of classroom experience that is at the centre of this research is told from various perspectives: those of each student, the teacher, and the researcher's own observations through meetings with the teacher. Thus the narrative inquiry here explored the ways in which the students and teacher were experiencing the world. The stories told in zones 2, 3, and, 4 and the subjective and inter-subjective data were analyzed using the approach of Connelly and Clandinin (1990). The stories were interconnected, so that the students and teacher were not only storytellers but also the characters in each other's stories. Because of this interconnectivity, it was important that all of their stories be considered along with the context in which they were composed, which led to interviewing the school principal. In terms of narrative research, the study of these individual stories falls in what can be described as the restory of the experiences in three dimensions, namely through interactions at the personal and social levels, through respecting continuity, and through place (Clandinin, 2006). To capture the truths of each perspective, the researcher entered the learning space with the teacher in an effort to create an empowering relationship involving connectedness through caring, mutual purpose, and intention (Connelly & Clandinin, 1990). By honouring the individual experiences while discovering the social, cultural, and institutional narratives within them (Clandinin & Rosiek, 2007), then, this study was able to tell a multifaceted story of the participants' paths on their mindfulness journey.

Participatory Research

This type of research is grassroots-driven, using local knowledge as a foundation upon which to build (Cornwall & Jewkes, 1995). At the beginning of the study, the researcher sat down with the participating teacher and discussed her current practice, thereby developing a mutual understanding of such key concepts as mindfulness and compassionate behaviour and of the mindfulness programming available for use in classrooms. The use of a participatory approach in this study recognized the value of the teacher-participant's local knowledge (van der Meulen, 2011) given her deep connection to her school community and understanding of her students. The discussions also helped to build a partnership with the teacher so that her role could extend beyond "doing research on" to "being part of" the research process in a collaborative environment (Ducharme, LeBlanc, Bourassa, & Chevalier, 2011). As a result, the decision was made to use the MindUP program (for which see Table 1) as a basis for the teacher's planning of her mindfulness unit. As the unit progressed, she adapted the program to include collaborative games and other ideas from a school-wide program called Tribes. Because of her knowledge and passion for the program, the teacher was able to weave the two programs together in order to create a meaningful experience for herself and her students.

Empirical Data Collection

Compassionate behaviours that were outward and observable were measured to yield empirical data from the perspectives of zones 5 and 6. The outward zone 6 perspective was that of the teacher collecting data on her students' compassionate behaviours over the course of the study. The zone 5 inner perspective was observed through the Mindfulness Attention Awareness Scale adapted for children (MAAS-C), a 15-item survey of mindful states that students self-report using a Likert-type scale to indicate the frequency with which they find themselves in a given state (Lawlor, Schonert-Reichl, Gadermann, & Zumbo, 2014). This survey was completed at the beginning and end of the data collection and analysed for statistically significant variations.

The data collected relating to the upper right quadrant were intended to provide a useful perspective on observable behaviour. These data thus added an observable dimension to the small, classroom-sized sample, providing a glimpse into what the students did in addition to the MAAS-C. The small sample clearly represented a limitation of the survey methodology, as did the teacher questionnaire; nevertheless useful data were obtained from these perspectives.

Systems Theory

The final perspectives considered in this study related to the wider system. Zone 7 was examined through an email interview with the school principal and zone 8 through a review of school, district, and provincial policies that promoted compassion in classrooms. The interview with the principal provided an understanding of school-wide programming and practices, situating them within the larger system. In drafting questions for this interview, Marrero's (2007) integral affective education report card was used as a means to determine the position of the school along the affective line of development and to map where the school fell within the larger system.

Through policy analysis, the elements that function together to make up the system (from classroom to school to district to province) and to achieve the common purpose of educating the children in the district can be explored (Betts, 1992). This study accordingly examined the interconnectedness of nationally and internationally influential school, district, and provincial policies.

The Research Problem

This research is founded on the notion that classrooms can be places of compassion for students and education professionals alike. When a classroom community becomes more compassionate, the learning therein becomes enriched and more meaningful for all involved. Given this obviously significant benefit, the question becomes how best to create this type of environment in today's diverse classrooms.

The Research Questions

The articulation of the research problem went through several iterations in the effort to define the parameters of the study and the exact nature of compassionate learning environments. In the process, an overarching research question emerged regarding whether mindfulness practice can foster compassionate attitudes and behaviours in a classroom community. This research question was then examined from the perspective of each AQAL quadrant to yield four questions, as illustrated below.

Data Collection

As discussed above, this study began with a meeting in which the teacher-participant and researcher together explored mindfulness programming for the classroom and built a relationship by sharing experiences. The teacher was provided with a trial for www.headspace.com a mindfulness application to help her to initiate her own personal mindfulness practice, which is a prerequisite to teaching mindfulness to others. A participatory method was employed over several subsequent meetings throughout the data collection process in order to plan for the incorporation of practices designed to promote mindfulness and compassion in the classroom. During the first meeting, collecting data relating to behaviour was also discussed; the teacher was provided with a checklist of compassionate behaviours rated on a Likert-type scale that she completed for each student once a week as the data were collected. The specific compassionate behaviours involved a given student

- Recognizing the feelings of others;
- Expressing care for others;
- Showing concern through kind thoughts, words, or actions;
- Being helpful and giving;
- Demonstrating good listening skills; and
- Being patient.

Table 2. Research questions in AQAL

Upper Left Quadrant (Interior Subjective)	Upper Right Quadrant (Interior Objective)
How does compassion developed through mindfulness practices impact students' attitudes toward the classroom community?	Can mindfulness practice in the classroom have an observable impact on students' compassionate behaviours?
Lower Left Quadrant (Exterior Subjective)	**Lower Right Quadrant (Exterior Objective)**
How is compassion embodied in a classroom community?	How do compassion and mindfulness in the classroom align with school and provincial policies?

Also during these meetings, non-negotiable elements of the mindfulness unit for this study were introduced. These included at least two minutes of daily sitting mediation, student journaling involving reflection on mindfulness practice, and using prompts adapted from the MindUP curriculum materials. The prompts included:

- What am I #1 at?
- How can I use my strengths and talents to help my classmates?
- If I were an apple tree, what would be my roots?
- What are the things/people/relationships in my life that make me strong and help me grow?
- Who values me?
- Who do I breathe easy with?
- What is it about this person that makes it so easy just to be me with them?
- What are some other things that make me happy?
- What bugs me? how can I deal with it?
- What can I actually control?
- What do I stand for?
- What are the most important things to me?
- How am I going to use them to make the world a better place?

The teacher and researcher also established an online reflective diary for the process that helped the teacher to remain connected with the researcher.

Assumptions

An assumption underlying this study is that, while the teaching of compassion and compassionate behaviours is not the primary goal of most teachers, they nevertheless as part of their teaching employ practices that promote the creation of compassionate communities. It was accordingly further assumed that mindfulness is not usually taught in any specific targeted manner, that most teachers do not actively seek to remedy the lack of compassion in their classroom communities, and that some teachers, those whose interpersonal line has not developed, do not see lack of compassion as a problem at all. It was also recognized that, because classroom systems are strongly driven by students' academic achievements, the absence of clear links between the development of compassionate classroom communities and increased achievement in such contexts as reading comprehension or number sense has meant that notions such as mindfulness are often dismissed as "nice to think about."

Limitations and Delimitations

The most obvious delimitation of this study is the omission of the zone 1 perspective from the upper-left quadrant, which relates to students' exterior reflections of their own interior views. This perspective is most commonly explored through phenomenology, but this delimitation arose in part owing to the time constraints associated doctoral research and also in part owing to the readiness of the students participating in the study. A second delimitation of this study concerns the time frame in which data were collected, specifically the seven weeks following the first term of the academic year, during which the teacher became sufficiently acquainted with her students to be able to compare their behaviour and demeanour during and after mindfulness. The study was further delimited in its focus on a single classroom. Qualitative research of this sort generally involves collecting rich data that allow for the creation of empathetic descriptions of the classroom being studied (Johnson & Onwuegbuzie, 2004).

The researcher's involvement with the research participants and the interpretations of the qualitative data both represent limitations of this research. To address these limitations, the researcher worked closely with the teacher to ensure the clarity of her narrative and used a reflective researcher journal throughout the analysis to follow up on observations. The small sample size was, as noted above, another limitation of the study; indeed, it was below that which would traditionally be considered sufficient for application of the scientific method (Flyvbjerg, 2006). A small sample, however, was the proper context for developing the meaningful narrative that was central to this work.

EXPLORING THE ISSUES

In the initial presentation of the findings, the organizational structure of the quadrants of AQAL provided a convenient means to present the themes that arose from each of the distinct data sets collected for the distinct perspective represented by each quadrant as seen in Table 3.

The quadrants seem tidy when presented in this way, but this tidiness obscures the ways in which these themes arise together and influence and are influenced by one another. In other words, this representation fails to depict the organic nature of a phenomenon like compassion or the manner in which it is cultivated within a community made up of individuals as well as collective thoughts, actions, and behaviours that are in turn shaped by the systems in which they reside. A considerably more sophisticated application of the integral model was needed to explore the interplay among the stories behind the findings.

Analysis of the Findings

The findings were analysed first by looking at how the individual quadrants of AQAL informed one another, the aim being to explore the phenomenon of compassion in a way true to integral theory, which recognizes, acknowledges, and celebrates the interwoven nature of our being.

Table 3. Overview of themes explored in each quadrant

Upper Left Quadrant: Interior/Subjective	Upper Right Quadrant: Interior/Objective
Relationships and the interconnectedness of being The importance of family Feeling valued by the teacher Fostering friendships The positive effects of mindfulness Happiness A sense of calm Those troublesome activities Self-awareness and a role in the world Listening Mindful moments identified	The teacher noted a general increase in the following compassionate behaviours: patience recognizing the feelings of others being helpful or giving expressing care for others demonstrating good listening skills showing concern through kind thoughts, words, or actions Student Self Assessment Eight of eleven students showed improvement on the MAAS-C, and the class average improved 9.2 points
Lower Left Quadrant: Exterior/Subjective	**Lower Right Quadrant: Exterior/Objective**
Teacher's self-awareness A democratic classroom community Student engagement	Programs Activities Expectations and philosophies

UL and UR: Individual Interior Perceptions and Exterior Behaviours

From the perspectives of the Upper Left and Upper Right Quadrants, the students' behaviours were explored through the teacher's eyes and through their own writing as they learned mindfulness in the classroom. The teacher tracked the six compassionate behaviours identified by Duffell (2008) in the Seeds of Compassion Curriculum. Table 4 shows the occurrences of these behaviours as identified by the students in their journals.

When the occurrences of these behaviours were then compared with the teacher's data regarding the students' growth, it became apparent that the teacher and the students stories were similar. Thus, from the broad perspective of the overall class, the teacher's behaviour tracking and the students' writing tended to tell a similar story. Students wrote about their acts of kindness toward others and their ability to use their strengths and talents to help others, and the teacher also indicated an improvement in these same student behaviours. Similarly, the students' journals indicated that they understood at a basic level the importance of listening but recognized that it was a skill that they were still learning, and their teacher rated their listening skills as average and noted little improvement over the course of the study. Student journals also indicated various levels of understanding of such virtues as patience, as did behaviour tracking, which showed a dip in the average in the third week of the study—tellingly, this was the week of the school's reopening after winter break.

Triangulation of the teacher's observations with the students' writing demonstrated an increase in positive behaviours in the classroom as a result of observation and self-identification. The finding that the teacher was able to observe behaviours that the students had difficulty articulating is consistent with the work of Davidson and Begley (2012) on the emotional life of the human brain with respect to this stage of adolescent development.

UL and LL: Individual Perceptions and the Classroom Community

From these perspectives, it was possible to assess the teacher's reflections on her classroom's collective journey through learning mindfulness (represented by the LL quadrant) as it related to the students' individual journeys (represented by the UR). In this way, the interrelationships between individuals and the collective and the ways in which they communicate were assessed as well as the teacher's individual journey in her relationships with her class.

Having engaged in reflective practice before the research commenced, the teacher soon after embarking on her mindfulness journey began to question the efficacy of her classroom practices in light of this new paradigm. One of the first reflective moments that she recorded concerned the visual behaviour-tracking chart used in her classroom. Having become more mindful, one of her first actions was to change the descriptors on this chart to reflect the culture of mindfulness being created in the classroom. Thus

Table 4. Compassionate behaviour traits (from student journals)

	Compassionate Behaviour Traits					
	Patience	Empathy	Helpful/Giving	Caring	Listening/Attentive	Concern/Kindness
Class Cohort Total:	5	19	32	21	36	21

the descriptors "succeeding" and "thinking" were replaced with "master of mindfulness" and "stop, breathe, and think." Such changes were a result of the teacher's reflection on her own mindlessness and her concerns regarding the relationships in her classroom as well as her instinct to correct ineffective behaviours mindlessly.

Inspired by this reflection, the teacher shared her thoughts with the students and worked with them on ways to promote her mindfulness practice in the classroom. As one step, the teacher added a magnet representing herself to the classroom behaviour chart. Through discussion, the class determined the circumstances under which her magnet would move, and the teacher followed up each move by having a one-on-one discussion with the students in order to strengthen both their understanding of one another and their ability to act mindfully in the classroom community. The teacher's personal reflections had a direct impact on this community; thus the visual behaviour board evolved from serving as a kind of watchdog into an opportunity for communication and growth.

The teacher's mindful reflection recalls the Buddhist teachers interviewed by Kerochan, McCormick, and White (2007). For them, mindfulness served as a means to increase empathy and to make their teaching more meaningful. The teacher in the elementary classroom experienced such a shift early in the study, and throughout her depth of understanding in these respects continued to grow. This growth was expressed in her final journal entry describing mindfulness practice in her class: "we are significantly more focused." Her use of the word "we" also represented a shift in her reflections, for rather than emphasizing her own perspective of her classroom, she spoke of one classroom community.

UL and LR: Interior Perceptions and Systems Perspectives

These perspectives informed the researcher's perceptions of how the policies and practices of the school were realized in the minds of the students in the classroom studied. These perceptions were related to programming, activities, and the expectations or philosophies of the teaching staff.

Programming was described by the principal as a means to develop the conditions that foster compassionate behaviours. The core program used by school, known as Tribes, has four main components: mutual respect, appreciation, the right to participate/pass, and attentive listening. Although the students did not make explicit connections to this program in their journals, some of them did touch on the differences between hearing and attentive listening when offered such prompts as "is listening a skill or a talent?" or "why is listening important?"

The principal mentioned in her interview that one of the activities in which the school was participating, the Angel Tree program, encouraged compassionate behaviour. For this program, a tree was set up in the entryway of the school adorned with tags specifying gifts that students' families could purchase for someone in need. This activity was not, however, mentioned in the students' journals even when they received such prompts as "what are the most important things to me" and "how am I going to use them to make the world a better place?"

The principal of the school expected that staff members would work with all of the students in a compassionate manner. She stressed that compassion was a significant aspect of her own philosophy of education and a quality she looked for in hiring. The principal's expectation was reflected in the students' journals. Thus, when discussing their teacher, they recognized that she valued them, and they also mentioned the compassion of other teachers. There was something of a disconnect between the principal's description of compassionate practices and the activities in which the students engaged, but the philosophy of compassion as articulated by the principal and enacted by the staff were still quite evident in the students' writings. The disconnect may be attributable to a perceived conflict between the valorization of concepts like compassion on the one hand and individual rights on the other within society (Orr, 2014).

UR and LR: Individual Behaviours and the Classroom Community

The students' individual behaviours were observed in isolation, and their teacher noted signs of improvement in most cases, including increased levels of the compassionate behaviours that she was tracking and of mindful attentiveness as reported by the students themselves through the MAAS-C. The interaction between the UR and LL quadrants was apparent in the comparison of students who reported significant changes in their own mindfulness following the beginning of the study (one of whom reported a 14- and another a 16-point difference) with the teacher's behaviour tracking and her account of the classroom.

An interesting story thus emerged. In a meeting with the researcher after the winter break, the teacher discussed an activity that the class had recently completed for which small groups of students were asked to recreate an object using items in the classroom. One member of each group was shown the object and then reported back to the group, which worked together to recreate it. The activity initially caused considerable frustration, anxiety, and stress for the groups, and it took a full 35 minutes for the first one to complete the task. The next day, the teacher led the class through a reflection exercise that included thinking back on their mindfulness activities and discussion of the frustration of the previous day in relation to brain function and stress, after which the class came up with a plan to complete the task mindfully and tried again. This time, the first group completed the task in just 6 minutes, and the whole class was done in 18. The students thus showed that they were able to discuss their shared experience and to use their mindfulness strategies to seek improvement in their classroom activities. This exercise proved to be a turning point for the class.

UR and LR: Individual Behaviours and System Perspectives

The analysis of these two quadrants represents a second opportunity to find support for the anecdotal evidence provided by the principal. The Tribes program served to link the compassionate behaviours tracked by the teacher, which included respect through empathy, appreciation through caring and concern for others, passing/participating through patience and helpfulness, and attentive listening skills. The school had earned a reputation for the promotion of these behaviours through students' participation in the Tribes and in Peaceful Schools International programs. The expectation was that the baseline data for this study in regard to behaviour would be high, but in fact the students started out slightly above average in most categories including; student is patient, student recognizes the feelings of others, student is helpful or giving, student shows good listening skills, student shows that they care for others, and student shows concern through kind thoughts, words, or actions.

From this baseline, it would be difficult to determine whether the programming in which these students were immersed as part of the school culture served to develop the behaviours that, according to the principal, the program was designed to promote. Further data from the study did show that, from the teacher's perspective, mindfulness and the type of classroom discussion that she designed during this study, when combined with the Tribes program, increased these behaviours on the part of the students.

LL and LR: The Classroom Community within the System

In this dual-quadrant exploration, the classroom is approached as a holon. Thus the classroom community as described by the teacher in the LL is a holon that resides within the holon of the school as described by the principal in the LR, which in turn resides within the holons of the district and province. An examination of these two quadrants thus amounts to an exploration of the interconectedness of the various holons.

The school has responded to district and provincial policies regarding safe and caring schools and the competencies of a twenty-first century learner through its use of the Tribes program. The teacher was chosen to participate in this study in part because she was using the Tribes program in her classroom, which aligned with her philosophy of education. The teacher made reference both in her journal and in conversations to the Tribes program and its links to mindfulness. So also in her design of the unit plan for teaching mindfulness demonstrated her effort to extend classroom routines and practices that were originally designed with Tribes in mind to include mindfulness; that is, she leveraged her students' background knowledge from Tribes to enhance her teaching of mindfulness. Thus, for example, she encouraged her students to use the "appreciation statements" developed for the program to recognize mindful actions by others. Through these moments of interconection, the classroom fit into the school's concept of character education and twenty-first century learning, even as the school conformed to district and provincial protocols.

CONCLUSION AND IMPLICATIONS

This study has explored the transformation of a classroom community through the introduction of mindfulness training. The community was already functioning well before the study, being led by a teacher who clearly valued her students as partners in learning. This much was clear in an early meeting with the researcher when she stated, "my class needs something like this to help us come together." She designed learning tasks to meet her learners' needs and created a positive environment overall that was evident to the outside observer.

One of the most impactful changes in the classroom community was brought about by the introduction of mindfulness training for the teacher herself. She had demonstrated that she valued democratic principles in her teaching, but mindfulness activated their practice in the classroom, so that the teacher came to see herself as participant, a true partner in the community.

Throughout the study, most of the students in the class demonstrated growth in the upper right quadrant; that is, they engaged in a growing number of observable compassionate behaviours over the course of each week. In their own accounts, the students also reported increases in attention awareness, and their writing included reflections on how mindfulness had made them feel happier and calmer and had increased their ability to focus. The teacher noted this change in her reflections as well, remarking that the class had become increasingly intent on task completion. As a group, the teacher and the students developed strategies to retain their mindful awareness and to help others recognize mindless moments in themselves. Again, the class benefited from being led by a teacher who recognized that she herself had in the past not always been effective in teaching her students to regain and maintain their focus.

Implications

It will be useful to explore the implications of this study for practice through each of the quadrants, as these perspectives were informed by one another.

From the Upper Left Perspective

This perspective focuses on the impact of mindfulness on individuals. As mindfulness has garnered increasing interest, various claims have been made about its benefits. This study has shown that, although these claims may have merit, the efficacy of mindfulness in communities such as the classroom studied here in fact depends on individuals' needs and the culture in which it is introduced. This research was designed to explore ways of cultivating compassion in the classroom through mindfulness training, but it was found that the benefits of mindfulness varied among the individuals who comprised the classroom community. The compassionate behaviours that were tracked did improve, but this was not the only positive benefit that students reported, for in their journals they began to comment on the interconnectedness of being and positive feelings brought about through mindfulness.

Further study of students at this age level could focus on the key benefits to cultivate by taking into consideration individuals' developmental levels. Such an approach could help to shape best practices for educators seeking to develop mindfulness and compassion in themselves and their classrooms.

From the Upper Right Perspective

The upper left perspective focuses on sustained compassionate behaviours. During the study, only one significant decrease in the compassionate behaviours of the group was reported by the teacher. This decrease occurred, as has been seen, in the week following the school's winter break. Students had returned to class in January after having acquired only the three weeks of mindfulness learning before the break, and this was simply not enough time to realize long-term improvement in compassionate behaviours. Further research in this area is needed to establish a timeline for making these behaviours habitual among students. A longitudinal study following a class over the course of one or two school years would offer the opportunity to determine whether improvements in mindful and compassionate behaviours persist through the various breaks in the school year.

From the Lower Left Perspective

The lower left perspective focuses on the classroom community, before and after. The class that took part in this study was chosen in part because the teacher had already been recognized for her ability to create a positive classroom community, and in some ways the class already demonstrated a degree of mindfulness. Nevertheless, the introduction of explicit mindfulness instruction did change the classroom community. As the teacher reflected on her own practice and that of the students, she perceived that they had become more engaged in general, especially after mindful activities. This teacher's mindful approach in her classroom management involved small changes in the ways in which she approached her students that strengthened understanding and ultimately the relationships in the classroom. Thus the researcher observed that, based on the nature of her reflective practice, the teacher worked from at least a "green" level of development in terms of the colours described in integral theory. Indeed, most teachers who are interested in pursuing mindfulness in their classrooms would likely be at this level at a minimum. Research into identifying teachers who are seeking to improve their skills in building a classroom community but are not at a green developmental level could offer insight into the expanding the scope of mindfulness practice.

The Lower Right Perspective

This perspective contrasts the systemic conception with the actual situation on the ground. Relevant here is the subtle disconnect noted above between the principal's perceptions of the school community and the real world of the classrooms. As mindfulness comes to be integrated into a growing number of school contexts, such disconnects need be given careful consideration. In the present study, programming and events that the principal described as important for building compassion and compassionate behaviours in the school were not acknowledged in the journals of students; the prompts that were provided did not explicitly focus on these activities, but they were sufficiently open-ended that students might be expected to mention them had they had a deep or widespread impact. Further exploration of ways to forge explicit connections to such school-wide activities as fundraisers and social profit endeavours in classrooms could thus serve to leverage practices that promote mindfulness and compassion.

An appropriate first step in such research would be an exploration of the values that a school district intends to promote through school-wide activities and its purpose in doing so. Relevant in this context are such questions as whether activities should be coordinated to promote a specific intent or whether, as Marrero (2007) has argued, such an approach is nothing more than standard character education that serves essentially to indoctrinate young people.

Individuals who belong to a culture are often ignorant of its developmental level, since they have been programmed from birth to view the world from a specific perspective (Wilber, 2006). Each developmental level represents a distinct degree of tolerance and capacity for complexity, and each embeds particular pathologies. Effective mindfulness and compassion can be practiced at each level, provided that the values and limitations of each are taken into consideration. The programming chosen for character education by the school at which this study took place was the Tribes program, the mission statement of which reads as follows: "Tribes Learning Communities is a research-based process that creates a culture that maximizes learning and human development." This self-description locates Tribes programming on the "orange" level defined by integral theory, a level that is also consistent with the school district's publications. In these contexts, therefore, mindfulness programming could be delimited to the orange perspective for the sake of maximizing student performance through meditation.

Recommendations for Research

This study has explored the use of mindfulness in a classroom in which, as noted, the classroom community was for the most part strong and vibrant. Mindfulness thus served as a tool in this case to increase the observance of compassionate behaviours. The question remains whether this type of work could improve a classroom community that is facing serious challenges. The potential of mindfulness as a technique to help teachers struggling to connect with their students or to improve trust and positivity in strained classroom communities remains to be explored, as does the potential of sustained mindfulness learning to transform classrooms.

The disconnect noted between the principal's vision of the activities in the school and the interpretation of these activities by the students likewise represents an avenue for further study. It would also be of interest to determine whether an integral analysis of efforts by the staff to align school activities with the curriculum and with the needs of the community could help students to draw more explicit connections.

Implications for Integral Research

Esbjörn-Hargens (2010) has described research involving integral methodological pluralism (IMP) in terms of first-, second-, and third-person perspectives, and this is just what many IMP studies at the doctoral level do, explore three of the eight possible primordial perspectives. This delimitation is often reasonable in light of the time constraints and demands of doctoral research, but this study offers a different approach. Here seven of eight perspectives were explored through the use of a narrative that interwove them and was further informed by quantitative data and systems theory. IMP in this way made the narrative more powerful (Martin, 2008). The various perspectives revealed various dimensions of the truths explored here and helped the narrative to evolve. Despite the variety of perspectives integrated through IMP, however, this study may lack the depth of analysis to exploit to the full the perspective of the right hand quadrants with regard to this particular data set. In order to achieve greater depth, a research team that included methodologists under each of the "umbrellas" discussed above in the Research Design Overview above would be required.

The nature of this study was exploratory; it was designed to complement existing research on the practice of mindfulness in the classroom, most of which privileges the right hand quadrants. The narrative presented here focused on the students and teacher from the perspective of the left hand quadrants, but was enriched by consideration of both the upper and lower quadrants.

REFERENCES

Albrecht, N. J., Albrecht, P. M., & Cohen, M. (2012). Mindfully teaching in the classroom: A literature review. *Australian Journal of Teacher Education, 37*(12). doi:10.14221/ajte.2012v37n12.2

Betts, F. (1992). How systems thinking applies to education. *Educational Leadership, 50*(3), 38–41.

Britton, W. B., Lepp, N. E., Niles, H. F., Rocha, T., Fisher, N. E., & Gold, J. S. (2014). A randomized controlled pilot trial of classroom-based mindfulness meditation compared to an active control condition in sixth-grade children. *Journal of School Psychology, 52*(3), 263–278. doi:10.1016/j.jsp.2014.03.002 PMID:24930819

Clandinin, D. J. (2006). Narrative inquiry: A methodology for studying lived experience. *Research Studies in Music Education, 27*(1), 44–54. doi:10.1177/1321103X060270010301

Clandinin, D. J. (2007). Mapping a landscape of narrative inquiry: borderland spaces and tensions. In Handbook of narrative inquiry: Mapping a methodology (pp. 35–76). Thousand Oaks, CA: SAGE Publications Ltd. doi:10.4135/9781452226552.n2

Connelly, F. M., & Clandinin, D. J. (1990). Narrative inquiry. In J. Green, G. Camili & P. Elmore (Eds.), Handbook of complementary methods in education research (pp. 477–487). Mahwah, NJ: Lawrence Erlbaum.

Cook-Greuter, S. (2004). Making a case for the developmental perspective. *Industrial and Commercial Training, 36*(7), 275–281. doi:10.1108/00197850410563902

Cornwall, A., & Jewkes, R. (1995). What is participatory research? *Social Science & Medicine, 41*(12), 1667–1676. doi:10.1016/0277-9536(95)00127-S PMID:8746866

Davidson, J., Dunne, R., Eccles, J., Engle, J. S., Greenberg, A., Jennings, M., ... Vago, D. (2012). Contemplative practices and mental training: Prospects for American education. *Child Development Perspectives, 6*(2), 146–153. doi:10.1111/j.1750-8606.2012.00240.x PMID:22905038

Davidson, R. J., & Begley, S. (2012). *The emotional life of your brain: How its unique patterns affect the way you think, feel, and live, and how you can change them.* New York: Penguin.

Ducharme, D., Leblanc, R., Bourassa, M., & Chevalier, J. (2011). Participatory research in a school setting: A process of acculturation. *Online Submission. US-China Education Review B*, 868–877.

Duffell, E. (2008). *Curriculum grades k-2.* Retrieved from http://www.seedsofcompassion.org/why/curriculum/K-%20Compassion%20Lessons.pdf

Esbjörn-Hargens, S. (2006). Integral research: A multi-method approach to investigating phenomena. *Constructivism in the Human Sciences, 11*(1), 79–107.

Esbjörn-Hargens, S. (2010). An ontology of climate change. *Journal of Integral Theory and Practice, 5*(1), 143–174.

Flyvbjerg, B. (2006). Five misunderstandings about case-study research. *Qualitative Inquiry, 12*(2), 219–245. doi:10.1177/1077800405284363

Hurley, W. (2014). Enhancing a positive school climate with compassion and analytical selective-focus skills (COMPASS). *Journal of Education and Practice, 5*(7), 1–15.

Hutcherson, C., Seppala, E., & Gross, J. (2008). Loving-Kindness meditation increases social connectedness. *Emotion, 8*(5), 720-724.

Johnson, R. B., & Onwuegbuzie, A. J. (2004). Mixed methods research: A research paradigm whose time has come. *Educational Researcher, 33*(7), 14–26. doi:10.3102/0013189X033007014

Kabat-Zinn, J. (1994). *Wherever you go, there you are: Mindfulness meditation in everyday life.* New York: Hyperion.

Kabat-Zinn, J. (2003). Mindfulness-based interventions in context: Past, present, and future. *Clinical Psychology: Science and Practice, 10*(2), 144–156. doi:10.1093/clipsy.bpg016

Kabat-Zinn, M. (2009). *Everyday blessings: The inner work of mindful parenting.* Hachette Books.

Kegan, R. (1994). *In over our heads: The mental demands of modern life*. Cambridge, MA: Harvard University Press.

Kernochan, R. A., McCormick, D. W., & White, J. A. (2007). Spirituality and the management teacher: Reflections of three Buddhists on compassion, mindfulness, and selflessness in the classroom. *Journal of Management Inquiry, 16*(1), 61–75. doi:10.1177/1056492606297545

Langner, E. J., & Moldoveanu, M. (2000). Mindfulness research and the future. *The Journal of Social Issues, 56*(1), 129–139. doi:10.1111/0022-4537.00155

Lawlor, M. S., Schonert-Reichl, K. A., Gadermann, A. M., & Zumbo, B. (2013). A validation study of the Mindful Attention Awareness Scale adapted for children. *Mindfulness*. doi:10.100712671-013-0228-4

Loevinger, J. (1985). A revision of the Sentence Completion Test for ego development. *Journal of Personality and Social Psychology, 48*(2), 420–427. doi:10.1037/0022-3514.48.2.420 PMID:3981402

Marquis, A. (2008). *The integral intake: A guide to comprehensive idiographic assessment in integral psychotherapy*. New York: Taylor Francis.

Marrero, F. (2007). An integral approach to affective education. *Journal of Integral Theory and Practice, 2*(4), 1–23.

Martin, J. A. (2008). Integral research as a practical mixed-methods framework: Clarifying the role of integral methodological pluralism. *Journal of Integral Theory and Practice, 3*(2), 155–163.

McClain, L., Ylimaki, R., & Ford, M. P. (2010). Sustaining the heart of education: Finding space for wisdom and compassion. *International Journal of Children's Spirituality, 15*(4), 307–316. doi:10.1080/1364436X.2010.525624

Meiklejohn, J., Phillips, C., Freedman, M. L., Griffin, M. L., Biegel, G., Roach, A., ... Saltzman, A. (2012). Integrating mindfulness training into K-12 education: Fostering the resilience of teachers and students. *Mindfulness, 3*(4), 291–307. doi:10.100712671-012-0094-5

Noddings, N. (1995). Teaching themes of care. *Phi Delta Kappan, 76*, 675.

Onwuegbuzie, A. J., Slate, J. R., Leech, N. L., & Collins, K. M. (2009). Mixed data analysis: Advanced integration techniques. *International Journal of Multiple Research Approaches, 3*(1), 13–33. doi:10.5172/mra.455.3.1.13

Orr, D. (2014). In A mindful moral voice: Mindful compassion, the ethic of care and education. *Paideusis, 21*(2), 41–53.

Schonert-Reichl, K. A., & Lawlor, M. S. (2010). The effects of a mindfulness-based education program on pre- and early adolescents' well-being and social and emotional competence. *Mindfulness, 1*(3), 137–151. doi:10.100712671-010-0011-8

Snow, B. A. (2007). *Reflections on integral methodological pluralism*. John F. Kennedy University working document. Available at: http://www.kenwilber.com/blog/show/379

Vacarr, B. (2001). Voices inside schools: Moving beyond polite correctness: Practicing mindfulness in the diverse classroom. *Harvard Educational Review, 71*(2), 285–296. doi:10.17763/haer.71.2.n8p0620381847715

Van der Meulen, E. (2011). Participatory and action-oriented dissertations: The challenges and importance of community-engaged graduate research. *Qualitative Report, 16*(5), 1291–1303.

Wilber, K. (2000). *Integral psychology*. Boston: Shambhala Publications.

Wilber, K. (2005). Introduction to integral theory and practice. *AQAL: Journal of Integral Theory and Practice, 1*(1).

Wilber, K. (2006). *Integral spirituality*. Boston: Shambhala Publications.

Wilber, K. (2007). *A brief history of everything*. Boston: Shambhala Publications.

Wilber, K., Patten, T., Leonard, A., & Morelli, M. (2008). *Integral life practice: A 21st century blueprint for physical health, emotional balance, mental clarity, and spiritual awakening*. Boston: Integral Books.

ADDITIONAL READING

Rempel, K. (2012). Mindfulness for children and youth: A review of the literature with an argument for school-based implementation. *Canadian Journal of Counselling and Psychotherapy/Revue Canadienne de Counseling et de Psychothérapie, 46*(3).

Tebay, G. (2017). *Cultivating Compassion in the Classroom: Exploring the Phenomenon of Compassion in an Upper Elementary School Classroom Community*. Dissertation. University of Calgary.

Wilber, K. (2005). Introduction to integral theory and practice. *AQAL: Journal of Integral Theory and Practice, 1*(1).

KEY TERMS AND DEFINITIONS

AQAL: An acronym for "all quadrants, all levels, all lines, all states, all types," this approach organizes for integral thinking, combining as it does the essential elements of the theory to represent the holistic nature of the concept.

Classroom Community: The intricate network of relationships within a classroom involving the students, each student and the teacher, the group and the teacher, and the group within the school environment.

Compassion: Literally meaning "to experience together," compassion is the feeling that arises when one individual encounters the suffering of another and is motivated to relieve it.

Integral Theory: This theory, developed by Wilber, draws together various threads of accepted knowledge from major disciplines and synthesizes them into a single coherent framework.

Lower-Left Quadrant (LL): The exterior/subjective quadrant of AQAL that relates to relationships, culture, and collective decision making.

Lower-Right Quadrant (LR): The exterior/objective quadrant of AQAL that relates to collective, systemic understanding.

Mindfulness Practice: The work of developing the skill set necessary to pay purposeful attention to the present moment in a non-judgmental way.

Upper-Left Quadrant (UL): The interior/subjective quadrant of AQAL that relates to the inner workings of individuals.

Upper-Right Quadrant (UR): The interior/objective quadrant of AQAL that relates to the empirical factual domain.

Chapter 9
An Integral View of Mindfulness Practices and the Perception of Challenge Within a High School Setting

Anne Daniel
University of Calgary, Canada

ABSTRACT

The purpose of this chapter was to examine how mindfulness-based strategies are taught within four different classroom settings in a large urban high school and how they impact students' perceptions of challenge. Two different approaches toward mindfulness training were represented in the four classrooms: the first derived from an explicit, outcomes-based approach within a Yoga class setting with a focus on awareness of personal experience; the other was embedded and implicitly connected to the subject discipline of natural science with a focus on situated being. Integral methodological pluralism (IMP) was used to gather data from multiple viewpoints: phenomenological interviews, structural analysis of language frequency and comparisons, ethnographic observations, and hermeneutic interviews. Integral theory was used to analyze the data and identify the individual and cultural themes. Systemic influences are discussed in connection with these findings, and implications for implementation of mindfulness in relation to perception of challenge are explored.

INTRODUCTION

Educational stakeholders are charged with the exciting yet daunting task of preparing learners to become competent and contributing future members of a complex and ever-changing society (Robinson, 2009). The pace of transformation has accelerated to the point that attempts to isolate and teach skills and aptitudes best fit for prospective working environments have become futile. Educators are encouraged to reach beyond and focus on building more generalized capabilities that span across different fields of study and experiences (Dweck, 2010). Developing broad-based competencies pushes the educator to prepare classroom environments that ensure students will be both authentically challenged and well supported as they engage in situations designed to provoke higher-order thinking.

DOI: 10.4018/978-1-5225-5873-6.ch009

An Integral View of Mindfulness Practices and the Perception of Challenge Within a High School Setting

To do this effectively the educator must first foster internal structures that enable students to have the academic and emotional stamina to work through each challenging learning task. Dweck (2009) has identified, defined, and illustrated two contrasting types of personal mindsets that support or inhibit students in their engagements with challenging problem-based academic work. The first of these is the *growth mindset*: the attitude that intelligence can be developed and that challenges and setbacks are essential to the process of learning. The second, the *fixed mindset*, is the belief that intelligence or talent is a pre-set or fixed trait. This fixed mindset prompts individuals to work to protect their personal ideas of their intelligence or talents, and, as a result, students tend to avoid situations that require facing challenges or setbacks.

The goal of this study was to examine how challenge was experienced by the learner and how mindfulness practices might affect perceptions of challenge. Mindfulness is a state of mental awareness of the present moment, which involves the ability to acknowledge thoughts and feelings without judgment (Kabat-Zinn, 2009). Meditative practices have started to gain acceptance within Western society and are now starting to be employed within the classroom. And since mindfulness practices have been used to increase insight, self-actualization and compassion, this study aimed to evaluate the effects of mindfulness practices on teachers' and students' perceptions of challenge.

The purpose of this study was to explore how students perceived challenge and to examine the effects that mindfulness practices might have on developing comfort with challenge. In this research, mindfulness and the perception of challenge were viewed systemically, empirically, phenomenologically and ethnographically by employing the Integral theory model (Wilber, 2007). Integral theory attempts to consolidate diverse philosophies and theorists into one single framework. It endeavours to pull together a number of separate paradigms into an interconnected network of approaches.

While exploring mindfulness practices it was discovered there was a distinct contrast between two very different approaches to developing mindfulness. The yoga classes were based on Eastern practices, which stemmed mainly from Theravada traditions. This eastern form was taught using a clear scope and sequence outlined within the course syllabus. Yoga practices, meditation, and mindfulness were assessed using formative outcomes-based assessment practices. In contrast, the Natural Science classes used mindfulness approaches that focused more on biophilia, gratitude, circle protocols, and grounding rituals. Many of the mindfulness strategies were designed to enable students to connect more deeply and genuinely to the environment they were learning about and will eventually be caretakers of. Each mindfulness or meditative strategy was purposefully not assessed and was implicitly taught in tandem with the Natural Science program of study.

BACKGROUND

Selected Review of the Literature

The Integral Model

Integral theory was developed by Ken Wilber (Esbjörn-Hargens, 2010; Wilber, 2007, 2012) in an attempt to bring a wide range of theories and thinkers into productive discourse. Wilber proposed to organize all human knowledge and experience in a four-quadrant grid, divided along the axes of *interior–exterior* and *individual–collective*. The resulting *All-Quadrants-All-Levels* (AQAL, pronounced "ah-qwul") model is illustrated in Figure 1.

Each of the quadrants of the AQAL model is also associated with specific modes of inquiry and methodological traditions. Figure 2 illustrates some of the main categories, organized according to whether a phenomenon is examined from *inside* or from *outside*. For example, looking at the lower left quadrant, a hermeneutical study would entail examining one's own cultural situation (i.e., from *inside*), whereas an ethnographic study is more commonly associated with inquiries into other cultures (i.e., from *outside*).

Esbjörn-Hargens (2010) refers to the resulting eight regions as basic "methodological categories." The upper left quadrant contains the individual interior and the methodologies of phenomenology and

Figure 1. Wilber's AQAL model
Adapted from Integral Spirituality by K. Wilber (2006).

	Interior	Exterior
Individual	Consciousness: "What I experience" "I" Subjective realities (e.g. self and consciousness, states of mind, psychological development, mental models, emotions, will.)	Behaviour: "What we do" "It" Objective realities (e.g., brain and organism, visible biology, degrees of activation within body systems.)
Collective	Culture: "What we experience" "We" Intersubjective realities (e.g. shared values, culture and worldview, webs of culture, communication, relationships, norms, boundaries, customs.)	Systems: "What we do" "Its" Intersubjective realities (e.g., social systems and environment, visible social structures, economic systems, educational systems, political order)

Figure 2. Wilber's AQAL model, used to relate different research methodologies
Adapted from Integral Spirituality by K. Wilber (2006).

	Interior	Exterior
Individual	Zone 2 *structuralism* Zone 1 *phenomenology*	Zone 6 *empiricism* Zone 5 *autopoiesis*
Collective	Zone 4 *ethnomethodology* Zone 3 *hermeneutics*	Zone 8 *systems theory* Zone 7 *social autopoiesis*

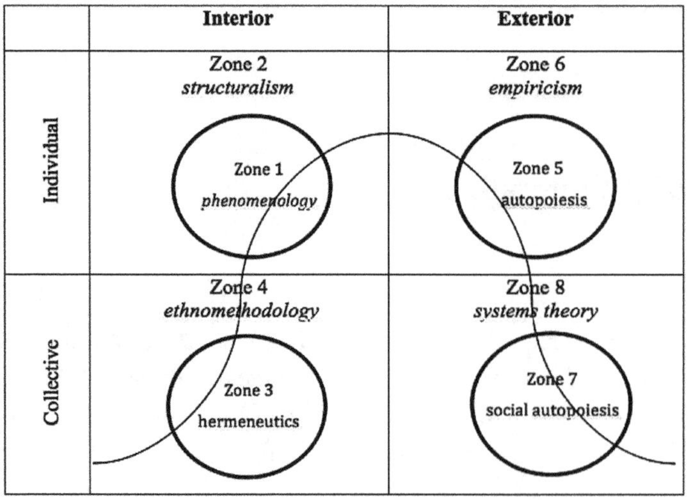

structuralism. The lower left quadrant, which is the quadrant that encapsulates the interior collective, will employ both hermeneutics and ethnomethodology. Autopoiesis and empiricism are used for the exterior of the individual in the upper right quadrant, and the lower right will use social autopoiesis and systems theory. In this chapter, the four quadrants and eight methodological categories of Integral theory are also useful for situating the research question and for expanding upon different aspects of the problem from different internal and external views (as illustrated in Figure 1).

The AQAL model is associated with "Integral methodological pluralism" (IMP), a framework for research in which an event or a phenomenon is understood as a *holon*—"a whole/part or a whole that is part of another whole" (Wilber, 2007, p. 34). IMP might be described as a "holonomic approach" that invites researchers to view a phenomenon within and across eight fundamental perspectives that align with eight fundamental methodologies (Esbjörn-Hargens 2010; Wilber, 2007). Or, in a yet different way, this conceptual framework emphasizes an assortment of fundamental perspectives that align themselves with postmodernist epistemologies and focuses on studying occurrences and knowledge created from the occurrence from all four quadrants (Martin, 2008).

Importantly, IMP involves most major methodologies within contemporary research. The model also aims to coordinate and triangulate different research approaches to support the most nuanced and robust understandings possible. To elaborate, Zone 1 and 2 in the upper left *individual–interior* ("Consciousness") quadrant are associated with phenomenological and structuralist methodologies (Wilber, 2007). Phenomenology is a mode of inquiry used to examine the direct experience of the insides of individual interiors, while structuralism studies the reoccurring patterns of direct experience, or the outsides of individual interiors. Zone 5 and 6 in the upper right *individual–exterior* ("Behavioural") quadrant are associated with phenomena that lend themselves to strategies associated with empiricism and autopoiesis. Autopoiesis is concerned with self-regulating behaviour (the insides of the individual exteriors), while empiricism is employed to investigate observable behaviours that occur on the outsides of individual exteriors (Wilber, 2007). As for Zones 7 and 8 in the lower right *collective–exterior* ("Systems") quadrant, these zones are, according to Esbjorn-Hargens (2010), associated with social-autopoiesis and systems theories. Their associated methodologies are used to explore self-regulating dynamics in systems (the insides of collective exteriors), and the functional-fit of parts within the observational whole (the outsides of the collective exteriors). Finally, Zones 3 and 4 in the lower left *collective–interior* ("Cultural") quadrant are affiliated with hermeneutics and cultural anthropology. These methodologies explore intersubjective understanding, or the insides of collective interiors, and recurring patterns of mutual understanding, or the outsides of collective interiors (Wilber, 2007).

Notably, the model is not intended to be a simple "sum" of perspectives and methodologies. Considered holistically, Integral ways of knowing transcend and include ideas held within each quadrant. It is precisely this quality that draws one to the framework, as it allows location and elaboration on research interests. The research questions from this study have been placed within the different quadrants which are illustrated briefly in Figure 3.

Mindfulness and Challenge in the Lower Right ("Systems") Quadrant

The lower right quadrant is the systems quadrant in which societal norms, expectations, and embedded practices are situated. The view from this quadrant enables the researcher to understand the inside (autopoietic systems) and outside (systems theory) of the exterior collective (Wilber, 2007). Recent events

Figure 3. An initial attempt to use the AQAL model to locate and elaborate my research interests
Adapted from Integral Spirituality by K. Wilber (2006).

	Individuality		
Interior	Consciousness Quadrant 1) Phenomenological view of challenge	Behavioural Quadrant 1) Empirical research about growth mindset 2) Empirical research on mindfulness practice	**Exterior**
	Cultural Quadrant 1) Scaffolding used within mindful classroom 2) Implementation of mindfulness practices in classroom	(Systems) Quadrant 1) Rise of Mindfulness practices within Canadian Society 2) Focus in Alberta on student engagement 3) Outcomes Based Assessment	
	Communality		

that might be located within this quadrant include the rise of the mindfulness movement, provincially mandated movement towards competencies-based understanding, and the crisis in student engagement throughout the province of Alberta.

Mindfulness in Western Culture

Maturana and Varela (1987) characterized autopoietic systems as organizations that define, maintain and reproduce themselves. Communication is the main element within a social system, this system is self-replicating and cannot exist outside of the network. Humans are another component of the social system and, since they are the source of the communication, they are then considered an essential internal component of the system (Fuchs & Hofkirchner, 2009). Communication around mindfulness has now entered into local school academic and social communication and has become a strong part of the vernacular in many areas of the larger community (Brown & Gerbarg, 2009).

The topic of mindfulness practices is centuries old and has a solid place in many different cultural, spiritual and religious practices. It is starting to gain traction within the secular world through its connection to social and societal well-being. The popularization of mindfulness has been associated with shifts in application, as understandings of mindful practices have adapted and changed from a deep religious and spiritual connection to a more secular, life-based practice. People are using mindfulness practices to enhance relationships, inform career decisions, and strengthen personal bonds with the social community around them. Secular benefits of mindfulness practices greatly benefit the organizations that embrace the practice (Weick & Putnam, 2006).

Connections between neuroscience and the benefits of meditation have boosted the popularity of mindfulness within Western society. In particular, greater attention has been given to this type of practice since the Dalai Lama was invited to the scientific conversation and allowed studies to be coordinated with the Buddhist masters who had had more than ten thousand hours of mindful meditative practice (Ricard, Lutz & Davidson, 2014). Just as any practice that continually stimulates areas of the brain, mindfulness uses and therefore cultivates areas within the brain that control self-perception and self-regulation. Evidence that meditation changes the structure of the brain is now supported through the field of neuroplasticity (Brown & Gerbarg, 2009). Mindfulness practices have been connected to salutary effects on the mind and the body (Bodhi, 2000). As a result of this empirical research, mindfulness strategies have begun to garner support within educational, medical, sociological and scientific communities. Brown and Ryan (2003) state that mindfulness practices have spread beyond, but not away from, primarily spiritual and religious communities.

Cognitive and intellectual engagement has been a provincial and jurisdictional goal within the setting of this research study. Rotgans and Schmidt (2011) define cognitive engagement as the ability and willingness to take on presented learning tasks. In their definition of cognitive engagement, Walker, Greene, & Mansell (2006) also include the level of effort students are willing to put forth, and the amount of resiliency they have while engaged within the task itself. Conventionally, cognitive engagement has been measured through a collection of stable traits; however, Rotgans and Schmidt (2011) propose that cognitive engagement is effected by context and learner autonomy and empowerment.

Developing broad-based competencies as required by the aforementioned change in curricular requirements in Alberta, pushes educators to prepare their classroom environments with the goal of ensuring students are well supported as they engage in situations that provoke higher order thinking. To do this effectively, the educator must also attend to fostering internal character traits that enable students to have the academic and emotional stamina to work through each challenging learning task. Attempting to develop the outlined competencies without attending to and nurturing qualities such as tenacity and resilience could be self-defeating. Educators must first build the scaffolding within the student to equip them for the paradigm shift in systemic educational goals.

Considerable research has been conducted on developing resilience and perseverance within a school based learner. Notably, Duckworth et al. (2011) defined resilience as the ability to embrace challenges, stay the course, and not get discouraged. Shechtman, DeBarger Dornsife, Rosier and Yarnall (2013) indicate that resilience is one of the most important qualities for a student to acquire. Deconstructing resilience quickly leads one to understand a student's personal mindset, which is one of the central components of this attribute. Dweck (2009) has identified, defined and illustrated two different types of personal mindsets. Growth mindset is the belief that intelligence can be developed, and that challenges and setbacks are essential to the process of learning. As Mercer and Ryan (2009) state, mindset is not a simple dichotomy and can be highly domain specific. Mindfulness practices could be helpful in fostering self-regulation necessary for creating consistency in growth mindset across many different domains.

Educators are moving to more progressive spaces in understanding of how to prepare students to navigate their future experiences. Building competencies rather than skills through the creation of learners with growth mindsets pushes researchers to seek strategies to help prepare competent students. The strategy proposed by this research was to examine how different mindfulness practices were used within two high school class based settings and the impact they had on students' perceptions of challenge.

Within the educational system in Alberta there is a push towards a more competency-based curriculum. This movement is in response to the understanding that current post-secondary and work environments are too complex to try to navigate with a skills-based curriculum. There has also been a noted decline in student engagement, which started to appear with middle school students and continued to decline throughout high school. It has been concluded that, for student engagement to increase, students need to be engaged in new ways. Problem-based, child-centered experiences have been proposed to re-engage the student and make the student the central agent of their learning (Willms, Friesen & Milton 2009). Such experiences would require the student to become more comfortable with dissonance within learning environments. Finally, mindfulness is becoming more understood and embraced within many different communities within the Canadian classroom. These systemic occurrences of Western culture embracing mindfulness and the call for deeper engagement within the student learner are situated in the lower right quadrant and provide a solid place to observe the need for mindfulness practices to foster growth mindset.

Mindfulness and Challenge in the Upper Right ("Behavioural") Quadrant

Having outlined the systemic supports and barriers to mindfulness and growth mindset, it is important to now compare and connect the behavioural upper right quadrant. This quadrant has historically been the heart of most educational research. Human responses to interventions and stimuli are measured, analysed, and reported within the upper right. It is beneficial for this study to examine the information within this quadrant because it provides the behavioural evidence from which the phenomena of mindset, challenge, and mindfulness extend. Within this quadrant, research about how to measure growth mindset is discussed. Three different mindfulness scales indicating the level a person has reached are explained. Finally, a mindset scale is discussed in relationship to student achievement.

Measurement of Mindfulness

Mindfulness is considered to be a flexible state of being aware of the present moment while also being able to understand new content and contexts. It refers to a level of consciousness that moves the individual away from autopilot and enables him/her to have clarity and perspective (Langer, 1989). Insights can be directed inward and outward and can influence the focus of the meditation. Whether the insight comes from an inward or outward source of stimuli, insight has an influence on the brain and how it understands different events (Brown & Ryan, 2003). The Mindfulness and Attention Awareness Scale (MAAS) has been used to measure focus and awareness (Bruin, Zijlstra, Bonne, Van de Weijer-Bergsma, & Bögels,, 2011). This scale is considered to be limited in that it does not allow for the measurement of other aspects of mindfulness, such as non-judgemental attitude, acceptance, insight, or dis-identification (Brown & Ryan, 2003). The Toronto Mindfulness Scale (TMS) is another scale that has been developed to measure one's level of mindfulness after being engaged in meditation. The scale is made up of ten different items to help differentiate between individuals who have meditated and individuals who did not engage in meditative practices (Shapiro, Astin, Bishop & Cordova 2005). Finally, the Kentucky Inventory of Mindfulness Scale (KIMS) relies on a conceptualization of mindfulness as applied in Dialectical Behavioral Therapy (DBT). KIMS is made up of thirty-nine separate items that are organized into four different scales.

These are only a few of the different mindfulness scales that are currently being used however, these scales are the most predominately mentioned when looking at the subject of overcoming challenge and becoming tenacious or resilient through the use of mindfulness practices. Since this study is concerned with the phenomenon of challenge, these three particular scales are the most conducive to measuring and analyzing this particular area of inquiry.

Standardized Academic Achievement and Mindset

Looking beyond the measurement of mindfulness, it would be prudent to look at the standardized level of student achievement and its connection to mindset. Blackwell et al. (2007) examined students transitioning into Grade 7 who were given a baseline assessment measuring their level of fixed or growth mindset. The 373 students were then monitored using summative math tests throughout the next two years. The students with growth mindset on average started to outperform the students who had a fixed mindset by an average by 8% each year (Dweck, 2010). Grant and Dweck (2003) studied college student achievement within a pre-med organic chemistry class. The researchers used math SAT scores for an assessment baseline to enable an examination of the influence that fixed or growth mindset had on the students' success in organic chemistry throughout the year and on the final exam. Students who had a fixed mindset struggled more to recover from a poor grade than students with a growth mindset. These results were tracked by questionnaires and by analysis of subsequent assignments and quizzes. This research creates a clear connection between growth mindset and student achievement.

Blackwell et al. (2007) also found that mindset theory interventions need to be customized to be successful. The messages must be precise and pinpoint how a certain mindset affects students in certain specific contexts. Dweck (2006) cautions against large group interventions, suggesting that messaging cannot come in the form of a blanketed approach. Although providing lectures about neuroscience and the brain's potential to change is valuable information, these presentations are not to be confused with actual intervention. The intervention occurs when people's characteristics, which are based in the brain, have the potential to be developed (Yeager & Walton, 2011). It would be highly ineffective to scale up and create a generic system-wide program consisting only of information packages or workshops regarding neurology of the brain and growth mindset (Yeager & Walton, 2011).

Yeager and Dweck (2012) also suggest that mindset interventions need to focus the message on how mindset is directly affecting the student within their specific context. The student must also be able to use personalized strategies to assist in internalizing the message quickly. However, Yeager and Dweck (2012) have also discussed how implicit theory interventions could be delivered on a larger scale if they were customized for different student populations. Gathering data about the specific goals and challenges within a particular learning community would be necessary before planning and implementing any larger scale intervention. The people facilitating the mindset intervention also need to have a solid understanding of the underlying psychology that the interventions are trying to instil and, therefore, partnerships would need to be established in order for interventions to truly work (Yeager & Walton, 2011).

Viewing mindfulness and mindset from the upper right confirms that there are tools for measuring both of these phenomena. However, there are no measures that directly connect the two. The tools previously discussed measure the four different mindfulness skills of observation, description, attention, and non-judgmental awareness, and these tools connect mindfulness to stress-reduction, and stress-reduction to student achievement. Measurements and studies that connect mindset to student achievement have also been discussed. These established measurements for mindset and mindfulness have been helpful in enabling researchers to use quantitative empirical data to validate their results (Brown & Ryan, 2003; Bruin, Zijlstra, Bonne, Van de Weijer-Bergsma, & Bögels,, 2011; Shapiro, Astin, Bishop & Cordova 2005). This study, which examines students' perceptions of challenge and how different attitudes toward mindfulness training impact their personal perceptions, was primarily situated within the two left quadrants. However, there was merit to also viewing the study's findings through the upper right to investigate the limits or possibilities of these quantitative tools to assist in the creation of sustainable mindfulness practice, which may have long-term benefits for the student.

Mindfulness and Challenge in the Upper Left ("Consciousness") Quadrant

Moving into the upper left, mindfulness practices and growth mindset were viewed through a phenomenological lens. This is where personal thoughts, perceptions, judgments, and emotions are most naturally situated. This quadrant highlights how students perceive challenge and the role it plays within their learning. Personal narratives were investigated after engaging in mindfulness practices. The research within this quadrant was essential because it sits at the heart of the concept of mindset and is the historic location of mindfulness.

Mindfulness Practices

Mindful practice have not been extensively explored and supported inside the curriculum of Western schooling. Albrecht, Albrecht and Cohen (2012) argue that one reason for this lack of support is that vague definitions of mindfulness are often left to personal interpretation, which in turn contributes to discomfort concerning the implementation of mindfulness within school-based settings. There are many definitions of mindfulness; however, some of the following are conducive when bridging mindfulness to growth mindset. Brown and Gerbarg (2009) propose that mindfulness is a way to assist in perceiving reality more lucidly in order to build an enhanced understanding of oneself and the surrounding environment, which will help one reach fulfillment. Mindfulness is a deliberate practice to move beyond embedded habits of the mind and become free of false perception; as a result, one can construct past and future experience in the present moment (Holland, 2004). Kabat-Zinn (2003) described mindfulness as paying attention in a particular way, in the present moment, non-judgmentally. Mindfulness can be operationally defined as the self-regulation of attention towards present-moment experience, complemented by an enquiring, open, and accepting stance. A definition more related to education describes mindful practice as *building habits of the mind* (Roeser, Skinner, Beers & Jennings, 2012). These habits enable one to gather data through the use of all senses, to be aware of and reflect on one's experience in an unprejudiced manner, to be adaptable when problem solving, and to control one's emotion.

Looking at themes and patterns invoked within these different definitions, one could settle on the understanding that mindfulness is purposeful, present-mindedness supported by past and future to help build deeper understanding of oneself and the surrounding environment. Mindfulness practice therefore is a perfect fit for developing student growth mindset, as it enables the student to embrace challenge and discredit false perceptions of their personal abilities. However, selecting operational methods for using mindfulness in the classroom is a daunting task for someone new to this process.

Rybak (2013) investigated how to acquire a sense of wellbeing through mental practices within a counseling situation. When participants used visualization and focus techniques, they experienced an evolutionary shift in perspective, transitioning from a mode of self-preservation to a broader and more compassion-based perspective. Mindfulness-based training and mental skill development enabled subjects to become more emotionally resilient (Rybak, 2013). Participants were able to form and strengthen new neural connections, which served to recalibrate responses to stimuli, thus creating new and more appropriate responses to uncertainty. Replacing anger with inquisitiveness and willingness enabled participants to see the uncertain situation as a chance to discover and learn something new. Participants flourished by moving towards accomplishing goals and weathering negative events (Rybak, 2013). Becoming coherent with their environment allowed the participant to work in a holistic manner to unite physical, emotional, intellectual and spiritual systems to appropriately address different life circumstances.

The use of modified Mindfulness-Based Stress Reduction (mMBSR) (Flook, Goldberg, Pringer, Bonus & Davidson, 2013) was helpful in building an awareness of the surrounding environment. Teachers benefited both personally and professionally from the reflective discipline that mindfulness practice promotes. Although mindfulness practice is grounded primarily in attention and awareness, Flook et al. (2013) found that it involves many measurable physiological and psychological benefits related to the reduction of physiological stress and increased differentiated activity within the brain. Implementation of the Cultivating Awareness and Resilience in Education (CARE) assisted teachers in dealing with the public pressure to broaden the educational agenda (Jennings, Snowberg, Coccia & Greenberg, 2011). The CARE professional development program used mindfulness practices to positively impact teacher wellbeing, motivational orientation, and feeling of self-efficacy.

Meditation is a specific mindfulness practice associated with decreased stress levels and has been used both inside and outside of the classroom environment. Holland (2004) suggests that a combination of two different forms of meditation (*Samatha* and *Vipassana*) and somatic education involving yoga is a powerful way to connect students to their own minds and bodies. The goal of this process is to embolden students to foster insight and overcome personal challenges. Samatha is a way of "settling the mind in a state of equipoise before applying it to the inquiry into the nature of reality" (Wallace, 2011, p. 89). It emphasizes sustained and controlled concentration as a means of attaining peacefulness and calm. A singular focus on a symbol, chant, or focal point enables a person to quiet the distractions of wandering thoughts and keep a centered focus and sense of momentary calm. Vipassana is similar to Samatha but emphasizes insight through the practice of deep concentration on a present moment (Holland, 2004). As one observes oneself, non-judgmental awareness and acceptance is created. Vipassana also involves the use of a focal point but, unlike Samatha, the focal point serves as a gentle anchor in which other phenomena can be observed and allowed to disperse.

Yoga breathing is another known strategy used to cultivate a point of focus, and can create a bi-directional relationship between the body and the mind. Yoga breathing, referred to as *pranayama,* is considered one of the Eight Limbs of Yoga that was systematized (Brown & Gerbarg, 2009). The life-force, life-air, vital breath—or strong-lung, as translated from Tibetan—creates control over, or expansion of, energy (Sovik, 1999). The manipulation of breath can affect an individual's level of consciousness and create a realization of enlightenment by eliminating karmic airs and creating pathways within the body (Brown & Gerbarg, 2009). The use of purposeful in and out breathing leads to culmination of four frames of reference—the focus on the body, feelings, mind, and mental qualities—and the ability to have clear-knowing and release (Holland, 2004).

Challenge in Developing Mindset

Students with a fixed mindset regard challenge, setbacks, and mistakes as indicators of a lack of cognitive ability (Dweck, 2007). Aronson, Fried and Good (2002) established that students with fixed mindsets respond negatively to under-par summative assessment and performance, and often never recover. Fixed mindsets associate hard work with low intelligence, believing that smart students shouldn't have to work hard to obtain information reference. Gifted learners reduce their effort and interest in learning tasks when they become challenging, and appear disinterested rather than cognitively incapable (Dweck, 2010). In a study by Good, Aronson and Inzlicht (2003), first-year college math students showed that brain activity was only heightened upon discovering whether an answer was correct or incorrect. If the answer was incorrect, students with a fixed mindset demonstrated little brain activity when correctional work was presented, which impeded their ability to learn from their mistakes.

In contrast, students with growth mindsets confront their deficiencies and correct them, as they understand that challenge is a necessary component of learning (Dweck 2007). Good, Aronson and Inzlicht (2003) discovered that brain activity increased significantly during work revisions in learners with growth mindsets, thus affording the learner extended opportunities to understand curricular concepts.

Development of Resilience

Development of a growth mindset influences students' levels of resilience (Dweck, 2006). Blackwell et al. (2007) found that highlighting students' potential to change is essential to developing resiliency. Adolescents internalize the social labels they have acquired and have great anxiety over issues of social status and peer exclusion (Birnbaum, Deeb, Segall, Ben-Eligyah & Diesendruck, 2010). However, Yeager and Walton (2011) indicate that adolescents are not trapped in a fixed mindset; they can be led to accept more of an incremental or growth mindset framework. Tangney, Stuewig and Mashek (2007) found that self-blaming attributions could be replaced with feelings of self-acceptance within a social context by interrupting the student's potentially negative interpretations of the situation.

The theory of "flow" is connected to growth mindset in its relationship to challenge. *Flow* is a theory that explains the phenomena of concentration and deep enjoyment. According to Csikszentmihalyi (1997), a person is considered to have entered into a state of flow when they are completely absorbed within an activity. Flow theory involves many different variables interacting within any environment in which a person is engaging in a task. Egbert (2004) described the flow experience as being "in the zone," "blinking out," or "having the touch." To create an environment conducive to producing flow there must be a balance of skill and challenge, opportunities for intense concentration, clearly-defined tasks, and goal statements (Egbert, 2004). The learner will then want to further explore the experience to analyze the learning and success that occurred throughout the activity. Snyder and Tardy (2001) state that group flow can occur as a dialogue between teacher and student, and individual flow can contribute to the level of group flow within the proper environment. Flow experience can transcend social class (Allison and Duncan 1988). Csikszentmihalyi (1997) suggests that activities that support flow can also transcend culture when activities are personalized to invoke an intense interest within the task.

Mindfulness and Challenge in the Lower Left ("Cultural") Quadrant

Mindfulness in the lower left quadrant is expressed mainly in how teachers create a classroom climate conducive to embracing both mindfulness practices and challenge. According to Dweck (2010), teachers need to ensure they are directly teaching mindset and how the brain has the capacity to change itself to positively impact a learner's mindset. Creating a challenge-based classroom, which embeds vernacular that encourages growth mindset, is discussed in the upper left quadrant. Proper scaffolding in the problem-based classroom is essential to the development of growth mindset.

Direct Teaching of Mindset

Dweck (2010) found that directly teaching students about incremental and entity theories, and how brains are trained by forming new neural pathways, could help develop growth mindset within the student and increase their overall grade point averages. Blackwell et al. (2007) demonstrate that a decline in ability could be reversed with incremental theory intervention through teacher messaging centering on the importance of taking on new challenges. Aronson, Fried and Good (2003) contend that directly teaching students about the theories behind mindset was an effective strategy. Students transitioning into junior high improved in math performance after learning about the expandability of intelligence (Dweck, 2006), while the gender gap in math and reading scores disappeared (Good, Aronson & Inzlicht, 2003). Good, Aronson and Inzlicht (2003) noticed that, after students were taught about the growth mindset, the greatest increases in academic achievement occurred in students who were at the greatest disadvantage or most susceptible to stereotypes. These students were exposed to both the incremental and reattribution intervention, which focus mainly on the malleability of intelligence. Pejorative statements had led to self-blame within these disadvantaged learners, and the development of growth mindset assisted in their understanding that one's cultural situation is variable and can be controlled and changed for the better (Good, Aronson & Inzlicht, 2003). Learners developed a fixed mindset if prone to making social comparisons; teachers could best support learners in their development of growth mindset by prompting the learner to internalize their own personal progress (Schroder, Moran & Donnellan, 2014).

Role of Feedback and Praise

Teacher practices can be conscientiously shaped to emphasize the dynamics of learning and knowing, which helps develop growth mindset. However, teachers and parents can also sometimes enforce entity theory and therefore enforce a fixed mindset with the misuse of praise. Mueller and Dweck (1998) found that praising the effort rather than the ability enabled students to move to a more incremental framework because effort was something they had control of. A classroom structured around emergent knowing—which includes insights into the background of the people behind the knowledge rather than focusing solely on statistically-driven objectified knowledge—is conducive to building a growth mindset within student learners (Davis, Sumara & Luce-Kapler, 2015).

Blackwell, Trzesniewski and Dweck. (2007) emphasize that learning tasks should allow the learner to become the central agent in their learning. The freedom to be creative and depart from structured plans in order to dwell on concepts of personal interest and importance encourages ownership and the formation of an incremental framework of understanding. Students also need to be provided the time to think deeply about questions posed throughout curricular explorations. Teachers should encourage the use of "yet" whenever limitations are identified in a learning situation. Dweck (2006) suggests that this particular word provides a powerful way to help students develop an understanding that learning is a lifelong process worthy of persistent effort. She further asserts that teacher messaging and curricular delivery has a profound impact on students' mindset. Incremental, or growth, mindset can be fostered if the teacher uses purposeful dialect, provides accurate information about brain growth, and focuses the classroom environment upon the idea of personal effort and not ability. The growth mindset is essential for generating authentically new and more deeply oriented academic understanding (Blackwell et al., 2007).

Jonas (2010) recapitulated Friedrich Nietzsche's and Jean-Jacques Rousseau's theories regarding pity and education. Educators altruistically try to alleviate student suffering in the classroom, which Jonas

(2010) deems detrimental to learning. Compassion, according to Jonas (2010), must be carefully employed because compassion can usurp necessary educational suffering that, if left uninterrupted, will effectively build autonomy and confidence within the learner. Jonas (2010) summarizes Nietzsche's stance that knowledge must hurt to be beneficial. Mintz (2008) argues that many educators try to mitigate struggle for their learners and protect students from challenge and tension. Students are rescued too often, which is detrimental to their learning. Within the struggle is the learning, and the movement between the known and unknown is where students internalize their understanding. Both Rousseau and Nietzsche regarded education as a social institution that molds human beings into a prefabricated form rather than fostering self-disciplined courageous and autonomous citizens (Jonas, 2010). Jonas (2010) summarizes Rousseau and Nietzsche's agreement that, to avoid pity, students need to achieve self-mastery, since much of the suffering we find in students is good for them and should not be alleviated—and sometimes should even be promoted. The goal is to see students' difficulties not as moments of suffering but of self-mastery (Mintz 2008)—experiences serving to create an individual who is more autonomous (Jonas, 2010). The goal of an educator must also be to develop self-mastery within herself so she can likewise support the development of the trait in her students.

Liu (2009) suggests that the use of selected teacher-taught strategies and feedback intertwined with instruction is the most effective way to reduce student misunderstanding. Feedback serves to tune and restructure metacognitive and domain-specific knowledge. Finally, Hattie, Biggs and Purdie (1996) note that specific teaching should decrease discrepancies between what is understood and what is not understood, and should situate itself around the processing, regulatory, and self-levels. Dweck (2006, 2007), Yeager and Walton (2011), and Yeager and Dweck (2012) have decidedly contrasted this notion by framing challenge in a different way. Within the traditional feedback chain, challenge is seen through a pathologic lens, promoting the notion that an effective teacher is obligated to successfully expunge any challenge the student might encounter. Hence, challenging work would be seen as a failure by the system and not embraced.

Problem-Based Learning

Students engaged in problem-based learning (PBL) apply their learning to real-world problems. Hmelo-Silver, Duncan, and Chinn (2007) argue that problems should be presented in authentic work-type situations so students can orient their learning on a skeleton of a real issue. Within a PBL-based classroom, tasks are authentic in their design and each task reflects the complexity of the natural environment in which the task would be present. The learner also needs to engage with and commit to the constructed process he used to solve the problem presented (Rotgans & Schmidt, 2011). Each step of the process is designed to challenge the learner's preconceived notions. Students are encouraged to work through a process that tests their ideas against alternate thoughts or solutions. Within PBL-based classrooms, ample opportunities are provided to support reflection and introspection of the knowledge generated and the pathways presented. The teacher is a facilitator of knowledge within a PBL scenario (Schmidt, Rotgans & Yew, 2011), and assists in the activation of previous knowledge to help students discover new understandings, ensuring the problem presented is logically and defensively solved.

Scaffolding Within IL and PBL

Problem-based learning (PBL) and inquiry-based learning (IL) are often mistaken for minimally-guided, constructivist learning. Raes, Schellens De Wever and Vanderhoven (2012) contend that all learning consists of the construction of knowledge, and that problem-based learning is far from laissez-faire. Kirscher, Sweller and Clark (2006) argue that minimally-guided instruction provides little to foster learning. However, Schmidt, Rotgans and Yew (2011) suggest that students in PBL and IL environments learn content as well as subject-specific reasoning skills and practices, which they then apply to real-world problems. This process requires the student to become a sense-maker developing an evidence-based platform on which to communicate their understanding (Belland, Glazewski & Richardson, 2011).

Zone of Proximal Development

The zone of proximal development (ZPD) is defined as "the distance between the actual development level as determined by independent problem solving and the level of potential development as determined through problem solving with adult guidance or in tandem with more capable peers" (Levykh, 2008, p. 83). Vygotsky's theory stands on the belief that learning leads development and where there is no struggle, there is no development (Harland, 2003). ZPD is a complex structure that is not just a sum of its parts. The parts are the participants within the learning equation, their interaction with their environment, and the type of learning tools and mediation used. ZPD is not only limited to the development of an intellectual self, but a conscious self as well (Harland, 2003).

Bodrova and Leong (2007) describe the zone of proximal development as the process of taking students lacking in self-regulation or "the ability to control emotion, attention and physiological responses to stimulation through cognitive and behavioural process and strategies" (Bodrova & Leong, 2007, p. 3). Self-regulation is needed for academic success and for bringing students into a process of mediation that increases their ability to self-regulate through planned opportunities and scaffolding. This process allows self-correcting and intrinsic-motivated improvement to occur, resulting in the creation of students who have more focused attention, deliberate memory, positive task orientation, and cultural tools (Hakkarainen & Bredikyte, 2008).

Vygotsky outlines how a struggle takes place between both the student and her learning environment as well as between her high and lower mental functions (Levykh, 2008). Vygotsky acknowledged the negative and emotionally-laden connection to both forms of struggles or tensions Levykh (2008), but felt that this strained relationship was necessary for growth. Struggles within Vygotsky's theory of proximal development created new formations of intellectual and emotional "super systems," which "penetrate the deepest layers of the culturally developed personality, and emerge in every stage and process of the child's cultural development" (Levykh, 2008, p. 87). These newly-developed capacities allow for higher-order systems that are deeply connected to context and environment and replace simple, elementary functions.

THEORETICAL PERSPECTIVES

Methods

The Research Problem

How mindfulness-based strategies are taught within school-based settings and how they impact students' perceptions of challenge.

The Research Questions

- What perceptions do students have about the role of challenge within their learning process?
- How do teachers teach and create a culture of mindfulness?
- How is student behaviour impacted by mindfulness?
- How does the system influence the development of mindfulness practices within the classroom setting?

Establishing a better understanding of how challenge is perceived by school students and of which mindfulness practices assist in building students' capacity to deal with challenges led me to use a qualitative multi-perspective, pluralistic approach. There are differences between contemporary meanings of "mixed-methods," "multi-methods" (or "multiple methods"), and Integral Methodological Pluralism research. For example, Creswell (2012) defines mixed-methods research as using and mixing both qualitative and quantitative methods in a single study and integrating the data. This definition is offered and often enacted without questioning the nature of the phenomenon under study or the epistemological positioning of the researcher. Similarly, multi-methods research typically involves qualitative and quantitative projects that are already comprehensive on their own, and then brought together to create an understanding of the essential components, which are then triangulated to form a comprehensive whole (Morse, 2003). Both mixed and multi-methods research have different definitions and processes that differ from IMP, in that IMP research study does not use triangulation or data integration, but is paradigmatic; it employs long-standing methodologies and weaves them together through the use of three integrative principles: nonexclusion, unfoldment, and enactment (Rentschler, 2006). In particular, IMP is mindful of diverse sensibilities concerning the nature of knowledge and of claims to truth, seeking not to collapse diverse perspectives into a singular insight but to generate more nuanced understandings by preserving the integrity of insights generated through varied modes of inquiry and interpretation.

To that end, qualitative research methods were used on the personal and cultural left side of the integral model, since these methods were developed to observe and explain happenings in natural or naturalistic settings. This type of research is thus well fitted to this study, which was undertaken in learning settings consisting of real children being asked to engage in real tasks. Data collection techniques included direct interviews, contextual descriptions, and close observation, which allowed the local context to be highlighted, not disregarded (Creswell, Klassen & Plano Clark, 2011).

The right-side exterior quadrants were not explored through a traditional diagnostic tool to test for mindfulness, but rather through the combination of the exterior ethnographic lens combined with the exterior structural lens. The two exterior lenses on the right side of the quadrants enabled me to see student behaviour from an external view.

Figure 4. Aligning research methods to research questions, and locating them in the "Zones" of the AQAL Model.

Question	Methodology	Data Collection and Analysis
What perceptions do students have about the role of challenge?	Phenomenology	Zone #1: Frayer Model and semi-structured interviews.
What perceptions do students have about the role of challenge?	Structuralism	Zone #2: In-depth phenomenological interviewing of participants focusing on past and present experience with the phenomenon. This will help to establish the essential experience with the phenomenon.
How can teachers embed mindfulness within scaffolding practices to foster comfort with challenge?	Hermeneutics	Zone #3: Hermeneutic interviews with participants and use of hermeneutic circle.
How can teachers embed mindfulness within scaffolding practices to foster comfort with challenge?	Ethnomethodology	Zone #4: Ethnographic observation and description and conversation analysis.

This research approach also permitted me to juxtapose the complementary ubiquity of certain factors involved within the known phenomena, and to search for crucial patterns of association of previously unknown processes and the range of their effects (Creswell et al., 2011). Methodologies were not siloed but cross-referenced in order to purposefully use the strengths of each associated method. The integration of data was essential within this study, and the desire to integrate this data was inspired by Wilber's integral pluralistic attitude. Qualitative research attitudes within this study also placed more emphasis on subjective experiences in social contexts, allowing more insight into how people think and feel about circumstances while avoiding passing judgment about whether the feelings are correct or valid (Creswell & Plano Clark, 2007).

By way of overview of methodologies that oriented and informed this research, Figure 4, outlines and connects research questions with established research methodologies and the associated methods that were employed.

Limitations and Delimitations

This study contained various limitations that were consistent with the multi-method research design chosen. The left side quadrants were mainly employed, which do not include empirical and systemic research. In an attempt to minimize the impact of this purposeful exclusion of the right quadrants by using those quadrants as informative speculative areas through which future research around challenge and mindfulness can be conducted. The scope of this study focused primarily on mindfulness-based classrooms within a high school implementing many of the high school re-design components. This type of learning environment readily presented mindfulness and challenge, making it a fruitful environment for research into this particular phenomena.

EXPLORING THE ISSUES

Figure 5 summarizes the research findings within the four-quadrant framework.

Figure 5. Research findings in quadrants

SUBJECTIVE	OBJECTIVE
What perceptions do students have about the role of challenge within their learning process? • Students reported their experience with challenge was necessary and that academic challenge took time and caused stress and anxiety. • Students connected mindfulness strategies to a positive change in perception challenge • Students increased their amount of mindfulness terminology	How is student behaviour impacted by mindfulness? • Students increase mindfulness vocabulary • Students learned different mindfulness techniques • Students in a classroom that used outcomes based assessment developed more mindfulness strategies
INTERSUBJECTIVE	INTEROBJECTIVE
How do teachers teach and create a culture of mindfulness? • Use of gratitude journals • Mindfulness meditation • Developing a Yoga practice • Learning about the historical background of Yoga and mediation • Discussing the importance of challenge • Use of outdoor environment • Use of breath work • Cultivating attention • Create a slower paced classroom • Assess four mindfulness skills	How does the system influence the development of mindfulness practices within the classroom setting? • Western secular culture restricted some historical Eastern mindfulness practices from being used • Traditional provincial assessment reporting practices caused program Yoga program attrition • Outcomes based assessment practices developed more mindfulness skills

LL Quadrant Themes and Discussion

Examining mindfulness through the LL interior and exterior cultural zones uncovered some tensions between the two different classroom cultures. The ethnographic study revealed many similarities between the two classrooms. Long introductions into classroom work, intentional language development, use of gratitude journals, and the use of outdoor learning spaces were some of the practices shared by both Yoga and Natural Science classrooms. The differences between the two classrooms outweighed the similarities, and were mainly marked by how purposefully mindfulness was taught. Within Yoga, mindfulness practices were outlined, scaffolded and assessed based on explicitly-stated curricular outcomes. The students also engaged in mindfulness activities more frequently and with longer duration in Yoga compared to Natural Science.

Hermeneutic interviews revealed different cultural themes, which were discussed by both teacher and student participants. These interviews uncovered the three different themes of attention, slowing down, and the celebration of challenge. Attention and the celebration of challenge were commonly and continually discussed, and had associated tasks and activities. Slowing down was a large theme because both classes used such a different paces than other classes. The teachers also continually discussed why slowing down was important and how they purposefully implemented a slow pace introduction.

Where the tensions lie are in the lack of differences within the hermeneutic interview responses. The pattern of responses and themes that emerged were not vastly different from one classroom culture to the next, bearing in mind that Yoga was taught with the explicit intent to systematically develop mindfulness skills, and Natural Science was aimed at developing an understanding of environmental conservation and stewardship. This contrast might prompt one to conclude there would be a significant difference in the participants' personal experiences across the two cultural climates. However, that was not the case. This issue becomes more amplified when adding in phenomenological and structuralistic analysis within the UL quadrant.

UL Quadrant Themes and Discussion

The main focus of the UL was the examination of how participants perceived challenge. The themes that emerged from this question were that challenge takes time, is necessary, and can cause stress and anxiety. Tensions appeared within the UL, especially within the student participants. Both teacher and student participants discussed the importance of having challenge; however, they reported to be concerned with how much time it took to overcome challenge, which was cited as the biggest source of stress. This gave the impression that the importance of challenge never really moved beyond a rhetorical level, in particular with the student participants. The students within both classroom cultures had developed a similar base of language; however, the Natural Science students seemed to attach their language more to natural spaces and real world and work experiences. This is somewhat surprising since the Yoga students had much more exposure to mindfulness strategies, but they didn't seem to have a practical base to attach it to. This could be attributed to the inability of Eastern-based practices to have traction within Western-based contexts.

On the matter of the contrasts between "Eastern and "Western" sensibilities Nisbett (2003) has discussed how the foundation of Western thought has a more developed sense of personal agency. This sense of individualism impacts socioeconomic and cultural factors, which in turn affects cognitive habits. Specifically, such habits of thought more strongly support tendencies toward individuality and objectivity within Western contexts. Consequently, there are stronger tendencies to notice and describe objects in isolation – tendencies that Nisbett has associated with an epistemology oriented toward scientific, positivistic approaches toward observing and theorizing about objects and their properties. Studies within school-based settings have not been immune from these tendencies. In contrast, Eastern ecosystems of thought arose in and contributed to societies that enact greater emphases on interdependent networks, social relationships, and relationships between objects, which gave rise to views and philosophies that invoke holism, cycles, recursions, change and flux while embracing dualities and conflicts within thought and reason.

These contrasts between the East and West cultural sensibilities were not conscientiously attended to in either classroom and therefore implicit tensions developed. Quite notably mindfulness practices, which are embedded within Eastern Yoga practices were not readily accessible to the high school student participants who embodied Western scientific ways of knowing and being. Therefore, ushering mindfulness into high school settings isn't the simple process of combining Eastern practices into Western subject matters. Both complementary and conflicting foundations of thought and would need to be consciously examined and understood before a successful fusion of sensibilities and practices could occur.

UR Quadrant Themes and Discussion

The UR quadrant explores student behaviours in an objective way. Student behaviour was observable through the exterior view of both the individual-focused UL ("Consciousness") and collective-focused LL ("Cultural") quadrants. The analysis of language unveiled distinctive and observable student behaviour.

The students in both classes demonstrated an increase in the number of overlapping mindfulness terms such as breath, focus, and consciousness within student interviews and within the level of description connected to the terminology. Throughout the term it was evident within the interview transcripts that students were discussing how they were transferring the mindfulness skills outside of the classroom and using them within real life.

The other observable behaviour was connected to the four different mindfulness skills of observation, description, attention, and non-judgmental awareness. Although students from both classes discussed observation, description and attention, only students within the Yoga classrooms discussed and used the term of non-judgmental awareness. Non-judgmental awareness is considered to be an essential skill within mindfulness and it has been defined as the ability to accept or allow without judgment, to allow reality to be as it is without judging, avoiding, changing, or escaping it (Kabat-Zinn, 2003). Brown and Ryan (2010) have connected non-judgmental awareness to a decrease in depression, stress, and anxiety; it is also the basis of many multifaceted therapies such as Mindfulness Based Stress Reduction (MBSR); Mindfulness Based Cognitive Therapy (MBCT); Dialectical Behaviour Therapy (DBT) and Acceptance and Commitment Therapy (ACT).

Both Natural Science and Yoga are part of Career and Technology Strategies, in which all students need at least 10 credits to meet graduation requirements; therefore, these courses are considered to have an equal amount of status since neither course is a core or considered to be more important than the other. Another notable behavior was the rate of student retention within the course. All student participants in Natural Science 10 had the intention of continuing in Natural Science 20 and 30. In comparison, only a third of the Yoga participants continued with Yoga 25/35. Yoga participants indicated they mainly enrolled in Yoga to help develop strategies to deal with feeling anxious and overwhelmed. The participants who were not registering in Yoga 25/35 did report an increase in their understanding of mindfulness strategies, however they did not feel that was enough of a reason to register in the course again.

When interviewed, the Natural Science 30 students stated they chose the Natural Science course first when completing their course selection, and three different Natural Science 30 participants were going to pursue a career related to Natural Science. The students within Natural Science discussed one of the reasons they continued to be involved with Natural Science was because of the "grounding effect" it had on them. The student participants indicated they also continued with Natural Science all three years because of the connection they felt with the natural environment around them, which helped build perspective about what was important and how to manage their feelings of being overwhelmed or anxious.

LR Quadrant Themes and Discussion

The LR quadrant explores the impact of the third person plural—viewing a phenomenon through the societal lens by expanding the view to include more complex systems (Wilber, 2007). Viewing the phenomenon through the LR ("Systemic") permitted observation on how the system connected, impacted, interrupted, and challenged research findings within the other three quadrants. There are many different systemic influences that could be considered within the LR ("Systemic") quadrant; however, there was a decision to focus on the three main systems that have the largest impact on teaching and learning within a Calgary public classroom. These systems are: overall public views of modern day Western society, the Alberta Ministry of Education, and the Calgary Board of Education.

The Relationships Between Findings in Each Quadrant

The dialogue between the left quadrant findings and the LR ("Systemic") influences gave rise to many new insights into findings. There was some naivety around the amount of impact the systemic view from the LR ("Systemic") had, but, after examining these findings, there was a realization that the system had been extremely present from the beginning. You can liken a systemic influence to an odourless, colourless gas; even though you can't really see or touch it, it can have a massive impact. Structuring my interview sessions around the students and teachers' schedules should have been the first hint of the deeply entrenched systemic influences. Students and teachers had different cycles of when they were extremely busy or stressed, and these periods were dependent on deadlines and reporting measures. Their responses and demeanour changed within these different times, and, therefore, the system was present.

The UL ("Consciousness") and LL ("Cultural") exterior view findings revealed similarity within the language of mindfulness but a difference in the true understanding of mindfulness strategies. The LR ("Systemic") enabled an understanding that this is probably partially due to the absence of outcomes-based assessment. Without using the power of purposeful task design and formative assessment practices, the learning can be restricted. This is not to say learning is only possible if the subject is held within a program of study. But it is important to be deliberate with task design and assess what the students know and what they will need next to move forward in their understanding.

UL ("Consciousness") interior findings of student perception of challenge revealed that there were tensions within the three themes. The LR ("Systemic") view of the influence of provincial reporting brought forth that the reporting practices and the publication of results has created some push and pull between the common ideology of students and the external expectations society places on them. Students knew they needed to embrace challenge but were stressed and anxious if it took too much time or if it would affect their marks.

The LL ("Cultural") findings uncovered mindfulness culture within the classroom. The culture created within both classrooms was deliberate and well received by both teacher and student participants. Accountabilities from the LR ("Systemic") did impact this culture. There were parameters within which the teaching of Eastern meditation and Yoga practice needed to sit. Within a secular system, the teaching *of* religion is permitted; however, actually teaching religious practices is not. This meant that discussions of the historic roots of Yoga and meditation practices were very guarded and redirected when needed.

IMPLICATIONS

Implications From the UI ("Consciousness") Quadrant: Play-Based Challenge and Assessment

The research question posed within the UL ("Consciousness") quadrant connected the perception of challenge to the structures present within the mindfulness classroom. The research findings indicated that both teachers and students needed to experience challenge to be able to build understanding and work towards mastery in all aspects of the educational process. However, participants expressed an awareness of time and conflicting ideas of necessity and linear time constraints. Stress and anxiety were also emotions involved with the experience of challenge.

Play-based Challenge

Serious play is movement coming from the innovator and maker communities. It is a way of using play to create solutions according to a design challenge. While engaged in the challenge, participants use the "how might we" question to guide their work and help increase communication, problem-solving, and innovative solutions. Bringing together mindfulness and a play-oriented approach to challenge could provide possibilities for developing more comfort with challenge through exposure to environments that promote risk taking in low-risk environments.

Implication From the LI ("Cultural") Quadrant: Curriculum Re-Design and Curricular Delivery Models

Currently, in high school the only curriculum that has outcomes that promote mindfulness strategies are Yoga and the CALM (Career and Life Management) curriculum. Mindfulness is not currently within the CALM curriculum, but self-regulation, stress management, and self-awareness currently reside within the personal wellness resources section of this particular curriculum, and mindfulness is essential to developing these skills. The issue is that there are not enough students enrolled in Yoga to have a large impact on the entire school population. However, every Alberta student needs to acquire three credits in CALM to receive their high school diploma. This is a positive factor in promoting mindfulness within an actual program of study; unfortunately, most of the student population takes CALM online over a two-week period without any opportunity to discuss what they are learning or engage in any hands-on learning opportunities. When taught face-to-face, CALM is often not considered to have as much priority as other subjects and is often taught from prescribed lesson plans that have not been currently revised, personalized, or informed by current assessment strategies.

Curriculum Re-Design

Alberta is re-designing all curriculum, which is an excellent opportunity to ensure mindfulness is introduced at an early age. Currently, mindfulness is being written into the wellness curriculum from Kindergarten to Grade 12. The issue of how to change the perception of importance of the wellness curriculum still remains. Often schools will silo health curriculum into one-off presentations or into a single period at the end of the week. A few questions arise from this dilemma. The goal of this focus is to ensure that all subjects are teaching disciplinary literacy and numeracy to enable recursion and increase student achievement within these subject areas. Personal growth and well-being is one of the competencies, which provides an opportunity for all subjects to teach this particular competency through their specific lens. However, it is not yet known how the competencies will be assessed within report card data, and thus it might not be something teachers will pick up within the front matter. Investigating the best delivery model for wellness—whether it be a cross-curricular approach or a separate subject that is considered as important as the core curriculums—should be considered an important task. Looking at the impact of extending a wellness curriculum through to Grade Twelve would be something important to investigate. Finally, another robust question concerns how students can better cultivate a practice of mindfulness if it is written within the new wellness curriculum from Kindergarten to Grade Twelve.

CONCLUSION

The analysis of findings led me to the conclusion that students' perceptions of challenge are characterized by different themes, which cause tensions. These tensions however can be minimized within a culture of mindfulness. Explicitly teaching the skills of mindfulness helps to create a better understanding of the practice and assessment is a necessary component within a mindfulness classroom. Students enjoy a culture of attention and slowing down within their day and the discussion of the importance of challenge helps students better understand what it is and how to approach it.

REFERENCES

Albrecht, N. J., Albrecht, P. M., & Cohen, M. (2012). Mindfully teaching in the classroom: A literature review. *Australian Journal of Teacher Education, 37*(12), 1–14. doi:10.14221/ajte.2012v37n12.2

Allison, M., & Duncan, M. (1988). Women, work, and flow. In M. Csikszentmihalyi & I. Csikszentmihalyi (Eds.), *Optimal experience* (pp. 118–137). Cambridge, UK: Cambridge University Press. doi:10.1017/CBO9780511621956.007

Aronson, J., Fried, C. B., & Good, C. (2002). Reducing the effects of stereotype threat on African American college students by shaping theories of intelligence. *Journal of Experimental Social Psychology, 38*(2), 113–125. doi:10.1006/jesp.2001.1491

Belland, B. R., Glazewski, K. D., & Richardson, J. C. (2011). Problem-based learning and argumentation: Testing a scaffolding framework to support middle school students' creation of evidence-based arguments. *Instructional Science, 39*(5), 667–694. doi:10.100711251-010-9148-z

Birnbaum, D., Deeb, I., Segall, G., Ben-Eliyahu, A., & Diesendruck, G. (2010). The development of social essentialism: The case of Israeli children's inferences about Jews and Arabs. *Child Development, 81*(3), 757–777. doi:10.1111/j.1467-8624.2010.01432.x PMID:20573103

Blackwell, L. S., Trzesniewski, K. H., & Dweck, C. S. (2007). Implicit theories of intelligence predict achievement across an adolescent transition: A longitudinal study and an intervention. *Child Development, 78*(1), 246–263. doi:10.1111/j.1467-8624.2007.00995.x PMID:17328703

Bodhi, B. (2000). *A comprehensive manual of Abhidhamma*. Seattle, WA: Buddhist Publication Society.

Branch, J., & Oberg, D. (2004). *Focus on inquiry*. Alberta, Canada: Alberta Learning.

Brown, R. P., & Gerbarg, P. L. (2009). Yoga breathing, meditation, and longevity. *Annals of the New York Academy of Sciences, 1172*(1), 54–62. doi:10.1111/j.1749-6632.2009.04394.x PMID:19735239

Bruin, E., Zijlstra, B., Van de Weijer-Bergsma, E., & Bögels, S. (2011). The Mindful Attention Awareness Scale for Adolescents (MAAS-A): Psychometric Properties in a Dutch Sample. *Mindfulness, 2*(1), 201–211. doi:10.100712671-011-0061-6 PMID:21909342

Creswell, J. W. (2012). *Educational research: Planning, conducting, and evaluating quantitative and qualitative research*. New York, NY: Pearson.

Csikszentmihalyi, M. (1997). *Finding flow: The psychology of engagement with everyday life.* Basic Books.

Davis, B., Sumara, D., & Luce-Kapler, R. (2015). *Engaging minds: Cultures of education and practices of teaching.* Routledge. doi:10.4324/9781315695891

Duckworth, A. L., Grant, H., Loew, B., Oettingen, G., & Gollwitzer, P. M. (2011). Self-regulation strategies improve self-discipline in adolescents: Benefits of mental contrasting and implementation intentions. *Educational Psychology, 31*(1), 17–26. doi:10.1080/01443410.2010.506003

Dweck, C. S. (2009). Even geniuses work hard. *Educational Leadership, 68*(1), 16–20. Retrieved from http://msan.wceruw.org/documents/resources_foreducators/Relationships/Even%20Geniuses%20Work%20Hard.pdf

Egbert, J. (2004). A study of flow theory in the foreign language classroom. *Canadian Modern Language Review, 60*(5), 549–586. doi:10.3138/cmlr.60.5.549

Esbjörn-Hargens, S. (2010). An ontology of climate change. *Journal of Integral Theory and Practice, 5*(1), 143–174. Retrieved from https://foundation.metaintegral.org/sites/default/files/Esbjorn-Hargens_Ontology.pdf

Flook, L., Goldberg, S. B., Pringer, L., Bonus, K., & Davidson, R. J. (2013). Mindfulness for teachers: A pilot study to assess effects on stress, burnout, and teaching efficacy. *Mind, Brain and Education: the Official Journal of the International Mind, Brain, and Education Society, 7*(3), 182–195. doi:10.1111/mbe.12026 PMID:24324528

Friesen, S. (2009). *What did you do in school today?* Toronto, Canada: Canadian Education Association. Retrieved from http://ccl-cca.ca/pdfs/otherreports/WDYDIST_National_Report_EN.pdf

Fuchs, C., & Hofkirchner, W. (2009). *Autopoiesis and critical social systems theory autopoiesis and critical social systems theory.* Academic Press. doi:10.1108/S1877-6361(2009)0000006007

Garrett, N. (1991). Technology in the service of language learning: Trends and issues. *Modern Language Journal, 75*(1), 74–101. doi:10.1111/j.1540-4781.1991.tb01085.x

Grant, H., & Dweck, C. S. (2003). Clarifying achievement goals and their impact. *Journal of Personality and Social Psychology, 85*(1), 541–553. doi:10.1037/0022-3514.85.3.541 PMID:14498789

Hakkarainen, P., & Bredikyte, M. (2008). The zone of proximal development in play and learning. *Cultural-historical Psychology, 4*(4), 2–11. Retrieved from http://psyjournals.ru/en/kip/2008/n4/Hakkarainen_full.shtml

Harland, T. (2003). Vygotsky's zone of proximal development and problem-based learning: Linking a theoretical concept with practice through action research. *Teaching in higher education, 8*(2), 263-272. Retrieved from http://www.researchgate.net/publication/233309078_Vygotsky's_Zone_of_Proximal_Development_and_Problem-based_Learning_Linking_a_theoretical_concept_with_practice_through_action_research

Hattie, J., Biggs, J., & Purdie, N. (1996). Effects of learning skills interventions on student learning: A meta-analysis. *Review of Educational Research, 66*(2), 99–136. doi:10.3102/00346543066002099

Hmelo-Silver, C. E., Duncan, R. G., & Chinn, C. A. (2007). Scaffolding and achievement in problem-based and inquiry learning: A response to Kirschner, Sweller, and Clark. *Educational Psychologist, 42*(2), 99–107. doi:10.1080/00461520701263368

Holland, D. (2004). Integrating mindfulness meditation and somatic awareness into a public educational setting. *Journal of Humanistic Psychology, 44*(4), 468–484. doi:10.1177/0022167804266100

Jonas, M. E. (2010). When teachers must let education hurt: Rousseau and Nietzsche on compassion and the educational value of suffering. *Journal of Philosophy of Education, 44*(1), 45–60. doi:10.1111/j.1467-9752.2010.00740.x

Kirschner, P. A., Sweller, J., & Clark, R. E. (2006). Why minimal guidance during instruction does not work: An analysis of the failure of constructivist, discovery, problem-based, experiential, and inquiry-based teaching. *Educational Psychologist, 41*(2), 75–86. doi:10.120715326985ep4102_1

Langer, E. J. (1989). *Mindfulness*. Boston, MA: Addison-Wesley.

Levykh, M. G. (2008). The affective establishment and maintenance of Vygotsky's zone of proximal development. *Educational Theory, 58*(1), 83–101. doi:10.1111/j.1741-5446.2007.00277.x

Liu, K. R. (2009). *Cooperative communications and networking*. Cambridge, MA: Cambridge University Press.

Martin, J. A. (2008). Integral research as a practical mixed-methods framework. *Journal of Integral Theory and Practice, 2*(3), 155–164. Retrieved from http://www.sunypress.edu/pdf/JITP_Index_Vol1_Vol6.pdf

Maturana, H., Varela, R., & Francisco, J. (1987). *The Tree of Knowledge*. Boston: Shambhala.

Mercer, S., & Ryan, S. (2009). A mindset for EFL: Learners' beliefs about the role of natural talent. *ELT Journal, 64*(4), 436–444. doi:10.1093/elt/ccp083

Mintz, A. (2008). *The labor of learning: A study of the role of pain in education* (Doctoral dissertation). Available from ProQuest Dissertations and Theses Full Text database. (UMI No. 3317653)

Morse, J. M. (2003). Principles of mixed methods and multimethod research design. Handbook of Mixed Methods in Social and Behavioral Research, 1, 189-208.

Mueller, C. M., & Dweck, C. S. (1998). Praise for intelligence can undermine children's motivation and performance. *Journal of Personality and Social Psychology, 75*(1), 33–52. doi:10.1037/0022-3514.75.1.33 PMID:9686450

Nisbett, R. E. (2003). *The geography of thought*. London, UK: Nicholas Brealey.

Raes, A., Schellens, T., De Wever, B., & Vanderhoven, E. (2012). Scaffolding information problem solving in web-based collaborative inquiry learning. *Computers & Education, 59*(1), 82–94. doi:10.1016/j.compedu.2011.11.010

Ricard, M., Lutz, A., & Davidson, R. J. (2014). Mind of the meditator. *Scientific American, 311*(5), 38–45. doi:10.1038cientificamerican1114-38 PMID:25464661

Robinson, K. (2009). Creativity in the classroom, innovation in the workplace. *Interview with Sir Ken Robinson.* Retrieved from http://www.Principalvoices.com/voices/ken-robinson-white-paper.html

Roeser, R. W., Skinner, E., Beers, J., & Jennings, P. A. (2012). Mindfulness training and teachers' professional development: An emerging area of research and practice. *Child Development Perspectives, 6*(2), 167–173. doi:10.1111/j.1750-8606.2012.00238.x

Rotgans, J. I., & Schmidt, H. G. (2011). Cognitive engagement in the problem-based learning classroom. *Advances in Health Sciences Education: Theory and Practice, 16*(4), 465–479. doi:10.100710459-011-9272-9 PMID:21243425

Rybak, C. (2013). Nurturing positive mental health: Mindfulness for wellbeing in counselling. *International Journal for the Advancement of Counseling, 35*(2), 110–119. doi:10.100710447-012-9171-7

Schroder, H. S., Moran, T. P., Donnellan, M. B., & Moser, J. S. (2014). Mindset induction effects on cognitive control: A neurobehavioral investigation. *Biological Psychology, 103,* 27–37. doi:10.1016/j.biopsycho.2014.08.004 PMID:25149141

Shapiro, S. L., Astin, J. A., Bishop, S. R., & Cordova, M. (2005). Mindfulness-based stress reduction for health care professionals: Results from a randomized trial. *International Journal of Stress Management, 12*(2), 164–176. doi:10.1037/1072-5245.12.2.164

Shechtman, N., DeBarger, A., Dornsife, C., Rosier, S., & Yarnall, L. (2013). *Promoting grit, tenacity and perseverence: critical factors for success in the 21st century.* Retrieved from http://www.ed.gov/edblogs/technology/files/2013/02/OET-Draft-Grit-Report-2-17-13.pdf

Snyder, B., & Tardy, C. (2001). That's why I do it: Flow and teachers' values, beliefs, and practices. *ELT Journal, 58*(2), 118–128.

Sovik, R. (1999). The science of breathing: The yogic view. *Progress in Brain Research, 122*(1), 491–505. doi:10.3389/fnhum.2014.00770 PMID:10737079

Tangney, J. P., Stuewig, J., & Mashek, D. J. (2007). Moral emotions and moral behavior. *Annual Review of Psychology, 58*(1), 345–372. doi:10.1146/annurev.psych.56.091103.070145 PMID:16953797

Walker, C. O., Greene, B. A., & Mansell, R. A. (2006). Identification with academics, intrinsic/extrinsic motivation, and self-efficacy as predictors of cognitive engagement. *Learning and Individual Differences, 16*(1), 1–12. doi:10.1016/j.lindif.2005.06.004

Wallace, B. A. (2011). *Minding closely: The four applications of mindfulness.* Boston, MA: Snow Lion Publications.

Weick, K. E., & Putnam, T. (2006). Organizing for mindfulness Eastern wisdom and Western knowledge. *Journal of Management Inquiry, 15*(3), 275-287. doi:291202 doi:10.1177/1056492606

Weick, K. E., & Putnam, T. (2006). Organizing for mindfulness Eastern wisdom and Western knowledge. *Journal of Management Inquiry, 15*(3), 275–287. doi:10.1177/1056492606291202

Wilber, K. (2007). *Integral spirituality.* Boulder, CO: Shambhala Publications.

Willms, J. D., Friesen, S., & Milton, P. (2009). *What did you do in school today? Transforming classrooms through social, academic, and intellectual engagement.* Retrieved from http://www.cea-ace.ca/sites/default/files/cea-2009-wdydist.pdf

Yeager, D. S., & Walton, G. (2011). Social-psychological interventions in education: They're not magic. *Review of Educational Research, 81*(2), 267–301. doi:10.3102/0034654311405999

KEY TERMS AND DEFINITIONS

Behavioral Engagement: It is connected to participation and being involved in social, academic, and extracurricular activities.

Emotional Engagement: It is connected to the positive and negative reactions to the people and physical structures that make up a school setting.

Fixed Mindset: The attitude that intelligence is a fixed trait you are born with and cannot change.

Growth Mindset: The attitude that intelligence is a malleable quality; it has potential that can be developed.

Chapter 10
Promising Futures:
An Integral Exploration of the Futures Thinking of High School Teachers

Roy A. Norris
Louis Riel School Division, Canada

ABSTRACT

Teachers spend their working days preparing young people for the times to come. Teachers also imagine a wide variety of ideas about possible, probable, and preferable futures. This chapter explores how teachers feel and think about the potential futures for themselves and their students, and how teacher perceptions of futures inform their teaching practices. The study sets integral theory as the basis for the methodological pluralism and analytical blending which are sustained throughout this trans-disciplinary study as a whole. The findings show that although high school teachers envision many possible futures, they are most likely to trust shorter term empiric predictions, and they rarely think about futures more than a few years away. Learning more about how often, how deeply, and how optimistically teachers envision possible futures matters because teachers are educating the people who will become adults in all versions of the near futures.

INTRODUCTION

This study explores the many ways that high school teachers imagine what many possible futures could be like, and how their perceptions of the futures are enacted in their lives and their teaching practices. High school teachers are the final teachers that children have before they become young adults, so knowing more about how these teachers think about possible futures and how they present those ideas to students is a research area worth exploring. Research into the ways that high school teachers think about possible futures could aid in understanding how schools adapt and change over time, and why those changes occur more easily for some teachers than for others.

DOI: 10.4018/978-1-5225-5873-6.ch010

Context

In 1997 the Organization for Economic Co-operation and Development (OECD) launched the Schooling for Tomorrow project (SfT) within the Centre for Educational Research and Innovation (CERI) (2010a). The project was launched due to a growing understanding in the late 1990s that the social and economic challenges facing OECD countries required a longer view into potential futures for education systems globally. The advent and uptake of the internet, growing world population and unprecedented social changes were moving at a faster pace than education reforms, and education systems were playing catch up. CERI has continued the work of the SfT project up to the present since the times are still changing at a much faster rate than are schools, and the gap between them is widening.

The site of the research was Riverview Collegiate (pseudonym), a technology-rich school where every student is required to bring a computer every day. This form of technology use is called 1-to-1 (as in, one computer per person), bring your own device (BYOD). 1-to-1 BYOD started at Riverview in 2010, and so far almost no research has been done at Riverview to see how teachers operate in a 1-to-1 BYOD school. My study on teacher perceptions of futures and how these perceptions are enacted within classes helps to provide groundwork for further study into the ways that 1-to-1 BYOD learning is changing teachers, how it is influencing Riverview Collegiate, and the Bison Crocus School Division as well.

Recently Riverview was recognized for the unique quality of the staff dynamic at Riverview Collegiate in the way that 1-to-1 BYOD has rolled out over the first four years. Riverview received a nationally recognized award from a Canadian educational organization in January 2015, which was covered by local media. Teachers at Riverview have accepted and included information technology use in their classes, and pedagogical changes connected to the use of technology have been incremental but steady. This study helps to explore of the habits of mind and perceptions of teachers that are allowing for the steady growth in uptake of technology use at the school.

Purpose

The purpose of this study was to discover how teachers feel and think about the potential futures for themselves and their students, and to explore how teacher perceptions of futures inform and are enacted in their teaching practices.

Significance

Knowing more about what kinds of futures are perceived by teachers may aid in developing programs similar to Riverview's in other contexts, and may also provide an original contribution to the fields of integral theory, change and change management in the educational sector, and futures research in a Canadian educational context. It may also open a wider discourse about the practicality, utility, and further development of integral methodological pluralism (IMP) as a guiding heuristic for multi-methods research. Martin (2008) has already begun the work of clarifying the role of IMP as a multi-method framework, and this study provides further research to compare with Martin (2008) and Esbjörn-Hargens (2008) who have previously employed the IMP approach in multi-method research studies.

Teachers spend the greatest amount of time with students in a school, and teachers' perceptions of futures are continually enacted in their classroom practices. Understanding more about how teachers perceive futures, especially within a school that is known provincially for being forward-thinking and future oriented may help to open the field to further study about the futures for Canadian secondary students.

BACKGROUND

Conceptions of Time and Educational Research on Time and Perception

All people in all cultures are subject to time. Time defines human existence: people think, act, and live within time. Theologians, philosophers, artists, and scientists work within time to try and describe time—to define it, to find its limits, and to measure it out—but their conclusions remain incomplete, and highly contradictory. The ineffable nature of time is aptly summarized by Augustine (397): "What, then, is time? If no one ask [sic] of me, I know; if I wish to explain to him who asks, I know not" (Bk. 11, Ch. 14). The mysteries of time, its essence, its origins, are still baffling in this current age. The crux of these problems is that defining time requires that there be something against which to measure time, but there is no correlative available, for time stands alone.

Although precise and complete *definitions* of time are mercurial, great physicists, writers, and thinkers have developed accurate and helpful *descriptions* of time. Newton described time as a "flow" (Falk, 2008, p. 127) while Einstein, in his theories of general and special relativity, postulated that time itself is changeable—time (and space as well) is relative to the absolute, which is the speed of light, or c. On May 29, 1919 Einstein's theories were tested by measuring the deflection of light from a distant star as it came into close alignment with the Sun during a total eclipse (Falk, 2008, p. 173). General relativity held that the light of the star ought to be deflected, and it was, thus proving general relativity. Einstein, at the age of 40, immediately became, and arguably remains, the world's most famous scientist.

Unfortunately, general and special relativity provide hardly any practical application for understanding the experiential temporality of the human condition. People never move fast enough (compared to c) for relativity to become a concern, so Newton's "flow" is a more pragmatic descriptor for conducting science that is social.

In *Flow: The psychology of optimal experience* (1990), Mihaly Csikszentmihalyi examines sets of activities that bring pleasure to subjects. Pleasurable activities vary greatly, but they all provide subjects with reasonable rigour, a sense of purpose, reward embedded in the process of the task, and a sense of accomplishment upon attaining a goal. Csikszentmihalyi (1990) further asserts that "flow" is the essential antecedent that leads to activities that people perceive as pleasurable.

Eva Hoffman's (2009) summation of flow is "…a sense that time is moving at the right, unforced pace" (p. 184). The flow of time is a subjective experience, and recognizing one's place within the flow of time is a precursor to happiness. The perception of time's flow from the future, to the present, and into the past is subjective, individual, and is ultimately an illusion. In the words of Einstein, as he wrote to the grieving family of his deceased friend Michele Besso: "…the distinction between past, present, and future is only a stubbornly persistent illusion" (as quoted in Calaprice, 2005, p. 73). Even for Einstein himself the physics of relativity was cold comfort when experiencing time's subjective flow, no matter how illusory it is. Einstein's physics trump Newton's, but Newton's perceptions of time as "flow" serve as a pragmatic and workable model of time, particularly time as it is experienced by people.

In her book *Time*, Eva Hoffman (2009) closely examines the subjective perceptions of time that help to define and to order the psychological interiority of the human mind. The mind can expand, shape, mould, recall, reframe, and anticipate time. This interiority gives people the capacity to reason, and helps them to make sense of their experiences. Past, present, and future are forms of time that seem completely undeniable, and somehow more "real" than "unreal."

Individuals and groups can share in their experiences of past, present, and future time, and deeply set social constructs about time form within cultures, as do languages, cultural mores, and cultural beliefs. Perceptions and conceptions of time are deeply embedded in the human psyche, so perceptions and beliefs about time must then also be scrutinized by those in the field of education (Duncheon & Tierney, 2013). It is not enough to assume that subjective perceptions of time are commonly shared within schools, or that these perceptions help to foster, to promote, or to enhance student learning. Students, parents, teachers, and school administrators operate within their own personal perceptions of time, within the range of their shared cultural beliefs about time, and within formalized school systems that stipulate limits of allowable time required for learning. Freire (2014) further points out that all educational practice occurs within a time and space context; learning cannot help but be bound within time and space (Freire, 2014, p.67). Therefore it stands to reason that the conceptions of time that are held by those in power will always dominate the lessons and the learning. Far too much is assumed by educators who go about their work without deeply considering the temporal nature of education and how their own ideas about time influence themselves and their students.

Futures Studies (FS), a History and Introduction

Futures Studies is a multi-disciplinary field of inquiry that draws upon a wide variety of research to consider possible, probable, and preferable (Fein & Hicks 2010) futures for all who live on planet Earth. Those in the field avoid using the colloquial singular term "future" and opt for the plural term "futures" to make clear the plurality of potential futures. The pluralistic understanding of futures studies opens up the territory for a broad spectrum of research forms, including many widely varying conceptual frameworks and methodologies (WFSF, 2002).

People have conceived of the passage of time for millennia and have therefore imagined the times to come, so futures thinking is an old phenomenon. Futures as an academic discourse in its currently recognizable form began to coalesce in the 1960s, arising from within the miasma of the industrial age, two catastrophic world wars, and several decades of futures-infused science fiction, most notably by H.G. Wells. Wells was already calling for the development of a scientific and rigorous study of futures as early as 1902 but it never came to fruition (Wagar, 1983). The murderously chaotic and economically vibrant first half of the 20th Century would have to pass by before anyone paid closer attention to futures studies.

By the beginning of the 1960s futures reached a critical mass in the post-war search for economic stability and social reconstruction. During this time Herman Kahn (1960) was an early futurist who came to prominence as an American war strategist and systems theorist, while in England Dennis Gabor, inventor of the hologram, (1963) was also writing on possible and probable futures.

Conferences and organizations dedicated to futures studies began to develop as a wide swath of scientists, artists, authors, philosophers and social reformers were drawn to futures studies, even as systems theory (Bertalanffy, 1962) and information age globalization (Nye, 2004) were emerging. Initially, those interested in futures studies had developed expertise in other fields, and futures was a secondary interest. Professional futurists such as Alvin Toffler (1980) arose in the 1970s and 80s, and then, after a decade and a half of growth and popular interest the field plateaued.

While futures studies was taking off in popular culture, academic work in the field was limited through the late 1970s, with the exception of those working on improving the initial Delphi (RAND, 2014) and Scenario (Lindgren & Bandhold, 2009) methodologies, and those whose primary interest was systems theory. A few academic journals were established and conferences persisted, but Universities were slow to add futures studies courses or programs to their offerings. Even so, futures studies managed to develop as a multi-disciplinary anomaly within a few schools.

Fs and Integral Futures: The Rise of Richard Slaughter

The University of Lancaster was an early adopter and in 1982, Richard Slaughter was awarded a Ph.D. in Futures Studies from Lancaster (Slaughter, 2011a). To the present day Slaughter has remained an active and prolific writer in the academic field of futures, tending the flame for over 35 years. His early work focussed upon the development of the T-Cycle (Slaughter, Naismith & Houghton, 2004) as a futures methodology, but in the mid-1990s Slaughter began to consider the diffusion of methods and conceptual frameworks within futures studies with some concern. Futures had always been widely divergent, lacking any readily agreed upon conceptual framework, and the academic work had become even more diverse through the 1980s and early 90s with several academics proposing new methodologies and lines of inquiry. Slaughter was concerned that the increasing diffusion of the field rendered it voiceless and impotent, and he began looking for ways to bring greater coherence to the field.

In 1995 Wilber introduced the concept of "flatland" as a way to show how western cultures had placed their attention on an "infinite ahead" and had given up on pre-scientific notions of an "infinite above" (1995, p.410). Three years later, Slaughter (1998) wrote "Transcending Flatland" to show how the entire field of futures studies had been founded on "empiricist notions of prediction, forecasting and control" (p.519) and to propose a way forward for futures studies that could draw upon ontologies and epistemologies beyond the rational/positivist tradition. This was the first paper linking integral theory with futures studies, and it was as informative as it was provocative. Slaughter (1998) asserted that by re-casting all meaning as rational/positivist the west had effectively chopped off individual and collective interior ways of knowing, leaving science and technology to blaze a trail ahead while culture, personality and spirit were ever more hollowed out and disregarded. This uneven tending to individual and societal growth over all four quadrants was seen by Wilber and Slaughter as the basis for the psychosis of western living: better technology and physical health than ever before, while mental health and societal decay also grew at unprecedented rates.

After providing a condensed version of the all quadrants all levels (AQAL) model, including re-productions of the original four quadrant diagrams that had appeared in Wilber's (1995) *Sex, Ecology, Spirituality*, Slaughter's conclusions bluntly spelled out how futures studies needed to change in the light of integral theory. Slaughter's direction is clear: futures studies has nothing at all to say about possible futures if it blindly ignores the upper and lower left quadrants, and those ways of knowing and telling. Furthermore, the futures do not arise solely from the external stimuli of rationality and systems processes of the right hand quadrants, but also from the interior individual and interior collective left hand quadrants (p. 532). In other words, the best way to draw people towards preferable futures is to have them look inside themselves and their cultures (UL, LL) and not only to develop scenarios and measure effects in an attempt to extrapolate (UR, LR).

Slaughter received criticism for proposing a meta-narrative/integral understanding of futures. Other researchers in futures were concerned about the validity of Wilber's (1995) model, and they feared being co-opted by Slaughter's work. Some in the integral community found fault with Slaughter's exegesis of Wilber's (1995) text. However, the initial surveying was done, and more work was afoot. Slaughter (2011b) has continued to defend and explain the role that integral futures has within futures studies, and recently summarized the position of integral futures in 2012, in the book *To See With Fresh Eyes*.

Teacher Education and Futures Studies

The majority of research that connects futures studies to education tends to focus on the great need for education systems to innovate via the uptake of information technology or it proposes curricula for students that will make them more hopeful for their futures. In both cases, teachers' perceptions of futures are left out of the equation. However, some work has been done in this area, most notably by UNESCO, as part of their teacher education program for sustainability education (Fien & Hicks, 2010). The UNESCO "Visions of the Future" heuristic is based upon Slaughter's work, so there is a traceable line of thought from Wilber, to Slaughter, to the UNESCO teacher education program for sustainability that relies on a futures perspective. (Fien & Hicks, "Introduction, References, Credits", 2010).

The discipline of futures has many proponents in the realm of education, including those who would like to see it formally embedded within K-12 curricula, primarily connected to subjects such as geography and sustainability (Hicks, 2007). UNESCO (2010) has also promoted futures education within curricula about sustainability. UNESCO includes their "Visions of the Future" within a multimedia teacher education program entitled "Teaching and Learning for a Sustainable Future" (Fien & Hicks, 2010). UNESCO has deliberately placed futures studies at the heart of their sustainable development curriculum efforts. The five UNESCO "Visions of the Future" are: 1) Business as usual 2) Edge of disaster 3) Authoritarian control 4) Technological miracles 5) Sustainable society. The UNESCO heuristic provides five externally focussed exterior/collective scenarios and lacks the subtlety of the interior/collective and interior/individual perspectives of integral futures, but it is a practical heuristic that is directly connected to addressing the ways that teachers envision possible, probable and preferable futures.

Futures thinking is tentatively connected to sustainability education in the Province of Manitoba through the Sustainability and Education Academy (SEDA) Domain framework for a whole system approach to education for sustainable development (SEDA). In the "Curriculum Teaching Learning" Domain of the framework the importance of futures thinking is mentioned, but the trail goes cold after that, with no further help with resources or definitions of what futures thinking is, or why it matters that teachers consciously focus on futures thinking.

The natural connections between envisioning hopeful futures and education for sustainable development are clear, strong, logical bonds. Further work could be done to strengthen teacher preparation and ESD curricula by more purposefully including futures thinking in teacher training and inservicing.

The strongest direct connections between futures studies and the perceptions of teachers has been conducted by the OECD's Centre for Educational Research and Innovation (CERI) (2010a) and the Schooling for Tomorrow (SfT) project. While the work is international in its scope, particularly strong work came out of Ontario (OECD 2006). As part of the SfT project, teachers were invited to consider scenarios regarding potential futures for education. Scenario planning (Lindgren & Bandhold, 2009) is one of the oldest and most respected futures studies methodologies, first introduced in the late 1950s and developed over decades to the point where the word "scenario" is now commonplace.

The goal of the SfT Phase III project in Ontario was to encourage longer-term thinking for strategic planning among teachers, and futures studies methodologies were at the heart of this professional development effort. The report concludes that scenario planning has promise as a mechanism to support change within an organization. This finding is significant since it means that both individuals and systems can be challenged to grow and think in longer-term ways.

More recently the CERI SfT project has moved away from trying to leverage system change through teacher development and has instead moved in the direction of publishing work using trend analysis. In the Introduction to *Trends Shaping Education* (OECD 2010) the authors point out that the trend analysis work is of benefit to teacher-educators and teachers for considering potential futures and to reflect on teaching practice and curriculum issues. Trend analysis is also a respected futures studies methodology, but by 2010 the application of futures methodology to aid in teacher preparation and readiness was much more oblique.

Futures, Complexity, and Curriculum Thought

Beyond the nuts and bolts of education systems and the formal teaching of a futures curriculum, reflecting upon what a futures studies theory of learning might look like is a worthwhile stop. Curriculum studies has, at its heart, the domain of learning and theories of learning. Brent Davis, Dennis Sumara and Rebecca Luce-Kapler (2015) organize a broad range of identified learning theories and theorists into a quadrant-like frame similar to that found in Wilber's (1995) integral model. While there is no direct connection between the Wilber quadrants and the four "moments" of education (Brent Davis, Dennis Sumara and Rebecca Luce-Kapler 2015), quadrants are used nonetheless to divide learning theory into four categories and Wilber's (1995) quadrants are implied. The use of the term "moment" is also a reference to time, and is apt since it does not favour or exclude any form of past/present/future time or delineate a specific duration of time. The historic learning theories that still dominate most education systems (positivist/rationalist) are placed in the UR quadrant, those which are "learner-centric" (constructivist/developmentalist) in the UL. The LL quadrant includes learning theory that has developed from critical theory, post colonialism and globalization, while the LR quadrant identifies learning theories emanating from wisdom traditions, systems theory, and complexity theory. The learning theory quadrant framework is much more involved that was just summarized, but the echoes of integral theory persist.

More interesting is the way that Davis, Sumara and Luce-Kapler (2015) have adapted the quadrants to develop a framework for understanding how learning theories relate with one another, much in the same way that Slaughter (2001) adapted the integral quadrants to create a knowledge cycle for integral futures. Slaughter (2001) developed an "integral cycle of knowledge" (p. 409). The cycle was initially developed by Wilber (1999), modified by Edwards (2000), and adapted to form a futures methodology by Slaughter (2001). As Figure 1 illustrates, the major innovation is that the cycle re-casts the four quadrants as domains within a cyclical process of knowledge building. Slaughter unpacks the knowledge cycle beginning in the UR quadrant, suggesting the use of an instrument (the desire to know, and a question arising) to establish a "known", then cycling to the UL for confirmation of the "known" within oneself. Thirdly, cycling to the LL for confirmation of the "known" within society and culture, and finally cycling to the LR to confirm the "known" within broader systems at play. If coherence is maintained after confirming the "known" through all four quadrants, the new "known" can be added to what is externally

Figure 1. The Integral Cycle of Knowledge
(Slaughter, 2001). Used with permission.

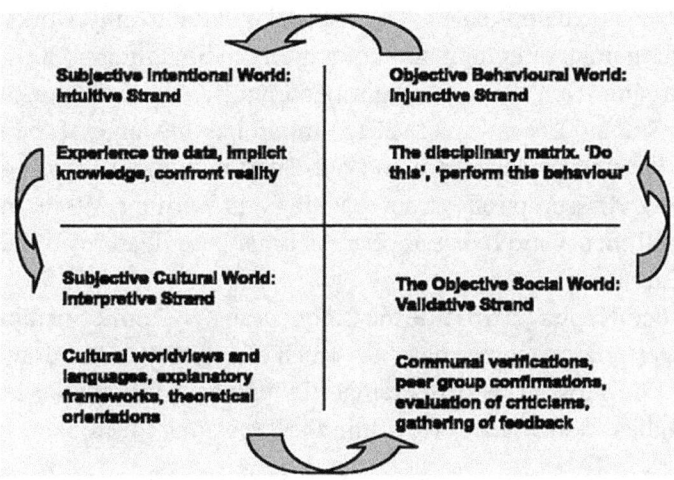

recognized as a stable known, which is simply called a fact. Such facts can then be used to create more questions, repeating the cycle each time in order to create knowing where there was none before.

Slaughter (2001) then applies the knowledge cycle to futures studies (see Figure 2) and provides four examples of how the process of knowledge creation works in integral futures. Slaughter applies four established futures methodologies (Forecasting, Delphi, Scenarios, and Causal Layered Analysis) to the cycle, explaining how each work.

Since all forms of futures methodologies can be mapped on to the four quadrant cycle with little difficulty, Slaughter's (2001) model of knowledge creation is shown to be generalizable.

I was struck at how similar the integral knowledge building cycle is to the inquiry cycle and the cycles present in action research (McNiff, 2013) and design-based research (McKenney & Reeves, 2012).

Figure 2. Knowledge creation cycle applied to integral futures studies to create a method
(Slaughter, 2001). Used with permission.

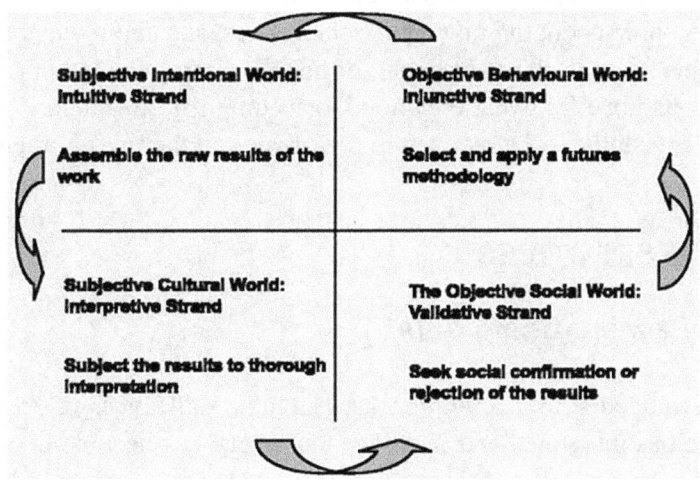

Furthermore, they clearly mirror the four "Moments" of Education described by Davis, Sumara and Luce-Kapler (2015). While there is some comfort in finding commonality between these methods for knowledge creation, this cyclical approach to the integral quadrants only works if it does not privilege any quadrant as the starting point or ending point of a cycle. In Slaughter's (2001) case, he inadvertently privileges knowledge arising from the upper right quadrant by starting the process in the upper right. Conversely, Davis, Sumara and Luce-Kapler (2015) minimize the value of the upper right hand quadrant by identifying it with stale, mechanistic and out-dated notions of learning accompanied by their concomitant pedagogies and assumptions about teaching and learning. While this is a concern, in both cases, portions of integral theory are being applied as organizing features to aid in coherence-making across vastly diverse disciplines.

Davis, Sumara and Luce-Kapler (2015) title the LR quadrant "Systemic Sustainability Education", and the connection to futures studies becomes clear: so much of futures studies draws heavily from systems theory and is embedded in most forms of sustainability education. Potential learning theories arising from integral futures studies would clearly fit within the "Systemic Sustainability Education" quadrant.

Summary

Time and the sub-domain of future time have been researched by scientists, philosophers, theologians, psychologists and many other knowledgeable and earnest intelligent people who have attempted to understand such a crushingly large concept through very limited conceptual frameworks. Historically, those who studied possible futures and who made predictions were considered seers, or prophets, or witches. They relied on the personal and subjective ways of knowing the world. Since the 1950s, weather forecasting, economic forecasting and even social forecasting have been adopted and legitimized by positivists, showing that predictions about the future can be made and can stand up to scientific rigor and measurement. However, the field of futures lacked significant coherence until all of these ways of perceiving potential futures were drawn together with Slaughter's (1998) development of integral futures.

Thinking about possible futures applies to education at every level, from system wide considerations right down to the moment-by-moment interactions between people in classrooms; those attempting to learn, and those attempting to teach. Perceptions of possible futures are present at every level; system wide, within school divisions, in schools, classes, and every teacher has ideas about the time that is to come. My study will not address the system wide concerns, but it will help to ferret out the spectrum of perceptions that teachers hold about their own potential futures, and about the potential futures for their students. In essence, this study is all about hope, for hope is simply the belief in a worthwhile future. Finding out what teachers hope for, what they hope to accomplish, may help to improve the odds that the better futures they envision may be realized in their lives and the lives of their students.

THEORETICAL PERSPECTIVES

Integral Theory as a Map (Using AQAL).

Ken Wilber (1995) developed a holistic approach to including all forms of knowledge building, and since the forms are seen as integrated and inclusive the theory has become known as integral theory. The simplest and most helpful diagram that explains the theory is a simple x and y axis that divides the

Figure 3. The All Quadrants, All Levels (AQAL) framework.
Adapted from Wilber (1995).

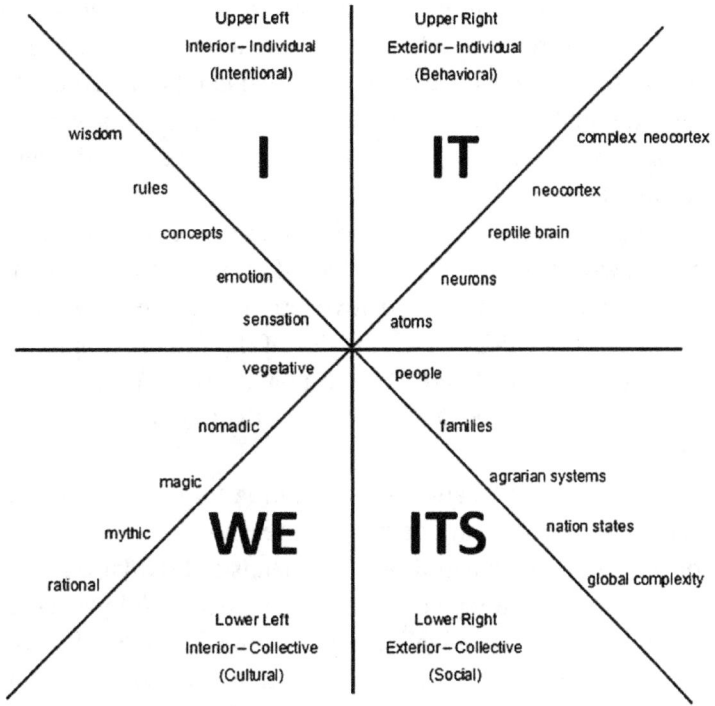

ground into four quadrants representing all quadrants and all levels (AQAL) of consciousness (see Figure 3). All forms of knowing and being known are then sorted on to the ground, divided by those which are more objective rather than subjective, and those which are more individual or communal in nature.

Integral theory is helpful because it attempts to include all of the ways that people go about deciding what is true (or false), good (or evil) and beautiful (or repulsive). Seeking the true, the good, and the beautiful echoes the ancient Greek philosophers, and is an entry point to begin finding the edges and contours of what constitutes reality, or, a start to understanding ontology from an integral perspective.

Getting a fix on the ontological stance of integral theory means including all other ontologies, and this can be maddening for those requiring discrete tolerances and definitions of ontology. Wilber (2013) explains that separating ontology from epistemology and methodology is artificial, since defining tolerances for "real" makes no sense without including the dynamics "knowing" and "learning". Integral theory has, therefore, been criticized for not providing a discrete ontology upon which an understanding of the "real" can be developed. Wilber (2013) counters this criticism by pointing out that ontology pervades integral theory:

Integral Theory has an extensive ontology—from "involuntary givens" to the 20 tenets, whose first tenet is: "Reality is composed neither of things nor of processes, but of holons." Holons, of course, are wholes that are parts of other wholes (as a whole atom is part of a whole molecule, a whole molecule is part of a whole cell, a whole cell is part of a whole organism, etc. They are whole/parts, or holons.) This is sometimes worded, "Reality is composed of perspectives that are holons". Since all of the items in all of the quadrants are holons, the Integral map is drenched in ontology (but, as I am maintaining, an ontology inseparable from epistemology and methodology, all interwoven aspects of the Whole—many subjects, many methods, many objects—or Who's, How's, and What's). (p. 4)

This explanation identifies integral ontology as a portion of a co-arising whole: reality comes into being with knowing and learning together. Therefore, the ontology of integral theory is also a plurality, accepting that there are many forms of real, and that real can be interpreted in many ways. Wilber (2014) offers the most elegant and simple explanation of an integral approach to ontology available as he is explaining that people are not all the same, and that life coaches of all kinds need to avoid providing one size fits all coaching advice:

But this is just another example of what an Integral approach in general does—namely, gets rid of a "one-size-fits-all" approach, which flattens the genuine differences between people and smooshes them all into the same category with the same unimaginative practice. The extraordinary differences between people have been one of the most significant discoveries of the Integral approach.

Again, we don't need to go overboard here. The complexities are immense, and it's easy to get lost in them. That's the point of the AQAL Framework—to use the fewest number of dimensions to explain the most amount of reality. (p. 96)

So integral theory does have an explanation and definition for reality; it is a shared sense of what is real, and it irreducibly co-arises along with knowing and learning.

Framing a reasonable definition of integral ontology leads to broader questions about the nature of consciousness, of awareness, and of intelligence. Here again the distinctions between human versus nonhuman consciousness, individual versus collective consciousness, universal consciousness, intelligence and volition are relaxed. Here again, this can be disorienting and even threatening to those who find that significant portions of their world-views depend on upholding these distinctions. It used to be that such ideas of universal consciousness were solidly in the domain of religion and theology, along with notions of spirit, and eternity; the scientific community could, at best, say that such hypotheses were unprovable, but more often dismissed them as nonsense.

However, scientists are busy working to explain the origins and nature of consciousness; Maturana and Varela (1980 & 1998) proposed an autopoietic, self-arising model of consciousness, Hofstadter (1999) hypothesized that self-referential "loops" in sufficiently complex systems give rise to self-awareness, while Laszlo (2012) goes further, proposing the existence of a universal consciousness he calls "Akasha". Such efforts represent a significant blending between ontological, epistemological and methodological paradigms that used to be considered discrete. Serious and earnest thinkers, be they theologians, scientists, shamans or pragmatists are more prone to consider the advantages of methodological plurality than ever before. René Girard (1987) points out the necessity of such pluralism if humanity is to advance:

In modern research, everything must take second place to the findings. We should not convert into stifling ideology a number of methodological principles that have been imposed by a particular state of knowledge and ought not to form a barrier to further progress.

Today's epigonal thinkers are all the more ready to stress these methodological taboos because they belong to the rearguard of the movement that they have joined and can only conceive of any threat to it as a regression to the past, in which they are still caught up. They interpret the historical moment they have witnessed in far too absolute a way and fail to see that a new breakthrough—perhaps made possible by the one they have too single-mindedly adopted—is abruptly bringing back into the field of theory everything that their own schema seemed to have eliminated for good. (p. 439)

This criticism is a lament about the short-sightedness of perpetuating discrete silos of research to the point that all things outside one's own scope of understanding must, by default, be assumed to be either unknowable, or nonsensical. Removing the barriers, relaxing the constraints, and attempting to remain open to a broader experience of consciousness is the goal. Integral theory encourages such openness, and IMP becomes the research methodology that reflects its holism.

Employing Integral Theory in This Study

Choosing integral theory (Wilber, 1995) makes sense for studying time, since integral theory is a meta-narrative theory that is expansive enough to include the highly abstract aspects of time study. The subject of time can be viewed and studied using integral theory, and the next four sections provide examples of how notions of time can be understood via the AQAL quadrants.

Upper Right (UR) Quadrant and Notions of Clock and Calendar Time

Clock and calendar notions of time fit well within the positivist tradition, viewing time as measurable, linear, scarce, divisible, and tradable (Duncheon & Tierney, 2013). This is the dominant, western, and empirical sense of time, imposed upon people world-wide and sold as a helpful tool for time navigation. What is often forgotten is that clock and calendar time are constructs, as surely as the alphabet itself is a construct; they all require wide adoption and conventional usage in order to gain any utility. These notions and aspects of time study fit well within the UR quadrant of the AQAL framework.

Upper Left (UL) Quadrant and Notions of Subjective Time Plasticity

Phenomenological notions of time being flexible, plastic, and of time passing, or speeding up or slowing down depending upon the conscious and unconscious state(s) of a subject within time are UL quadrant concerns, and obviously very different from clock and calendar time. In *Flow: The psychology of optimal experience* (1990), Mihaly Csikszentmihalyi makes connections to engagement and time that are germane in the UL quadrant. Anyone who has endured a boring class knows how time can stretch when one is under stimulated, but also that time flies when one is engaged. So, does time actually change perception, or does perception change time? Time questions such as this and the answers that arise belong in the UL quadrant.

Lower Left (LL) Quadrant and Notions of Socially Constructed Time

Social interaction and task completion trump mechanistic or individual/experiential notions of time in the LL quadrant. For example, How do people know when a party starts, or when it is over? Not because they look at a clock or because of our individual experiences in the group. Parties (and fights) start and end when the group deems they should start and end, irrespective of a clock, a calendar, day, night, or one's own circadian rhythm. Furthermore, they may start or end with a greater or lesser degree of certainty (Duncheon & Tierney, 2013). Sometimes it can be very difficult to know when the party started or ended, and it might happen at different times for different sub-groups. Social time constructs also account for the phenomenon of individuals remembering where they were when an important world event of shared cultural experience occurred. For example, many people recall place and time together when they remember the 9/11 attacks, the explosion of Space Shuttle Columbia, when the Berlin Wall fell, or when recalling the assassination of a world leader.

Lower Right (LR) Quadrant Notions of Complexity and Systems Time

Complex systems that are seemingly beyond human manipulation, control or enhancement play into all human notions of time, serving as markers and reminders of time's arrow. For example, volcanoes erupt, storms come to pass, seasons change, and shadows cross the wall. Also, trillions of living things (including people) seemingly come into existence (are born) and then seemingly cease to exist (they die). These broader, undeniable and seemingly immutable and autoregulatory time aspects (Trueit, 2012) fit perfectly into the LR quadrant of the AQAL framework. Time is a very big subject, so it needs a very big framework, and integral theory is big enough to tackle time study on many fronts.

Futures studies is a subdivision of time studies, and integral theory has been a dominant theoretical framework for futures researchers for over 20 years, beginning with the work of Richard Slaughter (2012). Slaughter's work adapts the AQAL quadrants to employ them as a knowledge cycle, allowing for a variety of futures methodologies to draw coherent findings about potential futures. By way of analogy, Slaughter (2012) employed integral theory to help interpret a wide spectrum of futures methodologies, so that the end result of any forecasting by any method became sensible and understandable knowledge creation. Using integral theory makes sense when studying time, and makes even better sense when trying to study futures and forecasting, because of the work of Richard Slaughter (2012). However, integral theory also makes sense to employ as the conceptual framework for the study as a whole.

Research Design Overview

A conceptual framework needs to draw upon the model that guides one's research and embody a harmony of theory, research, and experience (Bloomberg and Volpe, 2012). Studying the enacted perceptions of individuals within a group is a complex task, and lends itself to a multi-methods approach. I am hesitant to call it a "mixed" methods approach since the term "mixed" connotes an unwanted or confused sense, in the way that "mixed up" and "mixed breed" are negative terms. IMP is a multi-method approach, and I am using the term "multi" to express the positive plurality and retained distinction that the term affords (Brewer, 2005). Examples in use include the positive associations such as "multiculturalism" and "multi-talented". Integral theory and IMP are holistic and celebrate plurality, therefore even though "mixed" methods is more commonly understood, this study follows a multi-method approach.

Bricolage is also understood as a meaningful multi-method approach (Denzin & Lincoln 1994), where a variety of methodologies are drawn together by a "jack of all trades" bricoleur researcher in order to create a multi-faceted and rigorous qualitative study. IMP includes this form of research, but moves beyond the novel combining of methodologies in order to extract novel data and therefore arrive at novel conclusions. Bricolage is undoubtedly a powerful multi-methods approach that has also been adopted and adapted by pragmatist methodologies (Onwuegbuzie & Leech, 2005). However, the difficulty with bricolage is that there is no core, no centre, and no heart that draws together the competing pieces. In a thoughtful criticism of bricolage Hammersley (1999) points out that knowledge building requires purpose, and invokes the metaphor of "Neurath's Boat". Neurath explained that sailors on a boat could, over time, repair and replace portions of their wooden vessel on the open sea by substituting driftwood and flotsam for damaged or worn portions of the ship. However, the original design of the ship always needed to be considered, since the boat would collapse and sink if the realities of the material and design were not respected. Hammersley's proposition is that multi-methods research is more akin to high seas boatbuilding than the unbridled inquiry of the bricoleur. Figure 4 depicts the multi-method design of this study.

METHODS

The research design of this study employs integral theory in many ways, beginning with the conceptual framework upon which the study rests, and reaching into all aspects of the study, including the emphasis on methodological pluralism, a purposeful blending of methodologies in order to address the complexities of researching dispositions toward futures, the analysis of the material leading to conclusions and recommendations reflecting the holism of the research approach. The conceptual framework of the study is depicted in Figure 5, which is provided as an orienting feature to point out that the eight research questions fan out across the quadrants of integral theory in a deliberate and ordered way.

The Research Problem

Traditional high school education systems are increasingly under enormous pressure to change, evolve, or be dismantled. Understanding something of teachers' perceptions of the future represents a potential lever for positive change, but very little research exists that touches upon this area. Furthermore, the degree of fidelity between the espoused perceptions of teachers and their enacted professional practice regarding what the future holds is particularly important to determine, since high schools are increasingly using the new tools of the digital information age to educate young people who face an infinite multitude of potential futures.

The Research Questions

Having eight research questions in a study is unusual, but the nature of my conceptual framework and methodologies make it possible to pose a family of questions. Integral methodological pluralism (IMP) (Wilber, 2006) allows for a variety of questions that fan out across all four quadrants, or the quadrivia of integral theory (Wilber, 2006). A more detailed explanation of the integral conceptual framework and IMP methodology follows in Chapter Two. The eight research questions follow, each with a bracket to identify the predominant quadrant connected to the question:

1. How do teachers at Riverview perceive futures, and how are these perceptions enacted in their classes? (UR)
2. To what extent are teachers' perceptions of the future similar or different from one another, and how well do they correlate with the UNESCO Heuristic? (UR)
3. How much importance do teachers place upon their own perceptions of futures? (UL)
4. To what extent do teachers use their perceptions of the future to deliberately plan their professional and personal lives? (UL)
5. How long are the longest views, and how short are the shortest views of the future that teachers perceive and enact? (LL)

Figure 4. Flowchart showing the phases and components in the research design

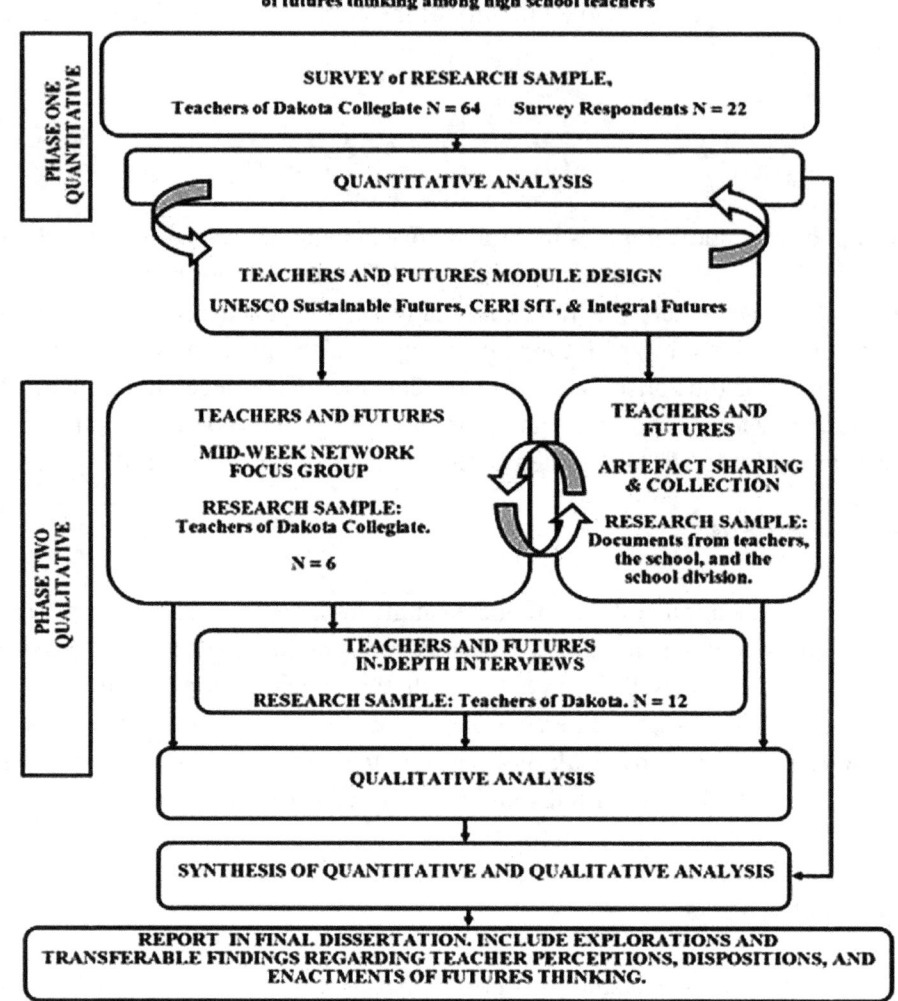

6. How do teachers express their perceptions of the future to their colleagues? (LL)
7. To what degree does working in a technology-rich Public High School influence teachers' perceptions of futures, and the enactment of these perceptions within their role as teachers? (LR)
8. In this incredible age of information access and globalization, how do teachers think about their own futures, and the futures of their students? (LR)

Data Collection

The teaching staff of Riverview Collegiate were invited to participate in this multi-method study in four distinct ways. Firstly, teachers responded to a voluntary survey that was conducted online. Secondly, a focus group of teachers was established, and operated as a Mid-Week Network professional learning group

Promising Futures

Figure 5. Research questions positioned on the AQAL quadrants, and showing the knowledge cycle beginning in the UR quadrant

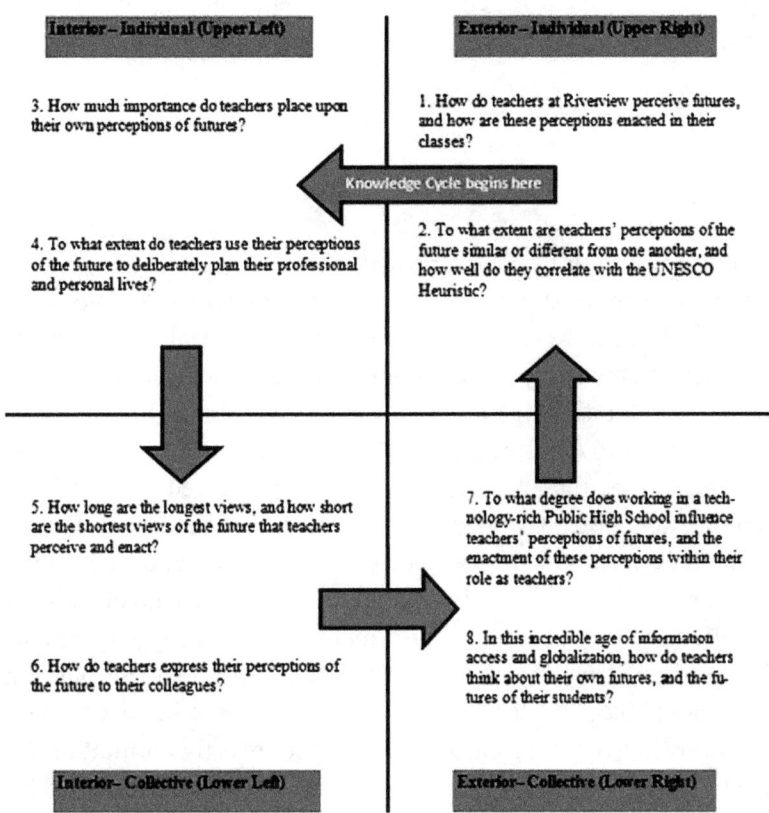

at Riverview Collegiate, with the mandate of learning about educational futures, and considering ways that the group's understandings of the futures impacts their practice as teachers. Thirdly, interviews were conducted with the eight teachers from the focus group and four more, for a total of twelve interviews. Within the focus group, teachers also provided samples of assignments, projects, units, tests, and other artefacts of teaching that are connected to their understandings of possible futures.

Assumptions

In my role as a high school teacher I am immersed in a culture of preparation; we prepare children for tests, exams, projects, and graduation. All of this preparation experience means that I hold several assumptions about possible futures. Firstly, I assume that the beliefs of teachers make a difference to the ways they teach, and therefore to the ways that students learn as well. Teachers' beliefs are shown to influence their uptake of educational innovation (Talbot & Campbell, 2014) and on the ways their beliefs impact student learning and students' beliefs as well (Phillips & Clarke, 2014). Secondly, preparing for the future is a common theme in all high schools; a random sampling of YouTube graduation speeches would bear this out. Thirdly, teachers prepare youth for the future in part by passing along the content and exercises of various subjects, but also in their lived experiences as adults interacting with teens (Renner,

2009). Fourthly, I also assume that teachers unwittingly transmit their implicit understandings of possible futures to their students. Finally, I assume that preparation for the future is often the overarching premise of secondary schooling for entire school systems on a global scale, whether implicit or explicit (Fullan & Langworthy, 2014).

Limitations and Delimitations

Limitations

This study includes limiting conditions which created the boundaries of the research. Firstly, the study is bound to one location. The entire study took place at Riverview Collegiate between September and June of the 2015-16 school year, and as such it can be seen as a case study. Therefore, it has the inherent advantages and limitations of case study research in that while it provides a thick description regarding teachers and futures thinking the findings and conclusions are also bound by the context and may be less transferrable. However, the overall trustworthiness of the study is not harmed by this limitation, and is addressed more fully in section 3.9. While this can be perceived as a limitation, the credibility of the study is borne out by a logical and sequential research design that led to lengthy, rich and detailed qualitative data sets that reflect the conclusions and recommendations of the study.

The second significant limitation is that I was the only researcher involved in the study, and I also work at Riverview Collegiate as a teacher. While there are advantages associated with practitioner research (Coupal, 2005) it can also be seen as a limitation, since researcher bias could lead to findings and conclusions that are less objective than studies where the researcher is new to the research site and has no pre-existing relationships with the participants. To address this limitation I frequently reminded participants about the two "hats" I wore, that of researcher, and that of teacher. This limitation was not that difficult to manage, since the research participants were all consenting adults, and I had no authority, power or control over them in my work at Riverview.

Thirdly, there were practical limitations to the study as well. The participants were very good about attending all of the MWN focus group sessions, but could not consistently schedule time to be involved in every meeting. Sometimes meetings went ahead with five teachers if someone was away.

Delimitations

As the researcher, I delimited the study in a variety of ways. Firstly, I chose that the teaching staff of Riverview Collegiate would be the only participants. This was a reasonable delimitation since the 1-to-1 BYOD pilot initiated by the Bison Crocus School Division was housed at Riverview Collegiate. Secondly, the study employed integral methodological pluralism, thereby including a variety of ideas and components from various research traditions. Thirdly, the scope of this study was delimited to an exploration of the perceptions of teachers. A further exploration of how the perceptions of teachers may or may not influence students and their perceptions of potential futures would require a follow up study as part of an integral program of research.

EXPLORING THE ISSUES

Analysis of Findings

Analysis and interpretation of the data from the qualitative phase followed the six step method described by Creswell (2012). Step 1 was to organize the data and transcribe it. A great deal of the work in a qualitative study revolves around this step, and this was certainly the case in this study. From November of 2015 to March of 2016 I recorded eight focus group sessions and twelve interviews, for a total of 20 transcripts. The recordings were transcribed by a transcription service described in section 3.8, and then I reviewed and corrected the transcripts by comparing them to the initial audio recordings. As I re-read transcripts and listened to the recordings, I also kept notes on paper about words or themes that seemed to appear most often, or which had significance for the participants.

Step 2 of Creswell's (2012) six steps involved coding the data, and in my case involved the use of a computer software program to aid in the coding. I opted to use NVivo as a data analysis tool since it was available to me as a University of Calgary Graduate Student, and since it also had a solid reputation among those who use CAQDAS on a regular basis. Using NVivo was relatively straightforward; input the transcripts in an organized fashion, employ a variety query functions available, and develop a coding structure based upon the transcripts, recordings and experience of the interviews and focus groups in the light of the eight research questions guiding the study.

During this time I also developed the "12 Word" and "15 Word" measures based on a combination of key word frequency queries, my own notation based on the data, and my initial coding. The initial "12 Word" and "15 Word" measures provided a way to apply the same analytical measure to each of the transcripts. This form of analysis helped me to see significant differences between respondents, particularly when the measures were presented as charts. The charts are included as appendices N and O. Creswell (2012) points out that "The object of the coding process is to make sense out of text data, divide it into text or image segments, label the segments with codes, examine codes for overlap and redundancy, and collapse these codes into broad themes" (p. 243). The broad themes began to emerge out of the "15 Word" measure, which then informed the next step of my analysis.

In Step 3 (Creswell 2102) of my analysis I used the codes I had developed to build description and themes. Trying to decide which ideas should be drawn together under one code or split apart over two or more codes was difficult at first. After more study, I learned about the "lumping" and "splitting" functions of codes in the works of Tracy (2013a) (2013b) and Saldana (2011). I also developed a coding structure of 4 code types, including Descriptive, Process, Emotion, and Structural codes (Saldana 2009). Thinking about the data through these four coding lenses helped me to finish my analysis of the data.

Creswell's (2012) Steps 4, 5, and 6 are about representing and reporting the findings, summary and interpretation, and considering the accuracy of the findings in a study. The discussion of themes is based on the themes and descriptions that emerged and were understood in the light of the eight research questions and complete Creswell's (2012) steps. Furthermore, tables, diagrams, charts, were constructed to aid in understanding the analysis and conclusions, however, for practical reasons these are not included in this chapter.

Discussion of Themes

After compiling the data in nVivo and running a variety of queries, I started to look at what was emerging in the findings as I began my analysis. It became clear that the types of findings that emerged from the survey were in fact different form either the focus group or interview findings, and drawing all three groups of findings together into meaningful conclusions would require a logical synthesis. Integral theory provides the underlying backdrop for the form of analysis that I used as I moved through the process of drawing information from data, knowledge from information, and ultimately arriving at a synthesis.

Drawing Together a Synthesis and Revealing Interconnected Themes

Drawing together the three sets of findings leads to a developing synthesis of the many ways that teachers at Riverview think about futures, and is illustrated in Figure 6. The teachers are a pragmatic group who accept completely that there is such a thing as a future time, and that people can change the future by acting in the present. Acting in the present to change the future is dominantly understood as the function of planning, and the teachers highly value planning.

However, the notion of planning only begins to create a common ground for anyone who would want to talk to the teachers about the benefit or need for much longer term planning. Planning, for the teachers, is seen as a cyclical process mostly, with an occasional goal that has a longer time frame. Teachers are good at thinking in 3-5 year timeframes, and this is due in part to the kinds of education programs they took as students and now reinforce as teachers themselves. The teachers begin to doubt the value of longer term planning that is a decade out or longer, and this is due to the many factors that crowd in, making long term visions, plans and goals seem far more improbable as they are forecast further and further into the future. Planning is a start, but planning alone, even long term planning, is not the kind of hopeful futures thinking that tackles problems such as world poverty, global warming, and the advent of robust artificial intelligence that can out-perform human intelligence.

When the teachers of Riverview do think about the longer term futures, they imagine that education systems and schools will continue on into the futures with minimal alteration, except that more assessment will be automated and courses of study will be much more focussed upon the unique learning needs of students. They do not envision futures where their jobs no longer exist, being replaced by either intelligent machines or the chaos of war, economic collapse, environmental degradation, or any other combination of factors. The possible futures they envision are also preferable for those who work within education institutions, and are hopeful and optimistic visions of futures that remain stable, supporting broad systems of state-sponsored and tax-funded universal education. The preferable futures the teachers of Riverview envision see life continuing on with a high degree of literacy and numeracy, renewals in curriculum that respect the lessons of history, and which maintain the central place of teachers as the main influencers of children sorted into age and ability based cohorts. This is a "happily ever after" vision of the future, to be sure, and I hope that the teachers predictions are accurate. If so, the future is friendly and stable.

Children under the influence of such teachers learn about the predictable advancement of time, and the assumed advancement of all things good, including peace, health, meaningful intellectual and physical challenges. Children are reassured that things are getting better, a little at a time, across many fields of study, in many ways, in many places. The predictable and cyclical school year, the semesters, courses, bells and weekends reinforce the notion that time is ordered, divided, harnessed and under control. The times themselves are not seen as volatile, uncertain, complex and ambiguous (VUCA).

Promising Futures

VUCA futures were invented by militaries to point to conceptions of time that are far more terrifying than the visions of futures that the Riverview teachers implicitly and explicitly share with teenagers who are emerging into adulthood. In fact, teachers defend against the terror of VUCA futures by reassuring students that no matter what the future holds, no matter how volatile, uncertain, complex or ambiguous, that the antidote to all of that is a good education.

The notion that teachers are purposefully teaching teenagers as a buttress against VUCA futures underlies the clock and calendar world of the school, the cellular nature of subject based classes, and the order that schools draw out of what would otherwise be chaos. In some ways, a

well-ordered school is a gem of any civilization, a tribute to order, learning, and good government. That teachers would like to keep things as they are, and only accept or reject minor changes to the institution is completely understandable.

Gaps and Contradictions in the Futures Thinking of Teachers

Yet, the irony is that in order to keep schools functioning as the best cultural defense against overwhelming VUCA futures may mean having to change schools completely. In other words, to keep schools the same, they may have to change. They may stay the same as respected and necessary systems for educating people, but may have to change to deal with new forms of volatility, uncertainty, complexity, and ambiguity that will emerge in the next decades and centuries.

As Figure 6 shows, the teachers express beliefs in futures that span out across the quadrants of integral theory, and the eight interconnected themes hold together to reinforce a science-friendly, secular and optimistic view of the status quo with incremental improvements over time. This is a healthy but short-sighted disposition towards futures, and three notable gaps in the futures thinking of the teachers need to be addressed.

Figure 7 highlights three gaps, or disconnects, in the futures thinking of Riverview teachers. The gaps illustrated in Figure 7 represent contradictions that arose regarding futures thinking as the eight interconnected themes were superimposed upon the AQAL quadrants. While it is clear that all eight of the themes overlap and are interconnected in the ways that teachers think about futures, the three gaps represent ways of thinking about futures that the teachers are missing. Considering these gaps and the contradictions they illuminate could help Riverview teachers to develop more comprehensive forms of futures thinking.

Gap 1 illustrates that while teachers trust scientific predictions, a UR quadrant idea and value, this belief is not well connected to their LR quadrant understandings that the futures will remain status quo. In particular, great advances in computer science and biology alone are now leading to applied science that is already challenging the status quo futures of schools. The predictions of scientists (which the teachers most trust) point to revolutions, not evolutions in education systems. The dizzying pace of advancements in CRISPR and AI alone illuminate possible and probable futures where human cognitive enhancements and replacements challenge the most robust theories of human learning and cognition. This gap in the futures thinking of teachers is perhaps a form of denial, since upheaval within school systems would likely be bad for teachers overall.

The second gap illustrated in Figure 7 is that while teachers expect the status quo in the most probable futures (LR), they view school system planning as a separate activity (LL). It is almost as though planning activities should occur only because they represent the status quo, and not because having plans and visions for futures may in fact change things. Teachers seem to value school division planning

Figure 6. Eight interconnected themes superimposed on the AQAL Quadrants.

Themes superimposed on the AQAL Quadrants

Interior – Individual (Upper Left) | Exterior – Individual (Upper Right)

- Personal planning matters
- Human choices do change futures
- We trust scientific forecasts
- No real concerns about future societal meltdown
- Teaching about planning matters
- Some things are way beyond human control
- We expect Status Quo Futures
- School and Division Planning Matters

Interior – Collective (Lower Left) | Exterior – Collective (Lower Right)

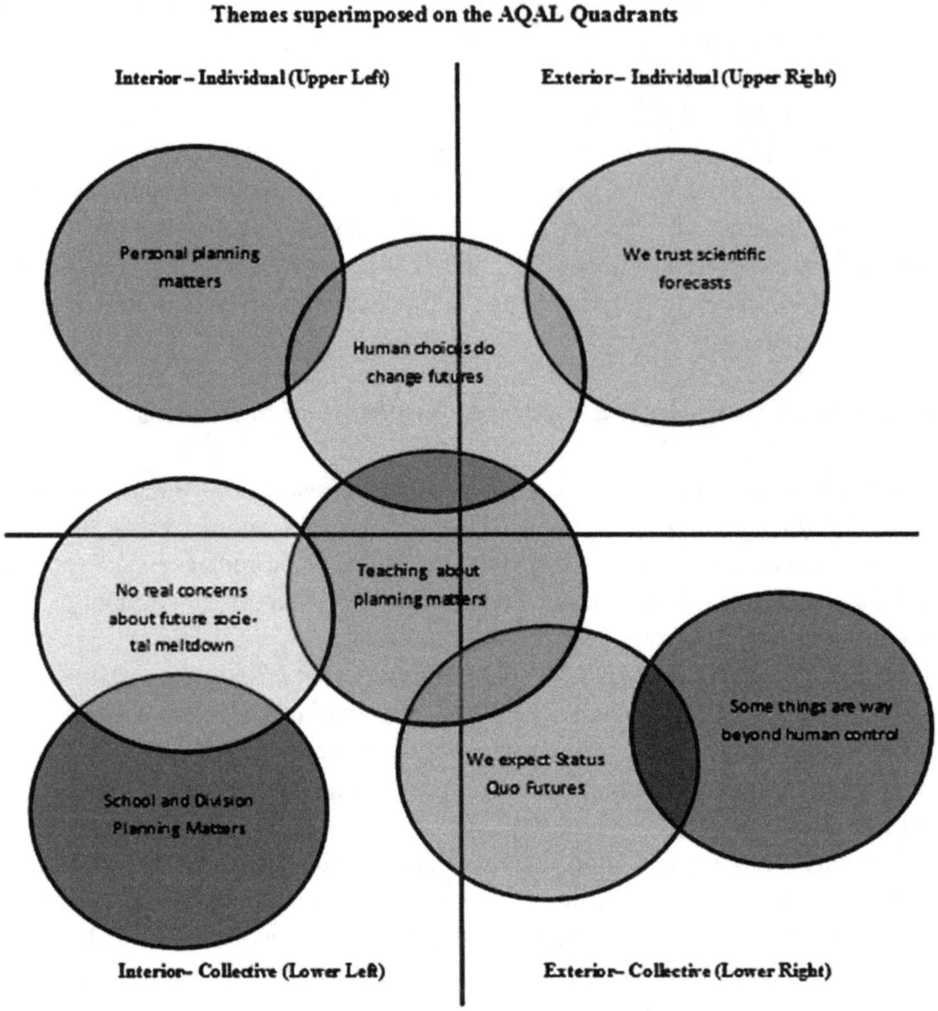

(LL) as a buttress against change forces from outside (LR) instead of as a catalyst for change within the system itself. As such, the teachers (and the systems in which they work) set themselves up to be the passive receivers of change, ever on the defensive against innovations in culture, technology, and teaching practice. This disconnect illustrates why school systems are inherently conservative, holding on to the past, managing the present, and preparing defenses against futures that include imposed change.

The third gap illustrates is that while personal planning matters, the lack of concern about adverse societal change mutes the value of personal planning. The subjective, UL plans a person makes are not believed to be important in the LL futures of cultures on the whole. This particular gap is overcome by the ways teachers link personal planning to their beliefs about personal agency, and the value of planning for one and all, but disconnecting "my" plans from "our" plans or "our" futures is an area of futures thinking where Riverview teachers could grow.

As an example of the third gap in action, a person who needs to get rid of used motor oil has an immediate problem (UL). Disposing of the oil into the city sewer solves the problem in the immediate for

Promising Futures

Figure 7. Analysis revealed gaps in the futures thinking of Riverview teachers

Three significant disconnects (gaps) in the futures thinking of Riverview teachers

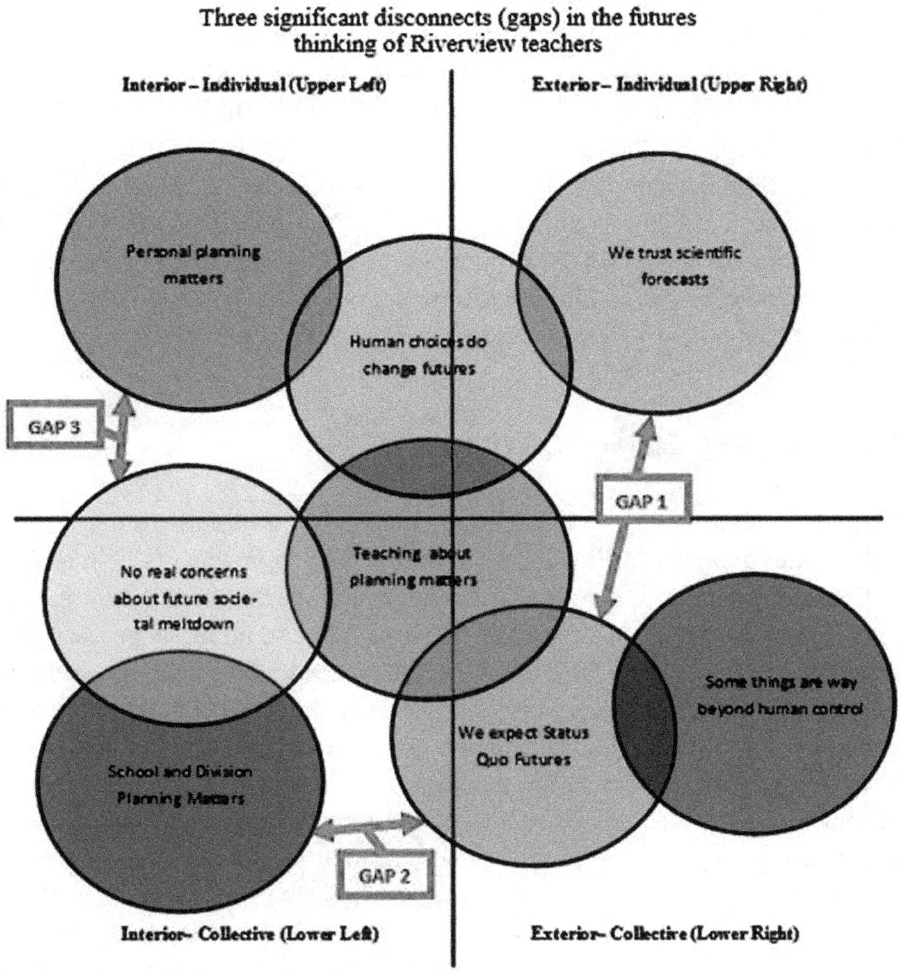

the individual (UL), but disregards the futures for culture (LL), society (LL) and the environment (LR). A person who closes the gap between personal planning (UL) and potential damage to societies (LL) is less likely to pour the oil down the sewer, and must plan ahead to dispose of the oil in a safe way (UR) that benefits all (UL,LL,LR and UR).

These three gaps are not intended as damning criticisms of the teachers, but rather point to gaps in their futures thinking where the teachers could grow. Creating better connections between all four quadrants where futures thinking is concerned would help teachers to develop more coherent and comprehensive views regarding the significance of futures thinking. This in turn would aid teachers as they perform the critical and vital work of educating young people to inhabit whatever form of futures emerge into the present. Much of education is about becoming prepared, and in this instance, this study itself can hopefully prepare teachers to consider many futures, in order to face whatever is realized in a not-so-distant present.

The survey, focus groups and interviews all worked together to confirm that teachers do think about long term futures as a form of planning, and see that envisioning long term futures has limited practical value, especially when there is so much to do and plan in the short term. Yet at the same time, the optimistic notion that the status quo in schools will continue, with improvements as the years go by is a version of a long term future that insulates students from the terrors of VUCA futures. The status quo vision of long term futures also leads to the system reproducing itself in every generation, as education always advertises itself as the best way for a person or a civilization to grapple with the chaos of possible VUCA futures.

This form of futures thinking among teachers, one that perpetuates the system and serves as the best antidote to chaos and societal melt-down, has worked well in Manitoba (and other jurisdictions) since it was established about 120 years ago. Yet the system has not always served all people well, and has done great harm in some cases, as any look into the experiences of indigenous peoples and school systems demonstrates. The world remains a VUCA world for many who do not benefit from the status quo system.

CONCLUSION AND RECOMMENDATIONS

The teachers who participated in this study envision a changing world with a status quo education system, and share this status quo vision of longer term futures with their students. Some of their sharing is overt, as they tell students to plan, to get ready for college or university, to stay in school, to prepare for whatever may come next. Some of what the teachers share is bound up in the process of schooling; the solid brick building, the regularity of the rhythm in a day, a month, and the September to June school year.

This study shows that teachers at Riverview do think about the future, but that long term envisioning of possible, probable and preferable futures is an under-valued skill set even within a high school staff that is progressive inclusive, and tech-rich. The mechanistic regularity of clock and calendar time, further amplified by school bells and schedules, has a way of anesthetizing teachers to the incredible economic and social changes that are occurring outside the doors of their schools. Everyone assumes that school will end in June, and pick up again in September, that the doors will be open, tax dollars will arrive to fund the work, and that parents will trust the system to do a good job of educating their children. These assumptions of a cyclical future are less credible than in the past, as forces of technology, economy, and a revival of neo-nationalism erode the foundations upon which public, secular, tax-funded universal education systems were built.

Teachers at Riverview and elsewhere would benefit from specific training in longer-term futures thinking. Professional development that focussed on futures that begin 50 years away at a minimum would help teachers look beyond the circumstances of their schools in the present and would help them to prepare children better for a world where rapid advances in technology and rapid degradation of viable living habitat are brought into the equation of education.

Teachers who were purposefully trained to think about preferable futures 50-100 years from now would also then be equipped to share this sort of longer term thinking with students, not as a unit, or a block of study, but as a continual attitude toward the ever-expiring present and the continual possibility of better times to come. Learning to think about longer term futures would create teachers who were positive and hopeful about the futures, and they would be less easily lulled into inaction by the reassuring rhythm of the calendar and the clock.

The conclusions I have drawn and five recommendations that follow serve as the summation of this study. The teachers at Riverview proved to be caring, responsive, and intellectually curious about the notions of time, futures, and potential futures for education systems. I was comforted to find that caring

Promising Futures

and intelligent people are in charge of helping teenagers to become young adults. I can only hope that my study reflects them accurately, honestly, and provides them some further direction to build into the lives of young people in even more dynamic and impactful ways.

Recommendations

So what should be done in the present to address the dearth of long-term futures thinking among teachers? What can be done to awaken teachers to their critical role in bringing about the most preferable of our probable futures? Teachers at Riverview do not accept that their futures are predetermined, and they do believe that choices in the present can bring about better futures, if they choose wisely.

However, people do require empowerment and direction in order to make wise choices. By way of a metaphor that has been extended throughout this work, the "doldrums" are a windless time and place; perhaps Neurath's boat seems to be stuck in the doldrums, lacking the wind to set a course, to set sail, and to set off. The following recommendations are practical and could be implemented with little difficulty, in order to allow teachers at Riverview, in the BCSD and beyond to set themselves to the task of forging preferable futures from the advantages and challenges of the present moment.

Recommendation 1: Teachers Should Learn About Long Term Futures Thinking in Teacher Preparation Programs

It is ironic that teacher preparation programs imagine all of the things young adults will need to teach children at some undetermined point in the future without providing them a course in navigating how to think about futures. Such a course would serve to cement the best aspects of the current industrial scale models of education in civilizations, while also pointing to the speed at which these monuments can fall to nothing.

Recommendation 2: Practicing Teachers Should Be Given In-Service Training to Learn About Long-Term Futures Thinking

Sadly, the pre-retirement seminar is about the closest thing to a futures presentation that many teachers receive in their careers. Also, new teachers are usually hired as substitutes or term teachers, so the longer term futures are almost never discussed with them because their employers consider them as valuable, but temporary help. Even teachers with significant job security rarely have an opportunity to envision or imagine futures, and this is because teachers are busy people with little time (scheduled or otherwise) to focus too far outside of the present. The nature of the work keeps teachers within an operational window of a few days to a few weeks, with a calendar to mark to significant events arising over the next few months.

Recommendation 3: Teachers Should Learn About Integral Theory as a way to map the Many Perspectives of Their Students, Colleagues, and Themselves

Since this study was about teachers and futures, there was never a need to explain anything about integral theory to any of the participants. Therefore it may seem surprising to include this recommendation within this study. However, I too was involved with the study as the researcher, and as a colleague to the participants. I knew how integral theory was woven throughout the study, and I could see how it was very beneficial to me as I tried to understand how teachers at Riverview perceived futures. This recommendation admittedly moves in the direction of being somewhat auto-ethnographical, bound deeply within the UL quadrant, as I try to justify that others would benefit from knowing more about integral theory because of how it benefitted me as a teacher and researcher throughout this study.

Recommendation 4: More Study Should be Done to Learn About the Ways That Students Envision Futures

This study explored the futures thinking of teachers, and this naturally leads one to wonder about the futures thinking of students. The participants of this study, and particularly those who identified as parents, pointed out that futures thinking is an activity that seems to develop after childhood. The participants perceived that teens exhibit a narrow window of time perception, meaning that adults have to do much of the futures thinking for teens. Whether or not this is the case bears further exploration. Teens at Riverview certainly are being taught very specific notions of futures in the implicit culture and nature of the way the school functions and in the explicit messages of teachers who frequently remind students that they are on a march towards graduation.

Recommendation 5: Futures Studies Material for Teachers, Including Imaginative Updated Education Scenarios, Should be Developed and Employed

One of the main barriers to thinking about distant futures is knowing where to start. The teachers at Riverview plan very little beyond a year, and since planning is the least imaginative and short term version of futures thinking they have few models for futures thinking that seem applicable.

CONCLUSION

The synthesis of themes, and their expression as the conclusions to the research study, arise from the application of integral theory to research problem, the development of the eight research questions, the literature review, methodology, data collection, findings, analysis, and the conclusions as well.

While it is true that integral theory has many detractors, it provides a way of trying to understand everything all at once, and all of the time. This ability to illuminate multiple perspectives simultaneously without melting ideas down into competing critiques and arguments is a great strength of integral theory. Integral theory, like other elegant ideas, is simple to understand for the beginner, yet reveals greater levels of complexity the longer that one studies how it works, what it means and why it persists. It serves as a theory to aid any and all intelligences that would grapple with the ancient ideas of the true, the good, and the beautiful.

Integral theory certainly has helped to shape my thinking, and aided me in trying to understand the moral, ethical, and intellectual vantage points of others, making me, in turn, a more integral person. For these reasons, as an unintentional self-experimenter writing an unintended auto-ethnography, I recommend that other teachers learn something of integral theory as a way to help make sense of their existence among the existence of others, and in the midst of all existence. This idea is large, and my words somehow make it seem silly, or obnoxious, or ostentatious. Perhaps this is what comes of earnestly trying to use anything finite to attempt to express anything infinite. As a final attempt to explain it, and a way that I explain integral to others, integral theory simply helps people find a bigger big, a smaller small, and a more together together. And we could all benefit from a deeper deepness, a more empathetic empathy, a more loving love, and a more reflective reflection.

REFERENCES

Augustine. (397). Neither time past or time future but the present only, really is. *The Confessions of St. Augustine Bishop of Hippo, Book 11* (Chapter XIV). Retrieved from http://www. leaderu.com/cyber/books/augconfessions/bk11.html

Bertalanffy, L. (1962). *Modern Theories of Development*. New York, NY: Harper Torchbooks.

Bloomberg, L. D., & Volpe, M. (2012). *Completing Your Qualitative Dissertation: A Roadmap from Beginning to End*. Los Angeles, CA: Sage.

Brewer, J. (2005). *Foundations of Multimethod research: Synthesizing Styles*. Newbury Park, CA: Sage.

Calaprice, A. (Ed.). (2005). *The New Quotable Einstein*. Princeton, NJ: Princeton University Press.

CERI. (2010a). *More about the schooling for tomorrow project*. Retrieved from http://www.oecd.org/site/schoolingfortomorrowknowledgebase/futuresthinking/scenarios/theschoolingfortomorrowscenarios.htm

Coupal, L. (2005). Practitioner-Research and the Regulation of Research Ethics: The Challenge of Individual, Organizational, and Social Interests. *Forum Qualitative Sozialforschung/Forum: Qualitative. Social Research*, 6(1). Retrieved from http://www.qualitative-research.net/index.php/fqs/article/view/528/1144

Creswell, J. W. (2012). *Quantitative Research Characteristics. In Educational research: Planning, conducting, and evaluating quantitative and qualitative research* (4th ed.). Toronto: Pearson.

Csikszentmihalyi, M. (1990). *Enjoyment and the quality of life. In Flow: The psychology of optimal experience* (pp. 43–70). Grand Rapids, MI: Harper & Row.

Davis, B., Sumara, D., & Luce-Kapler, R. (2015). Influences: Systemic Sustainability Education. In *Engaging Minds* (3rd ed.; pp. 243–245). New York, NY: Routledge. doi:10.4324/9781315695891

Denzin, N. K., & Lincoln, Y. S. (Eds.). (1994). *Introduction: Entering the field of Qualitative Research. In Handbook of Qualitative Research*. Thousand Oaks, CA: Sage.

Duncheon, J. C., & Tierney, W. G. (2013). Changing Conceptions of Time: Implications For Educational Research and Practice. *Review of Educational Research*, 83(2), 236–272. doi:10.3102/0034654313478492

Edwards, M. (2000). The Integral Cycle of Knowledge: Some thoughts on integrating Ken Wilber's Developmental and Epistemological Models. *Integral World*. Retrieved from http://www.integralworld.net/edwards2.html

Falk, D. (2008). *In Search of Time: Journeys Along a Curious Dimension*. Toronto: McLelland & Stewart.

Fein, J., & Hicks, D. (2010). *Visions of the Future*. Retrieved from http://www.unesco.org/education/tlsf/mods/theme_a/popups/mod03t04s01.html

Freire, P. (2014). *Pedagogy of hope: Reliving pedagogy of the oppressed*. New York, NY: Bloomsbury.

Fullan, M., & Langworthy, M. (2014). *Rich Futures in A Rich Seam: How New Pedagogies Find Deep Learning*. London, UK: Pearson.

Gabor, D. (1963). *Inventing the Future*. New York, NY: Alfred A. Knopf.

Girard, R. (1987). To Conclude. In *Things hidden since the foundation of the world* (S. Bann & M. Metteer, Trans.; pp. 433–447). Stanford, CA: Stanford University Press.

Hammersley, M. (1999). Not Bricolage but Boatbuilding: Exploring two metaphors for thinking about ethnography. *Journal of Contemporary Ethnography, 28*(5), 574–585. doi:10.1177/089124199129023569

Hoffman, E. (2009). *Time*. New York, NY: Picador.

Hofstadter, D. R. (1999). Gödel, Escher, Bach: An Eternal Golden Braid. (20th anniv. ed.). New York, NY: Basic Books.

Kahn, H. (1960). *On Thermonuclear War*. Princeton, NJ: Princeton University Press.

Laszlo, E. (2012). *The Ashaka Paradigm: Revolution in Science, Evolution in Consciousness*. Cardiff, CA: Waterside.

Lindgren, M., & Bandhold, H. (2009). *Scenario Planning: The Link Between Future and Strategy* (2nd ed.). New York, NY: Palgrave MacMillan.

Martin, J. A. (2008). Integral Research as a Practical Mixed-Methods Framework: Clarifying the role of Integral Methodological Pluralism. *Journal of Integral Theory and Practice., 2*(3), 155–164.

Maturana, H. R., & Varela, F. J. (1980). *Autopoiesis and Cognition: The Realization of the Living*. Boston, MA: Reidel. doi:10.1007/978-94-009-8947-4

Maturana, H. R., & Varela, F. J. (1998). *The Tree of Knowledge: The biological roots of human understanding* (R. Paolucci, Trans.). Boston, MA: Shambhala.

McKenney, S., & Reeves, T. C. (2012). *Conducting Educational Design Research*. New York, NY: Routledge.

McNiff, J. (2013). *Action Research: Principles and Practice* (3rd ed.). Florence, KY: Taylor and Francis. doi:10.4324/9780203112755

Nye, J. S. (2004). *Power in a Global Information Age*. New York, NY: Routledge.

OECD. (2006). *OECD/CERI Schooling for Tomorrow Phase III Interim Report (Draft) Ontario Ministry of Education*. Retrieved from http://www.oecd.org/edu/school/37362462.pdf

OECD. (2010). Introduction. *Trends Shaping Education*. Retrieved from http://www.oecd.org/edu/ceri/46447355.pdf

Onwuegbuzie, A. J., & Leech, N. L. (2005). On becoming a pragmatic researcher: The importance of combining quantitative and qualitative research methodologies. *International Journal of Social Research Methodology, 8*(5), 375–387. doi:10.1080/13645570500402447

Phillips, S. P., & Clarke, M. (2012). More than an education: The hidden curriculum, professional attitudes and career choice. *Medical Education, 46*(9), 887–893. doi:10.1111/j.1365-2923.2012.04316.x PMID:22891909

(2012). Prigogine: A New Sense of Order. InTrueit, D. (Ed.), *Studies in Curriculum Theory Series: Pragmatism, Postmodernism, and Complexity Theory: The Collected Works of William E. Doll, Jr* (p. 137). Florence, KY: Routledge.

RAND. (2014). Delphi. *Futures Methodologies.* Retrieved from http://www.rand.org /pardee/pubs/futures_method/delphi.html

Renner, A. (2009). Teaching Community, Praxis, and Courage: A Foundations Pedagogy of Hope and Humanization. *Educational Studies, 45*(1), 59–79. doi:10.1080/00131940802527209

Slaughter, R. (1998). Transcending Flatland: Implications of Ken Wilber's meta- narrative for futures studies. *Futures, 30*(6), 519–533. doi:10.1016/S0016-3287(98)00056-1

Slaughter, R. (2001). Knowledge creation, futures methodologies and the integral agenda. *Foresight, 3*(5), 407–418. doi:10.1108/14636680110697129

Slaughter, R. (2011a). *About us.* Foresight International. Retrieved from http://www.foresightinternational.com.au/richard-slaughter

Slaughter, R. (2011b). The Integral Futures Controversy: An Introduction. *Journal of Integral Theory and Practice, 6*(2), 105–111. Retrieved from http://integralfutures.com/ wordpress/wp-content/uploads/2011/11/RS_JITP_Intro.pdf

Slaughter, R. (2012) Introduction. *To See with Fresh Eyes: Integral Futures and the Global Emergency.* Brisbane, Australia: Foresight International. Retrieved from http://richardslaughter.com.au/wp-content/uploads/2012/06/To_See_With_Fresh_Eyes_Intro_ 051011.pdf

Slaughter, R., Naismith, L., & Houghton, N. (2004). *The Transformative Cycle.* Hawthorn, Australia: Swinburne University. Retrieved from http://richardslaughter.com.au/wp-content/ uploads/2008/06/AFI_Monograph_06.pdf

Talbot, J., & Campbell, T. (2014). Examining a teacher's negotiation through change: Understanding the influence of beliefs on behavior. *Teacher Development, 18*(3), 418–434. doi:10.1080/13664530.2014.927393

Toffler, A. (1980). *The Third Wave.* New York, NY: Bantam.

Wagar, W. W. (1983). H.G. Wells and the Genesis of Future Studies. *World Future Society Bulletin, 17*(1), 25-29. Retrieved from http://www.wnrf.org/cms/hgwells.shtml

WFSF. (2002). *About Us.* Retrieved From http://www.wfsf.org/about-us/futures-studies

Wilber, K. (1995). *Sex, Ecology, Spirituality: The Spirit of Evolution.* Boston, MA: Shambhala.

Wilber, K. (1999). *Eye to eye: the quest for the new paradigm. The Collected Works of Ken Wilber* (Vol. 3). Denver, CO: Shambhala.

Wilber, K. (2006). Integral Methodological Pluralism. In *Integral Spirituality: Startling New Role for Religion in the Modern and Post-Modern World*. Boston, MA: Shambhala.

Wilber, K. (2013). Response to Critical Realism in Defense of Integral Theory. In *Integral Post: Transmissions from the leading edge*. Retrieved from https://www.integrallife.com /integral-post/response-critical-realism-defense-integral-theory?page=0,0

Wilber, K. (2014). The Future of Buddhism. In *The Fourth Turning: Imagining the evolution of an Integral Buddhism*. Boston, MA: Shambhala.

KEY TERMS AND DEFINITIONS

1-to-1: An education technology practice and pedagogy that encourages a 1-to-1 ratio of computers to students in educational settings.

AQAL: Acronym for "all quadrants, all levels, all lines, all states, all types." This acronym aids by combining the five most essential components of integral theory into one word, and represents the holistic nature of integral theory, particularly as it is applied within any specific context or to any specific person.

Bring Your Own Device (BYOD): A policy decision whereby one must bring his or her own approved computer/tablet/ICT device to the school, as a condition set by the institution. Generally, BYOD leads to a shared-resource model where internet access and proprietary web content is provided by the institution employing a user-name and password, but access to these resources is through devices owned and maintained by the students.

Futures: The perceptions of the time that is to come that are created and expressed through the sets of values, beliefs, of individuals and of groups. Futures research emerged as an academic discipline beginning with the publication of *On Thermonuclear War* by Herman Kahn in 1960. Through the 1970s futurism was popularized by writers such as Alvin Toffler (1980). From the mid-1980s to the mid-1990s as researchers such as Richard Slaughter (1998), Francis P. Hutchinson (1996), and Wendell Bell (1997) brought a greater degree of synthesis and academic rigor to the field.

Integral Lines: Representative of all potential and known models of development, and are present within each of the four quadrants of integral theory.

Integral States: All potential human states, such as being awake, or being in deep sleep, in meditative states, the state of arousal, and all senses of emotional and psychological states. States are temporary, but if a state is sustained repeatedly or over a long duration of time then it ultimately impacts the person as a whole, altering one's levels of consciousness.

Integral Theory: A holistic theory that draws together all known forms of knowledge discovery and knowledge creation in an attempt to provide coherence and synthesis across all understandings of the universe, both as it is known, and unknown. The major theorist is Ken Wilber, a living American philosopher.

Lower Left Quadrant (LL): The plural/intersubjective domain, wherein the collective understandings of people are explored, developed and understood. The realm of social and communal understandings.

Lower Right Quadrant (LR): The plural/inter-objective domain, wherein the systems in which all things exist, the ways they interact and the complexities they face are made real. This is the realm of systems and complexity, and expands far beyond human control or knowledge.

Upper Left Quadrant (UL): The singular/subjective domain, wherein one ultimately experiences a reality and understanding that is completely unique and potentially indescribable to others, or which may sometimes be observed but not reliably interpreted by others. The realm of phenomenology and individual experience.

Upper Right Quadrant (UR): The singular/objective domain, wherein the facts of the world that one inhabits are explored and discovered. The realm of science and empiricism.

Chapter 11
Creating a Culture of Inclusion in Pre-Kindergarten:
An Integral Analysis of Beliefs, Understandings, and Practices of Early Childhood Educators

Natalie Anne Prytuluk
Edmonton Public Schools, Canada

ABSTRACT

The purpose of this study was to understand how beliefs, understandings, and pedagogical practices of early childhood educators affect, and are affected by, their relationships with children, classroom team members, parents, and colleagues, as they create an inclusive culture in a pre-kindergarten classroom. To explore this research problem from multiple perspectives, integral theory was selected as the conceptual framework, and a multi-methods exploratory sequential design was employed using integral methodological pluralism. Data about educational experiences, culture, behaviors, and systems, were collected from five early childhood educators in pre-kindergarten classrooms in four urban schools, followed by a questionnaire of classroom practices, document analysis, and a focus group. Findings revealed that important factors for creating an inclusive classroom culture included: early childhood educators' positive beliefs toward inclusion; a social constructivist theoretical perspective; and the ability to build strong relationships with children, parents, and colleagues.

INTRODUCTION

The provocation for this research study emerged from questions surrounding challenges to implement inclusive education within early childhood classrooms in the province of Alberta, Canada. In Alberta, the transition from segregated special education programs toward inclusive education is relatively new. A framework for inclusive education in all schools was not published by the Government of Alberta until 2010, and schools are still coping with what inclusive education looks like within the classroom. A Blue

DOI: 10.4018/978-1-5225-5873-6.ch011

Ribbon Panel on Inclusive Education in Alberta Schools (Alberta Teachers' Association, 2014) concluded that effective implementation of inclusion in Alberta has not been realized due to inadequate support and resources in the areas of shared vision, leadership, research and evidence, teacher professional growth, and community engagement. While these issues are not isolated to Alberta, they exemplify the problem of systemic change without providing adequate resources and time to connect policy to research and practice (Fixsen, Blasé, Metz & Van Dyke, 2013; Odom, Buyesse & Soukakou, 2011; Lieber, Hanson, Odom, Sandall, Schwartz, Horn, & Wolery, 2000). Despite these challenges, Alberta school districts continue to forge ahead to make inclusive education a reality in their schools and classrooms albeit with varying degrees of success.

Schools in the province are faced with considerable complexities in regard to inclusive education for students in grades 1 to 12, but inclusion becomes increasingly difficult to implement prior to kindergarten. While kindergarten is universally funded by the provincial government and available to every child, what is lacking for pre-kindergarten children are inclusive programs in which all children have access to an environment that is flexible and can respond to support a diversity of needs, rather than a segregated special education model that includes children who require specialized supports, interventions and services based on a medical diagnosis, and excludes those who don't (Leiber et al., 2000).

The main challenge to providing inclusive pre-kindergarten programs is that provincial grants are given to school boards to support children with medically diagnosed disabilities or delays and those who are learning English as a new language, making it financially difficult for school boards to create programming that is inclusive and representative of a range of learners. This funding model also requires a process of assessing, labeling and sorting children into those who are defined as normal and don't require support and those who are viewed as lacking, deficient and needing extra services to get them ready for school. This deficit based concept is grounded in principles of developmental psychology, and has come under fire from postmodernist thinkers as a limiting perspective that presents problematic assumptions about children and does not address the complexities of working with children and families in the 21st century (Manning, 2011; Pacini-Ketchabaw et al., 2010; Pence & Pacini-Ketchabaw, 2008). School boards must also make sense of conflicting government requirements that "educating children with special education needs in inclusive settings is the option of first choice" for families and the provision of "systematic and planned contact with children who do not have special education needs" is to be part of the program design (Alberta Education, 2006, p. 15).

These challenges, alongside changes in thinking about how young children learn and develop, have created a need for Alberta school boards to reconceptualize how programming prior to kindergarten is provided for children. What is emerging from this shift is juxtaposition between a traditional, medically informed, deficit based and segregated provision of pre-kindergarten programs for children with special education needs, and a postmodern, progressive vision of pre-kindergarten programs that represent a democratic, inclusive and strengths-based model for all children. Early Childhood Educators (ECEs) are in the midst of this disequilibrium and are key players to influence and be influenced by these discourses.

Problem Statement

In the province of Alberta, Canada, early childhood education is undergoing change to reconceptualize pre-kindergarten programming that is inclusive of all children in light of postmodern views and theoretical perspectives about diversity and the impact of experiences, relationships, environment and culture on learning. This thinking has created tensions between the view of difference as a deficit that needs to be fixed through interventions and support in a specialized education program, and difference as a natural and vital part of an inclusive school community. ECEs' beliefs, understandings and pedagogical practices are at the centre of this transformation because what they think and do in the classroom directly impacts children. Therefore, this research was guided by the following problem statement: What are the perspectives of ECEs as they experience the creation of inclusive programming in the early years?

Purpose

The purpose of this study was to understand how beliefs, understandings, and pedagogical practices of ECEs affect, and are affected by, their relationships with children, classroom team members, parents, and colleagues, as they create an inclusive culture in a pre-kindergarten classroom. My reason for engaging in this specific line of inquiry was to better understand ECEs' experiences of inclusion in a large urban public school system and how environments, practices and classroom culture are shaped to include all children. My assumption was that this research would lead to deeper insight into how inclusive early childhood programming can be realized and applied in other settings. While this study is context specific, the possibility exists that findings from this study have the potential to inform inclusive practices locally, provincially and perhaps internationally.

Setting and Situation of the Study

This study took place in five classrooms in four different schools with pre-kindergarten programs in a large urban Alberta school district. This school district was in the process of restructuring how early childhood programming before kindergarten is provided for children ages 2 years and 8 months to 5 years of age. At the time of this study, three models of programming in this district existed, and each relied on funding from Alberta Education based on eligibility criteria such as a medical diagnosis for severe or mild to moderate disability or delay, or an observational assessment or questionnaire to identify children who are English language learners (ELL). The three models were: 1) a segregated program for children identified as having severe disabilities or delays; 2) a community program located in high risk or vulnerable socioeconomic areas, and: 3) a new program model that combined aspects of the first and second model to provide programming that included a diverse group of children. Each program has its own challenges and strengths and this was being explored as part of the restructuring of what a new pre-kindergarten model could look like. ECEs working in these pre-kindergarten programs have their own assumptions, beliefs and understandings about inclusion and early childhood, providing a unique opportunity and context to situate this study.

The ECEs selected were a purposive sample based on recommendations from principals of schools that have pre-kindergarten programs. Principals were given a summary of the study, and approached teachers they believed would be good candidates, and obtained verbal consent from the ECE to share their contact information with the researcher via email. From the list of names put forward by the principals of these schools, five ECEs were invited to participate. The participants had a range of learners in their classroom, believed they had an inclusive classroom culture, and were excited to be part of the research study.

Rationale and Significance

ECEs in Alberta, Canada, are in the midst of a changing educational landscape in which the importance of early childhood is gaining recognition at all levels of government, community, school, and families. As school culture shifts to a postmodern perspective and reclaims social constructivist and democratic citizenship ideologies that shape a view of children as capable agents involved in creating their own continuum of learning and discovering, there will be disequilibrium as beliefs, understandings and pedagogies are questioned and challenged.

This research study offers a rich opportunity for in-depth exploration of inclusion in early childhood education within the context of system-wide change in one Alberta school district. Knowing more about what ECEs think and do in response to changing classroom culture provides original contributions to the fields of inclusion, diversity, early childhood education, change and change management in education, and the possibilities for using integral theory as a conceptual framework for educational research, and may lead to further research provincially and nationally. This work adds to established and current research in early childhood education and inclusive education, and provides a distinct perspective of inclusive early childhood programming in Alberta by exploring participants' experiences as they construct and actively collaborate in the research process.

Integral Theory as the Conceptual Framework

To make sense of how the construct of inclusion was perceived and enacted by teachers within an early childhood context required a broader view of the educational system as a holistic organism; one that must be examined consciously through intentional, behavioural, cultural and social perspectives. For this reason, Ken Wilber's integral theory was used as the conceptual framework for the ontological, epistemological and methodological organization of this study (Wilber, 2011, 2006; Wilber, Patten, Leonard & Morelli, 2008).

Wilber consolidated theories from great thinkers throughout history, uniting non-dual philosophies of the east with the critical philosophies of the west and organized them into four quadrants (Snow, 2007). Each of the quadrants represents a window into the interior and exterior view of experiences, culture, behaviour and systems of any phenomenon. "Like unique windows on the world, the quadrants offer four unique ways of looking at the same thing, each of which reveals different dimensions or qualities of that thing" (Brown, 2006, p.5). Within each quadrant, the researcher can examine phenomena internally and externally as well as from the individual and collective view, maximizing first, second and third person perspectives, for a deep and comprehensive approach to the research questions.

The upper left (UL) quadrant holds the psychological theories and looks at the individual first person perspective which includes both internal personal experiences and external reflections on those experiences; What do I believe? How is what I believe described by others?

The lower left (LL) quadrant holds the socio-cultural theories and looks at the collective first and second person perspective, both from the internal belief systems and relationships of a culture and the external worldview; What do we believe? How do others describe what we believe?

The upper right (UR) quadrant holds the behavioural theories and looks at the empirical and objective third person view both internally and from external observations; What do I observe? What do others observe me doing?

The lower right (LR) quadrant holds the systems theories and looks at the collective perspective from a third person objective internal and external view; What do we observe? What do others observe about us? Table 1 illustrates each of the quadrants and the theoretical perspectives each quadrant encompasses.

The Researcher

The personal and professional identity of the researcher and the experiences, biases and assumptions they bring into the research they are conducting cannot be ignored.

[T]he 'I' must be acknowledged- it really does matter where you as that researcher 'stand' relative to the process of your own fieldwork and ultimately to the subject of your study. That means not only whether you might consider yourself an 'insider' or and 'outsider' to the group that may be your focus but also the attitudes and/or preconceptions that you bring to that study. (Hoey, 2014, p. 4)

An important consideration in conducting this study was my relationship as a researcher to the people and places in the study. I entered into this research as both an insider and an outsider. As an insider, I have been an ECE for over seventeen years with this school board. I bring my own lived experiences of what it means to be an ECE, to work with diverse populations of children and families in a variety of communities in this city, and have felt frustration and joy, challenge, reward and intense passion for this work. I believe that it is our questions and wonders and inquiry that drive lifelong learning. Continuously questioning assumptions, observing and reflecting, and engaging in discourse continues to be an important part of my professional growth and has led me on an academic journey through a master of education degree and the pursuit of a doctorate to follow my inquiries.

While teachers may see themselves as researchers (Dietze & Kashin, 2016) and contributing to the knowledge base of a larger research community, positioning myself as a researcher could also position me to be perceived as an outsider rather than in collaboration with the participants to discover and learn together. Ideally, I viewed my role as researcher to be one of "observer as participant" which "implies that the researcher is first and foremost seen as an observer who could be engaged in the activities of the people being studied" (Belouin, 2010, p.1). This permitted me to gage the level of my involvement

Table 1. Integral theory four quadrant characteristics

Upper Left (UL) Interior- Individual (Intentional)	Upper Right (UR) Exterior- Individual (Behavioural)
Educational Experiences 1st person perspectives Experiential phenomena- phenomenology • Phenomenological inquiry: emotions, identity & beliefs	Educational Behaviours 3rd person perspectives Behavioural phenomena- autopoiesis • Behaviour analyses: cognitive, behavioural
Lower Left (LL) **Interior – Collective (Cultural)**	**Lower Right (LR)** **Exterior- Collective (Systems)**
Educational Culture 1st & 2nd person perspectives Cultural phenomena- hermeneutical phenomenology • Cultural & worldview investigation: educational, relational & philosophical	Educational Systems 3rd person perspectives Systems phenomena- social autopoiesis • Systems analysis: educational environment, policies, economics

Adapted from S. Esbjörn-Hargens (2009, 2007)

based on the level of trust and comfort of the ECE. Ensuring that it was clearly communicated that I was not there to observe the ECE, but rather to describe the environment, the culture and the rituals that occur within the classroom context in collaboration with the ECEs observations, was part of building a high level of trust. As both a colleague and a researcher, I was truly honoured to listen to the stories shared and felt a great deal of responsibility to guard the words that were disclosed and do my very best to accurately capture the information entrusted to me.

BACKGROUND

I used integral theory as the conceptual framework to organize related literature into themes connected to each research question within each quadrant perspective, as indicated in Figure 1.

UL: Educational Experiences in Inclusion and Early Childhood

This section explores literature related to how teachers experience inclusion and early childhood education, namely those deeply held beliefs or interpretations of the world maintained by members of a particular group (Hora & Millar, 2011). Davis et. al (2015) express that the biases teachers carry with them may enable or limit how they view their students, classroom and teaching practice. "Everyone is prejudiced, and most prejudices are absolutely necessary. They are the expectations, the beliefs, and the assumptions that are rooted in each person's unique-but-culturally-embedded histories" (p. 122). Themes from this section will explore how ECE's beliefs and understandings may impact the creation of an inclusive classroom culture.

Figure 1. Map of the literature review

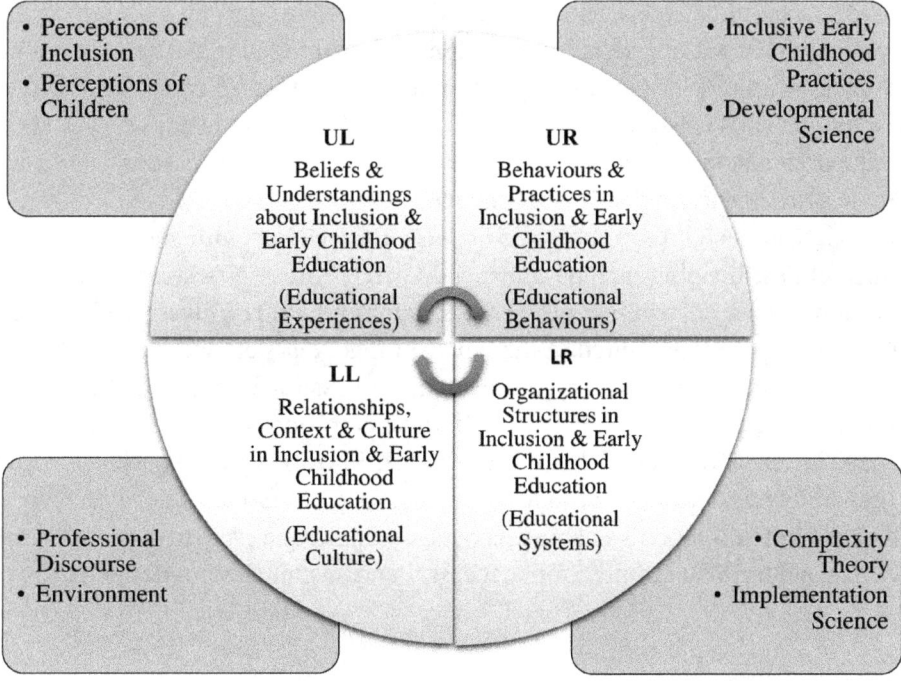

Perceptions of Inclusion

In the upper left quadrant of the integral theory framework are first person perspectives; what do individuals think and feel and how do they experience their world? It is important to situate what ECEs believe and understand about inclusion within the substantial body of research that has been written about teacher perception of inclusion and the impact on classroom practice. Not surprisingly, positive teacher attitudes toward inclusion appear to be the most important factor toward successful implementation of inclusion (McGhie,-Richmond, Irvine, Loreman, Cizman & Lupart, 2013; Hsieh & Hsieh, 2012; Clough & Nutbrown, 2004). Avramadis and Norwich (2002) also found the reverse to be true; that teacher resistance to inclusion created the largest barrier to implementation in schools.

Research by Pacini-Ketchabaw and Schecter (2002) highlight how difficult it is for teachers to challenge the concept of difference as deficiency and to construct an alternative view. In their three-year action research study with 39 teachers from two urban schools in the province of Ontario, Canada, they found teachers held different core narratives regarding their understanding of diversity. The four discourses commonly held by teachers were; difference as a deficit; the purpose of schooling as preparation for academic success; intercultural sensitivity as a pedagogical tool; and diversity as a curriculum of study. Their findings indicated that critical discourse through conversation and collaboration with colleagues, students, and the community, increased teacher's willingness to experiment with creating a classroom culture that successfully promoted the learning and inclusion of all, but the discourse of deficiency remained the predominant perspective.

In multiple studies, teachers clearly expressed the challenges of inclusion. Teachers want to do the very best for the students in their classroom but often feel guilty, inadequate or frustrated in accommodating children with diverse needs in their classroom. Concerns centre on lack of time for planning and collaboration, need for ongoing professional development and training, and lack of support and resources (ATA, 2014; Horne & Timmons, 2009). Perhaps the largest challenge identified by teachers was including children with emotional and behavioural difficulties (Nutbrown & Clough, 2004; Clough & Nutbrown, 2004; Avramidis & Norwich, 2002). Clough (1998, p.5) also identifies the danger of a child being physically included but socially or academically excluded if teachers do not have the skills, knowledge and positive attitude to structure appropriate inclusive learning environments and practices. Nutbrown and Clough (2004) also recognized the inclusion/exclusion factor of "yes but". These were teachers who valued inclusion in policy, "but" in practice had multiple reasons why it wouldn't work, highlighting a gap with transferring policy to practice.

Teachers who view inclusion favourably see benefits for students with and without disabilities. For children with disabilities, benefits include enhanced social skills, self-esteem, a sense of belonging, academic motivation and overall well-being (Horne & Timmons, 2009; Buysse, Skinner & Grant, 2001). For children with development measured in the normal range, teachers viewed benefits of inclusion as extending attributes of acceptance, empathy, caring and compassion for others and awareness of personal strengths (Hsieh & Hsieh, 2012; Leiber et al., 1997). In an empirical study of 130 urban early childhood teachers, Hsieh and Hsieh (2012) found that those who had a positive past experience with children with diverse needs, generally had a positive attitude toward inclusion as did teachers with more experience or related education. So how do schools enable teachers to experience a positive inclusive classroom and gain the experience and training required for successful and sustainable implementation of inclusion?

Several studies which explored teacher perception and attitude toward inclusion identified key themes that influence successful implementation of inclusion and are about the dynamics of changing cultures as well as changing individuals:

- Specialized instruction is important to address the individual learning needs of children so the experience of inclusion is positive (Odom, Buyesse & Soukakou, 2011; Avramidis & Norwich, 2002).
- Adequate system supports are necessary such as resources for professional development, coaching or mentoring, and time for planning (Odom, Buyesse & Soukakou, 2011; Horne & Timmons, 2009; Nutbrown & Clough, 2004; Avramidis & Norwich, 2002).
- Collaboration and communities of practice can lead to a shared responsibility for all children which is also an important perception toward successful inclusion (McGhie-Richmond et al. 2013; Odom, Buyesse & Soukakou, 2011).

Perceptions of Children

Early childhood professionals not only bring perceptions about inclusion into the classroom, they also bring a preconceived image of the child into their work with children. This image of the child influences how they relate to children, construct learning and knowing in the classroom environment, and develop and carry out practice.

A variety of theoretical, socio-cultural, political and economic perspectives of early childhood contribute to current views and beliefs of children and schooling (Hinitz, 2013, Kellett, 2013) and these beliefs may align or clash with the philosophy of inclusion. Kegan (1994) describes these competing approaches to education as fundamentalist (traditional) and humanist (holistic) philosophies.

A fundamentalist philosophical approach in education is defined by long standing traditions and customs that have been established and deemed appropriate and necessary by societal standards. Inherent in a traditional educational approach is the 'normalization' of the child. Olsson (2009) describes normalization as "representing, classifying and measuring of the child through the concept of 'developmentally' which has led to the inclusion and exclusion of certain ways of being a child" (p. 34). Developmentally appropriate practice is the dominant pedagogical discourse found in curriculum programs, assessment tools and resources to guide teaching and learning.

A humanist philosophical approach in education adopts a holistic perspective to develop the potential of all children by engaging children in the learning process and encouraging personal and collective responsibility for each other. Educators in a Reggio based classroom, for example, operate on the premise that all children have extraordinary potential, strengths, ideas, opinions and theories that are co-constructed alongside peers and adults in the child's world. This notion of special rights is also affirmed through research conducted by Nind, Flewitt and Payler (2014) which demonstrated that children with learning difficulties are able to convey preferences, patterns of resistance and choice as active meaning-makers within the social classroom environment. However, it takes a reflective and observant teacher who views children as capable, to respond to the multiple ways that children may communicate their opinions and ideas. Embracing a holistic image of the child, particularly children with diverse needs, allows educators to expect, invite, encourage and embrace diversity, difference, ambiguity and uncertainty (McCartney & Morton, 2013).

These philosophical approaches provide very different conceptions of child development and the organization of schooling. Understanding how early childhood professionals view the child strongly influences classroom practices as aligned with a holistic or traditional pedagogical approach, which in turn, affects how inclusion is realized in the classroom. The basis for this study was to explore what early childhood professionals believe and understand about young children, and how these views may be grounded in a traditional or holistic perspective.

UR: Educational Behaviours in Inclusion and Early Childhood

Within this quadrant the objective educational behaviours related to research in the area of inclusive early childhood practices are examined. This section focuses on evidence-base practices that shape positive educational outcomes for diverse learners.

Inclusive Early Childhood Practices

Based on a review of the multitude of practices used in inclusive and segregated early childhood settings, the Division for Early Childhood of the Council for Exceptional Children (DEC) and the National Association for the Education of Young Children (NAEYC) (2009) identified three major areas that define quality inclusive programming in early childhood alongside current research identifying evidence-based practices. While the term quality programming can be problematic, Pence and Pacini-Ketchabaw (2008) define quality early childhood programming as "emerging from diverse pedagogical, social, and cultural factors that interact within specific contexts" (p. 4). Three areas identified in quality inclusive early childhood programs are access, participation and support and are described as follows:

1. Access to a variety of diverse activities and environments to support the development of all children and enable them to take part in the learning reflects an accessible and inclusive setting. Universal Design for Learning (UDL) is one such approach that effectively meets the needs of all learners so they can experience success. UDL includes adapting and modifying the physical environment, using assistive technology, individualized assessment and evaluation, and using multiple strategies for instruction and learning (Katz, 2012; DEC/NAEYC, 2009; Conn-Powers, Cross, Traub, & Hutter-Pishgahi, 2006).
2. Participation using a variety of instructional and intervention approaches to engage all children in learning and play. Participation and engagement in the social context of school is an important goal to develop a sense of belonging which is at the heart of an inclusive program. Evidence abounds that immersing children in an environment that encourages child-initiated play alongside guided learning with rich, experiential and playful activities is an engaging and appropriate way to enhance attitudes, skills, and knowledge, but also leads to later success in school and life (CMEC, 2014; Miller & Almon, 2009; Hewes, 2006). Individualized instruction and interventions are required for some children to provide necessary supports so they can fully participate with their peers. Tiered models of intervention such as Response to Intervention (RTI) provide a framework to plan instruction, intervention and supports to meet diverse needs within the classroom (Odom, Buysse, & Soukakou, 2011; DEC/NAEYC, 2009).

3. Supports at the systems-level to implement high quality inclusion. Support consists of professional development including acquisition of evidence-based practices and collaboration with colleagues, parents and community partners (Odom, Buysse, & Soukakou, 2011; DEC/NAEYC, 2009; Lero, 2010; Odom, 2009; Devore & Russell, 2007; Cook & Odom, 2013). Building knowledge, skills and attitudes of early childhood professionals toward positive and effective inclusive practices is the foundation to quality inclusive early childhood programs.

Developmental Science

In reviewing developmental science, it is important to note there is controversy surrounding the principles of developmental practice in early childhood education as a limiting and problematic westernized perspective that defines what normal development is, and that it overlooks factors such as environment, culture and relationships (Pacini-Ketchabaw, Kummen & Thompson, 2010; Pacini-Ketchabaw, White & Armstrong de Almeida, 2006). This is where an integral approach to educational controversy such as development theory enables a holistic view of child development by including all perspectives. Whereas conventional approaches tend to emphasise the objective dimension of empirical science and rationality, and the holistic approaches tend to highlight both the subjective dimension of expression and self-inquiry and the intersubjective dimension of collaboration and meaning-making, an integral approach includes and values all three dimensions: objective, subjective, and intersubjective (Esbjorn-Hargens, 2007).

Therefore, it would be negligent to disregard emerging scientific research in child development, and important to review the objective perspective on brain development and how certain factors may impact the biological health and well-being of children. Consideration for, and connection to the other quadrants and in particular, socio-cultural theory, alongside biological neuroscience, psychiatry, developmental psychology, genetics, and pediatric medicine are examined to situate what practices ECEs are subscribing to and tension between beliefs, understandings and practices as they are enacted in the classroom.

Where we can see the merging of science and culture is the collapse of the modern belief that our genetic make-up is fixed and cannot be altered.

Exciting new studies reveal that most human traits and most diseases come not just from genetics and not just from environmental experience, but from a convergence of the two- a mixing of the two into what are called gene-environment interactions. It is this differential expression of the genetic code that turns out to be what really does guide our fate, our ability, and our potential as human beings (Boyce in AFWI 2013, p.11)

The lines are softening between environment, experiences, socio-cultural and biological traits, and are shifting modernist perspectives toward a more encompassing postmodern and pragmatic view of child development. This scientific research has important implications for practice. If early childhood professionals understand developmental neuroscience and their role in supporting the developing brain, they can better provide a classroom environment, which supports how children learn.

LR: Educational Systems in Inclusion and Early Childhood

Complexity Theory

Schools, school boards, and governments are complex systems that co-exist and influence each other with varying ideologies, structures and processes that are constantly in transition. Examining organizational structures and theories that frame the working environment of ECEs provides insight into policies, assumptions and worldviews that help or hinder how inclusive early childhood classroom cultures emerge. Complexity theory provides a broad view of educational systems as holistic organisms and is defined by three core components: 1. Self-organization of individuals and the inter-relationships created among them can potentially lead to new structures and behaviours, 2. System growth relies on continuous feedback, which influences the system both positively and negatively, and 3. New structures often emerge through the process of collaboration (Mason, 2008, Morrison, 2008). Collaboration provides a fluid, dynamic and iterative process that allows the system to discover meaningful practices in an authentic manner (Snyder, 2013). Systems also subscribe to ideologies that form organizing principles to guide development of policies and regulations (Dietz & Kashin, 2016). Through this process of feedback and collaboration, system policies and processes shift and change as new systems become the social norm.

Within the education system it is important to critically review policies as they reflect the dominant discourses. Typically, societal norms are situated within the policies themselves. By critically exploring policies we can view how power operates and transforms and reforms categories of inclusion and exclusion and societal consciousness regarding these constructs as they apply to the field of education (Pacini-Ketchabaw, White, & Armstrong de Almeida, 2006). In Alberta, the gaps in policy, funding, labeling and inclusion versus segregation, continue to be problematic. This is a complex problem that requires a systems approach to change from governmental levels through the layers of school boards, schools and classrooms. Rittel and Webber (1973) describe this as a wicked problem, one that will fight back at any attempt to change the system as is, and that will expose other issues and assumptions. To tame a wicked problem requires patience, a clear plan, and the support of those involved in bringing about change. Complexity theory helps orient the challenges and opportunities of creating an inclusive early childhood culture within this larger perspective. How policy is translated and then implemented in the classroom requires meaningfully connecting what this looks like in "real life". The next section will look at implementation science as a means to bridge research and practice.

Implementation Science

Implementation science is a new and developing field, which studies the integration of research and evidence into policy and practice. Eccles and Mittman (2006) describe implementation science as "the scientific study of methods to promote the systemic uptake of research findings and other evidence-based practices into routine practice" (p. 1). The goal is to understand how innovations in practice are adopted, maintained and sustained so that it becomes part of the educational culture. Addressing the research to policy to practice gap is part of the complexity of education systems. Relationships from the macro system of educational research to the microsystem of the individual ECE working in the classroom setting are complex and dependent on reciprocal communication, flexibility and adaptation of what research is identifying as evidence and what that means in practice. Limitations of implementation science are lack of consensus on the best scientific methodology for research, and because it is relatively new there is not a solid body of research to define what that methodology should be or how to disseminate findings. In addition, mixed methods are often used to provide an authentic viewpoint rather than precise empirical results, which has been criticised as lacking rigour (Fogarty International Center, 2013).

Implementation strategies to adopt and integrate evidence-based interventions and change patterns of practice within specific settings take time and often fail to be sustained (Cook & Odom, 2013). This is often due to resistance to change and lack of time to ingrain new ways of doing things. Although rigorous guidelines have been developed to identify evidence-based practices, attempting to put practices into action have proved difficult. Research may indicate a practice is ineffective, yet many professionals continue to use ineffective practices within the classroom (Hattie & Yates, 2014; Cook & Odom, 2013).

Summary

Relevant literature was organized thematically within the framework of integral theory beginning with the UL and research related to perceptions of inclusion and children in the educational context. In the LL educational culture was reviewed, specifically professional discourse and classroom culture and how we collectively engage in co-constructing understandings and knowledge. The UR provided an objective, empirical view of evidence-based practices in early childhood education and a review of findings in developmental science and how this relates to classroom practice. Finally, the LR provided a review of theory and research that impacts educational systems such as complexity theory and implementation science which has implications for how policy and research influence actualization of inclusive early childhood classroom cultures.

A detailed explanation of AQAL, the acronym that encompasses all developmental aspects of integral theory; quadrants, levels, lines, states and types, and how these elements are important considerations for this research study, is included in the study report, but is beyond the scope of this chapter.

METHODS

Research Design Overview

This study employed a multi-methods approach to investigate the research questions situated in Wilber's (2011, 2006) integral theory framework. As integral theory includes all valid forms of knowledge and research, it also includes all valid forms of methodologies. This methodological pluralism is known as integral methodological pluralism (IMP). For the purpose of this study, elements of phenomenology, ethnography and empiricism were used to answer the research questions.

The research questions, literature review and methodologies have all been organized within the four quadrants of integral theory to ensure the research problem was explored in a thorough and comprehensive manner. However, a caution when using the model of integral theory is that the researcher does not compromise the integrity of the study by doing a broad and superficial sweep of three different methodological perspectives rather than deeply exploring one aspect. I focused on being true to the research questions, which were best explored using phenomenological, ethnographic and empirical methods encompassed within each of the four quadrants. As an organizational tool, integral theory provided me robust overview of the issues, dynamics and challenges surrounding the research problem of inclusion in early childhood education.

The Research Questions

The purpose of this study was to understand how the beliefs, understandings and pedagogical practices of early childhood professionals affect the creation of an inclusive culture in a pre-kindergarten classroom. To meet this goal, four research questions were addressed:

1. What do ECEs believe and understand about creating a classroom culture that includes all children?
2. How are ECEs affected by, and how do they affect perspectives shared by children, classroom team members, colleagues, and parents in the creation of an inclusive classroom culture?
3. What pedagogical practices do ECEs use to include all children?
4. How are ECEs affected by system level structures and processes in the creation of an inclusive classroom culture?

Based on the conceptual framework of integral theory, the research questions can be viewed through the four quadrants of integral theory (Table 2) and organized as follows:

Data Collection Methods Overview

Once approval from the Research Ethics Board at the University of Calgary and the Research Proposal Review Committee with the participating school board was granted, ECEs in pre-kindergarten settings and selected by their principals, were invited to participate in this study by the researcher. The following methods were used for gathering data:

- Two semi-structured interviews were conducted with the participants. The first was to discuss beliefs, understandings and pedagogical practices and how ECEs monitor and reflect on what they think and do. The second was to discuss how ECEs respond to the range of perspectives offered by other players in the classroom context, how these perspectives shaped new beliefs and understanding and conversely, how the ECE may have impacted other's beliefs and understandings.
- Two to four scheduled times to volunteer in the classroom alongside the ECE were agreed upon. This provided me with the opportunity for deeper understanding of the classroom context and

Table 2. Research questions in the four quadrants. (Hereafter, each of the quadrants will referred to by its abbreviated name; UL (Upper Left), LL (Lower Left), UR (Upper Right) and LR (Lower Right).

	Interior	Exterior
Individual	**UL** **Educational Experiences** What do ECEs believe and understand about creating a classroom culture that includes all children?	**UR** **Educational Behaviours** What pedagogical practices do ECEs use to include all children?
Collective	**LL** **Educational Culture** How are ECEs affected by and how do they affect perspectives shared by children, classroom team members, colleagues, and parents in the creation of an inclusive classroom culture?	**LR** **Educational Systems** How are ECEs affected by system level structures and processes in the creation of an inclusive classroom culture?

culture and to create rich descriptions of the environment. Each visit was followed by collaborative discussion with the ECE to talk about what was observed by both the researcher and the ECE. Permission for my presence in the classroom was granted by the ECE and principal. As well, parents were informed of my visits and provided consent for my presence, and children were informed and asked for their consent for my presence in the classroom. However, for children who were non-verbal, implied consent was given by their reaction and acceptance of my presence in the classroom.

- Documentation in the form of research notes was kept to record items deemed important through informal conversations with participants that occurred during time volunteering in the classroom or follow up conversations to clarify data collected from interviews.
- A questionnaire was completed by the ECEs about the classroom environment and pedagogical practices that ECEs subscribe to. This was developed from information gathered from the two interviews, classroom visitations and the literature review.
- Samples of documentation that illustrated beliefs, understandings and pedagogical practices as they emerge in the classroom included photographs, displays, and publications such as class newsletters.
- A focus group of ECEs with leadership experience were invited to participate in a discourse on barriers and opportunities to inclusion in the pre-kindergarten classroom within the systems of school, community and government. Three ECEs with leadership experience and who were teaching or had taught pre-kindergarten in the school district were recruited through an email invitation to take part in the focus group.

Table 3 provides a summary of the research questions and methodologies used in this research study.

The five cases studied were situated within one urban Alberta public school district in the process of exploring the need to create inclusive pre-kindergarten options for children. At the time of this research study, there were three pre-kindergarten options; 1) Segregated programs for children with medically diagnosed disabilities or delays; 2) community programs located in socially and economically vulnerable communities and open to all children who live in the school attendance area; and 3) a new program which is a hybrid of the two previous models in which children identified as having a disability or delay and who are learning English as a new language are included into the classroom. The case studies and ECE participants were purposefully selected from schools offering one of the pre-kindergarten options in order to research distinct but similar pre-kindergarten classrooms and how ECEs in these contexts experienced inclusion and the creation of an inclusive classroom environment.

Data Analysis and Interpretation

Data were analyzed using data condensation and interpretation and compared with patterns predicted from theory and the literature review. This involved reducing the collected data to patterns and categories, which were interpreted by the researcher and then presented as a collective picture of patterns and categories discovered (Creswell, 2015). The term data condensation is used by Miles, Huberman & Saldana (2014) and refers to making data stronger by selecting, simplifying, organizing and transforming data as part of the analysis. Data condensation leads the researcher through a creative process in which final conclusions can eventually be made. NVIVO 11 software was used to assist with this process. Following

Table 3. Research questions, methodology and methods in the four quadrant integral model

	Interior	Exterior
Individual	**UL** **Educational Experiences** 1st person perspectives What do ECEs believe and understand about creating a classroom culture that includes all children? **Methodology:** phenomenology **Methods:** semi-structured interviews, thematic analysis, research journal	**UR** **Educational Behaviours** 3rd person perspectives What pedagogical practices do ECEs use to include all children? **Methodology:** empiricism **Methods:** classroom practices questionnaire, classroom visitations, statistical analysis
Collective	**LL** **Educational Culture** 1st and 2nd person perspectives How are ECEs affected by, and how do they affect perspectives shared by children, classroom team members, colleagues, and parents in the creation of an inclusive classroom culture? **Methodology:** ethnography, case study **Methods:** semi-structured interviews, thematic analysis, classroom visitations	**LR** **Educational Systems** 3rd person perspectives How are ECEs affected by system level structures and processes in the creation of an inclusive classroom culture? **Methodology:** empiricism **Methods:** focus groups, text and document analysis

the data gathering, the transcripts and field notes were uploaded into the NVIVO 11 pro software and coded to look for patterns and create themes.

Within ethnographic research, analysis consists of describing patterns of behaviours or practices and beliefs within the cultural group. Like phenomenology, ethnographers describe in a detailed, substantial and vivid manner what is happening within the cultural group to bring to life the events or process being studied and also include their own biases.

In analysing the data, I asked reflective questions such as; what views of inclusion does this text reveal? What tensions can be identified between the ECE's perspectives and how do they resolve those tensions? What metanarratives can be found in the text? How are the voices of ECEs positioned in relation to other voices such as children, classroom team members and parents? What issues arise and what issues are absent? To what beliefs and understandings do ECEs commit themselves to? How do these values emerge in the text and how are they linked? What contradictions are present? (adapted from Pacini-Ketchabaw & Armstrong de Almeida, 2006, p. 319).

For the questionnaire of inclusive pedagogical practices, the questionnaire responses were analyzed empirically to search for patterns and trends within the data. Data were also compared with themes from the cross case analysis to look for similarities and gaps in what was being actualized in the classroom. In order to do so, a summary of findings, patterns and themes was created including data from the questionnaire. The final component of data analysis was the focus group. Again this was a qualitative analysis using data condensation and interpretation to bring in the perspective of a wider group of participants invested in early childhood education. This was compared with an objective analysis of school board and government documents on policy, organizational structure and guides or regulations about early childhood or inclusion that may establish barriers or opportunities to how inclusive classroom culture is created.

Research Assumptions

First assumption, in my role as both teacher and leader in the education of children, I understood that my personal experiences enhanced my awareness, knowledge and sensitivity toward inclusive rather than segregated environments for the education of young children. I was cautious that this bias did not shape how I viewed and interpreted the data I collected, however I was mindful that we naturally identify with ideologies that resonate with our own ideas and beliefs and give us a sense of belonging (Cook-Greuter, 2013). I was conscious that my worldview was not necessarily shared by all participants, and I tried to allow the process and outcome of this study to unfold without being influenced by my assumption of inclusion.

Second, I assumed that I had the ability to separate my roles as researcher and professional so as not to bias how data were interpreted. Within this school district I am in a leadership role in early childhood education that is consultative and supportive, and I do not directly supervise any of the early childhood education staff involved in schools.

A third assumption was that participants involved in this research study answered truthfully, thoughtfully, and with candour and for various reasons, this may not have transpired.

Limitations

There were several limitations with this research study. Firstly, limitations to qualitative data collection and analysis arise as data collected in this study can never be truly objective. As much as I attempted to provide checks and balances to counteract bias, my personal values, beliefs and experiences colour the data that I collected and interpreted. Additionally, the study captured participant perceptions at particular points in time and was dependent on the context at that point in time. Participants may not have answered honestly, thoughtfully or with candour about their true beliefs, understandings and pedagogical practices. Additionally, because participants are coming from differing educational and cultural backgrounds and experiences, there could have been difficulty relating to or being able to contribute meaningfully to the interview questions.

Delimitations

To keep the scope of this study manageable, the following delimitations were noted. The research focused on one school district and five ECEs in pre-kindergarten classrooms within the school district. Other staff, who were not the ECE, such as principals, classroom team members, therapists, parents, or other teachers in the school were not directly part of this study. While there were twenty potential school locations that offered pre-kindergarten programming in this school district, only those ECEs who identified that they have inclusive classroom contexts, were willing to be part of this study, and were certificated teachers were invited to become involved in the research study. The focus group included current and former ECEs who volunteered to participate. Individuals who had not taught in a pre-kindergarten program were not part of the focus group. Data from the questionnaire was only collected from the five ECEs who were part of the study.

EXPLORING THE ISSUES

This study began with qualitative data as the first phase of data collection to understand multiple perspectives in response to the research questions. The first three research questions were the focus for the data collection in the initial phase:

1. What do ECEs believe and understand about creating a classroom culture that includes all children?
2. How are ECEs affected by, and how do they affect perspectives shared by children, classroom team members, colleagues, and parents in the creation of an inclusive classroom culture?
3. What pedagogical practices do ECEs use to include all children?

This first component of the study focused on the ECEs' interior life world situated in the UL subjective elements of educational experiences, and LL intersubjective elements of educational culture. In the UL, the ECE's educational experiences were explored and three categories emerged from the process of coding and data condensation (Miles et. al., 2014). These categories brought forward participant's thinking about their beliefs and understandings and their reflections on their thinking:

1. ECE Disposition and Role
2. Beliefs about Children
3. Inclusive Culture

In the LL, the ECEs experiences with educational culture and relationships were explored. Three categories emerged from coding and data condensation that encompassed how the ECE's experienced and reflected on creating an inclusive culture and the relationships that were important.

1. The Children
2. The Team
3. The Parents

Next, elements of the UL and LL influenced UR as participants reflected on and described their practices in relation to their beliefs, understandings and what was happening within classroom culture. Elements of UL and LL were intertwined with UR as researcher observations of pedagogical practices during classroom visitations were embedded within what ECEs were thinking about and what they were doing in the classroom context. Thus, three components of integral methodological pluralism are presented in the study findings; UL educational experiences, LL educational culture, and UR educational behaviours.

Creating a Culture of Inclusion in Pre-Kindergarten

In the UR, six categories of practices, which appeared to foster creation of inclusive classroom culture, were identified through coding and data condensation of the interviews and visitations. Embedded within these categories were specific strategies and resources the ECEs used to support their pedagogical practice and create a culture of inclusion within their pre-kindergarten classroom. The six categories of pedagogical practices are:

1. Routines and Structures
2. Play and Engagement
3. Environment
4. Curriculum and Authentic Learning
5. Differentiation
6. Purposeful Planning and Assessment

Table 4 provides a visual map outlining how the categories fit within the integral framework.

Cross Case Analysis of Case Studies and Questionnaire – UL, LL, UR

Quadrants

The purpose for analysing each case individually and then collectively was to deepen understanding of the research questions and enhance generalizability of the study to similar educational contexts (Miles et al., 2014). Using a process of analytic category development each case was analysed in depth by coding

Table 4. Coding categories in the integral model.

	Interior What meaning is being made in the life world?	Exterior What is happening in the system world?
Individual	**UL** **Educational Experiences** subjective elements *What do ECEs believe and understand about creating a classroom culture that includes all children?* **Coding Categories** 1. ECE Disposition and Role 2. Beliefs about Children 3. Inclusive Culture	**UR** **Educational Behaviours** objective elements *What pedagogical practices do ECEs use to include all children?* **Coding Categories** 1. Routines and Structure 2. Play and Engagement 3. Environment 4. Curriculum and Authentic Learning 5. Differentiation 6. Purposeful Planning and Assessment
Collective	**LL** **Educational Culture** intersubjective elements *How are ECEs affected by, and how do they affect perspectives shared by children, classroom team members, colleagues, and parents in the creation of an inclusive classroom culture?* **Coding Categories** 1. The Child 2. The Team 3. The Parents	**LR** **Educational Systems** interobjective elements *How are ECEs affected by system level structures and processes in the creation of an inclusive classroom culture?*

Adapted from Esbjörn-Hargens, (2009, 2007).

and creating a summary of individual findings, and then developing a series of "meta-matrixes" (Miles et al., 2014, p. 103) to further condense and compare patterns, and identify themes. The quantitative data from the completed questionnaires were analysed separately and then included into the meta-matrix to provide an objective third person perspective about what ECEs do to include all children. Next, the questionnaire findings were systematically compared to identify patterns across case analysis for congruency.

Each finding and related theme were then synthesized to provide a holistic understanding of what ECEs think and do to create inclusive culture in pre-kindergarten. Table 5 provides an overview of this analytic category development. Analysis, interpretation and discussion of each finding and thematic categories will be presented next using the organizational and conceptual framework of UL, LL and UR integral theory quadrants.

Discussion of Themes

UL, LL, UR Quadrants

The ECE's beliefs and understandings, intertwined within the classroom culture and relationships with others, influenced their pedagogy and the practices enacted in the classroom. The practices employed by the ECEs were rooted in social constructivists theory and influenced and actively transformed the behavioural and physical environment so all children could participate at their developmental level and experience success. Thus, the UR pedagogical practices, transcend and include the UL individual beliefs, understandings and experiences, and the LL relationships and collective culture, to reflect these beliefs, understandings and relationships though enactment of practices within an inclusive classroom culture. In other words, the practices described in the UR are based on a theoretical foundation of social constructivism on the part of the ECE and collective understanding by the culture sharing group to employ these practices with children in an inclusive classroom context.

LR Quadrant

LR collective was examined from a systems level perspective to answer the research question "How are ECEs affected by systems level structures and processes in the creation of an inclusive classroom culture?" A focus group of ECEs with leadership experience and a review of documents that guide and regulate early childhood and inclusion in school systems in the province of Alberta were analysed.

Investigation of educational systems in the LR was conducted in two parts. First, qualitative data was gathered by three focus group participants, and supplemented with reflections from the individual case studies to inform the impact of the exterior systems world in pre-kindergarten. This provided the interior participant experience with system level organizational structures.

Second, results from analysis of school board and provincial government documents provided exterior interobjective perspectives to reflect how policies, regulations and ideologies could impact inclusive culture in pre-kindergarten. Together these LR interior and exterior perspectives provided a well-rounded view of educational systems from the lens of an ECE.

The purpose for bringing in a focus group of ECEs not part of the original study, was to provide an interior interobjective perspective of LR educational systems and gain a deeper understanding of how ECEs are affected by systems such as school, school board or government structures.

Table 5. Analytic category development

Research Question	Finding Statement	Analysis	Thematic Category
UL What do ECEs believe and understand about creating a classroom culture that includes all children?	**Finding 1:** Inclusive culture is shaped by pedagogical beliefs and understandings.	All of the participants revealed that their beliefs and understandings were important to define what they believed about inclusion and how they viewed children, their theoretical understandings, and how they described the characteristics and role of an ECE in supporting young children's growth and learning.	**Theme 1:** *A child is a child: Beliefs about inclusion* **Theme 2:** *A social constructivist perspective* **Theme 3:** *Characteristics of an ECE*
LL How are ECEs affected by, and how do they affect perspectives shared by children, classroom team members, colleagues, and parents in the creation of an inclusive classroom culture?	**Finding 2:** Inclusive culture is built through relationships.	All of the participants strongly valued relationships with children, the team and parents and this was vital to creating an inclusive classroom culture. It was indicated by all the participants that collaboration, learning from each other, communication and connection were important to build inclusive classroom culture.	**Theme 4:** *Inclusive culture is about relationships*
UR What pedagogical practices do ECEs use to include all children?	**Finding 3:** Inclusive culture is defined by pedagogical practices.	There were many common practices described by the ECEs within Theme 5. These categories were synthesized from each individual case and questionnaire results and include: routines, environment, play, authentic learning, differentiation, purposeful planning While ECEs identified cultural, language, religious and ethnic differences as part of inclusion and diversity, a gap in understanding, knowledge, and ways to implement interculturality in the classroom was identified.	**Theme 5:** *Pedagogical practices define learning for all* **Theme 6:** *Meaningful connection to intercultural practices*

For the exterior LR perspective, an analysis of documents related to early childhood and inclusion from the provincial government of Alberta and the school board in which this study took place, were reviewed to provide contextual information and supportive evidence. Findings from the focus groups, document analysis and relevant individual case data were compared and synthesized into thematic categories. Table 6 provides an overview of analytic category development for the LR. Theme numbers are reflective of a continuation of themes 1 - 6 from the other three quadrants.

From the analysis of how inclusive cultures are supported or hindered by educational systems, two categories emerged. The first category reflected how ECEs experienced a supportive school system, and the second outlined system level barriers to creating an inclusive classroom culture. Educational experiences, culture and behaviours all interact with educational systems in a cyclical and reciprocal manner. For example, an ECE's beliefs, understandings and pedagogical practices within the context of her classroom culture and the relationships within the school culture may be positively or negatively influenced depending on the ideologies, structures and processes that are in place at the school, school board and government level. Table 7 shows findings and themes situated in all four quadrants, which influence the creation of inclusive culture in a pre-kindergarten class.

As identified in the UR findings, there is a gap in ECE's knowledge and understanding of intercultural practices to support children's language development and cultural identity in inclusive early childhood classrooms. There is also a gap in provision of supporting resources for ELLs as Alberta Education has online teacher resources for kindergarten but not for pre-kindergarten. And while resources for early childhood should span the continuum of children in pre-kindergarten through to kindergarten, there is not an approved curriculum framework specific to pre-kindergarten.

Table 6. LR analytic category development

Research Question	Finding Statement	Analysis	Thematic Category
LR How are ECEs affected by system level structures and processes in the creation of an inclusive classroom culture?	**Finding:** Inclusive culture is supported or hindered by systems For inclusive culture to work well in schools it must be supported through educational systems Alberta Education Documents Reviewed: Standards for the provision of ECS Special Education (2006) Funding Manual for School Authorities (2016) School Act (2015) Guide to Education (2016) Kindergarten Program Statement (2008)	**Supportive Leadership and Resources** Supportive principals and assistant principals – willingness to understand early childhood ideology Provide adequate staff, funds and access to resources- prioritize Pre-K Autonomy and trust Circles of support **School Culture** Operational items like schedule, participation- Pre-K valued or marginalized **Professional Learning** Collaboration and conversation for ECEs, team & leaders Challenge- not everyone ready to grow and change/isolation **Teacher Training** no specialization/ requirements for early childhood	**Theme 7:** *School system support*
		Inclusion and Diversity Definitions are not aligned. **Funding Model** Pre-K not an inclusive model, discrepancy with standards and inclusion, deficit view, north American norms/tools time spent on paperwork, assessment Funding is generous- allowing adequate support **Child vs Student** Children not residents of board, but K has universal access. Is Pre-K part of school culture or not? No Pre-K curriculum. **Changing demographics** More complexities- refugee, ELL population increasing- no Pre-K resources for ELL.	**Theme 8:** *Barriers to supporting inclusive culture*

In summary, system barriers that affect the creation of an inclusive classroom culture in pre-kindergarten include:

- Using the terms inclusion and diversity to describe two different populations is confusing and continues to identify differences through a new label.
- The current funding model only supports children with developmental delays and children who are ELL. Extensive time is spent by school system staff compiling assessments, reports, and paperwork to access funding. Pre-kindergarten in Alberta is not inclusive or universally accessible to all children.
- Changing demographics and a growing preschool population in Alberta communities shows a steady increase in foreign born children, and children with complex needs. Pre-kindergarten resources for ELL and a curriculum framework have not been approved at the government level to guide ECEs with programming, thus it is left up to schools or individual ECEs to determine what resources to use.
- From the thematic analysis, it was apparent that micro-level elements garnered from educational experiences, culture and behaviours are influenced by a macro-level educational systems perspective of inclusion and early childhood, and that the reverse is also true. What is interesting to note is how schools and school systems are doing their best to fit a square peg in a round hole. In other words, beliefs, understandings and pedagogical practices that include all children are driving

Table 7. LR findings and themes in the Integral model.

	Interior What meaning is being made in the life world?	Exterior What is happening in the system world?
Individual	**UL** **Educational Experiences (subjective)** *Finding 1*: *Inclusive culture is shaped by pedagogical beliefs and understandings* **Themes:** • A child is a child: Beliefs about inclusion • A social constructivist perspective • Characteristics of an ECE **Zone 1:** Beliefs and understandings **Zone 2:** Reflections about beliefs and understandings	**UR** **Educational Behaviours (objective)** *Finding 3*: *Inclusive culture is defined by pedagogical practices* **Themes:** • Pedagogical practices define learning for all • Meaningful connection to intercultural practices **Zone 5:** Practices described/observed **Zone 6:** Analysis of questionnaire
Collective	**LL** **Educational Culture (intersubjective)** *Finding 2*: *Inclusive culture is built through relationships* **Themes:** • Inclusive culture is about relationships **Zone 3:** Relational experiences **Zone 4:** Reflections on relationships	**LR** **Educational Systems (interobjective)** *Finding 4*: *Inclusive culture is supported or hindered by systems* **Themes:** • School system support • Barriers to supporting inclusive culture **Zone 7:** Experiences with systems **Zone 8:** Analysis of systems

Adapted from Esbjörn-Hargens, (2009, 2007)

school systems to find innovative ways to work around constraints in funding and lack of supportive resources to create inclusive pre-kindergarten programs in response to a growing preschool population. This can be verified by scanning school jurisdiction websites for pre-kindergarten programming, and the growing list of private early childhood services operators.

CONCLUSION AND IMPLICATIONS

Synthesis of Quadrant Interactions and Relationships

Throughout this study, each quadrant has been shown to transcend and include the findings and themes from the next quadrant in a reciprocal and cyclical manner. Wilber (2006) describes phenomena in the quadrants as tetra-arising, meaning that the interior and exterior perspectives in each quadrant together with all quadrants form a collective whole, and provide a comprehensive view of any life experience. Figure 2 represents the themes from this study as they interact and relate with one another through the quadrants followed by a description of these inter-quadrant relationships.

UL 1, 2, 3 ←→ LL 4

For an inclusive classroom culture to be actualized, the ECE must have a positive view of inclusion and operate from a world centric, social-constructivist perspective in what she believes about how children learn and this is turn affects the creation of an inclusive classroom culture through relationships with the child, team and parents. This reciprocal and collaborative exchange of beliefs and understandings blossoms into a culture sharing group with a common understanding of inclusion and early childhood pedagogy. Collaboration with colleagues supports discourse about beliefs and understandings, increasing UL personal reflection bringing forth new thinking.

UL 1, 2, 3 → UR 5

The pedagogical practices outlined in the research study could not be enacted by an ECE who did not have a social-constructivist perspective and a world centric level of consciousness. What ECEs think has a direct impact on what they do. This relationship between the UL and UR shows that you can't have one without the other. Beliefs and understandings directly reflect the classroom practices.

LR 7 ←→ UL 1, 2, 3

The ECEs were able to enact their ideologies of inclusion and early childhood because they were enabled by the school system to teach in this way. What ECEs believe and understand about teaching and learning is influenced by professional learning, guiding documents, policies and regulations, and the beliefs and understandings of leadership, such as principals. In turn, the ECEs can influence the beliefs and understandings of the system through the creation of exemplary inclusive pre-kindergarten programming.

LR 7 ←→ LL 4

Supportive school systems impact how school culture evolves. The correlation between the LL and the LR indicates that positive and collaborative school culture impacts positive and collaborative classroom culture. If pre-kindergarten is valued as part of the school culture, and the ECE feels supported, this builds a supportive network of relationships both inside and outside the classroom.

LR 7 → UR 5

When school systems provide adequate and qualified adult classroom support for pre-kindergarten, the ECE can enact pedagogical practices to support all children. Lack of adult support equals frustration that not all needs of the children are being met and impacts the well-being of the ECE. School systems must also provide materials and resources to support activities and the environment for an inclusive pre-kindergarten classroom.

Creating a Culture of Inclusion in Pre-Kindergarten

Figure 2. Quadrant interactions and relationships

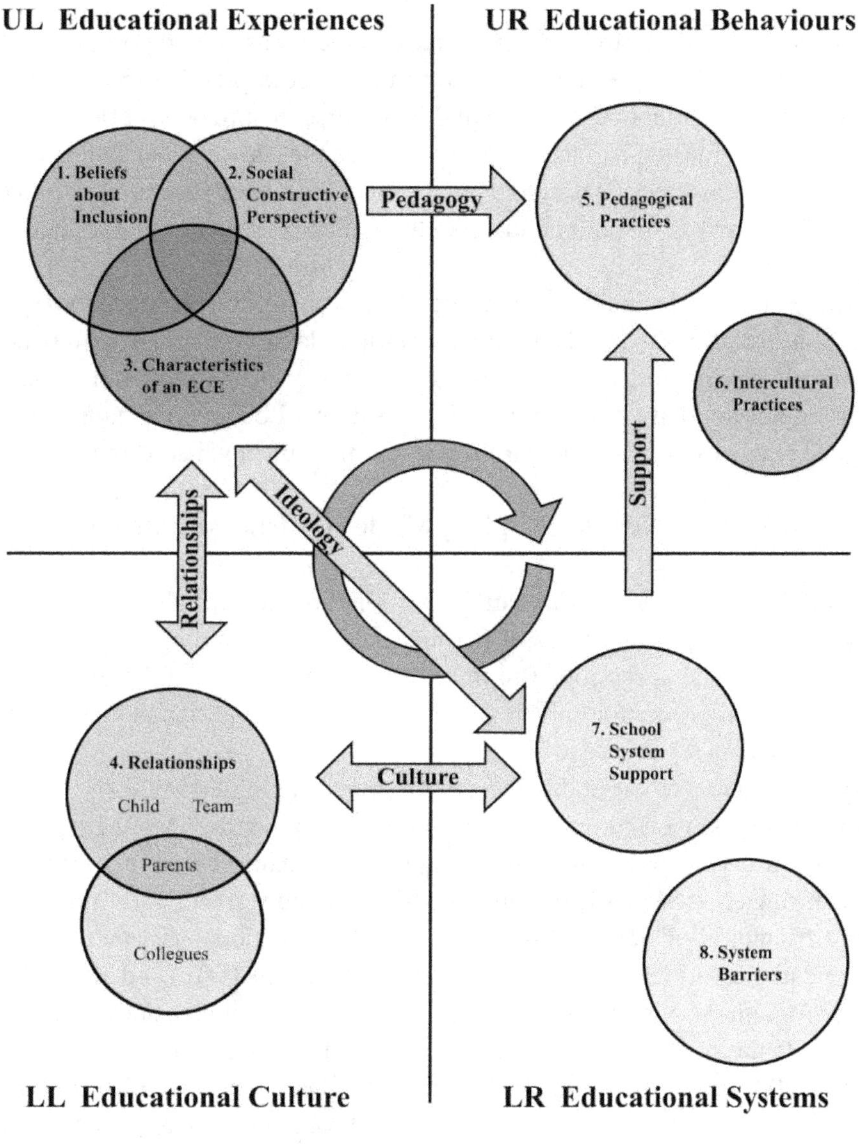

UR 6 & LR 8

These two themes represent the gaps or barriers identified in this study thus are depicted as separate from the interconnection between the other themes. Barriers to inclusive pre-kindergarten culture will be addressed in the recommendations below.

Recommendations

Based on the findings, analysis and conclusions of this research study, I offer recommendations that further support inclusive pre-kindergarten programming. Recommendations that follow are intended for consideration by school boards, policy makers at the government level, and future research.

Recommendation 1: Implementation of Reflective Professional Learning

Perhaps the most pervasive and obvious topic that emerged was the importance placed on professional learning that is collaborative and embedded in classroom practice to co-construct knowledge and understanding of early childhood research and ideologies in support of effective pre-kindergarten programming. ECEs want meaningful learning experiences that involve learning from and with others through a social constructivist lens. Reflective practice and facilitated discourse are an effective way to begin to shift beliefs and create common understandings (Pacini-Ketchabaw & Schecter, 2002; Pacini-Ketchabaw et al., 2010).

If we wish to have effective inclusive pre-kindergarten programming in our school system, it warrants schools and school jurisdictions to build an implementation plan for this type of embedded professional learning. It requires time, a mentor or specialist to facilitate the conversations, and money for release time to visit other classrooms and have collaborative conversations. I believe the gain from doing so would elevate pedagogical practices in pre-kindergarten classrooms to the level described in this research study.

Recommendation 2: An Inclusive Funding Model for Pre-Kindergarten

Given the current deficit-based funding model for pre-kindergarten which includes children who meet criteria as delayed, but excludes all others, it is time to explore a funding model for pre-kindergarten that is inclusive, equitable and accessible. But this is a complex recommendation, not amenable to easy solutions. While I would advocate for universal access to pre-kindergarten beginning at age three and a half, there are many challenges to consider.

The first is space in schools to meet the demand for programming. Many schools are overcrowded in areas where young families live and underserved in older communities. Managing space in schools or in community locations would be a time-consuming issue for many school jurisdictions.

The second is hiring qualified early childhood educators and staff to work in pre-kindergarten programs. It can be difficult to find qualified staff, particularly educational assistants or specialists such as Speech Language Pathologists (SLPs) and Occupational Therapists (OTs) and increasing the number of pre-kindergarten programs would put considerable pressure on schools to staff effectively.

The third is cost to the province. While it can be argued that intervening early sees reduced costs to society later (Rand, 2005), providing funding for all children would be at significant cost to the province and could be perceived as taking away jobs from the child care and private preschool sector.

Given these challenges, it is apparent that not all families know about and access available support for their child until kindergarten due to various reasons such as social vulnerabilities, lack of access to a family doctor or health centre, lack of awareness of programming for English language learners, or cultural stigma of having a child with perceived delays. Universal access to pre-kindergarten may provide that safety net to catch children who would benefit from early intervention, while still allowing parental choice to place their child in a pre-kindergarten program. Knowing what the research tells us about the importance of early experiences to set children up for success later in life, this is an educational service that would benefit society as a whole. That said, this is a complex and wicked problem and collaborative dialogue between school systems and government to navigate the best approach to fund and support inclusive pre-kindergarten classrooms is long overdue.

Recommendation 3: Adopting a Pre-Kindergarten Curriculum Framework

If we wish to have ECEs in our pre-kindergarten classes with beliefs and understandings that support a social constructivist approach and pedagogical practices that support learning for all, then we need a research and evidence-based framework to provide a common reference point for professional learning and reflection. While ECEs are free to determine the resources, and practices they will use in their classroom to facilitate teaching and learning, it is essential to have an ideological guide to shape the direction for learning and teaching in pre-kindergarten. It is important to note that this should not be a prescriptive, how-to manual, and must be based on theory, approaches to learning and best practices in the field of early childhood education. There is also a need to fill a gap in understanding interculturality and how to authentically support a growing English language learner population.

Currently in the province of Alberta there is a pre-kindergarten framework being piloted in schools and childcare centres (Makovichuk et al., 2014). Having a curriculum framework specific to pre-kindergarten would likely elevate the perception of pre-kindergarten as a valued part of the school system, but ECEs and school leadership would need to be vigilant that a traditional, academic focus would not creep down into a social-constructivist, play based pre-kindergarten program. Thus, a recommendation to adopt a pre-kindergarten curriculum framework for Alberta to guide pedagogical practice will help school systems support collaborative conversations within pre-kindergarten communities of practice.

Recommendation 4: Implications for Future Research

The importance of early childhood, early intervention and child development and the impact that building a strong foundation has on later mental and physical health, academic success and societal well-being cannot be denied. Continued research in the areas of pre-kindergarten, inclusion and how the education system can best support learning for all children at this formative stage in their development is critical. I suggest the following future studies could provide a more comprehensive understanding of creating inclusive classroom culture in pre-kindergarten:

- Based on the limitations of this study, the questionnaire of inclusive pedagogical practices could be revised and administered to a larger sample of ECEs in the province of Alberta to assess if similar findings would be revealed.
- A similar study could be designed to explore the beliefs, understandings and practices of school leaders in supporting inclusive pre-kindergarten programs within their school culture to better understand what school leaders think and do to facilitate effective pre-kindergarten programs.
- In the original study, eight characteristics that identified a personality typology of an ECE best suited to actualize a quality inclusive classroom culture were outlined. Further research to determine if these characteristics hold true and are generalizable in a larger population sample could be explored.
- Six pedagogical practices were identified by the ECEs in this study as important to include all children. Further research to determine if these practices are found in a larger population sample could be investigated.

While these recommendations are not exhaustive, they provide some direction for continued advocacy, research and support for inclusive pre-kindergarten programming in the province of Alberta, and beyond.

Researcher Reflections

It is through others that we develop into ourselves.(Vygotsky, 1981, p. 161)

This quote by Lev Vygotsky has guided me throughout this research study as I am forever changed by the relationships and experiences I have encountered along the way. I am not the same person who began this journey over three years ago. As I reflect on the past three and a half years, I think perhaps the most affirming part of conducting this research was experiencing the wonderful pre-kindergarten classrooms created by the ECEs and their team. Seeing joy, laughter, concentration, engagement in the children as they played with each other alongside adults confirmed that good things are happening for children in our pre-kindergarten programs.

This journey has also opened my awareness to integral theory and looking at things from multiple perspectives. While this was a complex framework to situate a study such as this, and there were times I simply wanted to go a more conventional research route, I do believe that I would not have revealed the depth of findings without considering interior and exterior perspectives of educational experiences, cultures, behaviours and systems. Integral theory is a unique way to approach any problem, and I appreciate how the relationships among and between the quadrants often reveal solutions or ideas I hadn't thought of. I now intuitively use this framework to think about things like work issues and life situations.

And now I am at that point in the journey where study has come to a close. So what now? In my current role in early childhood leadership, I plan to take what I have learned, and what I have recommended, to advocate for inclusive pre-kindergarten programming and to support ECEs by implementing a comprehensive professional learning plan that builds reflective practice. Ensuring schools have ECEs who view all children as capable and can create a culture of learning to provide rich experiences for our youngest children is a gift. I look forward to beginning this work.

Ultimately my hope is this study will tell a story, spark interest and wonder, and give pause for reflection about what we believe and understand about including all children in our classrooms, because a child is a child no matter what.

REFERENCES

Alberta Education. (2006). *Standards for the provision of early childhood special education.* Retrieved from http://education.alberta.ca/media/452316/ecs_specialedstds2006.pdf

Alberta Education. (2016). *Funding manual for school authorities: 2016/2017 school year.* Retrieved from https://education.alberta.ca/media/3272973/funding-manual-august-2016.pdf

Alberta Family Wellness Initiative. (2013). *Sharing the brain story: AFWI's knowledge mobilization strategy: Transforming research, policy, and practice in Alberta.* Retrieved online http://www.alberta-familywellness.org/system/files/report-files/Sharing%20the%20Brain%20Story%20Final%20jan%2027%2014.pdf

Alberta Teachers' Association. (2014). *Report of the blue ribbon panel on inclusive education in Alberta schools.* Retrieved from http://www.teachers.ab.ca/SiteCollectionDocuments/ATA/News-Room/2014/PD-170-1%20PD%20Blue%20Ribbon%20Panel%20Report%202014-web.pdf

Avramidis, E., & Norwich, B. (2002). Teachers' attitudes towards integration/inclusion: A review of the literature. *European Journal of Special Needs Education, 17*(2), 129–147. doi:10.1080/08856250210129056

Belouin, P. (2010). Ethnography: A short description of the roles available to researchers in the field [Web log comment]. Retrieved from http://belouin.com/blog/2010/03/ethnography-which-role-is-one-to-adopt-in-the-framework-of-an-ethnographic-study/

Brown, B. (2006). The four worlds of sustainability: Drawing upon four universal perspectives to support sustainability initiatives. *Integral Sustainability Centre*. Retrieved from http://nextstepintegral.org/wp-content/uploads/2011/04/Four-Worlds-of-Sustainability-Barrett-C-Brown.pdf

Buysse, V., Skinner, D., & Grant, S. (2001). Toward a definition of quality inclusion: Perspectives of parents and practitioners. *Journal of Early Intervention, 24*(2), 146–161. doi:10.1177/105381510102400208

Clough, P. (Ed.). (1998). *Managing inclusive education: From policy and practice*. London: Sage.

Clough, P., & Nutbrown, C. (2004). Special education needs and inclusion: Multiple Perspectives of preschool educators in the UK. *Journal of Early Childhood Research, 191*(2), 191–210. doi:10.1177/1476718X04043015

CMEC. (2014). *Early learning and development framework*. Retrieved from http://www.cmec.ca/Publications/Lists/Publications/Attachments/327/2014-07-Early-Learning-Framework-EN.pdf

Conn-Powers, M., Cross, A., Traub, E., & Hutter-Pishgahi, L. (2006). The universal design of early education: Moving forward for all children. *Beyond the Journal: Young Children on the Web*. Retrieved from http://journal.naeyc.org/btj/200609/ConnPowersBTJ.pdf

Cook, B. G., & Odom, S. L. (2013). Evidence-based practices and implementation science in special education. *Council for Exceptional Children, 70*(2), 135–144. doi:10.1177/001440291307900201

Cook-Greuter, S. (2013). Nine Levels Of Increasing Embrace. In *Ego Development: A Full-Spectrum Theory Of Vertical Growth And Meaning Making*. Independent Scholar Publication.

Creswell, J. W. (2015). Educational research: Planning, conducting, and evaluating, Quantitative and qualitative research (5th ed.). Pearson.

Davis, B., & Sumara, D. (2003). Why aren't they getting this? Working through the Regressive myths of constructivist pedagogy. *Teaching Education, 2*(14), 123–140. doi:10.1080/1047621032000092922

Davis, B., Sumara, D., & Luce-Kapler, R. (2015). *Engaging minds: Cultures of education and practices of teaching* (3rd ed.). New York, NY: Routledge. doi:10.4324/9781315695891

DEC/NAEYC. (2009). *Early childhood inclusion: A joint position statement of the Division for Early Childhood (DEC) and the national Association for the Education of Young Children (NAEYC)*. Chapel Hill, NC: The University of North Caroline, FPG Child Development Institute.

DeVore, S., & Russell, K. (2007). Early childhood education and care for children with disabilities: Facilitating inclusive practice. *Early Childhood Education Journal, 35*(2), 189–198. doi:10.100710643-006-0145-4

Dietze, B., & Kashin, D. (2016). *Empowering pedagogy for early childhood education*. Toronto: Pearson Canada Inc.

Eccles, M. & Mittman, B. (2006). Welcome to implementation science. *Implementation Science, 1*(1), 1-3. doi: 10 doi:1.1186/1748-5908-1-1

Esbjörn-Hargens, S. (2007). Integral teacher, integral students, integral classroom: Applying integral theory to education. *AQAL: Journal of Integral Theory and Practice, 2*(2), 1–41.

Esbjörn-Hargens, S. (2009). *An overview of integral theory: An all-inclusive framework for the 21st century*. Integral Institute, Resource paper No. 1, 1–24.

Fixsen, D., Blase, K., Netz, A., & Van Dyke, M. (2013). Statewide implementation of evidence based programs. *Council for Exceptional Children, 70*(2), 213–230. doi:10.1177/001440291307900206

Fogarty International Centre. (2013). *Frequently asked questions about implementation science*. National Institutes of Health. Retrieved from http://www.fic.nih.gov/News/Events/implementation-science/Pages/faqs.aspx

Hattie, J., & Yates, G. (2014). *Visible learning and the science of how we learn*. New York, NY: Routledge.

Hewes, J. (2006). *Let the children play: Nature's answer to early learning*. Early Childhood Learning Knowledge Centre, Canadian Council on Learning. Retrieved from http://www.ccl-cca.ca/pdfs/ECLKC/lessons/Originalversion_LessonsinLearning.pdf

Hinitz, B. F. (2013). *The hidden history of early childhood education*. New York, NY: Routledge. doi:10.4324/9780203814420

Hoey, B. (2014). A simple introduction to the practice of ethnography and guide to ethnographic fieldnotes. *Marshall University Digital Scholar,* 1–10. Retrieved from http://works.bepress.com/brian_hoey/12

Hora, M. T., & Millar, S. B. (2011). *A guide to building education partnerships: Navigating diverse cultural contexts to turn challenge into promise*. Sterling, VA: Stylus Publishing Inc.

Horn, E., & Wolery, R. (2000). Key influences on the initiation and implementation of inclusive preschool programs. *The Council for Exceptional Children, 67*(1), 83–98. doi:10.1177/001440290006700106

Horne, P., & Timmons, V. (2009). Making it work: Teachers' perspectives on inclusion. *International Journal of Inclusive Education, 13*(3), 273–286. doi:10.1080/13603110701433964

Hsieh, W., & Hsieh, C. (2012). Urban early childhood teachers' attitudes towards Inclusive education. *Early Child Development and Care, 9*(182), 1167–1184. doi:10.1080/03004430.2011.602191

Katz, J. (2012). *Teaching to Diversity: A three-block model of universal design for learning*. Winnipeg, Canada: Portage & Main Press.

Kegan, R. (1994). *In over our head: The mental demands of modern life*. Cambridge, MA: Harvard University Press.

Kellett, M. (2013). *Images of childhood and their influence on research*. Retrieved from http://www.sagepub.com/upm-data/59004_Clark_et_al.pdf

Lero, D. (2010). *Accessing inclusion quality in early learning and child care in Canada with the SpeciaLink child care inclusion practices profile and principles scale.* Canadian Council on Learning, University of Guelph.

Lieber, J., Hanson, M. J., Beckman, P. J., Janko, S., Marquart, J. M., Horn, E., & Odom, S. L. (1997). The impact of changing roles on relationships between professionals in inclusive programs for young children. *Early Education and Development, 8*(1), 67–82. doi:10.120715566935eed0801_6

Makovichuk, L., Hewes, J., Lirette, P., & Thomas, N. (2014). *Play, participation, and possibilities: An early learning and child care curriculum framework for Alberta.* Retrieved from www.childcareframework.com

Manning, D. (2011). *Separate but equal? A postmodern analysis of educational structures for individuals with disabilities* (Doctoral dissertation). Statesboro, GA: Georgia Southern University. (paper 563)

Mason, M. (2008). What is complexity theory and what are its implications for educational change? *Educational Philosophy and Theory, 40*(1), 35–49. doi:10.1111/j.1469-5812.2007.00413.x

McCartney, B., & Morton, M. (2013). Kinds of participation: Teacher and special educationperceptions and practices of 'inclusion' in early childhood and primary school settings. *International Journal of Inclusive Education, 17*(8), 776–792. doi:10.1080/13603116.2011.602529

McGhie-Richmond, D., Irvine, A., Loreman, T., Cizman, J. L., & Lupart, J. (2013). Teacher perspectives on inclusive education in rural Alberta, Canada. *Canadian Journal of Education, 36*(1), 195–239.

Miles, M. B., Huberman, A. M., & Saldana, J. (2014). *Qualitative data analysis: A methods sourcebook* (3rd ed.). Thousand Oaks, CA: Sage.

Miller, E., & Almon, J. (2009). Crisis in the kindergarten: Why children need to play in school. *Alliance for Childhood*, 1–72. Retrieved from http://www.allianceforchildhood.org/sites/allianceforchildhood.org/files/file/kindergarten_report.pdf

Morrison, K. (2008). Educational philosophy and the challenge of complexity theory. *Educational Philosophy and Theory, 40*(1), 19–34. doi:10.1111/j.1469-5812.2007.00394.x

National Association for the Education of Young Children (NAEYC). (2009). Developmentally Appropriate Practice in Early Childhood Programs Serving Children from Birth through. Retrieved from https://www.naeyc.org/sites/default/files/globally-shared/downloads/PDFs/resources/position-statements/PSDAP.pdf

Nilholm, C. (2006). Special education, inclusion and democracy. *European Journal of Special Needs Education, 21*(4), 431–445. doi: 10:1080/08856250600957905

Nind, M., Flewitt, R., & Payler, J. (2014). The social experience of early childhood for children with learning disabilities: Inclusion, competence and agency. *British Journal of Sociology of Education, 3106*, 653–670. doi:10.1080/01425692.2010.515113

Nutbrown, C., & Clough, P. (2004). Inclusion and exclusion in the early years: Conversations with European educators. *European Journal of Special Needs Education, 19*(3), 301–315. doi:10.1080/0885625042000262479

Odom, S. L. (2009). The tie that binds: Evidence-based practice, implementation science, and outcomes for children. *Topics in Early Childhood Special Education*, *29*(53), 53–61. doi:10.1177/0271121408329171

Odom, S. L., Buyesse, V., & Soukakou, E. (2011). Inclusion for young children with disabilities: A quarter century of research perspectives. *Journal of Early Intervention*, *33*(4), 344–356. doi:10.1177/1053815111430094

Olsson, L. M. (2009). *Movement and experimentation in young children's learning*. New York, NY: Routledge. doi:10.4324/9780203881231

Pacini-Ketchabaw, V., Kummen, K., & Thompson, D. (2010). Becoming intimate with developmental knowledge: Pedagogical explorations with collective biography. *The Alberta Journal of Educational Research*, *56*(3), 335–354.

Pacini-Ketchabaw, V., & Schecter, S. (2002). Engaging the discourse of diversity: Educators' frameworks for working with linguistic and cultural difference. *Contemporary Issues in Early Childhood*, *3*(3), 400–414. doi:10.2304/ciec.2002.3.3.7

Pacini-Ketchabaw, V., White, J., & Armstrong de Almeida, A. (2006). Racialization in early childhood: A critical analysis of discourses in policies. *International Journal of Education Policy, Research & Practice: Reconceptualizing Childhood Studies*, *7*.

Pence, A., & Pacini-Ketchabaw, V. (2008). *Discourses on quality care: The investigating 'quality' project and the Canadian experience*. Academic Press. http://dx.ci.org/10.2304/ciec.2008.9.3.241

Pound, L. (2006). *How children learn*. London, UK: Practical Preschool Books.

Rand: Labor and Population Research Brief. (2005). *Proven benefits of early childhood interventions*. Retrieved from http://www.rand.org/pubs/research_briefs/RB9145.html

Rittel, H., & Webber, M. (1973). Dilemmas in a general theory of planning. *Policy Sciences*, *4*(2), 155–169. doi:10.1007/BF01405730

Snow, B. A. (2007). *Reflections on integral methodological pluralism*. John F. Kennedy University working document. Retrieved from http://www.kenwilber.com/blog/show/379

Vygotsky, L. S. (1981). The genesis of higher mental functions. In J. V. Wertsch (Ed.), *The Concept of Activity in Social Psychology* (pp. 144–188). Armonk, NY: M.E. Sharpe.

Wilber, K. (2006). *Integral Spirituality: A startling new role for religion in the modern and postmodern world*. Boston: Shambhala Publications, Inc.

Wilber, K. (2011). *A Brief History of Everything*. Boston: Shambhala Publications, Inc.

Wilber, K., Patten, T., Leonard, A., & Morelli, M. (2008). *Integral life practice: A 21st century blueprint for physical health, emotional balance, mental clarity, and spiritual awakening*. Boston: Shambhala Publications, Inc.

KEY TERMS AND DEFINITIONS

Beliefs: Defined from an ethnographic view as how an individual perceives events and phenomena in the context of their cultural setting which is the school and classroom, and how this viewpoint and attitude influences ideas, values, emotions and perceptions of other members in that cultural setting.

Children With Diverse Needs: The government of Alberta defines children with "diverse needs" as children who require special education programming because of their behavioral, communicational, intellectual, learning, or physical characteristics or a combination of those characteristics, and children learning English as a new language who benefit from enhanced language programming to support growth and development. Postmodern thinking views diversity as an approach to building a learning community that is inclusive of varying identities and abilities so that difference "becomes part of the social structures and practices within the environment" and that children and families "do not feel stripped of their 'being and belonging' or put into marginalized situations."

Culture: This term is used in conjunction with both inclusion and classroom such as "culture of inclusion" and "classroom culture." From an ethnographic perspective, culture is defined as the beliefs, behaviors, and characteristics of a specific social group, in this case the ECEs. The ECEs are also part of a larger culture sharing group which encompasses people who are part of the immediate classroom context including children, and the classroom team who may consist of an educational assistant (EA), speech language assistant (SLA), speech language therapist (SLP), occupational therapist (OT), physical therapist (PT) or family-school liaison (FSL). The culture sharing group may also include those on the periphery, such as parents and other colleagues, whose beliefs and behaviours could influence how the classroom context is shaped.

Early Childhood Educators (ECEs): ECEs are defined as certificated teachers with the school board and directly responsible for designing the environment, learning and assessment of pre-kindergarten children within their individual classroom context. They may or may not have a specialization in early childhood education, but as professionals, they are responsible for learning about and acquiring dispositions, knowledge and skills to enhance their pedagogical practice with young children.

Pedagogical Practice: The ECE's approach to teaching and learning that guides their professional practice. This is unique to each ECE based on their beliefs, understandings, experiences and the image they hold of themselves and the child.

Pre-Kindergarten: Within Alberta, children are eligible for two years of pre-kindergarten programming beginning as young as 2 ½ years of age by September 1 of the school year if they have significant educational needs, or one year of pre-kindergarten programming at 3 ½ years of age if they have mild or moderate educational needs or if they are learning English as a new language. Pre-kindergarten funding is provided by the government of Alberta for various supports, services and educational programming for children who meet these eligibility criteria.

Understandings: Defined from an ethnographic view as; how an individual uses the cultural frame of the classroom to interpret their own understandings of early childhood and inclusion that emerge from day to day life in the classroom.

Section 3
Application of AQAL in Practice Beyond the School System

Chapter 12
An Integral Theory Approach to the Feedback System in Supervising Doctoral Students in the Nordic Higher Education Context

Cheryl Marie Cordeiro
University of Gothenburg, Sweden & The Norwegian Institute of Food, Fisheries and Aquaculture Research (Nofima), Norway

ABSTRACT

Feedback giving makes an important part in the context of higher education thesis writing, in particular, doctoral thesis writing supervision. In the past decade, European level standardization higher education policies have encouraged a pedagogy paradigm shift towards a more student-centered learning approach. Within the Nordic context of higher education, feedback giving from supervisor to student has often been studied from the perspective of the supervisor, as a small part of the overall doctoral degree program. This study uses findings from foundational pedagogy literature in the field of Nordic pedagogy studies in combination with empirical data findings from interviews, and maps elements of the doctoral thesis writing feedback system from an integral pluralism approach. The integral model of a feedback system to a doctoral thesis supervision is novel for the Nordic pedagogy literature and it is meant as complement to the current canon of literature on Nordic pedagogy.

INTRODUCTION

In the late 1990s, as part of a larger effort of the European Higher Education Area (EHEA) to standardize and ensure compatibility of higher-education qualifications in 48 European countries, education policy changes were made throughout the European Union (EU). This move was part of the Europe 2020 Strategy by the EU, with the stated goal that 40% of individuals between ages 30 and 40 will have attained higher

DOI: 10.4018/978-1-5225-5873-6.ch012

education by 2020 (EC, 2015). This move made the pursuit of higher education more interesting and attractive to young individuals, and recent statistics show an increase in enrolment in higher education within EU countries in general (Eurostat, 2016, 2013). Another effect of these policy changes was that a more student oriented teaching and learning process began to be emphasized. This shift in ideology towards a more student-centered learning approach is also reflected in pedagogic textbooks in the Nordic countries (Denmark, Norway, Sweden and Finland). With this ideological shift, the teaching-learning dialogic process of feedback was implemented within higher education programs. In particular, doctoral student supervision has come into focus, since the doctoral degree process-product is cognitively most demanding in terms of learning goals, yet heterogeneous in terms of context of discipline. It is not uncommon in the Nordic higher education context for a doctoral student in medical sciences to have group supervision throughout their doctoral studies and thesis writing years, whilst in the humanities, supervision takes place on a one-to-one supervisor-student basis (Lauvås & Handal, 2005).

In the Nordic countries, since the 1970s to the present, most Nordic books on pedagogy are written in their respective Scandinavian languages. There are three most influential books on pedagogy in the Nordic context that include the foundational works of: (i) Handal, Holmström and Thomsen (1973) on teaching at university level, covering academic and practical challenges, (ii) Elmgren and Henriksson (2010) university pedagogy in various facets from teaching to academic thesis writing, and (iii) Stigmar (2009) how to become a professional teacher in higher education. These three books were reviewed by Lauvås and Handal (2012) as means of tracking the evolution of the Nordic pedagogy tradition in the past fifty years.

Study Focus and Research Questions

With the pedagogic paradigm shift towards a more student-centered learning approach, this chapter focuses on the process of supervision and feedback in doctoral thesis writing, in the Nordic higher education context. This study uses an Integral Theory perspective to frame a student-centered approach to thesis feedback advising. Based on the literature of the foundational books reviewed by Lauvås and Handal (2012), and their practical advice on how to optimise the use and giving of feedback for master and doctoral students in their thesis writing (Lauvås & Handal, 2005), the four-quadrant model of Integral Theory is used to uncover knowledge gaps in current Nordic pedagogy literature and to complement these knowledge gaps with empirical data collected in the form of interviews. The respondents to this study are affiliated to Nordic institutions of higher education. Details of the respondents' profiles can be found in the methodology section of this study. The names and institutional affiliations of the eight respondents have been anonymised. The research questions investigated in this study include:

What practical facets of the feedback system are reflected in the Nordic context of higher education, specifically in doctoral thesis supervision?

In what ways can an Integral Theory framework contribute towards a more holistic student-centered feedback system at doctoral supervision level in the Nordic context of higher education?

LITERATURE REVIEW: FEEDBACK IN HIGHER EDUCATION THESIS SUPERVISION

The general study of higher education processes, in particular the doctoral degree program that includes its feedback system during thesis writing, has been done in relation to the perspective of the supervisor (Barnes & Austin, 2009; Dudley, 1984; Franke & Arvidsson, 2011; Pole, Sprokkereef, Burgess & Lakin, 1997; Stephens, 2014) and of the doctoral student (Hoskins & Goldberg, 2005; Ivankova & Stick, 2007; Zhou, 2015). Feedback in doctoral thesis writing is a foundational process of student cognitive development in the doctoral degree process. In the years of thesis writing, the student matures in conceptual ideas and perspectives. More importantly, the processes of academic writing teaches the student to express their concepts in rhetoric formulations that enable them to be part of the academic community, speaking/writing in the register of academic debate (Bitchener & Basturkmen, 2010; Odena & Burgess, 2017; Olmos-López & Sunderland, 2017; Phillips & Pugh, 2005).

In terms of theoretical coherence in the field of pedagogy in higher education however, scholars have acknowledged that relatively few studies have proposed an integrated model with a combined perspective overview that can provide practical advice (Gatfield, 2005; Grant, Hackney & Edgar, 2014; Loganbill, Hardy & Delworth, 1982). Studies on doctoral programs also tend rather to be discipline specific, lacking cross-disciplinary insight (Allen, Stebnicki & Lynch, 1995; Berman & Smyth, 2015; Carr, Lhussier & Chandler, 2010; Rafferty, 2001). While most studies cited in this literature review thus far pertain to an international perspective on higher education doctoral programs, the policy and ideological shift of perspectives of the Bologna Process within the European higher education context uncovers a relative lack of research literature with regards as to how doctoral programs are managed in the diverse European economies, in particular the process of doctoral thesis writing supervision (Elmgren & Henriksson, 2010; Lauvås & Handal, 2005). Pedagogy literature in general also identifies a knowledge gap for a systemic, integral conceptualization of the doctoral degree program and its academic thesis writing processes (Davis & Callihan, 2013; Schwartz-Shea & Bennett, 2003).

The doctoral degree program in this study is characterised by the perspective that elements that constitute a doctoral degree process, such as actors, institutions and environment for example, are dynamically related to each other. Acting dialogically, these elements form a doctoral degree program ecology that requires a systems view or integral approach of investigation and study.

Review of Systems Thinking and Integral Pluralism in Pedagogy

Within the scientific knowledge paradigm, the increasing influence of systems thinking began as a response to the limitations of Descartes's analytic reason. As an approach to a deeper understanding and managing complex transdisciplinary challenges, strong systems thinking influences saw scholars shift their perspective from viewing the parts to viewing the whole (Capra, 1997; Floyd, 2008). Pedagogy as a field is inherently cross-disciplinary and pluralistic in methodology. Each faculty and discipline have for example, differing standards and ways of approaching the similar challenges whether it is having students write a thesis monograph or produce a collection of journal articles as part of their doctoral paper series. A potential cohesive framework that would allow for the encompassing of cross-disciplinary research and mixed methods is through an integral worldview (Davis & Callihan, 2013; Esbjorn-Hargens & Zimmerman, 2009; Wilber, 2006, 2000), characterised by plurality in perspectives. In Integral Pluralism, existing theories across disciplines are interrelated, the comprehensive overview of which lends a deeper understanding of the subject of study. The integral framework used in this study is shown in Figure 1. It is grounded in the Pronoun referencing system of language in use. Consistent inquiry into each specific deictic ('pointer') function of pronouns leads to the mapping of the different types of knowledge zones and different perspectives.

The Pronoun referencing system perspectives illustrated in the quadrants can be seen as holons, moving from narrower (*I/You*) to broader perspectives (*It/Its*). The Individual Interior perspective is expressed in the Upper Left quadrant (UL, *singular subjective*) which are *I (intra)/You (extra)*. With regards to pursuing a doctoral degree, this quadrant from the student-centered learning approach would reflect the individual psyche and motivation for the individual to have begun the process of acquiring a doctoral degree. It could also map knowledge with regards to Self, such as an understanding of one's own cognitive learning and activity management styles. The perspectives expressed in the Lower Left quadrant (LL, *plural intersubjective*) are *We (intra)/They (extra)*. From the student-centered learning approach, this could reflect knowledge about the culture of the department and university in which the doctoral student is embedded. Whether it is research seminars for students by students or the extra-curricular activities that students are engaged in, this quadrant maps knowledge about activities and processes that lend support to the student as belonging to the in-group of university life and activities. The cultural eco-climate can be helped by the presence of dedicated supervisors and an efficient administration system that bolsters student activities. Crossing diagonally over to the top right quadrant, the Individual Exterior

Figure 1. The Pronoun referencing system in language, I(You), We(They), It, Its, maps into four quadrants that render four different types of knowledge zones
(Wilber 2000)

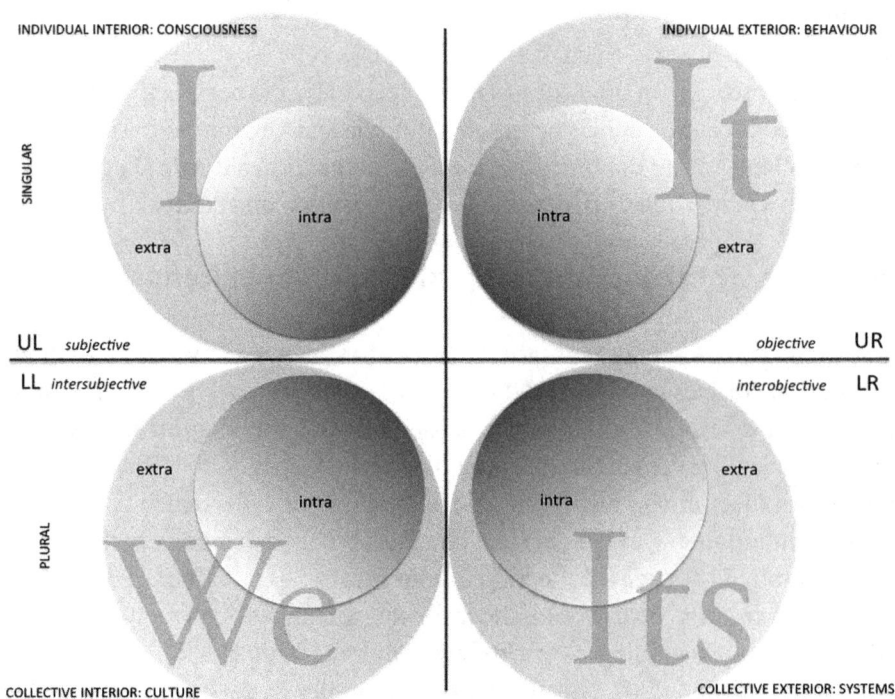

perspective is expressed in the Upper Right quadrant (UR, *singular objective*), which are *It (intra)/It (extra)*. The combined effects of elements from the UL and LL quadrants can be observed in terms of human behaviour most often captured in knowledge in the UR quadrant. This quadrant would capture knowledge about *how* feedback is given in the material processes of doing. Behind these activities are the administrative support functions towards a student-centered learning approach. These network activities and infrastructures are reflected in the Lower Right (LR, *plural interobjective*) quadrant. The LR quadrant would be the broadest perspective, encompassing all other perspectives. It is a system-of-systems type knowledge. Activities, policies and infrastructure at this level can have influence in lower order physio-spaces, such as the very practical question of whether a doctoral student can have their own room or if they sit in a shared space dedicated to doctoral students could be due to university workspace allocation policies. For the purposes of this study and in order to more coherently consolidate the data collected, the perspectives of *I, We, It/Its* will be investigated (sans intra/extra perspectives).

METHODOLOGY

Twenty doctoral students and their corresponding main supervisors (40 respondents in total) were approached in request to participate in this study. Of those approached, 8 respondents agreed to interviews if they remained anonymous in the event of published findings. This is due to mitigate or avoid identification purposes with regards to place of work and subject of research/teaching. The disciplinary background of the respondents can be broadly classified as belonging to humanities and social sciences.

The interviews took place in the context of higher education in the Nordic region over 2 months during the spring of 2017. They consist of 4 doctoral degree students of various nationalities and their corresponding main supervisors. 3 doctoral students were of nationalities outside of the Nordic countries. The doctoral students were at various stages of their doctoral degree completion. Most doctoral students were in their second and third years of a four-year program. The corresponding main supervisors to the doctoral students have all had extensive experience in doctoral supervision. All supervisors are professors in the field, having had more than a decade's experience in research supervision. The supervisors have also taught extensively at the university, at undergraduate and postgraduate levels. The interview was designed semi-structured, so as to capture as broad a perspective from the respondents' as possible. On average, the interview sessions timed 1 to 1 hour 30 minutes. The interviews were transcribed in accordance to the Gothenburg Transcription Standard version 6.4 (Nivre *et al.*, 2004) in Modified Standard Orthography (MSO). The reason for this is to be able to capture certain nuances in pauses when writing speech. The findings to this study are corpus driven.

EMPIRICAL FINDINGS: FEEDBACK ELEMENTS IN THE DOCTORAL DEGREE THESIS SUPERVISION PROCESS

Feedback in a doctoral degree thesis supervision process can be expressed in a tri-columned framework in Table 1. The table reflects combined findings from the Nordic foundational pedagogy texts (literature review), complemented from interview findings. Figure 2 illustrates how the findings from Table 1 can be mapped using an Integral Pluralism framework.

Table 1. Feedback system characterisation in the doctoral degree thesis writing supervision: A combined Nordic pedagogy literature review and empirical data analysis findings from 8 respondents

Research Environment		
Supervisor	**Doctoral Student**	**Institutional Support/Structure**
Credibility: Commitment to doctoral student thesis supervision	Credibility: Commitment to writing as part of the learning process	Workspace provision, hardware, software infrastructure availability
Truthfulness and accuracy in feedback	Proactive approach to feedback	Fostering culture of open communication
Research funding	Research funding	Scholarship, funding channels, facilitation, accessibility of information
Adequate Time allocation	Adequate Time allocation	Individual Study Plan (ISP), a mandatory document in the Nordic higher education context
Show contextual awareness	Show contextual awareness	Administrative support for student living, allowance for sick-leave and paternal/maternal leave
Encourage students to start writing early	Make writing habitual, not necessarily perfect	Foster culture of creative writing sessions
Communication style	Communication style	Institutional communication style
Teaching style	Learning style	Building architecture, classroom spatial design
Purpose, goal, expectation	Purpose, goal, expectation	Institutional purpose, goal, curriculum framework, assessment, evaluation procedures, examination procedures, policies, complaint channels, feedback channels
Encouragement of publishing	Honing academic writing skills, rhetoric style	Ease of access to information on publishing possibilities, library resources, scientific journal database accessibility
Interactivity	Interactivity	Institutional events, activities, interactivity with supervisors and students

EMPIRICAL FINDINGS AND DISCUSSION: AN INTEGRAL APPROACH TO FEEDBACK IN STUDENT-CENTERED LEARNING IN DOCTORAL DEGREE PROGRAMS

Upper Left Quadrant Findings

The UL quadrant pertains to the *singular subjective* perspective, with *I* type of knowledge. It pertains to intention and introspection of Self. The dominant theme of interest for the doctoral student respondents here seemed to be personal motivation. Feedback for individuals does not only come from their supervisors but from people around. In Text Example 1, doctoral student respondent $E, gave the example of how she pursued a doctoral degree based the motivation towards personal development.

Text Example 1

$E: i{ha}ve just had my final seminar and / at this point in time if you asked me why i started my phd in the first place < shakes head > / i must say i don{o}t know / i think i wanted to do something more than just be a stay at home mom / money is not an issue with us you know because < name of husband > has his own business and it{i}s going well / it gets a little stressful at times with the children / it gets that

way sometimes / but i can{no}t say that i am research inclined < shakes head > / no in fact / i{woul}d say the opposite / i{a}m not supermotivated to do research / it{i}s not in me to do it / but i just do it // you know / just because // no / i don{o}t think i will teach or go into research or academia after this / at least i don{o}t see me doing it

Text Example 1 is laced with a lot of uncertainties. The negative polarity *no,* in phrases such as "i don't know" and "but i cannot say that i am research inclined" indicate emotional and cognitive uncertainty. Still, intuitively, something was lacking and $E's personal feedback to herself was life goal oriented, expressed in the mental process words *think* and *wanted,* in "i *think* i *wanted* to do something more".

Personal motivation and Self feedback came for respondent $W (Text Example 2) as a conscious decision of a change of career from corporate to academic. Feedback that contributed to the beginnings of a doctoral degree program for $W was phrased as a manner of disappointment with the corporate world. He thought that academia might prove a more interesting career path, to which a doctoral degree would be a necessary prerequisite.

Text Example 2

$W: i was disillusioned with the corporate life / so when i saw that they had an opening for a phd position i applied / i thought it was something new to try and i{ha}d always wanted to pursue higher education anyway after my master thesis / so this was a good opportunity / i{a}m actually getting less in salary here as a phd student than when i was working in the corporation but i think i{a}m happier here

From a supervisor perspective, a student-learning approach meant greater focus on what students found beneficial in the learning process. Supervisors were committed to being there for their students. Watching their students learn and develop as individuals motivated them as supervisors. These cognitive reflections of supervisors can be mapped in the UL quadrant. Supervisors generally felt that even doctoral students, who are at an advanced stage in their learning goals, needed consistent guidance (feedback). Some spent hours of discussion time with the students. Supervisors also saw themselves in a mentorship role. The ideal relationship as some supervisor respondents described is to have a fairly close working relation with the student, with constant, open channels of communication. Two respondents in particular, felt that supervisors were responsible for cultivating students towards being well-rounded individuals, beyond simply equipping them with research skills. What could prove challenging is purpose and goal alignment in the doctoral thesis writing process. This was highlighted as something that needed to be discussed and then written down much like in contract format between supervisor and doctoral student. In the Nordic higher education context, this document is known as the Individual Study Plan (ISP), and can be used as a reference document for deliverables and activities to be covered by the doctoral student in a given project timeline. The ISP is negotiated every six months to which open channels of communication are important. The importance of supervisor-doctoral student goal alignment and expectations are reflected in Text Example 3, by supervisor respondent $T.

Text Example 3

$T: i think most important is to see that your student is in line with your thinking as a supervisor / in terms of goals, purpose and timeline / very important to get this information across in the very first meetings // even in this department we have different supervisory styles so to say / we have one professor here who has phd students as sort of disciples you know / so he has one method and he teaches his students that method which he has developed through his twenty years career / and then he expects his students to carry on that method / so with that type of supervisory role or purpose / students who do not understand this will come into big trouble with him / they disagree / they fight / and then you have a very unhappy situation of the student complaining to the department board or school administration and everything goes very bad // so very important / from the beginning / you need to set the guidelines / the expectations of what you are going to do as supervisor and as student

Lower Left Quadrant Findings

The LL quadrant pertains to the *plural intersubjective* perspective, with *We* type of knowledge, such as culture. All 8 respondents to this study cited the weekly group / department seminar as an activity and event for research culture fostering. Both the humanities and business administration faculties in which the respondents reside have as part of their higher education research program, a weekly seminar where works-in-progress from research faculty members can be shared and internally peer reviewed. Sometimes speakers with relevant expertise from the industry or from other universities are invited to present and share research findings and ideas. It is through such weekly seminars that constitute the basis of what the respondents thought was a 'research culture' at the university. These seminars also help bring faculty members closer together in terms of alignment of research interests, increasing the prospect of collaboration amongst the faculty members. These activities also provide opportunities for rich feedback sessions for the doctoral students. Depending on department funding and financial structure, some seminars are run as combined 'coffeetable sessions' or Nordic 'fika' sessions as part of the research culture and activities.

Two respondents who were main supervisors, cited lack of consistent high level of attendance from doctoral students as a challenge in terms of research culture fostering as part of the doctoral degree process. It is here that they felt that doctoral students could be more proactive in feedback seeking. The doctoral degree project timeline is pegged at 4 years, as such, students might not have as much time to devote to their thesis writing as some might assume. Department and institutional environments also play important roles in feedback for doctoral students on whether to stay or leave the doctoral degree program (Golde, 2000, 2005). Within most Nordic universities, seminar attendance is not mandatory unless written into the ISP by the supervisor. As such, it is often the case that with the pressures of completion of the doctoral thesis or of teaching commitments, faculty members tend to skip on attending seminars. It was pointed out by one respondent that there had been an internal departmental discussion on whether seminars should be made mandatory for all faculty members to attend. Some members felt that regardless of if the topic of the paper presented and discussed, seminar attendance would contribute greatly towards the overall feeling of solidarity and collegiality.

An Integral Theory Approach to the Feedback System in Supervising Doctoral Students

Upper Right Quadrant Findings

The UR quadrant pertains to the singular objective perspective, with *It* type of knowledge, such as the overall observable behaviour of people at the department/institution. Pertaining to the UR quadrant perspective would be interview findings indicating respondent thoughts on the supporting institutional structures and policies. A poignant theme from the supervisor respondents was change processes that affected department/institution culture of learning and teaching. Supervisor respondent $A in Text Example 4 speaks of change occurring in university processes and policies with regards to the recruitment of new doctoral students. $A has spent close to forty years as faculty at a Nordic university. In $A's perspective, change in administrative procedures towards greater centralisation and standardisation between the various faculties had cascading influences on the relations between supervisor and doctoral student. These changes needed to be communicated and managed between supervisor and doctoral student.

Text Example 4

$A: recruiting the right people / that / is difficult to answer and it's certainly a challenge // before around 2000 / before the administration changed then we had a different system of recruiting doctoral students where i believe was much better / the students needed to prove their interest in the subject by hanging around / they called it shadow students / and then after about six months a formal decision is taken usually by the supervisor and then the administrators get involved / today / it is more the administrators who administer the recruitment of the doctoral students / sometimes the supervisors don't even get to meet with the students / they're just told oh here you have a new student to handle / and oh <1 looks around >1 what a surprise / <2 >2 / and with this system too / it's more of a formal job application / the students need to meet certain criteria and be this and be that / before you could say that the doctoral student recruitment process was more egalitarian / anyone with interest could apply / of course you had to have some level of basic education and requirements yes / but still it was more open then and i would say anyone could more or less apply to become a phd student / but not so today / so it has been a change in the system and whether it is good or bad / well / both systems had their plus and minuses

@ <1 $A looks around >1

@ <2 laughing >2

The change processes described by $A could in part be said to be a reflection of the overall centralisation efforts of the European higher education system that resulted in regional standardisation policies. From a student-centered perspective, doctoral students are seen as employed in the national employment system that gives them greater income stability and work environment. In this sense, a doctoral position at the university would mean contracted employment to which the doctoral student is protected by labour unions and labour laws, which was not necessarily the case prior to 2000 in the Nordic countries.

Other topics that surfaced during the interviews from the supervisor respondents reflected practical issues, such as the seating arrangements of new doctoral students. Practical issues of concern was also allowance for life context changes such as when doctoral students due to personal reasons, needed to reduce the percentage of doctoral degree program participation from 100% to 70% or 50%. While the change of participation pace should not provide any real barriers to the completion of the doctoral degree program, it might affect surrounding resources such as supervision hours, office space availability for newly intended doctoral students in the following years. From the doctoral respondents' perspective, one respondent, $R (reflected in Text Example 5), had considered at worst case scenario, dropping out of the doctoral degree program due to what was deemed as a somewhat inflexible administrative system and too many uncertainties happening in concurrence.

Text Example 5

$R: i{ha}ve been feeling a little stressed lately / my grandmother is sick and my father wants me to go back to < name of country > to look after her because he doesn{o}t really have the time and all my other siblings are also out of the country // i{ha}ve tried to postpone going home but every time i speak to my parents / my mother is crying and threatening and my father is getting upset that i am not taking up my responsibility in the family / so i{ha}ve spoken to < name of supervisor > and he understands perfectly / i told him that this could take months up to half a year to settle with my family / and he said he would speak with the head of department and see if something can be sorted out / < > / i wanted to do forty percent time but i think that was a dead no / i understood that it had to be no less than sixty percent time / i also have some teaching this term and somebody will need to take care of that / so i really don{o}t know how this will go / i have to wait and see

@ < pauses with hesitation >

In $R's case, an inflexibility in the general doctoral degree program administration could be the main feedback was perceived as a discouragement for $R to continue with the doctoral degree program.

Lower Right Quadrant Findings

The LR quadrant pertains to the plural interobjective perspective, with *Its* type of knowledge, such as the overall behaviour of the network of institutions/organisations and supra-organisational bodies that might govern education policies and academic work environment. A theme that arose in the interview data with regards to the recent internationalisation efforts of the university that began in 2014. Some specific aims of the internationalisation effort included to increase recruitment of students from non-European Economic Area (EEA) countries, to intensify strategic international university collaborations that increases teacher and staff mobility both within the European Union (EU) and on the international arena, to increase participation in international networks and to intensify global university engagement in general.

From the interview data, challenges seem to have been faced mostly from the doctoral student respondents, especially those who have arrived in the Nordic countries to pursue a doctoral degree and who do not have working knowledge of the local language. Text Examples 6 and 7 from $D, lends differing perspectives to the challenges faced by foreign doctoral students in the Nordic region. $D did not have knowledge of the native language at first arrival for the doctoral program. This made it impossible him to access information in the doctoral student handbook, which was at the time only available to him in the native language of the Nordic country. Respondent $D began to notice the challenges faced by a lack of working knowledge of the native language early on from arrival, especially when faced with daily administration of confirming living accommodation and getting a personal identity number in order to open a bank account in the country (reflected in Text Example 6). There was then the additional challenge of encountering the use of higher academic seminars that $D had assumed would be conducted in English, but were in fact conducted in higher academic local language (reflected in Text Example 7).

Text Example 6

$D: i think one of the main problems that i{ha}ve faced as a doctoral student here at the university is that almost all official forms i need to fill in from housing arrangements to courses was in < name of native language > / and that is truly frustrating because it takes so much more time / i{ha}ve heard that the working language for doctoral students here is english but when you{ha}ve arrived and you{a}re faced with the daily practicalities / all administration seems to be taken in < name of native language > anyway / so it takes more time / do i didn{o}t know how to access the doctoral student handbook / how to get my identity card / how to set up my housing properly / i knew that being a foreign student / going to a different country was not going to be easy / but it has become very stressful due to this unexpected language barrier

Text Example 7

$D: i attended a mandatory module for doctoral students in my first year here / and i read in the doctoral handbook that you can use english throughout your doctoral degree / but then during this mandatory module / everything was in higher academic < name of native language > / i could barely grasp the concepts and ideas // i asked the lecturer afterwards if it was possible to switch to english / and he said that if he did that / all the native students wouldn't understand the course / so the course would continue in < name of native language > / so for some time / i was at a loss and felt mostly excluded from discussions / i was only starting basic < name of native language > language courses / so it was not enough to understand higher academic discussions / it was difficult

Some supervisor respondents acknowledged $D's perspective too, on the potential difficulties that foreign students might encounter when living and working in the Nordic countries. Accommodation shortage for foreign students in general has been acknowledged as a general challenge, where the supervisors could sometimes use informal means of their own network of friends in order to help students find accommodation. That the native Nordic language was used at doctoral seminars and feedback sessions was also acknowledged as a challenge, because there was little productivity in giving feedback in a language that the doctoral student could not understand.

The Doctoral Degree Process-Product System: An Integral Dialogic Model

Figure 2 illustrates the combined elements from Table 1 and findings from the empirical data collected for this study. The dialogic relations between these different perspectives pegged at different levels of analysis occurs between actors, between all quadrants and levels, so that an integral approach can be obtained even from the perspective of student-centered learning and feedback.

The different facets and levels of analysis range from individual student and individual supervisor perspective in the UL quadrant in Figure 2, to the departmental / faculty culture perspective in the LL

Figure 2. Integral approach to doctoral thesis feedback system

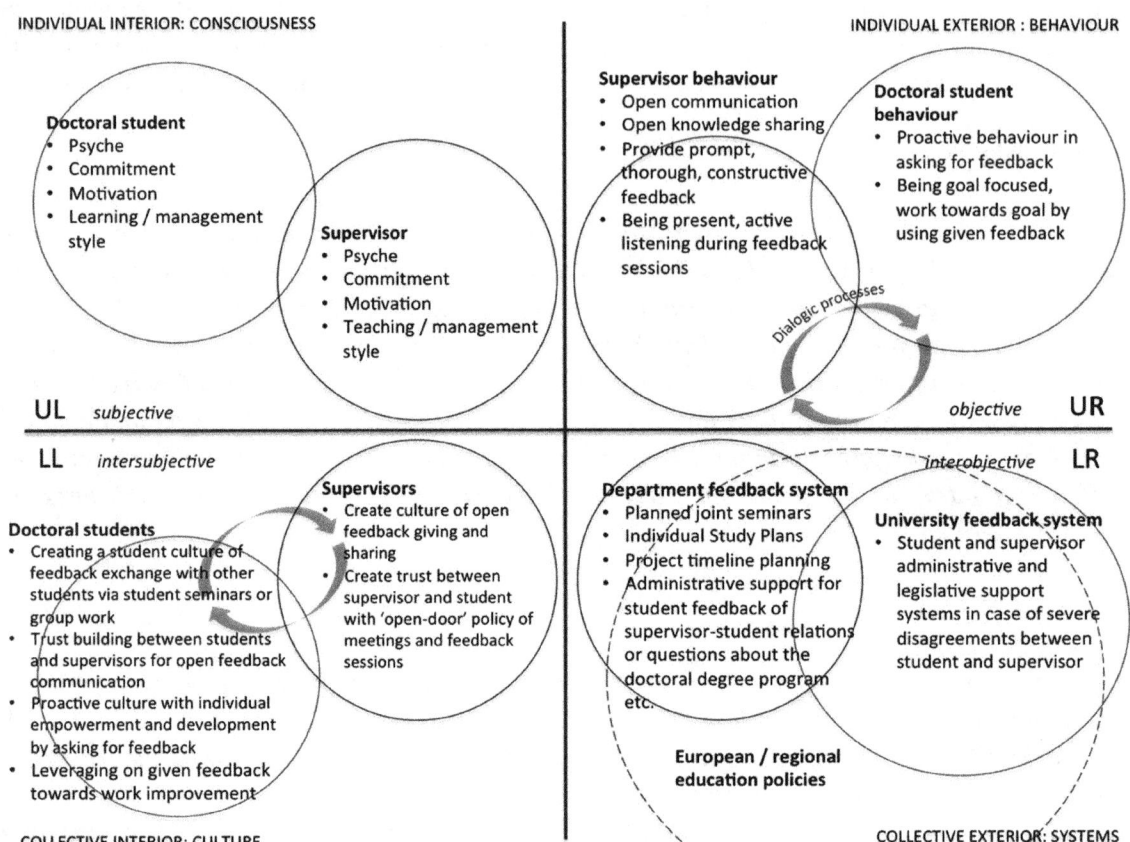

quadrant, institution perspective in the UR quadrant, and network of institution support perspective in the LR quadrant.

The red arrows drawn in circularity the quadrants in Figure 2 indicate the dialogic relations between the elements and individuals involved in the doctoral degree feedback system. An example of a direct correlation of elements across individuals and quadrants would be the ideas raised by supervisor respondent $T in Text Example 3 when speaking about the alignment of purpose and goals of the doctoral student and the supervisor. Open feedback and communication is crucial. A misalignment of purpose and goals between the two individuals might have the undesired effect of involving institution administration processes, in the event of a request of a change of supervisor or a change of field of study on the part of the doctoral student. If the doctoral student were of a foreign nationality, the effect of a misalignment between purpose and goals between doctoral student and supervisor could also involve global institutional networks in order to have the challenge addressed. If in the event of the situation raised by $R in Text Example 5, where the doctoral student might want to pursue part of the doctoral program back in their home country due to a personal situation, in a worst case scenario, international university networks might need to be activated in order to bolster the situation and lend support to the doctoral student. In is in these situations that national and regional higher education policies implemented might need to be taken into consideration, or a freer movement of students between universities would prove helpful.

Practical Application of the Model

The resulting Integral Pluralism model as illustrated in Figure 2, could potentially be applied in relation to further research studies within the field of Nordic pedagogy. The model is adaptive and reflects relativity in perspective. When taken as a whole, it reflects a comprehensive fabric for the feedback system dynamics of a doctoral degree program. Narrower research studies can be formulated by focusing on one or two specific quadrants. The integral model of feedback system in the doctoral degree thesis writing process reflects thought processes that can be taught in a systematic manner. The four quadrants map knowledge zones that constitute Nordic pedagogy in terms of the doctoral degree program. As such, depending on scope and purpose of the user, the model can be applied within a pedagogic teacher-discussion context, when designing for a doctoral degree program. It can also be used as a critical thinking tool, taught to students as a means of perspectivising research design for students to work with in positioning their own context of study.

CONCLUSION

This study focused on the feedback process in doctoral thesis writing supervision. In answer to the first research question of what practical facets of the feedback system were reflected in the Nordic context of higher education, findings from key foundational Nordic pedagogy books and academic journal articles were combined with interview data findings from 8 respondents on the topic of feedback in student-centered learning at doctoral degree level. These findings were systemically mapped using the Pronoun referencing system in language, that rendered an integral approach mapped into a four-quadrant model. In answer to the second research question, what has been found is that within the Nordic pedagogy literature, feedback is seldom seen as constituting of an ecological process of its own within the overall doctoral degree program. Rather, feedback giving is conceived as (a small) part of the doctoral thesis writing process (Elmgren & Henriksson, 2010; Lauvås & Handal, 2005). The Integral Pluralism approach illustrates that a much broader perspective of the success or failure of completion of a doctoral degree program might well hinge on appropriate, timely and accurate feedback through proper and established communication channels.

This study has also shown how regional policy changes towards European standardisation of higher education in order to increase movement of labour, require a big picture tool for analysis. The Integral view of how higher education programs can be perspectivised and studied, and specifically the Integral Methodological Pluralism model (illustrated in Figure 3) can effectively complement the knowledge and theoretical conceptualisation of the current academic literature, which has thus far focused on discrete acquisition of knowledge in individual quadrants only.

REFERENCES

Allen, H., Stebnicki, M., & Lynch, R. (1995). Training clinical supervisors in rehabilitation – a conceptual model for training doctoral-level supervisors. *Rehabilitation Counseling Bulletin, 38*(4), 307–317.

Barnes, B., & Austin, J. (2009). The Role of Doctoral Advisors: A Look at Advising from the Advisor's Perspective. *Innovative Higher Education, 33*(5), 297–315. doi:10.100710755-008-9084-x

Berman, J., & Smyth, R. (2015). Conceptual frameworks in the doctoral research process: A pedagogical model. *Innovations in Education and Teaching International*, *52*(2), 125–136. doi:10.1080/14703297.2013.809011

Bitchener, J., & Basturkmen, H. (2010). The focus of supervisor written feedback to thesis/dissertation students. *International Journal of English Studies*, *10*(2), 79-97.

Capra, F. (1997). *The web of life: A new synthesis of mind and matter*. London: Flamingo.

Carr, S. M., Lhussier, M., & Chandler, C. (2010). The supervision of professional doctorates: Experiences of the processes and ways forward. *Nurse Education Today*, *30*(4), 279–284. doi:10.1016/j.nedt.2009.03.004 PMID:20138411

Davis, N., & Callihan, T. (2013). Integral methodological pluralism in science education research: Valuing multiple perspectives. *Cultural Studies of Science Education*, *8*(3), 505–516. doi:10.100711422-012-9480-5

Dudley, H. (1984). Doctoral students and the supervisor's role. *British Medical Journal*, *288*(6416), 511. doi:10.1136/bmj.288.6416.511 PMID:20742178

EC. (2015). Attainment: Raising graduate numbers. *European Commission, Education and Training*. Retrieved from http://bit.ly/2mmlO9T

Elmgren, M., & Henriksson, A.-S. (2010). *Universitetspedagogik* [University pedagogy]. Uppsala, Sweden: Norstedts.

Esbjorn-Hargens, S., & Zimmerman, M. (2009). *Integral ecology: Uniting multiple perspectives on the natural world*. Boston: Integral Books.

Eurostat. (2013). Tertiary education statistics. *Eurostat*. Retrieved from http://bit.ly/2eJPfRL

Eurostat. (2016). Educational attainment statistics. *Eurostat*. Retrieved from http://bit.ly/2oTzCbs

Floyd, J. (2008). Towards an Integral renewal of systems methodology for futures studies. *Futures*, *40*(2), 138–149. doi:10.1016/j.futures.2007.11.007

Franke, A., & Arvidsson, B. (2011). Research supervisors' different ways of experiencing supervision of doctoral students. *Studies in Higher Education*, *36*(1), 7–19. doi:10.1080/03075070903402151

Gatfield, T. (2005). An investigation into PhD supervisory management styles: Development of a dynamic conceptual model and its managerial implications. *Journal of Higher Education Policy and Management*, *27*(3), 311–325. doi:10.1080/13600800500283585

Golde, C. M. (2000). Should I stay or should I go? Student descriptions of the doctoral attrition process. *The Review of Higher Education*, *23*(2), 199–227. doi:10.1353/rhe.2000.0004

Golde, C. M. (2005). The role of the department and discipline in doctoral student attrition: Lessons from four departments. *The Journal of Higher Education*, *76*(6), 669–700. doi:10.1353/jhe.2005.0039

Grant, K., Hackney, R., & Edgar, D. (2014). Postgraduate research supervision: An 'agreed' conceptual view of good practice through derived metaphors. *International Journal of Doctoral Studies*, *9*, 43–60. doi:10.28945/1952

Handal, G., Holmström, L.-G., & Thomsen, O. (1973). *Universitetsundervisning: Problem, empiri, teori Lund.* København: Studentlitteratur.

Hoskins, C., & Goldberg, A. (2005). Doctoral student persistence in counselor education programs: Student-program match. *Counselor Education and Supervision, 44*(3), 175–188. doi:10.1002/j.1556-6978.2005.tb01745.x

Ivankova, N., & Stick, V. (2007). Students' persistence in a distributed doctoral program in educational leadership in higher education: A mixed methods study. *Research in Higher Education, 48*(1), 93–135. doi:10.100711162-006-9025-4

Lauvås, P., & Handal, G. (2005). Optimal use of feedback in research supervision with master and doctoral students. *Nordisk Pedagogik, 25,* 177–189.

Lauvås, P., & Handal, G. (2012). Universitetsundervisning – problem, empiri, teori [University teaching – problems, findings, theory]. *The International Journal for Academic Development, 17*(1), 87–92. doi:10.1080/1360144X.2012.646533

Loganbill, C., Hardy, E., & Delworth, U. (1982). Supervision: A Conceptual Model. *The Counseling Psychologist, 10*(1), 3–42. doi:10.1177/0011000082101002

Nivre, J., Allwood, J., Grönqvit, L., Gunnarsson, M., Ahlsén, E., Vappula, H., . . . Ottesjö, C. (2004). *Gothenburg Transcription Standard 6.4.* University of Gothenburg. Retrieved from http://bit.ly/2hbMNoA

Odena, O., & Burgess, H. (2017). How doctoral students and graduates describe facilitating experiences and strategies for their thesis writing learning process: A qualitative approach. *Studies in Higher Education, 42*(3), 572-590.

Olmos-López, P., & Sunderland, J. (2017). Doctoral supervisors' and supervisees' responses to co-supervision. *Journal of Further and Higher Education, 41*(6), 727–740. doi:10.1080/0309877X.2016.1177166

Phillips, E. M., & Pugh, D. (2005). *How to get a PhD.* London: Continuum.

Pole, C., Sprokkereef, A., Burgess, R., & Lakin, E. (1997). Supervision of doctoral students in the natural sciences: Expectations and experiences. *Assessment & Evaluation in Higher Education, 22*(1), 49–63. doi:10.1080/0260293970220104

Rafferty, M. (2001). A conceptual model for clinical supervision in nursing and health visiting based upon Winnicott's (1960) theory of the parent-infant relationship. *Journal of Psychiatric and Mental Health Nursing, 8*(2), 153–161. doi:10.1046/j.1365-2850.2000.00277.x PMID:11146911

Schwartz-Shea, P., & Bennett, A. (2003). Introduction - Methodological pluralism in journals and graduate education? Commentaries on new evidence. *PS, Political Science & Politics, 36*(3), 371–372.

Stephens, S. (2014). The supervised as the supervisor. *Education + Training, 56*(6), 537–550. doi:10.1108/ET-10-2012-0095

Stigmar, M. (2009). *Høgskolepedagogik. Att vara professionell som lärare i högskolan* [Pedagogy for higher education. Being a professional teacher in higher education]. Stockholm, Sweden: Liber.

Wilber, K. (2000). *A theory of everything*. Boston: Shambhala.

Wilber, K. (2006). *Integral spirituality*. Boston: Shambhala.

Zhou, J. (2015). International students' motivation to pursue and complete a Ph.D. in the U.S. *Higher Education, 69*(5), 719–733. doi:10.100710734-014-9802-5

KEY TERMS AND DEFINITIONS

Bologna Process: The Bologna Process was signed by 29 European countries in 1999. Named after the University of Bologna where the Bologna declaration was signed, it was the result of a series of ministerial meetings and agreements between European countries to ensure comparability in the standards and quality of higher education qualifications. It supports freedom of movement of labor and inter-university transfers of students and staff between European countries.

EHEA: The European Higher Education Area (EHEA) is the result of the political will of 48 countries that over two decades have put together common tools to reform and standardize higher education on the basis of common values such as freedom of expression, autonomy for institutions, independent student unions, academic freedom, free movement of students and staff.

Europe 2020: The Europe 2020 strategy is the European Union's agenda for inclusive growth and job creation for the current decade. It emphasizes intelligent, sustainable growth eco-systems as a means to overcome weaknesses in Europe's economic development. It is for the purpose of improving European competitiveness in the following area such as (1) employment, (2) research and development (R&D), (3) climate change and energy, (4) education, and (5) poverty and social exclusion.

Feedback: Defined in this study in its broadest sense of a dialogic communication process, although it is analyzed from the niche field of Nordic pedagogy doctoral thesis supervision.

Integral Pluralism: A combined theoretical framework that integrates multiple perspectives, based on the understanding that all knowledge is interrelated to a greater or lesser proximity. It is an approach that can be used to study the increasing complexity of socio-cultural and economic phenomena in an era of interconnectedness.

Nordic Pedagogy: In this study, it refers specifically to the body of academic literature that studies pedagogy traditions and practices in the Nordic countries that include Denmark, Norway, Sweden, and Finland. Most Nordic pedagogy material are written in their native Scandinavian languages. One of the aims of this study is to provide readers with some insight into the Nordic pedagogy paradigm.

Student-Centered Learning: This is a paradigm shift that occurred in the early 2000s when European standardization policies began to be set in motion in order to facilitate cross-border education exchange particularly in higher education. What this meant in practice was an increase in centralization of administration for higher education degree programs, in view of a single European labor market in its heterogeneity of regional countries.

Chapter 13
An Integral Analysis of Wellbeing in Adults With Characteristics of High Functioning Autism

Janice Marie Beler
University of Calgary, Canada

ABSTRACT

Quality of life is generally assessed through objective measures including conditions relating to material living, productive activity, health measures, education levels, and economic standing. In contrast, wellbeing is a complex process involving subjective evaluation of the qualities and experiences that make life good. Research is plentiful with studies exploring autism and quality of life. Less information is available relating to wellbeing and autism, especially from first person perspectives. This research explored how autism characteristics shape understanding and experiences of wellbeing in individuals with characteristics of high functioning autism. The study made use of a multi-method research framework, integral methodological pluralism (IMP), based on Ken Wilber's integral theory, for gathering and understanding knowledge from diverse perspectives, styles, and methodologies. Findings contributed towards a more coherent and inclusive understanding of personal wellbeing in high functioning autism.

INTRODUCTION

As a whole, individuals with high functioning autism do not tend to have better life outcomes than those with more severe forms of autism (Hofvander, et al., 2009). Studies indicate that few individuals with autism live independently and that they experience higher levels of antisocial personality disorder, substance abuse problems, and mood and anxiety disorders. Despite having normal IQs, less than half are generally employed (Eaves & Ho, 2008), the majority have never been in a long-term relationship (Hofvander, et al., 2009), and a higher percentage of this population express suicidal thoughts (Eaves &

DOI: 10.4018/978-1-5225-5873-6.ch013

Ho, 2008). In general, people with high functioning autism are often unable to meet their potential and suffer a decreased quality of life (VanHeijst & Geurts, 2014).

Alberta's education system has seen a significant increase in the number of students diagnosed with, or exhibiting characteristics of, high functioning autism (Clarke, Dudley, Dutton, Emery, & Ghali, 2014). These students tend to be academically capable, but their prospects beyond school are often bleak. Increased understanding of their condition and strategies to support their needs are more likely to be implemented now than in previous years, but the current approach to accommodating these students' needs lacks consistency and reflects a reactive rather than proactive approach. To shift to a proactive position requires an inclusive, integrated perspective that focuses on the long-term implications of high functioning autism as well as the symptoms that manifest in the classroom. C.D. Ryff's model for psychological well-being (Ryff, 1989) was used to explore improved understanding of the long-term implications of high functioning autism, with IMP providing methodological framework for collecting data that reflected inclusive and integrated perspectives. All Quadrant (AQ) mapping was used to enhance the value of understanding from the literature review, establish the design framework and data collection methods for the research, and to enrich analysis and understanding from the study's findings.

Context

People with high functioning autistic characteristics tend to have strong skills in some areas, while being very low functioning in others. Common strengths often include skills and traits that are required for school success, including the ability to focus attention, memorize, master basic academic skills quickly and easily, and follow concrete instructions. It is not uncommon for the educational needs of these learners to be overlooked because they are capable of mastering basic curriculum. Important areas of deficit are generally not addressed in school, as they are not part of any current curriculum and possibly because most neurotypical learners naturally develop these essential skills without specific instruction. Weaknesses relating to perception, abstract thinking, understanding cause and effect, prioritizing, decision-making, and adapting to change are typical in the diagnosis. These are examples of skills that are pertinent to success, but are not identified as focus points in any particular curriculum.

Although existing research allows for speculation about what knowledge, skills and attitudes should be addressed in the successful education of learners with characteristics of high function autism, there seems to be little research examining the big picture of autism.

Purpose

This research sought to understand well-being in individuals with characteristics of high functioning autism, and to explore what this insight could reveal about educating Alberta learners on the autism spectrum. It was anticipated that a better understanding of participants' perceptions and experiences of well-being could have curricular implications. By examining multiple perspectives of the topic, rich and contextualized understanding offered valuable information towards improving the educational experiences and outcomes for learners on the autism spectrum.

Significance

An increasing number of families are facing diagnoses of high functioning autism in their children; our school systems are reporting record numbers of students experiencing the challenges of autism (Clarke, et al., 2014). Alberta's parents and teachers are facing a new reality in which they are expected to meet the diverse needs of this population who seem to be characterized by paradox, in that autistic individuals often exhibit a curious mixture of strength and challenges, obvious abilities and hidden disabilities. This study uncovered a better understanding of well-being in adults with high functioning autism characteristics, one that can be used to improve educational practice in Alberta schools.

THEORETICAL PERSPECTIVE

For the purposes of this research, Integral Theory (IT) was adopted as a philosophy that served to integrate different ways of knowing and being into as complete of an understanding of the topic as possible within the scope of the research study. The theoretical perspective was not intended to result in an "end-product"; rather it lent itself towards understanding the continuous process of growth and change evident in the core of the research questions. The perspective mirrored a process that seems to replicate the growth and change that is constant in the world. It provided an ontological and epistemological explanation for why simple questions and problems can be so elusive to capture and solve. In doing so, it accounted for both the complexity and richness of the research findings.

IT is an emergence theory. It is based in a holistic philosophy which promotes methodological diversity towards a richer understanding and practice for working with complex issues. It aims to be an all-inclusive framework that draws on key insights and understandings from many truths and perspectives (Esbjorn-Hargens, 2010). IT provided the ontological, epistemological and methodological foundation for gathering and interpreting information.

Integral Theory

Integral theory, as described by Ken Wilber, offers an approach to draw together an already existing number of separate paradigms into an interrelated network of approaches that are mutually enriching (Esbjorn-Hargens, 2010). Integral theory has developed into an emerging field of academic research, providing a methodology for a comprehensive approach towards uniting knowledge and experience towards better understanding and acting towards complex issues.

Wilber describes an integral map that helps by allowing knowledge and understanding seekers to "touch all bases", promoting the utilization of a more comprehensive range of resources for any situation. This map, referred to as All Quadrants All Lines (AQAL), is built around five elements: quadrants, levels, lines, states and types. The quadrant element was used as the basis for conducting the literature review, developing research methodology, collecting data, and analysing understanding in this research on well-being and high functioning autism.

BACKGROUND

Reviewing literature relating to a topic of study constitutes research in and of itself (Bloomberg & Volpe, 2012). A comprehensive literature search was completed with the goal of conducting a methodological examination of the topics pertinent to this study. Integral Methodological Pluralism (IMP) was used as a tool to ensure a balanced representation of perspectives for the scholarly review.

The Four Quadrants

Theorists working across wide ranges of disciplinary studies frame their research and data in terms of hierarchies that spiral forward in what appears to be increasing complexity, with each turn of the spiral including and transcending the previous one before it. Ken Wilber, recognizing broad similarities and patterns existing throughout a range of research fields, themes and topics, set out to study the phenomenon. He analysed a vast array of theories that extended beyond time, knowledge families and geography. What he found was that the different knowledge claims share common hierarchical ground. He saw a pattern that involved, among other things, at least eight paradigms that he considers foundational for gaining knowledge and understanding. These paradigms were developed into his version of Integral Theory. Integral Methodological Pluralism (IMP) is presented as the means by which integral theory can be enacted for research. Wilber believes the fundamental claim in his version of Integral Methodological Pluralism, the means by which he rationalizes integral theory can be enacted for research, is that these paradigms need be considered in research design and as the most comprehensive way for interpreting data for understanding. Central to his method are the quadrants.

Any occasion and phenomena possesses an inside and an outside, an individual and a collective dimension. These form the basic quadrant, shown in Figure 1.

Figure 1. All Quadrants model.
Adapted from Wilber (1995)
These four perspectives together represent a more comprehensive way to understanding, each contributing a complementary vision of the same phenomena. Each is a vital but different piece of the truth. Different from each other, but connected in their relationship and contribution to the subject. These four are expanded into eight when we consider that each quadrant can be looked at from zones of inside or outside perspectives, as shown in Figure 2. This study employed the quadrants and zones as a methodological tool. While it is not possible to consider all diverse perspectives and knowledge claims existing around the rapidly expanding studies of autism or well-being, the model offered a more balanced perspective for studying the complex connections and relationships between phenomena relating to autism and well-beng.

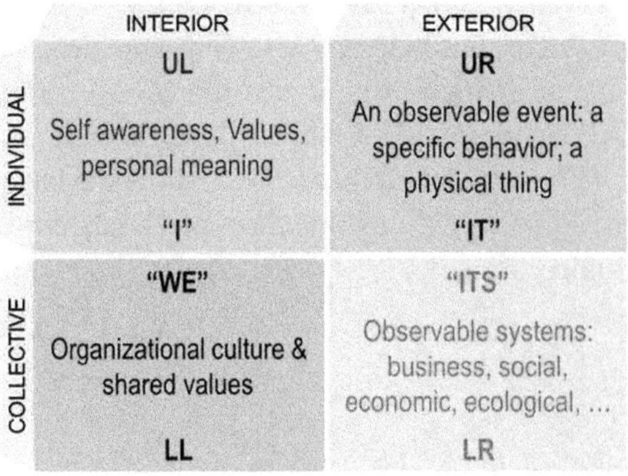

	INTERIOR	EXTERIOR
INDIVIDUAL	UL — Self awareness, Values, personal meaning — "I"	UR — An observable event: a specific behavior; a physical thing — "IT"
COLLECTIVE	"WE" — Organizational culture & shared values — LL	"ITS" — Observable systems: business, social, economic, ecological, ... — LR

Research Design and Scholarly Review

A simplified form of IMP's basic quadrant was employed as a method for gathering a more holistic collection and understanding of background knowledge pertinent to the topic of well-being in high functioning autism. Each of the four quadrants provided direction for gathering insight into the subject, as shown in figure 3.

Well-Being

Historically, research on well-being grew from two philosophical schools of thought - one that posits a hedonic focus to well-being and the other that emphasizes eudemonism as the path forward to well-being. Hedonic models advocate that the chief goal of a good life is to seek out pleasure and avoid pain. The pursuit of maximizing pleasure and minimizing pain is seen as the purpose of a life well lived. In

Figure 2. IMP framework.
Adapted from Esbjorn-Hargens (2010)

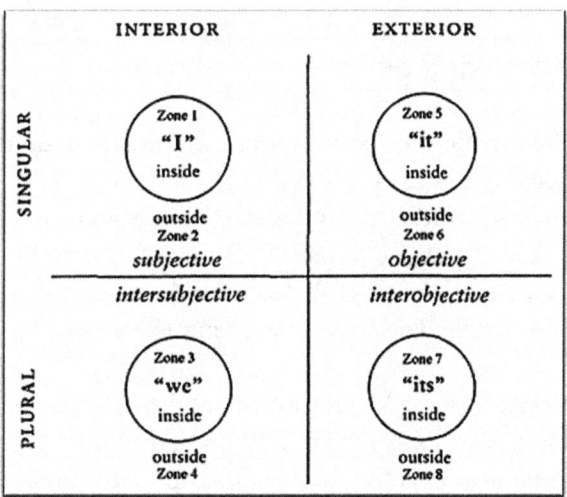

Figure 3. Selected review of research from a quadrant perspective

contrast, Eudemonic models hold that well-being lies in the actualization of human potential. Humans, as individuals and groups, hold final values and purpose in which they pursue and fill. Ryan & Deci noted that both of these philosophical positions alone cannot account for well-being (Ryan & Deci, 2001). They describe well-being as a complex construct that concerns optimal experience and functioning. It is composed in varying degrees of both hedonistic and eudemonic experiences. Models of well-being seem to fluctuate between perspectives of objective values and well-being as understood by an individual's psychology. Seven prominent theories of well-being, each taking some form of a balanced approach to these perspectives, were examined towards understanding the complexity inherent in the idea of well-being. Theories studied were *Liking/Wanting/Needing Theories*, *Multiply Discrepancy Theories*, *Top Down and Bottom Up Factor Models*, *Orientations to Happiness Models*, *Mental Health Continuum Models*, *Past/Present/Prospect Models* and the *Ryff Model of Psychological Well-Being* (Ryff, 1989). Well-being is an ideal, but an ideal that is rooted in our psychology. What people value needs to be put at the center of any theory of well-being. Ryff's Six-Factor Model of Well-Being model was selected for use in this study because it respects a balance between individual values and the ideals of the concept being explored. Additionally, it is accompanied by a scale that allowed for simplicity in identifying and measuring factors of well-being in participants along with a vast data base of participant measures from previous studies that could be used for comparison in understanding data results.

Ryff Model of Psychological Well-Being

This study used the Ryff model, which conceptualizes *well-being* as an individual's subjective experience relating to self- acceptance, quality ties to others, a sense of autonomy in thought and action, the ability to manage complex environments in order to suit personal needs and values, the pursuit of meaningful goals and a sense of life purpose, and the continued growth and development of the individual (Ryff, 1989). The Psychological Well-Being Scales (PWBS) were developed as a credible method for collecting empirical measures of well-being. The scales were simple for participants to complete and for the researcher to interpret.

The model was developed in effort to address fundamental challenges in studying and understanding well-being, which included a lack of tools for credibly measuring the concept. A review of literature relating to the topic and mental health, self-actualization, optimal functioning and developmental life span converged around the six core constructs of her model.

The Ryff model emphasizes an approach to understanding well-being that initially appears to relate more to eudemonic values of well-being. However, as evidenced in each of the popular theories examined in the literature review, connections between the two philosophies of well-being interact with each other in an ongoing swirl of ebb and flow to create the malleable nature of the phenomena.

Autism

Autism is a neurological developmental disorder characterized by impaired social interaction and communication as well as restricted interests and repetitive behavior. About one percent of the worldwide population is affected by the condition, and the proportion of autistic students in Calgary's school population mirrors this statistic (Ghali, et al., 2014). The prevalence of autism has been steadily increasing over the past two decades

Autism is a spectrum condition that can manifest with mild to severe symptoms.

Approximately forty-five percent of autism cases involve intellectual disability. Males are three times more likely to be effected than females. While the broad phenotype is specific to social communication and interaction challenges with restricted and repetitive patterns of behavior, more than seventy percent of individuals with autism have co-occurring medical, developmental, or psychiatric conditions. Sleep disorders, depression, anxiety, ADHD, tic disorders, and obsessive-compulsive disorder are the most common conditions accompanying autism.

A meta-analysis showed that individuals with autism have a mortality risk that is almost three times higher than that of unaffected people of the same age and sex. Up to eighty percent of adults with autism have poor or very poor outcomes in terms of independent living, educational attainment, employment, and peer relationships. Even for individuals without intellectual disability, adult social outcome is often unsatisfactory in terms of quality of life and achievement of occupational potential (VanHeijst & Geurts, 2014)

High functioning autism is at one end of the spectrum. Signs and symptoms are less severe, and people with high functioning autism usually have average to above-average intelligence. From an educational perspective, high functioning autism is challenging because of the diversity in intrapersonal strengths and challenges.

Cognitive Theories of Autism: Upper Right Quadrant

Leading the path in autism research has been an effort to elucidate the mechanisms underpinning the behavioral manifestations of autism (Lai, Lombardo, & Baron-Cohen, 2014). Genetics/biology, cognition, behavioral factors and an individual's environment have been implicated to some degree as either having a causal or symptomatic role—although the specific nature or role of each remains uncertain (Frith, Morton, & Leslie, 1991). Initial theories focused on single and primary cognitive deficits, but more recent theories acknowledge that there is likely a complex interplay between explanatory levels, which is represented in Figure 4.

Pellicano (Pellicano, 2011) suggests that a successful model of autism needs to address four key criteria:

1. The model must be universal; it needs to address autistic traits in all individuals on the spectrum, not just some of them.
2. It should be unique to the characteristics of individuals with autism, to distinguish between it and other developmental disabilities.
3. The model should explain causal precedence, addressing how the theory is a cause in the disorder rather than a symptom of the disorder.
4. It should provide an explanation that connects the severity of the described deficit to the behavioral symptoms of autism.

A successful cognitive or psychological theory of autism should also be able to integrate neurobiological theories. To date, no single theory has been proposed that stands to meet each of the above requirements, although there are prominent theories that contribute to our understanding of autism. For the purpose of this scholarly review, five prominent cognitive theories for autism were explored towards understanding what the upper right quadrant, through science and medicine, could contribute to understanding regarding autism. These were *Theory of Mind, Executive Dysfunction, Central Coherence, Empathizing-Systemizing,* and *Intense World* theories.

Figure 4. Causal model showing three levels of explanation.
Adapted from Frith et al., 1991.

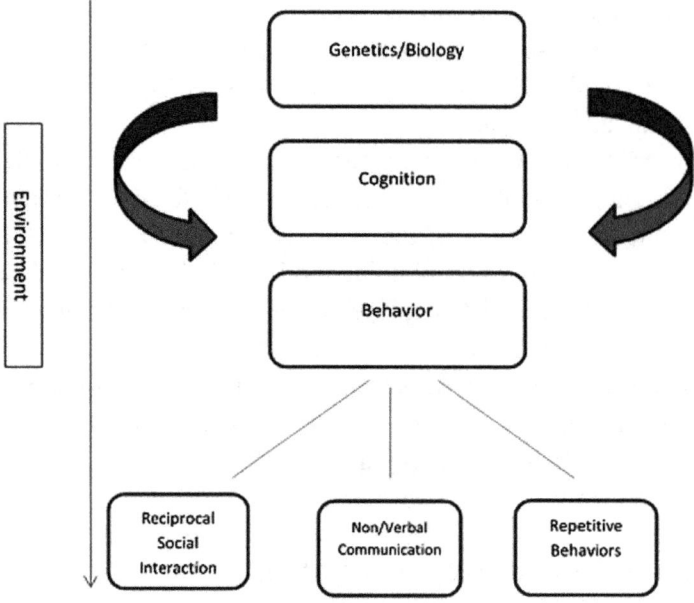

Autism is widely accepted as a neurological condition, and upper right quadrant understanding certainly lends some insight into the condition. However, the review of literature focusing on prominent cognitive theories of autism offered little conclusive data. Abnormalities in brain structure and function are described, but with exceptions in consistency and limitations in understanding the implications of such abnormalities. Rather, autism remains a condition that is defined largely by behavioral characteristics for which evidence has traditionally been sought from a medical and scientific perspective. This alone, and to date, has not brought us much closer to unlocking the mysteries of the condition. Exploring cognitive theories was valuable in helping to define and clarify the characteristics of autism that may influence well-being, but independently offered limited understanding regarding the complex nature underlying the topic of study.

The Role of Self in Autism: Upper Left Quadrant

It is established that theory of mind is affected in autism. It is also theorized that the ability to recognize mental states in oneself depends on the same psychological mechanisms (Cheng, Rolls, Gu, Shang, & Feng, 2015). If this is the case, autism likely involves mechanisms relating to the *theory of own mind*. The combination of weaknesses relating to theory of mind and theory of own mind may be associated with anxiety disorders, which are prevalent in autism. An inability to recognize the intent of others and reconcile it with self-awareness can impair systemizing strengths and create anxiety by contributing to an inability to predict what might occur in a personal environment. Lack of certainty and fear of the unknown are triggers for anxiety in most people. This alone supports the value of focusing on the development of self in autism. Without a strong sense of self, an individual is more likely to interpret experiences as occurring from an external locus of control. People with autism tend to experience difficulty distinguishing between self-controlled and externally-controlled action, indicating that they may exhibit abnormalities in their metacognition of agency (Zalla, Miele, Leboyer, & Metcalfe, 2015).

As Siegel observes, "Few ideas are both as weighty and as slippery as the notion of the self" (Hobson, 2010). Yet for all of its slipperiness, self-experience combines with worldly encounters that facilitate personal development and social engagement. Hobson suggests that we cannot presume that autistic people have the structure of self-experience that most people take for granted.

Facilitating the development of the recognition of self has implications not only for anxiety management and social connections, but for improving communication. Communication itself requires understanding of self. In essence, communication is the connection between self and other. An individual with limited understanding of self will be at a disadvantage in communication, which will impact the developmental trajectory of communication and likely result in further impairment over time (Hobson, 2010).

Research indicates that facilitating development of self through mindfulness practices is promising. It seems that mindfulness-based stress reduction (MBSR) techniques may be an effective intervention for reducing comorbid symptoms of depression, anxiety and distress in high functioning adults with Autism Spectrum Disorder (ASD). New techniques that help individuals with autism develop a sense of self will likely have a positive influence on well-being (Bogels, Hoogstad, Dun, Schutter, & Restifo, 2008).

Interpersonal Relationships and Autism: Lower Left Quadrant

At one point, there was an unsubstantiated belief that individuals with autism did not experience or were not affected by loneliness. More recent studies show that loneliness is an associated negative emotional experience for people with autism (Mazurek, 2013). Many building blocks of interpersonal relationships, such as communication, social cognition, and processing of emotional signals, are impaired in people with autism (Travis & Sigman, 1998). These challenges with developing interpersonal relationships are detrimental to the development of individuals with autism. Loneliness is associated with increased depression and anxiety as well as decreased life satisfaction and self-esteem. Yet we know that people with autism can and do develop meaningful relationships. Increasing social networks to decrease loneliness may have a significant impact on well-being for adults with autism (Mazurek, 2013).

At the core of most educational approaches to autism is the teaching of social skills. This can include encouraging specific social behaviors and social rules, which can be quite effective. However, Baron-Cohen suggests that we need to go further than the rote teaching of skills (Baron-Cohen, 2008). By themselves, these approaches tend to impose a rigid use of social skills, which can be detrimental since social rules are hard to specify in ways that cover all instances. He argues that it is equally important to teach about mental states (beliefs, thoughts, intentions, desires, and emotions).

Addressing social deficits and enhancing social skills early on seems to be an effective way of improving the quantity and quality of relationships for people with autism. In addition, it is likely to improve the developmental trajectory of people with characteristics of high functioning autism and may improve well-being outcomes.

Alberta Education and High Functioning Autism: Lower Right Quadrant

It is difficult to distinguish between supporting autistic learners and supporting other diverse learning groups. When one marginalized group benefits, others tend to benefit as well. This has always been the challenge of systems, how to fairly respect and tailor the rights and needs of individuals with the larger community that they are part of. Education in Alberta, specifically in relationship to autistic learners, has been no exception.

In Alberta, the 1970s and 1980s were a time of prescriptive teaching. The emphasis was on providing teachers with a list of skills and objectives that needed to be taught in a developmental sequence, with the ultimate goal being the students' "normalization" and attainment of skills most pertinent to independence and basic life skill functioning (Alberta Department of Education, 1982). Students who were not able to achieve or benefit from these prescribed learning goals were viewed as being deficit, being broken and in need of being fixed. The role of the education system was to repair the student in so much as possible, as evident by their ability to achieve the prescribed learning outcomes. While talk of inclusion was beginning to emerge, the emphasis was on integration. The term *integration* suggests that learners with special needs were to begin in seclusion and ideally progress towards assimilation with peers in a more natural environment. There was a program of studies outlining general objectives for special education, which were further developed into guides for teaching all learners with special needs. Learners with characteristics of high functioning autism were either expected to conform and master existing curriculum, or to be served by working on a curriculum for students with special needs, regardless of whether or not those outcomes matched their individual learning needs. For example, a student who was exhibiting behavior challenges that impaired their ability to be successful with regular curriculum, but was otherwise intelligent and academically capable, would likely simply fail school and not continue with their education. If learning or cognitive disability was suspected, the student would then be served by teaching directed from the Educable Mentally Handicapped or Trainable Mentally Handicapped Curriculum Guide (Alberta Education, 1982).

Between the early 1990s and 2005, Alberta began a paradigm shift which would have important implications for how we thought about teaching learners on the spectrum. The call for integration in Alberta had grown in strength. This approach still worked from the standpoint of the medical model and its emphasis on finding a remedy, or at least controlling deficits. The basic structure of this approach resembled the category used at the federal level in the United States called the "Disability Model" (Jahnukainen, 2011). Only now the model was applied with a single-minded goal to focus all efforts and resources on placing the disadvantaged child in a regular classroom regardless of what would be best for the child or the other students.

There was a call for intervention, integration and for special education to be structured as a supportive system to supplement regular education. This era saw the rise in the importance of the individualized program plan (IPP). Meaningful and substantial resources were dedicated to this cause, and it is worth noting that Alberta teachers reported a high level of satisfaction with their ability to meet the needs of children coded as special education students (Murgatroyd, 2013). This was the era of resource rooms—when most schools had access to special education teachers and were able to employ collaborative team-teaching approaches to meet unique learning needs.

With President Bush's 1990 proclamation of the Decade of the Brain project (America, 1990), public awareness of brain research brought forward a wealth of new research and understanding relating to autism. The condition was recognized socially and economically as a disability in the United States, and other nations soon followed suit. This era can be identified as a forerunner to the early 2000s commitment to social action and equity. Freire's *Pedagogy of the Oppressed*, published in 1970, was a beacon to a new generation motivated by a passion for justice and equity for all. It was not until the 1990s that these ideals were to become evident in Alberta Education's policies, publications, and practices.

In combination with the scientific insight gathered from the Decade of the Brain, autism benefited from the work of advocacy organizations and social justice fighters. It was here that the philosophy emphasizing a focus on ability over disability was born. This was a philosophy that would spread through the autistic community and facilitate progress in the way society viewed, valued, and worked with this population. In Alberta, this change in public consciousness culminated in the 2003 Alberta Education publication, *Teaching Students with Autism Spectrum Disorders*—just one document in a series providing information and strategies for differentiating instruction for students with a wide range of needs influencing their learning. These documents provided valuable support for teachers struggling to help their students achieve success. They remain in frequent use today.

The new millennium saw the emergence of a different way of thinking about challenge, one that moved past the boundaries of the deficit model. Part of this new way of thinking initiated the transition from the disability model to a strength-based model. Strength-based learning as a process advocates a focus on personal strengths and success in order to encourage the acquisition of knowledge and skills. This promising approach represented a gentler, more respectful philosophy in which all learners could be successful. At its core was the belief that each learner is a unique individual with unique talents and challenges. It further promoted the decentralization of traditional special education services in Alberta schools, and instead emphasized that each and every learner had the right to her development within the dynamics of the regular classroom. Resource rooms as a consistent part of the school geography faded. So too did the idea of the traditional regular education classroom.

All teachers were expected to be special education or inclusive education teachers. Differentiation and inclusive education became concepts that every teacher was expected to exemplify. This adaptation can be seen as a call to move towards 21st century learning, and is reflected in Alberta Education documents including Action Plan for Education (2008), Inspiring Education (2009), and Setting the Direction (2010).

Through this period, new understandings about autism continued to emerge at an impressive rate. Of equal interest was the changing perception of autism in the media and the general public. Public awareness had increased, and it seemed that the negative stigma associated with the condition had decreased (Martin, 2013). This new vision and a philosophy that truly reflected the values of the new millennium permeated Alberta schools and inspired its educators.

However significant challenges remained because, to be successful vision and philosophy must be accompanied by resources, skills and knowledge. As Alberta's previously advantageous economy experienced distress, resources required for supporting both students and school personnel in achieving the vision of inclusion begun to disappear. In addition, the previous era that sought to normalize students with special learning needs had also resulted in many universities moving away from teacher education programs specific to what had previously been acknowledged as special education. Teachers were left with diminished levels of support, a growing shadow of reduced efficacy regarding their ability to meet the standards of a philosophy that they truly believed in, and a curriculum that felt shallow because alone it often did not reflect the real learning needs of their students on the spectrum. While resources and levels of support are likely to remain a challenge in the near future, Alberta issued an order in 2015 that holds great promise towards providing curricular direction and is likely to enhance the education of all learners. It holds particular importance for students on the autism spectrum.

In 2015 Alberta issued a ministerial order on learning, a foundational policy framework that will provide an overview of goals and expectations for all Alberta Students (Alberta, Ministerial Order on Student Learning, 2015). This order, intended to facilitate the development of new curriculum, focused on "the three E's – engaged thinkers and ethical citizens with entrepreneurial spirit". It laid out ten competencies that are to be viewed as an interrelated set of attitudes, skills and knowledge in the journey toward personal excellence. Personal excellence for students is specified. The ten competencies are:

1. Critical Thinking
2. Problem Solving
3. Managing Information
4. Creativity and Innovation
5. Communication
6. Collaboration
7. Cultural and Global Citizenship
8. Personal Growth and Well-Being

There are two important aspects in these competencies that are of special importance for improving education for learners on the spectrum. First, personal excellence not only allows for but requires teaching to be reflective of individual strengths and needs. This compels teachers to move beyond the outcomes specified in programs of studies, outcomes that traditionally have not been too difficult for students on the high functioning side of the spectrum to achieve. This limited educators' responsibility to teach lessons that were not specified in curriculum but were essential to personal success for these learners. Next and as previously described, many of these competencies directly relate to areas that are generally described as personal deficits for learners on the spectrum. In particular, personal growth and well-being is specified as a core competency. Despite an influx of research being conducted to help us understand autism, consideration and exploration into how people with autism understand and experience personal well-being has traditionally been underrepresented in literature.

METHODS

The Research Problem

This research sought to understand well-being in individuals with high functioning autism characteristics (HFAC), and to explore what this insight could reveal about educating Alberta learners who are on the autism spectrum. Observations in the field suggested that despite being intellectually and academically capable, a disproportionate number of students with HFAC leave our schools without the competencies required for their personal success in the world outside of school.

The Research Questions

To shed light on the problem, the following research questions were addressed:

1. What was the nature and extent of high functioning autism characteristics of participants and subjects in the research study?
2. How did participants and subjects experience and describe the effects of autism on well-being?

3. What themes emerged as important to well-being for people with HFAC, and how do these themes compare with those of people who do not have HFAC?
4. What does this study suggest as far as new directions and improvements to our capacity to meet the learning needs of students who are on the autism spectrum?

Data Collection

As illustrated in Figure 5, data was collected from methodologies representing each of the four IMP quadrants. Understanding was gathered relating to the individual interior quadrant through a series of interview questions and conversations conducted with participants through email, and in two instances over telephone. Data collected relating to the individual exterior quadrant was derived from participants completing the Psychological Well-Being Scales (PWBS) and the Autism Quotient (AQ) Questionnaire (Baron-Cohen, 2008). The collective interior perspectives were represented through a series of duo-ethnographic conversations with the parents of an adult with HFAC. A learning support teacher with extensive experience in working with learners on the spectrum wrote a narrative analysis documenting her experiences and observations regarding the topic from inside Alberta schools, representing the collective exterior quadrant.

Assumptions

Based on observations in the field, the following assumption was made in the formulation of this study:
While being aware of the unique strengths and needs of their students with characteristics of high functioning autism, teachers believe that current curriculum alone is not sufficient in meeting the educational needs of these students. In these instances, teaching is adapted to meet student needs based on teacher background knowledge, personal beliefs, learning supports and educational policy.

Figure 5. Study methodologies by quadrant

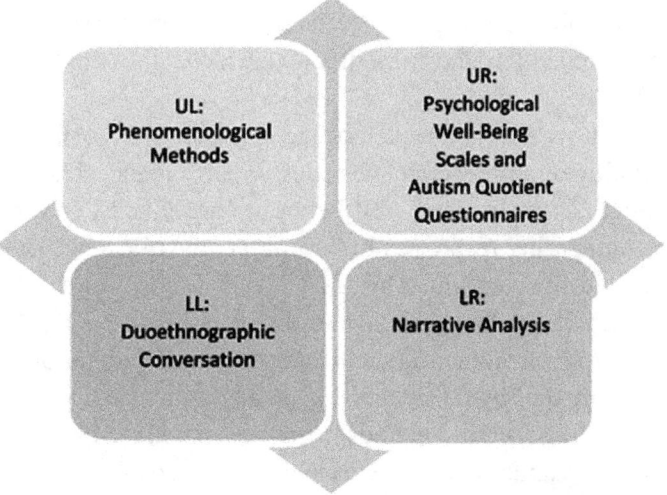

Limitations and Delimitations

Limitations

This study encountered the following limitations:

1. The nature, size and scope of this study limited the ability to make generalized assertions regarding the larger group of people with characteristics of high functioning autism.
2. The Psychological Well-Being Scales were not developed or referenced specifically for people on the autism spectrum.
3. Characteristics of high functioning autism can include challenges relating to communication and introspection, which might influence the quality of the data collected from participants.

Delimitations

Delimitations inherent in this study includes:

1. The choice to use the first element of the integral model only, which comprises the quadrants of integral methodological pluralism. IMP, derived from Integral Theory (Wilber, 2007), espouses multiple aspects to support gathering and understanding holistic understanding that include states, lines, levels and stages of development.
2. Analysis focused only on data/information that was available, even if other or additional analytical methods became available.

EXPLORING THE ISSUES

Analysis of Findings

There were four types of data collected in this study: Qualitative data from phenomenological interviews, duoethnographic conversations, and narrative inquiry. Qualitative data was gathered using measurement inventories (AQ and PWBS).

The Autism Quotient scales were used to determine participant eligibility for the study and then to define the quantity and quality of autism characteristics in participants. The Psychological Well-Being Scales were used as an initial assessment of well-being in participants, and then later to aid in the interpretation of results by comparing responses to baseline data collected from people not specifically identified as being on the autism spectrum. This data was derived from previous research using these scales in research independent from this particular study.

Understanding gathered from phenomenological interviews and duoethnographic conversations were transcribed and analyzed for themes by researcher's hand and then using NVivo software. Themes from both quantitative and qualitative research methods were then examined and responded to through a narrative analytical writing process undertaken by a teacher with extensive experience working with school staffs, administrators and students (neurotypical and autistic) in Alberta school divisions.

UR: Autism Quotient and Psychological Well-Being Scale Findings

All participants met study criteria for participation with Autism Quotient scores of 26 or above, with the mean average being 34.7. The average score in control groups was 16.4. Challenges consistent with autism characteristics relating to ability to shift attention, enhanced attention to detail, social skills, communication skills and imagination were measured in study participants.

The mean average for participant scores on the Psychological Well-Being Scales was 269.87, with a clear pattern of strengths and challenges in subjective well-being emerging. Personal growth and autonomy were identified as relative well-being assets, while reduced levels of satisfaction relating to self-acceptance and personal relationships were identified as detriments. Average scores on these scales for control groups were 404.62.

UL: Phenomenological Interview Findings

Numerous themes emerged from phenomenological interviews, revealing rich and intimate understandings regarding how participants thought about and experienced well-being. All participants described negative thoughts and experiences relating to self-acceptance, slow developing self-awareness, communication, personal relationships, and perception of self as detrimental to their well-being. However, the majority also described characteristics of autism as being an asset to their well-being. Table 1 summarizes the broad themes relating to well-being described and experienced by study participants.

LL: Duoethnographic Conversation Findings

Insight into the topic of well-being and high functioning autism was also enhanced by collecting data from the parents of a young adult with HFAC about their own observations and understanding of their son's well-being. Understanding was gathered initially via each parent completing a Psychological Well-Being Scale on behalf of their son from their own perspectives, as well as one for themselves. This information was additionally used to facilitate a series of conversations between the parents regarding the topic of well-being in their son. Both parents assessment of their son's well-being using the scales was consistent with findings from individual participants' self-assessments, with the mother scoring the son at 282, and the father scoring the son at 261. In addition to data from these scales, conversation between the parents identified themes on the topic. These included personal relationships, empathy, belonging, communication, repetition and routine, autism challenges and limitations, and life purpose/ meaning. There was evidence that parent assessment of their son's well-being was strongly influenced by each of their own individual perceptions and experiences of well-being.

LR: Narrative Analysis Findings

Of the initial themes identified through the UL, UR and LL quadrants of methodology from which they were gathered (UL: Phenomenology, UR: Qualitative Scales, LL: Duoethnography, LR: Narrative Analysis), 23 common themes were assigned to the quadrant they most closely inhabited. Within each quadrant of methodology, another IMP quadrant was superimposed, with data themes being matched to the quadrant most closely inhabited. In doing so, primary themes were identified. To be included as

Table 1. Participants making reference to themes in interviews (n=14)

	% of Participants Making Reference to Theme
Self-acceptance	100 (generally negative perceptions)
Communication	100 (generally negative perceptions)
Relationships	100 (generally negative perceptions)
Perceptions of Me	100 (generally negative perceptions)
Self-Awareness	93 (mixed positive/negative perceptions)
Autism Assets	93 (generally positive perceptions)
Prev. Shaping Exp	86 (generally negative perceptions)
Goals/Purpose	86 (generally positive perceptions)
Mental Health	86 (generally negative perceptions)
Advocacy	86 (generally positive perceptions)
Parental/Family	79 (mixed positive/negative perceptions)
EducationalSystem	79 (generally negative perceptions)
Social Expect.	79 (generally negative perceptions)
Work	79 (mixed positive/negative perceptions)
Physiological	71 (generally negative perceptions)
Bullying/Abuse	71 (generally negative perceptions)
Diagnosis	71 (generally negative perceptions)
Passion/Interests	64 (generally positive perceptions)
Significant Other	64 (generally negative perceptions)
Sensory	50 (generally negative perceptions)
Social System	43 (generally negative perceptions)
Resilience	36 (generally negative perceptions)
Mimic/Mask	36 (mixed positive/negative perceptions)

primary, the theme either needed to be identified in three research methodologies (phenomenology, rating scales and duoethnographic conversation), *or* inhabit each of the four quadrants in the methodology from which they were derived. A dozen themes emerged as primary. Of these primary themes, five were identified as integral themes because they were uncovered by each of the methodologies *and* they could be comfortably situated in each of the four IMP quadrants. These integral themes were: growth/ learning, balance/environmental mastery, awareness, communication, and relationships/belonging. Integral themes were further explored through narrative analysis from the perspective of a professional working in the educational system, representing the LR quadrant. These analyses lead to a series of recommendations towards improving the quality of education for learners with high functioning autism in Alberta schools. Three categories of recommendations emerged from narrative analysis specific to the collective exterior quadrant: recommendations for parents, professionals and school communities, system based recommendations, and recommendations for future research.

Discussion of Themes

UR Themes

Autism Quotient Scales

The Autism Quotient Scales were developed to assess domains of cognitive strengths and difficulties relating to high functioning autism (Baron-Cohen, Wheelwright, Skinner, Martin, & Clubley, 2001). Five categories of the autism phenotype are measured using these scales: communication, social skills, imagination, attention to detail and attention shifting. Each participant self-evaluated their own autism characteristics as being significant. As a group, participants in the study identified their most significant challenge relating to autism as being their ability to shift their attention. They identified imagination as being their least impaired trait of the five domains. Elevated scores on the AQ correlated with lower overall scores on the well-being scales. There was no specific connection between specific strengths or deficits in individual domains from the scales and specific perceived strengths or challenges in each of the correlates measured for well-being. Beyond scores of 26, higher AQ scores did not seem connected with lower well-being scores.

Psychological Scales of Well-Being

When compared with control groups from previous studies, results from these scales were not only significantly lower, but showed a more drastic discrepancy between strengths and weaknesses. A surprising pattern was evident in participants' self-assessment of personal well-being. Relative strengths emerged relating to continued personal growth and development and a sense of autonomy in thought and action. Significant challenges to personal well-being of participants were evident in areas relating to self-acceptance, establishment of quality ties with others, and the ability to manage complex environments to suit personal needs and values.

Autonomy as a strength is not surprising considering the characteristic profile of people on the spectrum. Continued growth and development as a strength to well-being was a surprise. This is an asset worth investigating as a potential strength of autism to be capitalized on.

Likewise, challenges relating to dissatisfaction with personal relationships are not new to study in the field of autism. However, it may be important that participants rated challenges connected with self-acceptance as even more significant to their overall well-being than relationships. Participants' assessment of their ability to manage complex environments to suit their personal needs and values was also disproportionally low, being rated as almost as significant of a challenge to their personal well-being as developing close relationships was.

UL Themes

A total of 23 themes significant to well-being in adults with high functioning autism characteristics were identified. Each theme warrants intensive study and analysis, but for the scope of this study, were narrowed down. Twelve primary themes were defined for further discussion.

Advocacy

Advocacy referred to the process of participants informing people about autism in order to influence how individuals and groups understand and interact with people on the spectrum. Most participants believed that advocacy was important because it benefited their personal relationships. It was also identified as important because it improved their ability to be happy and productive in work and school environments.

Autonomy

Participants described autonomy as their ability to self-direct and self-govern. It seemed to entail being aware of one's own person, thoughts and values, and maintaining a loyalty to these when part of a bigger group. It was the second most common well-being strength identified by the well-being scales. This study suggested that participants' strengths in autonomy often came at the expense of their ability to connect with the world around them, an outcome that had implications on every aspect of their well-being.

Assets of Autism

Assets directly connected to characteristics participants associated with autism were: ability to attend to detail, logic and analytic skill, academic skills, work ethic, creativity and innovation, and acceptance of others. Many participants described the value of being able to use these strengths to navigate around perceived weaknesses. Participants emphasized the importance of learning how to situate themselves into environments and contexts that cast their autism traits in a positive light, as opposed to environments where their characteristics limit their opportunities and well-being.

Bullying and Abuse

A majority of participants described incidents of bullying or abuse that continued to affect their personal well-being long after the events ended. Trauma ranged from feeling unacknowledged, undervalued, and suffering from a lack of nurturing to full out physical assault. Each participant who initiated discussion concerning this theme described their experiences as having such negative effects on their sense of self-worth that it continues to hinder their ability to accept themselves. It was often described as either causing or contributing to an overwhelming sense of depression and anxiety.

Diagnosis

Of the 16 participants who participated in this study, half had received a formal diagnosis of autism. Diagnosis was a contentious issue among participants, with an approximate equal distribution between people thinking it was a positive thing and people thinking it was not. People supporting the process expressed that they were grateful because the diagnosis helped them to understand and accept themselves. It provided an explanation for the challenges they faced and described this new understanding as being useful for navigating around personal challenges. This group tended towards describing a liberating feeling from diagnosis. In contrast, participants who did not support the diagnosis process had a very negative construct regarding the topic. They tended to view diagnosis as a limitation, one that impaired their ability to accept themselves. It was often described in terms of being associated with a sense of hopelessness and failure. All participants who received a formal diagnosis, along with participants who initiated the process but were unable to see it through to completion, described a very frustrating and negative experience regarding working with the medical and educational systems that were required for diagnosis.

Growth and Learning

Participants spoke of this topic with an overwhelming sense of positivity and optimism. There was some disagreement regarding the value of the formal education system and teacher practices, and some described traditional teaching environments and strategies as being ineffective for them. Additionally, many participants described school as the first setting in which they experienced the bullying and abuse that was so detrimental to their well-being.

In spite of their differing experiences within the educational system, the majority of participants identified the development of their ability to "self-teach" as being instrumental to their success and well-being. Many participants did not come to view their learning as a personal strength until their adult years. It was typically described as something slow to develop, but that picked up steam over time. This particular asset is one that many participants believed continues to enrich their lives, helps them to overcome obstacles, and offers them hope for the future.

Relationships and Belonging

Early relationships with parents and family seemed to have a profound effect on participants' ability to develop subsequent relationships later in life. Participants who described positive relationships with their families presented a greater inclination towards valuing relationships and described putting more effort into developing supporting skills for and cultivating relationships. Participants who described poor early connections and experiences with family tended towards being pessimistic about the nature of people and the value of relationships. They presented as being more inclined to withdraw socially and holding other people responsible for their own feelings of unfulfilled interpersonal needs.

Most participants indicated a desire to engage in close relationships, specifically to find a significant other. All described their autism characteristics as hindering their ability to develop relationships. There also seemed to be a pattern of difficulty in moving past poor relationship experiences, with more of a general reluctance to move forward and form new relationships than might be expected in people who do not have autism characteristics.

A preference, or need, for time alone also seemed to impair the ability to pursue relationships for many participants. Participants frequently expressed that the demands of developing and maintaining close relationships were both exhausting and anxiety provoking, indicating that despite the desire for personal relationships with others, they found it easier not to have the relationship. While this information was uncovered through the interview process, it was not reflected through scale and questionnaire results. There was no visible connection between participants in elevated scores relating to social skills or communication challenges on the autism quotient and relatively lower scores relating to meaningful relationships on the well-being scales.

Balance and Environmental Mastery

Challenges relating to life balance and environmental mastery can be traced to the autism characteristic of restricted ability to shift attention and strengths relating to seeing detail (sometimes at the expense of seeing the bigger picture). These characteristics were described as sometimes impairing their ability to function productively and comfortably within the environment they were in. Many participants described their ability to excel at a single task or topic of focus as being an asset, but that this asset was easily compromised by challenges with sharing attention and focus with other tasks or domains that were also important for well-being.

Autism is characterized by repetitive and restrictive patterns of thought and behavior. Routine and repetition appeared important for the well-being and success of many participants, but it seemed that there was a tendency for participants to become trapped within the routine. What could be a strategy for regulation sometimes became a habit that challenged participants' sense of well-being.

Mental Health

Many participants vividly described situations of crippling depression and anxiety, along with an overwhelming sense of loneliness. One third of participants reported that they had seriously entertained suicidal thoughts. Mental health challenges were seen as being exasperated by participant difficulties with navigating a system that was often described as requiring the very skills they were deficient of and that were creating crisis' within their lives. Mental health issue described by some participants were initiated or compounded by a sense of personal isolation, poor self-acceptance, social anxiety, limited mental flexibility and a tendency to become easily overwhelmed.

Communication

All participants described a preference for clear, concrete and literal styles of communication. This is the way most participants expressed themselves throughout interviews and conversations, and it was clear that their receptive language skills were based on the same style of communication. Non-verbal, abstract and figurative language was often equated with ambiguity that reduced the effectiveness of communication between participants and people around them. Some participants described communication challenges as creating disconnect between them and the world around them. This disconnect seemed to influence higher levels of personal autonomy, but at the expense of quality relationships. It is also possible that the lack of confidence participants felt regarding their communication skills also contributed to a sense of anxiety.

Awareness of Self and Others

This theme seemed closely connected with the themes of growth and learning, advocacy and acceptance. The majority of participants described this topic with a sense of optimism. These participants tended to describe awareness as their first step on the path for improving their lives. It was perceived as a tool to help them harness their own strengths and to improve their weaknesses.

Most participants did not describe a slow and gradual path to awareness. Rather, for most, awareness occurred rapidly at some point in their young adult years. Participants described their younger selves as overcome by the challenges and frustrations associated with their autism characteristics, unable to see beyond the details of their personal sense of dissatisfaction. Experience and increasing levels awareness that came from age and experience were often described as the impetus for improving their self-acceptance, which was among the most significant challenges to the well-being of the study participants.

An Integral Analysis of Wellbeing in Adults With Characteristics of High Functioning Autism

Self-Acceptance

In contrast with self-awareness, self-acceptance was not described in positive or optimistic light. There seemed little grey area around this theme. Participants described the phenomena as something that they had either achieved or not achieved – and the majority claimed that they had not. Curiously, while awareness was seen as a first step on a path towards improving well-being, self-acceptance was seldom described as an on-going process. Participant self-assessment of personal awareness did not translate to a greater sense of self-acceptance. This study suggested that a poor sense of self-acceptance remained as among the most significant challenges to the well-being of individuals on the spectrum.

LL Themes

The parents of an adult son with characteristics of high functioning autism individually contributed third person perspectives of their son's well-being by completing the Psychological Well-Being Scales on his behalf, and then participated in a series of conversations about his well-being. Results from the scales showed similar assessments between parents of their son's relative well-being strengths and weaknesses, although the mother's score for the son's overall well-being was somewhat higher than the father's. Their responses presented a profile clearly matched by the well-being profiles of study participants who completed the same scales from first person perspectives, with the notable exception of them both evaluating their son as having far greater relative satisfaction relating to his level of self-acceptance than other participants did.

Conversations between parents were rich and consisted of varying perspective between the two. Themes that emerged as significant challenges to their son's well-being, indicated by the frequency addressed in conversation, were: relationships, empathy, belonging, repetition and routine, and autism challenges and limitations. Themes that emerged as assets to their son's well-being were: continuous growth and learning, intelligence and academics, goal-setting, and life purpose and meaning.

While there were many issues that both parents agreed upon regarding their son's well-being, there were also differences in their perspectives. The father tended to focus more on his son's challenges with personal relationships, limited interests and hobbies, and level of overall happiness. The mother put more emphasis on the role of her son's personal strengths and autism assets, with concerns about his challenges relating to balance, awareness and mental health. While both parents expressed concern for their son's well-being, the mother tended to take a more optimistic and proactive perspective. The father was less positive about the state of his son's well-being, and was less confident in how to support his progress in the future.

These differences clearly reflected the ways each parent perceived and experienced their own personal well-being, which was measured by their first-person responses to the well-being scales. While the father emphasized the value of personal relationships for his own well-being, the mother put more value in areas relating to growth, achievement and personal purpose than on relationships. Autism creates significant challenges to domains of well-being that the father values as being very important to his own well-being. Conversely, characteristics of high functioning autism can potentially contribute to success in areas that the mother valued more. Individual values and perceptions regarding well-being profoundly influenced how the parents interpreted and supported the development of well-being in their son, and had implications for how they parented their son as individuals and as a couple.

CONCLUSION AND IMPLICATIONS

Implications

The inclusive nature of this integral study resulted in a breadth of understanding with implications for further in-depth study. For the scope of this study, the five integral themes of growth and learning, balance and environmental mastery, awareness, communication, and relationships and belonging were explored from the lower right quadrant perspective of educational institutions and high functioning autism. From this narrative analysis, recommendations for educational practice and future research emerged.

LR Themes: Recommendations for Practice

Recommendations for Parents, Professionals and School Communities

1. Recognize that positive relationships between teachers and students with autism will be critical for the student's growth and well-being, now and into the future.
2. Understand the importance of perspective and context in defining whether autism characteristics will be reflected as strengths or challenges.
3. Teach strategies to improve metacognition in students with autism.
4. Strive to understand that inflexible, self-centered patterns of behavior on the part of students with autism are likely the result of combined impairment in the student's awareness of self and others as well as difficulty in shifting attention. Focusing on developing awareness is likely to be more beneficial than emphasizing the elimination of undesirable behavior itself.
5. From a young age, teach children to distinguish between supporting details and important ideas to help them achieve balance and meet the demands of daily living.
6. Draw attention to the importance of life balance; teach strategies for promoting balance relating to awareness, attention and techniques for managing multiple obligations and expectations in their environments.
7. Recognize the likelihood that communication challenges in students with autism are more significant than they appear.
8. Recognize that the unsocial behavior of students with HFAC, who may appear fully capable of developing relationships, does not necessarily reflect a lack of desire or need for close personal relationships.
9. Provide a safe and structured environment in which young people can pursue their interests alongside peers in a social academic environment, limiting the requirement for students with autism to socialize only during breaks in busy, unstructured environments.

System Based Recommendations

1. That information regarding teaching skills for working in groups, critical thinking, and combining and transferring existing knowledge and skills towards innovation and problem-solving be organized and systematically presented to teachers such that this knowledge can supplement existing curriculum instead of becoming new curriculum.

2. Speech Language Pathologist (SLP) support to be made available for students with autism as early as possible and should extend to include the duration of the student's school years if beneficial.
3. Schools be funded to be proactive in providing supports for teaching skills and assisting in the development of relationships for students with autism.

Recommendations for Future Research

1. Work is done towards identifying the foundational skills that are essential to a student's ability to work in groups, think critically, and to combine and transfer knowledge and skills towards innovation and problem-solving.
2. To explore how education focusing on improving self-awareness and awareness of others in young people with autism influences self-acceptance later in life.
3. To explore possible connections between an improved awareness of self and others and satisfaction in personal relationships for people with autism.
4. Future research focus expands beyond the skills and conditions required for developing relationships in individuals with autism, to the challenges inherent in utilizing these skills.

CONCLUSION

This study contributed knowledge and understanding relating to how well-being is perceived and experienced in adults with characteristics of high functioning autism. This understanding was accompanied with recommendations for improving education towards meeting the unique needs of this growing group of learners in Alberta schools.

Specifically, this study suggests that schools in Alberta are not focused on identifying or teaching the skills and attributes identified as most important to the well-being of HFAC learners. The contribution that schools do make to learning and development relating to the well- being needs of these learners is indirect and supplementary to current curriculum and practices. While schools in Alberta are meeting the needs of students with HFAC in terms of teaching academic skills and specific outcomes from programs of study, this study suggests that formal attention needs to be focused on ensuring that these learners have the opportunity to develop to their full potential.

Educational content that should be pertinent to learning, growth and development for these learners is notably absent on an official level. Strategies and practices to support the specific learning needs of students with characteristics of high functioning autism tend to be sporadic and uncoordinated, dependent on the knowledge and advocacy of parents and/or individual professionals.

It is recommended that the school system formally recognize and respect learning that enhances the ability of these individuals to develop awareness of self and others, self-acceptance, the ability to manage and balance multiple demands, communication skills and strategies, and skills for developing relationships.

In today's world the population affected by the characteristics of high functioning autism has grown greatly in number, and our knowledge regarding the condition is expanding almost to match the pace of our increasing diagnoses. A clear assessment of autism characteristics as having both strengths and challenges was expressed eloquently by Hans Asperger in 1944:

The good and bad in a person, their potential for success or failure, their aptitudes and deficits – they are mutually conditional, arising from the same source. Our therapeutic goal must be to teach the person how to bear their difficulties. Not to eliminate them for him, but to train the person to cope with special challenges with special strategies; to make the person aware not that they are ill, but that they are responsible for their lives. (Asperger, 1944)

Asperger was part of a clinical world that studied the earliest documented cases and occurrences of high functioning autism. The condition was initially recognized and interpreted through the lens of a medical model that focused on physical conditions and mental illness, with an emphasis on therapeutic intervention.

While the condition still maintains a close connection with medical and health sciences, its prevalence should earn it more recognition in education. Education holds promise and potential, for both individuals and society, to identify and promote growing levels of awareness, knowledge, and acceptance. High functioning autism deserves the attention of Alberta Education and its efforts in helping individuals and groups recognize and achieve the ability connected with the disability.

REFERENCES

Alberta Education. (1982). *Educable mentally handicapped: Curriculum guide.* Author.

Alberta Government. (2015). Ministerial Order on Student Learning. An Order to Adopt or Approve Goals and Standards Applicable to the Provision of Education in Alberta. Edmonton, Canada: Author.

Asperger, H. (1944). Die autistischen psychopathen im kindersalter [Autistic Psychopaths in Childhood]. *Archiv für Psychiatrie und Nervenkrankheiten, 117*(1), 76–136. doi:10.1007/BF01837709

Baron-Cohen, Wheelwright, Skinner, Martin, & Clubley. (2001). The autism spectrum quotient (AQ): Evidence from Asperger Syndrome/high functioning autism, males and females, scientists and mathematicians. *Journal of Autism and Developmental Disorders*, 5–17. PMID:11439754

Baron-Cohen, S. (2008). *Autism and Asperger syndrome.* New York: Oxford University Press.

Bloomberg & Volpe. (2012). *Completing your qualitative dissertation* (2nd ed.). Thousand Oaks, CA: Sage Publications.

Bogels, Hoogstad, & Dun, Schutter, & Restifo. (2008). Mindfulness training for adolescents with externalizing disorders and their parents. *Behavioural and Cognitive Psychotherapy*, 193–201.

Cheng, R., & Gu, S. (2015). Autism: Reduced connectivity between cortical areas involved in face expression, theory of mind, and sense of self. *Brain, 138*(5), 1382–1393. doi:10.1093/brain/awv051 PMID:25795704

Clarke, Dudley, Dutton, Emery, & Ghali. (2014). *Laying th foundation for policy: Measuring local prevalence for autism spectrum disorder.* Calgary: The School of Public Policy, University of Calgary.

Dugas, M. J., Gosselin, P., & Ladouceur, R. (2001). Intolerance of Uncertainty and Worry: Investigating Specificity in a Nonclinical Sample. *Cognitive Therapy and Research*, *25*(5), 551–558. doi:10.1023/A:1005553414688

Durayappah, A. (2010). The 3P Model: A General Theory of Subjective Well-Being. *Journal of Happiness Studies*. doi:10.100710902-010-9223-9

Eaves & Ho. (2008). Young adult outcomes of autism disorders. *Journal of Autism and Developmental Disorders*, 739–747.

Esbjorn-Hargens, S. (2010). An ontology of climate change: Integral pluralism and the enactment of multiple objects. *Journal of Integral Theory and Practice*, 143-174.

Frith, M., Morton, J., & Leslie, A. M. (1991). The cognitive basis of a biological disorder: Autism. *Trends in Neurosciences*, *14*(10), 433–438. doi:10.1016/0166-2236(91)90041-R PMID:1722361

Ghali, Dudley, Dutton, Zwicker, McMorris, Emery, & Clarke. (2014). *Laying the foundation for policy: Measuring local prevalence for autism spectrum disorder*. Calgary: University of Calgary School of Public Policy.

Grupe, D. W., & Nitschke, J. B. (2013). Uncertainty and Anticipation in Anxiety: An integrated Neurobiological and Psychological Perspective. *Nature Reviews. Neuroscience*, *14*(7), 488–501. doi:10.1038/nrn3524 PMID:23783199

Hobson. (2010). Explaining Autism: Ten reasons to focus on the developing self. *Autism*, 391-407.

Hofvander, D., & Chaste, N., & Stahlberg. (2009, June 10). *Psychiatric and psychosocial problems in adults with normal intelligence autism spectrum disorders*. Retrieved from Pubmed: http://www,ncbi.nlm.nih.gov/pubmed/19515234

Jahnukainen. (2011). Different strategies, different outcomes? The history and trends of inclusive and special education in Alberta (Canada) and Finland. *Scandinavian Journal of Educational Research*, 489-502.

Martin, D. (2013). *The ever-changing social perception of autism spectrum disorders in the United States*. Academic Press.

Mazurek. (2013). Lonliness, friendship, and well-being in adults with autism spectrum disorders. *Autism*, 223-32.

Murgatroyd, S. (2013). *Rethinking equity and creating a great school for all*. Edmonton: Collaborative Media Group Inc.

Pellicano, E. (2011). Cogniton, development and education: Psychological models of autism. In *Researching the Autism Spectrum*. Cambridge, UK: Cambridge University Press.

America Proclamation. (1990). *Decade of the Brain*. Proclamation No. 6158.

Ryan & Deci. (2001). On happiness and human potentials: A review of research on hedonic and eudaimonic well-being. *Annual Review of Psychology*, 144-66.

Ryff, C. (1989). Happiness is everything, or is it? Explorations on the meaning of psychological well-being. *Journal of Personality and Social Psychology*, *57*(6), 1069–1081. doi:10.1037/0022-3514.57.6.1069

Travis & Sigman. (1998). Social deficits and interpersonal relationships in autism. *Mental Retardation and Developmental Disabilities*, 65-72.

Van Heijst & Geurts. (2014). Quality of life in autism across the lifespan: A meta-analysis. *Autism*, *19*(2), 1–37. PMID:24443331

Wilber, K. (2007). *A Brief History of Everything*. Shambhala.

Zalla, Miele, Leboyer, & Metcalfe. (2015). Metacognition of agency and theory of mind in adults with high functioning autism. *Journal of Autism and Developmental Disorders*, 126–138. PMID:25482271

KEY TERMS AND DEFINITIONS

All Quadrant All Lines (AQAL) Framework: A tool to assist with interpretation and understanding of knowledge and phenomena through the lens of integral theory. Specific aspects of the framework include quadrants, levels, stages, waves, states, lines, and types.

Autism Quotient (AQ) Scales: A questionnaire tool developed to measure the degree to which an adult with normal intelligence has autism. Categories of traits measured involve communication, social skills, imagination, attention switching, tolerance of change and attention to detail.

High Functioning Autism Characteristics (HFAC): High functioning autism is a neurodevelopmental disorder marked by social impairment, communication difficulties, and restricted, repetitive and stereotyped patterns of behavior in individuals with average to above average IQs. Prior to the implementation of the newest *Diagnostic and Statistical Manual of Mental Disorders* (DSM-5), it was synonymous with Asperger's Syndrome. HFAC refers to the qualities and traits most commonly connected with high functioning autism. The starting point for HFAC in this research was based on the categories identified in the UR AQ scales, and then were further developed and described using methodology representing each of the other quadrants.

Integral Methodological Pluralism (IMP): A construct for applying integral theory to research and analysis.

Integral Theory: A metatheory that provides a framework towards integrating human knowledge and understanding beyond traditionally compartmented topics, disciplines, and geography. In this chapter, references to integral theory are based on the work and conceptualizations of Ken Wilber.

Lower Left (LL) Quadrant: Focuses on dimensions of phenomena relating to the interior collective. Duoethnography was chosen as methodology for this quadrant, with themes from data connecting with participant relationships, community, and personal interactions with others.

Lower Right (LR) Quadrant: The LR quadrant examined elements of the research connected with the exterior collective. The representing methodology, espoused in understanding connected to well-being and social systems, focused on a narrative analysis exploring the issue of wellbeing and high functioning autism in Alberta schools, healthcare, and social support systems.

Psychological Wellbeing Scales (PWBS): An instrument developed for the purpose of obtaining a measurement of theoretically-derived constructs of psychological wellbeing. Domains measured include autonomy, self-acceptance, environmental mastery, personal growth, positive relationships with others, and purpose in life.

Quadrant Framework: The quadrant model included as part of the AQAL framework, which was used as the primary tool in guiding the literature review, developing the research methodology and assisting in data analysis for this research.

Upper Left (UL) Quadrant: Represents the interior individual dimensions of the quadrant. Phenomenology was used as the research methodology relating to this quadrant. Themes connected with this quadrant focused on the thoughts, beliefs, and values of individual participants.

Upper Right (UR) Quadrant: This quadrant examines perspectives representing the exterior individual perspective. It is based in quantitative understandings of the phenomena. UR understanding was collected using referenced questionnaires and scales. Participant themes connected with the UR quadrant included physical aspects of the experience of wellbeing and autism.

Wellbeing: The individual and subjective phenomena and lived experiences that people connect with value and happiness in life. Wellbeing is a complex construct that is composed in varying degrees of both hedonistic and eudemonic experiences. Research specific to the wellbeing of people with autism, from a first-person perspective, was underrepresented in the literature review.

Chapter 14
The Development of Creativity:
Integral Analysis of Creative Adolescents and Young Adults – Abstract, Introduction, Background, Theoretical Perspectives

Krystyna Czeslawa Laycraft
University of Calgary, Canada

ABSTRACT

The purpose of this chapter was to investigate creativity in adolescents and young adults and its role in psychological development. For this qualitative research, hermeneutic phenomenology/ontology linked with the narrative/biography methodology was chosen. To interpret the data, the pattern models of creativity were generated, by applying the concepts of complexity science, especially self-organization, with the theory of positive disintegration and the psycho-evolutionary theory of emotions. It was discovered that the process of creativity in young people is intertwined with the strong emotions of passion, curiosity, enthusiasm, and delight. These emotions are the driving forces that generate order and complexity not only in the creative process but also in overall psychological development. The presence of these strong emotions often contributes to lesser tension in young people's development, including a greater ability to integrate their experiences, to take their psychological development into their own hands, and to find direction for their future.

INTRODUCTION

In order to locate the research topic in the overall context of existing literature and research, I review the main theories concerning the process of creativity and its relation to human development. They are Merleau-Ponty's phenomenology of perception, Piaget's theory of knowledge development, Heidegger and Gadamer's hermeneutic phenomenology, Dilthey's theory of understanding human life, Dąbrowski's theory of positive disintegration, Vygotsky's theory of social development, and the neurophenomenology of Varela. In searching for explanatory frameworks, I focus on the main concepts of chaos theory and self-organization and how they can be applied to emotional processes.

The review of the literature demonstrates the complexity of creativity and its role in human development. Wilber's Integral Theory provides an excellent conceptual framework for the journey through the different areas of study.

DOI: 10.4018/978-1-5225-5873-6.ch014

The Development of Creativity

The main purpose of the study is to investigate the role of creativity during the periods of adolescence and young adulthood, especially as it relates to psychological development. The research investigates whether adolescents spontaneously use the process of creativity to gain the capacity to differentiate and integrate their own inner experiences in order to achieve internal dynamic order and find direction for their future.

Creativity is an expression of our unique perspective toward situations or problems. Abraham Maslow refers to a self-actualizing (SA) type of creativeness that stresses highly valuable traits like boldness, courage, freedom, spontaneity, integration, and self-acceptance (Maslow, 1968, p. 145). This description aligns with Rogers' idea that people become creative by going within themselves and developing trust in their own thoughts and feelings. The resulting authenticity allows individuals to live by their truest values and to express themselves in their own unique ways. With this sensitive openness to their world, they are able to form new relationships with their environment and become the individuals from whom creative products and creative living emerge (Rogers, 1961/1989, p. 193). This is why we need more creativity! By introducing creative programs to our schools in a deliberate and coherent manner, we could help young people develop their ability to question, to make connections, to express their thoughts and feelings, to innovate, and to reflect critically.

Research on creativity is, by necessity, in-depth, personal, and small-scale; therefore, a number of similar studies carried out across Canada would be needed in order to assess the value of including more creativity in the education of young people. It is reasonable to anticipate that the significance of creativity would be demonstrated as a result of these studies.

BACKGROUND

Wilber's Integral Theory (2008) serves as a map of the literature on creativity and its role in human development. According to Integral Theory, there are four major perspectives that must be studied when we are challenging ourselves to fully comprehend any phenomena of reality: the subjective (intentional), intersubjective (cultural), objective (behavioral), and interobjective (social).

The Upper-Left Quadrant: Subjective

In the upper-left quadrant, Merleau-Ponty's Phenomenology of Perception, Dąbrowski's Theory of Positive Disintegration, and Piaget's Theory of Knowledge Development are placed. This quadrant represents the intentional first-person perspective. Phenomenology is the study of the structure of human consciousness as experienced from the first-person point of view, and concerns perception, thought, memory, imagination, emotion, and desire, will, embodied action, and social activity.

The French philosopher Maurice Merleau-Ponty (1908-1961) was the first phenomenologist to identify the body itself as the conscious subject of experience responding to the world by its faculty of sense. Central to Merleau-Ponty's philosophy is his emphasis on the foundational role of perception (Merleau-Ponty, 2004a, 2004b). He claims that sense-perception is fundamental to being in the world and is essential to the creative and aesthetic activities of human beings. The artist's body is "not a chunk of space or a bundle of function but that body which is an intertwining of vision and movement" (Merleau-Ponty, 2004b, p. 294). Vision and movement are essential to both life and art.

Next, I introduce Dąbrowski's theory of positive disintegration, which describes patterns and explains mechanisms of human development, placing great emphasis on emotional development. Kazimierz

Dąbrowski (1902-1980), like the humanistic psychologists Carl Rogers and Abraham Maslow, believes that every human being has the potential for personality development. But Dąbrowski proposes a different kind of development: development through discontinuous psychical levels. This process is not harmonious, peaceful and painless; it requires the experience of sadness, depression, anxiety, and various internal and external conflicts. However, the process still allows for the experience of enthusiasm, delight, and ecstasy (Dąbrowski, 1972, 1996; Dąbrowski et al., 1970).

In this same quadrant, I've placed Piaget's theory of knowledge development. Jean Piaget (1896-1980), a pioneer of constructivist thought, views the development of human knowledge as a continuous struggle. For him, the human being is a complex system trying to adapt to a complex environment. He postulates the existence of two functional invariants: *organization* and *adaptation*. Organization refers to the tendency to catalog various experiences by integrating parts into wholes and wholes into more comprehensive wholes. This is true of perception, memory, language competence, and creativity. As we organize we also adapt—that is, we tend to adjust our physical and intellectual world in increasingly more flexible ways (Piaget, 1962).

The Lower-Left Quadrant: Intersubjective

In the lower-left quadrant, representing the second-person cultural perspective, I've placed the ideas of the German philosopher Wilhelm Dilthey (1833-1911), who emphasized the importance of situating the human subject in historical and cultural contexts. In his book *Philosophy of Life*, Dilthey proposed that human studies have to be based on the relationship between *experience, expression,* and *understanding* (Dilthey, 1976, p. 177). Through experiences and understanding, individuals are able to comprehend a complex whole of life, which contains not only their lived experiences but also the experiences of the society and history of which they are apart. Dilthey's work provided a general foundation for developmental psychology. During the course of his development, the subject is able to evaluate his interests, perceptions, and ideas and to judge the value of various life options. One of the characteristics of development is the creation of new values that had not yet existed, called creative processes (Dilthey, 2010).

On the border of the subjective and intersubjective quadrants, the hermeneutic phenomenology of Heidegger and Gadamer is placed. Martin Heidegger (1889-1976), a German philosopher, synthesizes phenomenology with hermeneutics. Heidegger's main focus is on the structure of Being and for him, the task of hermeneutics is to understand the mystery of Being. Influenced by Dilthey, Heidegger argues that Being is not separate from the world, but is a formation of historically lived experience, which includes cultural and social contexts. To understand Being, the interpreter has to participate in the structure of being, immersing herself in the cycle of meaning and interpretation in order to increase her depth of understanding. In his article, *The Origin of the Work of Art,* Heidegger treats poetry and art as expressive works for interpreting the nature of truth, language, thinking, and Being. He claims that to understand the origin of the artwork we must consider not only the work itself but also the process of creation, i.e., the activity of the artist (Heidegger, 2008).

In his influential work *Truth and Method*, Hans-Georg Gadamer (1900-2002) extends Heidegger's work into practical application by exploring the role of language, the nature of questioning, the phenomenology of human conversation, and the understanding of the visual and literary arts. He claims that our relationships with artworks are deep and promote self-understanding, and that self-understanding always occurs through understanding something other than oneself, such as the unity and integrity of the other (Gadamer, 1975/1989, p. 83).

The Integration of Four Perspectives: Intentional, Cultural, Behavioral, and Social

The work of Russian psychologist Lev Vygotsky (1896-1934) combines all four perspectives: the individual, cultural, behavioral, and social. Through his work, Vygotsky tried to answer the question of how humans, in their short life trajectory, have advanced so far beyond their initial biological endowment and in such diverse directions (Vygotsky, 1981). He saw that, in order to arrive at an adequate answer, it would be necessary to look at not only individuals but also the social and material environment with which they interacted in the course of their development. The development of the human being could not be seen as an isolated trajectory, but in relation to historical change on a variety of levels: on the individual level, the institutional level (which concerns family, school, workplaces, etc.), and on the wider cultural level in which institutions are embedded.

The Integration of Three Perspectives: Intentional, Behavioral, and Dynamical System Theory

Another Integral and interdisciplinary approach to the study of human consciousness is neurophenomenology (Varela, Thompson & Rosh, 1993; Varela, 1992), which combines three different fields: (i) first-person data from the careful examination of experience with specific first-person methods; (ii) formal model and analytical tools from the dynamical system theory, grounded in an embodied-enactive approach to cognition; and (iii) neurophysiological data from the measurement of large-scale, integrative processes of the brain.

The Lower-Right Quadrant: Interobjective

To continue the review of the literature, I introduce a section on complexity science with particular emphasis on the concepts of chaos theory (Lorenz, 1993; Li & Yorke, 1975; May, 1976). These concepts include sensitivity to initial conditions, positive and negative feedback, bifurcation points and attractors, and self-organization (Haken, 1987; Prigogine, 1980; Prigogine & Stengers, 1984; Prigogine, 1997).

Self-organization is not a single theory or a conceptual model; it is rather an idea that explains the process of the spontaneous emergence of new patterns, changes, and novelties in a variety of systems, whether physical, chemical, or biological. Recently, principles of self-organizing dynamic systems have been introduced to developmental psychology, especially to emotional development and brain development (Izard et al., 2000; Lewis, 1997, 2000a, 2000b, 2005a, 20005b; Thelen & Smith, 1994).

THEORETICAL PERSPECTIVES

Only after experiencing many stages of understanding and interpretation was I able to grasp the emerging patterns of psychological development and creativity of young people. Therefore, I proposed that the process of adolescent development could be modeled by the theory of positive disintegration (TPD) combined with the idea of self-organization and the psycho-evolutionary theory of emotions (Laycraft, 2009, 2011, 2012).

The Theory of Positive Disintegration

Positive disintegration is a fundamental process in an individual's development stimulated by tension, inner conflict, and anxiety. Development involves a disorganization of mental structure, which then supports the formation of more complex, more organized, more adaptive, and more creative organization (Dąbrowski, 1972, 1996, 2015). The lower level of functioning must break down ("disintegrate") before it can be replaced by a new organization of a higher level. This is a self-organizing process that deals with the increasing complexity of the mental structure as it differentiates and incorporates more and more from all basic mental life—especially emotions, thoughts, imagination, and memories—and then integrates these elements by constructing connections between these elements (Dąbrowski et al., 1970).

The theory of positive disintegration is especially useful for understanding the tumultuous psychological development of gifted and creative adolescents.

Creative and gifted people display symptoms of increased psychic excitability, nervousness, and psychoneuroses. On the one hand, increased psychic excitability is one of the basic causes of inner tension and conflict within oneself and one's environment. On the other hand, this increased excitability creates a condition for a broader, deeper, and more complex pattern of experience. Nervousness and psychoneurosis symptoms are necessary forms of human growth and are signs of the beginning of an advancing process of positive transformations (Dąbrowski, et al., 1970).

Parents and educators need to know these signs and should create conditions in which gifted children and adolescents are less susceptible to unnecessary tension operating on lower levels of mental functioning by facilitating the development of the more complex, richer and higher levels. The process of complex growth helps young people take their development into their own hands. There is much less tension and mental disorder on the higher levels where better conditions are formed which give rise to protection and prophylaxis against serious mental disorder or suicide (Dąbrowski, 1972).

According to Dąbrowski, positive disintegration is a multilevel development where each level represents a qualitatively distinct, relatively stable and coherent developmental structure characterized by a distinctive set of developmental dynamisms that interact with each other, creating a unique pattern of behavior.

Developmental dynamisms are instinctual-emotional-cognitive forces fueling and shaping human development.

The positive disintegration includes five clearly distinguishable levels: (a) primary integration, (b) unilevel disintegration, (c) spontaneous multilevel disintegration, (d) organized multilevel disintegration, and (e) secondary integration (Dąbrowski et al., 1970; Dąbrowski, 1996).

I proposed that adolescent development could be modeled by a sequence of patterns of organization (attractors) as developmental potential (a control parameter) changes:

- The early period of adolescence described by the unilevel disintegration as a limit cycle attractor or two fixed-point attractors,
- The middle period of adolescence described by the spontaneous multilevel disintegration as a chaotic attractor, and
- The late adolescence and young adulthood described by the organized multilevel disintegration as an emerging order. (Laycraft, 2011, 2012) (See Figure 1).

The Unilevel Disintegration

Changeable feelings, fluctuations of moods, conflicting courses of action, circular patterns of thoughts, indecision, doubt, and social influences characterize the unilevel disintegration. As Dąbrowski states, "All these phenomena and internal sensations occur on one plane only; there are no inner conflicts between the consciousness of the 'higher' and the 'lower.' There is only one level of activity" (Dąbrowski, 1972; p. 104). It is "a structure without structure " (Dąbrowski, 1996; p. 33).

This pattern of behavior is observed in early adolescence when young people can only think about isolated characteristics of the self ("I am intelligent, gifted, But then I see myself as a fool") and can be described by the two fixed-point attractors or the limit cycle attractor (Laycraft, 2011).

On this level, the individual experiences an internal disturbance and becomes aware of some internal "noise" in her organism. These irregularities begin to direct her attention inwards. The collision of various subconscious forces creates excessive internal tensions, conflicts, ambivalent attitudes, conditions of excitement, and depression. In general, this level is characterized by a total lack of internal organization and of any directionality in their disorders (Dąbrowski, 1972, pp. 103-106).

The Spontaneous Multilevel Disintegration

The phase transition between the unilevel disintegration and the spontaneous multilevel disintegration is characterized by an abrupt change from horizontal (the limit cycle attractor) to vertical motion (the chaotic attractor) when the developmental potential approaches the third factor (the autonomous processes) (Laycraft, 2011). This is "the dynamic factor of *hierarchization of values*" (Dąbrowski, 1972; p. 106). According to Dąbrowski,

Figure 1.

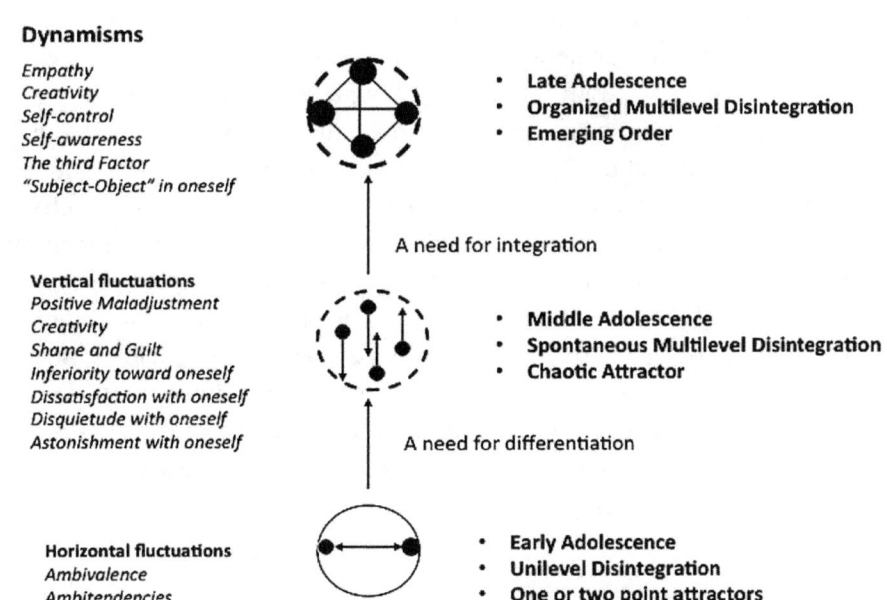

The appearance of a split between the 'lower' and the 'higher' marks the emergence of a vertical direction in development which pushes from within, as it was, and is strongly felt but not entirely clear to the individual as its nature, hence the name 'spontaneous.' (Dąbrowski, 1996, p. 35)

The spontaneous multilevel disintegration is characterized by an extensive differentiation of psychological structure, an increasing role of inner conflict, and a gradual decrease in the frequency of external conflict. Internal conflicts reflect a hierarchical structure of cognitive and emotional life: "what is" versus "what ought to be." It is proposed that this level of development describes the behavior of middle adolescents (Laycraft, 2009).

The process of the differentiation of the mental structure is global and influences the whole mental structure. Differentiation is the result of interaction between the five forms of overexcitability that can be viewed as channels through which information flows, such as sensations, feelings, experiences, images, ideas, hopes, and desires (Piechowski, 1999).

In most of our participants, these channels are open wide, and the abundance and diversity of feelings, thoughts, images, and sensations lead to conflict and tension that create a far-from-equilibrium state. The rapid flow of energy links the components of the mental structure into coherent, higher order forms. These higher-order arrangements are developmental dynamisms and through them, the abrupt changes in human behavior can be observed (Dąbrowski et al., 1970; Dąbrowski, 1973; Dąbrowski, 1996). Developmental dynamisms act as loops of positive feedback. They push the mental structure further into a chaotic state and create instability that becomes strong enough to shatter the pre-existing organization.

According to Dąbrowski, "the instability and partial or even complete disorganization of behavior are necessary in the process of development from a lower level to higher level of mental functioning" (Dąbrowski, 1996, p. 11).

The Organized Multilevel Disintegration

The next level, the organized multilevel disintegration, is a further expansion of the spontaneous multilevel disintegration, and there is some overlap between these two levels. The characteristic feature of this level is the conscious transformation of oneself, facilitating a synthesis that leads to increased stabilization of the hierarchy of value. There are existential, philosophical and transcendental conflicts. Behavior changes towards self-perfection and emotional relationships become deep and enduring (Dąbrowski, 1996, Dąbrowski, Kawczak, & Piechowski, 1970, Dąbrowski & Piechowski, 1977 a,b).

This level of development, which is characterized by lesser tension and a greater ability to systemize experiences, describes the behavior of older adolescents and young adults. Often during late adolescence and early adulthood individuals choose an interest that will later become a central theme in their lives. This level is characterized by openness to external experiences, sensitivity, and identification with others. It can be compared to "dissipative structures," which maintain their existence by interacting with their environment and maintaining the flow of energy into and out of the system (Prigogine, 1980; Prigogine & Stengers, 1984; Prigogine, 1997). Mental structure transforms itself into a new ordered state of increased complexity and therefore stability.

The Development of Creativity

Self-Organization

Self-organization explains the process of a spontaneous emergence of new patterns in systems. These can be physical, chemical, or biological. Recently, principles of self-organizing dynamic systems have been introduced to developmental psychology and have proved to be influential in the study of emotional development, as well as the relationship between cognition and emotion (Izard, et al., 2000).

Self-organization has been studied by the Russian-Belgian chemist Ilya Prigogine, who introduced the concept of *dissipative structures* (Prigogine, 1980, 1987; Prigogine & Stengers, 1984). Such structures must interact with the environment continually, maintaining a flow of energy in and out of the system. Prigogine stressed the importance of openness and strong thermal instability of the system in the process of the formation of dissipative structure.

Prigogine and Stengers write, "at equilibrium, molecules behave as essentially independent entities; they ignore one another. However, non-equilibrium wakes them up and introduces a coherence quite foreign to equilibrium. This is the concept of 'order through fluctuations'" (Prigogine & Stengers, 1984).

Self-organization is a process whereby an open, nonlinear, and complex system, in a state of high entropy, acquires a new internal state without interference from the outside. This means that a system undergoing self-organization does not receive any directions about the nature of structure originating in it. When self-organization is in effect, the external influence has a global nature. It is a source of instability and a turbulent state, which triggers the internal processes and gives rise to phase transitions. New states, patterns or behaviors emerge spontaneously as a function of the inner dynamics of nonlinear interactions between the system's components. In a state of non-equilibrium, the rapid flow of energy links its components into more ordered and complex patterns. We can say that complexity is situated between order and disorder when the system finds itself at the "edge of chaos." In this state, the system is displaying intelligent behavior in adapting to environmental stimuli. A complex system is capable of change, adaptation, and growth (Bertugli, & Vaio, 2005). The human brain is an example of a complex adaptive system in which single neurons interact in simple ways while their collective neural network produces highly complex properties such as creativity and consciousness.

Psycho-Evolutionary Theory of Emotion

Plutchik's psycho-evolutionary theory of emotions (Plutchik, 1980, 1994, 2003) is a Darwinian position that treats emotions as adaptive reactions to the basic problems of life. But Plutchik goes beyond Darwin's idea by specifying these life problems and by introducing the concept that primary emotions must come in pairs of opposites: one for adapting to a positive situation (an opportunity), and one for negative, problematic situation (an obstacle).

Plutchik proposes that there are exactly four problems in life: *identity*, *temporality*, *hierarchy*, and *territoriality*.

Identity concerns membership in social groups and is a problem of two opposite primary emotions: *acceptance* (taking in) and *rejection* (expelling).

Temporality leads to the development of social institutions, such as the family, friendship networks, social communities, and others. *Joy* and *sadness* are adaptive emotions to the positive and negative experiences of temporality.

Hierarchy is a broad concept whose meaning includes power, influence, authority, and prestige. *Anger* and *fear* are the adaptive reactions to the positive and negative experiences of hierarchy.

Territoriality is also a universal problem of life. Territory requires exploration and an ability to plan, monitor, expect, and anticipate. Opposed to the behavior of opening territory through exploration is orientation, with its implied surprise and loss of control. The most generic subjective terms for these two emotions are *anticipation* and *surprise*.

The central idea of Plutchik's theory is that emotions have a purpose in the lives of individuals.

Plutchik proposes that beyond the eight primary emotions, all other emotions are derivative states occurring as a combination of the primary emotions. His theory is based on self-organizing processes where a primary emotion is activated and then recruits other emotions. When two emotions are joined, they produce a secondary emotion; when three are joined, a tertiary emotion, and so on. Similar to color theory, the combining of these primary emotions produces a variety of emotions. They form emotional patterns that stabilize and describe personality traits. Plutchik also introduces the concept of intensity in emotions. For example, rage, vigilance, ecstasy, admiration, terror, amazement, grief, and loathing all represent emotions with high-intensity levels. Anger, anticipation, joy, trust, fear, surprise, sadness, and disgust all represent medium levels of intensity. Finally, annoyance, interest, serenity, acceptance, apprehension, distraction, pensiveness, and boredom represent low-intensity levels of the primary emotions (Plutchik, 1980).

METHODS

The Research Problem

In the research on creativity and human development, I have used *narrative/biography methods*. The biographical method rests on individuals' subjectively gained knowledge and the understanding of their life experiences. Such understanding rests on an interpretive process that leads a researcher to enter the emotional life of participants (Denzin, 1989). This research was focused on the participants' own formative stories, situated in the broader context of their lives. The aim of the first phase of the study was to listen, record, and reflect upon their stories about their lives and creativity.

The Research Questions

To understand the process of development and creativity I studied how young people interpret their lives and derive meaning from what they experience. Most of the questions started with "what," "how" and "why," and hermeneutic phenomenology/ontology was highly suited to answering these kinds of questions about human issues and concerns. A set of research questions was grouped into six focal areas: cognitive awareness, emotional access, interpersonal skills, moral capacity, spiritual experience, and self-identity.

Data Collections

The participants were interviewed in-person for two hours, at a time and place of their choice, for the purpose of documenting their biographical stories and identifying their life-turning points with respect to their psychological development and the process of creativity in the context of their day-to-day lives. The first interview was in the form of an interpretive conversation and encouraged participants to reflect on their experiences in order to determine the deeper meanings of those experiences, particularly their feelings, thoughts, dreams, life choices, and memories.

During the second interview, participants were asked to read, review, and edit the transcripts from the first interview. Following the principles of hermeneutic phenomenology, I worked with the participants in the attempt to bring life to their experiences through the use of imagination and attention to language (Laverty, 2003).

As a process of the interpretation of the data of this research, I created pattern models of creativity of young people by applying the concept of self-organization to Dąbrowski's theory of positive disintegration and Plutchik's psycho-evolutionary theory of emotions. At the bottom of the interpretive hierarchy, I placed each participant's "Life Story" as a simple presentation of data from the interviews. I call it the "iconic reference," which includes landscapes or portraits of their lives. The next two stages of the interpretive process are the "indexical reference," where, by applying the theory of positive disintegration, I started to recognize, understand, and analyze the psychological development of participants. The fourth stage contains a creative approach—the "symbolic reference." Finally, I generated the pattern models of the developmental dynamisms and creativity by applying the idea of self-organization and the theories of emotions (Figure 2).

Assumptions

The use of the hermeneutic phenomenology requires the ability to be reflective, insightful and sensitive to language, and constantly open to experience (van Manen, 1997). The goal is to be reflective in the experience without bringing in preconceived notions about what will be found in the investigation (Laverty, 2003). For the hermeneutic phenomenologist, the biases and assumptions are not bracketed, but rather are embedded and essential to the interpretive process.

Figure 2.

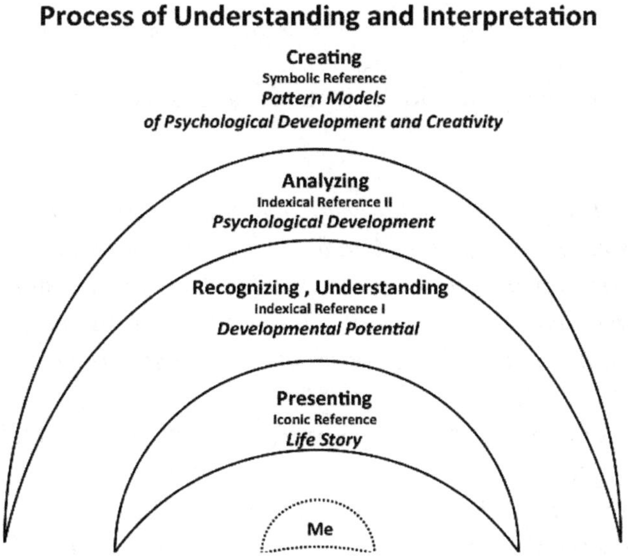

Process of Understanding and Interpretation

Creating
Symbolic Reference
Pattern Models
of Psychological Development and Creativity

Analyzing
Indexical Reference II
Psychological Development

Recognizing, Understanding
Indexical Reference I
Developmental Potential

Presenting
Iconic Reference
Life Story

Me

Limitations and Delimitations

The major limitations of conducting qualitative research are that it is time-consuming and dependent on the skills of the researcher. The researcher has to act as an interviewer, observer, facilitator, communicator, and interpreter of data.

The delimitations for choosing qualitative research are its flexibility and freedom. The research is not restricted to specific questions and can be adjusted during interviews as new information emerges. Interviews can be designed with open-ended questions. Methods are flexible and can be used with a wide range of participants. Data can be collected in an atmosphere that is not only casual and stress-free, but also safe and trustful.

EXPLORING THE ISSUES

Analysis of Findings

I present here the whole process of understanding and interpreting the psychological development and creativity of one of the seven participants involved in this study. First, I introduce the life story of this participant. Next, by applying the concepts of the theory of positive disintegration, the participant's psychological development is recognized, understood and analyzed. And finally, the pattern models of developmental dynamisms and creativity are generated.

Alasdair MacEwan: The Young Composer

Alasdair MacEwan is a nineteen-year-old graduate of Westmount Charter School. As I have learned from his teacher, Alasdair is a special person who has the ability to combine his interests in music, science, and mathematics to produce very interesting school projects.

Life Story

When Alasdair was seven or eight years old, he took piano lessons but quit after two or three years. He said in the interview,

I decided I didn't want to play how my teacher wanted to play. I wanted to play how I wanted to play. It was not worth taking lessons so I stopped. In Grades 7, 8, and 9, I was in a band. In Grade 10, I joined the choir, jazz band, and orchestra...I never could decide what I liked. I started off with bass clarinet, then French horn, bassoon, and lastly tuba. I also bought several instruments on my own and taught myself how to play the guitar, trumpet, flute, and viola. I even took organ lessons for a while.

In Grades 9 and 10, Alasdair was constantly depressed and started to get treatment for depression. In the middle of Grade 10, he ended up having his first "manic period," during which his doctor diagnosed him with bipolar disorder. "*Grade 10 was a pretty horrible year for me. I got very bad marks. That was because I was either depressed or manic and couldn't concentrate at all,*" Alasdair shared. During this period, he was very scared about what would happen, and he was having suicidal thoughts:

I was very afraid that I wouldn't be able to check in. I had to talk to my mom because I was afraid that I was going to do something awful. It was a very unspecific fear. It was not fear of something—it was fear in general. Something in my brain was triggered that made me afraid.

Alasdair's situation was so serious that his mother and grandmother decided to put him in a different school. One of his grandmother's friends knew the principal at Westmount Charter School, "so we went for an interview and they said, 'Can you start tomorrow?' So I was given a schedule and started classes there. Everything worked out great," he said.

The students and teachers of his new school accepted him and he found that the students there embraced strangeness: "If you were different, it wasn't seen as a bad thing. They thought it was good you had something different to offer. The teachers were understanding and genuinely nice people. People there were generally welcoming."

Alasdair felt healthier and was able to open himself up to other people and to his interest. He shared, "I hadn't been seeing a psychiatrist for a while because I'd been feeling much better…I met a friend online and got on right away. We were pretty much like brother and sister…"

In Grade 12, Alasdair combined a variety of his interests into some challenging school projects. One of them was about paralleling the development of physics with some historical changes in the field of music.

PSYCHOLOGICAL DEVELOPMENT

Developmental Potential

Alasdair's developmental potential is rich in three forms overexcitability (OE): emotional, imaginational, and intellectual, which can be seen in his diverse interests, which include music and science.

The signs of Alasdair's emotional OE are in his excessive shyness, feeling depressed, feeling of loneliness, the need for acceptance and security, and exclusive relationships. His tendency to dream can be the sign of enhanced imaginational OE. Finally, the diversity of his interests, which include music, science, mathematics, and writing novels, are indicators of his intellectual OE.

The Unilevel Disintegration: Early Adolescence

Alasdair's early adolescence can be described by the unilevel disintegration of the theory of positive disintegration. Because of his enhanced emotional overexcitability, he experienced strong fluctuations of opposing feelings, intense highs and lows of mood, and conflicting courses of action, which were diagnosed as symptoms of bipolar disorder. He also experienced forms of *depression* related to feelings of inferiority, shame and guilt, fear of death, and suicidal tendencies.

Model of Depression

Depression is a state of mind that is characterized by a lack of active energy exchange between the individual and his environment. It involves the four main negative primary emotions of *distress/sadness, anger, disgust/rejection,* and *fear,* which interact and combine with each other (Izard, 1977). Distress is the key emotion in the pattern of depression. Anger, disgust, and contempt (a secondary emotion of anger combining with disgust) comprise the hostility triad, which represents violent behavior directed toward the self. Fear acts in the opposite direction. It motivates the depressed individual to remove himself from the distressing situation and serves as a check against excessive inner-directed hostility and thus decreases the chances of suicidal behavior (Izard, 1977, p.320). Alasdair experienced constant fluctuations between anger (destruction—moving toward) and fear (protection—moving away from hostility).

The feeling of fear brought a feeling of readiness and willingness for change. By being aware of those feelings and allowing himself to recognize what he lacked, Alasdair was ready to make the decision to accept his mother help and support.

Emotions like rejection (expelling) and despair/sadness (losing/decreasing energy), when combined with each other, bring a feeling of *misery* and *loneliness*. In this situation, the individual feels worthless and the boundary of the self shrinks dangerously into *the point attractor*. During this time, Alasdair felt rejected by his peers and teachers and was extremely lonely (Figure 3).

The negative emotions of anger, sadness, rejection, shame, dislike, loneliness, and depression produce "psychic entropy" in the mind. In this state, the individual cannot use his attention to effectively deal with external tasks because he is busy using this energy to reflect on himself (Csikszentmihalyi, 1997, p. 22). During his early adolescence, Alasdair could not concentrate on his schoolwork and had no interest in it. Even choosing instruments was a problem for him. According to the theory of positive disintegration, disturbances such as hesitation, mental and emotional disequilibrium, increased sensitivity, and temporary lack of interest in the outside world are essential for human development. In these cases, the individual is not really aware and conscious of what is going on inside of him and feels some internal "noise" (Dąbrowski, 1972, p. 103). But this "noise" is strong enough to make the individual shift his attention inwards.

The Spontaneous Multilevel Disintegration: Late Adolescence

Alasdair, by accepting the support and help from his mother, was willing to change schools and, consequently, he experienced new emotions.

Hayes (1994) makes the distinction between social and emotional willingness. On the social level, willingness involves openness to the experience of being with others. On the emotional level, willingness involves openness to whatever internal events follow from togetherness.

Fortunately, people from his new school offered him support, friendliness, and understanding. This new condition of support, acceptance, and understanding became a stabilizing factor to his negative

Figure 3.

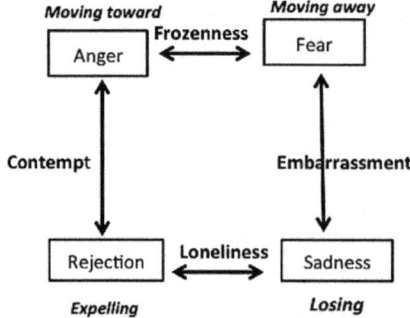

feelings. Alasdair started to reorganize his mental structure and his relationship to his own life. He was escaping the dangerous point attractor of his thoughts, feelings, and behavior, and approaching a new and healthier mental state. The boundary of his self was starting to open and expand.

Alasdair was experiencing new emotions like acceptance, joy, and interest. Because he felt accepted by others, he opened himself up and started to accept others. He also opened himself up to different areas of science and art.

Acceptance *of* oneself and others and acceptance *by* others acts as a positive feedback, which brings changes in one's mental state. Acceptance involves one's sense of identity (TenHouten, 2009) and has a tendency to recruit other emotions such as joy and interest. These three emotions create a richness of feelings such as openness, receptivity, friendliness, love, resourcefulness, and optimism, which are essential for the psychological growth of young people (see Figure 4). In other words, these positive emotions create a chaotic attractor, which can take on an infinite number of forms and patterns of life dynamics.

During his middle and late adolescence, Alasdair also experienced dynamisms such as

- Astonishment with oneself (*"I often stop and think back and wonder, was that a valid thought? Was that something that makes sense?"*)
- Dissatisfaction with oneself (*"I see more flaws in myself than I see flaws in others. It constantly leads me to think that they are better than I am."*)
- Shame (*"Walking down the hall, I feel ashamed for no reason."*) and
- Guilt (*"I was talking to one of my friends one day. He was being silly about something and I told him off. Later, I went back and apologized because I felt guilty about it."*).

Astonishment with oneself is the first phase in the authentic observation of oneself and the beginning of the desire to change. It is a feeling that some of one's mental and emotional qualities are surprising, unexpected, or strange (Dąbrowski, 1973; Dąbrowski & Piechowski, 1977a). This dynamism can be expressed by a combination of two primary emotions: *surprise/astonishment* and *anticipation*. These two emotions create a state of *confusion* and *conflict*, which starts to create a state of disequilibrium in the young psyche.

Dissatisfaction with oneself is one of the strongest dynamisms of the first phase of the spontaneous multilevel disintegration. It is a critical and condemning attitude toward oneself accompanied by a state of anxiety and disappointment (Dąbrowski, 1973; Dąbrowski & Piechowski, 1977a). It can be expressed by four primary emotions: *anticipation, surprise, fear,* and *sadness*. Strong dissatisfaction with oneself is one of the indicators of accelerated development and expresses a strong determination for change.

Figure 4.

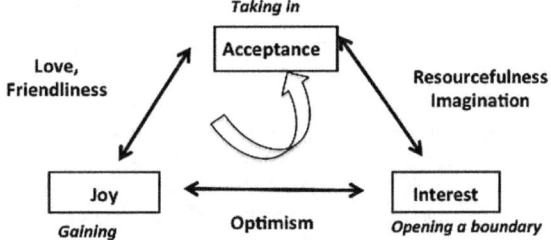

These dynamisms create states of self-observation, self-reflection, self-awakening, and self-criticism. They are the primary product of emotional overexcitability, and intellectual overexcitability enhances the development of self-awareness (Dąbrowski, 1996) (see Figure 5).

In the second phase of the spontaneous multilevel disintegration, the self-conscious emotions appear. They include *embarrassment*, *shame*, *guilt*, and *pride*. These emotions require the ability to evaluate one's self and to infer the mental states of others (Dabrowski, 1996).

Izard (1977) writes that in feeling shame an individual experiences a heightened degree of self-consciousness and self-awareness. Shame creates a psychological instability and the boundary of self becomes more permeable. The instability and permeability of the self in shame provides a strong motivation for the individual to want to know himself. Thus, one of the positive functions of shame is to increase self-knowledge (Izard, 1977, p. 410).

Guilt occurs in situations where one feels personally responsible for something, and it stimulates a great deal of thought as one begins to reflect on the wrongdoing and how she can set things right again. The emotion of guilt plays a role in the development of personal and social responsibility (Izard, 1977, p. 427).

In the third phase of the spontaneous multilevel disintegration, *positive maladjustment* emerges. This dynamism is characterized as a conscious and selective rejection of the standards and attitudes of one's social environment that are conflicting with one's growing awareness of higher values. The individual is in the process of adapting to a higher hierarchy of values, and developing attitudes of autonomy and authenticity (Dąbrowski, 1973; Dąbrowski & Piechowski, 1977a). The primary emotions of this dynamism are rejection of a lower hierarchy of values, acceptance of a higher hierarchy of values, anticipation in the process of developing these higher values, and anger in response to seeing the lower values in a social environment. A combination of anticipation and acceptance creates the secondary emotion of sagacity or resourcefulness. Sagacity can be defined as "keenness and soundness of judgment in the estimation of persons or conditions and in the adaptation of means of ends" (Oxford, p. 2620). A combination of anger and rejection creates the secondary emotion of contempt, which involves "the feeling or action of the person toward someone or something considered low, worthless, or beneath notice (Webster, p. 300) (see Figure 6).

Figure 5.

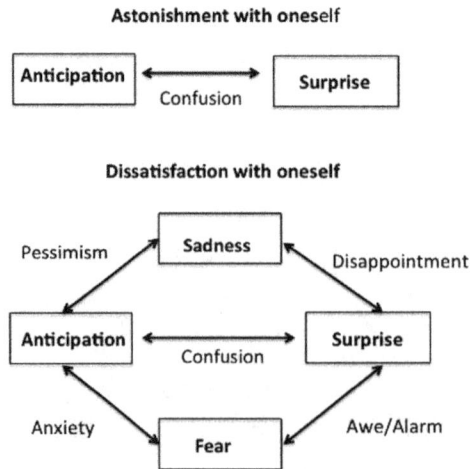

Figure 6.

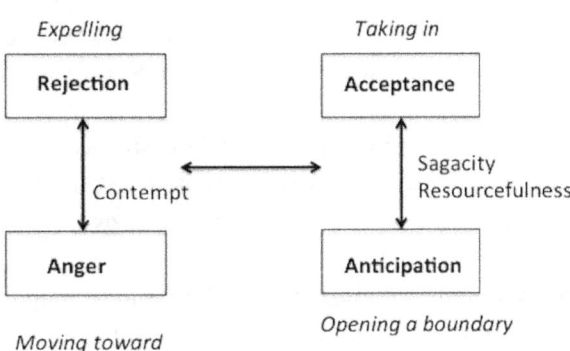

The interview with Alasdair was conducted six days after the Stanley Cup riot in Vancouver. This is how he expressed his feeling of positive maladjustment:

I have a sense of disappointment in my fellow people. I think that in general, we are pretty crappy species. We kill each other for any good reason. We go out and do horrible things and then we make excuses for that. We go out and destroy beautiful things in nature all the time and then put ugly things in their place. Some of the reactions afterward when people were going and volunteering to help out and repair things alleviate some of that. But it still leaves a little bit of a bitter taste in my mouth.

During his middle and late adolescence, Alasdair was actively involved in creative activities. He composed music and wrote a novel. His creativity arose from his enhanced excitability and his sensitivity to his internal and external worlds. It became a channel for his anxiety and depression and gave him a feeling of flow and satisfaction.

The Process of Creativity

By observing and studying gifted and creative people, Dąbrowski proposed that creative dynamisms emerge at the spontaneous multilevel disintegration. They arise from above-average sensitivity and develop under conditions of emotional turmoil, mental tension, and internal conflict. Creative dynamisms help in differentiation and then integrate a richness of emotions.

I present here a pattern model of the creativity of Alasdair, whose main passion was a composing music. First of all, Alasdair had to find the idea for his composition. He opened himself to a variety of ideas (*interest*—open a boundary) and immersed himself in this process (*acceptance*—taking in). A combination of interest and acceptance creates a secondary emotion of imagination or inspiration (TenHouten, 2009). He says, "I took an idea from a piece of Bach. Another one was from folk music, or expressing the movement of cat…"

Quite often, he was struggling with choosing an idea and engaged himself in daydreaming. Alasdair mentioned that during his daydreaming his mind jumped from one idea to another.

The next phase was to integrate his ideas. He describes, "If I really wanted to work on one, I'd listen to a piece of music a few times and see if I picked up something that I could use."

Near the end of his creative process, Alasdair felt what was right to do:

I couldn't do much by pausing and thinking about where I was going with it. It flowed easily when working but it was hard to explain. It was one of the best feelings that I knew because it was a combination of knowing that was something I created. It was just me. It might be what drew me back to it.

The feeling of *flow/attraction* is the result of the self-organization of the primary emotions of acceptance, surprise, and joy. Acceptance and surprise create the emotional experience of *curiosity*, and in a combination with joy can create the experience of *joyful curiosity*, which attracts the individual to an activity (Figure 7).

Creative dynamisms of the spontaneous multilevel disintegration help to reorganize a disintegrated mental structure and to build a new reality through an expanded awareness. It is a starting point for the transition to the next level of development.

Discussion of Themes

The following are the themes that arose from the analysis of the seven participants' stories in response to the research questions:

T1: Creativity helps individuals in the turbulent period of adolescence by serving as an outlet for their increased tensions and their inner and external conflicts.

T2: Creativity promotes conditions that are optimal for the prevention of the serious mental disorder.

T3: Creativity helps individuals in the process of cognitive, emotional, and spiritual development.

T4: Creativity helps individuals in the process of identity formation and in finding direction toward their future goals and plans

The following participants' statements, taken from their interviews, illustrate these themes.

Figure 7.

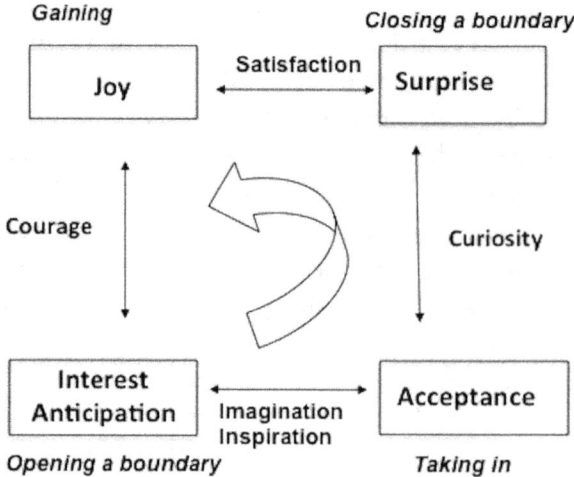

The Development of Creativity

T1

- *"When I get into a crowd of people cruising around me, I feel like I am suffocating. Drawing or distracting myself with art was a way of coping with my space."* (Stephannie)
- *"The best part is when everything goes quiet and I draw or paint. My mind checks out and I can see things as they are."* (Marsha Park)

T2

- *"I was obsessed with something but was scared at the same time. By working through my art and my ideas, I began to understand what I was going through and coping with it by reversing it a little bit – because I am not so bad anymore."* (Stephannie)
- *"It happens in my writing and in my art too. Sometimes, I feel like I am connected to some form of energy, like this "Chi" energy. I just feel like a stream going through everything, like invisible but you know it's there. You just feel it. It just vibrates."* (Marsha Park)
- *"I just fell in love with the circus. I was amazed by what the human body is capable of doing. I was completely in awe."* (Krista Jennings)
- *"If I don't enjoy the process and it is leading me into the ego direction, I don't want to do it. I only want to be closer to my being, to my soul."* (Eton)

T3

- *"I started getting interested in non-objective art as a way of expressing something deeper, something spiritual, something mystical, something that is not in this world...I became really process-oriented. I wanted to really focus on the process. It was a sort of moving meditation, doing repetitive movements, trying to draw circles over and over again."* (Eton)
- *"When I perform, it is really me, and it takes what I train very hard to do and brings so much creativity into it. I really connect with the audience and express myself doing something that I love doing."* (Krista Jennings)

T4

- *"If I hadn't been an artist, I would never have figured out who I am."* (Stephannie)
- *"I poured my heart and soul into it. I was determined to be the best artist. I was competitive because I loved it."* (Eton)

The Integral Model: An Analysis of Perspectives

By applying the integral model, the impacts of creativity on the individual and on others are discussed. In the subjective and objective quadrants, two modes of mental processing are placed: the mindful mode and the default mode. Both modes are essential for creative thinking. During the process of creativity, individuals are alternatively active and passive; they are constantly oscillating between these two modes.

The mindful mode, characterized by a high degree of attention, response flexibility, openness, and receptivity, activates the middle regions of the prefrontal cortex, including the orbitofrontal, anterior cingulate, and ventral and medial prefrontal cortex (Siegel, 2007).

The default network mode is active during passive "rest" periods when individuals are not focused on the external, but rather on their internal environment (Raichle et al., 2001). It can be understood as multiple interacting subsystems (the medial temporal lobe, the medial prefrontal and the posterior cingulate cortex), which integrate self-referential information, facilitate perception and cognition and provides a social context or narrative in which events become personally meaningful (Schilbach et al., 2008).

I can also look at the impacts of creativity from the intersubjective and interobjective perspectives. Creative products such as performance pieces, paintings, writing, compositions, or even school projects, are available at the cultural and social levels and can influence and inspire others in a variety of ways. Cultural and social influences play a decisive role in the process of creativity and development of young people, who are highly sensitive to the values, opinions, and expectations of their parents, teachers, and peers (see Figure 8).

CONCLUSION AND IMPLICATIONS

1. Wilber's Integral Model was a useful conceptual framework for integrating a variety of disciplines and theories into a meaningful map. By integrating the theory of positive disintegration with theories of emotions and the concepts of complexity science, the unique patterns of the developmental processes of the seven participants emerged, bringing a more integral understanding of the complex process of the emotional development of adolescents.
2. Following Heidegger and Gadamer's idea, the researcher immersed herself in the circular movement of understanding and interpreting the psychological development and creativity of young

Figure 8.

Subjective - Intentional	Objective – Behavioral
The Mindful Mode of Cognitive Processing	The Mindful Mode of Cognitive Processing
• Openness & receptivity to the external world	• Activation of the middle regions of prefrontal cortex
• Response flexibility, Insights, Intuition	
The Default Network Mode	The Default Network Mode
• Passive "rest" periods focusing on the internal world	• Activation of the medial temporal lobe and the medial prefrontal cortex.
• Helps to integrate self-referential information	
Intersubjective – Cultural	Interobjective – Social
• Creative products are available to others at the cultural and social level	
• Sensitivity of young people to external (cultural and social) influences	

people. This was a multistage and very productive process of finding new meanings generated through "deep" interviews, the journals of the participants, and their products. The researcher's experiences as an artist, scientist, and educator played an essential role during this process. Her openness, sensitivity, and understanding of art and the process of creativity helped her to connect with participants on a deeper level and gain their honesty and trust.

3. The participants of this study were very open and willing to talk on a deep level, sharing their feelings, thoughts, memories, beliefs, decisions, spiritual convictions, and ideas about their creative process. From the interviews, the researcher learned that, during their early and middle adolescence, the participants experienced internal conflicts, anxieties, and depression. Fortunately, these young people had somebody (a parent, teacher, or friend) who accepted them and helped them bifurcate to higher psychological level.

4. This study demonstrated that a condition of acceptance activates the process of development to more complex, richer, and higher levels characterized by lesser tension. Acceptance (taking in) is a strong positive emotion that involves one's sense of identity. Acceptance helps young individuals connect with the outside world. Their patterns of behavior, thoughts, and feelings change and become healthier. Young people are then able to open themselves to their interests and to other people. They begin to experience new emotions such as joy, friendliness, surprise, resourcefulness, curiosity, and delight. Activated emotions act as a flow of energy, which becomes the driving force for their creativity and psychological development.

5. This study shows why it is of enormous importance to encourage creativity in schools:
   a. For early and middle adolescents, creativity very often becomes a refuge, a retreat, and a way of escaping an unfriendly or brutal environment.
   b. Creativity allows young people to learn about themselves, connect them to something meaningful and introduces purposes and values in their lives.
   c. Creativity helps them in emotional, cognitive, and spiritual growth and empowers them to make life choices that bring joy, satisfaction, and fulfillment.
   d. Creativity helps them grow into resourceful, optimistic, sanguine, open-minded, confident, and prideful human beings.
   e. Creativity helps them to become open and sensitive not only to human issues and to other human beings, but often to wider problems of the natural world.

6. The researcher's main contribution to research on the creativity and psychological development of young people demonstrates that both are self-organizing processes emerging spontaneously purely as a function of the inner dynamics of interactions between the system's components in a far-from-equilibrium state. Creativity is a self-organizing process, created and maintained by complex emotions such as enthusiasm, curiosity, resourcefulness, delight, and satisfaction. These emotions are the driving forces that generate order in the psyche of young people. Similarly, the psychological development of young people is a self-organizing process, which differentiates, and then integrates, the internal elements such as emotions, thoughts, imagination, and memory. The long-term processes of psychological development and the short-term processes of creativity are intertwined in a cyclical and dynamical relationship. Creativity is a temporary experience generating the context in which emotional, cognitive, and spiritual development takes place. Psychological development, on the other hand, creates the conditions for creativity by adjusting the internal environment toward openness, sensitivity, and receptivity.

REFERENCES

Abraham, F. D. (1995). Introduction to dynamics: A basic language: a basic metamodeling strategy. In F. D. Abraham & A. R. Gilden (Eds.), *Chaos theory in psychology* (pp. 31–49). Westport, CT: Greenwood Press.

Abraham, R. H., & Shaw, C. D. (1984). *Dynamics: The geometry of behavior*. Santa Cruz, CA: Aerial Press.

Bertugli, C. S., & Vaio, F. (2005). *Nonlinearity, chaos and complexity: The dynamics of natural and social systems*. Oxford University Press.

Briggs, J., & Peat, F. D. (1990). *Turbulent mirror*. New York: Harper Collins Perennial Library.

Csikszentmihalyi, M. (1997). *Finding flow: The psychology of engagement with everyday life*. Basic Books.

Dąbrowski, K. (1972). *Psychoneurosis is not an illness*. London: Gryf Publications Ltd.

Dąbrowski, K. (1973). *The dynamics of concepts*. London: Gryf Publications Ltd.

Dąbrowski, K. (1996). *Multilevelness of emotional and instinctive functions*. Lublin: Towarzystwo Naukowe Katolickiego Uniwersytetu Lubelskiego.

Dąbrowski, K. (2015). *Personality shaping through positive disintegration*. Red Pill Press.

Dąbrowski, K., Kawczak, A., & Piechowski, M. (1970). *Mental growth through positive disintegration*. London: Gryf Publication Ltd.

Dąbrowski, K., & Piechowski, M. M. (1977a). Theory of levels of emotional development: Vol. 1. *Multilevelness and positive disintegration*. New York: Dabor Science Publications.

Dąbrowski, K., & Piechowski, M. M. (1977b). Theory of levels of emotional development: Vol. 2. *From primary integration to self-actualization*. New York: Dabor Science Publications.

Denzin, N. K. (1989). *Interpretive biography: Qualitative research methods series 17*. Sage University Press. doi:10.4135/9781412984584

Dilthey, W. (1976). *Dilthey selected writings*. Cambridge University Press.

Dilthey, W. (2010). *Understanding the human world*. Princeton University Press.

Edelman, G. M. (2004). *Wider than the sky: The phenomenal gift of consciousness*. New Haven, CT: Yale University Press.

Gadamer, H. G. (1975/1989). *Truth and method*. London: Continuum.

Gleick, J. (1988). *Chaos: Making a new science*. New York: Penguin.

Hayes, S. C. (1994). Content, context, and the types of psychological acceptance. In S. C. Hayes, N. S. Jacobson, V. M. Follette, & M. J. Daugher (Eds.), *Acceptance and change: Content and context in psychotherapy* (pp. 13–32). Reno, NV: Context Press.

Heidegger, M. (1962). *Being and time*. New York: Harper Perennial Modern Thought.

Heidegger, M. (2008). On the origin of the work of art. In D. F. Krell (Ed.), *Basic Writings* (pp. 143–212). New York: Harper Collins.

Izard, C. E. (1977). *Human Emotion*. New York: Plenum Press. doi:10.1007/978-1-4899-2209-0

Izard, C. E., Ackerman, B. P., Schoff, K. M., & Fine, S. E. (2000). Self-organization of discrete emotions, emotion patterns, and emotion-cognitive relations. In M. D. Lewis & I. Granic (Eds.), *Emotion, development, and self-organization* (pp. 15–36). Cambridge University Press. doi:10.1017/CBO9780511527883.003

Kelso, J. A. (1995). *Dynamic patterns, the self-organization of brain and behavior*. Cambridge, MA: MIT Press.

Laverty, S. M. (2003). Hermeneutic phenomenology and phenomenology: A comparison of historical and methodological considerations. *International Journal of Qualitative Methods*, *2*(3), 21–35. doi:10.1177/160940690300200303

Laycraft, C. K. (2009). Positive maladjustment as a transition from chaos to order. *Roeper Review: A Journal on Gifted Education*, *31*, 113-122.

Laycraft, C. K. (2011). Theory of positive disintegration as a model of adolescent development. *Nonlinear Dynamics Psychology and Life Sciences*, *15*(1), 29–52. PMID:21176438

Laycraft, C. K. (2012). *The Development of creativity: A study of creative adolescents and young adults* (Doctoral dissertation). University of Calgary, Calgary, Alberta. Retrieved from http://these.ucalgary.ca/handle/11023/166

Lewis, M. D. (1995). Cognition-emotion feedback & self-organization of developmental paths. *Human Development*, *38*(2), 71–102. doi:10.1159/000278302

Lewis, M. D. (1997). Personality self-organization: Cascading constraints on cognition-emotion interaction. In A. Fogel, M. C. Lyra, & J. Valsiner (Eds.), *Dynamics and indeterminism in development and social processes* (pp. 193–216). Hillsdale, NJ: Lawrence Erlbaum.

Lewis, M. D. (2000a). The promise of dynamic systems approaches for an integrated account of human development. *Child Development*, *71*(1), 36–43. doi:10.1111/1467-8624.00116 PMID:10836556

Lewis, M. D. (2000b). Emotional self-organization at three time scales. In M. D. Lewis & I. Granic (Eds.), *Emotion, development, and self-organization* (pp. 37–69). Cambridge, UK: Cambridge University Press. doi:10.1017/CBO9780511527883.004

Lewis, M. D. (2005a). Self-organizing individual differences in brain development. *Developmental Review*, *25*(3-4), 252–277. doi:10.1016/j.dr.2005.10.006

Lewis, M. D. (2005b). Bridging emotion theory and neurobiology through dynamic system modeling. *Behavioral and Brain Sciences*, *28*(02), 169–245. doi:10.1017/S0140525X0500004X PMID:16201458

Li, T. Y., & Yorke, J. A. (1975). Period three implies chaos. *The American Mathematical Monthly*, *82*(10), 985–992. doi:10.1080/00029890.1975.11994008

Lorenz, E. N. (1993). *The essence of chaos*. Seattle, WA: University of Washington Press. doi:10.4324/9780203214589

Maslow, A. H. (1968). *Toward a psychology of being*. Melbourne: D. Van Nostrand Company.

May, R. (1976). Simple mathematical models with very complicated dynamics. *Nature, 261*(5560), 459–467. doi:10.1038/261459a0 PMID:934280

Merleau-Ponty, M. (2004a). Cezanne's doubt. In T. Baldwin (Ed.), *Maurice Merleau-Ponty: Basic Writing* (pp. 272–290). New York: Routledge Taylor & Francis Group.

Merleau-Ponty, M. (2004b). Eye and mind. In T. Baldwin (Ed.), *Maurice Merleau-Ponty: Basic Writing* (pp. 290–324). New York: Routledge Taylor & Francis Group.

Oxford English Dictionary, The Compact Edition. (1971). Oxford, UK: Oxford University Press.

Piaget, J. (1962). *Science of education and the psychology of the child*. New York: Viking Press.

Piechowski, M. M. (1999). Overexcitabilities. In M. Runco & S. Pritzker (Eds.), *Encyclopedia of creativity* (Vol. 2, pp. 325–334). San Diego, CA: Academic Press.

Plutchik, R. (1980). *Emotion: A psycho-evolutionary synthesis*. New York: Harper & Row.

Plutchik, R. (1994). *The psychology and biology of emotion*. Harper Collins College Publishers.

Plutchik, R. (2003). *Emotions & life: Perspectives from psychology, biology, and evolution*. Washington, DC: American Psychological Association.

Prigogine, I. (1980). *From being to becoming: Time and complexity in the physical science*. San Francisco, CA: W.H. Freeman and Company.

Prigogine, I. (1997). *The end of certainty. Time, chaos and the new laws of nature*. New York: The Free Press.

Prigogine, I., & Stengers, I. (1984). *Order out of chaos*. New York: Bantam Books.

Raichle, M. E., MacLeod, A. M., Snyder, A. Z., Powers, W. J., Gusnard, D. A., & Shulman, G. L. (2001). A default mode of brain function. *Proceedings of the National Academy of Sciences of the United States of America, 98*(2), 676–682. doi:10.1073/pnas.98.2.676 PMID:11209064

Rogers, C. R. (1961/1989). *On becoming a person: A therapist's view of psychology*. Boston: Houghton Mifflin Company.

Schilbach, L., Eickhoff, S. B., Rotarska-Jagiela, A., Fink, G. R., & Vogeley, K. (2008). Mind at rest? Social cognition as the default mode of cognizing and its putative relationship to the "default system" of the brain. *Consciousness and Cognition, 17*(2), 457–467. doi:10.1016/j.concog.2008.03.013 PMID:18434197

Siegel, D. J. (2007). *The mindful brain: Reflection and attunement in the cultivation of well-being*. New York: W. W. Norton & Company.

TenHouten, W. D. (2009). *A general theory of emotions and social life*. New York: Routledge, Taylor and Francis Group.

Thelen, E., & Smith, L. B. (1994). *A dynamic system approach to the development of cognition and action*. MIT Press.

Van Manen, M. (1997). *Researching lived experience: Human science for an action sensitive pedagogy* (2nd ed.). London, Canada: The Althouse Press.

Varela, F. J. (1992). *Ethical know-how: Action, wisdom, and cognition*. Stanford, CA: Stanford University Press.

Varela, F. J., Thompson, E., & Rosh, E. (1993). *The embodied mind: Cognitive science and human experience*. Cambridge, MA: The MIT Press.

Vygotsky, L. S. (1971). *The psychology of art*. Cambridge, MA: The MIT Press.

Vygotsky, L. S. (1978). *Mind in society: The development of higher psychological processes*. Cambridge, MA: Harvard University Press.

Vygotsky, L. S. (1981). The genesis of higher mental functions. In J. V. Wertsh (Ed.), *The concept of activity in Soviet psychology*. Aemonk, NY: Sharpe.

Webster's New World Dictionary of American English. (1988). New York: Webster's New World.

Wilber, K. (2008). *The integral vision*. Boston, MA: Shambhala.

ADDITIONAL READING

Laycraft, K. C. (2013). *Creativity as an order through emotions: A study of creative adolescents and young adults* (2nd ed.). Victoria, BC: Promontory Press.

Laycraft, K. C. (2014). Toward the pattern models of creativity: Chaos, complexity, creativity. In B. S. Don Ambrose & K. M. Pierce (Eds.), *A critique of creativity and complexity* (pp. 269–290). Sense Publishers.

KEY TERMS AND DEFINITIONS

Developmental Dynamisms: Are instinctual-emotional-cognitive forces fueling and shaping emotional development.

Developmental Potential: Is an original endowment that determines what level of development a person reaches if the physical and environmental conditions are optimal.

Overexcitability (OE): Is defined as a higher than average capacity for experiencing inner and external stimuli, and is based on a higher than average responsiveness in the nervous system. There are five forms of psychic overexcitability: psychomotor, sensual, imaginational, emotional, and intellectual.

Positive Disintegration: Is a fundamental process in an individual's development stimulated by tension, inner conflict, and anxiety. Development involves a disorganization of mental structure, which then endorses the formation of more complex, more organized, more adaptive, and more creative organization.

Positive Maladjustment: Is a conscious and selective rejection of the standards and attitudes of one's social environment that are conflicting with one's growing perception of higher values. The primary characteristics of this dynamism are a rejection of a perceived lower hierarchy of values, acceptance of a higher hierarchy of values, anticipation in the process of developing these higher values, and anger in response to seeing the lower values in a social environment.

Self-Actualizing (SA) Creativeness: Refers to a type of creativity that stresses highly valuable traits like boldness, courage, freedom, spontaneity, integration, and self-acceptance.

Self-Organization: Is the spontaneous emergence of new patterns, changes, and novelties in a variety of systems, whether physical, chemical, or biological. Recently, principles of self-organizing dynamic systems have been introduced to developmental psychology, especially to emotional development and brain development.

Chapter 15
Post-Adult Education Alternatives in 45 Years of Learning/Teaching:
An Integral-Informed Autoethnographic Reflection

R. Michael Fisher
University of Calgary, Canada

ABSTRACT

The author critically examines the directional trends that education has gone through in the last 45 years of his teaching and learning experiences, primarily in Alberta, Canada (1972-2017). He argues that, formerly, Alberta was at the leading edge of positive progressive change, before neoliberal ideology invaded Education. Through use of autoethnographic reflection and sociocultural and political contextualization of his educational experiences, the author elaborates the necessity of adopting a holistic-integral alternative path to research and teaching outside of institutionalized mainstream education systems. His emphasis on the affective domain, for example the importance of fear in education, is accompanied by his applications of developmental notions of "post-adult," transdisciplinary, and integral theoretical work. The purpose of the chapter is to demonstrate, through his own life, a model of potential guidance for teachers, who are questioning how best to negotiate their own careers within the challenges of 21st century neoliberalism and cascading global crises.

INTRODUCTION

A Narrative-Based Integral Methodology

If I am going to promote an *integral education* beyond merely a holistic or integrative education of multiple perspectives, I feel obligated to apply integral methodology. Likewise, I ought to performatively write integrally as well—as much as I am capable. Although this chapter is not action research nor a

DOI: 10.4018/978-1-5225-5873-6.ch015

best example of action research in my teaching history for 45 years, it is an acting upon my own life as a teacher/learner for the purpose of my own growth, healing and potential transformation. I want to be a better teacher and person, in a better world.

For the past 60 years in North America (at least), the field of Education has universally been greatly impacted in a positive way by two influences: *reflective practice* and *action research*. Teachers have become classroom researchers, and like this chapter for me, they are encouraged to put themselves under the lens of investigation and critique (both positive and negative). There is more to good education and development of a quality teacher than merely delivering content effectively and/or be a nice caring person.

I have set out an integral methodology guideline for myself for this chapter. The guideline begins by foregrounding self-reflectivity to the point of creating a "study" using autoethnographic principles, whereby I attempt to research *myself* as intimately interrelated with the *culture* in which I teach and learn. Context is important, to make this not an autobiography—all about me. Yet, the structuration is a narrative-based personal "story" about a specific learning/teaching journey. Ultimately, the chapter's purpose is to better understand Education historically, especially in Alberta and beyond, and offer my journey as a model of potential guidance for other teachers, who are negotiating their careers in the context of a 21st century of global cascading crises.

What is not usual about my interest in Education is the emphasis on the affective domain. Leitch and Day (2000) make a critical point, that reflective practice and action research methodologies for teachers and educational researchers have been overly dominated by rational cognitive models and theories. These two researchers argue that there needs to be a better 'balance' and integration of the "role of emotion in understanding and developing the capacities for reflection which facilitate personal, professional and ultimately system change" (p. 179). In other words, their critique is that we have not been attentive enough on the impact that emotion has on determining the quality by which teachers, in particular, research themselves using reflective practice and action research approaches.

Since 1989 my special focus has been on the so-called emotion named "fear." I mean to emphasize that my study is transdisciplinary, and thus I have concluded that *'fear'* today is not what it used to be—that is, as it was (and still is) typically framed in a more traditional disciplinary methodological container—primarily, that of Philosophy, Psychology and Medicine. Education as a field has largely been dependent on psychology to tell it what it is supposed to think about human affect. My work challenges that assumption.

The most important role of transdisciplinary research and thinking has been its emphasis on "integrating epistemics (i.e., [diverse] ways of knowing)" and the deeper analysis of "world views" that shape the researcher (Scholz, 2017, p. 1). I have wanted to know what shaping worldviews lie deep below the surface of people and cultures and how they determine not only the behavior of fear as an emotion (e.g., fears, phobias)—but how they determine the very way we perceive and understand *fear itself*—and, concomitantly the way we perceive ourselves. All of which determines how we practice *fear management* and educate ourselves (e. g., our children) about fear itself. I will weave this affective thread of inquiry and findings (as a fearologist[1]) throughout the narrative in this chapter.

The strong case about the cognitive rationalist bias in reflective practices and action research is likely due (in part) to being afraid of emotion—and, in particular, being afraid of fear itself. To keep things simple for the moment, I am suggesting that there's a good reason why most narratives of teachers and educational researchers, using these popular reflective action-based methods of analysis, end up as rather low quality. According to Heikkinen et al. (2012), there needs to be systematic (integral) principles brought into narrative inquiry research overall—but especially in the field of Education. They suggest five principles to be applied when doing reflective practices like narrative inquiry: (a) *historical continuity*, (b) *reflexivity*, (c) *dialectics*, (d) *workability* and, (e) *evocativeness*. These five also ensure cognitive and rationally dominating modes do not overtake the interpretive investigation and quality of the actual narratives produced. How to get higher quality *"authentic narratives"* (Heikkinen et al., p. 5) out of teachers is an interest of mine too. I want them to reflect courageously into deeper than usual places—entering into territories they are often very uncomfortable to explore, reveal and share. Often this has to do directly with emotion, with unconscious cherished worldviews and a fear of change—a fear of exposure and vulnerability, an authentic confrontation with the world they live in and what is happening globally as in crises of ecological and social disorder. I know that teachers, like anyone else, carry 'shadows' of injury (and denial of such) that are part of the culture and their upbringing. These greatly influence the quality of their teaching and development and maturation as a teacher—myself included.

The last thing to say about my integral methodology in this chapter is that I too am going to try to follow and 'balance' these five principles (*a la* Heikkinen) to ensure (or at least pursue) *high quality* (i.e., "authentic narratives") in my autoethnographic "story." It was exciting to map the five principles onto the Wilberian (Integral Theory) quadrant analysis (e.g., Wilber, 1995). And, it turns out the five map nicely across all four epistemic quadrants/perspectives and one principle is generic enough to cover all the quadrants: (a) *historical continuity* (lower right or "its" perspective), (b) *reflexivity* (upper left or "I" perspective), (c) *dialectics* (all quadrants), (d) *workability* (upper right or "it" perspective), (e) *evocativeness* (lower left or "we" perspective). Due to space limitations, I cannot go into greater detail on these for this chapter; but suffice it to say they have provided me with a new integral approach to writing about myself as a teacher/learner. At times I'll make their use explicit but mostly they will be utilized implicitly.

What Is a Post-Adult?

Among other things, (critical) *integral theory* and thinking is decidedly evolutionary, historical, and developmental. The "critical" part is my own specialty addition to Wilber's Integral Theory[2] and other integralists' work. One reason for my emphasis is that I come from a poor working class background going back as far as we have histories in Russia/Germany and Belgium. All were peasants working for the owning classes and elites, I imagine. I'm a son of an immigrant family with grade eight schooling and the first of the generations to attend post-secondary education—which is remarkable because I really quite despised most all my K-12 schooling in Calgary. But that's another story. Being from the oppressed and marginalized by classism, I have always been a fighter of the middle-class 'norms.' I didn't fit in the way the 'average' person was supposed to be. I just wanted to be a long-haired rock star since the age of 14. I played drums and sang lead but mostly back-up harmony. We played The Beatles' tunes and other songs of revolution.

I grew out of that fantasy soon enough and attended a technical training institute in Edmonton to try to make a career in what I loved—Nature. I'll get to that below. What really happened in my very passionate life seems to have followed a developmental trajectory of "stages," not that I knew it at the time, only upon reflection. Around 1989, I discovered an amazing psychology book by Keen (1983) called the *Passionate Life: Stages of Loving*. It mapped in a meaningfully accurate way my growth. Keen thought it was a universal path. The five stages are: (1) *child*, (2) *rebel*, (3) *adult*, (4) *outlaw* and, (5) *lover*. Wow. That model showed that "adult" was only the middle of a developmental spectrum in the potential human life-cycle. Keen argued most everyone stops at that stage of development—and, societies generally do not encourage post-adult stages. My experience told me at the time that I was well into the *outlaw* stage with all its excitement and struggles—and thus, my attraction to critical theory in general. It is a theory that explains social conflict—that is, struggles that are at the core of the formation of social order and function. Over the decades I have noticed that what nearly everyone overlooks (or suppresses) when they read Wilber's Integral Theory, especially these days, is that it is a (North American) late-branch of the European (Frankfurt) Critical Theory (very leftist) schools of thought (see Crittenden, 1997). I'll return to this Keenian model at the end to explain culture and Alberta's Education system and especially why I get into trouble so easily.

A STORY OF "CLASH" IN ALBERTA EDUCATION: MY LATE 20s

Although I track out my 45 years of learning/teaching in and out of the province of Alberta, Canada, between 1972–2017 in this chapter, it is educative to begin with a critical story of my first two years of school teaching in a rural district, grades 5–8 at Raymond School (pseudonym), in southern Alberta. After this story, I offer autoethnographic reflections and cultural contexts for why things clashed in my early school teaching career and why I had to retire early, while pursuing radical alternative forms of education.

I like to believe that by the time I secured my first public teaching position at Raymond school that I was already well on my way to becoming an integral and transdisciplinary thinker ('out of the box')—and, an activist searching to transform society and myself. Like most of the keenest of teachers that go into public school teaching careers, I was determined to offer rich in depth, memorable, relevant and respectful learning relationships with young people like I did *not* have in my K–12 public schooling experience. This rebellious corrective attitude can take a new teacher far. However, like all good things it has a shadow-side too, as I was to learn quickly where the fault lines lie by my choice to join the institutional public system in September of 1980.

Sure there were several unpleasant signs of clash during my Bachelor of Education (after) degree at The University of Calgary. I was registered as "a mature student" then (1978), another influential story I'll return to later. Yet, I was totally ready at age 28 to shake the world, and if that was to be in the heart of rural 'Bible-belt' Alberta, so be it. My student teaching prior went great for the most part and I had received lots of kudos for my creative and alive teaching approach. So, after being assigned a grade 5-6 class with no elementary teacher training (I was a secondary science major), it was a lot of "fun" trying to adapt. The eight-grade, four-room school needed a "science" person and that was me. Then I realized I had to teach science across grades 5–8, which was challenging enough; but add on slew of other courses the situation was intense. By mid-second year I was teaching 11 different courses across four grades.

I thrived for the most part in that preposterous challenge. I was young. As well to my advantage the staff, principal and I got on well. Though, I thought things would go downhill fast (and they slowly started to) when the local fundamentalist Christian minister visited my classroom unannounced at the end of a school day. It was like the second week. He was super friendly at first. Then he questioned my teaching evolutionary theory in my life science courses. Wanted to know if I go to church. Uh ha. I knew where that would go. My dad's side of the family were rural Christian evangelicals for the most part. But the Pastor wasn't the only one questioning what I was doing to shape their young people's minds. Some parents also talked to me with worry. One girl in grade five went home crying (apparently) because she thought I was telling her "humans came from apes." She really liked me but natural selection theory went against everything her family and community of the religious believed.

Yet, these were not nearly as significant to my teaching career as was that day, about 7:45 am on a Tuesday morning before school started. The principal came to my room and said there is a call from head office. The Assistant Superintendent wanted to talk with me. So, I walked down the hall, closed the office door and that's when it began. "I heard you on CBC radio yesterday morning. You are facilitating an Alternative Education Conference in Olds next month. Let me remind you that you are a public school teacher. It is a conflict of interest... ".

I don't remember much after those cutting words, and I was immediately on defense and interrupted her berating with "I disagree. This is not a conflict of interest. The alternative and public approaches to education are complementary." She disagreed and hung up on me because she got a clear message that I would not relent on my values and views. I listened to her economic arguments and that's about all. She had no reasonable or educational argument to make against alternative education and its value. She merely didn't want to lose $$/student to an alternative system. That worldview and value system totally disgusted me.

I pretty much knew her slamming the phone down on my ear was a sign that I wouldn't be around long in that county school district. A few nightmarish dreams of working at the school in months following the phone call, and after putting in an exhausting teaching year more, it was late 1981 and I'd chose to give my retirement notice. People were shocked. I taught two years. I realized that I loved teaching but couldn't stand schools. I was voted runner up for "Best First Year Teacher" in the entire county and I was handing in my resignation. Now, there's a tension that was never resolved. The Assistant Superintendent and I really liked each other before that phone call. Regardless, my first wife and I went ahead and held the first Alberta Conference on Alternative Education in 1981, in Olds, AB.

Dr. John Friesen, an educational philosopher at The University of Calgary and a Mennonite attended and gave one of the presentations. I really liked his open-mindedness about learning/teaching when I was in my last year of the Bachelor program. He graciously accepted my bold invitation. The only problem coming onto my doorstep was not having another job to go to. But 1982 (i.e., after June) was my year of freedom—and some major life crises of transformation—for fully exploring alternatives in (mostly) adult education. I was beginning to ask: "What does the term "adult" mean, anyways?" Intuitively, at age 30, I sure didn't want to be one, if they behaved in the ways I had experienced in this society and at the school district administration level.

About three years after retiring, I researched, wrote and self-published a small book on Waldorf (or Rudolf Steiner) Education as an alternative to complement the dominant public education philosophies (Fisher, 1985). I sent a few copies to the assistant superintendent hoping maybe we could also warm-up to each other again and even do some collaboration. I was naive. She responded with a nasty letter after reading it. She basically said, "Why do you have to criticize the public school system in this book? Why don't you just focus on the positive that a Waldorf approach has to offer?" I wrote back answers to her question, more than once. I said I wanted to balance good critique with good offerings of other ways—the negative and positive. She never returned a reply to any of my letters. I found it so hypocritical how she was discouraging my critical thinking, when the very curriculum she and I worked on in science education, while I was a teacher in the district, was all about how to improve critical thinking and inquiry in our young people facing a challenging future world of complexity and ecological crises.

THE WILD 1970s: MY ECO-INTEGRAL GROWING UP

The 1960s had accumulated plenty of collective trauma that I vaguely remember, like President J. F. Kennedy's publicized assassination in Dallas, TX. There were the civil rights protests and sometimes violent riots in the US and the Cuban Missile Crisis, but I think mostly I was too young to take it in. The best early 1970s summer jobs I had were working for Alberta Provincial Parks as a Park Interpreter in Cypress Hills Provincial Park. What fun. I learned how to teach in front of large audiences and guide people on nature tours. There were ups and downs too, and I learned about myself as a teacher and human being. I ended up not going back another summer because I was too critical of tourists asking the same 'dumb' questions on nature trails and taking pictures rather than really paying attention with all their senses to what Nature had to teach them. It was a great experience teaching young kids, seniors, and those disable-bodied and several groups of mentally challenged adults. I learned how to keep a four-year old child, stung by several wasps on the trail hike, in a state of calm by being calm, while his parents were totally freaking out.

My first encounter, as far as I can recall, with transdisciplinarity and integral thinking came after I quit my job in Edmonton with an environmental consulting company. It was a great job right after my diploma at Northern Alberta Institute of Technology in Ecological Sciences (1972-74). The problem was that my boss was very corporate. It was paradoxical, I thought at the time, he was being paid high bucks by the coal strip mining company we were studying and supposed to deliver a scientific (non-biased) environmental impact assessment to the Alberta government. Of course, all staff were also being paid from the same corporate purse, including me the wildlife technician.

I soon learned of the corruption that plagued the industry of environmental consulting. It was insulting to work for them. So off I went to do a BSc. in Environmental Biology (1977-78) at The University of Calgary. Although, I had no form of training in the field of Education, the innate activist-educator in me was already writing and publishing critical educative articles in the Calgary newspaper on pollution and urban planning (Fisher, 1976, 1977, 1979). I was ready to advance my post-secondary schooling and pursue more power/knowledge in order to critique and positively influence society's growth and sustainable ethics.

Luckily, I received two years of credit for my diploma and quickly moved on to take senior classes in advanced evolutionary topics. I'll never forget the mind-blowing experience of taking a 500-level "Mammology" class with Dr. Valerius Geist, an internationally recognized big game (wild sheep) expert, and a professor in the Environmental Design department. His breadth of eclectic knowledge opened my eyes and mind in terms of how to think in transdisciplinary and integral ways. The reading package for the course was primarily his latest unpublished manuscript. I remember the day vividly of finally getting down to the library and signing out the typed paper copy of his book to become. Three huge binders labeled "*Life Strategies*," some 1000 pages or more, that drew me into an intriguing adventure of how someone could collect research from so many different areas and synthesize them, taking many perspectives, and creating a universal "biological theory of health." I knew this was what I wanted to do, and eventually I purchased the expensive published version (Geist, 1978). I bought five copies and sold them or gave them to people. I thought I found the evolutionary bible and 'the way' to design an entirely different and healthy society of sustainability.

Great as that time was in biological sciences, I explored the softer sciences, taking an advanced course in cultural anthropology. Was that ever a mind-shattering ecstatic experience. Because for the first time I read the pioneering work of Erich Jantsch (1976), an eminent evolutionary systems theorist. His complex holistic models were amazing. I had through Jantsch been exposed to the more invisible interiority of life-systems beyond straight-up empirical biology—through autopoesis and emanating from something Jantsch called "consciousness." It opened the world of possible perspectives on reality and myself, and my careers to come. The short of that encounter with Jantsch is that it led me on to read Gregory Bateson (1972, 1979), an incredibly insightful evolutionary systems anthropologist/epistemologist—and, that led to other thinkers of post-adult stages of consciousness (e.g., Ken Wilber), and on and on. It's remarkable that during my initial research for this chapter, I was searching on the topic "transdisciplinary university," thinking about how my chapter might influence and potentially help turn-around (if that's possible for a massive dinosaur) the contemporary neoliberal university. The first author to come up in my research was Erich Jantsch. He'd written a few papers on interdisciplinarity and going beyond that to transdisciplinarity in higher education (e.g., Jantsch, 1972). He was way ahead of his time, and because of that an *outlaw*—not without its costs. Listen to a biographer's description of Jantsch's end of life:

Jantsch was without a job for the last few years of his life, living in an "apartment in Berkeley: dark and depressing room, with massage parlors above and below; a typewriter, a plant, and scattered copies of his favorite newspaper, Neue Zurcher Zeitung. It was here that he finished his last book, The Self-Organizing Universe. He made a living and supported his mother "by giving lectures all over the world, through writing, and by relying on a few friends....Jantsch died on December 12, 1980 in Berkeley, California, "alone and lonely, abandoned by friends, misunderstood by colleagues." His ashes were scattered over the Pacific Ocean.[3]

I'm indebted to his path alone with integrity and pursuit of understanding the self-organizing creative universe from a systems perspective. By the late 1970s, I was understanding what systems theory and the evolution of consciousness was really about and how radical it was (still is), and how it ought to be foundationally informing the nature of education in the shaping of healthy, sane and sustainable societies. That was the end of the radical 1970s, and I had switched to do a Bachelor of Education (after) degree (1979-80) so that I could influence children, their worldviews and their values appropriate for the next generations and the challenging if not fearful future coming.

I specialized in Secondary Science but mostly loved the radical Environmental Education literature, Futures Studies, and Paulo Freire's Critical Pedagogy notions. I wish I had space to talk about professor Tad Guzzie, who taught Religious Education at The University of Calgary, and how he introduced me to William James, Carl J. Jung and other thinkers who extended my interior consciousness into exploring dreams and trance-states as possible realities that exist. There's all too many threads to link in this short chapter, but you likely get the sense of how I was influenced at the time by deep cultural and spiritual infusions and changes in the Eco-Movement.

So, I arrived with a lot of critique to my first public school teaching job in 1980 (the above "Clash" story). I was still evolving from *rebel* to *adult* but much of what I loved learning about was stretching me beyond adult to post-adult, what Keen called the *outlaw*. The entire field of ecology with its activists and philosophers (e.g., Bateson) really were mature outlaws. They were my heroes and implicit mentors, not the schoolteachers and education professors at university. I found the latter very boring for the most part. This led me to become an 'outsider' amongst my peers. These days, when I reflect back, I think I was more of a 'geek' than I would ever admit then.[4] No one seemed to understand me; I couldn't find my 'tribe.' Not that I thought I was all that brilliant. I wasn't very tolerant of them either. Yet, they were all understandable but I didn't want to understand things anymore the way they did. They were behind the times, too far. I was pretty judgmental and they must have known. So, "clash" was the theme of those years during the bachelor's degree and after into the funky "new age" 1980's.

AQUARIAN CONSPIRACY: NEW PARADIGM OF THE 1980s

While finishing off my brief teaching career in public schools, my wife at the time and I had a child. We also joined a conscious learning community called Common Ground. It was led by a charismatic older woman[5] who had reading groups at her humble rented home in the country. I in awe around her worldly knowledge and wisdom and found out she had been on a long healing journey, traveling to many places around the globe. I realized how local my own life-experiences had been. She was greatly influenced by the "new age" and "ecological" and organic farming resistance movements in California and elsewhere. She bought us copies of a catalytic book by Marilyn Ferguson (1980) called *Aquarian Conspiracy* and I learned about what old and new paradigms of politics, of gender, of health, of spirituality and education might be. It was a 'heady' and ideal time of growth and development for the whole community and we were sure that we could change the world for the better. It was the first time I had joined a consciousness and social movement *per se*. Our vision in that community was based on 'think globally, act locally.' The number of courses and workshops in new physics, altered realities, bodywork, authentic relationships, energy healing, and learning to learn were phenomenal. We did it all ourselves. 'We took the future in our own hands.'[6] It was so important that we not fear the future, if we wanted to be well prepared for it (Fisher, 1984). We taught and learned, critiqued ourselves and changed. And, of course, like all such conscious communities they have inner conflicts and after nine years of thriving the project fell apart and a lot of people were disgruntled.

After I retired from school teaching I imagined a living could be made doing full-time wildlife art, and to my surprise it actually could. With that third career now blooming, we had a second child and pressures were growing to find more lucrative work. Yet, I was endlessly curious to keep learning everything I could about consciousness and human potential. One day in The University of Calgary bookstore I picked up a book entitled *Up From Eden* by Ken Wilber (1981). I'd not heard of this dude. The book's table of contents was absolutely fascinating to me, as it was fresh because I had not read a lot about transpersonal philosophy or psychology that he advocated at the time. In this book, his darkest one of all his career as a philosopher, Wilber told the universal 'big story' of human cultural evolution in a way that made sense and was not taught by any other author I had read, and I had read a lot of books by then. I studied his "spectrum of consciousness" model in another book he'd written earlier (when he was 23 years old) (Wilber, 1977). Then I read more. I couldn't get enough of this thinker/teacher. Many years later he began to call himself no longer a transpersonalist but an integralist—eventually he developed Integral Theory and by then had an enormous following of fans around the world. Wilber's work was post-adult education, delving into and informed by the postformal stages of cognition/thinking (e.g., see Gidley, 2017). My notion of what a human being was and could be totally got rewired, in a good way. I can't thank Wilber enough for being my 'teacher' from afar.

My wife and I began a group in Olds to start a Waldorf School, of which I wanted to bring in ideas of Ken Wilber. I sent off an application to enter the masters program in transformative education and leadership to the California Institute of Integral Studies. I had heard it was the place to study for people like me that wanted an alternative higher education experience. And Ken Wilber apparently taught there now and then as well. I received a go from CIIS and a $500 scholarship. Unfortunately, the fates of being a father with family and not enough income made it impossible to follow that dream.

I was really getting into Wilber's early work but noticed that even the Green-sensitive[7] and open-minded Common Ground community showed little interest. A few had severe postmodern critiques of Wilber's philosophy. I was on my own with it and didn't know enough to argue back. While changing baby's diapers and staying up most of the night walking a crying baby girl and doing fine art work, I found time to punch away on my old manual typewriter a unique and passionate application of the foundations of a book, using the framing of Wilber's spectrum theory of consciousness applied to mainstream education curriculum (Fisher, 1983). That manuscript lies covered with dust in a dark drawer of my file cabinet to this day. I keep wondering if I could resurrect it.

Our progressive learning community invited in famous Canadian futurists like Ruben Nelson to talk about how paradigm shifts take place in organizations and society. He was the co-founder of The Canadian Transformation Network out of Ottawa and predicted Alberta would be a leader of this shift. Nelson introduced us to the Assistant Deputy Minister of Education at the time, Des Berghoffer, and we found his writings and educational philosophy advanced beyond anything in higher education we had seen before. The man really cared about a sustainable future, and had a vision, of which I typically find missing in all bureaucrats and most educational leaders today. It really seemed like a transformative (r)evolution in education was happening right in our area and province and we all wanted to be co-participants if not leaders. Of course, reality hit. Berghoffer left his job or maybe he was pushed out *via* an increasing conservative government and voting public? We lost touch with him. Nelson went on to business consulting and disappeared too, until he ran for politics in Alberta but then he became harder and harder to connect with. In reflecting on all this, I must say that I have never known for Alberta to be so progressive as it was in those days. What happened?

THE 1990s: A TIME TO LEAD THINGS MY WAY

What I've learned about change and transformation theories is that they are grand, but they are also resisted like mad by the *status quo*. Nothing moves forward without many steps backwards and a lot of pain and disappointment, especially when one is trying to change progressively within the context of basically conservative and fear-based societies. I have never lived and worked in California, so my experience is that most places are pretty conservative in North America—at least, in Alberta and even W. Canada where I mostly have been. To my mind, progressive educators and activists are too often unrealistically over-expectant of the positive possibilities of progression—and, often end-up very depressed with what actually happens in institutional systems.

Unfortunately, the State-controlled systems of Education are characteristically very conservative and fear-based (e.g., Fisher, 1998, 2003a, 2003b, 2007a). I know that because of comparisons with my investment into other careers in Environmental Management, Health, Rehabilitation, and Adult Education—the latter, which is outside of strict government regulations and tends to be freer of social norms. Although, adult education *via* Continuing Education had lost its radical political strength and legitimation for transformation. This was mainly because of the new climate of neoliberalism since the mid-1990s (e.g., see Giroux, 2014).

To counter all the conservative apolitical and ahistorical trending and emphasis on economics and credentialism, I started my own institute and learning community to try to do things different that were really liberating (Fisher, 1996).[8] It all began when I moved from Olds back to Calgary (my hometown) in 1988. I finished a successful year of grad school in Educational Psychology (Rehabilitation Studies) and accumulated great field experience from several years working with troubled youth and their families at Quest Ranch, just west of Cremona, AB. I had gained therapeutic skills there and knew how to work with people of all kinds, especially care staff, who were mostly fearful and resistant to change the traditional program from behavioral (i.e., punishment) control to a therapeutic community approach. I brought in transpersonal psychology, and Sam Keen's developmental map, and Joseph Campbell's mythological work to create a hero's identity map for these youth, whereby they could see their "rebel" in a new frame of both challenging the "adult" and potentially healing and growing beyond the adult stage to "outlaw." They really liked that concept and their motivation to improve their lives was enhanced.

I taught an adult continuing education course called "Basics to the Path of Fearlessness" as a personal growth and liberation initiative for post-adult development at the University of Calgary between 1992–95. We did some 'wild' things in that class, as it truly helped several people get beyond a life-style they were living based on fear, the *status quo*, and just boring. And, there were some people who hated it and me and dropped out after the first or second class. They complained to officials but never talked to me. The Continuing Education administration didn't like that I was upsetting a few people and they cancelled the course. I can pretty much guarantee there are no such risky courses offered in Continuing Education like that anymore, anywhere, at least not in Canada in mainstream universities.

During this time, emotions and deep motivations (especially, unconscious fear) became my main focus of research and influenced my teaching/learning from the mid-1980s to late 1990s. I co-founded the In Search of Fearlessness Project (1989-) as a global (not-for-profit) liberation movement. Fear seemed the greatest limiting factor in all of society as far as I was concerned, and I wasn't the only one I knew of expressing those concerns as such in the field. Critics in education (e.g., Wieder, 1978; Palmer, 1998) and sociologists (e.g., Furedi, 1997; Glassner, 1999) were some of the people I read at the time but they never took fear studies to the level of depth and seriousness I did. They pointed to an ever-growing "culture of fear" as context for much of Western cultures in the modern world. I kept asking how are teachers in schools and higher education going to prepare themselves for this new world so fearful? The Cold War ended in 1989–90 but the decade of the 1990s was conflicted as ever with new smaller wars and terrorism on the rise. This was all symptomatic of what would lead up to the tragedy of 9/11, 2001.

I pursued a rigorous study of Ken Wilber's Integral Theory, even attended the very first conference in San Francisco, CA in 1995 on Wilber's work. Wilber had sent me his unpublished manuscript for *Sex, Ecology and Spirituality* in 1994 and asked me for written feedback. This book (Wilber, 1995) was incredibly influential to my thinking about many things. I was pretty high at that point. I was also teaching a few "Introduction to Ken Wilber" courses at the In Search of Fearlessness Center in downtown Calgary. Few attended and no one really got it then, virtually no one had heard of this guy and didn't much care. Calgary was not San Francisco or Boulder, CO.

Pursuing my writing and critique on fear and its (mis-)uses (beginning with Fisher, 1984), I began my most systematic articulation with a series of technical papers devoted to clarification of a critical integral "spectrum" theory of 'fear' that was transdisciplinary (e.g., Fisher, 1995a, 1995b). I have published over 70 technical papers in this series. Most people back then couldn't understand these works and were even annoyed that I was making the topic of "fear" more serious and complex than they thought it ought to be. One person from the "new age" movement of the time saw one of my technical papers and said "the print is too small and reading it makes my head hurt." End of story—that was enough to make them not read it further. I thought that was impatient, if not intolerant. Those times were incredibly stimulating intellectually—I was on a roll. I was able to create a 'fear' vaccine curriculum process of praxis[9] that really worked for many people.

However, like all good things that are liberating there are forces that work to oppress it. The Fearlessness Project (Calgary) ended abruptly in 1998 due to lack of funds and internal conflict. I couldn't stand the hypocrisy of the Board of Directors of the non-profit society that tried to control how I wanted to lead the organization as unpaid Director of the Center itself. Vested interests and personalities clashed. I own my own share of anger that I probably didn't manage all that well at times. So more than a little exhausted and broke, my wife then (Barbara Bickel) and I left to attend The University of British Columbia to pursue graduate school. I started with an Master of Arts in Adult Education and loved studying transformative learning theories (e.g., Mezirow, 1990) and also critical pedagogy/andragogy. It was a great time also to introduce Wilber's integral approach into my study of conflict for my thesis. But my peers, faculty and supervisors didn't get it either—or didn't choose to get it—as they were mostly postmodernists and leftists very critical of Wilber's grand theory narrative of evolution. There was little respect from them. They didn't much like developmental hierarchy theories period. I had to figure out how to negotiate all that and so I stayed low to the margins—didn't talk about my radical integral ideas about fear ('fear') and fearlessness, that is, not until my doctorate degree.

TURN OF THE 21ST CENTURY: MY 50s ONWARD

Things really came together for me during the heat of the turn of the century, despite the fact of so much excessive fear that was created because of the Y2K scare and the general apocalyptic terror of the turn of the millenium, when many people carried a sense that the world was going to end. I predicted all the fear breeding before 2000 was just a symptom of greater fears below—ones left over and post-traumatic from the growing ecological disasters, wars, AIDS epidemic, etc. Despite the young people starting to create "NO FEAR! logo-wear and 'fighting back,' I felt society overall was quickly unravelling. For my part, I believed it had to before it would ever transform itself into something less fear-based. Years later, Barber's (2003) book on the collapse of "Fear's Empire" in America was pretty much saying the same thing as I was thinking much earlier. However, what positively came together for me was the theoretical puzzle linking my study of fear, of Ken Wilber's integral work and my sharp focus as a curriculum designer for the 21st century, in a world challenged by cascading global crises. I'll get to that connection in a moment.

As graduate school proceeded my question was basically: How are we going to equip our future school teachers (and professors) with adequate knowledge and meta-skills to be able to manage fear/terror and how to create high quality education for students of all ages? I graduated with an MA in 2000 and began my dissertation in Curriculum and Instruction completed in 2003. I had a graduate assistantship to create a Ken Wilber Study Group and had a couple progressive co-supervisors, who thank goodness, let me do pretty much what I wanted to in my doctoral program as long as it was academically original and rigorous. It was great for the most part and receiving a prestigious fully-funded Social Sciences and Humanities Research award for three years made it a lot sweeter. I started the first Ken Wilber and Integral Education Newsletter in Canada on my website (2001-03), I turned my office into an art studio and I began studying the "culture of fear" in every possible angle I could think of. I created art installations[10] in the student union art gallery a few times, did art performances and was giving talks at conferences on the nature and role of fear in education and leadership.

Wilber's (2000) book *A Theory of Everything* was the practical book on his work that I had been waiting for. He integrated Clare Graves's work in developmental (futurist) psychology and cultural evolution, while working with some of Grave's students, who began Spiral Dynamics[11] integral theory and technology (SDi). I took the Level 1 and 2 Training in SDi. In a nutshell, SDi and Wilber made sense of culture value-memes and how they carry, with great power, a particular (and developmental) worldview consciousness structure with beliefs and values that can be identified, measured and passed on analogous to gene-coding but more easily. Green values-meme was the structure and worldview of the Ecological/Environmental Movement and Feminism, and Civil Rights—all of which were background contexts that I grew up and into, including what hippies all loved. My views on Education were completely coloured by this values-meme, and equally by my transdisciplinary study of fear (and 'fear')—see my design for a new field of 'Fear' Studies (Fisher, 2006, 2018).

The inspiring 'story' that SDi theory tells is how Green[12] value-meme is only one in a spectrum of about nine equally important v-memes available to human consciousness—ranging from the most primal Beige value-meme to nondual Coral value-meme. Wilber has modified this spectral schema over the years to fit more his own theory; nonetheless, there was something that Graves, Beck and Cowan and Wilber all agreed on, and that was that there were six value-memes (and/or worldviews) that were "first-tier" and then there was a developmental jump (potential) in consciousness required (like over an abyss, or "quantum leap")—and, this was to "second-tier."[13] The latter tier was very similar to the educational psychology work coming out on postformal thinking (e.g., Robert Kegan et al.). I found this all met the same criteria, more or less, as Keen's "outlaw" stage or my own work on fear management systems (FMS) theory, in which I identified there are nine FMS in the evolution of humanity since the beginning of recorded history (see Fisher, 2010). I was attempting then (and still am) to create an entirely new second-tier curriculum of *fear education* (analogous to sex education, moral education, spiritual education).

The back-up for my integral approach, which I argued was no longer fear-based because it was second-tier (FMS-7, Yellow v-meme), came from the writings of Graves, Beck and Cowan and Wilber. They all agreed that there was in the quantum leap from first-tier systems (v-memes) to second-tier systems (v-memes) an identifiable distinction in the driving meta-motivational forces in individuals, groups and institutions. The leap was from a fear-based structure (which Maslow, 1968 called "deficit" motivation based on fear) to one that is no longer driven by fear as the primary motivator (Maslow called "growth" motivation based on love).[14] I now had the answer and basis for what I called a *fearlessness* curriculum and pedagogy where the very notion of "critical thinking" and "critical theory" needed to be deconstructed and reconstructed (e.g., Fisher, 2011). Implications of my theory for integral, holistic and integrative approaches to education have been hinted at but as yet I have not written those full critiques.

It was a huge project then (still is), and one that Wilber and the Integral Circles have largely ignored. I learned the hard way that there is a power/knowledge (political and ideological) structure everywhere, even in the Integral Movement and it prevents some 'voices' from being heard, while it foregrounds and promotes others. You may have watched the futurist sci-fi movie trilogy "The Matrix" by the Wachowski Bros. (1999-2003). It is an incredible story and tells of how this 'Fear' Matrix of our world works.[15] If you don't conform to the Program (The Matrix) you will be deleted (marginalized). Being naive about these things is not going to help anyone. From this experience I learned that all movements, even second-tier ones need to be continually critiqued from inside and outside. I attempted to do that when I systematically analyzed Ken Wilber's critics and how Wilber responded to them in Fisher (1997)—and, it turned out Wilber and others around him did not want to hear what I had to say.[16] Integral educators that came along in the last 20 years also were not at all interested in my critical integral theory and ideas about fear management /education.

EPILOGUE

This brings this version of my 45-year teaching/learning story to a close. I wish to critique my contribution in the space that remains, rather than try to summarize it neatly. I notice that the five criteria for a high-quality narrative (Heikkinen et al, 2007) that I mentioned at the beginning of the methodology section are very applicable to my writing. My interest is that this writing (story) is itself integrally-informed and integrated with what it is I am promoting—that is, transdisciplinarity as action research and an integral approach. How much action research is in this chapter is debateable, it is more an invisible phenomenon. I simply never did serious action research all these years with all the rigor required. It was implicit that people (myself included) were changing and transforming because of what I facilitated.

By contrast, the fear and fearlessness research within this story is very rigorous and transdisciplinary in that I utilized critical educators,' artists,' sociologists,' political scientists,' anthropologists' perspectives among others. It is obvious that I refuse to delimit the meaning of "fear" within Psychology/Psychiatry for example. I go beyond the clinical perspective and make the topic relevant across all aspects of society, although I probably could have done a better job talking about the spiritual perspective—and, especially in regard to my own spirituality. I rate myself four out of five points for using the principle of *reflexivity* in the analysis, as it seems I am always talking about myself reflectively and what I have learned over these 45 years, although I left out the spiritual dimension explicitly. I rate the *historical continuity* principle as very high because of the constant historical and cultural context I bring into my own history, views, value systems and my aims in educational research and teaching/learning.

As for the principle of *workability* I would rate myself lowest (2.5 out of five) in that I never covered much of the very specific ways or methods to apply my fear management systems theory and the integral approach to education overall. It turns out, within the confines of space provided, I preferred theoretical and intellectual speculation with history. Although, I have presented a few cases studies (in communities).[17] In some sense, that focus is somewhat contradictory to my interest in bringing in the affective and emotional dimension to narrative inquiry—a point, I made early on in the paper as I critiqued narratives generally and educational research. On this same grounds, I would give myself only a 3.5 out of five for the principle of *evocativeness*—well, maybe I'd go as high as a 4.5 actually, or maybe five, because I think this whole narrative of my 45 years is radical and challenging to the readers. Whether you know it or not, I am evoking a spirit of fearlessness and an imperative to become "unplugged" from the 'Fear' Matrix (e.g., Fisher, 2009). I only briefly mentioned 9/11 and post-9/11 as contexts directly. Fact is, this context continues to be very important in my work but that deserves more attention than I could give it here. But as to how evocative or not this chapter and my life is, that I will only know when readers give me direct feedback, which I welcome.[18]

Regarding the last principle *dialectics* I am not so sure. I like to think I am a true blue dialectical thinker when it comes to integral development and evolution. The story I wanted to write about was just too complex and demanding to wrestle with for one chapter. If I wrote a book on my 45 years I'd think a lot more about this. I will say however, that the section on "fear-based" vs. "love-based" implied and stated (e.g., Maslow's theory of motivation) is the core foundation of my dialectics—with "fearlessness" as the operating motivational force running between fear and love (see Fisher, 2017). Yet, that's all another long conversation I wish educators of every stripe would undertake.

Overall, this is a fairly good example of an integral story. If anything, perhaps my teaching/learning life will serve as a model for what you as a teacher/researcher and life-long learner will strive for and/or be cautious of beyond naiveté. Perhaps, it will act as an authentic mirror and remind you of all that you are already doing that is part of the Fearlessness Movement,[19] even if you've not heard of it.

REFERENCES

Barber, B. (2003). *Fear's empire: War, terrorism, and democracy*. New York: W. W. Norton.

Bateson, G. (1972). *Steps to an ecology of mind: Collected essays in anthropology, psychiatry, evolution, and epistemology*. Chicago, IL: University of Chicago Press.

Bateson, G. (1979). *Mind and nature: A necessary unity*. New York: Hampton Press.

Beck, D., & Cowan, C. (1996). *Spiral dynamics: Mastering values, leadership and change*. Cambridge, MA: Blackwell.

Crittenden, J. (1997). Foreword: What is the meaning of "Integral?" In *The eye of spirit: An integral vision for a world gone slightly mad* (pp. vii–xii). Boston, MA: Shambhala.

Ferguson, M. (1980). *The Aquarian conspiracy: Personal and social transformation in the 1980s*. Los Angeles, CA: J. P. Tarcher.

Fisher, R. M. (1976, January). Air pollution in Calgary. *Calgary Herald*, 17.

Fisher, R. M. (1977, October). Mechanized monsters invade creek. *Calgary Herald*, 15.

Fisher, R. M. (1979, September). Support positive planners. *Calgary Herald*, 26.

Fisher, R. M. (1983). *Appropriate education: Education as if the human being mattered*. Unpublished.

Fisher, R. M. (1984, June). Future not to be feared. *Olds Optimist*, 10.

Fisher, R. M. (1985). *The Waldorf experience: Education as an art*. Old, Canada: Janus Alternatives.

Fisher, R. M. (1995a). *An introduction to defining 'fear': A spectrum approach*. Technical Paper No. 1. Calgary, Canada: In Search of Fearlessness Research Institute.

Fisher, R. M. (1996). Dare to contradict, dare to distinguish; Into the flaming heart of the. In *Search of Fearlessness Project*. Calgary, Canada: In Search of Fearlessness Research Institute.

Fisher, R. M. (1997). A guide to Wilberland: Some common misunderstandings of the critics of Ken Wilber and his work on transpersonal theory prior to 1995. *Journal of Humanistic Psychology*, *37*(4), 30–73. doi:10.1177/00221678970374005

Fisher, R. M. (1998). *Culture of 'fear': Toxification of landscape-mindscape as meta-context for education in the 21st century*. Technical Paper No. 7. Vancouver: In Search of Fearlessness Research Institute.

Fisher, R. M. (2003a). *A report on the status of fear education*. Technical Paper No. 15. Vancouver: In Search of Fearlessness Research Institute.

Fisher, R. M. (2003b). *Fearless leadership in and out of the 'Fear' Matrix* (Unpublished dissertation). Vancouver: The University of British Columbia.

Fisher, R. M. (2006). Invoking 'Fear' Studies. *Journal of Curriculum Theorizing, 22*(4), 39–71.

Fisher, R. M. (2007a). *Education and the culture of fear: A review*. Technical Paper No. 25. Vancouver: In Search of Fearlessness Research Institute.

Fisher, R. M. (2007b). *Ken Wilber and the education literature: Abridged annotated bibliography*. Retrieved from http://www.pathsoflearning-net/resources_writings _Ken_Wilber.pdf

Fisher, R. M. (2009). *"Unplugging" as real and metaphoric: Emancipatory dimensions to* The Matrix *film trilogy*. Technical Paper No. 33. Carbondale, IL: In Search of Fearlessness Research Institute.

Fisher, R. M. (2010). *The world's fearlessness teachings: A critical integral approach to fear management/education in the 21st century*. Lanham, MD: University Press of America.

Fisher, R. M. (2011). A critique of critical thinking: Towards a critical integral pedagogy of fearlessness. *NUML: Journal of Critical Inquiry, 9*(2), 92–104.

Fisher, R. M. (2017). Radical love, is it radical enough? *International Journal of Critical Pedagogy, 8*(1), 261–281.

Fisher, R. M. (2018). *'Fear' Studies, 12 years later: Progress and barriers*. Technical Paper No. 74. Calgary, Canada: In Search of Fearlessness Research Institute.

Fisher, R. M. (1995b). *An introduction to an epistemology of 'fear': A fearlessness paradigm*. Technical Paper No. 2. Calgary, Canada: In Search of Fearlessness Research Institute.

Fisher, R. M., & Subba, D. (2016). *Philosophy of fearism: A first East-West dialogue*. Xlibris.

Furedi, F. (1997). *Culture of fear: Risk and the morality of low expectation*. London, UK: Cassell.

Geist, V. (1978). *Life strategies, human evolution, environmental design: Toward a biological theory of health*. New York: Springer-Verlag. doi:10.1007/978-1-4612-6325-8

Gidley, J. (2017). *Postformal education: A philosophy for complex futures*. New York: Springer.

Giroux, H. A. (2014). *Neoliberalism's war on higher education*. Chicago, IL: Haymarket Books.

Glassner, B. (1999). *The culture of fear: Why Americans are afraid of the wrong things*. New York: Basic Books.

Heikkinen, H. L. T., Huttunen, R., Syrjala, L., & Pesonen, J. (2012). Action research and narrative inquiry: Five principles for validation revisited. *Educational Action Research, 20*(1), 5–21. doi:10.1080/09650792.2012.647635

Jantsch, E. (1972). Inter- and transdisciplinarity university. *Higher Education, 1*(1), 7–37. doi:10.1007/BF01956879

Jantsch, E. (1976). Evolving images of man: Dynamic guidance for the mankind process. In E. Jantsch & C. H. Waddington (Eds.), *Evolution and consciousness: Human systems in transition*. New York: Addison-Wesley.

Keen, S. (1983). *The passionate life: Stages of loving*. New York: Harper and Row.

Leitch, R., & Day, C. (2000). Action research and reflective practice: Towards a holistic view. *Journal of Educational Action Research*, 8(1), 179–193. doi:10.1080/09650790000200108

Maslow, A. (1968). *Toward a psychology of being*. New York: Van Nostrand Reinhold.

Mezirow, J. (1990). *Fostering critical reflection in adulthood: A guide to transformative and emancipatory learning*. San Francisco, CA: Jossey-Bass.

Palmer, P. (1998). *The courage to teach: Exploring the inner landscapes of others*. New York: Harper and Row.

Scholz, R. W. (2017). The normative dimension in transdisciplinarity, transition management, and transformation sciences: New roles of science and universities in sustainable transitioning. *Sustainability*, 9(6), 1–35. doi:10.3390u9060991

Schwandt, T. A. (2007). *The SAGE dictionary of qualitative research* (3rd ed.). London: SAGE. doi:10.4135/9781412986281

Wieder, C. G. (1978). *Fear and force versus education: A study of the effects of coercion on learning*. Branden Press.

Wilber, K. (1977/82). *Spectrum of consciousness*. Wheaton, IL: Theosophical Publishing House.

Wilber, K. (1981). *Up from Eden: A transpersonal view of human evolution*. New York: Anchor/Doubleday.

Wilber, K. (1995). *Sex, ecology and spirituality: The spirit in evolution* (Vol. 1). Boston, MA: Shambhala.

Wilber, K. (2000). *A theory of everything: An integral vision for business, politics, science, and spirituality*. Boston, MA: Shambhala.

KEY TERMS AND DEFINITIONS

Fearlessness: A paradigm, a fear management system, an integral-level second-tier consciousness structure that no longer is motivated by fear as primary; is a historical movement to contradict and "managed" excess fear accumulation in living systems and is a behavioral attitude and set of virtues and practices that are aligned with courageous but transcend it because there is a deep desire to know everything (integrally) about the nature and role of fear as a troubling, complex and contextual cultural and sociopolitical phenomenon.

ENDNOTES

1. A fearologist participates in the study of fearology.
2. Somewhere around early 2000, Wilber decided to label his own approach Integral Theory—both with caps to distinguish it from other forms of integral theory. I mostly utilize Wilber's work but also do not conform my own work necessarily within his strict Integral Theory and rules.
3. Retrieved from http://leahmacvie.com/blog/erichjantsch/
4. As I reflect back, I had two impressive and consistent practices which served me well to grow in my thinking and be a better teacher. The first was that I read beyond the field of Education. In fact, I had a disciplined reading practice where I would go to the U of C library "Recent Journals" stacks and scan virtually every journal across every discipline. I was looking for any title of an article, or particular author that stood out. I would often read it and/or photocopy it and keep it in files. I collected thousands of these articles and they really expanded my vocabulary and connected webs of ideas and intelligence. The second was to write and publish articles that had little or nothing to do with what I was studying in Education or as demanded by my assignments. I basically did this to keep my mind alive and to practice being a writer, meaning to be a good communicator. I still do these practices at times, although much less so than back then.
5. I acknowledge gratefully Jean Robertson especially for her leadership and the assistant support of the late Prosper Williams.
6. I quote these words as there were a number of large gatherings our Common Ground community attended all around W. Canada and in the USA, which more or less were part of a generic movement at the time called "Taking the Future in Our Own Hands." Upon reflection today, that slogan is exactly what the best of the emancipatory W. adult education movements were about in the late 19th and early 20th century of workers/unions adult education movements, and the civil rights adult education movements.
7. "Green" refers to the Eco-movement worldview and values in general, but it will also be refined below by the theory of Spiral Dynamics (see Beck and Cowan, 1990) and Wilber's interpretation of value-meme theory and cultural evolution.
8. This took the form of the In Search of Fearlessness Research Institute (1991-), which offers a platform for inter- and transdisciplinary research, teaching and publishing on fear and fearlessness. Archives of some of this Project can be found at https://fearlessnessmovement.ning.com/forum/in-search-of-fearlessness-isof-project-archives.
9. The six 'fear' vaccines are: (1) Good Information on fear and fearlessness, (2) Liberation Peer Counseling as learning how we are hurt and heal, (3) Community-building, (4) Sacred Warriorship, (5) Spontaneous Creation-making and, (6) Vision Quest.
10. The largest one was called "Platinum 'Fear'—*plat du jour*" which consisted of 71 collage art pieces (9 X 9 in.), which looked at how society produces and consumes fear ('fear') and makes it a habit to do so.
11. E.g., see Beck and Cowan (1990).
12. According to SDi theory these colors are arbitrarily assigned to the value-memes, other than cooler and warmer colors,,which represent the communal and individual v-memes respectively. It just happens that "green" value-meme fits nicely with the Eco-Green Movement overall.

13 I am horribly simplifying this all but it is worth noting that there is also a "third-tier" consciousness and worldview (with its own v-memes).
14 See Fisher (2010), pp. 70, 75.
15 See Fisher (2003), as The Matrix film narrative and characters became the foundational part of my dissertation, as I was attempting to create a performative piece of curriculum that demonstrated how the 'Fear' Matrix (my term) actually works—and, to create a new meta-myth for our times, of which this sci-fi trilogy offers in great emancipatory (albeit, postmodern) ways.
16 I have several personal correspondence letters with Wilber at the early stages and into the editing of this article (1994-1996). Wilber basically thought my paper was excellent in scholarship and accurate, except he thought I gave all his critics too much ink again. Oh, and he did *not* acknowledge (or likely appreciate) at the same time that I labeled his pattern of responses to most critics of his work as "unnecessarily arrogant" (Fisher, 1997, p. 30).
17 One project that deserves a chapter on its own is my founding of the Center for Spiritual Inquiry and Integral Education (2009-16) in southern Illinois, as an alternative higher education online program.
18 I'd be glad to discuss this material. Contact: r.michaelfisher52@gmail.com.
19 For more information on this see https://fearlessnessmovement.ning.com/.

Chapter 16
Reimagining Sustainability Leadership:
Integral Action Research in a Non-Profit Organization

Justin Robinson
Royal Roads University, Canada

ABSTRACT

This research explored how the stakeholders of Integral Without Borders (IWB)—an international think tank and NGO focused on applying integral metatheory to sustainable development—might reimagine sustainability leadership to increase their collective capacity for wise and transforming action in the world. Applying an integral action research methodology in the context of an action research engagement model, eight individual interviews, two focus groups, and an open space lab were conducted with participation from an international cohort of IWB's stakeholders. The study identified fertile territories from which the possibility space for sustainability leadership might be expanded, specifically "four Rs" of integral transformation praxis: (1) revive, (2) reidentify, (3) recode, and (4) reconfigure. Recommendations relevant to IWB's specific leadership goals and development as an organization were also proposed.

INTRODUCTION

Context

This study focused on implicit and explicit dimensions of Integral Without Borders' sustainability leadership. Integral Without Borders (IWB) is a non-profit society[1] incorporated in British Columbia (BC), Canada that operates like an informally structured community of development practitioners and social change activists working in a number of countries around the globe (IWB, What we do, n.d.). IWB fosters impact by "supporting practitioners and organizations to bring greater clarity, depth, and rigor to their global development efforts" (IWB, Vision and purpose, n.d.). The board is committed to helping

DOI: 10.4018/978-1-5225-5873-6.ch016

agents of social and environmental change generate deep transformation, by providing "support for the advance of an integral approach" within their initiatives (IWB, Vision and purpose, n.d.).

At the nucleus of this global community is the IWB board consisting of eight people: one currently based in Vancouver, one in Latin America, one in the California, two in the United Kingdom (UK), two in Norway, and Ken Wilber, the originator of Integral Metatheory (IM), in Boulder, Colorado. Wilber is less involved operationally and acts more as a special advisor to the board. Periodically, additional field-based volunteers participate in specific projects and engagements from other locations.

Unlike many international development organizations, IWB does not focus on a single issue or methodological approach to change. Instead, it seeks to positively impact a broad range of issues and approaches through the application of IM: a framework that bears significant potential as a source of robust solutions to the multidimensional, interlocking, complex dilemmas currently faced by the human species (Hedlund, Esbjörn-Hargens, Hartwig and Bhaskar, 2016; Stein, 2105, 2016, in review; Edwards, 2010). In practice, IM has been used in numerous contexts to expand the possibilities for positive change. For example, IM has been applied in the areas of climate adaptation and mitigation (Esbjörn-Hargens, 2010; O'Brien & Hochachka, 2010), international development (Hochachka, 2008), psychotherapy (Witt, 2014), addiction (du Plessis, 2013), organizational development (Laloux, 2014), education (Stein, 2009, 2013), and other fields. One of IWB's principal interests is how an approach informed by IM might produce or enable transformations at the level of planetary systems and culture, leading to a more just and sustainable future for humanity.

In the months leading up to and during the study, IWB was in transition. Four new directors joined the board, two stepped down, and the long-standing Executive Director moved out of her role (although she continues to serve on the board of the organization). As these shifts took effect internally with IWB, unprecedented worldwide geopolitical, cultural, and technological changes also surfaced the possibility—or perhaps more appropriately, the necessity—of rethinking how IWB can best contribute to planetary transformation. Specifically, IWB's intent participating in this integral action research project was to harness these internal and external shifts to build energy and capacity for bringing-into-being the highest possibilities for "what sustainability leadership actually is or could be in today's moment" (G. Hochachka, personal communication, March 1st, 2017).

Purpose

This project brought together different perspectives from within IWB's orbit. Inquiry participants included IWB board members, current and past members of the organization's global community of practitioners, and individuals who supported the organization's work. Together these participants explored the question: "How might the stakeholders of IWB reimagine sustainability leadership in a way that increases their collective capacity for wise and transforming action in the world?"

There were several challenges with framing the inquiry project this way. To address one of the most obvious, it is important to acknowledge that the very phrase "sustainability leadership" is suspect: *Leadership* is notoriously challenging to define. It is a topic that is "vast, amorphous, slippery, and, above all, desperately important" (Bennis, 2007, p. 2). Perhaps the nature of *sustainability* is even more resistant to clarification. Mulvihill and Milan (2007) observed that the word is fraught with paradox and futility, and that "many use it reluctantly, lamenting the lack of better terms to frame discussion" (p. 658). The inherent contradictions of many sustainability initiatives, they suggested, tells us that a sustainable human presence on the planet is not only something we don't know how to bring about—it is something we are currently incapable of imagining.

We should not trick ourselves into thinking that we can understand our normative commitment to sustainability leadership when we do not have a clear sense of what it looks like in practice or what it requires of us. Kenneth Burke (1984) concluded that, when "the conditions of living have undergone radical changes since the time when [our] scheme of duties and virtues was crystallized, the serviceability of [our] orientation [i.e. our responses to situations, implied before-the-fact in how we have grown to understand—or fail to understand—them] may be impaired" (p. 21). Surely there has never been a time in history to which such a statement was more applicable. As Stein (2016) noted:

some argue that the species as a whole faces an impending identity crisis as the unchecked proliferation of informational and biological technologies create abrupt discontinuities in the intergenerational fabric of the lifeworld, catapulting us out of history and into forms of life that are incongruent and incomprehensible. (p. 36)

For this and other reasons, we face not just a crisis, but a "metacrisis"—a rapidly evolving set of interlocking, planetary, multidimensional issues that exist on multiple time scales and pose deep existential and moral problems for the human species—constituting a crucible that humanity may not survive, and most assuredly will not survive in its current embodiment (Hedlund, Esbjörn-Hargens, Hartwig, & Bhaskar, 2016).

For the purposes of this inquiry, "sustainability leadership" was taken to entail the realization of adequate response(s) to the metacrisis, for it is this—and not just more harmonious coupling of anything resembling existing economic systems with ecological systems—that may be required for humanity to continue as a going concern. Such a response has never before been *imagined*. Hence, the verb *reimagine* as applied to sustainability leadership in the main inquiry question risked obscuring the very nature of what was being pursued, in that the objective was not necessarily to modify something that already exists but to enact something that has never existed. The inquiry invited IWB's stakeholders to translate-into-existence a future in which sufficient planetary transformation has occurred, such that the paradoxes of our species' quest for continued existence have been transcended. Arguably, this moment in history presents us with the possibility of thinking about planetary transformation and sustainability leadership in unprecedented ways.

Role of the Researcher

As an action researcher, my role in this project was to collaborate with the stakeholders of IWB to help them not only imagine an adequate planetary response to the metacrisis, but also make discoveries concerning their collective role in enacting that response. For this project, I served as a facilitator, attempting to hold the space for a deep and powerful inquiry about the future that is possible for the human species, and about the most authentic way for the stakeholders of IWB to participate in midwifing that future. I have no official role with the organization beyond that of a researcher, although I completed some minor volunteer activities after embarking on the project in the fall of 2016.

Starting in October 2016, IWB's cofounder, Gail Hochachka, and I engaged in several conversations about what inquiry parameters would best serve IWB. Based on these discussions, I produced a concept paper in December 2016 that Hochachka shared and discussed internally with IWB's directors. She and I continued to collaborate, evolving the research question several times during the early part of 2017. The act of reimagining sustainability leadership was ultimately selected as the core of the inquiry; we felt that such a focus not only had the potential to generate useful knowledge within the field, but would also reflect valuable information back to IWB concerning how the organization can best express its commitments and support practitioners in this historical moment.

Significance

The unfolding of this particular moment in history has important implications for humanity, and for our collective fate as we hurtle through space-time together on this little blue rock. Our species is currently confronting numerous global crises—dynamic, evolving challenges involving complex nonlinear systems that transcend national boundaries, which our existing development paradigms and measurement infrastructures are incapable of adequately comprehending, let alone resolving (Stein, 2015). These include the breakdown of democratic institutions, epistemological confusion, nuclear proliferation, significant and poorly understood risks associated with rapid technological change, the rise of nationalism, economic inequality, global warming, and disruption to ecosystems, the food supply, and human health.

In such a world, the very nature of sustainability leadership, and of what is required for it to be effective, may be changing. In other words, it is conceivable that the current global situation demands an entirely new idea of what sustainability leadership is, how to carry it out, and what its outcomes or objectives ought to be. As IWB's stakeholders opened themselves to deep inquiry about this situation, or to some form of 'metanoia' (an ancient Greek word for transformation, meaning something like 'to go beyond the mind') they were well positioned to generate insights that could help to redefine sustainability leadership. It is within this big-picture context that stakeholders of IWB, taking inspiration from Lewin (1947), undertook to enact a "field" that would pull them collectively into a deeper emergent expression—one that is relevant, timely, and in some sense equal to the challenges currently faced by our species.

An important factor in this inquiry was IWB's relationship to the larger ecosystem of organizations and individuals working with or contributing to the evolution and application of IM. IWB is a somewhat unusual member of this ecosystem in the sense that its main emphasis is on realizing the emancipatory potentials of IM at the cultural and systemic levels (or in integral nomenclature, within the "lower quadrants"), rather than on transforming individual consciousness. Hochachka (2015) referred to its work as "the integral you don't see" because it involves activism conducted in corners around the globe, mostly by people who wouldn't participate in the academic discourses where integral perspectives reflecting an "upper left [quadrant] bias" have tended to take prominence. In other words, IWB is occupying a distinct position within the integral space and has a significant contribution to make within the community of practitioners and researchers who constitute that space. In particular, given Ken Wilber's role on the board of the organization, its impact can be directly viewed as a part of his legacy. In short, the work of IWB offers a sense of what is possible when Wilber's ideas are applied in the context of international development or social change activism.

BACKGROUND

Systems Analysis

The ability to thrive in complexity, or to "see" systems and work with them effectively, has been identified as a hallmark of post-conventional (or "integral") consciousness (Wilber, 2000; Brown, 2011; Torbert et al., 2004; Cook-Greuter, 2013). This is the very consciousness that IWB's offerings seek to foster and encourage within change agents and sustainability leaders. A quick review of the resources on IWB's website (IWB, Resources, n.d.) reveals a range of sophisticated and creative approaches for working with complexity and mapping system dynamics. Indeed, IM's quadrants and their associated "quadrivia" (or methodological perspectives from which to engage reality) disclose different phenomena within human systems and can help illuminate the ways in which those phenomena arise together (Wilber, 2006d). Perhaps as a consequence of IM's usefulness as a framework for addressing systems change, the organization often attracts practitioners involved in very complex, multi-jurisdictional and/or multi-stakeholder initiatives that require systems leadership. Several types of stakeholders have an important influence on the IWB's ability to fulfill its purpose. In Figure 1, these stakeholders are organized as agents, targets, sponsors, and champions/supporters; some stakeholders occupied multiple roles in this inquiry.

Figure 1. Diagram of IWB's stakeholder ecosystem
(Robinson, 2018, p. 25)

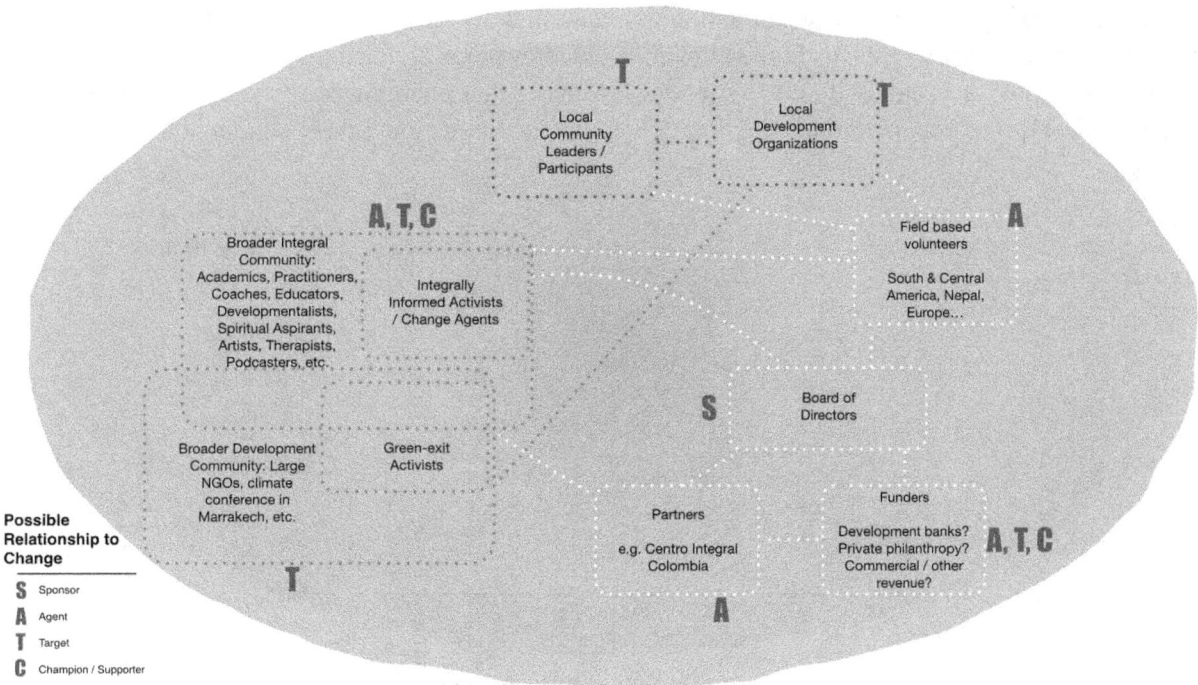

THEORETICAL PERSPECTIVES

Integral Metatheory: Its impact on IWB and the Systems It Is Part of

Meadows (2008) believed that the most powerful leverage points to intervene in a system involve transcending and transforming "shared ideas in the minds of society", including our "deepest set of beliefs about how the world works" (pp. 162-163)[2]. Any metatheoretical endeavor—and IM is no exception—is concerned with precisely such leverage points (Edwards, 2010). Thus, not to account for IM as a force acting within and upon IWB-as-a-system would be to disregard an important dynamic in this analysis. Wilber (2017) described IM as "psychoactive for virtually all of its elements and dimensions" meaning that studying it and engaging with it transforms people (and hence, systems those people are part of) in a multiplicity of important ways (p. 47).

An ultrashort summary of some of IM's major components—its five major archetypal patterns—is appropriate here. This summary highlights important aspects of the shared "map" that IWB's stakeholders use to navigate the "territory" of social change work, and of practices which bring that territory into being, thus influencing IWB's stakeholders' opportunity set for interacting with the systems they are part of (Wilber, 2006b, p. 3).

Archetypal Pattern 1: The Four Quadrants

IM understands all events within the universe in terms of two equiprimordial polarities present since the beginning of time: interior-exterior and individual-collective. Taken together as a matrix as in Figure 2, these two polarities give us four irreducible "quadrants" or dimensions of reality: psychological, cultural, material (or behavioral), and systemic. IM insists that phenomena in each of these quadrants can only be detected with methodologies specific to that quadrant, and that evaluating claims about the

Figure 2. The four quadrants.
Adapted from Integral spirituality: A startling new role for religion in the postmodern world by Ken Wilber, p. 20, ©2007. Printed with permission

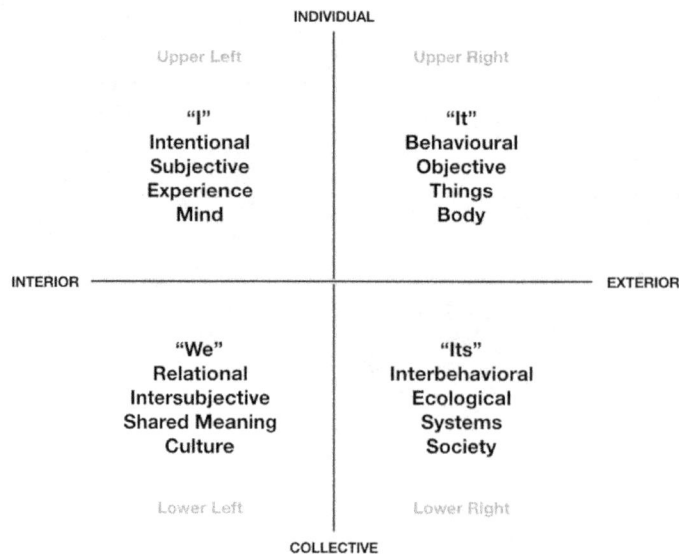

nature of phenomena in a particular quadrant requires using validity conditions innate to that quadrant (Wilber, 2006b). The four quadrants present us with eight methodological families or "zones", two in each quadrant, that IM holds as a basic minimum to gain an understanding of what is taking place in any given moment (see Figure 3).

While many approaches to sustainability or social change have attempted to reduce issues to a single quadrant—as in critical / social constructionist approaches which tend to view change strictly in terms of the lower left quadrant—IM insists that reality "tetra-arises" (Wilber, 2006a), which is to say that the four quadrants constantly and recursively emerge together in patterns of mutual influence and constraint. Hence an informed and effective approach to change must take all four quadrants seriously. Change agents familiar with IM often find the four quadrants immediately relevant and applicable as a framework for assessing complex situations in terms of multiple facets and identifying specific areas to address in the light of a "big picture" perspective (Brown, 2007, 2011). Dozens of patterns for applying the quadrants to change initiatives and mapping the relationships between them have been identified (Esbjörn-Hargens, 2014).

Archetypal Pattern 2: Developmental Levels (or Stages of Complexity)

IM recognizes that a pervasive pattern, observed in domains as diverse as biology, chemistry, culture, economics, technology, and psychology is that individuals and groups tend to increase in complexity over time. While such evolution can at times be gradual, there are also junctures when entirely new stages or levels seem to emerge in the history of a society, a population, or an individual; in such moments the new stage that appears is somehow qualitatively distinct from the previous one; its components have been reorganized into a new structure with different ways of metabolizing energy or information (Wil-

Figure 3. The eight methodological zones.
Adapted from Integral spirituality: A startling new role for religion in the postmodern world by Ken Wilber, p. 37, ©2007. Printed with permission

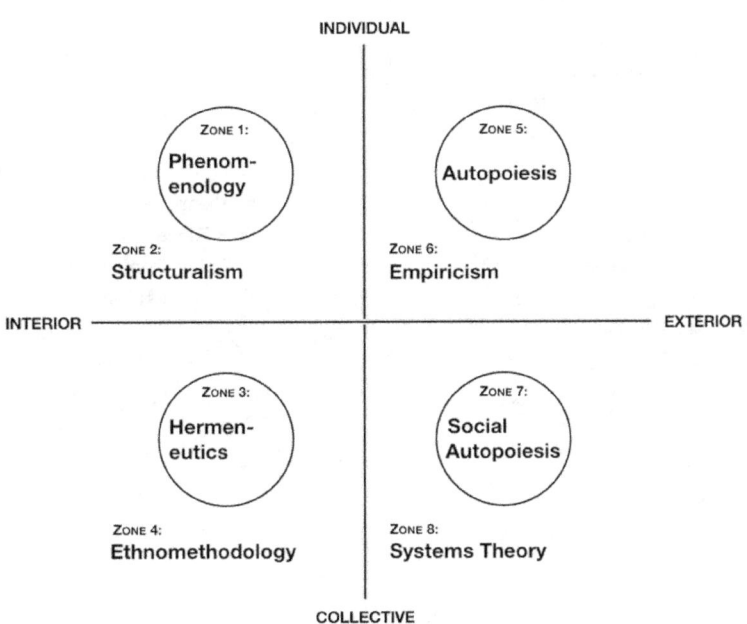

ber, 2006c, p. 80). This phenomenon is what famously led Piaget (1971), for example, to comment that a seven-year old is not generally an incrementally more intelligent four-year old, but rather an entirely different mind, a completely distinct embodiment of intelligence. Piaget (1971) also noted that children tend to progress through stages of cognitive complexity that are *predictable.* Although with immense variation, predictable stages of evolution can clearly be identified in each of the four quadrants, with correlates in each of the other three (as broadly indicated in Figure 4).

Developmental stages are important to sustainability leadership in a number of ways. First, leaders operating from mature developmental stages or "action logics" are able to see, know, and do things that other leaders cannot and seem to be better equipped to reliably foster large-scale systems transformations (Torbert et. al, 2004; Brown, 2011). Second, understanding the dynamics that inform worldviews at each developmental stage is useful for designing messages and experiences that will motivate participation in sustainability initiatives from individuals occupying those stages (Leonard, 2004; Brown, 2011). Third, leaders with a sense of how systems and organizations advance through stages may be better positioned to invite healthy and resilient progression of a whole system from one stage of complexity to the next (Brown, 2011).

Figure 4. Developmental levels.
Adapted from Integral spirituality: A startling new role for religion in the postmodern world by Ken Wilber, p. 22, ©2007. Printed with permission

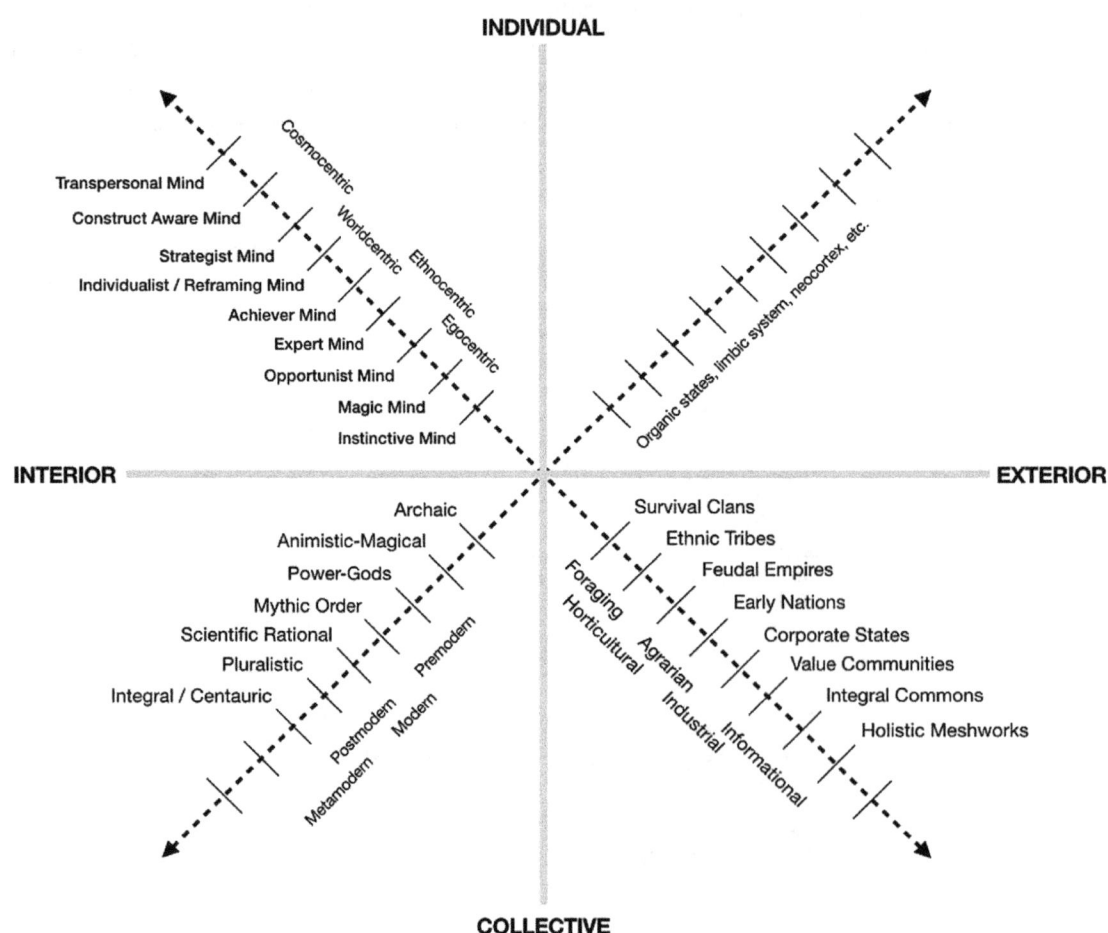

Archetypal Pattern 3: Developmental Lines (or Domains of Complexity)

Within any individual, culture, or society, numerous "lines" or growth trajectories are simultaneously unfolding and interacting with each other. Each of these lines may be at varying stages of development. Perhaps the most well-known explication of this principle is Gardner's (1983, 1993) theory of multiple intelligences, which proposed between seven and nine distinct "streams" or lines of intelligence that an individual can exhibit, whereby they may be exceptionally skilled in one line but not-so-developed along another. Mapping multiple intelligences, or any combination of lines in the Upper Left quadrant, tells us something about an individual's "integral psychograph" (Wilber, 2000), as in Figure 5. In addition to lines in the upper left quadrant, it is possible to observe subcultures that produce artefacts reflecting varying levels of complexity within a culture (distinct lines in the lower left quadrant), sectors of the global economy exhibiting different levels of maturity (distinct lines in the lower right quadrant), and so forth.

Archetypal Pattern 4: States

Regardless of their developmental stage, brains, minds, cultures, and social systems can each occupy various "states"—reflecting the overall energy, quality, mood, reactivity, or equilibrium that they exhibit. Different states lead to very different outcomes, no matter which quadrant you are looking at. Typically, practitioners working with IM have tended to focus on states in the upper left quadrant. An important question here is whether, by training their minds to perceive increasingly subtle phenomena with greater clarity, they can produce different leadership outcomes. Increasingly within the integral community, practices for working with states in the lower left quadrant are also being explored (Patten, 2013; see also the anthology, *Cohering the integral we space*, by Gunnlaugson & Brabant, 2016, for a range of approaches and perspectives by different practitioners).

Figure 5. Integral psychograph (lines of development in the upper left quadrant).
Adapted from Integral spirituality: A startling new role for religion in the postmodern world by Ken Wilber, pp. 10, 25, ©2007. Printed with permission

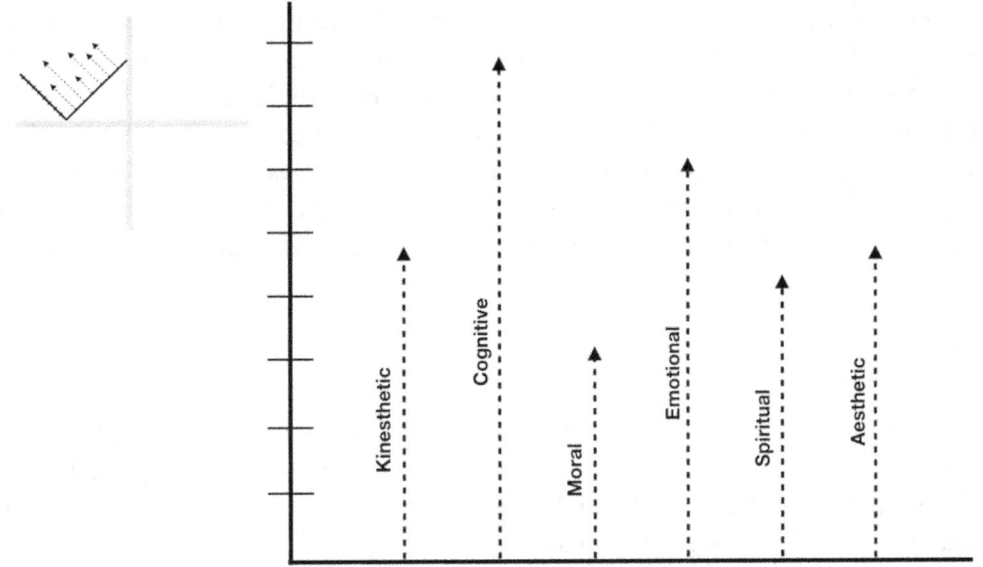

Archetypal Pattern 5: Types

IM recognizes that different entities of the same class often exhibit patterns whereby they can be organized according to type, for example: masculine / feminine; Monera / Protista / Fungi / Plantae / Animalia; introverted / extroverted; metals / nonmetals; and so forth. Not a great deal has been written about how this aspect of IM applies to sustainability leadership, although leaders (not limited to the integral community) often engage with typological tools within the upper left quadrant—for example, Myers Briggs, Enneagram, Motivation Factor, the Big Five, and so on—to better understand themselves and the people they work with.

RESEARCH DESIGN OVERVIEW

For this research, I used a multi-method approach, consisting of several qualitative methods that were adapted to the needs of IWB's stakeholders. More detail is presented about these methods in the sections that follow, however, in brief: I interviewed eight individuals with meaningful connections to IWB, seeking a deep understanding of their experiences and their relationship to the inquiry questions. I hosted two focus groups—one that convened an eclectic group of activists and integral practitioners to explore the main inquiry question in a broad sense, and one that brought together IWB's core team to focus specifically on the organization's future. And I conducted an open space lab at a gathering of social change agents organized by IWB in Guatemala. This research adhered to the Tri-Council Policy Statement: *Ethical Conduct for Research Involving Humans* (TCPS, 2010) and was approved by the Royal Roads University Research Ethics Board.

Integral Action Research

Action research is not one thing. As Rowe et al. (2013) noted it is "a loose term covering a variety of approaches for social research within organizations and other social systems" (p. 17). These approaches have nonetheless been broadly generalized as espousing (1) "research *in* action, rather than research *about* action", (2) "a collaborative, democratic partnership" that invites active participation by members of the system being studied in generating the inquiry and its outcomes, and (3) "a sequence of events and an approach to problem-solving" involving iterative cycles of action and reflection (Coghlan & Brannick, 2014, p. 6). I adopted IAR as the methodology for this study: an embodiment of AR that is congruent with and informed by IM's AQAL[3] framework and postmetaphysical approach. I emphasized three areas of compatibility between AR and IM: integration of first-, second- and third-person perspectives, an enactive stance, and an emancipatory predisposition. I discuss the importance of these areas in the paragraphs that follow.

Integration of Perspectives

AR has an explicit interest in integrating first-, second-, and third-person knowledge, and in the paradigms (i.e., practices, injunctions, validity conditions) that give rise to each (Floyd, 2012; Teehankee, 2017; Torbert et. al, 2004; Rowe et. al, 2013). Having first been conceived by Kurt Lewin in the context of deeply pragmatic inquiry concerning organizational change, AR linked awareness and motivation with performance and results from the beginning (Burnes, 2004). As with IM's four quadrants, AR thus acknowledges both exterior and interior dimensions of social reality, concerning itself with action and its practical outcomes, yet emphasizing subjectivities, cultural contexts, and embodied knowledge as irreducible elements of action and the outcomes it gives rise to (Coghlan & Brannick, 2014; Stringer, 2014). In this sense, AR moves to transcend the "split between the knower and the known", uniting 'in here' and 'out there' into a single process or event (Coghlan & Brannick, 2014, p. 51).

Enactive Stance

A move to unify the knower and the known is compatible with IM's principle of "enactment"—that is, the stance that reality is "brought forth" as specific practitioners carry out specific injunctions to generate specific data. This is reflected in the intuition of one of IWB's cofounders (the sponsor of this research) concerning IAR, which she distinguished as a process in which participants are "very aware that the observer and observed co-arise, such that nothing is not-already-unified from the perspective being taken" (G. Hochachka, personal communication, February 9th, 2017).

Enaction (or "tetra-enaction" as Wilber, 2006b, has called it) is the moment-by-moment, co-creative, participatory emergence of reality, taking place within four irreducibly enmeshed dimensions of reality: subjective, objective, intersubjective, and interobjective. As Wilber (2006b) explained, *who* is performing the observation is *inseparable from the reality that is enacted:*

Subjects do not perceive worlds but enact them. Different states of subjects bring forth different worlds. For AQAL, this means that a subject might be at a particular [level] of consciousness, in a particular [line] of consciousness, in a particular state of consciousness, in one quadrant or another. That means that the phenomena brought forth by various types of human inquiry will be different depending on the quadrants, levels, lines, states, and types of the subjects bringing forth the phenomena. A subject at one [level] of consciousness will not enact and bring forth the same worldspace as a subject at another [level]; and similarly, with quadrants, [lines], states, and types. (p. 27).

While IM does not—contrary to certain versions of constructivism—deny that there is *something* 'out there' which we can know, it is deeply attuned to the ways in which what is known co-arises with the observer's interiority (Indeed, as previously noted, IM views all phenomena as a tetra-arising of the four quadrants). In a sense, all reality mirrors the awareness within which it arises back to itself. IM offers a very detailed map of how structures and states, as well as types, of consciousness affect what we know and what we *can* know (Wilber, 2000; Esbjörn-Hargens, 2010).

Emancipatory Predisposition

One additional feature of action research is notable in terms of its compatibility with an integral approach. Action research is inherently normative and is often concerned with the emancipatory potentials of action (Coghlan & Brannick, 2014; Walker, 2009; Wittmayer and Schäpke, 2014). By its very nature, in other words, it involves an attempt to create a better lifeworld; one that is more free, just, desirable, and sustainable for its inhabitants (Reason & Bradbury, 2001). Similarly, IM is seen by its proponents as having the potential to be an "an emancipatory, visionary, and transformational force vis-a-vis our complex twenty-first-century challenges" (Hedlund et al., 2016). In this sense, both integral researchers and action researchers are interested in innovation and cohesive development within social systems.

METHODS

The Research Problem

This research was guided by the following problem: "How might the stakeholders of IWB reimagine sustainability leadership in a way that increases their collective capacity for wise and transforming action in the world?"

The Research Questions

The five research questions that informed the inquiry are as follows:

1. How is sustainability leadership currently showing up (being enacted) in the world?
2. What is the future that IWB's stakeholders are committed to bringing about through sustainability leadership?
3. How would sustainability leadership need to show up (be enacted) in the world to bring that future into being?
4. What could sustainability leadership be, in this historical moment?
5. What is the role of IWB's stakeholders in enacting the highest possibilities of sustainability leadership?

Research Design and Data Collection

This research sought to understand how the stakeholders of IWB might reimagine sustainability leadership in a way that could increase their collective capacity for wise and transforming action in the world. Data were enacted in this research through eight interviews, two separate focus groups, and a (Spanish language) open space lab. These techniques are representative of only the methodological families of Zone 1 (e.g. phenomenology) and Zone 3 (e.g. hermeneutics) raising the issue of whether this research falls short of addressing the putative injunctions of IMP to integrate first-, second-, and third-person data-perspectives. However, Hedlund (2010) noted that defining integral research as only research that utilizes mixed methods is problematic because it could lead to a "default privileging of *span over depth*" and be prohibitive to researchers in terms of time, resources, and methodological expertise (p. 8). Instead, Hedlund proposed that research which, first, has an integral/enactive disposition woven through multiple phases, and second, involves "at least some reflexive disclosure of aspects of the epistemological and methodological conditions of enactment" meets minimum conditions to qualify as integral research (p. 10). He also theorized that:

If effectively constructed, [such a] definition of Integral Research can be enacted as a psychoactive attractor—exerting a developmental pull on researchers—thereby supporting increasingly optimal, integral performances in the domain of research. Therefore, such a definition could possibly increase the already marked transformative potential of Integral Research for the researcher her/himself (p. 9).

Elsewhere, I have attempted to demonstrate epistemological and methodological reflexivity by considering how my own history and perspective, influenced by cultural and societal factors, and situated within a specific moment of planetary evolution, contributed to the way this research unfolded (Robinson, 2018).

For the purposes of this study, the stakeholders of IWB were defined as individuals who: were part of the IWB's core team, *and/or* had contributed to IWB's initiatives, *and/or* had chosen to participate in IWB-convened gatherings or online courses, *and/or* were somehow in IWB's "orbit" through professional engagement and/or relationships. Research participants also demonstrated an active interest in social change and/or sustainability leadership through their vocational and/or volunteer undertakings. As these criteria suggest, potential participants were identified through purposive sampling; they were seen to embody circumstances directly relevant to the inquiry questions, and thus to be in a position to contribute meaningfully to the creation of knowledge that advances the aims of this research (Creswell, 2013; Palys, 2008). However, specific methods entailed circumstances that required combining purposive sampling with other selection strategies; in particular, snowball sampling was used in the selection of interview participants.

I facilitated three large group methods that supported data triangulation, approaching inquiry questions from different angles with three quite distinct groups of participants. Two of these were focus groups—the first of which took place in Vancouver. Participants in this first focus group were invited to assemble at one of the participant's homes where the research took place following a meal. In total, nine individuals participated in this focus group: four members of IWB's board and five others professionally engaged in some combination of environmental activism, social innovation, and/or large-scale systems change—typically all three.

The open space lab was conducted in Spanish, at an IWB-convened multi-day gathering of social change practitioners in Guatemala. IWB advertised this gathering to its international email list, shared the event on its social media channels, and asked Latin American members of its network to spread the word to their contacts in sustainability-related fields. Fourteen individuals participated in the open space lab, representing Canada, Colombia, El Salvador, France, Guatemala, Paraguay, and the United States. Two translators helped me conduct the open space lab.

The third large group method—a second focus group—was conducted online using an online meeting tool, with participation restricted to IWB's core operating team—all board members with one exception, plus a key field volunteer. All seven invitees participated in this focus group, which involved an exploration of the organization's future, and of specific issues that its members felt drawn to explore.

Scope and Limitations of the Inquiry

This inquiry was exceedingly broad and open-ended, asking not how to address a specific issue or challenge within the domain of sustainability leadership, but what it could mean for IWB's stakeholders to reimagine the entire field, building their capacity for wise, transforming collective action in the process. As such, it adopted an expansive view: one which sought to take account of the biggest possible picture. While such an approach might misleadingly create the impression of 'limitlessness' in its scope, in fact the opposite is true. Countless specifics were ignored entirely or given much less than the treatment they deserve in this study, as was necessary in order to focus on broad generalizations and to draw conclusions about how the overall "shape" of sustainability leadership might be improved. Readers should also be cautioned that, given the immensity of the topic under investigation, any attempt to paraphrase it—this one included—is liable to fall short not only at the level of details but at the level of the whole.

Although qualitatively expanding the range and types of actions possible within the domain of sustainability leadership was a central goal of this study, offering specific prescriptions concerning those actions was not. Consequently, the broad contours inside of which inquiry and experimentation could lead to paradigm-level innovation, and where IWB's stakeholders seem well positioned to make important contributions, were explored. The specific actions and concrete practices that might be carried out within those contours were not. Again, this is a study focused on provoking the imagination and expanding the overall set of opportunities available to individuals participating in sustainability leadership. Hence it is only fitting that the stakeholders of IWB, in a word, use their imaginations, to create the next actions that they will take together.

EXPLORING THE ISSUES

Analysis of Findings

I adopted a thematic approach to analysis, which was appropriate for this research because it disclosed patterns that informed a nuanced understanding of how sustainability leadership is—and could be—enacted by IWB's stakeholders (Glesne, 2016). I coded data using the MAXQDA software application. I began by reviewing all the transcripts and making note of frequent topics of conversation and possible codewords. I then commenced the 'first round' of coding, making a conscious effort to "be overgenerous in judging what is important to code," so as not to "foreclose any opportunity to learn from the field by prematurely settling in on what is or is not relevant" (Glesne, 2016, p. 198). Following the initial round, I journaled using Saldaña's "codeweaving" technique (as cited in Glesne, 2016, p. 200) and experimented with various visual arrangements, particularly "metapatterning" the codes in constellations reflecting the four quadrants as outlined in IM (Hedlund, 2010). Juxtaposing the codes in this way produced insights that significantly altered the coding system I used in subsequent rounds of coding.

Discussion of Themes

Blessed with what I assert is a remarkably rich and uncommon data set from which to proceed, in this section I outline the major findings of this study: five themes that emerged through systematic analysis of the texts enacted through the course of eleven qualitative research moments. These themes are presented in Table 1 and subsequently discussed below.

Theme 1: IWB as an Attractor for Integral Social Transformation Praxis

Research participants envisaged IWB as an attractor for integral social transformation praxis. Participants agreed IWB has carried out its role by embodying a clarified vision of socio-cultural change, convening and developing community, and nurturing praxis. They surmised that developments within the arena of social innovation, as well as increasing acceptance towards integrative approaches by sustainability practitioners, suggest that the resonance between the organization and the field it serves is deepening.

Table 1. Themes and subthemes

Emphasis	Theme	Subthemes
IWB	Theme 1: IWB as an attractor for integral social transformation praxis. (To what extent can IWB be a beacon for sustainability practitioners seeking to nurture their integrative intuitions?)	*Subtheme 1.1: Embodying clarity.* (IWB embodies a robust and coherent theory of social change.) *Subtheme 1.2: Nurturing praxis within community.* (IWB fosters a community of praxis characterized by depth and care.) *Subtheme 1.3: A seed that might flower.* (Is IWB prepared to realize a deeper expression of its commitments?)
IWB	Theme 2: Embodying IWB's commitments. (How can IWB embody its vision with aliveness, audacity, and precision?)	*Subtheme 2.1: Focus.* (What IWB stands for.) *Subtheme 2.2: Relationships.* (How IWB can meet the world where it is at.) *Subtheme 2.3: Structures.* (What structures can energize and elevate IWB.) *Subtheme 2.4: Resources.* (How IWB attracts and honours resources.)
IWB and Sustainability Leadership	Theme 3: Funding integral transformation praxis. (How can adequate approaches for funding integral sustainability leadership be identified and realized?)	*Subtheme 3.1: Can existing funding models sustain integral praxis?* (To be compatible with integral approaches, funding models need to reflect a different definition of value, including how it is created and measured.)
Sustainability Leadership	Theme 4: Transforming power structures. (Sustainability leadership involves transforming power structures in a way that fosters a more just, creative, and secure existence.)	*Subtheme 4.1: Economic criticalization.* (Late capitalism presents an opening for new forms of sustainability leadership.) *Subtheme 4.2: Consciously owning the "destroyer" role.* (Sustainability leadership calls for the wisdom to engage issues of destruction and loss so that liberating structures can emerge.) *Subtheme 2: Beyond systems thinking.* (Deep structural change is more than systems change.)
Sustainability Leadership	Theme 5: Interiority. (How can sustainability leadership attend to interior dimensions of reality, including developmental complexity, being-with one another, and altered states?)	*Subtheme 5.1: Developmental complexity.* (Sustainability leadership benefits from embracing developmental hierarchies.) *Subtheme 5.2: New ways to be together.* (Demonstrating new paradigms for coexistence is a central element of sustainability leadership.) *Subtheme 5.3: Causal leadership.* (Extremely subtle phenomena have important consequences that blend into all aspects of sustainability leadership.)

(Robinson, 2018, p. 100)

Theme 2: Embodying IWB's Commitments

Closely linked to the notion of IWB being an attractor for integral social transformation praxis, participants expressed a desire to cultivate aliveness and fluid collaboration within IWB. They demonstrated eagerness to foster conditions that support the organization in being a profound expression of its commitments and in generating meaningful impact. They explored "focus," "relationships", "structures", and "resources" as important conditions for facilitating this deeper embodiment.

Theme 3: Funding Integral Transformation Praxis

From a broad perspective, participants spoke about funding integral transformation praxis as a puzzle for which solutions, in large part, have yet to be enacted.

Some participants implied that funding integral praxis seems to involve a chicken-and-egg predicament, in the sense that it takes "money to change the mindsets of people and show a different way", yet the mindsets that need to be changed in order to increase funding for integral projects are those of funders themselves.

These questions were reflected in participants' more immediate concerns regarding what IWB should become, and how to ensure it has adequate resources to fulfill its commitments. One participant acknowledged broader acceptance and incorporation of IM in the field, but did not necessarily equate this with increased capacity for impact on IWB's part.

The chicken-and-egg question of resourcing new structures from within an old paradigm that is incompatible with those new structures is complex and interesting. On the whole, participants painted what could be described as a provocative picture of sustainability leadership for this moment—one that could help inspire the field to reach beyond conventional thinking and approaches in important and impactful ways.

Theme 4: Transforming Power Structures

Participants expressed a commitment to support the development of deep structures that go beyond existing power structures to foster creativity, "thriveability", and flourishing. Considering sustainability leadership broadly, one participant underlined "the capacity to discover and support enabling structures and...to encourage and support self-organizing generativity" on multiple scales.

Participants connected these approaches with a desire to see humanity—as well as non-human species—liberated from harms brought about by the dominant techno-economic regime. Many participants were energized by the work of "creating something new that makes the other thing obsolete" and the perception of being part of a "shift from...business as usual".

Thus, participants, both explicitly and implicitly, appealed to the relevance of Integral Methodological Pluralism (IMP) and other integrative approaches in enacting sweeping shifts, which they saw as timely, exciting, and deeply necessary. Nonetheless, they continued to be challenged by the paradoxical nature of bringing into existence that which has never existed within the sphere of social reality.

Theme 5: Interiority

Participants stressed that the best performances of sustainability leadership vividly engage the interior (i.e. psychological, spiritual, cultural, relational) dimensions of the situations they aim to transform. They understood working with interiority in a skillful, integrated way as an indisputably important part of enacting sweeping changes to society.

Participants contended that imaginal and aesthetic practices can effectively shift reality in significant ways; they saw them as an opening for the emergence of new discoveries, attractors, values, and opportunities for responding to complex problems. In many cases, participants believed that these less tangible approaches offered a far more fertile starting point than traditional frameworks for social change.

Development is held by IM to occur within all quadrants, including the lower left, cultural sphere (Wilber, 2016; 2006c). Hence, participants unsurprisingly expressed the belief that this historical moment both demands and makes possible the emergence of radical and profound new ways to be together. They described developing new paradigms for coexisting with other beings as a core imperative of contemporary sustainability leadership.

On the whole, participants expressed many ideas and sentiments regarding the need to discover new frames and practices for coexisting, and shared the belief that IWB could make an important contribution in this area.

Conclusions: Fertile Areas for Integral Transformation Praxis

The thematic analysis concluded with the identification of four Areas. Taking inspiration from the familiar "Four Rs" of waste management, these concluding themes are offered as the "Four Rs" of Integral Transformation Praxis—Revive, Reidentify, Recode, and Reconfigure. These Four Rs are summarized in Table 2 and subsequently discussed.

Area 1: Revive

Throughout the study, participants considered consciousness not simply as an indicator of change, but as a central factor in sustainability leadership with the power to birth new possibilities and effect the unfolding of realities. Participants regarded consciousness as profoundly relevant within social change work—from the way collectively embodied states and values inform patterns of coexistence, as in Subthemes 4.3 and 5.2; to the impact of developmental complexity on leadership performances, as in Subtheme 5.1; to the influence of different states of consciousness on creativity and agency, as in Subtheme 5.3.

Area 2: Reidentify

Amongst all participants, I observed strong commitments to invent and live sacred narratives of coexistence that are relevant to this historical moment; and to enact creative, liberating performances of culture, communication, and collaboration. These commitments take on special significance in light of

Table 2. The "Four Rs" of integral transformation praxis

Areas of Praxis	Definition
Area 1: Revive	Demonstrating that consciousness "matters"; which is to say, demonstrating that consciousness is not reducible to our physical circumstances; it both enables and acts as a constraint on outcomes in social change work and sustainability leadership, and cannot be separated from those outcomes.
Area 2: Reidentify	Embodying the mystery of coexistence in this historical moment; which is to say, living and collaborating from a place of inquiry concerning our identity as a species, and co-creating narratives and ethical understandings that grasp the full complexity of our collective being.
Area 3: Recode	Transforming how value is understood and measured; which is to say, enacting a more integral framework for 'seeing' value and goodness.
Area 4: Reconfigure	Co-creating platforms for resourcing integral transformation praxis; which is to say, fostering an ecosystem of support for social change initiatives that weave together multiple time cycles, emphasize structural transformation, and increase impact by enabling collaboration between practitioners and perspectives from all four quadrants.

(Robinson, 2018, p. 131)

two considerations: first that prevailing paradigms of sustainability leadership are plagued by a number of internal contradictions, at least in part because they reflect inadequate theories concerning the meaning of collective existence, limiting and distorting opportunities for action available to change agents (Edwards, 2010; Kauffman, 2016). and second, that a principal function of metatheories is to furnish humanity with "languages of transformation" out of which new narratives and new patterns of collective identity can be born (Stein, 2016). Expressions of Area 2 might involve facilitating shared inquiry within groups of people concerning the uncertainties of coexistence and what it means to be part of the human species during this time in history.

Area 3: Recode

Participants, as noted in Theme 4, demonstrated a commitment to upgrading unjust or oppressive power structures. In Subtheme 4.3, participants interpreted this task not only as taking action to alter the processes by which power is enacted and distributed within society, but as a matter of transforming the ontological and axiological assumptions that underpin civilization's most basic institutions and practices.

As Subtheme 1.1 suggested, IWB's stakeholders can help to transform the field of sustainability leadership by *clarifying* the underlying nature of current contradictions and by transcending them in creative ways to produce elegant, surprising outcomes. One of IM's important contributions to distinguishing how new structures within the lower quadrants emerge is that it makes what has often been invisible—the paradigms encoded into society at the most fundamental levels—visible (Edwards, 2010).

Transforming social value means transforming how it is measured (Stein, 2015). Numerous entry points exist for the stakeholders of IWB to become involved in this activity of "recoding". These include: making IMP accessible to individuals involved in the creation of measurement infrastructures, developing innovations in measurement, advocating for the transformation of measurement infrastructures within the field of international development, or simply creating projects that reflect more integral ways of attending to and observing reality, and sharing those projects with others.

Area 4: Reconfigure

Area 4 asks: how can the entire Integral community creatively engage the paradoxes of "building the new models that make the old ones obsolete" and resource its projects effectively? How can its members work together and with others in the world to co-create robust, efficient, "enabling structures" that "encourage and support self-organizing generativity" on multiple scales? Area 4 suggests that we can reimagine sustainability leadership by reconfiguring the ways we collaborate on, fund, and support initiatives in order to integrate multiple time scales and bring together practitioners from all four quadrants.

Thus, "Reconfigure," is in a relationship of tension with the third Area of "Recode". Where in Area 3, we explored the possibility of reimagining sustainability leadership as transforming the underlying encoding of society, Area 4 is concerned with the specific issue of how to adequately resource that kind of activism from within a system built from the 'old' code. The paradox-laden question of enabling integral transformation praxis with financial capital-measured-in-terms of the very paradigm it aims to transform is central to Area 4.

RECOMMENDATIONS AND IMPLICATIONS

Recommendations

This section outlines four recommendations that surfaced through a consideration of the selected literature, study findings, and conclusions. Participants in this study viewed IWB, as discussed in Subtheme 1.3, as a "seed that might flower", a wonderful possibility that has been cared for and incubated, but hasn't yet fully emerged into its potential. The recommendations presented here are designed to support and challenge IWB's core team in creating conditions that will enable the organization to take root, thrive, and unfurl surprisingly potent expressions of its commitments; they are written as injunctions that, if followed, are intended to increase the collective capacity of its members for wise and transforming action in the world. To put it another way, these recommendations form the basis of a minimal organizational development framework, conceived in the context of IWB's specific needs as a non-profit focused on international development in the integral community, faced with the entrepreneurial challenge of how to resource its commitments. They are summarized in Table 3 and subsequently discussed.

Recommendation 1: Engage a Process to Agree Upon and Articulate a Clear Organizational Focus

As Subtheme 2.1 stated, members agreed that it would serve the organization to clarify what it stands for. There are numerous reasons why this point in IWB's trajectory was a particularly appropriate moment for members to engage in such a process: new members on the board; the consensus that the organiza-

Table 3. Study Recommendations

Recommendation	Questions to Hold	Possible Resources	Polarities to Hold
Recommendation 1: Engage a process to agree upon and articulate a clear organizational focus.	What is IWB taking a stand for? What does IWB value? Why does IWB exist? What is IWB's promise to the world?	Mission, vision, values. Brand architecture. Organizational story or manifesto.	Polarity between *focus* and *freedom*. Saying yes to a singular path means saying no to many that are potentially valuable and similar in nature.
Recommendation 2: Conceive of, select, and develop projects.	What projects: -align with IWB's focus (*Rec. 1*)? -embody team members' passions and strengths? -build capacity? -have surprising impact? -inspire others and attract resources?	Design thinking. Crowdsourcing. Partnerships with external organizations. Decision criteria and timeline. SMART goal setting.	Polarity between *action* and *knowledge*. We learn through implementation.
Recommendation 3: Conduct an "opportunity identification" process to explore sources of capital for IWB's projects and operations.	Who could contribute to the transformation of structures and processes involved in funding social change? How could IWB and its backers enact new procedures for funding integral transformation praxis?	Existing and potential funding partners. Business model canvas. CFO expertise / mindset. Fundraising expertise. Brainstorming. AQAL map.	Polarity between *discovery* and *creation*. Opportunities and possible futures do not exist in the world or in our awareness, but in the interplay between the two. They are *enacted*.
Recommendation 4: Establish structures that provide refuge, foster deep collaboration, and make development unavoidable.	How might members of IWB be liberated to do the most important work they've ever done with their lives? How can IWB influence factors that support deep collaboration and unlock the genius of its team?	Interaction rhythms. Liberating structures (Lipmanowicz & McCandless, 2014).	Polarity between *structure* and *agency*. Polarity between *agency* and *communion*.

(Robinson, 2018, p. 142)

tion can achieve more through the "disciplined pursuit of less"; the feeling that the next steps for the organization need to "be grounded in [the] wishes and [the] thinking" of younger members; and a set of unique historical conditions that seem to suggest the potential—at a planetary scale—for revolutionary social change, or what Wilber (2006a) has called an "increase in authenticity" (p. 55).

Thus, undertaking a process to clarify and articulate IWB's focus was proposed as the first recommendation, given the manner in which it could impact on the quality of the projects that emerge (Recommendation 2) and the funding opportunities that are enacted (Recommendation 3).

Recommendation 2: Conceive of, Select, and Develop Projects

It was recommended that IWB conceive of, select, and develop projects to pursue. Members of the organization were encouraged to do this subsequent to carrying out Recommendation 1, so that they could hold the organization's focus in the forefront of their minds while brainstorming and evaluating possible projects to enact. It was also suggested that they focus on creating projects that will energize them, foster deep and broad collaboration, and encourage collective and individual development. It was recommended that they do this *before* carrying out Recommendation 3, because having projects specific projects to connect to and communicate about will make their exploration of structures and processes for funding integral praxis more creative and generative.

It is worth noting that even the process of creating projects could be carried out in a way involving radical collaboration and designed to foster learning. Approaches such as crowdsourcing and inquiry beyond the boundaries of the organization seem potentially worthy of exploration.

Recommendation 3: Conduct an "Opportunity Identification" Process to Explore Sources of Capital for IWB's Projects and Operations

An atypical organization conducting atypical work, such as IWB, may be in the position to develop atypical funding partnerships and platforms that would be otherwise inaccessible to conventional nonprofits. However, a certain combination of financing expertise, broad familiarity with emerging edges in social change praxis, and divergent thinking could prove helpful in identifying and opening new revenue channels that could hypothetically be 'right before the eyes' of IWB's stakeholders but which they have not yet made use of. For these reasons, it was recommended that stakeholders of IWB undertake an "opportunity identification" process to explore sources of capital for their projects and operations.

Recommendation 4: Establish structures That Provide Refuge, Foster Deep Collaboration, and Make Development Unavoidable

To foster opportunities for individual transformation, organizational development, and deep collaboration, it was proposed that IWB deliberately implement structures to make those things unavoidable. The word "structures" was specifically intended to connote: interaction rhythms (Nonaka, 1994), processes for determining and accomplishing goals, measures, and meaningful roles and accountabilities.

Organization Implications

It is notable that although the recommendations for further organizational action could be considered relatively simple in the context of the research questions that informed this study, these recommendations are appropriate for the organization at this point in its trajectory and given the study's findings. The study's concluding Areas for integral praxis will serve as frames for orienting discussion amongst IWB's core team as they carry out recommendations 1, 2, and 4. Recommendation 3 flows directly from Area 4. The concluding Areas present a number of opportunities for reimagining sustainability leadership in this historical moment. The specific role IWB will play in doing that, and the way they will enact that role in the coming years, is best supported by the recommendations in this study.

This study is in no way the final story on sustainability leadership. It does not address myriad details—technical and otherwise—but instead has tried to paint a picture in very broad strokes. The goal of this inquiry has been to offer some contours or frames in which new approaches to sustainability leadership could be imagined. It contributes to research by bringing together a range of ideas in interesting ways. There is no known answer to the ecological crisis, so it should be discussed in ways that can help to break our thinking out of its conventional patterns. This research has attempted to do that.

This study's exploration of how sustainability leadership can be enacted by IWB's stakeholders has broader implications for individuals and organizations within the field of sustainable development. The "four Rs" of integral transformation praxis presented at the end of chapter four offer a useful important framework for any organization looking to clarify and deepen its impact in today's moment. Greater inclusion of these four areas in social change work has the potential to help transform how sustainability leadership is conducted at various scales today and in the future.

Implications for Future Inquiry

The findings of this study present a number of openings for future inquiry that could lead to valuable knowledge in the context of social change practice. For example, Subtheme 5.3, "causal leadership" invites future inquiry about how individuals and groups with state training or state capacities practice sustainability leadership; what do they see, know, and do that differentiates their work, and its outcomes, from others?

Subtheme 4.2, "owning the destroyer role" also provides a rich context for inquiry about integral transformation praxis. What experiences do integral practitioners have of engaging roles and conversations around death and destruction that have been transformational and empowering? What communication practices would serve our species' need to confront its mortality, and how can this need be articulated in resonant ways?

The question of changing society's fundamental agreements and practices concerning what value is and how to measure it—explored from various angles in several of the findings in this study—is a robust area for future inquiry.

And finally, future studies could explore how IWB has responded to the recommendations in this research, and how their response is impacting the integral community and/or the broader field of sustainability leadership.

CONCLUSION

In summary, this chapter considers the perils, paradoxes, and possibilities of planetary transformation in our perplexing and unprecedented historical moment. Looking through an integral lens, very preliminary steps toward enacting a new, more adequate form of sustainability leadership were considered. This study identifies areas to include in an enactment of sustainability leadership for today's moment: "reviving"—breathing consciousness back into sustainability leadership; "reidentifying"—championing transformational inquiry concerning our collective existence; "recoding"—changing how value is measured and understood; and "reconfiguring"—creating new structures to enable and resource integral transformation praxis.

REFERENCES

Bennis, W. (2007). The challenges of leadership in the modern world: Introduction to the special issue. *The American Psychologist, 62*(1), 2–5. doi:10.1037/0003-066X.62.1.2 PMID:17209674

Brown, B. C. (2007). *The four worlds of sustainability: Drawing upon four universal perspectives to support sustainability initiatives.* Retrieved May 9, 2018 from: http://nextstepintegral.org/wp-content/uploads/2011/04/Four-Worlds-of-Sustainability-Barrett-C-Brown.pdf

Brown, B. C. (2011). *Conscious leadership for sustainability: How leaders with late-stage action logics design and implement sustainability initiatives* (Doctoral dissertation). Fielding Graduate University.

Burke, K. (1984). *Permanence and change: An anatomy of purpose* (3rd ed.). Berkeley, CA: University of California Press.

Burnes, B. (2004). Kurt Lewin and the planned approach to change: A re-appraisal. *Journal of Management Studies, 41*(6), 977–1002. doi:10.1111/j.1467-6486.2004.00463.x

Canadian Institutes of Health Research, Natural Sciences and Engineering Research Council of Canada, and Social Sciences and Humanities Research Council of Canada. (2014). *Tri-Council policy statement: Ethical conduct for research involving humans.* Retrieved from: http://www.pre.ethics.gc.ca/pdf/eng/tcps2-2014/TCPS_2_FINAL_Web.pdf

Coghlan, D., & Brannick, T. (2014). *Doing action research in your own organization* (4th ed.). Thousand Oaks, CA: Sage.

Cook-Greuter, S. R. (2013). *Nine levels of increasing embrace in ego development: A full-spectrum theory of vertical growth and meaning making.* Retrieved from: http://www.cook-greuter.com/Cook-Greuter%209%20levels%20paper%20new%201.1%2714%2097p%5B1%5D.pdf

Creswell, J. W. (2013). *Qualitative inquiry & research design: Choosing among five approaches* (3rd ed.). Thousand Oaks, CA: SAGE.

Du Plessis, G. P. (2013). *The import of integral pluralism in striving towards an integral metatheory of addiction.* Paper presented at the 3rd Biannual Integral Theory Conference, Redwood City, CA.

Edwards, M. G. (2010). *Organisational transformation for sustainability: An integral metatheory*. New York, NY: Routledge. doi:10.4324/9780203859933

Esbjörn-Hargens, S. (2010). An ontology of climate change: Integral pluralism and the enactment of multiple objects. *Journal of Integral Theory and Practice*, 5(1), 143–174.

Esbjörn-Hargens, S. (2014). *Tetradynamics: Quadrants in action*. Sebastopol, CA: MetaIntegral Publishers.

Floyd, J. (2012). Action research and integral futures, a path to embodied foresight. *Futures*, 44(10), 870–882. doi:10.1016/j.futures.2012.09.001

Gardner, H. (1983). *Frames of Mind: The Theory of Multiple Intelligences*. New York: Basic Books.

Gardner, H. (1993). *Multiple intelligences: The theory in practice: A reader* (2nd ed.). Boston, MA: Basic Books.

Glesne, C. (2016). *Becoming qualitative researchers: An introduction* (5th ed.). Boston, MA: Pearson.

Gunnlaugson & Brabant. (Eds.). (2016). *Cohering the integral we space: Engaging collective emergence, wisdom and healing in groups*. Integral Publishing House.

Hedlund, N. (2010). Integrally researching integral research: Enactive perspectives on the future of the field. *Journal of Integral Theory and Practice.*, 2(5), 1–30.

Hedlund, N., Esbjörn-Hargens, S., Hartwig, M., & Bhaskar, R. (2016). Introduction: On the deep need for integrative metatheory in the twenty-first century. In Metatheory for the 21st century: critical realism and integral theory in dialogue (pp. 1-34). New York: Routledge.

Hochachka, G. (2008). Case studies in integral approaches in international development: An integral research project. *Journal of Integral Theory and Practice*, 3(2), 58–108.

Hochachka, G. (2015, July). *The integral you don't see: Activism at the frothy edge.* Presentation given at the 4th Biannual Integral Theory Conference, Sonoma, CA.

Integral Without Borders. (n.d.). *Vision and purpose*. Retrieved January 15th, 2017 from: https://integralwithoutborders.net

Integral Without Borders. (n.d.). *What we do*. Retrieved January 15th, 2017 from: https://integralwithoutborders.net

Kauffman, S. (2016). *Humanity in a creative universe*. New York: Oxford University Press.

Laloux, F. (2014). *Reinventing organizations: A guide to creating organizations inspired by the next stage in human consciousness*. Brussels: Nelson Parker.

Leonard, A. (2004). *Integral communication* (Doctoral dissertation). University of Florida. Retrieved May 9th, 2018 from: http://www.integral-life-practice.com/wp-content/uploads/2011/06/integral-communication_by_adam_b_leonard.pdf

Lewin, K. (1947). Frontiers in group dynamics: Concept, method and reality in social science; social equilibria and social change. *Human Relations*, 1(1), 5–41. doi:10.1177/001872674700100103

Lipmanowicz, H., & McCandless, K. (2014). *The surprising power of liberating structures: Simple rules to unleash a culture of innovation*. Liberating Structures Press.

Meadows, D. (2008). *Thinking in systems: A primer*. White River Junction, VT: Chelsea Green Publishing.

Mulvihill, P. R., & Milan, M. J. (2007, August). (2007/8). Subtle world: Beyond sustainability, beyond information. *Futures, 39*(6), 657–668. doi:10.1016/j.futures.2006.11.006

Nonaka, I. (1994). A Dynamic Theory of Organizational Knowledge Creation. *Organization Science, 5*(1), 14–37. doi:10.1287/orsc.5.1.14

O'Brien, K., & Hochachka, G. (2010). Integral Adaptation to Climate Change. *Journal of Integral Theory & Practice, 5*(1). Retrieved from http://aqaljournal.integralinstitute.org/Public/JITP_5(1).pdf#page=100

Palys, T. (2008). Purposive sampling. In L. M. Given (Ed.), *The Sage Encyclopedia of. Qualitative Research Methods* (Vol. 2, pp. 697–698). Los Angeles: Sage.

Patten, T. (2013). *Enacting an integral revolution: How can we have truly radical conversations in a time of global crisis?* Paper presented at the third biannual Integral Theory Conference, Burlingame, CA. Retrieved from: http://www.terrypatten.com/sites/default/files/ITC2013.Patten.pdf

Piaget, J. (1971). *Biology and Knowledge*. Chicago: University of Chicago Press.

Reason, P., & Bradbury, H. (2001). *Handbook of action research: Participative inquiry and practice*. New York: Sage.

Robinson, J. (2018). *Reimagining sustainability leadership for this historical moment* (Unpublished master's thesis). Royal Roads University, Canada.

Rowe, W., Graf, M., Agger-Gupta, N., Piggot-Irvine, E., & Harris, B. (2013). Action Research Engagement: Creating the Foundation for Organizational Change. ALARA monograph series no.5.

Societies Act 2015 (BC) s. 2.2.1 (CA).

Stein, Z. (2009). Educational crises and the scramble for usable knowledge. *Integral Review, 2*(5), 354–367.

Stein, Z. (2016). Beyond nature and humanity: Reflections on the emergence and purpose of metatheories. In Metatheory for the 21st century: critical realism and integral theory in dialogue. New York: Routledge.

Stein, Z. (in review). On realizing the possibilities of emancipatory metatheory: beyond the cognitive maturity fallacy, toward an education revolution. In Metatheory for the anthropocene: emancipatory praxis for planetary flourishing: critical realism and integral theory in dialogue (vol. 2). New York: Routledge.

Stein. (2015). *Desperate measures: Global crises of measurement and their metatheoretical solutions*. Paper presented at the 4th Biannual Integral Theory Conference, Sonoma, CA.

Stringer, E. T. (2014). *Action research* (4th ed.). Thousand Oaks, CA: Sage.

Teehankee, B. (2017). Institutional entrepreneurship: Transforming management education for participatory development in the Philippines. In H. Bradbury & ... (Eds.), *Cooking with action research: Stories and resources for self and community transformation*. Portland, OR: AR.

Torbert, B., Cook-Greuter, S., Fisher, D., Foldy, E., Gauthier, A., Keeley, J., ... Tran, M. (2004). *Action inquiry: The secret of timely and transforming leadership*. San Francisco, CA: BerrettKoehler Publishers.

Walker, M. (2009). Capabilities, flourishing and the normative purposes of action research. In S. Noffke & B. Somekh (Eds.), *Handbook of educational action research*. Thousand Oaks, CA: Sage. doi:10.4135/9780857021021.n28

Wilber, K. (2000). *Integral psychology: Consciousness, spirit, psychology, therapy*. Boston: Shambhala.

Wilber, K. (2006a). *Excerpt A: An integral age at the leading edge*. Retrieved May 9th, 2018 from: http://www.kenwilber.com/Writings/PDF/ExcerptA_KOSMOS_2003.pdf

Wilber, K. (2006b). *Excerpt B: The many ways we touch—three principles helpful for any integral approach*. Retrieved May 9th, 2018 from: http://www.kenwilber.com/writings/read_pdf/84

Wilber, K. (2006c). *Excerpt C: The ways we are in this together: Intersubjectivity and interobjectivity in the holonic kosmos*. Retrieved May 9th, 2018 from: http://www.kenwilber.com/writings/read_pdf/85

Wilber, K. (2006d). *Integral spirituality: A startling new role for religion in the modern and postmodern world*. Boston: Integral Books.

Wilber, K. (Speaker). (2015, October 28). *Being vs. knowing: Ending the debate between epistemology and ontology* [Video file]. Retrieved May 9, 2018 from: https://integrallife.com/being-vs-knowing-ending-debate-between-epistemology-and-ontology/

Wilber, K. (2016). Miracle of we. In O. Gunnlaugson & M. Brabant (Eds.), *Cohering the integral we space: Engaging collective emergence, wisdom and healing in groups*. Integral Publishing House.

Wilber, K. (2017). *The religion of tomorrow: A vision for the future of the great traditions—more inclusive, more comprehensive, more complete*. Boulder, CO: Shambhala.

Witt, K. (2014). Defensive states and states of healthy response in integrally informed psychotherapy: An interpersonal neurobiological contribution to shadow. *Journal of Integral Theory and Practice*, *9*(2), 35.

Wittmayer, J. M., & Schäpke, N. (2014). Action, research and participation: Roles of researchers in sustainability transitions. *Sustainability Science*, *9*(4), 483–496. doi:10.100711625-014-0258-4

KEY TERMS AND DEFINITIONS

Action Research: Action research is a general term that refers to research developed with and/or by the people being studied and involves both taking and reflecting on actions to solve problems or create desired change.

Integral Action Research: In this study, the phrase *integral action research* is used to represent a form of action research that (1) is broadly informed by integral metatheory, (2) emphasizes the integration of first-, second-, and third-person perspectives, (3) takes an enactive stance on reality in which the observer and the observed are understood to be part of the same process, and (4) adopts an emancipatory predisposition.

Integral Metatheory (IM): IM proposes organizing principles concerning theories about reality, and offers a framework for understanding how particular theories disclose and account for phenomena in the ways that they do, on what terms they should be evaluated, and how they relate to each other.

Integral Without Borders (IWB): IWB is an international think tank and NGO focused on applying integral metatheory to international development. IWB is incorporated in British Columbia (BC), Canada as a non-profit society, and operates as an informally structured community of development practitioners and social change activists working in a number of countries around the globe.

Sustainability Leadership: Sustainability leadership has been problematic and challenging to define, but for the purposes of this study was taken to entail the realization of adequate responses to the metacrisis.

Transformation: A term used in this study to indicate deep or revolutionary change, particularly involving structures in the lower left (cultural) and lower right (systems) quadrants.

ENDNOTES

[1] Under the Societies Act in BC, a society is a legal entity that may be formed for "one or more lawful purposes, including, without limitation, agricultural, artistic, benevolent, charitable, educational, environmental, patriotic, philanthropic, political, professional, recreational, religious, scientific, social or sporting purposes". (Societies Act, 2015)

[2] Meadows called these deep shared beliefs "paradigms", however I have avoided that term here because it is inconsistent with Wilber's (2006a) view of paradigms—not as ideas but as practices and injunctions that enact data or disclose aspects of reality.

[3] AQAL is an acronym for "All Quadrants, All Levels" and is shorthand for "a theoretical framework [IM] that explicitly honours and includes" all five archetypal patterns described earlier in this chapter: "all quadrants, all levels, all lines, all states, all types" (Wilber, 2006a, p. 88).

Chapter 17
Integral Post-Analysis of Design-Based Research of an Organizational Learning Process for Strategic Renewal of Environmental Management

A. Faye Bres
University of Calgary, Canada

ABSTRACT

This chapter is based on a design-based research study of organizational learning and on a subsequent integral analysis of how and why organizational learning did, and did not, occur in the study. Integral theory is applied to deepen the understanding of how human organizations learn and adapt as complex adaptive systems made up of nested, operationally closed groups and individuals. The level of development and learning potential of an organization, as holon, can be understood as an emergent property resulting from the coordination of function and action of the unities that make up the system, even given that the levels of development and learning potentials of the groups and individuals in an organization are not consistent across the organization. The advantages of combining complexity and integral theory are explored, as both are understood to provide different, complementary interpretations of whole human systems.

INTRODUCTION

Application of Complexity Theory provides researchers with a rigorous and varied scientific perspective to investigate human organizations. It is, essentially, a "theory of everything" that integrates knowledge from a wide variety of sciences including ecology, evolutionary biology, and physics. Complexity Theory has a remarkable quality of clarifying, of making sense at a whole system level without requiring a deep reductionist focus on the details. The "sense" becomes transparent as we grow to understand each

DOI: 10.4018/978-1-5225-5873-6.ch017

unique complex system, as complex systems generate their own coherence. Through their capacity to self-organize, complex systems actual *make* "sense", and we can see that sense more clearly through application of Complexity Theory. The theory, however, can be intimidating to the uninitiated because of its jargon, and reductionist because it is rooted hard scientific research. To apply Complexity Theory effectively in research on human systems, we need to be sensitive to its limitations in dealing with soft topics such as culture, personal perspectives, and consciousness.

Integral Theory too is a "theory of everything", but where Complexity Theory is firmly rooted in a positivistic and objective perspective of hard sciences; Integral Theory also includes subtle and subjective perspectives of "interiors". Integral Theory provides a holistic analytical tool that invites us to consider all perspectives, from all academic disciplines, when looking at a system. It also invites us to consider explicitly how a system grows and develops.

In this chapter, a study of organizational learning is presented as an example of how modeling of a human organization as a complex system can be used to understand its ability to adapt to changing conditions. At the time of the study, Complexity Theory was applied alone as the theoretical framework; and the study is reinterpreted here with an Integral Theory lens to consider how the two theories together could provide a more inclusive and comprehensive view.

THEORETICAL FRAMEWORK

Before proceeding to a description of the design and methods of the study, an introduction to the Complexity theoretical framework is provided, along with an brief explanation of the gaps in the theory that could be addressed by applying Integral Theory as a secondary lens.

In the study presented, Complexity Theory was selected with the expectation that it could provide framework for modeling and interpretation of an organization as a learning system: a complex collective human organization undergoing adaptation, development or learning.

Morin (1992) points out that in studying complexity, the focus is not on creating a general theory that covers everything from atoms to stars and cells to societies. It is rather to consider such phenomena in a richer way, "in the light of the complexity of system and organization" (p. 42). Complex systems of all types share the quality of "self-organization"; it is through their functioning as a complex system that they adapt and change over time in a form of co-evolution with dynamic changes in the environments in which they exist. As Morin explains, order is achieved *through an act of ordering*. Complexity research looks not at order, but at the process or act of ordering, at *organization*. And "organization is not an institution, but a continually generative and regenerative activity" (Morin, 1992, p. 43). Through their dynamic internal functions and the interactions of their many diverse parts, complex systems all exhibit the characteristic of self-organization. Rather than dissecting and analyzing the ordered structure of the system, complexity gives a researcher the opportunity to see how an organization functions on a macro level, and then focus in on aspects of the system that are of special interest.

Every complex system is unique, and it is in its unique composition and the interactions of its parts that coherence is generated. This quality of uniqueness makes it both challenging to study such systems, and at the same time provides a structure to research that includes a special key: though each system is entirely unique, they all exhibit similar properties. These properties are key to unlocking mysteries

Figure 1. 10 common properties of complex systems
Based on Mitleton-Kelley (1998), Cilliers (1998), Bres (2016)

1. A complex system is made up of many elements, both similar and diverse
2. The elements interact in a dynamic and nonlinear way
3. The system experiences "feedback"
4. The system is hierarchically ordered and nested, elements are made up of other elements
5. Boundaries in the system are open to exchanges and signals, but operationally closed
6. The elements are interdependent and they have influence over each other
7. The system co-evolves with its environment
8. The system experiences self-organization
9. The system displays emergence, properties at one level are generated through interactions at a lower level
10. The history of the system is embedded in its structure

of all complex systems. The system *makes* its own sense. Though it may hold infinite mysteries in its expression, there are things you can be sure you will find in any complex system that are like the fundamental laws of physics.

Common Properties of Complex Systems

The theory is commonly criticized because there is no firm consensus on the basic principles of the theory (Cilliers, 1998). This lack of consensus is undoubtedly associated with the fact that complexity principles are recognized in many different fields of study, and the theoretical evolution has not been coordinated between the disciplines.

The common principles of complexity are of great interest as they provide the keys to interpreting and understanding complex systems. Two key sources were used in this study to generate a list of common principles (Figure 1). Mitleton-Kelley (1998) suggests that all complex systems demonstrate the following: self-organization, emergence, connectivity, interdependence, feedback, far from equilibrium conditions, space of possibilities, co-evolution, historicity & time, path-dependence, and creation of new order. Cilliers (1998) offers the following list of characteristics of complex systems: complex systems consist of large numbers of elements; these elements undergo dynamic interactions; there are many of these interactions, they are rich, each element is influenced by many others; the interactions are non-linear, therefore small changes can be associated with large scale change; interactions are generally 'close,' though long-range interactions can also occur; interactions involve positive and negative feedback loops; complex systems are 'open' and their boundaries or borders are often difficult to distinguish; they operate under far-from-equilibrium conditions; they have 'history,' time is irreversible and the influences of a system's past effects its current conditions; the individual elements of the system are 'unaware' of what happens on a higher or emergent level, and they are only aware of local conditions.

Theoretically, all of these characteristics should be observed in any complex system, however interpretation is highly specific to the system in question. For example, the term "history" has a very different connotation when ascribed to a biological organism versus a social system. "Interdependence" means something very different in biochemical terms than in human interactions. In this research project, the interpretations of the properties in the organization being studied were a key focus of interpretation of data, and lead to a deep understanding of a whole system without requiring detailed analysis of all of its parts.

Human Complex Adaptive Systems

Among scientists there is still widespread skepticism that human systems function as natural complex adaptive systems, that complexity serves as anything more than a metaphor when applied to social systems (Morgan, 2006). This criticism is rooted in the assumption that humans are somehow separate from or above nature. Identifying human organizing as different from other natural forms of organizing may be central to the decoupling that appears to have occurred between humans and the natural environment, and the unfortunate tendency of humans to cause harm to the environments upon which they depend for survival.

Maturana and Varela's work (1998) on the biological roots of human cognition emphasizes that human cognition has evolved on earth through processes of self-organization; processes that are similarly expressed in all complex systems. Human social organizations are extensions of human cognitive evolution, where our social interactions generate social structures with operational features that support our existence, a process of autopoiesis. Human systems are not merely metaphorically similar to natural systems, they represent an advanced and recent emergence of order in the process of complex systems adaptation and development at this place and time in our evolving world. The philosophy, theory and concepts for studying human systems are rich and evolving themselves, and though there is still much learning to be done in the area, the understandings being developed in cognitive science, organization theory, Complex Adaptive Systems Theory, and other related scholarly explorations provides rich fodder for those interested in exploring human potential for growth and adaptation.

Letiche (2000) takes a similar approach to understanding how human systems differ from non-human systems. He emphasises that "Complexity Theory is conceptualized as a product of human consciousness that can be used to understand human consciousness" (Letiche, 2000, p. 546). Knowledge is social, and the emergence of knowledge in society is a function of human interactions, human experience. Letiche suggests that "(T)raditional scientific concepts and research paradigms only suffice so long as a higher level of organization than the one they refer to is not achieved" (p. 546). In other words, complexity science could transcend the scientific paradigm. Complexity provides an entirely different ontology, one based on the emergence of understanding and knowledge that is socially defined. Letiche (2000) criticises many theorists for applying concepts derived from various disciplines to human social interactions without acknowledging human experience as being an emergent phenomenon in itself. He suggests that many theorists, seem to ignore the 'experience' of the human subject in complex organizations.

The central issue that appears to distinguish human systems from non-human complex systems is the human ability to differentiate the 'self,' which allows humans to interact with their environment *reflexively* (Allen, 1998). This feature is in direct contrast to the point in Cilliers' (1998) list of features of complex systems (see above), which states that individual elements in a system are 'unaware' of organization at the emergent level. It appears that human self awareness and consciousness may actually create an interference of sorts that disrupts a human system's capacity to self-organize.

Goldspink and Kay (2010) argue that failure to recognize this unique feature of human systems limits our ability to understand social Organizations as complex systems, and they develop a definition of *reflexive emergence* to clarify:

Reflexive emergence operates where the agents of the system, like humans, have a capacity to distinguish self from other and therefore to interact reflexively with their environment. This reflexivity results in a unique feedback path between the emergent structure and the individual agents—each agent being an

Integral Post-Analysis of Design-Based Research of an Organizational Learning Process

observer of the structure he/she contributes to producing and the process of observation contributes to what emerges.(p. 58)

In human systems, non-reflexive emergence can occur through pre-linguistic structural coupling of agents, which Goldspink and Kay (2010) still consider social as it happens between humans. These kinds of emergences result from local interactions and preserve the quality of non-human systems in that the individual elements are not 'aware' of the structures or macro level patterns of which they are a part. When linguistic capacity, and thus the capacity for abstraction, is exercised, the nature of emergence changes. The agents become more plastic, more structurally flexible, and reflexivity changes the way that the system responds. The system has enhanced capacities for generating and supporting higher order structures. In these systems, the agents are aware of the structures and patterns emerging from their interactions, an interaction Gilbert (2002) calls *second order emergence*. This feedback between macro and micro phenomena is not seen in non-reflexive (non-human, mechanical, physical) systems.

Goldspink and Kay's (2010) ideas relate to Maturana and Varela's (1998) model of social cognitive evolution of animals (including humans), which involves both ontogenic (during the developmental changes of individuals) and phylogenic (over many generations of individuals) changes. The reflexive activities of the individuals involved in the creation of social structures can be interpreted as a unique feature of human complex systems, an internal feedback loop (Goldspink & Kay, 2010) that allows for structural changes on the ontogenic level. Because of the reflexive nature of individual humans, human systems may be able to change much faster than evolution has allowed in the past. Unlike the slow change in the social behaviour of animals as they adapt, which tends to ensure maintenance of environmental coupling, human social systems appear to have changed so quickly that they have become uncoupled from the environment, with disastrous effects of maladaptation in human societies. Human Organizations may be able to achieve coupling with the environment if the reflexive function is intentionally controlled or disciplined through *learning*, in a way that is consistent with the natural conditions of emergence as far as we currently understand them.

Complexity-Based Organizational Learning

There is a considerable amount of research literature that applies complexity thinking to organizational learning. R. L. Flood (2009) seeks to transcend Peter Senge's classic work on learning organizations by applying concepts that go beyond the traditional scientific approach associated with predict and control management. He discusses the conflict between traditional systems-based organizational learning, specifically the model developed and promoted by Senge, and complexity thinking. Managers cannot expect actions to be realized exactly as intended when they are carried out over an extended period of time through multiple complex interactions with unpredictable outcomes. As Flood remarks, "anyone who honestly believes they have everything under control is seriously out of touch with what is going on" (p. 91). The best the manager can hope to do is to understand short term local interactions. Long-range planning, when based on fixed implementation, is inconsistent with complexity. This does not of course mean that long-range planning should be abandoned, but rather that there must be constant monitoring of and adaptation to emerging changes and conditions if the intended outcome is not to be derailed by some small local disturbance. Managers need to be aware that the perception of certainty can kill adaptability (Flood, 2009). Organizational learning should be designed to deal with uncertainty, and to improve adaptability or dynamic capability.

Integral Post-Analysis of Design-Based Research of an Organizational Learning Process

Zollo and Winter (2002) define "dynamic capability" as "a learned and stable pattern of collective activity through which the Organization systematically generates and modifies its operating routines in pursuit of improved effectiveness" (p. 340). The have developed a theory of organizational learning intended to support the development of dynamic capability through the careful evolution of operating routines. They look at bridging the gap between behaviorist models of learning, which focus on the accumulation of tacit knowledge, and cognitivist models, which focus more on the articulation and codification of knowledge supported by intentional learning. Tacit knowledge is readily accumulated in situations where routine, relatively predictable activities are frequently repeated—a form of unintentional learning. Zollo and Winter propose a model to identify when such learning can be enhanced through deliberate learning, which would consist in articulation and codification of knowledge resulting in the formal definition of 'operational routines.' They carefully reflect on the potential problems of articulation and codification, and the apparent paradox between creating structured routines and developing dynamic capability. The emphasis is on the actual activity of individuals, who are invited to go through the process of analysing their experiences in a group in order to try to define their routines. The deliberate cognitive process of articulating and codifying this information is a learning exercise that allows the individuals and groups to reflect deeply on their past experiences, and reveals the complexity of the tasks that they are seeking to codify. The objective is not to *change operational routines to be better*, but rather to *enhance adaptive capacity*. Despite the apparent paradox between the structured activity of codifying a routine and the dynamic nature of adaptation, it is understood that the *process* of codifying enhances learning (Zollo & Winter 2002). If the Organization has a defined method of identifying and analysing potential and emerging sources of environmental information and feedback, it can establish a learning cycle that will allow it to be more adaptive over time.

What Is Organizational Learning, and Who Is Doing the Learning?

Individual human learning is a cognitive function and, as organizations lack a brain, there are obviously some very significant differences between individual human learning and organizational learning. Education research concerning neurological function or individual behaviour modification as learning is clearly not applicable at the organizational level. Simon (1991) suggests that an organization can only learn through the learning of its members, or by adding new members who bring new knowledge with them. Argyris and Schön (1978) and Hedberg (1981) also suggest that it is the individuals that make up the Organization that do the actual learning.

Popper and Lipshitz (2000) recognize the functional correlations between individual human learning and organizational learning. There are organizational level processes and structures in Organizations that act to collect, analyse, store, disseminate and use information in a way that allows the Organization itself to learn. Through the operation of "Organizational Learning Mechanisms" and through the actions of individuals in the Organization, the ability to learn is institutionalized. Organizational learning also involves the dissemination of information between individuals and units in an Organization, which takes place at various *levels* of information processing (Popper & Lipshitz, 2000). Note that "levels" here refer to an organizational hierarchy, not to be confused with integral, developmental levels in Wilber's work.

These *levels* are also addressed in Crossan, Lane and White's model of organizational learning (1999). Their "4I" method involves capturing the intuitive, tacit learning that occurs as individuals in an Organization conduct their work activities. Once this knowledge is identified, it is sent forward into the institution through a systematic process of interpretation and implementation. This is consistent with the idea that creative ideas are generated by people, not Organizations, but Organizations can still learn if those ideas are institutionalized (Nonaka & Takeuchi, 1995; Simon, 1991; Crossan et al., 1999). The learning of the individuals and groups becomes embedded into the institution through implementation of organizational structures, policies, procedures and strategies.

Marsick and Watkins' (1990) educational model of informal learning recognizes that learning occurs at multiple levels: individual, group, and Organizational. Learning involves mutual construction of new norms as individuals learn in group or Organizational settings. At the individual level, informal learning often involves the development of skills and knowledge. At the group level the construction of knowledge and norms can occur through collective action. At the organization level, norms and mutually constructed knowledge become embedded in systems, policies, processes, and services. The tenets of this model merge with the ideas of transformational learning, where the individual is stimulated to learn by critical analysis of shared norms and values (Mezirow, 1997), as well as organizational learning according to the 4I model (Crossan et al., 1999), where learning at an individual level is fed forward into an institution. These ties between organizational learning literature and education research literature were applied in this study.

Another interesting potential contribution to organizational learning research from Education research is Vygotsky's concept of the Zone of Proximal Development (ZPD). A learner's developmental stage is defined not only by her current cognitive capabilities, but also by her potential to advance in development under the guidance of a more capable person. Assessing the learner's stage of development allows for the definition of what the learner is capable of learning next, and design of learning challenges that are achievable to the learner. As individual learning can be scaffolded (Wood, Bruner, & Ross, 1976) with the support of a "capable person", organizational learning of an operational group in an organization may be scaffolded by identifying other groups (or even individuals) in the organization that have already developed structures and processes for similar challenges encountered in the activity of the organization. In the study described in this chapter, this concept became more important as an understanding emerged of how the levels of development (as defined in Wilber's AQAL model) varied in different individuals in the organization, and in different collective groups in functional and operational units in an organization. The potential for self-scaffolding in an organization was recognized as a characteristic of the organization's complex functioning, and a part of its adaptive capacity.

Integral Theory

Integral Theory, like Complexity theory, is a "theory of everything". Unlike Complexity Theory, it was developed by a single theorist (Ken Wilber), it is highly consistent and unified, and it includes a concise and clear Theoretical map. And where Complexity Theory struggles to differentiate human from non-human and individual from collective, Integral Theory seamlessly unites such dualities into a single framework: the All Quadrants, All Levels or AQAL framework (Figure 2).

Wilber uses this simple AQAL quadrangle to order an interpretation of human knowledge and wisdom developed through a very wide range sources, from scientific disciplines to individual and collective experiences. Two axes delineate the quadrants: Individual and collective, and interior/subjective and exterior/objective. The quadrants are not separations, but rather distinctions of parts which make up wholes or "holons", each having expressions in all quadrants. For example, an organization includes individuals and groups, each with interior and exterior qualities and characteristics. The quadrants can be understood as intention and behaviour of individuals (upper left and right), and cultural and social

Figure 2. Wilber's AQAL model
(adapted from Wilber, 2007, p. 22)

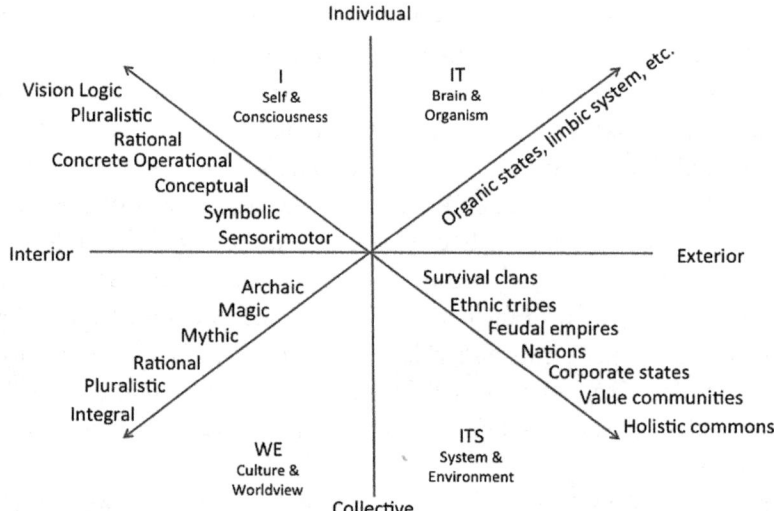

systems of groups (Lower left and right). The model invites us to consider that no part of a system exists on its own, and focus on singular perspectives generates incomplete understanding. We are invited to consider spiritual and phenomenological understanding of human intentions, psychological and neurological interpretations of individual behaviours, hermeneutic and cultural perspectives of groups of individuals, and structural investigation of human social systems. Similar to complexity theory, the AQAL model seeks to provide a generalized map of the order and characteristics of whole systems and their parts, assembled in a hierarchical pattern. Each quadrant exhibits a pattern of growth and development over a set of levels that are defined in a way that they can be interpreted according to the aspects.

Though the AQAL graphic is simple, its application is infinitely complex; as is apparent when one enters the extensive literature Wilber has generated to develop and explain the model. As in complexity theory, the aim is not to explicate all of everything, but to provide a framework to guide our understanding and learning.

Where Complexity Theory focuses primarily on modern western objective science, Integral theory recognizes subjective and interpretivist perspectives from a wide range of cultures and historical periods as all contributing depth and breadth to human understanding and wisdom. Interestingly, both complexity theory and Integral theory have deep foundations in evolutionary biology. But where complexity theory tends to emphasize the unpredictability and randomness in evolution, Integral Theory explicates a clear hierarchical order to development. Both theories recognize the self-organizing nature of complex systems, but Integral Theory carefully delineates the order of "levels of development" that can be used to understand a directionality in growth. The concept is consistent with Complexity, which addresses the topic through the concept of systems nesting.

The stages of human individual development are familiar to and widely accepted by education researchers in terms of individual development through childhood, and to a lesser degree in Adult Education, but much less so in organizational development research. Similar models have been developed by multiple theorists in the past, including Freud, Piaget, and Kegan, and others, which have all been synthesized into an integral model presented by Wilber. Wilber goes beyond a simple description of

Integral Post-Analysis of Design-Based Research of an Organizational Learning Process

individual childhood development (both internal individual and cultural), and applies the model of development to external and collective development from evolution of species, to evolution of social, collective and organizational systems. The defining feature of all development according to Wilber is the concept of "include and transcend", whereby at each stage of development the holon undergoing development includes the learnings of all previous stages of development, and transcends their limitations by taking a higher or broader, more inclusive perspective. Worldviews develop from Archaic, Magic, Mythic, Rational, Pluralistic to Integral. Cognitive levels evolve from Sensorimotor, Symbolic, Conceptual, Concrete Operational, Rational, Pluralistic, to Vision Logic. These and other hierarchies of developmental growth are modeled by Wilber to provide a comprehensive interpretive tool for assessing levels of development of both individuals and groups.

STUDY DESIGN AND METHODOLOGY: DESIGNING THE RESEARCH PROCESS

The case study presented here was of The City of Calgary and its response to a major flooding event that occurred in June of 2013. With a focus on the environmental management function of the organization, the study looked at what was learned about the interactions between the organization and its environment during the flood, and at potential ways to institutionalize enhancements to adaptive capacity of the organization by "feeding forward" or formalizing naturally emergent adaptive processes and structures. A Design-Based Research methodology was used to design and test an organizational learning process aimed at formalizing naturally emerging organizational processes for adaptation.

Research Topic: How Can We Apply Complexity Theory and Concepts of Adaptation to Human Systems?

The purpose of the study was to observe and characterize the complex adaptive systems function of an organization with the goal of designing mechanisms for the support and continued development of its adaptive capacity. Organizational adaptation was interpreted as an organizational process of learning. The initial assessment of the problem suggested that a complexity-based adaptive model of organizing would be an enhancement complementary to existing systems-based (Deming, 1986), "predict and control" environmental management approaches. The assumption was that a bottom-up approach to organizing, focusing on applying common principles of complex system function to achieve self-organization, could help establish a "coupled" relationship between the organization and its environment, where the organization would co-adapt with the dynamic changing nature of that environment. This research investigated whether this intuition was valid, and how complexity thinking could be useful in establishing organizational adaptation as a complement to existing environmental management processes.

Wilber's Integral Theory AQAL model was not used in the design or analysis of the study as it was conducted. Though it was identified as a potential informing theory, the initial grounding in Complexity Theory was considered adequate, and as a novice researcher in a PhD program, incorporation of the AQAL model was simply too overwhelming given the already ambitious scope of the research project. The Complexity framework delineated the study to an objective, external view (the Lower Left quadrant of Wilber's AQAL model), and focused on how the organization as a collective responded to changes in the environment *structurally* (e.g. With responses in policy, organizational structure, and management processes). The underlying expectation was that changes in structure made in response to environmental changes could potentially improve the organization's adaptive capacity as its "learning" was embedded in the structure of the system. It was hoped that taking this focused, objective view would make the research project more manageable, but in retrospect the reductionism of the approach may have created as many problems in the research design as it avoided.

Individual behaviour in the learning units (individuals, business units, work units) was clearly a factor in the complex systems function of the organization, but was not the focus of analysis. Culture, also, was recognized as a significant factor in the ability of the organization to learn. Both culture and behaviour, however, were considered to be only influencing factors in organizational learning, and the internal phenomenological experience of the individual actors in the system was left completely of the scope of the study, partially because of the potential implications for research ethics. The "learning" was interpreted, as per Complexity Theory, as an actual *structural* change in the *organization*. This included changes in policies, procedures, roles, infrastructure, or business processes; all external and collective in the Lower Right quadrant of the AQAL model.

Introduction to Design-Based Research Methodology

Design-based research (DBR) is a methodology developed by educational researchers that focuses both on improvement of practice and development of learning theory (Anderson & Shattuck, 2012). The approach involves designing a "learning intervention", working with practitioners in a naturalized learning setting, and testing and improving the intervention over several iterations. Through iterative adjustment of various design aspects of the learning intervention, the researcher provides experimental evidence of the effectiveness of the intervention in a naturalized setting, which enhances validity (Brown, 1992). As in much action research, the researcher aims to impact learning, not merely to study it (Barab and Squire, 2004). At the same time the approach is focused on the production and development of teaching and learning theory (Cobb, diSessa, Lehrer, & Schauble, 2003). DBR focuses on characterizing situations rather than controlling variables, and also focuses on social interactions, which is key this study's focus on self-organization (Barab & Squire, 2004). It is slowly gaining popularity, and is being used effectively in a wide range of settings, though currently it is used mostly in K-12 settings (Anderson & Shattuck, 2012).

The method was selected because of its compatibility with a complexity-based theoretical framework, and because of the appropriateness of its pragmatic approach in the study, which aimed to investigate potential enhancements to The City of Calgary's environmental management systems. The participants were interested in the potential for practical application in their work, not only theoretical-based research, which is grounded in explanatory approaches and merely describes, explains and predicts, without being of practical use (van Aken, 2004).

Gowin's Vee

To facilitate consistency and coherence in the research design, Gowin's Vee (Novak & Gowin, 1984) was applied, as illustrated below in Figure 3. This heurism was developed specifically for educational research methods that investigate the phenomenon of knowledge formation through naturalistic, qualitative studies. The Vee heurism brings rigor to such studies, requiring the researcher to maintain consistency in epistemology through alignment of worldview, philosophy, theory, and concepts in all phases of the research. The Vee was applied as a tool during the design of the research to focus the research topic, select a specific research subject, and identify coherent research questions and select an appropriate method. The model was then used to address the methodological side of the study, aligning the design of data collection and analysis with theory and concepts, leading to the development of findings and knowledge claims, from specifics to generalizations.

Doing a PhD is as much about learning to be a researcher as it is about gaining and developing knowledge in a disciplinary field. A traditional approach to research requires a PhD student to demonstrate the ability to maintaining consistency between the research and Theory, and work with other academic researchers in the field. While this is critical in disciplinary research, the focus on consistency with theory proved to be problematic in this complexity based study. As will be discussed later in this chapter, the focus on consistency in application of theory distracted from a key aspect of Complexity Theory itself: that a complex system generates its own unique and irreducible consistency. Relying on Theory and established research to provide objectivity and validity may actually interfere with the ability of researchers to see what the system has to teach them. It is much more important to ensure consistency with the nature of the complex system being investigated than with the theory and existing research.

Description of the Project

In June of 2013, the city of Calgary experienced a massive flooding event of the Bow and Elbow rivers. With respect for the suffering and loss that the flood caused to Calgarians, the emergency situation, with its disruption of normal operating conditions, stimulated many positive events in community action and creative, innovative actions by individuals and groups working in The City. As established structures, both physical (infrastructure) and organizational, were destabilized, damaged and destroyed, dynamic interaction between the many elements that make up the system created opportunities for adaptation, emergence, and self-organization. The flood took place only a few weeks before The Calgary Stampede, a world class Rodeo and Agricultural Fair in which Calgarians take enormous pride. The event venue was among the areas impacted severely by the flood, as were many residential areas, the river park system,

Figure 3. Alignment of the Conceptual and Methodological Aspects of the Study
(Adapted from Novak and Gowin, 1984)

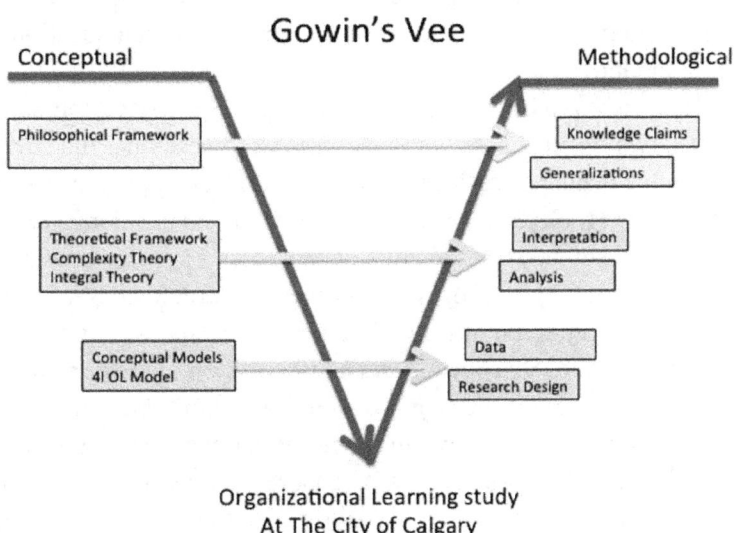

bridges, roads, businesses and a significant portion of the down town. The flood was defining for the city, with Calgarian citizens and businesses volunteering in a massive effort to assist in the emergency response and recovery, working along with City personnel and provincial emergency workers on everything from evacuations of zoo animals and people from the rising waters, stabilizing bridges, pumping out buildings to draining the fair grounds and facilities in time for the Stampede.

The research project aimed to study the unique and far-from-equilibrium conditions and non-standard interactions that occurred between various system elements such as business units, facilities, individuals, leaders, government agencies, the media, the public, and infrastructure elements. These unique interactions in non-standard operational conditions resulted in emergence of structural changes in the system as the City adapted to changes in its environment. With an understanding of adaptation as a form of organizational learning, this study sought to identify what was learned during the flood about the relationship between The City and its environment, and to design a "feed-forward" organizational learning process to capture, formalize and integrate the adaptations into the structure of the organization. Careful analysis of the changes in interactions, relationships, and activities during the dynamic conditions of the flooding event and recovery were recognized as an example of co-adaptation between The City and its environment.

Based on a research proposal presented to The City, a 16-month researcher position was created in the Strategic Services Division of the Environment and Safety Management business unit at the City of Calgary. In addition to formal research activities, I was able to participate in a professional capacity on number of ongoing projects in the department, which allowed development of professional relationships with the participants and an opportunity to experience the dynamics and interactions in the work environment, and of The City as a complex adaptive system.

The study involved collecting large amounts of raw data from multiple data sources including semi-structured interviews, a journal of reflections, notes from informal discussions with participants, audio recordings of workshops, and reviews of documents and records. In Design Based Research studies, it is typical that large amounts of data are collected, and often not all the data collected are analysed (Collins, Joseph, & Bielaczyc, 2004). A surplus of data is appropriate to a study grounded in complexity thinking, as it is understood that the researcher cannot predetermine which data will prove to be important. Managing the large amount of data from multiple sources presented a significant challenge, but was simplified by focusing carefully on what was needed to address the problems at hand in the research. As Miles, Huberman and Saldana (2014) affirm, focusing on the research questions is key to preventing 'overload' in data collection and analysis.

Data collection and analysis was a highly interactive process. Spending time with participants, taking part in Strategic Services Division business planning and strategy sessions, and engaging in project work and conversations with project managers and leaders all provided the opportunity to become immersed in the Organization. Conversations took place regarding organizational problems, functions and structures, and current and past projects; ideas about complexity theory, adaptation, and organizational learning were discussed; and information about City of Calgary processes, culture, history, and structures was shared. While the details in the data proved to be of limited value in analysis, what emerged was a rich view of the system as it functioned on a day-to-day basis, and an impression of the current and historical context of the Organization. The consistency of the Organization, its culture, behaviour, action, and structures became apparent. The research did not involve modeling this consistency, but being immersed in this process of observation and interaction was essential to coherent, contextualized analysis. As the research project evolved, the methods were refined align the study with the consistency of the Organization.

The First Iteration

A project team was assembled from individuals at different functions in the Environment and Safety Management group at The City. The first iteration of the study involved an investigation of the activities of Waste and Recycling department during the 2013 flood. To re-establish access in the emergency zone and eliminate potential health and safety hazards, the Waste and Recycling department had to coordinate removal and disposal of approximately 100,000 tonnes of waterlogged debris and flood generated waste from impacted neighborhoods. Waste and Recycling staff worked hand in hand with individuals from the Roads department, Bylaw Enforcement, Emergency services, private service companies, and members of the public.

The project team conducted a series of interviews with individuals at all levels of the Waste and Recycling division of The City. We were looking for examples of operational learnings that were fed forward to "higher" levels in the organization, examples of adaptation that could be tracked through the organizational learning process from intuitive learning at the level of operations to institutionalize changes in processes and structures. There was no shortage of interesting stories collected by the project team of creative, "adaptive" behaviours during the emergency flood conditions. Since Calgary has a "bin" system for domestic waste collection utilizing specialized side loader trucks with robotic arms, Waste and Recycling did not have the equipment necessary to conduct the modified tasks of flood waste removal. This required a unique coordinated effort with the Roads Department and private contractors to obtain and operate the necessary equipment for the task (dump trucks, front and rear loaders, roll off trucks and bins). Given the highly siloized and specialized nature of service provision at The City of Calgary, this created an unprecedented organizational challenge; one that was met with remarkable co-operation and flexibility.

As the interview data was analysed, principles of Complex Systems were considered to allow interpretation of the Complex System Properties as identified in Figure 1. For example, an image of the nesting of the organization, with individuals functioning across different bounded organizational units was generated. Individuals functioning as "superintendents" could effectively coordinate their activates across departmental boundaries (Waste and Recycling and Roads) because of the commonalities between their functional roles as superintendents, despite the differences in departmental functions and organizational boundaries. Equipment operators could translate their specialized knowledge to perform similar operational activities (moving materials) across strongly siloized organizational boundaries (moving waste as opposed to moving road building materials).

Analysis of emergent communications networks was particularly interesting, as a model of dynamic interactions, fluidity of operational roles, and resource sharing grounded in interdependence was generated, along with an interpretation of the nature of signal/boundaries in the system. The importance of diversity in individual capacity and knowledge was identified as key in the response, as well as the importance of flexibility of organizational structure, and diversity in equipment and infrastructure. Evidence of history embedded in the system was observed, both as a unifying factor (as different parts of the organization had shared history), and a disrupting factor (as these same parts had histories that had not been shared).

Some Key Findings From the First Iteration

As data from interviews with Waste and Recycling representatives directly involved in the flood response was analysed, the stories of cooperation and innovation were abundant, and were interpreted as Complex System Functioning. What was lacking however, was evidence that these impromptu operational and organizational modifications resulted in any long term structural changes in the organization. When asked about how the innovations translated into lasting change, the most common response was "It didn't. Things migrated back to how they were before, only with an exhausted supply of resources.

This result was a challenging surprise. The issue was not an absence of evidence of complex system functioning, but rather the complex system was not integrating in the way that was anticipated in the research design; the changes experienced during the flood appeared to be temporary mitigations rather than actual structural adaptations.

Also, there was an almost complete lack of reference in the interviews to the flood as a natural, environmental event. Descriptions of the event were consistently given in operational terms; references to water levels and flow without mention of a "river", and a strong focus on the operational impacts. Although this may not be surprising given the positions of those being interviewed, it put into question the interpretation in the research design of the event as an interaction between an organization and its environment. The distinction was subtle, but it created a sense that the research proposal was somehow out of alignment with the situational context of the event as experienced by the complex system.

A Redirection in the Research

The analysis at the end of the first iteration of the study lead to the conclusion that adhering rigidly to the original research design would impose an unacceptable bias. The data collected did not confirm that the City, as a complex organization, had adapted structurally to the flood through a bottom up/feed forward mechanisms outlined in the 4I conceptual model of organizational learning. This does not mean that The City did not adapt, but the original design of the research was put into question. There was a strong sense that imposing the 4I learning process on the organization would violate its natural tendencies.

With a genuine commitment to the principles of complexity the decision was made to modify the research design; to ensure that the study was conducted in a way that was consistent with the integrity of the system under investigation. Every complex system is unique, and its characteristics are emergent qualities. A system's capacity and mechanisms for adaptation is also unique, and forcing a learning design that appeared to be inconsistent with how The City of Calgary adapted during the flood would have been a violation of both the integrity of the system and of the theoretical framework for the study. A different approach was required to understand, model and support the organization's adaptive capacity, with careful attention to the complex characteristics of The City.

The analysis of the first iteration had revealed some important findings. The established, pre-flood organizational structures were very strong, so much so that the system appeared to resist change as the emergency event passed. There was a strong tendency to "return to normal" that limited adaptive structural change. Exploring the nature of this tendency was beyond the scope of the study, but initial analysis suggested that it was linked to siloization, behaviours of individuals in the system related to power issues, rigidity in organization structure as the system resisted change (partly because change requires expenditure of resources and creates uncertainty), and organizational culture and habits. Reflecting on the data through the integral theory AQAL model it is clear that the scope of the research design, with its AQAL Lower Right quadrant emphasis on Complexity Theory and organizational structures, was too restrictive to get a full understanding of the adaptive nature of the organization.

The Second and Third "Iterations": Exploring The City's Adaptive Capacity

The study continued with significant modifications to the original proposal. Rather than focusing on feeding forward of learning according to the 4I model of organizational learning, the team shifted towards a concept of building adaptive capacity in the organization. As Zolo and Winter (2002) describe, the objective is not to *change operational routines to be better*, but rather to *enhance adaptive capacity*.

The first phase of the study had provided extensive data on which to base interpretations of The City of Calgary as a complex system, specifically understanding how the 10 basic properties of complex systems (Figure 1) manifested in this particular human organization. These interpretations were used for evaluation in two separate projects that explored how to scaffold organizational development (learning) in the organization as it addressed problems which required adaptive, structural changes. This represented a fundamental change in the research, including a redefinition of the research questions. The emphasis shifted from "how can a complexity based organizational learning intervention be applied" to "what is the nature of complex system function at The City, and how can understanding of the system (through interpretation of its properties as per Figure 1) inform design of new organizational structures to deal with "problems" or "issues" experienced in the Environmental Management function of the system". The shift was messy, and lacked the level of control one might hope for in a clean research study, but it opened the research team to a very rich learning experience, and generated practical applications that were consistent with the unique nature of The City as a living system. The team completed two projects resulting in two design proposals.

The first project looked at how to design a corporate level environmental management system for business units in the organization that did not yet have their own systems in place. These were business units that had relatively low potential for environmental impacts (mostly administrative or planning rather than operational functions), and therefor had not had any regulatory requirements which justified the expense of developing full environmental management systems. It was recognized that these business units could have "influence" over decisions and actions associated with environmental impacts, and that some common corporate systems could be established to provide The City with confidence that the issues were addressed, at least from a perspective of basic due diligence. The project would also serve to strengthen unity in the system by aligning the activities of Business Units that were structurally and functionally separate. The second project involved design of a proposed Strategic environmental management system intended to improve alignment between the various operational business units that had each developed independent environmental management systems. While meeting the needs of the system the team recognized the potential for enhancing the system's adaptive capacity in two ways; by enhancing interdependence within the system, and promoting coupling between the system and its environment.

In both of these projects, the goal was similar: select a significant structural change that has been identified by the organization as being required and provide a design solution that applied principles of complexity theory. In both cases, analysis of problem in the context of the organization focused on investigating actual observed complex systems processes that could be supported to strengthen the adaptive capacity of the organization.

THEORY AND PRACTICE, COMPLEXITY AND INTEGRAL THEORY INTERPRETATIONS FROM THE RESEARCH

When studying human systems in applied, practical research, we have an opportunity to explore the nature of the system, both with the objective of advancing theory and of influencing positive change in the system. While it is interesting to test and confirm theoretical predictions, such research presents even more valuable opportunities practical applications. Complexity and Integral Theory each provide useful theoretical frameworks in themselves, but they may actually be more valuable when applied together. Complexity Theory, as a scientific approach, provides an objective scientific view of a whole that is reasonably manageable because of its inherent reductions. And Integral Theory provides a method of opening interpretations of the data beyond the limits of Complexity Theory to look at the subjective. Common properties of Complex Systems are expressed in human systems, but understanding them requires a deep examination and interpretation of the specific and unique system under investigation; the sense of the system cannot be reduced because it is an emergent expression of the system itself. Human systems are made up of individuals and groups, and they have both external objective expressions and internal subjective ones.

Four examples are provided here of key findings from this Complexity Theory based study that can be more deeply understood with application of Integral Theory.

1. The Nested Structure of an Organization: Providing Insight Into the Complex Functioning and Adaptive Capacity of a System

Complexity Theory looks at "nesting" in terms of the functional, operational and structural aspects of the system. As both an analytical tool and a practical sense making exercise, mapping of the City of Calgary as a nested set of unities proved to be invaluable to the research project. At the beginning of the study individuals, work teams, divisions, business units and departments were mapped according to the formally established "organization chart" as posted on the website of The City of Calgary. As the study progressed, it was noticed that the hierarchic order of the organization was not a representation of functional nesting so much as a hierarchy of control. In an organizational chart, a departmental manager has power over his subordinates, he is not "made up" of subordinates in the way a kidney is made up of cells and a body is made of organs. A more accurate understanding of the functional/operational hierarchical nature of the organization would place a manager as an individual with a specific function, within a higher order functional unity (department) made up of many elements (manager, operators, administrators etc.)

Through analysis of what people and groups were actually *doing* in their workplace activities both during the flood and under standard conditions, the organizational map was reinterpreted as a dynamic series of operations and interactions of both individuals and collectives. The maps themselves were not used as "representations" for practical purposes in the research, but the analytical process of generating the maps of fluid, dynamic relationships and operations resulted in a deeper understanding of the complex system as a series of functional, operational unities. These unities were understood as functional collectives of individuals; and the makeup of the functional unities was observed to be dynamic as individuals can belong to multiple different functional collectives.

For example, superintendents have an operational function that appears bounded in the functional groups that they supervise (ie Superintendent of Waste Collection Services or of Roads Construction).

Integral Post-Analysis of Design-Based Research of an Organizational Learning Process

During the emergency conditions of the flood, superintendents from different business units were placed in the emergency zone where operators of different business units were working together in unique, non-standard operational situations. The Superintendents, who would not normally be working with each other across functional groups, performed new functional operations during the dynamic and changing environment of the flood, functional operations of coordination of action between different departments. The formal nested organizational structures were transcended through the capacities of individuals, often because of the unique personal characteristics of those individuals and because of the non-standard and dynamic requirements of the organization during far from equilibrium conditions.

A full understanding of the dynamic nature of system nesting as layers of function and operation of individuals in the organization was beyond the scope of the study, and perhaps largely beyond the scope of our current understanding of human systems as complex systems. The recognition of the discord between the formal organizational chart and the operational nesting maps opened the research to an issue already identified and dealt with in Integral Theory. Integral Theory, like Complexity Theory, recognizes nesting as a key property of human systems, but its focus is on developmental levels as understood from multiple theories ranging from evolutionary development of life forms from uni-cellular to multi-cellular organisms, to individual human development from infancy through to adulthood. Integral Theory distinguishes between Growth Hierarchies and Power Hierarchies, and warns us of the potential harm in confusing the two (Wilber, 2017).

2. Growth Hierarchies vs Power Hierarchies: the Effects of Violating Operational Closure

From our understanding of biological complex systems of bodies with organs and cells, the operational closure of nested unities is critical; a system feature that co-emerges with the interdependent nature of the unity as a system forms through autopoiesis (Maturana and Varela, 1986). Each organ or cell performs its function without operational interference from outside; based on its own coherent and consistent nature. A kidney does not control its cells, it is made up of its cells, each one doing what it knows how to do in a way that supports the system that sustains it while unknowingly contributing to the emergent qualities of the whole. A cell does not know how to perform kidney function, it knows how to perform its cellular function, and through its interdependent unification with other cells it contributes to emergent functions of the collective. And the organ does not make decisions for the cells, the cells generate the emergent function of the organ.

In human organizations, this operational closure is equally important, each nested unity performing its functions independently. This is the natural or "growth" hierarchy of a human system, not to be confused with a "power" hierarchy where an individual at a "higher" level in the organizational chart has authority and control over subordinates. The emergent function and efficiency of a whole human organization depends on individuals being able to fulfill their role. If a manager had to attend to all the operational details of all their subordinates, the system would be impossible to manage. People know how to do their jobs; managers coordinate between the people. This operational closure can be violated when individuals in higher positions on an organization chart *control* the operational activities of lower positions without respect for operational closure.

It is suggested here that the power hierarchy violation of operational closure in nested human systems is a key factor in why human organizations may fail to adapt, and part of the cause of the harmful relationships human systems have established with their natural environments.

During the flood at the City of Calgary, we saw examples of operational closure being respected as technically experienced operations staff did their work with minimal control by managers or other operational unities. In part, the interference was eliminated because the situation was simply too complex for the managers to exert power, and also because the culture of the system in the situation encouraged everyone to fulfill their roles to the best of their abilities in the circumstances of the emergency situation. The system exhibited a high capacity for adaptation during the flood, as it was freed from the effects of power control.

During normal operating conditions, individuals are not afforded the luxury (or responsibility) of adapting or modifying their activities; they are expected to follow the established rules. When circumstances returned to normal following the flood, long established control features of the organization returned, and the burst of adaptive behaviour of the system was suppressed in favor of the status quo. This is sensible from a resource management perspective, as change costs resources. There were also, however, indications that resistance to change was actually the result of power issues of individuals in management roles.

During the second iteration of the research project, power issues in different groups and organizations interfered with decisions on design options. A series of environmental management processes were carefully designed that were consistent with existing organizational structures and processes and systematically aligned with principles of complexity, but they were rejected through a decision making process by what appeared to be a rather transparent issue of power and control among competing interests in the organization. An Integral analysis would suggest that this group was behaving according to an amber or tribal level of development; more interested in preserving their own power in the organization than in participating with other groups in an inclusive process designed for enhancing the adaptability of the entire system. Recognizing that there was a specific group involved in operational process as designed that simply did not want to cooperate with the project, an alternate proposal was designed by the project team with minor operational adjustments that simply did not involve the operational unity that was resistant to the design. This was not intended as a deception, but rather as an opportunity to respect the operational closure of the resisting group. If the design was accepted and implemented by the organization, the expectation was that the processes would eventually become fully integrated to the benefit of the whole organization.

3. Defining "Better" in the Design Selection Processes in Organizational Development: Integral "Levels of Development" as a Tool to Transcend Value Judgments

In trying to design improvements to the environmental management system at The City of Calgary, or to make "adaptive" changes, the research team was challenged with the task of deciding what design options were actually "better". Though this judgment frequently seems to be common sense, it is exceedingly difficult to look past our own biases and perspectives, especially in a competitive organization. Complexity Theory and evolution is firmly grounded in the concept of acausality; in the idea that, though there is a general trend towards increasing complexity in self organizing systems, the options as a system evolves are limitless and one way is not necessarily better than another. Acausality is a challenging perspective to take as a researcher, designer, manager, or any other "agent". The approach taken in this study was to be reflexive and avoid value judgments, while focusing on enhancing the capacity of the organization (The City) to self-organize by generating and selecting options that strengthened the complex system function as outlined in Figure 1. Design options were analysed to see which ones were associated with higher levels of diversity in the system, or which ones fostered an improvement in interdependence and connectivity in the system. The selection process for design options was objectified by allowing decisions to be made through the normal decision-making and approval processes in the organization, with the assumption that this would be the best reflection of the complex system's natural function.

While this approach worked well enough in the context of the study, it was difficult to demonstrate or verify its merits, to measure its effectiveness, or to explain the approach to those uninitiated in complexity theory, evolution theory, or non-dual philosophy. Wilber's Integral model of Levels of Development provides an alternative approach that is consistent with acausality and non-duality, but more explicit in its definition of direction of development. This is valuable not only as a communication tool, but also as a tool to facilitate Scaffolding (Wood, Bruner, & Ross, 1976) in organizational learning.

4. Understanding System Interdependence Through the Concepts of "Levels of Development" and "Include and Transcend"

Clearly it is not realistic as an organization to expect that all parts of the system can be lifted up to the same level of development, as defined in Wilber's levels hierarchy. Our knowledge of how to increase levels of development in an organization, especially given that those levels are not the same in all parts of the organization, is limited. The relationship between organizational levels of development and the levels of development of the individuals that make up the organization is also not clearly understood. Even Frederick Laloux's extensive work in applying integral analysis to organizations is mostly descriptive, and only fully descriptive of the teal level of development in organizations. It does not explore the growth hierarchy at all levels and all quadrants. Laloux has suggested that an organization can only sustain a teal level of development if members of the leadership team are themselves at teal, and he does not provide a clear model of how to deal with the highly varied distribution of levels of development of all individuals in the organization (Laloux, 2014).

As human systems become more interconnected, the potential for interference of operational closure and for power and control issues increases, as does the importance of elevating levels of development to ensure inclusivity. Inclusivity is a feature which increases with each level in Wilber's developmental hierarchy. It is therefor helpful to organizational developers to focus on improving the level of development in functional areas that are involved in defining and maintaining organizational interdependence. If areas are identified where the level of development is low (i.e. where a culture of inclusivity is low) they may seek to bound that part of the system operationally in a way that will have less impact on the rest of the organization while still allowing it to fulfill its operational function without outside interference. Or, they may identify system mechanisms that promote interdependence as a means to stimulate increase in inclusivity and level development.

Throughout the research project, the team was actively looking to identify opportunities to strengthen interdependence; a key common property of Complex Systems. In the second iteration of the research project with the City of Calgary, it was realized that the system for budgeting resources, so critical to any organization human or biological, could be utilized as a mechanism for generating a practical system for defining interdependence. At the time of the study, the budgeting process was still highly competitive, with departments and projects vying for limited resources. There was, however, a system wide movement to shifting the budgeting process to a corporate wide "results based" process that was designed to coordinate action more effectively and strategically across organizational boundaries. Rather than each department setting its own goals and objectives, the emerging process was focused on generating alignment through common, city-wide strategies, and a hierarchical system to align actions in the organization, and budgets, to these strategies. This system was identified in the research as a potential process for strengthening a clearly defined, structured interdependence between siloized operational unities in the organization; and a potential for aligning environmental management strategies across the organization. Operational groups could increase their access to resources by coordinating their activities with other groups, strengthening the case for budgets by demonstrating that their activities would contribute to the goals of all parts of the organization. The budgeting process could be used by the Strategic Services Division of Environmental Management as a formal mechanism for creating unity in corporate wide environmental policy. In the past, various departments at the City had highly siloized and independent environmental management systems; and incorporating environmental policy and strategy in the budgeting procedures provided an opportunity to generate unity and interdependence across the system.

This is an example of structural change (AQAL Lower Right quadrant) that could be used to strengthen the state of interdependence in an organization. Given more time, and an experienced transdisciplinary team of researchers, it would be interesting to conduct an integral analysis to inform design and implementation of a comprehensive unification program at The City, and to determine whether and how this could improve the adaptive capacity of the organization. An integral analysis would encourage researchers to focus on all quadrants of the holon. For example, a deep cultural analysis (Lower Left Quadrant) could provide a nuanced understanding of cohesion of the system, such as how a culture of "dedication to providing excellent service to the public" could be leveraged to enhance a sense of unity and interdependence.

ACADEMIC PROCESS LIMITATIONS: INTERPRETATION FROM THE STUDY

Design-Based Research is focused on solving problems. DBR projects seek to generate practical ways of applying theory by aligning the theory to practice in the full context of a "real situation", further refining and generating the theory itself through a kind of co-creation. As this study demonstrated, the context of the situation should take precedence over theory, and too much focus on theory in design can actually introduce biases in research. Once the research team identified the biases in the design, we could focus on interpreting the theory through the system; understanding The City of Calgary as a complex system and working with its properties to support its natural capacity to adapt rather than imposing a designed intervention to "improve" the system. The validity of this approach was strengthened as the team developed several recommendations for both modifications to the system and implementation ideas that made sense to the practitioners working in the system, and were aligned with processes and structures that had naturally emerged in the system.

Upon reflection of this study, three issues were identified in the academic process that were restrictive, encouraging reductionism and limiting academic freedom. Though this is only a personal interpretation, the issues are raised here as a potential for improvements to academic processes. The three issues were funding, the timing of research design and the ethics approval process, and theoretical focus.

This project was funded by the proponent, The City of Calgary. It was surprising to me how many comments and opinions I encountered from academic researchers that suggested that direct corporate funding may distort the results of research to align with the goals of the organization. Funding from

Integral Post-Analysis of Design-Based Research of an Organizational Learning Process

traditional academic agencies such as the Social Sciences and Humanities Research Council of Canada (SSHRC) or the Natural Sciences and Engineering Research Council of Canada (NSERC) is recognized as supporting credible, objective academic research, whereas corporately funded research is suspected of potential for bias. In fact, alignment with the goals of the organization was exactly the objective of this research as such goals, regardless of external value judgments, are very real factors in the structure, culture and behaviour of the organization under study. It was my experience in this research that my own theoretical bias, demonstrated when the proposed organizational learning intervention designed prior to interaction with the organization proved to be inconsistent with the nature of the complex organization being studied, was a much bigger problem in the research than any bias derived from the corporation.

To meet requirements in the ethics approval process and the PhD Dissertation Proposal approval process, I was required to complete the research design prior to any contact with the participants (members of the organization involved in the research). The intention, from an academic integrity perspective, is that these approvals are essential for the protection of the research participants, for assurance of academic objectivity in the research, and for the protection of the reputation of the University. But predesigning the intervention and the research proposal without the involvement of the participants increased the chances of incompatibility between the designs and the organization under study. Careful pre-planning of research should improve the success of the research, but it may in some cases just further encourage a researcher to see exactly that for which they looking.

Focusing on theoretical consistency in research design, and consistency with established disciplinary literature is currently an imperative in most PhD programs. Students are learning how to conduct academically acceptable research, and must demonstrate the consistency of their research both internally and with accepted disciplinary methods and literature. In this study, Gowin's Vee was used to demonstrate this consistency between Theory, Concepts, and Methods during the design and initial execution of the research process. The focus on Complexity Theory, however, limited the perspective of the research to the lower right quadrant of the AQAL model, as Complexity Theory is firmly positivist due to its grounding in scientific disciplines. As the study progressed, it became clear that a purely external collective view of a complex system is not a full view, and that interpretations of the system could be better informed if all of the quadrants of the AQAL model were considered.

Three recommendations are presented

- Bias in research should not be confused with bias in the system being studied. While researcher bias is something that needs to be identified (and potentially eliminated), system bias is a natural expression of the level of development of the system. An integral analysis of levels of development of a system may enhance interpretation of why it functions as it does.
- Specifics of research design and methodology should be flexible, and be modified as a study progresses to maintain consistency with the system being studied. The unique nature of the system will become increasingly apparent as the study progresses.
- Throughout the data collection and analysis phase of a study, the researcher should maintain an open stance by considering theoretical models that are appropriate to what is observed in the system. A diversity of theoretical models, from all quadrants of the AQAL model, may be required to make sense of the system.

CONCLUSION

Academia is still deeply rooted in an old rationality that we desperately need to transcend. As Morin (1992) explains,

The old rationality was content to fish for order in the sea of nature. But it caught no fish—only fishbones! By allowing us to conceive of organization and existence, the new rationality allows us to perceive not only the fish, but the ocean as well – that is to say, that which can never be caught. (p. 42)

Application of the new "rationality" to which Morin refers is intended in Complexity Theory, but the grounding in hard sciences still limits Complexity researchers to incomplete external and objective perspectives. Design based and Action research methods too are intended to transcend traditional methods, but ingrained academic processes limit us in fully realizing their goals. And Integral Theory seeks to transcend, with intention and mindfulness aimed at opening all theories and methods.

A synthesis of the concepts of "emergence" in Complexity with "transcendence" in Integral Theory provides researchers with a new and powerful tool to not only understand, but potentially influence, human collective development. The two concepts are similar, but just different enough that integrating them could be a genuine and significant step forward in academic research. They represent a theoretical integration of the self-organizing potential of nature and the intentional development of humans, with a clear and obvious understanding that humans and nature are not separate. Complexity Theory gives researchers a tool to understand how systems develop themselves, so that we can study how to strengthening the adaptive capacity of the system. Integral Theory provides a map of levels of system development so we can study nudge that development in the right direction.

With each attempt to integrate another theory or a different perspective, we transcend limitations and biases that are not perceivable at the level prior to integration. And as research methods develop more nuanced and rich perspectives through theoretical integration, we reach more deeply into the potential of actively and consciously participating in human evolution. What kinds of unique research could be realized if we were to fully align the two theories? What kinds of questions should we be asking? And what kinds of research methodologies should we be developing? The complex systems themselves have the answers deeply imbedded in their structures, we need keys to open our understanding, and to provide us with options for actions that are better informed to work coherently within our human systems as they continue to evolve. Application of both Integral Theory and Complexity Theory would have provided an exceptionally powerful framework: one that would be well worthwhile developing through theoretical work aligning the two approaches to be tested in future studies.

REFERENCES

Allen, P. M. (1998). Evolving complexity in social science. In G. Altman & W. A. Koch (Eds.), *Systems: New paradigms for the human sciences*. New York: Walter de Gruyter. doi:10.1515/9783110801194.3

Anderson, T., & Shattuck, J. (2012). Design-Based Research: A decade of progress in education research. *Educational Researcher, 41*(1), 16–25. doi:10.3102/0013189X11428813

Argyris, C., & Schön, D. A. (1978). *Organizational learning: A theory of action perspective*. Reading, MA: Addison-Wesley.

Barab, S., & Squire, K. (2004). Design-based research: Putting a stake in the ground. *Journal of the Learning Sciences*, *13*(1), 1–14. doi:10.120715327809jls1301_1

Bres, A. F. (2016). *From Management to Adaptation: Designing an Organizational Learning Process for Strategic Renewal of Environmental Management at The City of Calgary* (Unpublished doctoral dissertation). The University of Calgary, Calgary, Alberta, Canada.

Brown, A. L. (1992). Design experiments: Theoretical and methodological challenges in creating complex interventions in classroom settings. *Journal of the Learning Sciences*, *2*(2), 141–178. doi:10.120715327809jls0202_2

Cilliers, P. (1998). *Complexity and postmodernism: Understanding complex systems*. London: Routledge.

Cobb, P., Confrey, J., diSessa, A. A., Lehrer, R., & Schauble, L. (2003). Design experiments in educational research. *Educational Researcher*, *32*(1), 9–13. doi:10.3102/0013189X032001009

Crossan, M. M., Lane, H. W., & White, R. E. (1999). An organizational learning framework: From intuition to institution. *Academy of Management Review*, *24*(3), 522–537. doi:10.5465/amr.1999.2202135

Deming, W. E. (1986). *Out of the crisis*. Cambridge, MA: Massachusetts Institute of Technology, Center for Advanced Engineering Study.

Flood, R. L. (2009). *Rethinking the fifth discipline: Learning within the unknowable*. London: Routledge.

Goldspink, C., & Kay, R. (2010). Emergence in organizations: The reflexive turn. *Emergence*, *12*(3), 47–63.

Hedberg, B. (1981). How Organizations Learn and Un-Learn. In P. C. Nystrom & W. H. Starbuck (Eds.), *Handbook of organizational design* (Vol. 1, pp. 3–27). New York: Oxford University Press.

Holland, J. H. (2012). *Signals and boundaries: Building blocks for complex adaptive systems*. Cambridge, MA: Massachusetts Institute of Technology.

Laloux, F. (2014). *Reinventing Organizations: A Guide to Creating Organizations Inspired by the Next Stage of Human Consciousness*. Nelson Parker.

Letiche, H. (2000). Phenomenal complexity theory as informed by Bergson. *Journal of Organizational Change Management*, *13*(6), 545–557. doi:10.1108/09534810010378579

Marsick, V. J., & Watkins, K. (1990). *Informal and incidental learning in the workplace*. London, New York: Routledge.

Maturana, H. R., & Varela, F. (1998). *The tree of knowledge: The biological roots of human understanding*. Boston, MA: Shambhala. (Original work published 1987)

Mezirow, J. (1997). Transformative learning: Theory to practice. *New Directions for Adult and Continuing Education*, *1997*(74), 5–12. doi:10.1002/ace.7401

Miles, M., Huberman, A., & Saldana, J. (2014). *Qualitative data analysis: A methods sourcebook*. Thousand Oaks, CA: Sage Publications.

Mitleton-Kelly, E. (2003). *Complex systems and evolutionary perspectives on organisations: The application of complexity theory to organisations*. Oxford, UK: Pergamon.

Morgan, G. (2006). *Images of organization*. Thousand Oaks, CA: Sage.

Morin, E. (1992). From the concept of system to the paradigm of complexity. Journal of Social and Evolutionary Systems, 15(4), 371-384.

Nonaka, I., & Takeuchi, H. (1995). *The Knowledge-creating company*. New York: Oxford University Press.

Novak, J. D., & Gowin, D. B. (1984). *Learning how to learn*. New York: Cambridge University Press. doi:10.1017/CBO9781139173469

Popper, M., & Lipshitz, R. (2000). Organizational learning: Mechanisms, culture, and feasibility. *Management Learning*, *31*(2), 181–196. doi:10.1177/1350507600312003

Prigogine, I. (1980). *From being to becoming: Time and complexity in the physical sciences*. San Francisco: Freeman.

Senge, P. M. (2006). *The fifth discipline: The art and practice of the learning organization (Revised and updated edition)*. New York: Doubleday/Currency.

Simon, H. A. (1991). Bounded rationality and organizational learning. *Organization Science*, *2*(1), 125–134. doi:10.1287/orsc.2.1.125

Stengers, I. (2000). *The invention of modern science* (D. W. Smith, Trans.). Minneapolis, MN: University of Minnesota Press.

van Aken, J. E. (2004). Management research based on the paradigm of the design sciences: The quest for field-tested and grounded technological rules. *Journal of Management Studies*, *41*(2), 219–246. doi:10.1111/j.1467-6486.2004.00430.x

Wilber, K. (1995). *Sex, ecology, spirituality: The spirit of evolution*. Boston, MA: Shambhala.

Wilber, K. (2006). *Integral spirituality*. Boston: Integral Books.

Wilber, K. (2017, January 2). *Trump and post-truth world*. Retrieved from http://integrallife.com

Wood, D., Bruner, J., & Ross, G. (1976). The role of tutoring in problem solving. *Journal of Child Psychology and Psychiatry, and Allied Disciplines*, *17*(2), 89–100. doi:10.1111/j.1469-7610.1976.tb00381.x PMID:932126

Zollo, M., & Winter, S. G. (2002). Learning and the evolution of dynamic capabilities. *Organization Science*, *13*(3), 339–351. doi:10.1287/orsc.13.3.339.2780

KEY TERMS AND DEFINITIONS

Adaptive Capacity: The ability or potential of an organization to respond successfully to changes in its environment. The ability to adapt is a feature of complex systems, associated with its ability to maintain coherence in changing conditions.

Emergence: A feature in a complex system that is generated through the dynamic interactions between the parts of a system at one level, and is realized at the next level of organization without intentionality or causality. For example: evasive maneuvers of a school of fish are generated through the actions of individuals, who are unaware of how their own actions contribute to the action of the school.

Nesting: A structural feature of complex systems, where the system is made of parts that are made of parts, in a hierarchical organization.

Operational Closure: A boundary characteristic of a unity as it functions, executing its operations in a system as determined by its own structure and organization (i.e., without external or environmental control).

Organizational Learning: Traditionally defined as the process of creating and transferring knowledge within an organization. In this study, Organizational learning is equated with system adaptation. As an organization experiences and responds to environmental change, structural modifications may occur at different levels in the organization, including changes in understanding of individuals and groups, and structural changes in organizational processes.

Structure: A stable ordered pattern generated by complex system as it fulfills its function. In an organization, structures include such things policies, processes, or procedures, or patterns of communication and interaction. Structures may be formal or informal. Structures also include physical entities such as buildings and roads.

Unity: A bounded, whole entity that performs a distinct function within a system. A unity defines itself as separate from and coupled with its environment.

Compilation of References

(2012). Prigogine: A New Sense of Order. InTrueit, D. (Ed.), *Studies in Curriculum Theory Series: Pragmatism, Postmodernism, and Complexity Theory: The Collected Works of William E. Doll, Jr* (p. 137). Florence, KY: Routledge.

Abraham, F. D. (1995). Introduction to dynamics: A basic language: a basic metamodeling strategy. In F. D. Abraham & A. R. Gilden (Eds.), *Chaos theory in psychology* (pp. 31–49). Westport, CT: Greenwood Press.

Abraham, R. H., & Shaw, C. D. (1984). *Dynamics: The geometry of behavior*. Santa Cruz, CA: Aerial Press.

Ackroyd, J., Anderson, M., Burg, C., & Martin, B. (2007). *Physics*. Toronto: Pearson Canada.

ACT. (2011). *The condition for college and career readiness*. ACT, Inc. Retrieved from http://www.act.org/research/policymakers/cccr11/pdf/ConditionofCollegeandCareerReadiness2011.pdf

Adler, P. S., & Borys, B. (1993). Materialism and idealism in organizational research. *Organization Studies*, *14*(5), 657–679. doi:10.1177/017084069301400503

Advanced Placement. (2015). *College Board/International*. Retrieved from http://international.collegeboard.org/programs/advanced-placement

Akin, A. (2012). Self-Compassion and Automatic Thoughts. *Hacettepe University Journal of Education*, 421–10.

Akiyama, T., Li, J., Kubota, J., Konagaya, Y., & Watanabe, M. (2012). Perspectives on sustainability assessment: An integral approach to historical changes in social systems and water environment in the Ili river basin of central Eurasia, 1900–2008. *World Futures*, *68*(8), 595–627. doi:10.1080/02604027.2012.693852

Alberta Education. (1982). *Educable mentally handicapped: Curriculum guide*. Author.

Alberta Education. (2006). *Standards for the provision of early childhood special education*. Retrieved from http://education.alberta.ca/media/452316/ecs_specialedstds2006.pdf

Alberta Education. (2016). *Funding manual for school authorities: 2016/2017 school year*. Retrieved from https://education.alberta.ca/media/3272973/funding-manual-august-2016.pdf

Alberta Family Wellness Initiative. (2013). *Sharing the brain story: AFWI's knowledge mobilization strategy: Transforming research, policy, and practice in Alberta*. Retrieved online http://www.albertafamilywellness.org/system/files/report-files/Sharing%20the%20Brain%20Story%20Final%20jan%2027%2014.pdf

Alberta Government. (2015). Ministerial Order on Student Learning. An Order to Adopt or Approve Goals and Standards Applicable to the Provision of Education in Alberta. Edmonton, Canada: Author.

Alberta Teachers' Association. (2014). *Report of the blue ribbon panel on inclusive education in Alberta schools*. Retrieved from http://www.teachers.ab.ca/SiteCollectionDocuments/ATA/News-Room/2014/PD-170-1%20PD%20Blue%20Ribbon%20Panel%20Report%202014-web.pdf

Compilation of References

Albrecht, N. J., Albrecht, P. M., & Cohen, M. (2012). Mindfully teaching in the classroom: A literature review. *Australian Journal of Teacher Education, 37*(12). doi:10.14221/ajte.2012v37n12.2

Alisat, L. (2013). *Gifted boys' experience of giftedness in alternative high school settings: Implications for practice and programming* (Doctoral Dissertation). Retrieved from http://theses.ucalgary.ca/bitstream/11023/548/2/ucalgary_2013_%20alisat_laurie.pdf

Allen, H., Stebnicki, M., & Lynch, R. (1995). Training clinical supervisors in rehabilitation – a conceptual model for training doctoral-level supervisors. *Rehabilitation Counseling Bulletin, 38*(4), 307–317.

Allen, P. M. (1998). Evolving complexity in social science. In G. Altman & W. A. Koch (Eds.), *Systems: New paradigms for the human sciences*. New York: Walter de Gruyter. doi:10.1515/9783110801194.3

Allison, M., & Duncan, M. (1988). Women, work, and flow. In M. Csikszentmihalyi & I. Csikszentmihalyi (Eds.), *Optimal experience* (pp. 118–137). Cambridge, UK: Cambridge University Press. doi:10.1017/CBO9780511621956.007

Alloy, L. B., Black, S. K., Young, M. E., Goldstein, K. E., Shapero, B. G., Stange, J. P., ... Abramson, L. Y. (2012). Cognitive vulnerabilities and depression versus other psychopathology symptoms and diagnoses in early adolescence. *Journal of Clinical Child and Adolescent Psychology, 41*(5), 539–560. doi:10.1080/15374416.2012.703123 PMID:22853629

Altass, P., & Wiebe, S. (2017). Re-imagining Education Policy and Practice in the Digital Era. *Journal of the Canadian Association for Curriculum Studies, 15*(2), 48–63.

America Proclamation. (1990). *Decade of the Brain*. Proclamation No. 6158.

Anderson, L. W., & Krathwohl, D. (2001). *A taxonomy for learning and assessing: A revision of Bloom's taxonomy of educational objectives*. New York: Longman.

Anderson, T., & Shattuck, J. (2012). Design-Based Research: A decade of progress in education research. *Educational Researcher, 41*(1), 16–25. doi:10.3102/0013189X11428813

Andrews, B. (2014). *The soul only avails: Teaching as a spiritual act*. Retrieved from: http://uuneedham.org/wp-content/uploads/2014/02/Teaching-as-a-Spiritual-Act.pdf?x34068

Argyris, C., & Schön, D. A. (1978). *Organizational learning: A theory of action perspective*. Reading, MA: Addison-Wesley.

Arnett, J. J. (2000). Emerging adulthood: A theory of development from the late teens through the twenties. *American Psychologist, 55*(5), 469–480. doi: 066X.55.5.469 doi:10.1037//0003

Aronson, J., Fried, C. B., & Good, C. (2002). Reducing the effects of stereotype threat on African American college students by shaping theories of intelligence. *Journal of Experimental Social Psychology, 38*(2), 113–125. doi:10.1006/jesp.2001.1491

Asperger, H. (1944). Die autistischen psychopathen im kindersalter [Autistic Psychopaths in Childhood]. *Archiv für Psychiatrie und Nervenkrankheiten, 117*(1), 76–136. doi:10.1007/BF01837709

Augustine. (397). Neither time past or time future but the present only, really is. *The Confessions of St. Augustine Bishop of Hippo, Book 11* (Chapter XIV). Retrieved from http://www.leaderu.com/cyber/books/augconfessions/bk11.html

Avramidis, E., & Norwich, B. (2002). Teachers' attitudes towards integration/inclusion: A review of the literature. *European Journal of Special Needs Education, 17*(2), 129–147. doi:10.1080/08856250210129056

Bahamas Ministry of Education. (2015). *Vision 2030: A shared vision for education in the Commonwealth of The Bahamas*. Retrieved from http://media.wix.com/ugd/29b6ce_3065a2357e31432f839d0eecea6dee3e.pdf

Ballard, D., Reason, P., & Coleman, G. (2010). Using the AQAL framework to accelerate responses to climate change. *Journal of Integral Theory and Practice, 5*(1).

Bangser, M. (2008). *Preparing High School Students for Successful Transitions to Postsecondary Education and Employment*. National High School Center.

Barab, S., & Squire, K. (2004). Design-based research: Putting a stake in the ground. *Journal of the Learning Sciences, 13*(1), 1–14. doi:10.120715327809jls1301_1

Barber, B. (2003). *Fear's empire: War, terrorism, and democracy*. New York: W. W. Norton.

Barnes, B., & Austin, J. (2009). The Role of Doctoral Advisors: A Look at Advising from the Advisor's Perspective. *Innovative Higher Education, 33*(5), 297–315. doi:10.100710755-008-9084-x

Barnett, R. (2000). *Realizing the university in an age of supercomplexity*. Maidenhead, UK: Society for Research into Higher Education and Open University Press.

Baron-Cohen, Wheelwright, Skinner, Martin, & Clubley. (2001). The autism spectrum quotient (AQ): Evidence from Asperger Syndrome/high functioning autism, males and females, scientists and mathematicians. *Journal of Autism and Developmental Disorders*, 5–17. PMID:11439754

Baron-Cohen, S. (2008). *Autism and Asperger syndrome*. New York: Oxford University Press.

Barrett, R. (2006). *Building a values-driven organization: A whole system approach to cultural transformation*. Butterworth-Heinemann. doi:10.4324/9780080461687

Bassett, P. F. (2005, September). Reengineering schools for the 21st century. *Phi Delta Kappan, 76–78*, 83. Retrieved from http://eric.ed.gov/?id=EJ725351

Bateson, G. (1972). *Steps to an ecology of mind: Collected essays in anthropology, psychiatry, evolution, and epistemology*. Chicago, IL: University of Chicago Press.

Bateson, G. (1979). *Mind and nature: A necessary unity*. New York: Hampton Press.

Baum, S., Ma, J., & Payea, K. (2013). *Education Pays 2013: The Benefits of Higher Education for Individuals and Society*. The College Board. Retrieved from http://trends.collegeboard.org/sites/default/files/education-pays-2013-full-report.pdf

BC Ministry of Education. (2012a). *Enabling innovation: Transforming curriculum and Assessment*. Retrieved from: http://www.bced.gov.bc.ca/irp/docs/ca_transformation.pdf

BC Ministry of Education. (2012b). *Overview to BC's curriculum transformation plans*. Retrieved from: http://www.bced.gov.bc.ca/irp/docs/overview.pdf

BC Ministry of Education. (2014a). *Transforming curriculum and assessment: Physical and health education – Draft*. Retrieved from: https://curriculum.gov.bc.ca/sites/curriculum.gov.bc.ca/files/pdf/phe_learning_standards.pdf

BC Ministry of Education. (2014b). *Transforming curriculum and assessment: Social studies – Draft*. Retrieved from: https://curriculum.gov.bc.ca/sites/curriculum.gov.bc.ca/files/pdf/ss_learning_standards.pdf

Beck, D., & Cowan, C. (1996). *Spiral dynamics: Mastering values, leadership and change*. Cambridge, MA: Blackwell.

Beck, D., & Cowan, C. (1996). *Spiral Dynamics: Mastering Values, Leadership and Change*. Malden, MA: Blackwell Publishers, Inc.

Belland, B. R., Glazewski, K. D., & Richardson, J. C. (2011). Problem-based learning and argumentation: Testing a scaffolding framework to support middle school students' creation of evidence-based arguments. *Instructional Science*, *39*(5), 667–694. doi:10.100711251-010-9148-z

Belle-Isle, R. (1986). Learning for a new humanism. *International Schools Journal, 11*, 27–30. Retrieved from http://www.johncattbookshop.com/books/international-schools-journal

Belouin, P. (2010). Ethnography: A short description of the roles available to researchers in the field [Web log comment]. Retrieved from http://belouin.com/blog/2010/03/ethnography-which-role-is-one-to-adopt-in-the-framework-of-an-ethnographic-study/

Benefiel, M. (2003). Irreconcilable foes? The discourse of spirituality and the discourse of organizational science. *Organization*, *10*(2), 383–391. doi:10.1177/1350508403010002012

Bennet, M. (2004). Becoming interculturally competent. In J. Wurzel (Ed.), *Toward multiculturalism: A reader in multicultural education* (pp. 62–77). Newton, MA: Intercultural Resource Corporation. Retrieved from http://www.idrinstitute.org/allegati/IDRI_t_Pubblicazioni/1/FILE_Documento.pdf

Bennett, M. (1986). A developmental approach to training for intercultural sensitivity. *International Journal of Intercultural Relations*, *10*(2), 179–196. doi:10.1016/0147-1767(86)90005-2

Bennis, W. (2007). The challenges of leadership in the modern world: Introduction to the special issue. *The American Psychologist*, *62*(1), 2–5. doi:10.1037/0003-066X.62.1.2 PMID:17209674

Bent, M. (2009). *A peaceful partnership? A case study of three IB English A1 teachers' conceptions of peace education at an IB World School in Peru* (Doctoral Dissertation). Retrieved from ProQuest Dissertations and Theses Global. (Order No. MR59633)

Berman, J., & Smyth, R. (2015). Conceptual frameworks in the doctoral research process: A pedagogical model. *Innovations in Education and Teaching International*, *52*(2), 125–136. doi:10.1080/14703297.2013.809011

Bernstein, B. (2000). *Pedagogy, symbolic control and identity* (revised ed.). Lanham, MD: Rowman and Littlefield.

Bertalanffy, L. (1962). *Modern Theories of Development*. New York, NY: Harper Torchbooks.

Bertugli, C. S., & Vaio, F. (2005). *Nonlinearity, chaos and complexity: The dynamics of natural and social systems*. Oxford University Press.

Bethel, K. (1999). *Educational reform in the Bahamas. In Educational Reform in the Commonwealth Caribbean*. Washington, DC: Organization of American States. Retrieved from http://www.educoea.org/Portal/bdigital/contenido/interamer/BkIACD/Interamer/Interamerhtml/Millerhtml/mil_beth.htm

Betts, F. (1992). How systems thinking applies to education. *Educational Leadership*, *50*(3), 38–41.

Birnbaum, D., Deeb, I., Segall, G., Ben-Eliyahu, A., & Diesendruck, G. (2010). The development of social essentialism: The case of Israeli children's inferences about Jews and Arabs. *Child Development*, *81*(3), 757–777. doi:10.1111/j.1467-8624.2010.01432.x PMID:20573103

Bitchener, J., & Basturkmen, H. (2010). The focus of supervisor written feedback to thesis/dissertation students. *International Journal of English Studies*, *10*(2), 79-97.

Blackwell, L. S., Trzesniewski, K. H., & Dweck, C. S. (2007). Implicit theories of intelligence predict achievement across an adolescent transition: A longitudinal study and an intervention. *Child Development*, *78*(1), 246–263. doi:10.1111/j.1467-8624.2007.00995.x PMID:17328703

Blatner, A. (2004). The developmental nature of consciousness transformation. *Revision*, *26*(4), 2–7. doi:10.3200/REVN.26.4.1-14

Bloomberg & Volpe. (2012). *Completing your qualitative dissertation* (2nd ed.). Thousand Oaks, CA: Sage Publications.

Bloomberg, L. D., & Volpe, M. (2012). *Completing your qualitative dissertation a road map from beginning to end* (2nd ed.). London, UK: Sage Publications, Inc.

Bloomberg, L. D., & Volpe, M. (2012). *Completing your qualitative dissertation: A road map from beginning to end*. Thousand Oaks, CA: SAGE.

Bloomberg, L. D., & Volpe, M. (2012). *Completing Your Qualitative Dissertation: A Roadmap from Beginning to End*. Los Angeles, CA: Sage.

Bluth, K., Roberson, P.N.E., & Gaylord, S.A. (2014). A pilot study of a mindfulness intervention for adolescents and the potential role of self-compassion in reducing stress. *Explore (New York, NY)*.

Bluth, K., & Blanton, P. W. (2014). The influence of self-compassion on emotional well-being among early and older adolescent males and females. *The Journal of Positive Psychology*, 1–12. PMID:25750655

Bluth, K., Gaylord, S. A., Campo, R. A., Mullarkey, M. C., & Hobbs, L. (2015). Making friends with yourself: A mixed methods pilot study of a mindful self-compassion program for adolescents. *Mindfulness*, *6*(6), 1–14. PMID:27110301

Bodhi, B. (2000). *A comprehensive manual of Abhidhamma*. Seattle, WA: Buddhist Publication Society.

Bogels, Hoogstad, & Dun, Schutter, & Restifo. (2008). Mindfulness training for adolescents with externalizing disorders and their parents. *Behavioural and Cognitive Psychotherapy*, 193–201.

Bourdieu, P. (2011). *Outline of a Theory of Practice*. Cambridge, UK: Cambridge University Press.

Bradbury, H. (1998). *Learning with the natural step: Cooperative ecological inquiry through cases, theory and practice for sustainable development (PhD)*. Boston: Boston College.

Branch, J., & Oberg, D. (2004). *Focus on inquiry*. Alberta, Canada: Alberta Learning.

Braskamp, L., Braskamp, D., & Engberg, M. (2014). *Global perspective inventory (GPI): Its purpose, construction, potential uses, and psychometric characteristics*. Retrieved from https://gpi.central.edu/supportDocs/manual.pdf

Braun, A., Ball, S., Maguire, M., & Hoskins, K. (2011). Taking context seriously: Towards explaining policy enactments in the secondary school. *Discourse (Berkeley, Calif.)*, *32*(4), 585–596. doi:10.1080/01596306.2011.601555

Breines, J. G., & Chen, S. (2012). Self-compassion increases self-improvement motivation. *Personality and Social Psychology Bulletin*, *38*(9), 1133–1143. doi:10.1177/0146167212445599 PMID:22645164

Bres, A. F. (2016). *From Management to Adaptation: Designing an Organizational Learning Process for Strategic Renewal of Environmental Management at The City of Calgary* (Unpublished doctoral dissertation). The University of Calgary, Calgary, Alberta, Canada.

Brewer, J. (2005). *Foundations of Multimethod research: Synthesizing Styles*. Newbury Park, CA: Sage.

Briggs, J., & Peat, F. D. (1990). *Turbulent mirror*. New York: Harper Collins Perennial Library.

Britton, W. B., Lepp, N. E., Niles, H. F., Rocha, T., Fisher, N. E., & Gold, J. S. (2014). A randomized controlled pilot trial of classroom-based mindfulness meditation compared to an active control condition in sixth-grade children. *Journal of School Psychology*, *52*(3), 263–278. doi:10.1016/j.jsp.2014.03.002 PMID:24930819

Compilation of References

Broderick, P. C. (2013). *"Learning to BREATHE": A Mindfulness Curriculum for Adolescents to Cultivate Emotional Regulation, Attention, and Performance*. New Harbinger Publications, Inc.

Broderick, P. C., & Metz, S. (2009). "Learning to BREATHE": A pilot trial of a mindfulness curriculum for adolescents. *Advances in School Mental Health Promotion*, *2*(1), 35–46. doi:10.1080/1754730X.2009.9715696

Brown, B. (2006). The four worlds of sustainability: Drawing upon four universal perspectives to support sustainability initiatives. *Integral Sustainability Centre*. Retrieved from http://nextstepintegral.org/wp-content/uploads/2011/04/Four-Worlds-of-Sustainability-Barrett-C-Brown.pdf

Brown, B. C. (2007). *The four worlds of sustainability: Drawing upon four universal perspectives to support sustainability initiatives*. Retrieved May 9, 2018 from: http://nextstepintegral.org/wp-content/uploads/2011/04/Four-Worlds-of-Sustainability-Barrett-C-Brown.pdf

Brown, B. C. (2011). *Conscious leadership for sustainability: How leaders with late-stage action logics design and implement sustainability initiatives* (Doctoral dissertation). Fielding Graduate University.

Brown, A. L. (1992). Design experiments: Theoretical and methodological challenges in creating complex interventions in classroom settings. *Journal of the Learning Sciences*, *2*(2), 141–178. doi:10.120715327809jls0202_2

Brown, K. W., & Ryan, R. M. (2003). The benefits of being present: Mindfulness and its role in psychological well-being. *Journal of Personality and Social Psychology*, *84*(4), 822–848. doi:10.1037/0022-3514.84.4.822 PMID:12703651

Brown, R. P., & Gerbarg, P. L. (2009). Yoga breathing, meditation, and longevity. *Annals of the New York Academy of Sciences*, *1172*(1), 54–62. doi:10.1111/j.1749-6632.2009.04394.x PMID:19735239

Bruce, C., Davis, B., Sinclair, N., McGarvey, L., Hallowell, D., Drefs, M., ... Woolcott, G. (2017). Understanding gaps in research networks: Using "spatial reasoning" as a window into the importance of networked educational research. *Educational Studies in Mathematics*, *95*(2), 143–161. doi:10.100710649-016-9743-2

Bruin, E., Zijlstra, B., Van de Weijer-Bergsma, E., & Bögels, S. (2011). The Mindful Attention Awareness Scale for Adolescents (MAAS-A): Psychometric Properties in a Dutch Sample. *Mindfulness*, *2*(1), 201–211. doi:10.100712671-011-0061-6 PMID:21909342

Bunnell, T. (2006). The growing momentum and legitimacy behind an alliance for international education. *Journal of Research in International Education*, *5*(2), 155–176. doi:10.1177/1475240906065600

Bunnell, T. (2009). The International Baccalaureate in the USA and the emerging 'culture war'. *Discourse (Abingdon)*, *30*(1), 61–72. doi:10.1080/01596300802643090

Burke, K. (1984). *Permanence and change: An anatomy of purpose* (3rd ed.). Berkeley, CA: University of California Press.

Burnes, B. (2004). Kurt Lewin and the planned approach to change: A re-appraisal. *Journal of Management Studies*, *41*(6), 977–1002. doi:10.1111/j.1467-6486.2004.00463.x

Buysse, V., Skinner, D., & Grant, S. (2001). Toward a definition of quality inclusion: Perspectives of parents and practitioners. *Journal of Early Intervention*, *24*(2), 146–161. doi:10.1177/105381510102400208

Cacioppe, R. (2000). Creating spirit at work: reNvisioning organization development and leadership – Part II. *Leadership and Organization Development Journal*, *21*(2), 110–119. doi:10.1108/01437730010318200

Cacioppe, R., & Albrecht, S. (2000). Using 360 degree feedback and the integral model to develop leadership and management skills. *Leadership and Organization Development Journal*, *21*(8), 8. doi:10.1108/01437730010379249

Cacioppe, R., & Edwards, M. G. (2005a). Adjusting blurred visions: A typology of integral approaches to organisations. *Journal of Organizational Change Management, 18*(3), 230–246. doi:10.1108/09534810510599399

Cacioppe, R., & Edwards, M. G. (2005b). Seeking the holy grail of organisational development: A synthesis of integral theory, spiral dynamics, corporate transformation and action inquiry. *Leadership and Organization Development Journal, 26*(2), 86–105. doi:10.1108/01437730510582536

Calaprice, A. (Ed.). (2005). *The New Quotable Einstein*. Princeton, NJ: Princeton University Press.

Cambridge Assessment International Education. (2017). *Cambridge IGCSE curriculum*. Retrieved from http://www.cambridgeinternational.org/programmes-and-qualifications/cambridge-secondary-2/cambridge-igcse/curriculum/

Cambridge, J. (2002). Global product branding and international education. *Journal of Research in International Education, 1*(2), 227–243. doi:10.1177/147524002764248158

Canadian Institutes of Health Research, Natural Sciences and Engineering Research Council of Canada, and Social Sciences and Humanities Research Council of Canada. (2014). *Tri-Council policy statement: Ethical conduct for research involving humans*. Retrieved from: http://www.pre.ethics.gc.ca/pdf/eng/tcps2-2014/TCPS_2_FINAL_Web.pdf

Capra, F. (1997). *The web of life: A new synthesis of mind and matter*. London: Flamingo.

Carlgren, D. (2017). *Integral exploration of the engagement of a scientific community of students in a school conference* (Unpublished dissertation). University of Calgary, Calgary, Alberta, Canada.

Carroll, G. (2003). The reification of international education. *IB Research Notes, 3*(4), 2–5. Retrieved from http://www.bath.ac.uk/ceic/ibru/

Carr, S. M., Lhussier, M., & Chandler, C. (2010). The supervision of professional doctorates: Experiences of the processes and ways forward. *Nurse Education Today, 30*(4), 279–284. doi:10.1016/j.nedt.2009.03.004 PMID:20138411

CASEL. (2013). *Effective social and emotional learning programs: Preschool and elementary school edition. Collaborative for Academic, Social and Emotional Learning*. KSA-Plus Communications Inc. Retrieved from: www.casel.org

CERI. (2010a). *More about the schooling for tomorrow project*. Retrieved from http://www.oecd.org /site/schoolingfortomorrowknowledgebase/futuresthinking/scenarios/theschoolingfortomorrowscenarios.htm

Charmaz, K. (2014). *Constructing Grounded Theory: a practical guide through qualitative analysis* (2nd ed.). London: Sage.

Cheng, R., & Gu, S. (2015). Autism: Reduced connectivity between cortical areas involved in face expression, theory of mind, and sense of self. *Brain, 138*(5), 1382–1393. doi:10.1093/brain/awv051 PMID:25795704

Chen, X., Christmas-Best, V., Titzmann, P. F., & Weichold, K. (2012). Issue editor's notes: Youth success and adaptation in times of globalization and economic change. *New Directions for Youth Development, 135*(135), 1–10. doi:10.1002/yd.20022 PMID:23097358

Chesterman, D. (2001). Learning from research perspectives in collaborative working. *Career Development International, 6*(7), 378–383. doi:10.1108/EUM0000000006058

Choi, B. C., & Pak, A. W. (2006). Multidisciplinarity, interdisciplinarity and transdisciplinarity in health research, services, education and policy: 1. Definitions, objectives, and evidence of effectiveness. *Clinical and Investigative Medicine. Medecine Clinique et Experimentale, 29*(6), 351–364. PMID:17330451

Choudhury, S., Charman, T., Bird, V., & Blakemore, S. (2007). Development of action representation during adolescence. *Neuropsychologia, 45*(2), 255–262. doi:10.1016/j.neuropsychologia.2006.07.010 PMID:16962147

Cilliers, P. (1998). *Complexity and postmodernism: Understanding complex systems.* London: Routledge.

Clandinin, D. J. (2007). Mapping a landscape of narrative inquiry: borderland spaces and tensions. In Handbook of narrative inquiry: Mapping a methodology (pp. 35–76). Thousand Oaks, CA: SAGE Publications Ltd. doi:10.4135/9781452226552.n2

Clandinin, D. J. (2006). Narrative inquiry: A methodology for studying lived experience. *Research Studies in Music Education, 27*(1), 44–54. doi:10.1177/1321103X060270010301

Clarke, Dudley, Dutton, Emery, & Ghali. (2014). *Laying th foundation for policy: Measuring local prevalence for autism spectrum disorder.* Calgary: The School of Public Policy, University of Calgary.

Clough, P. (Ed.). (1998). *Managing inclusive education: From policy and practice.* London: Sage.

Clough, P., & Nutbrown, C. (2004). Special education needs and inclusion: Multiple Perspectives of preschool educators in the UK. *Journal of Early Childhood Research, 191*(2), 191–210. doi:10.1177/1476718X04043015

CMEC. (2014). *Early learning and development framework.* Retrieved from http://www.cmec.ca/Publications/Lists/Publications/Attachments/327/2014-07-Early-Learning-Framework-EN.pdf

Cobb, P., Confrey, J., diSessa, A. A., Lehrer, R., & Schauble, L. (2003). Design experiments in educational research. *Educational Researcher, 32*(1), 9–13. doi:10.3102/0013189X032001009

Coghlan, D., & Brannick, T. (2014). *Doing action research in your own organization* (4th ed.). Thousand Oaks, CA: Sage.

Colman, A. M. (Ed.). (2006). *Oxford Dictionary of Psychology* (2nd ed.). Oxford, UK: Oxford University Press.

Conley, D. T. (2008). Rethinking college readiness. *New Directions for Higher Education, 144*(144), 3–13. doi:10.1002/he.321

Conley, D. T. (2011). *Redefining College Readiness* (Vol. 5). Eugene, OR: Educational Policy Improvement Center.

Conley, D. T. (2014). *Getting ready for college, careers, and the common core: What every educator needs to know.* San Francisco, CA: Jossey-Bass.

Connelly, F. M., & Clandinin, D. J. (1990). Narrative inquiry. In J. Green, G. Camili & P. Elmore (Eds.), Handbook of complementary methods in education research (pp. 477–487). Mahwah, NJ: Lawrence Erlbaum.

Connely, M., & Clandinin, J. (1990). Stories of Experience and Narrative Inquiry. *Educational Researcher, 19*(5), 2–14. doi:10.3102/0013189X019005002

Conn-Powers, M., Cross, A., Traub, E., & Hutter-Pishgahi, L. (2006). The universal design of early education: Moving forward for all children. *Beyond the Journal: Young Children on the Web.* Retrieved from http://journal.naeyc.org/btj/200609/ConnPowersBTJ.pdf

Cook, B. G., & Odom, S. L. (2013). Evidence-based practices and implementation science in special education. *Council for Exceptional Children, 70*(2), 135–144. doi:10.1177/001440291307900201

Cook-Greuter, S. R. (2013). *Nine levels of increasing embrace in ego development: A full-spectrum theory of vertical growth and meaning making.* Retrieved from: http://www.cook-greuter.com/Cook-Greuter%209%20levels%20paper%20new%201.1%2714%2097p%5B1%5D.pdf

Cook-Greuter, S. (2013). Assumptions Versus Assertions: Separating Hypotheses from Truth in the Integral Community. *Journal of Integral Theory and Practice, 8*(3&4), 227–236.

Cook-Greuter, S. (2013). Nine Levels Of Increasing Embrace. In *Ego Development: A Full-Spectrum Theory Of Vertical Growth And Meaning Making.* Independent Scholar Publication.

Cook-Greuter, S. R. (1999). *Postautonomous ego development: A study of its nature and measurement (Ph.D.)*. Cambridge, MA: Harvard University.

Cook-Greuter, S. R. (2004). Making the case for a developmental perspective. *Industrial and Commercial Training*, *36*(7), 275–281. doi:10.1108/00197850410563902

Cornwall, A., & Jewkes, R. (1995). What is participatory research? *Social Science & Medicine*, *41*(12), 1667–1676. doi:10.1016/0277-9536(95)00127-S PMID:8746866

Coupal, L. (2005). Practitioner-Research and the Regulation of Research Ethics: The Challenge of Individual, Organizational, and Social Interests. *Forum Qualitative Sozialforschung /Forum: Qualitative. Social Research*, *6*(1). Retrieved from http://www.qualitative-research.net/index.php/fqs/article/view/528/1144

Craton, M., & Saunders, G. (1998). *Islanders in the stream: A history of the Bahamian people, Volume two: From the ending of slavery to the twenty-first century*. Athens, GA: The University of Georgia Press.

Creswell, J. W. (2015). Educational research: Planning, conducting, and evaluating, Quantitative and qualitative research (5th ed.). Pearson.

Creswell, J. W., & Plano Clark, V. L. (2011). *Designing and conducting mixed methods research*. Retrieved from https://books.google.com/

Creswell, J. W. (2012). *Educational research: Planning, conducting, and evaluating quantitative and qualitative research*. New York, NY: Pearson.

Creswell, J. W. (2012). *Quantitative Research Characteristics. In Educational research: Planning, conducting, and evaluating quantitative and qualitative research* (4th ed.). Toronto: Pearson.

Creswell, J. W. (2013). *Qualitative inquiry & research design: Choosing among five approaches* (3rd ed.). Thousand Oaks, CA: SAGE.

Crittenden, J. (1997). Foreword: What is the meaning of "Integral?" In *The eye of spirit: An integral vision for a world gone slightly mad* (pp. vii–xii). Boston, MA: Shambhala.

Crocker, J., & Canevello, A. (2008). Creating and undermining social support in communal relationships: The role of compassionate and self-image goals. *Journal of Personality and Social Psychology*, *95*(3), 555–575. doi:10.1037/0022-3514.95.3.555 PMID:18729694

Crossan, M. M., Lane, H. W., & White, R. E. (1999). An organizational learning framework: From intuition to institution. *Academy of Management Review*, *24*(3), 522–537. doi:10.5465/amr.1999.2202135

Crotty, M. (1998). *The Foundations of Social Research: Meaning and perspective in the research process*. London: SAGE Publications.

Csikszentmihalyi, M. (1990). Enjoyment and the quality of life. In *Flow: The psychology of optimal experience* (pp. 43–70). Grand Rapids, MI: Harper & Row.

Csikszentmihalyi, M. (1990). *Flow: The psychology of optimal experience*. New York: Harper Collins Publisher.

Csikszentmihalyi, M. (1997). *Finding flow: The psychology of engagement with everyday life*. Basic Books.

Cunnien, K. A., Martin Rogers, N., & Mortimer, J. T. (2009). Adolescent work experience and self-efficacy. *The International Journal of Sociology and Social Policy*, *29*(3/4), 164–175. doi:10.1108/01443330910947534 PMID:19750144

Dąbrowski, K. (1972). *Psychoneurosis is not an illness*. London: Gryf Publications Ltd.

Dąbrowski, K. (1973). *The dynamics of concepts*. London: Gryf Publications Ltd.

Dąbrowski, K. (1996). *Multilevelness of emotional and instinctive functions*. Lublin: Towarzystwo Naukowe Katolickiego Uniwersytetu Lubelskiego.

Dąbrowski, K. (2015). *Personality shaping through positive disintegration*. Red Pill Press.

Dąbrowski, K., Kawczak, A., & Piechowski, M. (1970). *Mental growth through positive disintegration*. London: Gryf Publication Ltd.

Dąbrowski, K., & Piechowski, M. M. (1977a). Theory of levels of emotional development: Vol. 1. *Multilevelness and positive disintegration*. New York: Dabor Science Publications.

Dąbrowski, K., & Piechowski, M. M. (1977b). Theory of levels of emotional development: Vol. 2. *From primary integration to self-actualization*. New York: Dabor Science Publications.

Dai, X. (2009). Intercultural personhood and identity negotiation. *China Media Research, 5*(2), 1–12. Retrieved from http://www.thefreelibrary.com/Intercultural+personhood+and+identity+negotiation.-a0215410902

Davidson, J., Dunne, R., Eccles, J., Engle, J. S., Greenberg, A., Jennings, M., ... Vago, D. (2012). Contemplative practices and mental training: Prospects for American education. *Child Development Perspectives, 6*(2), 146–153. doi:10.1111/j.1750-8606.2012.00240.x PMID:22905038

Davidson, R. J., & Begley, S. (2012). *The emotional life of your brain: How its unique patterns affect the way you think, feel, and live, and how you can change them*. New York: Penguin.

Davidson, R., & Begley, S. (2012). *The emotional life of your brain: How its unique patterns affect the way you think, feel and live – and how you can change them*. London: Penguin Books.

Davis, B. & Sumara, D. (2008). Complexity as a theory of education. *Transnational Curriculum Inquiry, 5*(2).

Davis, B., & Sumara, D. (2008). Complexity as a theory of education. *Transnational Curriculum Inquiry, 5*(2), 33–44. Retrieved from http://ecs210.uregina.wikispaces.net/file/view/Complexity+as+a+Theory+of+Education.pdf

Davis, B., Sumara, D., & Luce-Kapler, R. (2013). Engaging minds: Cultures of education and practices of teaching (3rd ed.). New York, NY: Routledge.

Davis, T. M., & Murrell, P. H. (1993). Turning teaching into learning: The role of student responsibility in the collegiate experience. *Higher Education Report*, 8. Retrieved from http://files.eric.ed.gov/fulltext/ED372703.pdf

Davis, B., & Sumara, D. (2003). Why aren't they getting this? Working through the Regressive myths of constructivist pedagogy. *Teaching Education, 2*(14), 123–140. doi:10.1080/1047621032000092922

Davis, B., Sumara, D., & Luce-Kapler, R. (2015). *Engaging minds: Cultures of education and practices of teaching*. Routledge. doi:10.4324/9781315695891

Davis, N. T., & Callihan, L. P. (2013). Integral methodological pluralism in science education research: Valuing multiple perspectives. *Cultural Studies of Science Education, 8*(3), 505–516. doi:10.100711422-012-9480-5

Dawson-Tunik, T. L., Commons, M., Wilson, M., & Fischer, K. W. (2005). The shape of development. *European Journal of Developmental Psychology, 2*(2), 163–195. doi:10.1080/17405620544000011

Dean, K. L. (2004). Systems thinking's challenge to research in spirituality and religion at work: An interview with Ian Mitroff. *Journal of Organizational Change Management, 17*(1), 11–25. doi:10.1108/09534810410511279

DEC/NAEYC. (2009). *Early childhood inclusion: A joint position statement of the Division for Early Childhood (DEC) and the national Association for the Education of Young Children (NAEYC)*. Chapel Hill, NC: The University of North Caroline, FPG Child Development Institute.

Decety, J., Chen, C., Harenski, C., & Kiehl, K. A. (2013). An fMRI study of affective perspective taking in individuals with psychopathy: Imagining another in pain does not evoke empathy. *Frontiers in Human Neuroscience*, *7*, 489. doi:10.3389/fnhum.2013.00489 PMID:24093010

Deming, W. E. (1986). *Out of the crisis*. Cambridge, MA: Massachusetts Institute of Technology, Center for Advanced Engineering Study.

Dent, E. B. (1999). Complexity science: A worldview shift. *Emergence*, *1*(4), 5–19. doi:10.120715327000em0104_2

Denzin, N. K. (1989). *Interpretive biography: Qualitative research methods series 17*. Sage University Press. doi:10.4135/9781412984584

Denzin, N. K., & Lincoln, Y. S. (Eds.). (1994). *Introduction: Entering the field of Qualitative Research. In Handbook of Qualitative Research*. Thousand Oaks, CA: Sage.

Derrida, J. (1984). Deconstruction and the other. An interview with Jacques Derrida. In R. Kearney (Ed.), *Dialogues with contemporary continental thinker*. Manchester, UK: Manchester University Press.

Design-Based Research Collective. (2003). Design-based research: An emerging paradigm for educational inquiry. *Educational Researcher*, *32*(1), 5–8. doi:10.3102/0013189X032001005

DeVore, S., & Russell, K. (2007). Early childhood education and care for children with disabilities: Facilitating inclusive practice. *Early Childhood Education Journal*, *35*(2), 189–198. doi:10.100710643-006-0145-4

Dietze, B., & Kashin, D. (2016). *Empowering pedagogy for early childhood education*. Toronto: Pearson Canada Inc.

Dilthey, W. (1976). *Dilthey selected writings*. Cambridge University Press.

Dilthey, W. (2010). *Understanding the human world*. Princeton University Press.

Divecha, S. (2014). *A climate for change: An exploration towards Integral Action Loops to apply our knowledge for sustainability success* (Ph.D.). Adelaide Business School, The University of Adelaide. Retrieved from https://greenmode.files.wordpress.com/2015/03/simon-divecha-thesis-reviews-print.pdf

Divecha, S. (2014). *A climate for change: An exploration towards Integral Action Loops to apply our knowledge for sustainability success (Ph.D.)*. Adelaide Business School, The University of Adelaide.

Divecha, S., & Brown, B. C. (2013). Integral sustainability: Correlating action logics with sustainability to provide new insights into the dynamics of change. *Journal of Integral Theory and Practice*, *8*(3-4), 13.

Doherty, C., & Mu, L. (2011). Producing the intercultural citizen in the International Baccalaureate. In F. Dervin, A. Gajardo, & A. Lavanchy (Eds.), *Politics of interculturality* (pp. 165–188). Newcastle upon Tyne, UK: Cambridge Scholars Publishing.

Drake, B. (2004). International education and IB Programmes: Worldwide expansion and potential cultural dissonance. *Journal of Research in International Education*, *3*(2), 189–205. doi:10.1177/1475240904044387

Du Plessis, G. P. (2013). *The import of integral pluralism in striving towards an integral metatheory of addiction*. Paper presented at the 3rd Biannual Integral Theory Conference, Redwood City, CA.

Ducharme, D., Leblanc, R., Bourassa, M., & Chevalier, J. (2011). Participatory research in a school setting: A process of acculturation. *Online Submission. US-China Education Review B*, 868–877.

Duckworth, A. L., Grant, H., Loew, B., Oettingen, G., & Gollwitzer, P. M. (2011). Self-regulation strategies improve self-discipline in adolescents: Benefits of mental contrasting and implementation intentions. *Educational Psychology*, *31*(1), 17–26. doi:10.1080/01443410.2010.506003

Dudley, H. (1984). Doctoral students and the supervisor's role. *British Medical Journal*, *288*(6416), 511. doi:10.1136/bmj.288.6416.511 PMID:20742178

Duffell, E. (2008). *Curriculum grades k-2*. Retrieved from http://www.seedsofcompassion.org/why/curriculum/K-%20Compassion%20Lessons.pdf

Dugas, M. J., Gosselin, P., & Ladouceur, R. (2001). Intolerance of Uncertainty and Worry: Investigating Specificity in a Nonclinical Sample. *Cognitive Therapy and Research*, *25*(5), 551–558. doi:10.1023/A:1005553414688

Duncheon, J. C., & Tierney, W. G. (2013). Changing Conceptions of Time: Implications For Educational Research and Practice. *Review of Educational Research*, *83*(2), 236–272. doi:10.3102/0034654313478492

Dunne, J., Williams, R., & Martinez, N. (2002). Food-web structure and network theory: The role of connectance and size. *Proceedings of the National Academy of Sciences of the United States of America*, *99*(20), 12917–12922. doi:10.1073/pnas.192407699 PMID:12235364

Dunne, S., & Edwards, J. (2010). International schools as sites of social change. *Journal of Research in International Education*, *9*(1), 24–39. doi:10.1177/1475240909356716

Durayappah, A. (2010). The 3P Model: A General Theory of Subjective Well-Being. *Journal of Happiness Studies*. doi:10.100710902-010-9223-9

Durlak, J. A., Dymnicki, A. B., Taylor, R. D., Weissberg, R. P., & Schellinger, K. B. (2011). The impact of enhancing students' social and emotional learning: A mata-analysis of school-based universal interventions. *Child Development*, *82*(1), 405–432. doi:10.1111/j.1467-8624.2010.01564.x PMID:21291449

Dweck, C. S. (2006). *Mindset: How we can learn to fulfill our potential*. New York: Ballentine Books.

Dweck, C. S. (2009). Even geniuses work hard. *Educational Leadership*, *68*(1), 16–20. Retrieved from http://msan.wceruw.org/documents/resources_foreducators/Relationships/Even%20Geniuses%20Work%20Hard.pdf

Eaves & Ho. (2008). Young adult outcomes of autism disorders. *Journal of Autism and Developmental Disorders*, •••, 739–747.

EC. (2015). Attainment: Raising graduate numbers. *European Commission, Education and Training*. Retrieved from http://bit.ly/2mmlO9T

Eccles, M. & Mittman, B. (2006). Welcome to implementation science. *Implementation Science, 1*(1), 1-3. doi: 10 doi:1.1186/1748-5908-1-1

Eckersley, R. (1999). Dreams and expectations: Young people's expected and preferred futures and their significance for education. *Futures*, *31*(1), 73–90. doi:10.1016/S0016-3287(98)00111-6

Edelman, G. M. (2004). *Wider than the sky: The phenomenal gift of consciousness*. New Haven, CT: Yale University Press.

Edmunds, J. A. (2012). Early colleges: A new model of schooling focusing on college readiness. *New Directions for Higher Education*, *158*(158), 81–89. doi:10.1002/he.20017

Education Act, §§46–17 & 29 (2001).

Edwards, M. (2000). The Integral Cycle of Knowledge: Some thoughts on integrating Ken Wilber's Developmental and Epistemological Models. *Integral World*. Retrieved from http://www.integralworld.net/edwards2.html

Edwards, M. G. (2005). The integral holon: A holonomic approach to organisational change and transformation. *Journal of Organizational Change Management, 18*(3), 269–288. doi:10.1108/09534810510599425

Edwards, M. G. (2009). *Organizational transformation for sustainability: An integral metatheory*. London, UK: Routledge.

Edwards, M. G. (2010). *Organisational transformation for sustainability: An integral metatheory*. New York, NY: Routledge. doi:10.4324/9780203859933

Edwards, M. G. (2013). Misunderstanding metatheorizing. *Systems Research and Behavioral Science*.

Egbert, J. (2004). A study of flow theory in the foreign language classroom. *Canadian Modern Language Review, 60*(5), 549–586. doi:10.3138/cmlr.60.5.549

Elmgren, M., & Henriksson, A.-S. (2010). *Universitetspedagogik* [University pedagogy]. Uppsala, Sweden: Norstedts.

Erikson, E. H. (1963). *Childhood and Society* (2nd ed.). New York, NY: W. W. Norton & Company, Inc.

Esbjörn-Hargens, S. (2007). Integral teacher, integral students, integral classroom: Applying integral theory to education. *AQAL: Journal of Integral Theory and Practice, 2*(2), 72–103. Retrieved from https://foundation.metaintegral.org/JITP

Esbjörn-Hargens, S. (2009). An overview of Integral Theory. *IntegralPost*. Retrieved from https://integrallife.com/integral-post/overview-integral-theory

Esbjörn-Hargens, S. (2009). *An overview of integral theory: An all-inclusive framework for the 21st century*. Integral Institute (Resource Paper No. 1).

Esbjörn-Hargens, S. (2009). *An overview of integral theory: An all-inclusive framework for the 21st century*. Integral Institute, Resource paper No. 1, 1–24.

Esbjörn-Hargens, S. (2009). *An overview of integral theory: An all-inclusive framework for the 21st century*. Integral institute: Resource paper no. 1, 1–24.

Esbjörn-Hargens, S. (2010). An ontology of climate change: Integral pluralism and the enactment of multiple objects. *Journal of Integral Theory and Practice*, 143-174.

Esbjörn-Hargens, S. (2011). *Integral teacher, Integral students, Integral classroom: Applying Integral theory to education*. Retrieved from http://nextstepintegral.org/wp-content/uploads/2011/04/Integral-Education-Esbjorn-Hargens.pdf

Esbjörn-Hargens, S. (2005). Integral ecology: The what, who, and how of environmental phenomena. *World Futures: The Journal of General Evolution, 61*(1), 5–49. doi:10.1080/02604020590902344

Esbjörn-Hargens, S. (2006). Integral research: A multi-method approach to investigating phenomena. *Constructivism in the Human Sciences, 11*(1), 79–107.

Esbjörn-Hargens, S. (2007). Integral teacher, integral students, integral classroom: Applying integral theory to education. *AQAL: Journal of Integral Theory and Practice, 2*(2), 1–41.

Esbjörn-Hargens, S. (2008). Integral ecological research: Using IMP to examine animals and sustainability. *Journal of Integral Theory and Practice, 3*(1), 15–60.

Esbjörn-Hargens, S. (2010). An ontology of climate change. *Journal of Integral Theory and Practice, 5*(1), 143–174.

Esbjörn-Hargens, S. (2010). An ontology of climate change: Integral pluralism and the enactment of environmental phenomena. *Journal of Integral Theory and Practice, 5*(1), 183–201. Retrieved from https://foundation.metaintegral.org/JITP

Esbjörn-Hargens, S. (2010a). Executive editor's introduction. *Journal of Integral Theory and Practice, 5*(1), 4.

Esbjörn-Hargens, S. (2010b). An overview of integral theory: An all-inclusive framework for the twenty-first century. In S. Esbjörn-Hargens (Ed.), *Integral theory in action: applied, theoretical, and constructive perspectives on the AQAL model*. New York: SUNY Press.

Esbjörn-Hargens, S. (2010c). An integral overview of climate change: Why truth is not enough. *Journal of Integral Theory & Practice, 5*(1), 1–42.

Esbjörn-Hargens, S. (2010d). An ontology of climate change: Integral pluralism and the enactment of multiple objects. *Journal of Integral Theory and Practice, 5*(1), 143–174.

Esbjörn-Hargens, S. (2014). *TetraDynamics: Quadrants in action*. Sebastopol, CA: MetaIntegral Foundation.

Esbjörn-Hargens, S. (2014). *Tetradynamics: Quadrants in action*. Sebastopol, CA: MetaIntegral Publishers.

Esbjorn-Hargens, S., & Zimmerman, M. (2009). *Integral ecology: Uniting multiple perspectives on the natural world*. Boston: Integral Books.

Eurostat. (2013). Tertiary education statistics. *Eurostat*. Retrieved from http://bit.ly/2eJPfRL

Eurostat. (2016). Educational attainment statistics. *Eurostat*. Retrieved from http://bit.ly/2oTzCbs

Falk, D. (2008). *In Search of Time: Journeys Along a Curious Dimension*. Toronto: McLelland & Stewart.

Farland-Smith, D. (2012). Development and field test of the modified Draw-a-Scientist test and he Draw-a-Scientist rubric. *School Science and Mathematics, 112*(2), 109-116. doi:.1949-8594.2011.00124.x doi:10.1111/j

Fein, J., & Hicks, D. (2010). *Visions of the Future*. Retrieved from http://www.unesco.org/ education/tlsf/mods/theme_a/popups/mod03t04s01.html

Ferguson, M. (1980). *The Aquarian conspiracy: Personal and social transformation in the 1980s*. Los Angeles, CA: J. P. Tarcher.

Finfgeld, D. L. (2003). Metasynthesis: The state of the art, so far. *Qualitative Health Research, 13*(7), 893–904. doi:10.1177/1049732303253462 PMID:14502956

Fisher, R. M. (1983). *Appropriate education: Education as if the human being mattered*. Unpublished.

Fisher, R. M. (1984, June). Future not to be feared. *Olds Optimist*, 10.

Fisher, R. M. (1995a). *An introduction to defining 'fear': A spectrum approach*. Technical Paper No. 1. Calgary, Canada: In Search of Fearlessness Research Institute.

Fisher, R. M. (1995b). *An introduction to an epistemology of 'fear': A fearlessness paradigm*. Technical Paper No. 2. Calgary, Canada: In Search of Fearlessness Research Institute.

Fisher, R. M. (1998). *Culture of 'fear': Toxification of landscape-mindscape as meta-context for education in the 21st century*. Technical Paper No. 7. Vancouver: In Search of Fearlessness Research Institute.

Fisher, R. M. (2003a). *A report on the status of fear education*. Technical Paper No. 15. Vancouver: In Search of Fearlessness Research Institute.

Fisher, R. M. (2003b). *Fearless leadership in and out of the 'Fear' Matrix* (Unpublished dissertation). Vancouver: The University of British Columbia.

Fisher, R. M. (2007a). *Education and the culture of fear: A review*. Technical Paper No. 25. Vancouver: In Search of Fearlessness Research Institute.

Fisher, R. M. (2007b). *Ken Wilber and the education literature: Abridged annotated bibliography*. Retrieved from http://www.pathsoflearning-net/resources_writings _Ken_Wilber.pdf

Fisher, R. M. (2009). *"Unplugging" as real and metaphoric: Emancipatory dimensions to* The Matrix *film trilogy*. Technical Paper No. 33. Carbondale, IL: In Search of Fearlessness Research Institute.

Fisher, R. M. (2018). *'Fear' Studies, 12 years later: Progress and barriers*. Technical Paper No. 74. Calgary, Canada: In Search of Fearlessness Research Institute.

Fisher, R. M. (1976, January). Air pollution in Calgary. *Calgary Herald*, 17.

Fisher, R. M. (1977, October). Mechanized monsters invade creek. *Calgary Herald*, 15.

Fisher, R. M. (1979, September). Support positive planners. *Calgary Herald*, 26.

Fisher, R. M. (1985). *The Waldorf experience: Education as an art*. Old, Canada: Janus Alternatives.

Fisher, R. M. (1996). Dare to contradict, dare to distinguish; Into the flaming heart of the. In *Search of Fearlessness Project*. Calgary, Canada: In Search of Fearlessness Research Institute.

Fisher, R. M. (1997). A guide to Wilberland: Some common misunderstandings of the critics of Ken Wilber and his work on transpersonal theory prior to 1995. *Journal of Humanistic Psychology*, *37*(4), 30–73. doi:10.1177/00221678970374005

Fisher, R. M. (2006). Invoking 'Fear' Studies. *Journal of Curriculum Theorizing*, *22*(4), 39–71.

Fisher, R. M. (2010). *The world's fearlessness teachings: A critical integral approach to fear management/education in the 21st century*. Lanham, MD: University Press of America.

Fisher, R. M. (2011). A critique of critical thinking: Towards a critical integral pedagogy of fearlessness. *NUML: Journal of Critical Inquiry*, *9*(2), 92–104.

Fisher, R. M. (2017). Radical love, is it radical enough? *International Journal of Critical Pedagogy*, *8*(1), 261–281.

Fisher, R. M., & Subba, D. (2016). *Philosophy of fearism: A first East-West dialogue*. Xlibris.

Fish, S. (1990). How to recognize a poem when you see one. In D. Bartholomae & A. Petrosky (Eds.), *Ways of Reading: An Anthology for Writers* (2nd ed.; pp. 178–191). Boston, MA: Bedford Books of St. Martin's Press.

Fixsen, D., Blase, K., Netz, A., & Van Dyke, M. (2013). Statewide implementation of evidence based programs. *Council for Exceptional Children*, *70*(2), 213–230. doi:10.1177/001440291307900206

Flood, R. L. (2009). *Rethinking the fifth discipline: Learning within the unknowable*. London: Routledge.

Flook, L., Goldberg, S. B., Pringer, L., Bonus, K., & Davidson, R. J. (2013). Mindfulness for teachers: A pilot study to assess effects on stress, burnout, and teaching efficacy. *Mind, Brain and Education: the Official Journal of the International Mind, Brain, and Education Society*, *7*(3), 182–195. doi:10.1111/mbe.12026 PMID:24324528

Floyd, J. (2008). Towards an Integral renewal of systems methodology for futures studies. *Futures*, *40*(2), 138–149. doi:10.1016/j.futures.2007.11.007

Floyd, J. (2012). Action research and integral futures, a path to embodied foresight. *Futures*, *44*(10), 870–882. doi:10.1016/j.futures.2012.09.001

Flyvbjerg, B. (2006). Five misunderstandings about case-study research. *Qualitative Inquiry*, *12*(2), 219–245. doi:10.1177/1077800405284363

Fogarty International Centre. (2013). *Frequently asked questions about implementation science*. National Institutes of Health. Retrieved from http://www.fic.nih.gov/News/Events/implementation-science/Pages/faqs.aspx

Forman, M., & Esbjörn-Hargens, S. (2008). *The academic emergence of integral theory: Reflections on and clarifications of the 1st Biennial Integral Theory Conference*. Retrieved 4 April, 2014, from http://www.integralworld.net/forman-hargens.html

Foucault, M. (1997). Subjectivity and Truth. In *Ethics: Subjectivity and Truth* (pp. 87–92). New York: The New Press.

Franke, A., & Arvidsson, B. (2011). Research supervisors' different ways of experiencing supervision of doctoral students. *Studies in Higher Education*, *36*(1), 7–19. doi:10.1080/03075070903402151

Freire, P. (2014). *Pedagogy of hope: Reliving pedagogy of the oppressed*. New York, NY: Bloomsbury.

Friesen, S. (2009). *What did you do in school today?* Toronto, Canada: Canadian Education Association. Retrieved from http://ccl-cca.ca/pdfs/otherreports/WDYDIST_National_Report_EN.pdf

Frith, M., Morton, J., & Leslie, A. M. (1991). The cognitive basis of a biological disorder: Autism. *Trends in Neurosciences*, *14*(10), 433–438. doi:10.1016/0166-2236(91)90041-R PMID:1722361

Fuchs, C., & Hofkirchner, W. (2009). *Autopoiesis and critical social systems theory autopoiesis and critical social systems theory*. Academic Press. doi:10.1108/S1877-6361(2009)0000006007

Fullan, M., & Langworthy, M. (2014). *Rich Futures in A Rich Seam: How New Pedagogies Find Deep Learning*. London, UK: Pearson.

Furedi, F. (1997). *Culture of fear: Risk and the morality of low expectation*. London, UK: Cassell.

Gabor, D. (1963). *Inventing the Future*. New York, NY: Alfred A. Knopf.

Gadamer, H. G. (1975/1989). *Truth and method*. London: Continuum.

Gardner, H. (1981). *The quest for mind*. Chicago, IL: University of Chicago Press.

Gardner, H. (1983). *Frames of Mind: The Theory of Multiple Intelligences*. New York: Basic Books.

Gardner, H. (1993). *Multiple intelligences: The theory in practice: A reader* (2nd ed.). Boston, MA: Basic Books.

Garrett, N. (1991). Technology in the service of language learning: Trends and issues. *Modern Language Journal*, *75*(1), 74–101. doi:10.1111/j.1540-4781.1991.tb01085.x

Gatfield, T. (2005). An investigation into PhD supervisory management styles: Development of a dynamic conceptual model and its managerial implications. *Journal of Higher Education Policy and Management*, *27*(3), 311–325. doi:10.1080/13600800500283585

Gay, L., Mills, G., & Airasian, P. (2006). *Educational research: Competencies for analysis and applications*. Columbus, OH: Pearson.

Geertz, C. (1973). *The Interpretation of Cultures*. New York, NY: Basic Books.

Geist, V. (1978). *Life strategies, human evolution, environmental design: Toward a biological theory of health*. New York: Springer-Verlag. doi:10.1007/978-1-4612-6325-8

Germeijs, V., & Verschueren, K. (2007). High school students' career decision-making process: Consequences for choice implementation in higher education. *Journal of Vocational Behavior*, *70*(2), 223–241. doi:10.1016/j.jvb.2006.10.004

Ghali, Dudley, Dutton, Zwicker, McMorris, Emery, & Clarke. (2014). *Laying the foundation for policy: Measuring local prevalence for autism spectrum disorder*. Calgary: University of Calgary School of Public Policy.

Gidley, J., & Hampson, G. (2008). Integral approaches to school educational futures. In Alternative Educational Futures: Pedagogies for Emergent Worlds. Sense Publishers.

Gidley, J. (2017). *Postformal education: A philosophy for complex futures*. New York: Springer.

Gigliotti-Labay, J. (2010). *Fulfilling its mission? The promotion of international mindedness in IB DP programmes* (Doctoral Dissertation). Retrieved from ProQuest Dissertations and Theses Global. (Order No. 3438266)

Girard, R. (1987). To Conclude. In *Things hidden since the foundation of the world* (S. Bann & M. Metteer, Trans.; pp. 433–447). Stanford, CA: Stanford University Press.

Giroux, H. A. (2014). *Neoliberalism's war on higher education*. Chicago, IL: Haymarket Books.

Gladwin, T. N., Kennelly, J. J., & Krause, T. N. S. (1995). Shifting paradigms for sustainable development: Implications for management theory and research. *Academy of Management Review*, *20*(4), 874–907. doi:10.5465/amr.1995.9512280024

Gladwin, T. N., Kennelly, J. J., & Krause, T. N. S. (1996). Toward eco-moral development of the Academy of Management. *Academy of Management Review*, *21*(4), 912–914. doi:10.5465/amr.1996.15867658

Glaser, B. D., & Strauss, A. K. (1967). *The Discovery of Grounded Theory*. Chicago: Aldine.

Glassner, B. (1999). *The culture of fear: Why Americans are afraid of the wrong things*. New York: Basic Books.

Gleick, J. (1988). *Chaos: Making a new science*. New York: Penguin.

Glesne, C. (2016). *Becoming qualitative researchers: An introduction* (5th ed.). Boston, MA: Pearson.

Glouberman, S., & Zimmerman, B. (2002). Complicated and complex systems: What would successful reform of Medicare look like? In P.-G. Forest, G. P. Marchildon, & T. McIntosh (Eds.), Romanow Papers: Changing Healthcare in Canada, Vol. 2. Toronto: University of Toronto Press.

Golde, C. M. (2000). Should I stay or should I go? Student descriptions of the doctoral attrition process. *The Review of Higher Education*, *23*(2), 199–227. doi:10.1353/rhe.2000.0004

Golde, C. M. (2005). The role of the department and discipline in doctoral student attrition: Lessons from four departments. *The Journal of Higher Education*, *76*(6), 669–700. doi:10.1353/jhe.2005.0039

Goldspink, C., & Kay, R. (2010). Emergence in organizations: The reflexive turn. *Emergence*, *12*(3), 47–63.

Goleman, D. (1995). *Emotional intelligence: Why it can matter more than IQ*. New York: Bantam Books.

Goleman, D. (2006). *Social intelligence: The revolutionary new science of human relationships*. New York: Random House Publishing.

Goleman, D., & Senge, P. (2014). *The Triple Focus*. Florence, MA: More Than Sound.

Compilation of References

Gómez, S. V. (2008). *From functional literacy and development to integral literacy and sustainable development. In Signposts to literacy for sustainable development.* Hamburg, Germany: UNESCO Institute for Lifelong Learning.

Gordon, G., & Esbjörn-Hargens, S. (2007). Are we having fun yet? An exploration of the transformative power of play. *Journal of Humanistic Psychology, 47*(2), 198–222. doi:10.1177/0022167806297034

Gouy-Pailler, C., Achard, S., Rivet, B., Jutten, C., Maby, E., Souloumiac, A., & Congedo, M. (2007). Topographical dynamics of brain connections for the design of asynchronous brain-computer interfaces. *Proceedings, Annual International Conference of the IEEE: Engineering in Medicine and Biology Society,* 2520-2523.

Grant, H., & Dweck, C. S. (2003). Clarifying achievement goals and their impact. *Journal of Personality and Social Psychology, 85*(1), 541–553. doi:10.1037/0022-3514.85.3.541 PMID:14498789

Grant, K., Hackney, R., & Edgar, D. (2014). Postgraduate research supervision: An 'agreed' conceptual view of good practice through derived metaphors. *International Journal of Doctoral Studies, 9,* 43–60. doi:10.28945/1952

Graves, C. (1970). Levels of Existence: An Open System Theory of Values. *Journal of Humanistic Psychology, 10*(2), 131–155. doi:10.1177/002216787001000205

Greene, J. (2006). Toward a methodology of mixed method social inquiry. *Research in the Schools, 13*(1), 93–98.

Grupe, D. W., & Nitschke, J. B. (2013). Uncertainty and Anticipation in Anxiety: An integrated Neurobiological and Psychological Perspective. *Nature Reviews. Neuroscience, 14*(7), 488–501. doi:10.1038/nrn3524 PMID:23783199

Gudykunst, W. (1994). *Bridging Differences, Effective intergroup communication.* London, UK: Sage.

Gunnlaugson & Brabant. (Eds.). (2016). *Cohering the integral we space: Engaging collective emergence, wisdom and healing in groups.* Integral Publishing House.

Haggis, T. (2008). "Knowledge must be contextual": Some possible implications of complexity and dynamic systems theories for educational research. *Educational Philosophy and Theory, 40*(1), 158–176. doi:10.1111/j.1469-5812.2007.00403.x

Haigh, M. (2013). AQAL Integral: A holistic framework for pedagogic research. *Journal of Geography in Higher Education, 37*(2), 174–191. doi:10.1080/03098265.2012.755615

Hakkarainen, P., & Bredikyte, M. (2008). The zone of proximal development in play and learning. *Cultural-historical Psychology, 4*(4), 2–11. Retrieved from http://psyjournals.ru/en/kip/2008/n4/Hakkarainen_full.shtml

Hall, C. W., Row, K. A., Wuensch, K. L., & Godley, K. R. (2013). The role of self-compassion in physical and psychological wellbeing. *The Journal of Psychology, 147*(4), 311–323. doi:10.1080/00223980.2012.693138 PMID:23885635

Hammersley, M. (1999). Not Bricolage but Boatbuilding: Exploring two metaphors for thinking about ethnography. *Journal of Contemporary Ethnography, 28*(5), 574–585. doi:10.1177/089124199129023569

Handal, G., Holmström, L.-G., & Thomsen, O. (1973). *Universitetsundervisning: Problem, empiri, teori Lund.* København: Studentlitteratur.

Harland, T. (2003). Vygotsky's zone of proximal development and problem-based learning: Linking a theoretical concept with practice through action research. *Teaching in higher education, 8*(2), 263-272. Retrieved from http://www.researchgate.net/publication/233309078_Vygotsky's_Zone_of_Proximal_Development_and_Problem-based_Learning_Linking_a_theoretical_concept_with_practice_through_action_research

Harwood, R., & Bailey, K. (2012). Defining and evaluating international-mindedness in a school context. *International Schools Journal, 31*(2), 77–86. Retrieved from http://www.johncattbookshop.com/books/international-schools-journal

Hattie, J., Biggs, J., & Purdie, N. (1996). Effects of learning skills interventions on student learning: A meta-analysis. *Review of Educational Research, 66*(2), 99–136. doi:10.3102/00346543066002099

Hattie, J., & Yates, G. (2014). *Visible learning and the science of how we learn.* New York, NY: Routledge.

Hayden, M. C., & Thompson, J. J. (2013). International mindedness: Connecting concepts to practice. In L. Stagg (Ed.), International mindedness: Global perspectives for learners and educators (pp. 185–204). Academic Press. Retrieved from http://urbanepublications.com

Hayes, S. C. (1994). Content, context, and the types of psychological acceptance. In S. C. Hayes, N. S. Jacobson, V. M. Follette, & M. J. Daugher (Eds.), *Acceptance and change: Content and context in psychotherapy* (pp. 13–32). Reno, NV: Context Press.

Haywood, T. (2007). A simple typology of international-mindedness and its implications for education. In M. C. Hayden, J. Levy, & J. J. Thompson (Eds.), *The handbook of research in international education* (pp. 78–89). London, UK: Sage.

Healey, M., & Jenkins, A. (2006). Strengthening the teaching-research linkage in undergraduate courses and programs. *New Directions for Teaching and Learning, 107,* 45–55. doi:10.1002/ti.244

Hedberg, B. (1981). How Organizations Learn and Un-Learn. In P. C. Nystrom & W. H. Starbuck (Eds.), *Handbook of organizational design* (Vol. 1, pp. 3–27). New York: Oxford University Press.

Hedlund, N., Esbjörn-Hargens, S., Hartwig, M., & Bhaskar, R. (2016). Introduction: On the deep need for integrative metatheory in the twenty-first century. In Metatheory for the 21st century: critical realism and integral theory in dialogue (pp. 1-34). New York: Routledge.

Hedlund-de Witt, N. (2013). *Coding: An overview and guide to qualitative data analysis for integral researchers.* Integral Institute (Resource Paper No. 1). Retrieved from https://foundation.metaintegral.org/JITP

Hedlund, N. (2010). Integrally researching integral research: Enactive perspectives on the future of the field. *Journal of Integral Theory and Practice., 2*(5), 1–30.

Hedlund, N. H. (2010). Integrally researching integral research: Enactive perspectives on the future of the field. *Journal of Integral Theory & Practice, 5*(2).

Heidegger, M. (1962). *Being and time.* New York: Harper Perennial Modern Thought.

Heidegger, M. (2008). On the origin of the work of art. In D. F. Krell (Ed.), *Basic Writings* (pp. 143–212). New York: Harper Collins.

Heikkinen, H. L. T., Huttunen, R., Syrjala, L., & Pesonen, J. (2012). Action research and narrative inquiry: Five principles for validation revisited. *Educational Action Research, 20*(1), 5–21. doi:10.1080/09650792.2012.647635

Hendricks, C. (2017). *Improving Schools Through Action Research: A Reflective Practice Approach* (4th ed.). Pearson.

Hewes, J. (2006). *Let the children play: Nature's answer to early learning.* Early Childhood Learning Knowledge Centre, Canadian Council on Learning. Retrieved from http://www.ccl-cca.ca/pdfs/ECLKC/lessons/Originalversion_Lessonsin-Learning.pdf

Heyward, M. (2002). From international to intercultural: Redefining the international school for a globalized world. *Journal of Research in International Education, 1*(1), 9–32. doi:10.1177/147524090211002

Hill, I. (2000). Internationally-minded schools. *International Schools Journal, 20*(1), 24–37. Retrieved from http://www.johncattbookshop.com/books/international-schools-journal

Hill, I. (2013). The emergence of international-mindedness. *International School, 15*(2), 9–11. Retrieved from http://www.johncatt.com/downloads/pdf/magazines/ismag/is15_2/is15_2.pdf

Hill, I. (2002). The history of international education: An International Baccalaureate perspective. In M. C. Hayden, J. J. Thompson, & G. Walker (Eds.), *International education in practice: Dimensions for schools and international schools* (pp. 16–25). Oxford, UK: Routledge.

Hill, I. (2006). Do International Baccalaureate programs internationalize or globalize? *International Education Journal, 7*(1), 98–108. Retrieved from http://www.johncattbookshop.com/books/international-schools-journal

Hinitz, B. F. (2013). *The hidden history of early childhood education.* New York, NY: Routledge. doi:10.4324/9780203814420

Hirschi, A., Niles, S. G., & Akos, P. (2011). Engagement in adolescent career preparation: Social support, personality and the development of choice decidedness and congruence. *Journal of Adolescence, 34*(1), 173–182. doi:10.1016/j.adolescence.2009.12.009 PMID:20074789

Hmelo-Silver, C. E., Duncan, R. G., & Chinn, C. A. (2007). Scaffolding and achievement in problem-based and inquiry learning: A response to Kirschner, Sweller, and Clark. *Educational Psychologist, 42*(2), 99–107. doi:10.1080/00461520701263368

Hobson. (2010). Explaining Autism: Ten reasons to focus on the developing self. *Autism*, 391-407.

Hochachka, G. (2005). Integrating interiority in community development. *World Futures: Journal of General Evolution, 61*(1N2), 110-126.

Hochachka, G. (2015, July). *The integral you don't see: Activism at the frothy edge.* Presentation given at the 4th Biannual Integral Theory Conference, Sonoma, CA.

Hochachka, G. (2008). Case studies in integral approaches in international development. *Journal of Integral Theory and Practice, 3*, 58–108.

Hochachka, G. (2008). Case studies in integral approaches in international development: An integral research project. *Journal of Integral Theory and Practice, 3*(2), 58–108.

Hoey, B. (2014). A simple introduction to the practice of ethnography and guide to ethnographic fieldnotes. *Marshall University Digital Scholar*, 1–10. Retrieved from http://works.bepress.com/brian_hoey/12

Hoffman, E. (2009). *Time.* New York, NY: Picador.

Hoffman, M. L. (2008). Empathy and prosocial behaviour. In M. Lewis, J. M. Haviland-Jones, & L. F. Barrett (Eds.), *Handbook of emotions* (3rd ed.; pp. 440–455). New York, NY: Guilford.

Hofstadter, D. R. (1999). Gödel, Escher, Bach: An Eternal Golden Braid. (20th anniv. ed.). New York, NY: Basic Books.

Hofvander, D., & Chaste, N., & Stahlberg. (2009, June 10). *Psychiatric and psychosocial problems in adults with normal intelligence autism spectrum disorders.* Retrieved from Pubmed: http://www,ncbi.nlm.nih.gov/pubmed/19515234

Holland, D. (2004). Integrating mindfulness meditation and somatic awareness into a public educational setting. *Journal of Humanistic Psychology, 44*(4), 468–484. doi:10.1177/0022167804266100

Holland, J. H. (2012). *Signals and boundaries: Building blocks for complex adaptive systems.* Cambridge, MA: Massachusetts Institute of Technology.

Hooker, S., & Brand, B. (2010). College knowledge: A critical component of college and career readiness. *New Directions for Youth Development, 127*(127), 75–85. doi:10.1002/yd.364 PMID:20973075

Hope, N., Koestner, R., & Milyavskaya, M. (2014). The Role of Self-Compassion in Goal Pursuit and Wellbeing Among University Freshmen. *Self and Identity*, 1–15.

Hora, M. T., & Millar, S. B. (2011). *A guide to building education partnerships: Navigating diverse cultural contexts to turn challenge into promise*. Sterling, VA: Stylus Publishing Inc.

Horn, E., & Wolery, R. (2000). Key influences on the initiation and implementation of inclusive preschool programs. *The Council for Exceptional Children*, *67*(1), 83–98. doi:10.1177/001440290006700106

Horne, P., & Timmons, V. (2009). Making it work: Teachers' perspectives on inclusion. *International Journal of Inclusive Education*, *13*(3), 273–286. doi:10.1080/13603110701433964

Hoskins, C., & Goldberg, A. (2005). Doctoral student persistence in counselor education programs: Student-program match. *Counselor Education and Supervision*, *44*(3), 175–188. doi:10.1002/j.1556-6978.2005.tb01745.x

Howe, K. R. (1998). Values in evaluation and social research. *Evaluation and Program Planning*, *23*(3).

Hsieh, W., & Hsieh, C. (2012). Urban early childhood teachers' attitudes towards Inclusive education. *Early Child Development and Care*, *9*(182), 1167–1184. doi:10.1080/03004430.2011.602191

Hurley, W. (2014). Enhancing a positive school climate with compassion and analytical selective-focus skills (COMPASS). *Journal of Education and Practice*, *5*(7), 1–15.

Husserl, E. (1990). *On the Phenomenology of the Consciousness of Internal Time (1893–1917)* (J. B. Brough, Trans.). Dordrecht: Kluwer. (Original work published 1928)

Hutcherson, C., Seppala, E., & Gross, J. (2008). Loving-Kindness meditation increases social connectedness. *Emotion*, *8*(5), 720-724.

IBO. (2013). *What is an IB education?* Cardiff, UK: International Baccalaureate Organization. Retrieved from http://www.ibo.org/globalassets/digital-tookit/brochures/what-is-an-ib-education-en.pdf

IBO. (2015). *Diploma Programme: From principles into practice*. Cardiff, UK: International Baccalaureate Organization. Retrieved from http://www.follettibstore.com/main/home

IBO. (2016). *Facts and figures*. Retrieved from http://www.ibo.org/about-the-ib/facts-and-figures/

Ingersoll, R. E., & Marquis, A. (2014). Understanding Psychopathology: An Integral Exploration. Pearson Higher Ed.

Integral Without Borders. (n.d.). *Vision and purpose*. Retrieved January 15th, 2017 from: https://integralwithoutborders.net

Integral Without Borders. (n.d.). *What we do*. Retrieved January 15th, 2017 from: https://integralwithoutborders.net

Irwin, R. R. (1996). Narrative competence and constructive developmental theory: A proposal for rewriting the *Bildungsroman* in the postmodern world. *Journal of Adult Development*, *3*(2), 109–125. doi:10.1007/BF02278776

Ivankova, N., & Stick, V. (2007). Students' persistence in a distributed doctoral program in educational leadership in higher education: A mixed methods study. *Research in Higher Education*, *48*(1), 93–135. doi:10.100711162-006-9025-4

Izard, C. E. (1977). *Human Emotion*. New York: Plenum Press. doi:10.1007/978-1-4899-2209-0

Izard, C. E., Ackerman, B. P., Schoff, K. M., & Fine, S. E. (2000). Self-organization of discrete emotions, emotion patterns, and emotion-cognitive relations. In M. D. Lewis & I. Granic (Eds.), *Emotion, development, and self-organization* (pp. 15–36). Cambridge University Press. doi:10.1017/CBO9780511527883.003

Jahnukainen. (2011). Different strategies, different outcomes? The history and trends of inclusive and special education in Alberta (Canada) and Finland. *Scandinavian Journal of Educational Research*, 489-502.

Jantsch, E. (1972). Inter- and transdisciplinarity university. *Higher Education*, *1*(1), 7–37. doi:10.1007/BF01956879

Jantsch, E. (1976). Evolving images of man: Dynamic guidance for the mankind process. In E. Jantsch & C. H. Waddington (Eds.), *Evolution and consciousness: Human systems in transition*. New York: Addison-Wesley.

Jarrell, M. G. (2000). Focusing on focus group use in educational research. *Annual Meeting of the Mid-South Educational Research Association*.

Joas, H. (1996). *The creativity of action*. Chicago: University of Chicago Press.

Johnson, R. B., & Onwuegbuzie, A. J. (2004). Mixed Methods Research: A Research Paradigm Whose Time Has Come. *Educational Researcher*, *33*(7), 14–26. doi:10.3102/0013189X033007014

Jonas, M. E. (2010). When teachers must let education hurt: Rousseau and Nietzsche on compassion and the educational value of suffering. *Journal of Philosophy of Education*, *44*(1), 45–60. doi:10.1111/j.1467-9752.2010.00740.x

Kabat-Zinn, J. (1994). *Wherever you go, there you are: Mindfulness meditation in everyday life*. New York: Hyperion.

Kabat-Zinn, J. (2003). Mindfulness-based interventions in context: Past, present, and future. *Clinical Psychology: Science and Practice*, *10*(2), 144–156. doi:10.1093/clipsy.bpg016

Kabat-Zinn, M. (2009). *Everyday blessings: The inner work of mindful parenting*. Hachette Books.

Kahn, H. (1960). *On Thermonuclear War*. Princeton, NJ: Princeton University Press.

Kaput, J., Bar-Yam, Y., Jacobson, M., Jakobson, E., Lemke, J., & Wilensky, U. (2005). *Planning documents for a national initiative on complex systems in K-16 education*. Retrieved October 31, 2014 from http://www.necsi.edu/events/cxedk16/cxedk16.html

Katz, J. (2012). *Teaching to Diversity: A three-block model of universal design for learning*. Winnipeg, Canada: Portage & Main Press.

Kauffman, S. (2016). *Humanity in a creative universe*. New York: Oxford University Press.

Keen, S. (1983). *The passionate life: Stages of loving*. New York: Harper and Row.

Kegan, R. (1994). *In over our head: The mental demands of modern life*. Cambridge, MA: Harvard University Press.

Kegan, R. (1994). *In over our heads: The mental demands of modern life*. Cambridge, MA: Harvard University Press.

Kegan, R. (1994). *In Over Our Heads: The Mental Demands of Modern Life*. Cambridge, MA: Harvard University Press.

Kellett, M. (2013). *Images of childhood and their influence on research*. Retrieved from http://www.sagepub.com/upm-data/59004_Clark_et_al.pdf

Kelso, J. A. (1995). *Dynamic patterns, the self-organization of brain and behavior*. Cambridge, MA: MIT Press.

Kernochan, R. A., McCormick, D. W., & White, J. A. (2007). Spirituality and the management teacher: Reflections of three Buddhists on compassion, mindfulness, and selflessness in the classroom. *Journal of Management Inquiry*, *16*(1), 61–75. doi:10.1177/1056492606297545

Kerpelman, J. L., Eryigit, S., & Stephens, C. J. (2008). African American adolescents' future education orientation: Associations with self-efficacy, ethnic identity, and perceived parental support. *Journal of Youth and Adolescence*, *37*(8), 997–1008. doi:10.100710964-007-9201-7

Kessler, R. C., Berglund, P., Demler, O., Jin, R., Merikangas, K. R., & Walters, E. E. (2005). Lifetime prevalence and age-of-onset distributions of DSM-IV disorders in the national comorbidity survey replication. *Archives of General Psychiatry*, *62*, 93–602. PMID:15939837

Kim, Y. Y. (2008). Intercultural personhood: Globalization and a way of being. *International Journal of Intercultural Relations*, *32*(4), 359–368. doi:10.1016/j.ijintrel.2008.04.005

Kind, P., Jones, K., & Barmby, P. (2007). Developing attitudes towards science measures. *International Journal of Science Education*, *29*(7), 871–893. doi:10.1080/09500690600909091

King, P., & Baxter Magolda, M. (2005). A developmental model of intercultural maturity. *Journal of College Student Development*, *46*(6), 571–592. doi:10.1353/csd.2005.0060

Kirschner, P. A., Sweller, J., & Clark, R. E. (2006). Why minimal guidance during instruction does not work: An analysis of the failure of constructivist, discovery, problem-based, experiential, and inquiry-based teaching. *Educational Psychologist*, *41*(2), 75–86. doi:10.120715326985ep4102_1

Koestler, A. (1976). The ghost in the machine (2nd ed.). London, UK: Hutchison.

Koestler, A. (1967). *The ghost in the machine*. London: Hutchinson.

Kohlberg, L. (1969). Stage and sequence: The cognitive developmental approach to socialization. In D. Goslin (Ed.), *Handbook of socialization: Theory and research*. New York: Rand McNally.

Kohlberg, L. (1981). *The philosophy of moral development: Moral stages and the idea of justice*. San Francisco, CA: Harper & Row.

Kohls, M. (2014). *The unintended quest: An examination of transcendence and personal change in high-risk non-traditional athletes* (Doctoral Dissertation). Retrieved from ProQuest Dissertations and Theses Global. (Order No. 3643109)

Kuhn, L. (2008). Complexity and educational research: A critical reflection. *Educational Philosophy and Theory*, *40*(1), 177–189. doi:10.1111/j.1469-5812.2007.00398.x

Kuhn, T. (1970). *The Structure of Scientific Revolutions* (2nd ed.). Chicago: University of Chicago Press.

Kuhn, T. (1970). *The structure of scientific revolutions*. Chicago: University of Chicago Press.

Küpers, W. (2005). Phenomenology and integral pheno-practice of embodied well-be(com)ing in organizations. *Culture and Organization*, *11*(3), 221–231. doi:10.1080/14759550500204142

Küpers, W. (2008). Embodied "inter-learning": An integral phenomenology of learning in and by organizations. *The Learning Organization*, *15*(5), 388–408. doi:10.1108/09696470810898375

Lai, C., Shum, M., & Zhang, B. (2014). International mindedness in an Asian context: The case of the International Baccalaureate in Hong Kong. *Educational Research*, *56*(1), 77–96. doi:10.1080/00131881.2013.874159

Laloux, F. (2014). *Reinventing organizations: A guide to creating organizations inspired by the next stage in human consciousness*. Brussels: Nelson Parker.

Laloux, F. (2014). *Reinventing Organizations: A Guide to Creating Organizations Inspired by the Next Stage of Human Consciousness*. Nelson Parker.

Landrum, N. E., & Gardner, C. L. (2005). Using integral theory to effect strategic change. *Journal of Organizational Change Management*, *18*(3), 247–258. doi:10.1108/09534810510599407

Landrum, N. E., Gardner, C. L., & Boje, D. M. (2013). A values-based and integral perspective of strategic management. *The Journal of Values Based Leadership*, *6*(1), 9.

Langer, E. J. (1989). *Mindfulness*. Boston, MA: Addison-Wesley.

Langner, E. J., & Moldoveanu, M. (2000). Mindfulness research and the future. *The Journal of Social Issues*, *56*(1), 129–139. doi:10.1111/0022-4537.00155

Laske, O. E., & Maynes, B. (2002). Growing the top management team. *Journal of Management Development*, *21*(9), 702–727. doi:10.1108/02621710210441685

Laszlo, E. (2007). *Science and the akashic field: An integral theory of everything*. Inner Traditions/Bear & Co.

Laszlo, E. (2012). *The Ashaka Paradigm: Revolution in Science, Evolution in Consciousness*. Cardiff, CA: Waterside.

Laszlo, E., & Woolfson, D. (2011). The WorldShift 2012 declaration: A declaration of global emergency and emergence. In E. Laszlo & A. Combs (Eds.), *Thomas Berry, Dreamer of the Earth: The Spiritual Ecology of the Father of Environmentalism*. Inner Traditions International.

Lauvås, P., & Handal, G. (2005). Optimal use of feedback in research supervision with master and doctoral students. *Nordisk Pedagogik*, *25*, 177–189.

Lauvås, P., & Handal, G. (2012). Universitetsundervisning – problem, empiri, teori [University teaching – problems, findings, theory]. *The International Journal for Academic Development*, *17*(1), 87–92. doi:10.1080/1360144X.2012.646533

Laverty, S. M. (2003). Hermeneutic phenomenology and phenomenology: A comparison of historical and methodological considerations. *International Journal of Qualitative Methods*, *2*(3), 21–35. doi:10.1177/160940690300200303

Lawlor, M. S., Schonert-Reichl, K. A., Gadermann, A. M., & Zumbo, B. (2013). A validation study of the Mindful Attention Awareness Scale adapted for children. *Mindfulness*. doi:10.100712671-013-0228-4

Laycraft, C. K. (2009). Positive maladjustment as a transition from chaos to order. *Roeper Review: A Journal on Gifted Education*, *31*, 113-122.

Laycraft, C. K. (2012). *The Development of creativity: A study of creative adolescents and young adults* (Doctoral dissertation). University of Calgary, Calgary, Alberta. Retrieved from http://these.ucalgary.ca/handle/11023/166

Laycraft, C. K. (2011). Theory of positive disintegration as a model of adolescent development. *Nonlinear Dynamics Psychology and Life Sciences*, *15*(1), 29–52. PMID:21176438

Leary, M. R., Tate, E. B., Adams, C. E., Allen, A. B., & Hancock, J. (2007). Self-compassion and reactions to unpleasant self-relevant events: The implications of treating oneself kindly. *Journal of Personality and Social Psychology*, *92*(5), 887–904. doi:10.1037/0022-3514.92.5.887 PMID:17484611

Lee, I. H., Rojewski, J. W., & Hill, R. B. (2013). Classifying Korean adolescents' career preparedness. *International Journal for Educational and Vocational Guidance*, *12*, 25–45. doi:10.1002/j.2164-5884.1933.tb00117.x

Lee, M., Leung, L., Wright, E., Yue, T., Gan, A., Kong, L., & Li, J. (2014). *Research Summary: A study of the International Baccalaureate Diploma in China: Programme impact on student preparation for university studies abroad*. Cardiff, UK: International Baccalaureate Organization. Retrieved from http://www.ibo.org/globalassets/publications/ib-research/dp/chinasummaryinenglishweb.pdf

Leitch, R., & Day, C. (2000). Action research and reflective practice: Towards a holistic view. *Journal of Educational Action Research*, *8*(1), 179–193. doi:10.1080/09650790000200108

Leonard, A. (2004). *Integral communication* (Doctoral dissertation). University of Florida. Retrieved May 9th, 2018 from: http://www.integral-life-practice.com/wp-content/uploads/2011/06/integral-communication_by_adam_b_leonard.pdf

Lero, D. (2010). *Accessing inclusion quality in early learning and child care in Canada with the SpeciaLink child care inclusion practices profile and principles scale*. Canadian Council on Learning, University of Guelph.

Letiche, H. (2000). Phenomenal complexity theory as informed by Bergson. *Journal of Organizational Change Management*, *13*(6), 545–557. doi:10.1108/09534810010378579

Levykh, M. G. (2008). The affective establishment and maintenance of Vygotsky's zone of proximal development. *Educational Theory*, *58*(1), 83–101. doi:10.1111/j.1741-5446.2007.00277.x

Lewin, K. (1939). Field theory and experiment in social psychology: Concepts and methods. *American Journal of Sociology*, *44*(6), 868–896. doi:10.1086/218177

Lewin, K. (1947). Frontiers in group dynamics: Concept, method and reality in social science; social equilibria and social change. *Human Relations*, *1*(1), 5–41. doi:10.1177/001872674700100103

Lewis, M. D. (1995). Cognition-emotion feedback & self-organization of developmental paths. *Human Development*, *38*(2), 71–102. doi:10.1159/000278302

Lewis, M. D. (1997). Personality self-organization: Cascading constraints on cognition-emotion interaction. In A. Fogel, M. C. Lyra, & J. Valsiner (Eds.), *Dynamics and indeterminism in development and social processes* (pp. 193–216). Hillsdale, NJ: Lawrence Erlbaum.

Lewis, M. D. (2000a). The promise of dynamic systems approaches for an integrated account of human development. *Child Development*, *71*(1), 36–43. doi:10.1111/1467-8624.00116 PMID:10836556

Lewis, M. D. (2000b). Emotional self-organization at three time scales. In M. D. Lewis & I. Granic (Eds.), *Emotion, development, and self-organization* (pp. 37–69). Cambridge, UK: Cambridge University Press. doi:10.1017/CBO9780511527883.004

Lewis, M. D. (2005a). Self-organizing individual differences in brain development. *Developmental Review*, *25*(3-4), 252–277. doi:10.1016/j.dr.2005.10.006

Lewis, M. D. (2005b). Bridging emotion theory and neurobiology through dynamic system modeling. *Behavioral and Brain Sciences*, *28*(02), 169–245. doi:10.1017/S0140525X0500004X PMID:16201458

Lieber, J., Hanson, M. J., Beckman, P. J., Janko, S., Marquart, J. M., Horn, E., & Odom, S. L. (1997). The impact of changing roles on relationships between professionals in inclusive programs for young children. *Early Education and Development*, *8*(1), 67–82. doi:10.120715566935eed0801_6

Lindfors, P., Solantaus, T., & Rimpelä, A. (2012). Fears for the future among Finnish adolescents in 1983–2007: From global concerns to ill health and loneliness. *Journal of Adolescence*, *35*(4), 991–999. doi:10.1016/j.adolescence.2012.02.003 PMID:22353240

Lindgren, M., & Bandhold, H. (2009). *Scenario Planning: The Link Between Future and Strategy* (2nd ed.). New York, NY: Palgrave MacMillan.

Lindsay, E. K., & Creswell, J. D. (2014). Helping the self help others: Self-affirmation increases self-compassion and pro-social behaviors. *Frontiers in Psychology*, *5*, 1–9. doi:10.3389/fpsyg.2014.00421 PMID:24860534

Lipmanowicz, H., & McCandless, K. (2014). *The surprising power of liberating structures: Simple rules to unleash a culture of innovation*. Liberating Structures Press.

Li, T. Y., & Yorke, J. A. (1975). Period three implies chaos. *The American Mathematical Monthly*, *82*(10), 985–992. doi:10.1080/00029890.1975.11994008

Liu, K. R. (2009). *Cooperative communications and networking*. Cambridge, MA: Cambridge University Press.

Locander, W. B., Hamilton, F., Ladik, D., & Stuart, J. (2002). Developing a leadership-rich culture: The missing link to creating a market-focused organization. *Journal of Market-Focused Management*, *5*(2), 149–163. doi:10.1023/A:1014048111158

Loevinger, J. (1976). *Ego development: Conceptions and theories*. San Francisco: Jossey-Bass Inc.

Loevinger, J. (1985). Revision of the sentence completion test for ego Development. *Journal of Personality and Social Psychology*, *48*(2), 420–427. doi:10.1037/0022-3514.48.2.420 PMID:3981402

Loganbill, C., Hardy, E., & Delworth, U. (1982). Supervision: A Conceptual Model. *The Counseling Psychologist*, *10*(1), 3–42. doi:10.1177/0011000082101002

Longe, O., Maratos, F. A., Gilbert, P., Evans, G., Volker, F., Rockliff, H., & Rippon, G. (2010). Having a word with yourself: Neural correlates of self-criticism and self-reassurance. *NeuroImage*, *49*(2), 1849–1856. doi:10.1016/j.neuroimage.2009.09.019 PMID:19770047

Lorenz, E. N. (1993). *The essence of chaos*. Seattle, WA: University of Washington Press. doi:10.4324/9780203214589

Luo, A. (2009). Supporting participation in communities of practice by scientists from developing countries—The case of high energy physics. *Proceedings of the American Society for Information Science and Technology*, *45*(1), 1–11. doi:10.1002/meet.2008.1450450288

Lynam, A. (2014). *Embracing developmental diversity: Developmentally aware teaching, mentoring, and sustainability education* (Ph.D.). Prescott College in Sustainability Education. UMI Dissertation Publishing.

MacBeth, A., & Gumley, A. (2012). Exploring compassion: A meta-analysis of the association between self-compassion and psychopathology. *Clinical Psychology Review*, *32*(6), 545–552. doi:10.1016/j.cpr.2012.06.003 PMID:22796446

Makovichuk, L., Hewes, J., Lirette, P., & Thomas, N. (2014). *Play, participation, and possibilities: An early learning and child care curriculum framework for Alberta*. Retrieved from www.childcareframework.com

Manning, D. (2011). *Separate but equal? A postmodern analysis of educational structures for individuals with disabilities* (Doctoral dissertation). Statesboro, GA: Georgia Southern University. (paper 563)

Marquis, A. (2008). *The integral intake: A guide to comprehensive idiographic assessment in integral psychotherapy*. New York: Taylor Francis.

Marrero, F. (2007). An integral approach to affective education. *Journal of Integral Theory and Practice*, *2*(4), 1–23.

Marshall, P. (2012). The meeting of two integrative metatheories. *Journal of Critical Realism*, *11*(2), 188–214. doi:10.1558/jcr.v11i2.188

Marsick, V. J., & Watkins, K. (1990). *Informal and incidental learning in the workplace*. London, New York: Routledge.

Martin, D. (2013). *The ever-changing social perception of autism spectrum disorders in the United States*. Academic Press.

Martin, J. A. (2008). Integral research as a practical mixed-methods framework. *Journal of Integral Theory and Practice*, *2*(3), 155–164. Retrieved from http://www.sunypress.edu/pdf/JITP_Index_Vol1_Vol6.pdf

Martin, J. A. (2008). Integral research as a practical mixed-methods framework: Clarifying the role of integral methodological pluralism. *Integral Research as a Practical Mixed-Methods Framework*, *32*(2), 155–164.

Martin, J. A. (2008). Integral research as a practical mixed-methods framework: Clarifying the role of integral methodological pluralism. *Journal of Integral Theory and Practice*, *3*(2), 155–163.

Martin, J. A. (2008). Integral Research as a Practical Mixed-Methods Framework: Clarifying the role of Integral Methodological Pluralism. *Journal of Integral Theory and Practice.*, *2*(3), 155–164.

Maslow, A. H. (1968). *Toward a psychology of being*. Melbourne: D. Van Nostrand Company.

Mason, M. (2008). What is complexity theory and what are its implications for educational change? *Educational Philosophy and Theory*, *40*(1), 35–49. doi:10.1111/j.1469-5812.2007.00413.x

Maturana, H. R., Thompson, & Varela, F. J., (1987). The tree of knowledge: The biological roots of human understanding. Boston: Shambhala Publications Inc.

Maturana, H. R., & Varela, F. (1998). *The tree of knowledge: The biological roots of human understanding*. Boston, MA: Shambhala. (Original work published 1987)

Maturana, H. R., & Varela, F. J. (1980). *Autopoiesis and Cognition: The Realization of the Living*. Boston, MA: Reidel. doi:10.1007/978-94-009-8947-4

Maturana, H. R., & Varela, F. J. (1998). *The Tree of Knowledge: The biological roots of human understanding* (R. Paolucci, Trans.). Boston, MA: Shambhala.

Maturana, H., Varela, R., & Francisco, J. (1987). *The Tree of Knowledge*. Boston: Shambhala.

May, R. (1976). Simple mathematical models with very complicated dynamics. *Nature*, *261*(5560), 459–467. doi:10.1038/261459a0 PMID:934280

Mazurek. (2013). Lonliness, friendship, and well-being in adults with autism spectrum disorders. *Autism*, 223-32.

McAlpine, K. (2015). *Doing the right thing to protect children in Tanzania: An explanatory theory of the basic psychological process of doing the right thing and a practical theory to enable more and better protection of children* (Doctoral Dissertation). Retrieved from ProQuest Dissertations and Theses Global. (Order No. 3688840)

McCartney, B., & Morton, M. (2013). Kinds of participation: Teacher and special educationperceptions and practices of 'inclusion' in early childhood and primary school settings. *International Journal of Inclusive Education*, *17*(8), 776–792. doi:10.1080/13603116.2011.602529

McCauley, C. D., Drath, W. H., Palus, C. J., O'Connor, P. M. G., & Baker, B. A. (2006). The use of constructive-developmental theory to advance the understanding of leadership. *The Leadership Quarterly*, *17*(6), 634–653. doi:10.1016/j.leaqua.2006.10.006

McCaulley, M. H. (1990). The Myers-Briggs Type Indicator: A measure for individuals and groups. *Measurement & Evaluation in Counseling & Development*, *22*(4), 181–195. doi:10.1080/07481756.1990.12022929

McClain, L., Ylimaki, R., & Ford, M. P. (2010). Sustaining the heart of education: Finding space for wisdom and compassion. *International Journal of Children's Spirituality*, *15*(4), 307–316. doi:10.1080/1364436X.2010.525624

McGhie-Richmond, D., Irvine, A., Loreman, T., Cizman, J. L., & Lupart, J. (2013). Teacher perspectives on inclusive education in rural Alberta, Canada. *Canadian Journal of Education*, *36*(1), 195–239.

McGregor, S. L. T. (2015a). Integral dispositions and transdisciplinary knowledge creation. *Integral Leadership Review*, *15*(1). Retrieved from http://integralleadershipreview.com/12548-115-integral-dispositions-transdisciplinary-knowledge-creation/

McGregor, S. L. T. (2015b). The Nicolescuian and Zurich approaches to transdisciplinarity. *Integral Leadership Review, 15*(2). Retrieved from http://integralleadershipreview.com/13135-616-the-nicolescuian-and-zurich-approaches-to-transdisciplinarity/

McKenney, S., & Reeves, T. C. (2012). *Conducting Educational Design Research*. New York, NY: Routledge.

McKenzie, M. (2004, October). *Prep for the planet: Effective internationalism in practice*. Paper presented to the Education for International Mindedness Conference, Düsseldorf, Germany. Retrieved from https://scholar.google.com

McKinnon, D. (2009). Uncovering and understanding the spirituality and personal wholeness of school educators (Doctoral Dissertation). Retrieved from ProQuest Dissertations and Theses Global. (Order No. 304832727)

McNiff, J. (2013). *Action Research: Principles and Practice* (3rd ed.). Florence, KY: Taylor and Francis. doi:10.4324/9780203112755

Meadows, D. (2008). *Thinking in systems: A primer*. White River Junction, VT: Chelsea Green Publishing.

Meiklejohn, J., Phillips, C., Freedman, M. L., Griffin, M. L., Biegel, G., Roach, A., ... Saltzman, A. (2012). Integrating mindfulness training into K-12 education: Fostering the resilience of teachers and students. *Mindfulness, 3*(4), 291–307. doi:10.100712671-012-0094-5

Mercer, S., & Ryan, S. (2009). A mindset for EFL: Learners' beliefs about the role of natural talent. *ELT Journal, 64*(4), 436–444. doi:10.1093/elt/ccp083

Merleau-Ponty, M. (2004a). Cezanne's doubt. In T. Baldwin (Ed.), *Maurice Merleau-Ponty: Basic Writing* (pp. 272–290). New York: Routledge Taylor & Francis Group.

Merleau-Ponty, M. (2004b). Eye and mind. In T. Baldwin (Ed.), *Maurice Merleau-Ponty: Basic Writing* (pp. 290–324). New York: Routledge Taylor & Francis Group.

Merriam, S. (2009). *Case Studies as Qualitative Research. In Qualitative research: A guide to design and implementation* (pp. 26–43). San Francisco, CA: Jossey-Bass. Retrieved from http://www.aea267.k12.ia.us/system/assets/uploads/files/1527/qualitative_research.pdf

Merrill, K., Braskamp, D., & Braskamp, L. (2012). Assessing individuals' global perspective. *Journal of College Student Development, 53*(2), 356–360. doi:10.1353/csd.2012.0034

Metz, S. M., Frank, J. L., Reibel, D., Cantrell, T., Sanders, R., & Broderick, P. C. (2013). The effectiveness of the "Learning to BREATHE" program on adolescent emotion regulation. *Research in Human Development, 10*(3), 252–272. doi:10.1080/15427609.2013.818488

Mezirow, J. (1990). *Fostering critical reflection in adulthood: A guide to transformative and emancipatory learning*. San Francisco, CA: Jossey-Bass.

Mezirow, J. (1997). Transformative learning: Theory to practice. *New Directions for Adult and Continuing Education, 1997*(74), 5–12. doi:10.1002/ace.7401

Miles, M. B., Huberman, A. M., & Saldana, J. (2014). *Qualitative data analysis: A methods sourcebook*. Los Angeles, CA: Sage Publications.

Millar, C. C., Choi, C. J., Russell, E. T., & Kim, J. N. B. (2005). Open source communities: An integrally informed approach. *Journal of Organizational Change Management, 18*(3), 259–268. doi:10.1108/09534810510599416

Miller, E., & Almon, J. (2009). Crisis in the kindergarten: Why children need to play in school. *Alliance for Childhood*, 1–72. Retrieved from http://www.allianceforchildhood.org/sites/allianceforchildhood.org/files/file/kindergarten_report.pdf

Mintz, A. (2008). *The labor of learning: A study of the role of pain in education* (Doctoral dissertation). Available from ProQuest Dissertations and Theses Full Text database. (UMI No. 3317653)

Mitleton-Kelly, E. (2003). *Complex systems and evolutionary perspectives on organisations: The application of complexity theory to organisations*. Oxford, UK: Pergamon.

Montuori, A. (2013). *Complex Thought, An overview of Edgar Morin's intellectual journey*. Retrieved from https://metaintegral.org/sites/default/files/Complex_Thought_FINAL.pdf

Morgan, G. (2006). *Images of organization*. Thousand Oaks, CA: Sage.

Morin, E. (1992). From the concept of system to the paradigm of complexity. Journal of Social and Evolutionary Systems, 15(4), 371-384.

Morin, E. (2008). *On complexity*. Cresskill, NJ: Hampton Press.

Morrison, K. (2008). Educational philosophy and the challenge of complexity theory. *Educational Philosophy and Theory, 40*(1), 19–34. doi:10.1111/j.1469-5812.2007.00394.x

Morse, J. M. (2003). Principles of mixed methods and multimethod research design. Handbook of Mixed Methods in Social and Behavioral Research, 1, 189-208.

Mueller, C. M., & Dweck, C. S. (1998). Praise for intelligence can undermine children's motivation and performance. *Journal of Personality and Social Psychology, 75*(1), 33–52. doi:10.1037/0022-3514.75.1.33 PMID:9686450

Mulvihill, P. R., & Milan, M. J. (2007, August). (2007/8). Subtle world: Beyond sustainability, beyond information. *Futures, 39*(6), 657–668. doi:10.1016/j.futures.2006.11.006

Murgatroyd, S. (2013). *Rethinking equity and creating a great school for all*. Edmonton: Collaborative Media Group Inc.

Murray, T. (2009). What is the integral in integral education? From progressive pedagogy to integral pedagogy. *Integral Review, 5*(1), 96–134. Retrieved from http://integral-review.org/pdf-template-issue.php?pdfName=vol_5_no_1_murray_what_is_the_integral_in_integral_education.pdf

National Association for the Education of Young Children (NAEYC). (2009). Developmentally Appropriate Practice in Early Childhood Programs Serving Children from Birth through. Retrieved from https://www.naeyc.org/sites/default/files/globally-shared/downloads/PDFs/resources/position-statements/PSDAP.pdf

National Education Committee. (2015). *Vision 2030: A shared vision for education*. Retrieved from http://media.wix.com/ugd/29b6ce_3065a2357e31432f839d0eecea6dee3e.pdf

Neal, J. A., Lichtenstein, B. M. B., & Banner, D. (1999). Spiritual perspectives on individual, organizational and societal transformation. *Journal of Organizational Change Management, 12*(3), 175–186. doi:10.1108/09534819910273757

Neblett, N. G., & Corina, K. S. (2006). Adolescents' thoughts about parent's jobs and their importance for adolescents' future orientation. *Journal of Adolescence, 29*(5), 795–811. doi:10.1016/j.adolescence.2005.11.006 PMID:16427693

Neely, J. E., Schallert, D. L., Mohammed, S. S., Roberts, R. M., & Chen, U. (2009). Self-kindness when facing stress: The role of self-compassion, goal regulation, and support in college students' wellbeing. *Motivation and Emotion, 33*(1), 88–97. doi:10.100711031-008-9119-8

Neff, K. D. (2003a). Self-compassion: An alternative conceptualization of a healthy attitude toward oneself. *Self and Identity, 2*(2), 85–101. doi:10.1080/15298860309032

Neff, K. D. (2003b). Development and validation of a scale to measure self-compassion. *Self and Identity*, *2*(3), 223–250. doi:10.1080/15298860309027

Neff, K. D. (2011). *Self-compassion: The proven power of being kind to yourself*. New York: Harper Collins.

Neff, K. D., & Beretvas, S. N. (2013). The role of self-compassion in romantic relationships. *Self and Identity*, *12*(1), 78–98. doi:10.1080/15298868.2011.639548

Neff, K. D., Hsieh, Y. P., & Dejitterat, K. (2005). Self-compassion, achievement goals, and coping with academic failure. *Self and Identity*, *4*(3), 263–287. doi:10.1080/13576500444000317

Neff, K. D., Kirkpatrick, K., & Rude, S. S. (2007). Self-compassion and its link to adaptive psychological functioning. *Journal of Research in Personality*, *41*(1), 139–154. doi:10.1016/j.jrp.2006.03.004

Neff, K. D., & McGeehee, P. (2010). Self-compassion and psychological resilience among adolescents and young adults. *Self and Identity*, *9*(3), 225–240. doi:10.1080/15298860902979307

Neufeld, G., & Maté, C. (2005). *Hold on to your kids: Why parents need to matter more than peers*. Toronto: Vintage Canada.

Newsome, S., Waldo, M., & Gruszka, C. (2012). Mindfulness group work: Preventing stress and increasing self-compassion among helping professionals in training. *Journal for Specialists in Group Work*, *37*(4), 297–311. doi:10.1080/01933922.2012.690832

Nicolescu, B. (1997). *La Transdisciplinarité*. Paris, France: Rocher. Retrieved from http://perso.club-internet.fr/nicol/ciret

Nicolescu, B. (2001). *Manifesto of transdisciplinarity*. Albany, NY: State University of New York Press.

Nikolayenko, O. (2011). Adolescents' hopes for personal, local, and global future: Insights from Ukraine. *Youth & Society*, *43*(1), 64–89. doi:10.1177/0044118X09351281

Nilholm, C. (2006). Special education, inclusion and democracy. *European Journal of Special Needs Education*, *21*(4), 431–445. doi: 10:1080/08856250600957905

Nind, M., Flewitt, R., & Payler, J. (2014). The social experience of early childhood for children with learning disabilities: Inclusion, competence and agency. *British Journal of Sociology of Education*, *3106*, 653–670. doi:10.1080/01425692.2010.515113

Nisbett, R. E. (2003). *The geography of thought*. London, UK: Nicholas Brealey.

Nivre, J., Allwood, J., Grönqvit, L., Gunnarsson, M., Ahlsén, E., Vappula, H., . . . Ottesjö, C. (2004). *Gothenburg Transcription Standard 6.4*. University of Gothenburg. Retrieved from http://bit.ly/2hbMNoA

Noddings, N. (2005). *Educating citizens for global awareness*. New York, NY: Teachers College Press.

Noddings, N. (1995). Teaching themes of care. *Phi Delta Kappan*, *76*, 675.

Nonaka, I. (1994). A Dynamic Theory of Organizational Knowledge Creation. *Organization Science*, *5*(1), 14–37. doi:10.1287/orsc.5.1.14

Nonaka, I., & Takeuchi, H. (1995). *The Knowledge-creating company*. New York: Oxford University Press.

Novak, J. D., & Gowin, D. B. (1984). *Learning how to learn*. New York: Cambridge University Press. doi:10.1017/CBO9781139173469

Nurmi, J. E. (1991). How do adolescents see their future? A review of the development of future orientation and planning. *Developmental Review*, *11*(1), 1–59. doi:10.1016/0273-2297(91)90002-6

Nutbrown, C., & Clough, P. (2004). Inclusion and exclusion in the early years: Conversations with European educators. *European Journal of Special Needs Education*, *19*(3), 301–315. doi:10.1080/0885625042000262479

Nye, J. S. (2004). *Power in a Global Information Age*. New York, NY: Routledge.

O'Brien, K. (2012). Global environmental change II: From adaptation to deliberate transformation. *Progress in Human Geography*, *36*(5), 667–676. doi:10.1177/0309132511425767

O'Brien, K., & Hochachka, G. (2010). Integral adaptation to climate change. *Journal of Integral Theory & Practice*, *5*(1).

O'Brien, K., & Hochachka, G. (2010). Integral Adaptation to Climate Change. *Journal of Integral Theory & Practice*, *5*(1). Retrieved from http://aqaljournal.integralinstitute.org/Public/JITP_5(1).pdf#page=100

O'Connell, M. E., Boat, T., & Warner, K. (2009). *National research council (US) and institute of medicine (US) committee on the prevention of mental disorders and substance abuse among children, youth, and young adults: Research advances and promising interventions*. Washington, DC: National Academies Press.

O'Fallon, T. J. (2010). *The collapse of the Wilber Combs matrix: The interpenetration of the state and structure stages*. Paper presented at the 2010 Integral Theory Conference, JFK University. Retrieved from http://www.pacificintegral.com/docs/statestagesofallon.pdf

Odena, O., & Burgess, H. (2017). How doctoral students and graduates describe facilitating experiences and strategies for their thesis writing learning process: A qualitative approach. *Studies in Higher Education*, *42*(3), 572-590.

Odom, S. L. (2009). The tie that binds: Evidence-based practice, implementation science, and outcomes for children. *Topics in Early Childhood Special Education*, *29*(53), 53–61. doi:10.1177/0271121408329171

Odom, S. L., Buyesse, V., & Soukakou, E. (2011). Inclusion for young children with disabilities: A quarter century of research perspectives. *Journal of Early Intervention*, *33*(4), 344–356. doi:10.1177/1053815111430094

OECD. (2006). *OECD/CERI Schooling for Tomorrow Phase III Interim Report (Draft) Ontario Ministry of Education*. Retrieved from http://www.oecd.org/edu/school/37362462.pdf

OECD. (2010). Introduction. *Trends Shaping Education*. Retrieved from http://www.oecd.org/edu/ceri/46447355.pdf

Olmos-López, P., & Sunderland, J. (2017). Doctoral supervisors' and supervisees' responses to co-supervision. *Journal of Further and Higher Education*, *41*(6), 727–740. doi:10.1080/0309877X.2016.1177166

Olsson, L. M. (2009). *Movement and experimentation in young children's learning*. New York, NY: Routledge. doi:10.4324/9780203881231

Onella, J.-P., Saramaki, J., Hyvonen, J., Szabo, G., Lazer, D., Kaski, K., ... Barabasi, A.-L. (2007). Structure and tie strengths in mobile communication networks. *Proceedings of the National Academy of Sciences of the United States of America*, *104*(18), 7332–7336. doi:10.1073/pnas.0610245104 PMID:17456605

Onwuegbuzie, A. J., & Leech, N. L. (2005). On becoming a pragmatic researcher: The importance of combining quantitative and qualitative research methodologies. *International Journal of Social Research Methodology*, *8*(5), 375–387. doi:10.1080/13645570500402447

Onwuegbuzie, A. J., Slate, J. R., Leech, N. L., & Collins, K. M. (2009). Mixed data analysis: Advanced integration techniques. *International Journal of Multiple Research Approaches*, *3*(1), 13–33. doi:10.5172/mra.455.3.1.13

Oral, S. B. (2013). An integral approach to interdisciplinary research in education. *International Journal of Educational Research, 4*(1), 1–13. Retrieved from http://www.journals.elsevier.com/international-journal-of-educational-research/

Orr, D. (2014). In A mindful moral voice: Mindful compassion, the ethic of care and education. Paideusis, 21(2), 41–53.

Ostrom, E., & Cox, M. (2010). Moving beyond panaceas: A multi-tiered diagnostic approach for social-ecological analysis. *Environmental Conservation, 37*(4), 451–463. doi:10.1017/S0376892910000834

Oxford Dictionaries. (2013). Retrieved from https://www.oxforddictionaries.com/

Oxford English Dictionary, The Compact Edition. (1971). Oxford, UK: Oxford University Press.

Pacini-Ketchabaw, V., White, J., & Armstrong de Almeida, A. (2006). Racialization in early childhood: A critical analysis of discourses in policies. *International Journal of Education Policy, Research & Practice: Reconceptualizing Childhood Studies, 7*.

Pacini-Ketchabaw, V., Kummen, K., & Thompson, D. (2010). Becoming intimate with developmental knowledge: Pedagogical explorations with collective biography. *The Alberta Journal of Educational Research, 56*(3), 335–354.

Pacini-Ketchabaw, V., & Schecter, S. (2002). Engaging the discourse of diversity: Educators' frameworks for working with linguistic and cultural difference. *Contemporary Issues in Early Childhood, 3*(3), 400–414. doi:10.2304/ciec.2002.3.3.7

Palmer, P. (1998). *The courage to teach: Exploring the inner landscapes of others*. New York: Harper and Row.

Palys, T. (2008). Purposive sampling. In L. M. Given (Ed.), *The Sage Encyclopedia of. Qualitative Research Methods* (Vol. 2, pp. 697–698). Los Angeles: Sage.

Paterson, B. L., & Canam, C. (2001). *Meta-study of qualitative health research: A practical guide to meta-analysis and meta-synthesis* (Vol. 3). London, UK: Sage Publications, Inc. doi:10.4135/9781412985017

Patten, T. (2013). *Enacting an integral revolution: How can we have truly radical conversations in a time of global crisis?* Paper presented at the third biannual Integral Theory Conference, Burlingame, CA. Retrieved from: http://www.terrypatten.com/sites/default/files/ITC2013.Patten.pdf

Pauchant, T. C. (2005). Integral leadership: A research proposal. *Journal of Organizational Change Management, 18*(3), 211–229. doi:10.1108/09534810510599380

Paulson, D. S. (2002). *Competitive business, caring business: An integral business perspective for the 21st century*. New York: Paraview Press.

Paulson, D. S. (2008). Wilber's integral philosophy: A summary and critique. *Journal of Humanistic Psychology, 48*(3), 364–388. doi:10.1177/0022167807309748

Pellicano, E. (2011). Cogniton, development and education: Psychological models of autism. In *Researching the Autism Spectrum*. Cambridge, UK: Cambridge University Press.

Pence, A., & Pacini-Ketchabaw, V. (2008). *Discourses on quality care: The investigating 'quality' project and the Canadian experience*. Academic Press. http://dx.ci.org/10.2304/ciec.2008.9.3.241

Phillips, E. M., & Pugh, D. (2005). *How to get a PhD*. London: Continuum.

Phillips, S. P., & Clarke, M. (2012). More than an education: The hidden curriculum, professional attitudes and career choice. *Medical Education, 46*(9), 887–893. doi:10.1111/j.1365-2923.2012.04316.x PMID:22891909

Piaget. (1930). *The child's conception of physical causality* (M. Gabain, Trans.). Kegan Paul, Trench, Trubner & Co.

Piaget, J. (1954). *The construction of reality in a child*. New York: Basic Books. doi:10.1037/11168-000

Piaget, J. (1962). *Science of education and the psychology of the child*. New York: Viking Press.

Piaget, J. (1971). *Biology and Knowledge*. Chicago: University of Chicago Press.

Piechowski, M. M. (1999). Overexcitabilities. In M. Runco & S. Pritzker (Eds.), *Encyclopedia of creativity* (Vol. 2, pp. 325–334). San Diego, CA: Academic Press.

Pielke, R. A. (Ed.). (2013). *Climate vulnerability: Understanding and addressing threats to essential resources*. New York: Academic Press.

Pielstick, C. D. (2005). Teaching spiritual synchronicity in a business leadership class. *Journal of Management Education*, *29*(1), 153–168. doi:10.1177/1052562903260027

Plutchik, R. (1980). *Emotion: A psycho-evolutionary synthesis*. New York: Harper & Row.

Plutchik, R. (1994). *The psychology and biology of emotion*. Harper Collins College Publishers.

Plutchik, R. (2003). *Emotions & life: Perspectives from psychology, biology, and evolution*. Washington, DC: American Psychological Association.

Pole, C., Sprokkereef, A., Burgess, R., & Lakin, E. (1997). Supervision of doctoral students in the natural sciences: Expectations and experiences. *Assessment & Evaluation in Higher Education*, *22*(1), 49–63. doi:10.1080/0260293970220104

Pommier, E. A. (2011). The compassion scale. *Dissertation Abstracts International. A, The Humanities and Social Sciences*, *72*, 1174.

Poole, M. S., & Van de Ven, A. H. (1989). Using paradox to build management and organization theories. *Academy of Management Review*, 562-578.

Poole, M. E., & Cooney, G. H. (1987). Orientations to the future: A comparison of adolescents in Australia and Singapore. *Journal of Youth and Adolescence*, *16*(2), 129–151. doi:10.1007/BF02138916 PMID:24277319

Popova, M. (2014). *Wisdom in the age of information*. Retrieved 5 Nov 2017, https://vimeo.com/105692521

Popper, M., & Lipshitz, R. (2000). Organizational learning: Mechanisms, culture, and feasibility. *Management Learning*, *31*(2), 181–196. doi:10.1177/1350507600312003

Potek, R. (2012). *Mindfulness as a school-based prevention program and its effect on adolescent stress, anxiety and emotion regulation* (Doctoral Dissertation). Retrieved from ERIC. (ED537610)

Pound, L. (2006). *How children learn*. London, UK: Practical Preschool Books.

Presley, S. (2014). *How leaders engage in complexity leadership: Do action logics make a difference?* (Doctoral Dissertation). Retrieved from ProQuest Dissertations and Theses Global. (Order No. 3611483)

Prigogine, I. (1980). *From being to becoming: Time and complexity in the physical science*. San Francisco, CA: W.H. Freeman and Company.

Prigogine, I. (1980). *From being to becoming: Time and complexity in the physical sciences*. San Francisco: Freeman.

Prigogine, I. (1997). *The end of certainty. Time, chaos and the new laws of nature*. New York: The Free Press.

Prigogine, I., & Stengers, I. (1984). *Order out of chaos*. New York: Bantam Books.

Raes, A., Schellens, T., De Wever, B., & Vanderhoven, E. (2012). Scaffolding information problem solving in web-based collaborative inquiry learning. *Computers & Education*, *59*(1), 82–94. doi:10.1016/j.compedu.2011.11.010

Raes, F. (2011). The effect of self-compassion on the development of depression symptoms in a non-clinical sample. *Mindfulness*, *2*(1), 33–36. doi:10.100712671-011-0040-y

Rafferty, M. (2001). A conceptual model for clinical supervision in nursing and health visiting based upon Winnicott's (1960) theory of the parent-infant relationship. *Journal of Psychiatric and Mental Health Nursing*, *8*(2), 153–161. doi:10.1046/j.1365-2850.2000.00277.x PMID:11146911

Raichle, M. E., MacLeod, A. M., Snyder, A. Z., Powers, W. J., Gusnard, D. A., & Shulman, G. L. (2001). A default mode of brain function. *Proceedings of the National Academy of Sciences of the United States of America*, *98*(2), 676–682. doi:10.1073/pnas.98.2.676 PMID:11209064

RAND. (2014). Delphi. *Futures Methodologies*. Retrieved from http://www.rand.org /pardee/pubs/futures_method/delphi.html

Rand: Labor and Population Research Brief. (2005). *Proven benefits of early childhood interventions.* Retrieved from http://www.rand.org/pubs/research_briefs/RB9145.html

Reams, J. (2005). What's integral about leadership? A reflection on leadership and integral theory. *Integral Review*, *1*, 118–131.

Reason, P., & Bradbury, H. (2001). *Handbook of action research: Participative inquiry and practice.* New York: Sage.

Renert, M. A. (2011). *Living mathematics education* (Doctoral dissertation). University of British Columbia, Vancouver, Canada.

Renner, A. (2009). Teaching Community, Praxis, and Courage: A Foundations Pedagogy of Hope and Humanization. *Educational Studies*, *45*(1), 59–79. doi:10.1080/00131940802527209

Resnik, J. (2009). Multicultural education – Good for business but not for the state? The IB curriculum and global capitalism. *British Journal of Educational Studies*, *57*(3), 217–244. doi:10.1111/j.1467-8527.2009.00440.x

Ricard, M., Lutz, A., & Davidson, R. J. (2014). Mind of the meditator. *Scientific American*, *311*(5), 38–45. doi:10.1038cientificamerican1114-38 PMID:25464661

Riedy, C. (2005). *The eye of the storm. An Integral perspective on sustainable development and climate change response (Ph.D.).* Sydney, Australia: University of Technology. Retrieved from http://adt.lib.uts.edu.au/public/adtNNTSM20050603.101829/

Riedy, C. (2008). An integral extension of causal layered analysis. *Futures*, *40*(2), 150–159. doi:10.1016/j.futures.2007.11.009

Riedy, C. (2011). Futures of the climate action movement: Insights from an integral futures approach. *Journal of Futures Studies*, *15*(3), 33–52.

Rittel, H., & Webber, M. (1973). Dilemmas in a general theory of planning. *Policy Sciences*, *4*(2), 155–169. doi:10.1007/BF01405730

Ritzer, G. (1992). Metatheorizing in sociology: Explaining the coming of age. *Metatheorizing*, *6*, 7–26.

Rizvi, F., & Lingard, B. (2000). Globalization and education: Complexities and contingencies. *Educational Theory*, *50*(4), 419–426. doi:10.1111/j.1741-5446.2000.00419.x

Roberts, B. (2003). What should international education be? From emergent theory to practice. *International Schools Journal, 22*(2), 69–79. Retrieved from http://www.johncattbookshop.com/books/international-schools-journal

Robinson, J. (2018). *Reimagining sustainability leadership for this historical moment* (Unpublished master's thesis). Royal Roads University, Canada.

Robinson, K. (2009). Creativity in the classroom, innovation in the workplace. *Interview with Sir Ken Robinson*. Retrieved from http://www.Principalvoices.com/voices/ken-robinson-white-paper.html

Robledo, M. A. (2013). Building an integral metatheory of management. *European Management Journal, 32*(4), 535–546. doi:10.1016/j.emj.2013.10.008

Roeser, R. W., Skinner, E., Beers, J., & Jennings, P. A. (2012). Mindfulness training and teachers' professional development: An emerging area of research and practice. *Child Development Perspectives, 6*(2), 167–173. doi:10.1111/j.1750-8606.2012.00238.x

Rogers, C. R. (1961/1989). *On becoming a person: A therapist's view of psychology*. Boston: Houghton Mifflin Company.

Rojewski, J. W., & Kim, H. (2003). Career choice patterns and behavior of work-bound youth during early adolescence. *Journal of Career Development, 30*(2), 89–108. doi:10.1177/089484530303000201

Ross, M. (2011). *The evolution of education: Use of biofeedback in developing heart intelligence in a high school setting* (Doctoral Dissertation). Retrieved from ProQuest Dissertations and Theses Global. (Order No. NR81527)

Rotgans, J. I., & Schmidt, H. G. (2011). Cognitive engagement in the problem-based learning classroom. *Advances in Health Sciences Education: Theory and Practice, 16*(4), 465–479. doi:10.100710459-011-9272-9 PMID:21243425

Rowe, W., Graf, M., Agger-Gupta, N., Piggot-Irvine, E., & Harris, B. (2013). Action Research Engagement: Creating the Foundation for Organizational Change. ALARA monograph series no.5.

Ryan & Deci. (2001). On happiness and human potentials: A review of research on hedonic and eudaimonic well-being. *Annual Review of Psychology*, 144-66.

Rybak, C. (2013). Nurturing positive mental health: Mindfulness for wellbeing in counselling. *International Journal for the Advancement of Counseling, 35*(2), 110–119. doi:10.100710447-012-9171-7

Ryff, C. (1989). Happiness is everything, or is it? Explorations on the meaning of psychological well-being. *Journal of Personality and Social Psychology, 57*(6), 1069–1081. doi:10.1037/0022-3514.57.6.1069

Scharmer, O., Arthur, W. B., Day, J., Jaworski, J., Jung, M., Nonaka, I., & Senge, P. (1999). Illuminating the blind spot: Leadership in the context of emerging worlds. Academic Press.

Schenck, D., Coles, J., Fraquelli, L., Airzee, S., & Wishy, A. (2011). Blackawton Bees. *Biology letters, 7*(2), 168-172.

Schilbach, L., Eickhoff, S. B., Rotarska-Jagiela, A., Fink, G. R., & Vogeley, K. (2008). Mind at rest? Social cognition as the default mode of cognizing and its putative relationship to the "default system" of the brain. *Consciousness and Cognition, 17*(2), 457–467. doi:10.1016/j.concog.2008.03.013 PMID:18434197

Schmid, K. L., Phelps, E., & Lerner, R. M. (2011). Constructing positive futures: Modeling the relationship between adolescents' hopeful future expectations and intentional self regulation in predicting positive youth development. *Journal of Adolescence, 34*(6), 1127–1135. doi:10.1016/j.adolescence.2011.07.009 PMID:22118506

Scholz, R. W. (2017). The normative dimension in transdisciplinarity, transition management, and transformation sciences: New roles of science and universities in sustainable transitioning. *Sustainability, 9*(6), 1–35. doi:10.3390u9060991

Schonert-Reichl, K. A., & Lawlor, M. S. (2010). The effects of a mindfulness-based education program on pre- and early adolescents' well-being and social and emotional competence. *Mindfulness*, *1*(3), 137–151. doi:10.100712671-010-0011-8

Schroder, H. S., Moran, T. P., Donnellan, M. B., & Moser, J. S. (2014). Mindset induction effects on cognitive control: A neurobehavioral investigation. *Biological Psychology*, *103*, 27–37. doi:10.1016/j.biopsycho.2014.08.004 PMID:25149141

Schwandt, T. A. (1994). Constructivist, interpretivist approaches to human inquiry. In N. K. Denzin & Y. S. Lincoln (Eds.), *Handbook of Qualitative Research* (pp. 118–137). Thousand Oaks, CA: Sage.

Schwandt, T. A. (2007). *The SAGE dictionary of qualitative research* (3rd ed.). London: SAGE. doi:10.4135/9781412986281

Schwartz-Shea, P., & Bennett, A. (2003). Introduction - Methodological pluralism in journals and graduate education? Commentaries on new evidence. *PS, Political Science & Politics*, *36*(3), 371–372.

Schwindt, E. (2003). The development of a model for international education with special reference to the role of host country nationals. *Journal of Research in International Education*, *2*(1), 67–81. doi:10.1177/1475240903002001607

Seefried, M. (2006, October). *Scholastic communities and democracy: The role of ethics in international education*. Speech presented at IB Africa/Europe/Middle East Regional Conference. Retrieved from http://www.ibo.org/contentassets/7adb995cb97e43ed8216a173aa4bcffe/ethics-in-international-education-en.pdf

Seginer, R. (2003). Adolescent future orientation: An integrated cultural and ecological perspective. *Online Readings in Psychology and Culture*, *6*(1). doi:10.9707/2307-0919.1056

Seginer, R. (2008). Future orientation in times of threat and challenge: How resilient adolescents construct their future. *International Journal of Behavioral Development*, *32*(4), 272–282. doi:10.1177/0165025408090970

Seginer, R., & Halabi-Kheir, H. (1998). Adolescent passage to adulthood: Future orientation in the context of culture, age, and gender. *International Journal of Intercultural Relations*, *22*(3), 309–328. doi:10.1016/S0147-1767(98)00010-8

Seginer, R., & Lilach, E. (2004). How adolescents construct their future: The effect of loneliness on future orientation. *Journal of Adolescence*, *27*(6), 625–643. doi:10.1016/j.adolescence.2004.05.003 PMID:15561307

Sen, A. (1999). The possibility of social choice. *The American Economic Review*, *89*(3), 349–378. doi:10.1257/aer.89.3.349

Senge, P. M. (2006). *The fifth discipline: The art and practice of the learning organization (Revised and updated edition)*. New York: Doubleday/Currency.

Shapiro, S. L., Astin, J. A., Bishop, S. R., & Cordova, M. (2005). Mindfulness-based stress reduction for health care professionals: Results from a randomized trial. *International Journal of Stress Management*, *12*(2), 164–176. doi:10.1037/1072-5245.12.2.164

Shechtman, N., DeBarger, A., Dornsife, C., Rosier, S., & Yarnall, L. (2013). *Promoting grit, tenacity and perseverence: critical factors for success in the 21st century*. Retrieved from http://www.ed.gov/edblogs/technology/files/2013/02/OET-Draft-Grit-Report-2-17-13.pdf

Siegel, D. (2013). *Brainstorm: The power and purpose of the teenage brain*. New York: Penguin Books.

Siegel, D. J. (2007). *The mindful brain: Reflection and attunement in the cultivation of well-being*. New York: W. W. Norton & Company.

Simon, H. A. (1991). Bounded rationality and organizational learning. *Organization Science*, *2*(1), 125–134. doi:10.1287/orsc.2.1.125

Singh, M., & Qi, J. (2013). *21st century international mindedness: An exploratory study of its conceptualisation and assessment*. Cardiff, UK: International Baccalaureate Organization. Retrieved from http://www.ibo.org/globalassets/publications/ib-research/singhqiibreport27julyfinalversion.pdf

Singh, P. (2002). Pedagogising knowledge: Bernstein's theory of the pedagogic device. *British Journal of Sociology of Education*, *23*(4), 571–582. doi:10.1080/0142569022000038422

Skelton, M. (2007). International mindedness and the brain: The difficulties of becoming. In M. C. Hayden, J. J. Thompson, & J. Levy (Eds.), *The SAGE handbook of research in international education* (pp. 379–389). London, UK: Sage. doi:10.4135/9781848607866.n32

Slaughter, R. (2011a). *About us*. Foresight International. Retrieved from http://www.foresightinternational.com.au/richard-slaughter

Slaughter, R. (2012) Introduction. *To See with Fresh Eyes: Integral Futures and the Global Emergency*. Brisbane, Australia: Foresight International. Retrieved from http://richardslaughter.com.au/wp-content/uploads/2012/06/To_See_With_Fresh_Eyes_Intro_051011.pdf

Slaughter, R. (2001). Knowledge creation, futures methodologies and the integral agenda. *Foresight*, *3*(5), 407–418. doi:10.1108/14636680110697129

Slaughter, R. (2011b). The Integral Futures Controversy: An Introduction. *Journal of Integral Theory and Practice*, *6*(2), 105–111. Retrieved from http://integralfutures.com/ wordpress/wp-content/uploads/2011/11/RS_JITP_Intro.pdf

Slaughter, R. A. (1998). Transcending flatland: Implications of Ken Wilber's meta narrative for futures studies. *Futures*, *30*(6), 519–533. doi:10.1016/S0016-3287(98)00056-1

Slaughter, R. A. (2002). Futures studies as a civilizational catalyst. *Futures*, *34*(3-4), 349–363. doi:10.1016/S0016-3287(01)00049-0

Slaughter, R. A. (2003). *Integral Futures: A new model for futures enquiry and practice*. Indooroopilly, Australia: Foresight International. Retrieved from http://www.foresightinternational.com.au

Slaughter, R., Naismith, L., & Houghton, N. (2004). *The Transformative Cycle*. Hawthorn, Australia: Swinburne University. Retrieved from http://richardslaughter.com.au/wp-content/ uploads/2008/06/AFI_Monograph_06.pdf

Snow, B. A. (2007). *Reflections on integral methodological pluralism*. John F. Kennedy University working document. Available at: http://www. kenwilber. com/blog/show/379

Snow, B. A. (2007). *Reflections on integral methodological pluralism*. John F. Kennedy University working document. Retrieved from http://www.kenwilber. com/blog/show/379

Snyder, S. (2013). The simple, the complicated, and the complex: Educational reform through the lens of complexity theory. In *OECD Education Working Papers* (No. 96). Paris, France: OECD Publishing. doi:10.1787/5k3txnpt1lnr-en

Snyder, B., & Tardy, C. (2001). That's why I do it: Flow and teachers' values, beliefs, and practices. *ELT Journal*, *58*(2), 118–128.

Societies Act 2015 (BC) s. 2.2.1 (CA).

Sovik, R. (1999). The science of breathing: The yogic view. *Progress in Brain Research*, *122*(1), 491–505. doi:10.3389/fnhum.2014.00770 PMID:10737079

Spence, K. K., & McDonald, M. (2010). Linking Developmental Action Logics to transformational leadership behaviours. *Journal of Integral Theory and Practice, 5*(4), 94–111.

Sriprakash, A., Singh, M., & Qi, J. (2014). *A comparative study of international mindedness in the IB Diploma Programme in Australia, China and India*. Cardiff, UK: International Baccalaureate Organization. Retrieved from http://www.ibo.org/globalassets/publications/ib-research/dp/international-mindedness-final-report.pdf

Stein, Z. (2016). Beyond nature and humanity: Reflections on the emergence and purpose of metatheories. In Metatheory for the 21st century: critical realism and integral theory in dialogue. New York: Routledge.

Stein, Z. (in review). On realizing the possibilities of emancipatory metatheory: beyond the cognitive maturity fallacy, toward an education revolution. In Metatheory for the anthropocene: emancipatory praxis for planetary flourishing: critical realism and integral theory in dialogue (vol. 2). New York: Routledge.

Stein. (2015). *Desperate measures: Global crises of measurement and their metatheoretical solutions*. Paper presented at the 4th Biannual Integral Theory Conference, Sonoma, CA.

Steinberg, L., Vandell, D., & Bornstein, M. (2010). *Development: Infancy through adolescence*. Retrieved from https://books.google.com/

Steingard, D. S. (2005). Spiritually-Informed management theory. *Journal of Management Inquiry, 14*(3), 227–241. doi:10.1177/1056492605276841

Stein, Z. (2009). Educational crises and the scramble for usable knowledge. *Integral Review, 2*(5), 354–367.

Stengers, I. (2000). *The invention of modern science* (D. W. Smith, Trans.). Minneapolis, MN: University of Minnesota Press.

Stephens, S. (2014). The supervised as the supervisor. *Education + Training, 56*(6), 537–550. doi:10.1108/ET-10-2012-0095

Stern, N. H., & Treasury, U. K. (2007). *The economics of climate change: the Stern review*. Cambridge, UK: Cambridge Univ Pr. doi:10.1017/CBO9780511817434

Stewart, C. C. (2008). Integral scenarios: Reframing theory, building from practice. *Futures, 40*(2), 160–172. doi:10.1016/j.futures.2007.11.013

Stigmar, M. (2009). *Högskolepedagogik. Att vara professionell som lärare i högskolan* [Pedagogy for higher education. Being a professional teacher in higher education]. Stockholm, Sweden: Liber.

Strauss, A. L., & Corbin, J. M. (2008). Basics of qualitative research: Techniques and procedures for developing grounded theory (3rd ed.). London, UK: Sage Publications.

Stringer, E. T. (2014). *Action research* (4th ed.). Thousand Oaks, CA: Sage.

Talbot, J., & Campbell, T. (2014). Examining a teacher's negotiation through change: Understanding the influence of beliefs on behavior. *Teacher Development, 18*(3), 418–434. doi:10.1080/13664530.2014.927393

Tangney, J. P., Stuewig, J., & Mashek, D. J. (2007). Moral emotions and moral behavior. *Annual Review of Psychology, 58*(1), 345–372. doi:10.1146/annurev.psych.56.091103.070145 PMID:16953797

Tarc, P. (2009). What is the 'international' in the International Baccalaureate? Three structuring tensions of the early years (1962–1973). *Journal of Research in International Education, 8*(3), 235–261. doi:10.1177/1475240909344679

Tarc, P., & Beatty, L. (2012). The emergence of the International Baccalaureate Diploma in Ontario: Diffusion, pilot study and prospective research. *Canadian Journal of Education, 35*(4), 341–375. doi:10.5116/ijme.4dfb.8dfd

Tasset, T. (2010). An integral exploration of leadership. *Journal of Integral Theory and Practice*, *5*(2), 96–116.

Taylor, B. C., Irvin, L. R., & Wieland, S. M. (2006). Checking the map: Critiquing Joanne Martin's metatheory of organizational culture and its uses in communication research. *Communication Theory*, *16*(3), 304–332. doi:10.1111/j.1468-2885.2006.00272.x

Teehankee, B. (2017). Institutional entrepreneurship: Transforming management education for participatory development in the Philippines. In H. Bradbury & ... (Eds.), *Cooking with action research: Stories and resources for self and community transformation*. Portland, OR: AR.

TenHouten, W. D. (2009). *A general theory of emotions and social life*. New York: Routledge, Taylor and Francis Group.

The Government of The Bahamas. (2011). *Bahamas General Certificate of Secondary Education (BGCSE)*. Retrieved from http://www.bahamas.gov.bs

Thelen, E., & Smith, L. B. (1994). *A dynamic system approach to the development of cognition and action*. MIT Press.

Thompson, J. J. (1998). Towards a model for international education. In M. C. Hayden & J. J. Thompson (Eds.), *International education: Principles and practice*. London, UK: Kogan Page.

Toffler, A. (1980). *The Third Wave*. New York, NY: Bantam.

Torbert, B., Cook-Greuter, S., Fisher, D., Foldy, E., Gauthier, A., Keeley, J., ... Tran, M. (2004). *Action inquiry: The secret of timely and transforming leadership*. San Francisco, CA: BerrettKoehler Publishers.

Tourki, Y., Keisler, J., & Linkov, I. (2013). Scenario analysis: A review of methods and applications for engineering and environmental systems. *Environment Systems & Decisions*, *33*(1), 3–20. doi:10.100710669-013-9437-6

Travis & Sigman. (1998). Social deficits and interpersonal relationships in autism. *Mental Retardation and Developmental Disabilities*, 65-72.

United Nations Educational Scientific and Cultural Organization (UNESCO). (1995). *Declaration and integrated framework of action on education for peace, human rights and democracy*. Paris, France: UNESCO. Retrieved from http://unesdoc.unesco.org/images/0011/001128/112874e.pdf

Urich, T. R., & Mackenzie, D. G. (1985). Educating students for life after high school: Where does vocational education fit? *NASSP Bulletin*, *69*(481), 89–94. doi:10.1177/019263658506948114

Vacarr, B. (2001). Voices inside schools: Moving beyond polite correctness: Practicing mindfulness in the diverse classroom. *Harvard Educational Review*, *71*(2), 285–296. doi:10.17763/haer.71.2.n8p0620381847715

van Aken, J. E. (2004). Management research based on the paradigm of the design sciences: The quest for field-tested and grounded technological rules. *Journal of Management Studies*, *41*(2), 219–246. doi:10.1111/j.1467-6486.2004.00430.x

Van de Ven, A. H. (1989). Nothing is quite so practical as a good theory. *Academy of Management Review*, *14*(4), 486–489. doi:10.5465/amr.1989.4308370

Van de Ven, A. H., & Poole, M. S. (2000). Toward a general theory of innovation processes. In A. H. Van de Ven, H. L. Angle, & M. S. Poole (Eds.), *Research on the Managment of Innovation: The Minnesota Studies*. New York: Ballinger, Harper and Row.

Van der Meulen, E. (2011). Participatory and action-oriented dissertations: The challenges and importance of community-engaged graduate research. *Qualitative Report*, *16*(5), 1291–1303.

van Eijnatten, F. M. (2004). Chaordic systems thinking; Some suggestions for a complexity framework to inform a learning organization. *The Learning Organization, 11*(6), 430–449. doi:10.1108/09696470410548791

Van Heijst & Geurts. (2014). Quality of life in autism across the lifespan: A meta-analysis. *Autism, 19*(2), 1–37. PMID:24443331

Van Manen, M. (1997). *Researching lived experience: Human science for an action sensitive pedagogy* (2nd ed.). London, Canada: The Althouse Press.

Varela, F. J. (1992). *Ethical know-how: Action, wisdom, and cognition.* Stanford, CA: Stanford University Press.

Varela, F. J., Thompson, E., & Rosch, E. (1992). *The embodied mind: Cognitive science and human experience.* London: MIT Press.

Varela, F., Maturana, H., & Uribe, G. (1974). Autopoiesis: The organization of living systems, its characterization, and a model. *Bio Systems, 5*(4), 187–196. doi:10.1016/0303-2647(74)90031-8 PMID:4407425

Volckmann, R. (2005). Assessing executive leadership: An integral approach. *Journal of Organizational Change Management, 18*(3), 289–302. doi:10.1108/09534810510599434

Volckman, R. (2014). Generativity, Transdisciplinarity, and Integral Leadership. *The Journal of New Paradigm Research, 20*(3-4), 248–265.

Voros, J. (2008). Integral futures: An approach to futures inquiry. *Futures, 40*(2), 190–201. doi:10.1016/j.futures.2007.11.010

Vuolo, M., Mortimer, J. T., & Staff, J. (2013). Adolescent precursors of pathways from school to work. *Journal of Research on Adolescence, 24*(1), 145–162. doi:10.1111/jora.12038 PMID:24791132

Vygotsky, L. S. (1971). *The psychology of art.* Cambridge, MA: The MIT Press.

Vygotsky, L. S. (1978). *Mind in society: The development of higher psychological processes.* Cambridge, MA: Harvard University Press.

Vygotsky, L. S. (1981). The genesis of higher mental functions. In J. V. Wertsch (Ed.), *The Concept of Activity in Social Psychology* (pp. 144–188). Armonk, NY: M.E. Sharpe.

Vygotsky, L. S. (1981). The genesis of higher mental functions. In J. V. Wertsh (Ed.), *The concept of activity in Soviet psychology.* Aemonk, NY: Sharpe.

Wacker, J. G. (1998). A definition of theory: Research guidelines for different theory-building research methods in operations management. *Journal of Operations Management, 16*(4), 361–385. doi:10.1016/S0272-6963(98)00019-9

Wacker, J. G. (2008). A conceptual understanding of requirements for theory-building research: Guidelines for scientific theory building. *The Journal of Supply Chain Management, 44*(3), 5–15. doi:10.1111/j.1745-493X.2008.00062.x

Waddock, S. A. (2001). Corporate citizenship enacted as operating practice. *International Journal of Value-Based Management, 14*(3), 237–246. doi:10.1023/A:1017548722646

Wagar, W. W. (1983). H.G. Wells and the Genesis of Future Studies. *World Future Society Bulletin, 17*(1), 25-29. Retrieved from http://www.wnrf.org/cms/hgwells.shtml

Waite, M. (Ed.). (2012). *Paperback Oxford English Dictionary* (7th ed.). Oxford, UK: Oxford University Press.

Walker, G. (2004). International Education and the International Baccalaureate. *Phi Delta Kappa Fastbacks, 522*, 7–34. Retrieved from http://pdkintl.org/

Walker, C. O., Greene, B. A., & Mansell, R. A. (2006). Identification with academics, intrinsic/extrinsic motivation, and self-efficacy as predictors of cognitive engagement. *Learning and Individual Differences*, *16*(1), 1–12. doi:10.1016/j.lindif.2005.06.004

Walker, M. (2009). Capabilities, flourishing and the normative purposes of action research. In S. Noffke & B. Somekh (Eds.), *Handbook of educational action research*. Thousand Oaks, CA: Sage. doi:10.4135/9780857021021.n28

Wallace, B. A. (2011). *Minding closely: The four applications of mindfulness*. Boston, MA: Snow Lion Publications.

Wallis, S. E. (2010). Toward a science of metatheory. *Integral Review*, *6*(3).

Warin, J., & Muldoon, J. (2009). Wanting to be 'known': Redefining self-awareness through an understanding of self-narration processes in educational transitions. *British Educational Research Journal*, *35*(2), 289–303. doi:10.1080/01411920802043000

Watkins, A., & Wilber, K. (2015). *Wicked & Wise: How to Solve the World's Toughest Problems*. Chatham, UK: Urbane Publications.

Watkins, A., & Wilber, K. (2015). *Wicked and wise: How to solve the world's toughest problems*. Chatham, UK: Urbane Publications.

Webster's New World Dictionary of American English. (1988). New York: Webster's New World.

Weick, K. E., & Putnam, T. (2006). Organizing for mindfulness Eastern wisdom and Western knowledge. *Journal of Management Inquiry*, *15*(3), 275-287. doi:291202 doi:10.1177/1056492606

Weick, K. E., & Putnam, T. (2006). Organizing for mindfulness Eastern wisdom and Western knowledge. *Journal of Management Inquiry*, *15*(3), 275–287. doi:10.1177/1056492606291202

Welp, L. R., & Brown, C. M. (2013). Self-compassion, empathy, and helping intentions. *The Journal of Positive Psychology*, *9*(1), 54–65. doi:10.1080/17439760.2013.831465

Wenger, E. (1998). *Communities of practice: Learning, meaning and identity*. Cambridge, UK: Cambridge University Press. doi:10.1017/CBO9780511803932

WFSF. (2002). *About Us*. Retrieved From http://www.wfsf.org/about-us/futures-studies

Whetten, D. A. (1989). What constitutes a theoretical contribution? *Academy of Management Review*, *14*(4), 490–495. doi:10.5465/amr.1989.4308371

Wieder, C. G. (1978). *Fear and force versus education: A study of the effects of coercion on learning*. Branden Press.

Wilber, K. (1995). Sex, ecology, spirituality: The spirit of evolution. Boston, MA: Shambhala, P. 802, where Carol Gilligan's 1982 book In a different voice (Cambridge: Harvard University Press) is specifically discussed.

Wilber, K. (2005). Introduction to integral theory and practice. *AQAL: Journal of Integral Theory and Practice*, *1*(1).

Wilber, K. (2006a). *Excerpt A: An integral age at the leading edge*. Retrieved May 9th, 2018 from: http://www.kenwilber.com/Writings/PDF/ExcerptA_KOSMOS_2003.pdf

Wilber, K. (2006b). *Excerpt B: The many ways we touch—three principles helpful for any integral approach*. Retrieved May 9th, 2018 from: http://www.kenwilber.com/writings/read_pdf/84

Wilber, K. (2006c). *Excerpt C: The ways we are in this together: Intersubjectivity and interobjectivity in the holonic kosmos*. Retrieved May 9th, 2018 from: http://www.kenwilber.com/writings/read_pdf/85

Compilation of References

Wilber, K. (2013). Response to Critical Realism in Defense of Integral Theory. In *Integral Post: Transmissions from the leading edge*. Retrieved from https://www.integrallife.com /integral-post/response-critical-realism-defense-integral-theory?page=0,0

Wilber, K. (2017, January 2). *Trump and post-truth world*. Retrieved from http://integrallife.com

Wilber, K. (Speaker). (2015, October 28). *Being vs. knowing: Ending the debate between epistemology and ontology* [Video file]. Retrieved May 9, 2018 from: https://integrallife.com/being-vs-knowing-ending-debate-between-epistemology-and-ontology/

Wilber, K. (1977/82). *Spectrum of consciousness*. Wheaton, IL: Theosophical Publishing House.

Wilber, K. (1981). *Up from Eden: A transpersonal view of human evolution*. New York: Anchor/Doubleday.

Wilber, K. (1995). *Sex, ecology and spirituality: The spirit in evolution* (Vol. 1). Boston, MA: Shambhala.

Wilber, K. (1995). *Sex, ecology and spirituality: The spirit of evolution*. Boston, MA: Shambala Publications.

Wilber, K. (1995). *Sex, ecology, spirituality*. Boston, MA: Shambhala.

Wilber, K. (1995). *Sex, ecology, spirituality: The spirit of evolution*. Boston, MA: Shambhala.

Wilber, K. (1995). *Sex, Ecology, Spirituality: The Spirit of Evolution*. Boston, MA: Shambhala.

Wilber, K. (1996). *A brief history of everything*. Boston, MA: Shambhala.

Wilber, K. (1999). *Eye to eye: the quest for the new paradigm. The Collected Works of Ken Wilber* (Vol. 3). Denver, CO: Shambhala.

Wilber, K. (2000). *A theory of everything*. Boston: Shambhala.

Wilber, K. (2000). *Integral psychology*. Boston: Shambhala Publications.

Wilber, K. (2000). *Integral psychology: Consciousness, spirit, psychology, therapy*. Boston, MA: Shambhala.

Wilber, K. (2000a). *A Brief History of Everything* (2nd ed.). Boston, MA: Shambhala Publications, Inc.

Wilber, K. (2000a). *A theory of everything: an integral vision for business, politics, science, and spirituality*. Boston, MA: Shambhala Publications.

Wilber, K. (2000b). *A theory of everything: An integral vision for business, politics, science, and spirituality*. Boston: Shambhala.

Wilber, K. (2005). Introduction to integral theory and practice. *AQAL Journal of Integral Theory and Practice*, *1*(1), 38.

Wilber, K. (2006). Integral Methodological Pluralism. In *Integral spirituality*. Boston, MA: Integral Books.

Wilber, K. (2006). Integral Methodological Pluralism. In *Integral spirituality: A startling new role for religion in the modern and post-modern world*. Boston, MA: Shambhala.

Wilber, K. (2006). Integral Methodological Pluralism. In *Integral Spirituality: Startling New Role for Religion in the Modern and Post-Modern World*. Boston, MA: Shambhala.

Wilber, K. (2006). *Integral spirituality*. Boston, MA: Shambhala Publications.

Wilber, K. (2006). *Integral Spirituality: A Startling New Role for Religion in the Modern and Postmodern World*. Boston, MA: Integral Books.

Wilber, K. (2006). *Integral spirituality: A startling new role for religion in the modern and postmodern world*. Boston: Integral Books.

Wilber, K. (2006). *Integral Spirituality: A startling new role for religion in the modern and postmodern world*. Boston: Shambhala Publications, Inc.

Wilber, K. (2007). *Integral Spirituality*. Boston, MA: Integral Books.

Wilber, K. (2007). *The integral vision: A very short introduction to the revolutionary integral approach to life, god, the universe, and everything*. Shambhala Publications.

Wilber, K. (2008). *The integral vision*. Boston, MA: Shambhala.

Wilber, K. (2014). The Future of Buddhism. In *The Fourth Turning: Imagining the evolution of an Integral Buddhism*. Boston, MA: Shambhala.

Wilber, K. (2016). *Integral meditation: Mindfulness as a path to grow up, wake up, and show up in your life*. Boulder, CO: Shambala Publications.

Wilber, K. (2016). Miracle of we. In O. Gunnlaugson & M. Brabant (Eds.), *Cohering the integral we space: Engaging collective emergence, wisdom and healing in groups*. Integral Publishing House.

Wilber, K. (2017). *The religion of tomorrow: A vision for the future of the great traditions—more inclusive, more comprehensive, more complete*. Boulder, CO: Shambhala.

Wilber, K., Patten, T., Leonard, A., & Morelli, M. (2008). *Integral life practice: A 21st century blueprint for physical health, emotional balance, mental clarity and spiritual awakening*. Boston, MA: Integral Books.

Wilber, K., Patten, T., Leonard, A., & Morelli, M. (2008). *Integral life practice: A 21st Century Blueprint for Physical Health, Emotional Balance, Mental Clarity, and Spiritual Awakening*. Boston, MA: Integral Books.

Wilber, K., Patten, T., Leonard, A., & Morelli, M. (2008). *Integral life practice: A 21st century blueprint for physical health, emotional balance, mental clarity, and spiritual awakening*. Boston: Integral Books.

Willms, J. D., Friesen, S., & Milton, P. (2009). *What did you do in school today? Transforming classrooms through social, academic, and intellectual engagement*. Retrieved from http://www.cea-ace.ca/sites/default/files/cea-2009-wdydist.pdf

Witt, K. (2014). Defensive states and states of healthy response in integrally informed psychotherapy: An interpersonal neurobiological contribution to shadow. *Journal of Integral Theory and Practice, 9*(2), 35.

Wittmayer, J. M., & Schäpke, N. (2014). Action, research and participation: Roles of researchers in sustainability transitions. *Sustainability Science, 9*(4), 483–496. doi:10.100711625-014-0258-4

Wood, D., Bruner, J., & Ross, G. (1976). The role of tutoring in problem solving. *Journal of Child Psychology and Psychiatry, and Allied Disciplines, 17*(2), 89–100. doi:10.1111/j.1469-7610.1976.tb00381.x PMID:932126

Yarnell, L. M., & Neff, K. D. (2013). Self-compassion, interpersonal conflict resolutions, and wellbeing. *Self and Identity, 12*(2), 146–159. doi:10.1080/15298868.2011.649545

Yeager, D. S., & Walton, G. (2011). Social-psychological interventions in education: They're not magic. *Review of Educational Research, 81*(2), 267–301. doi:10.3102/0034654311405999

Young, J. E. (2002). A spectrum of consciousness for CEOs: A business application of Ken Wilber's Spectrum of Consciousness. *The International Journal of Organizational Analysis, 10*(1), 30–54. doi:10.1108/eb028943

Yuen, C. (2013). *Mathematics anxiety learning phenomenon: Adult learner's lived experience and its implications for developmental mathematics instruction* (Doctoral Dissertation). Retrieved from ProQuest Dissertations and Theses Global. (Order No. NS23075)

Zalla, Miele, Leboyer, & Metcalfe. (2015). Metacognition of agency and theory of mind in adults with high functioning autism. *Journal of Autism and Developmental Disorders*, 126–138. PMID:25482271

Zelazo, P. D., & Lyons, K. E. (2012). The potential benefits of mindfulness training in early childhood: A developmental social cognitive neuroscience perspective. *Child Development Perspectives*, *6*(2), 154–160. doi:10.1111/j.1750-8606.2012.00241.x

Zhou, J. (2015). International students' motivation to pursue and complete a Ph.D. in the U.S. *Higher Education*, *69*(5), 719–733. doi:10.100710734-014-9802-5

Zollo, M., & Winter, S. G. (2002). Learning and the evolution of dynamic capabilities. *Organization Science*, *13*(3), 339–351. doi:10.1287/orsc.13.3.339.2780

About the Contributors

Veronika Bohac Clarke is Associate Professor in the Werklund School of Education at the University of Calgary in Alberta, Canada. She has been using the Integral Model in teaching and research since 2001. She has designed and coordinated a Master's level program in Integral Curriculum Development, with two cohorts graduating. Bohac Clarke also co-designed and coordinated a doctoral program in Curriculum – Integral Theory, which recently graduated a cohort of 10 students.

* * *

Avis Beek has been a Science and Mathematics Specialist teacher for twenty five years. She taught in the public school system in Nunavut, Canada, volunteered with NGO's in Malawi and Greece and has taught in international schools in Bahrain, Malaysia, Japan, and the Czech Republic. Her research and pedagogy focus on fostering respectful intercultural understanding through education.

Janice Beler has been a teacher for over 25 years. Throughout her career she has had the opportunity to work in western Canada with students between preschool and grade 12. She has worked as a classroom teacher, resource teacher, consulting teacher, and learning support teacher. Currently she is supporting teachers as they work with students who exhibit challenging behaviors. She lives in Lethbridge, Alberta with her husband and two sons.

A. Faye Bres has a background in environmental science, and worked for 15 years as a consultant developing and auditing management systems for clients in power generation, forestry and pulp, hazardous and industrial waste management, mining, oil and gas, and manufacturing. Having reached the limits of "systems based management" models, she recently completed a PhD on Complex Adaptive Systems theory at The University of Calgary. Her research was participatory and design based, and explored the adaptive capacity of The City of Calgary as it learns and self-organizes in its dynamic and ever changing natural and institutional environments. She is expanding her interests beyond only Environmental Management to a transdisciplinary, complexity based approach to addressing "wicked problems" experienced in human organizations and societies.

Dave Carlgren is currently a physical science educator in the private school system in Calgary, Alberta, Canada. His interests in educational research span from epistemological and ontological considerations to teacher preparation, technology, and science education.

About the Contributors

Cheryl Marie Cordeiro has a PhD in general linguistics from the University of Gothenburg. She is currently Principal Investigator in the RJ Flexit 2015/18 programme, a project funded by the Bank of Sweden Tercentenary Foundation (Riksbankens Jubileumsfond, RJ). She worked as a Research Scientist at the User Experience and Industrial Design Group at ABB AB Corporate Research in Västerås, Sweden. She is currently faculty member at the Centre for International Business Studies (CIBS), School of Business, Economics and Law at the University of Gothenburg. She has a Master of Science in Information Studies (2001) from the Nanyang Technological University (NTU) of Singapore, and a Master of Arts in the English Language (2000) from the National University of Singapore (NUS).

Kathleen Kellock has been teaching for 25 years, in both elementary and secondary education. After teaching in Canada for seven years, she moved to the Commonwealth of The Bahamas where she is now living and has been working for the last 18 years. Currently, she teaches high school geography and environmental science. Her research interests are in college readiness and geography education.

Krystyna C. Laycraft is a graduate of the University of Warsaw (Master of Science in Theoretical Physics) and of the University of calgary (PhD in Education). She shares her time between art, science, and teaching. She gives lectures and workshops on applications of Complexity Science in creativity, psychology, neuroscience, and education. She is a member of the Society for Chaos Theory in Psychology and Life Sciences. For more information on her work and teaching, view her websites: www.krystynalaycraft.com and www.krystynalaycraft.academia.edu.

Natalie Anne Prytuluk recently completed her doctorate through the University of Calgary focused on early childhood education, inclusion and integral theory. Throughout her twenty-nine year career in education as a teacher, senior manager in Alberta Education, and school leader with Edmonton Public Schools, Dr. Prytuluk has focused on supporting young children through evidence based practices and research. She is a past recipient of the Alberta Excellence in Teaching award, and the Alberta Teachers' Association Advocate for Young Children award. Dr. Prytuluk is currently the Director of Early Years with Edmonton Public Schools.

Justin Robinson consults in the areas of leadership, learning, and organizational development. He is the creator of the Integral Breakthrough Design Lab, a totally unconventional three-day exploration of integral theory, design thinking, and action-oriented inquiry for executives and entrepreneurs. Justin is passionate about socio-technical transformation and planetary ethics in the Anthropocene. He is the director of the award-winning documentary film, Pipeline Wars: A Burning Debate About Our Future.

Garette Tebay is a teacher and administrator in Alberta, Canada. She has spent most of her career working with students in caring classrooms. This led her to develop research around the development of classroom communities that foster compassion in students and teachers. In working to creating caring space full of loving-kindness she hopes to change the world, even if for just one kid.

Bernita Wienhold-Leahy, EdD, is an educator and trained teacher of Mindful Self-Compassion. She has worked for more than a decade with adolescents and young adults in an educational setting and endeavours to bring mindful self-compassion in the community, schools, and professions to build resilience and well-being in others. Bernita currently works in the Faculty of Education at Thompson Rivers University.

Index

1-to-1 209, 224, 236

A

action research 48, 62, 215, 244, 339-340, 351, 357-358, 366-367, 381, 392, 404
activism 360, 369, 374
adaptive capacity 388-389, 391-392, 396-398, 402, 404, 407
adolescents 76, 109-116, 118-120, 122-123, 125-128, 134-145, 151, 153-154, 192, 314-315, 318, 320
Alberta 88, 186-187, 200, 202, 238-241, 248, 251, 256-257, 263, 269, 288-289, 295-300, 302, 309-310, 312, 339-340, 342-344, 347
All Quadrant All Lines (AQAL) Framework 312
AQAL 20-22, 45, 48, 50-53, 56, 58, 60, 62-63, 77-78, 86, 92-93, 116-118, 126, 128, 136-138, 161-165, 168, 170, 180-181, 183-186, 197, 212, 216-220, 223, 227-228, 236, 249, 289, 312-313, 366-367, 389-392, 397, 402-403
Autism Quotient (AQ) Scales 312

B

B.A.I.S.S. 133
Behavioral Engagement 207
beliefs 5, 24, 29, 90, 104, 109-112, 114, 119, 122, 126, 211, 223, 227-228, 236, 238, 240-241, 243, 245, 247, 250, 252-254, 256-257, 260, 262-263, 269, 295, 299, 313, 350, 362
Bologna Process 273, 286
Bring Your Own Device (BYOD) 209, 236

C

children 106, 113, 122, 143, 154, 162, 164-165, 167, 196, 208, 223, 226, 230-231, 238-242, 244-247, 249, 251-253, 256-257, 260, 262-264, 269, 276, 289, 296, 318, 340, 345, 364
children with diverse needs 244-245, 269
classroom 2, 10, 56, 71-72, 78, 87, 100-101, 105, 116, 134, 144, 146, 149-151, 155, 160-163, 165-177, 180, 182-183, 187-188, 190-194, 198-201, 203, 210, 238, 240-241, 243-258, 260, 262-263, 269, 288, 296-297, 340, 342
classroom community 160-161, 163, 166, 168, 171-176, 180
college and career readiness 109-110, 114, 116-118, 120, 125-128
Commonwealth of The Bahamas 109-111, 116, 118, 123, 126-128
communities of practice 87, 89, 93-94, 102, 108, 263
compassion 134-136, 139-141, 143, 145-147, 149, 151-152, 154-155, 160-165, 167-173, 175-176, 180, 183, 194, 244
complexity 2, 5, 11, 17, 20, 25, 34-35, 47, 49-50, 53, 56, 58, 65, 68, 72-73, 78, 87, 89, 91-92, 94, 96, 100, 108, 113, 115, 176, 194, 214, 220, 227, 232, 237, 248-249, 286, 289-290, 292, 314, 317-318, 320-321, 343, 361, 363-365, 373, 383-394, 396-401, 403-404
conceptual framework 56, 60, 62-63, 65, 68, 73, 77, 118, 160, 185, 212, 220-221, 238, 241, 243, 250, 256, 314
conference 70, 87-89, 94-95, 99, 102-103, 343, 348
critical theory 11, 214, 342, 350

D

David Conley 115, 126
depression, 144, 200, 293, 295, 316
developmental dynamisms 318, 320, 323-324, 337
developmental potential 318-319, 325, 337
diversity 10, 65, 69, 72-73, 76-77, 79-80, 117, 125, 135, 239, 241, 244-245, 269, 289, 293, 320, 325, 395, 401
doctoral degree program 271, 273, 277-280, 283
dynamisms 318, 320, 323-324, 327-330, 337

E

Early Childhood Educators (ECEs) 239, 269
EHEA 271, 286
emergence 5, 10, 15, 69, 90, 92, 94, 108, 289, 297, 317, 320-321, 338, 367, 372-373, 385-387, 393-394, 404, 407
Emotional Engagement 207
emotions 114, 135, 137-142, 144, 147-148, 151, 153, 163-165, 190, 201, 269, 295, 314, 317-318, 321-323, 325-330, 348
enactive stance 366-367, 381
Europe 2020 271, 286
European higher education context 273
experiences 2, 7, 10, 45-46, 53, 66, 68-69, 75-76, 91, 94, 100, 102, 105, 109, 111, 115, 118-119, 126-128, 139, 141-143, 163, 166, 168, 182, 187-188, 194, 197, 199, 211, 219, 223, 230, 237-243, 247, 253-254, 256-257, 262, 264, 269, 287-288, 292, 294, 299, 301, 304-305, 313-316, 319-323, 328, 339, 364, 366, 377, 388-389, 407

F

Fearlessness 348-352, 354
feedback 10, 72, 89, 92, 95-96, 98-102, 105, 108, 193-194, 248, 271-273, 275-278, 280-283, 286, 317, 320, 327, 348, 351, 385-388
feedback system 271-273, 282-283
fixed mindset 183, 189, 191-193, 207
future 7, 20, 23-24, 70-72, 78, 97-98, 100, 104-105, 109-116, 119, 122, 125-128, 155, 182, 187, 190, 197, 210-211, 213-214, 216, 221, 223-224, 226-227, 230-231, 261, 263, 297, 302, 305, 307-309, 314-315, 343, 345-347, 349, 358-359, 366, 369, 377, 404
futures 34, 110, 112-114, 116, 120, 127, 208-216, 220-221, 223-224, 226-232, 236, 345

G

growth mindset 11, 134, 142, 147, 153, 155, 183, 187-190, 192-193, 207

H

High Functioning Autism Characteristics (HFAC) 298, 312
high school 109-116, 118, 120-123, 125-128, 135-136, 145-146, 182, 187-188, 197, 199, 202, 208, 221, 223, 230
higher education 109, 113, 116, 122, 271-273, 275, 277-279, 282-283, 286, 345, 347-348
holon 25, 30, 42, 174, 185, 383, 391, 402
hope 1, 35, 142-143, 216, 226, 231, 264, 305, 387, 397

I

inclusive 4, 56-58, 94, 120, 161, 216, 230, 238-241, 243-244, 246, 248-258, 260-264, 269, 286-288, 297, 308, 384, 391, 400
integral action research 357-358, 366, 381
Integral Education 339, 349
Integral Lines 236
integral metatheory 357-358, 362, 381-382
Integral Methodological Pluralism (IMP) 48, 52, 63, 145, 165, 177, 182, 209, 221, 249, 287, 290, 312, 372
Integral Pluralism 118, 271, 273, 275, 283, 286
Integral States 236
integral theory 2-3, 19-25, 30-31, 33-35, 45-46, 48-49, 52, 60, 63, 65-66, 73, 78, 80, 86-87, 92, 105, 116-118, 134, 136-138, 141, 144-147, 160-161, 165, 170, 175-176, 180, 182-183, 185, 208-209, 212, 214, 216-221, 226-227, 231-233, 236, 238, 241, 243-244, 249-250, 256, 264, 271-272, 287, 289-290, 312, 314-315, 341-342, 346, 348, 350-351, 383-384, 389-391, 397-399, 404
Integral Without Borders (IWB) 357, 382
Integrally Informed Research 68, 86
intercultural understanding 65, 70-71, 79, 86
International Baccalaureate 65-66, 79, 86, 115, 123
International Baccalaureate Diploma Program 86
international education 67, 70-72, 76, 78-79, 86, 120
international mindedness 65-80, 86
international school 66, 69-70, 86

K

Ken Wilber 2, 19, 21, 63, 66, 73, 80, 92, 116, 126, 137, 183, 216, 236, 241, 287, 289-290, 312, 345-349, 351, 358, 360, 362-365, 389

L

Lower Left (LL) Quadrant 56, 102, 219, 241, 312

Index

Lower Right (LR) Quadrant 220, 242, 312

M

metacrisis 359, 382
metatheory 63, 92-93, 312, 357-358, 362, 381-382
mindfulness 11, 70, 134-141, 143-146, 148-151, 153-155, 160-163, 165-177, 181-183, 185-192, 196-203, 295, 404
mindfulness practice 135, 139-140, 148-149, 151, 155, 160-163, 168-169, 172, 176, 181, 189-191
models 21, 23, 25-26, 34, 42, 70, 89, 91, 102, 202, 231-232, 236, 240, 251, 291-292, 314, 323-324, 340, 345, 374, 388, 390
multi-methods 134, 145, 196, 209, 220-221, 238, 249

N

narrative 8, 10, 53-54, 92, 105, 142, 160, 165-166, 170, 177, 299-302, 308, 312, 314, 322, 332, 340-341, 349, 351
National School 66, 86
nesting 390, 395, 398-399, 407
networks 5, 87, 89, 199, 280, 282, 295, 321, 395
NEW PARADIGM 171, 346
Nordic pedagogy 271-272, 283, 286

O

Ontological pluralism 46, 63
open space 357, 366, 368-369
operational closure 399-401, 407
organizational learning 383-384, 387-389, 391-392, 394-397, 401, 403, 407
outlaw stage 342
Overexcitability (OE) 325, 337

P

paradigm 29, 42, 47, 91-92, 108, 171, 187, 271-273, 286, 296, 346-347, 354, 372, 374, 386
paradigms 25, 27, 29, 47, 52, 58, 63, 89-90, 92, 145, 183, 218, 289-290, 346, 360, 366, 373-374, 386
paradox 42, 289, 358, 388
parents 58, 70, 76, 95, 101, 103, 110-112, 116, 118, 121-123, 125-128, 134, 137, 139, 193, 211, 230, 232, 238, 240, 252-253, 260, 269, 280, 289, 299, 301-302, 305, 307-309, 318, 332, 342, 344
Participatory Research 166

pedagogical practice 255, 263, 269
pedagogy 11, 105, 236, 256, 260, 271-273, 275, 283, 286, 296, 345, 349-350
perceptions 24, 46, 69, 109-111, 113, 115, 120, 122, 125-128, 137, 141, 146, 171-172, 176, 182-183, 187, 189-190, 196, 203, 208-211, 213, 216, 220-221, 224, 236, 244-245, 249, 253, 269, 288, 301, 307, 316
planetary transformation 358-359, 378
planning 113-116, 123, 126, 150, 167, 189, 213-214, 226-229, 232, 244, 344, 387, 394, 397
positive disintegration 314-315, 317-318, 323-326, 337
positive maladjustment 328-329, 338
post-adult 339, 341-342, 345-346, 348
Post-Modernism 91, 108
praxis 349, 357, 370-374, 376-378
pre-kindergarten 238-240, 250-251, 253-258, 260-264, 269
privilege 65, 72, 76, 79, 216
psychological development 49, 63, 314-315, 317-318, 322-325
Psychological Wellbeing Scales (PWBS) 313

Q

Quadrant Framework 214, 313

R

relationships 23-24, 30, 56, 60, 74, 99-100, 103-105, 114, 123, 137-140, 143-145, 150, 162, 171-172, 175, 180-181, 186, 199, 201, 224, 238-241, 247-248, 254, 256-257, 259-261, 264, 290, 293, 295, 301-309, 312-313, 315-316, 320, 325, 342, 346, 363, 369, 371, 394, 398-399
research paradigms 52, 58, 63, 386

S

science 4, 11, 17, 47, 87-89, 91-92, 94-101, 103-105, 108, 110, 115, 163, 182-183, 198-200, 210-212, 227, 237, 247-249, 293, 314, 317, 324-325, 327, 342-343, 345, 386, 390
science education 87-89, 97, 104-105, 343
Self-Actualizing (SA) Creativeness 338
self-compassion 134-150, 152-155
self-organization 248, 314, 317, 321, 323, 330, 338, 384-386, 391-393
social constructivist 238, 241, 262-263

Stage-Based Development 68
structure 20-23, 30-31, 48, 66, 102, 104, 138, 165, 170, 187, 195, 225, 244, 253, 278, 294-296, 315-316, 318-321, 327, 330, 337, 350, 354, 363, 384, 386-387, 391-392, 394-396, 398, 403, 407
student-centered learning 271-272, 274-276, 281, 283, 286
supervision 271-273, 275, 280, 283, 286
sustainability 19-20, 23-28, 30-35, 42, 60, 86, 92, 101, 110, 114, 213, 216, 344, 357-361, 363-364, 366, 368-370, 372-374, 377-378, 382
sustainability leadership 357-360, 364, 366, 368-370, 372-374, 377-378, 382

T

teacher 2, 4, 14, 62, 73, 78, 88, 95, 100, 121, 145-146, 150, 155, 160, 163, 165-175, 177, 180, 191-194, 198-199, 201, 208-209, 213-214, 216, 223-224, 231-232, 239, 244-245, 253, 257, 272, 280, 297, 299-300, 305, 324, 340-344, 346, 352
technology 34, 56, 76, 110, 122, 128, 149, 200, 209, 212-213, 228, 230, 236, 344, 350, 363
the psycho-evolutionary theory of emotions 314, 317
the theory of positive disintegration 314, 317-318, 323-326
theoretical framework 56, 63, 220, 286, 384, 392, 396
transdisciplinarity 14-16, 18, 48, 60, 344-345, 351

transformation 20, 27-28, 72, 75, 78, 119, 140, 174, 182, 240, 320, 340, 343, 347, 357-360, 370-374, 376-378, 382
triangulation 31, 33-34, 42, 118, 171, 196, 369

U

understandings 15, 35, 78, 185-186, 194, 196, 223-224, 227, 236, 238, 240-241, 243, 247, 249-250, 252-254, 256-257, 260, 262-263, 269, 289, 297, 301, 313, 386
unity 79-80, 316, 397-400, 402, 407
Upper Left (UL) Quadrant 92, 219, 241, 313
Upper Right (UR) Quadrant 56, 219, 241, 313

W

wellbeing 134-136, 141, 143-144, 155, 163, 190-191, 287, 312-313
Wilber 2-4, 9, 19-23, 30-32, 48-55, 60, 63, 65-66, 69, 73, 77-78, 80, 92, 109, 114, 116-119, 121, 126, 128, 136-139, 141, 143-144, 161, 164-165, 176, 180, 183-186, 197, 200, 212-214, 216-219, 221, 236, 241, 249, 259, 273-274, 287, 289-290, 312, 314-315, 341-342, 345-351, 358, 360-365, 367, 373, 376, 388-391, 399, 401

Purchase Print, E-Book, or Print + E-Book

IGI Global books are available in three unique pricing formats:
Print Only, E-Book Only, or Print + E-Book. Shipping fees apply.

www.igi-global.com

Recommended Reference Books

ISBN: 978-1-5225-2145-7
© 2017; 408 pp.
List Price: $210

ISBN: 978-1-5225-2334-5
© 2017 ; 375 pp.
List Price: $195

ISBN: 978-1-5225-1718-4
© 2017; 457 pp.
List Price: $270

ISBN: 978-1-5225-0672-0
© 2017; 678 pp.
List Price: $295

ISBN: 978-1-5225-2630-8
© 2018; 209 pp.
List Price: $145

ISBN: 978-1-5225-1621-7
© 2017; 173 pp.
List Price: $135

Do you want to stay current on the latest research trends, product announcements, news and special offers?
Join IGI Global's mailing list today and start enjoying exclusive perks sent only to IGI Global members.
Add your name to the list at **www.igi-global.com/newsletters**.

Publisher of Peer-Reviewed, Timely, and Innovative Academic Research

IGI Global
DISSEMINATOR of KNOWLEDGE

www.igi-global.com   Sign up at www.igi-global.com/newsletters   facebook.com/igiglobal   twitter.com/igiglobal   linkedin.com/igiglobal

Ensure Quality Research is Introduced to the Academic Community

Become an IGI Global Reviewer for Authored Book Projects

The overall success of an authored book project is dependent on quality and timely reviews.

In this competitive age of scholarly publishing, constructive and timely feedback significantly expedites the turnaround time of manuscripts from submission to acceptance, allowing the publication and discovery of forward-thinking research at a much more expeditious rate. Several IGI Global authored book projects are currently seeking highly qualified experts in the field to fill vacancies on their respective editorial review boards:

Applications may be sent to:
development@igi-global.com

Applicants must have a doctorate (or an equivalent degree) as well as publishing and reviewing experience. Reviewers are asked to write reviews in a timely, collegial, and constructive manner. All reviewers will begin their role on an ad-hoc basis for a period of one year, and upon successful completion of this term can be considered for full editorial review board status, with the potential for a subsequent promotion to Associate Editor.

If you have a colleague that may be interested in this opportunity, we encourage you to share this information with them.

www.igi-global.com

Celebrating 30 Years of Scholarly Knowledge Creation & Dissemination

InfoSci®-Books

A Collection of 4,000+ Reference Books Containing Over 87,000 Full-Text Chapters Focusing on Emerging Research

This database is a collection of over 4,000+ IGI Global single and multi-volume reference books, handbooks of research, and encyclopedias, encompassing groundbreaking research from prominent experts worldwide. These books are highly cited and currently recognized in prestigious indices such as: Web of Science™ and Scopus®.

Librarian Features:
- No Set-Up or Maintenance Fees
- Guarantee of No More Than A 5% Annual Price Increase
- COUNTER 4 Usage Reports
- Complimentary Archival Access
- Free MARC Records

Researcher Features:
- Unlimited Simultaneous Users
- No Embargo of Content
- Full Book Download
- Full-Text Search Engine
- No DRM

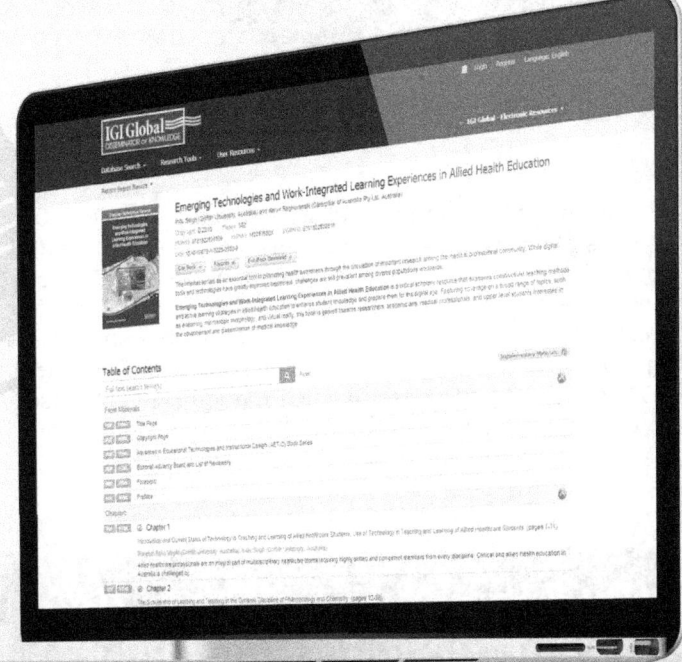

To Find Out More or To Purchase This Database:
www.igi-global.com/infosci-books

eresources@igi-global.com • Toll Free: 1-866-342-6657 ext. 100 • Phone: 717-533-8845 x100

www.igi-global.com

IGI Global Proudly Partners with

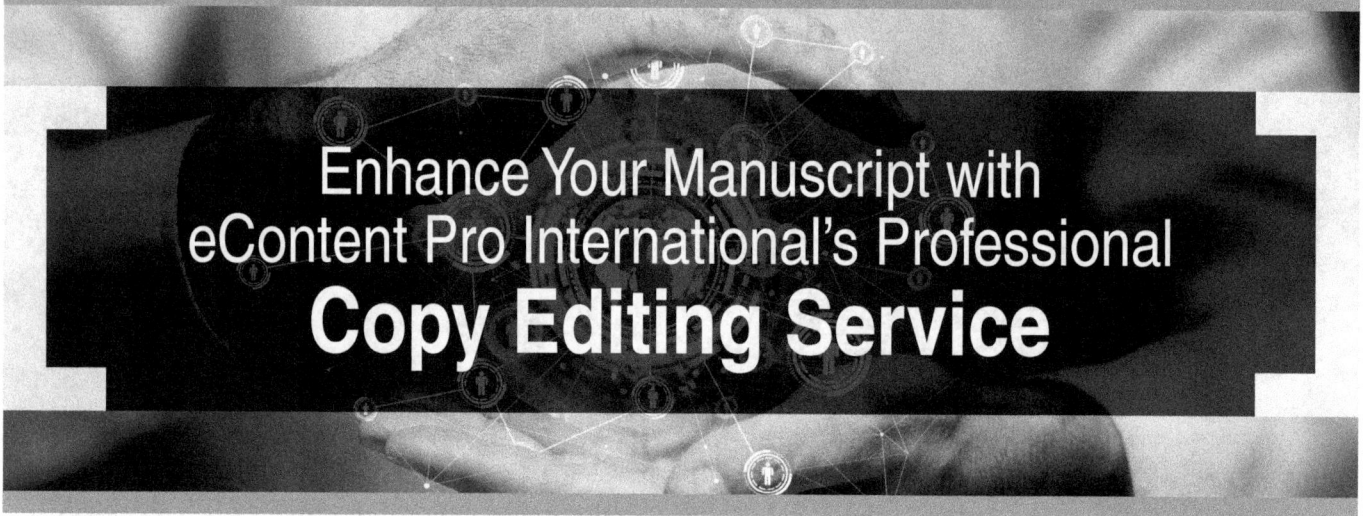

Expert Copy Editing

eContent Pro International copy editors, with over 70 years of combined experience, will provide complete and comprehensive care for your document by resolving all issues with spelling, punctuation, grammar, terminology, jargon, semantics, syntax, consistency, flow, and more. In addition, they will format your document to the style you specify (APA, Chicago, etc.). All edits will be performed using Microsoft Word's Track Changes feature, which allows for fast and simple review and management of edits.

Additional Services

eContent Pro International also offers fast and affordable proofreading to enhance the readability of your document, professional translation in over 100 languages, and market localization services to help businesses and organizations localize their content and grow into new markets around the globe.

IGI Global Authors Save 25% on eContent Pro International's Services!

Scan the QR Code to Receive Your 25% Discount

The 25% discount is applied directly to your eContent Pro International shopping cart when placing an order through IGI Global's referral link. Use the QR code to access this referral link. eContent Pro International has the right to end or modify any promotion at any time.

Email: customerservice@econtentpro.com

econtentpro.com

Information Resources Management Association

Advancing the Concepts & Practices of Information Resources Management in Modern Organizations

Become an IRMA Member

Members of the **Information Resources Management Association (IRMA)** understand the importance of community within their field of study. The Information Resources Management Association is an ideal venue through which professionals, students, and academicians can convene and share the latest industry innovations and scholarly research that is changing the field of information science and technology. Become a member today and enjoy the benefits of membership as well as the opportunity to collaborate and network with fellow experts in the field.

IRMA Membership Benefits:

- **One FREE Journal Subscription**
- **30% Off Additional Journal Subscriptions**
- **20% Off Book Purchases**
- Updates on the latest events and research on Information Resources Management through the IRMA-L listserv.
- Updates on new open access and downloadable content added to Research IRM.
- A copy of the Information Technology Management Newsletter twice a year.
- A certificate of membership.

IRMA Membership $195

Scan code or visit **irma-international.org** and begin by selecting your free journal subscription.

Membership is good for one full year.

www.irma-international.org

CPSIA information can be obtained
at www.ICGtesting.com
Printed in the USA
LVHW101911021019
632991LV00005B/5/P